Listed Buildings

AUSTRALIA AND NEW ZEALAND
The Law Book Company Ltd
Sydney : Melbourne : Perth

CANADA AND U.S.A.
The Carswell Company Ltd
Agincourt, Ontario

INDIA
N. M. Tripathi Private Ltd
Bombay
and
Eastern Law House Private Ltd
Calcutta and Delhi
M.P.P. House
Bangalore

ISRAEL
Steimatzky's Agency Ltd
Jerusalem : Tel Aviv : Haifa

Listed Buildings:
The Law and Practice
of
Historic Buildings, Ancient
Monuments, and Conservation
Areas

by

Roger W. Suddards   and   **June M. Hargreaves**
Solicitor, L.M.R.T.P.I.,   *Chartered Town Planner,*
C.B.E., D.L., F.S.V.A. (Hon.)   *M.B.E., M. Univ [York] Dip. T.P.,*
M.R.T.P.I.

with contributions by

David Hicken   and   **Chris Allen**
B.A. (Hons.) B.T.P., D.M.S.,   *F.C.A.*
M.B.I.M., M.R.T.P.I.

and a Foreword by

Sir Desmond Heap
LL.M., Hon. LL.D.

LONDON
SWEET & MAXWELL
1996

Second Edition 1988
Third Edition 1996

Published in 1996 by
Sweet & Maxwell Limited
of 183, Marsh Wall, London E14 9FT
Computerset by Interactive Sciences Ltd, Gloucester
Printed in Great Britain by
Hartnolls Ltd, Bodmin

No natural forests were destroyed to make this product; only farmed timber
was used and re-planted.

ISBN 0 421 43260 8

A CIP Catalogue record for this book is available from the British Library.

Foreword

By

Sir Desmond Heap, LL.M., Hon. LL.D.

Once upon a time there lived a lady and her name was Teresa Gorman. (Come to think of it, it still *is* her name because she is, happily, still with us, "once upon a time" being merely an evocative way of beginning a Foreword; or so I like to think!). Mrs Teresa Gorman is also an M.P.; she sits for the Parliamentary Constituency of Billericay in Essex. Mrs Gorman achieved much publicity earlier this year when it was revealed that she and her husband had bought, for a considerable sum, a very old house called Old Hall Farm in Essex which Mrs Gorman had then proceeded, at further great expense, to repair (because it was some 300 years old and in bad shape) improve, restore and thoroughly up-date in order to render it fit for modern living by no less an occupant than the Honourable Member for Billericay.

For all of this Mrs Teresa Gorman found herself facing some 66 prosecutions in a Magistrates' Court for some 66 alleged offences under the Planning Acts of 1990. Why was this so? The answer is simple; Mrs Gorman, when she bought Old Hall Farm and (more importantly) when she proceeded to modernise it, did not realise that she was tampering with "a Grade II Listed Building." What a pity! If only the lady had first purchased and then carefully read a copy of Mr Roger Suddard's and Miss June Hargreaves eloquent and informative book on "Listed Buildings" she would have known better.

Mrs Gorman's case shows just how easy it is for property buyers and developers to run into deep trouble with the law, with quite dire consequences (including heavy fines and terms of imprisonment), when they start tinkering with a listed building. The Planning (Listed Buildings and Conservation Areas) Act 1990 is no arcane piece of legislation; it is a lively Parliamentary Pronouncement greatly to be reckoned with.

And that is exactly what Mr Roger Suddards and Miss June Hargreaves now do in this, their Third Edition of his popular work on Listed Buildings. Their Third Edition is both timely and welcome because the battle to achieve a fair balance between the past, the present and the future of our built environment continues with increased spate. It is a battle between the entrepreneurs who want more and more cleaned and boned sites on which they can make new beginnings and those who rely on the comfort of the known, the familiar, the urban scene as they have understood it, man and boy, for I simply don't know how many years. Both sides should have copies of this Third Edition which I warmly commend to their attention. They should read, mark, learn and inwardly digest the contents of this New Edition. It is true that, after doing all this, they may well be none the wiser but they will, at least, be better informed and their clashing arguments (sometimes passionate, sometimes intemperate) may thereby benefit from the opportunity of being conducted in a cooler and more informed climate of opinion.

Earlier this week Mr John Major, the Prime Minister, won his political battle to retain his place in Parliament. On Wednesday last, July 5, 1995, he made a radical reshuffle of his Cabinet. Amongst other changes Mrs Virginia Bottomley, after six years as Health Secretary, becomes the new National Heritage Secretary. As Secretary for Health Mrs Bottomley would not lift a little finger to save Bart's Hospital in London, founded by the medieval monk Rahere some 800 years ago, from destruction as a hospital.

It will be interesting (will it not?) to see if she will now, as Heritage Secretary, fight tooth and nail to preserve the old place as a Grade I Listed Building. Like Mrs Gorman, Mrs Bottomley should have a copy of Mr Roger Suddard's and Miss June Hargreaves Third Edition for which I wish all good fortune and success; it deserves no less in these taxing and testing days for the built environment.

The Atheneam,
Pall Mall,
London.
July 8, 1995.

Preface

To be writing a Preface is like leaving for a holiday. This third edition of Listed Buildings has taken so long and has become so much larger that I feel as if I need a holiday! The intention remains the same—to present in one book a comprehensive statement of the law and the practice relating to historic buildings, be they listed, in a conservation area, or be they ancient monuments. The law is stated as at today—January 1, 1995, with occasional later minor amendments. I hope we have achieved that accurately.

The task has been the easier—and I am sure the resolution has been made more sure—by the co-option as a co-author of June Hargreaves, a Chartered Town Planner and formerly the Assistant City Planning Officer of York. I have had not merely the skills of the enormous experience of June, but also her enthusiasm of the subjects. This has been wonderful and I have no doubt that if we persuade her to take over the editorship of the next edition, she will produce a splendid new version.

But my thanks in no way are limited. So many people have been involved in this edition. As with the first two editions, my former secretary, Beryl Hull, has done a wonderful job. She has typed out the whole of the draft but invited so many corrections and improvements that I am greatly indebted to her. My thanks, also, must go to Ian Beesley, who has taken two wonderful photographs for the front and inside covers of the book.

My colleagues in the production of this book have been so helpful and made so many suggestions which have become reality. David Hicken, a Chartered Town Planner in Maidstone, Kent, has produced an invaluable chapter on problem operations and features; it is so good to have another practical town planner with such an interest in listed buildings being able to support the publication by very realistic suggestions. His long experience in both local government and private practice is a great assistance to us.

I was very sad that in the intervening years between the second and this edition my old friend, Philip Hardman of Grant Thornton, has died. In his place, however, there has emerged Chris R. Allen, FCA, who practices as a principal in a VAT consultancy service from Headington in Oxford. Chris has written the invaluable VAT chapter, which is so important as a subject in considering listed buildings.

Our colleagues have been very helpful in this edition. Two solicitors from the firm of Hammond Suddards have been much involved: Richard Wade-Smith and Mrs. Shona Emmott. We have been very grateful for their help. It was also very helpful to have the services of a solicitor, Neil K. Stanley, and a legal assistant Tim J. Ratledge, who were both involved in the early research with this book. The work of Peter Wilbraham now as principal of his firm in Leeds has been very useful in this edition, for which we are most grateful.

Finally, we must thank once again that great authority of town planning law—Sir Desmond Heap—who has read this draft edition and contributed again such useful thoughts and a welcome Foreword, for which we are immensely grateful.

I have had the benefit of being a Commissioner of English Heritage: this has been so very helpful. We were sad to lose from English Heritage the services of Miss Jennifer Page, CBE, the Chief Executive, who has done so much for heritage generally. Her influence and that of the Chairman, Mr. Jocelyn Stevens, have been of enormous value to me, and I am most grateful to them and the many members of English Heritage for their encouragement.

But finally, to my dear wife, who has put up with it all once again. Without her patience and understanding I would neither have started nor finished this volume.

January 1, 1995

Roger W. Suddards
Salts Mill,
Saltaire,
Bradford.

Contents

6. Problem Operations and Features—The Nuts and Bolts of Listed Building and Conservation Area Control

7. "Problem Buildings": Redundancy, Neglect and Disrepair

8. Ancient Monuments and Archaeology

9. Value Added Tax—("VAT")

10. Churches

11. Rights of Entry

Table of Cases

Table of Statutes

[References in **bold** type indicate where the text of the statute is printed]

Table of Statutory Instruments

Table of Circulars

Table of Abbreviations

AAI	Areas of Archaeological Importance
AHF	Architectural Heritage Fund
AMAAA	Ancient Monuments and Archaeological Areas Act
CAC	Conservation Area Consent
CLA	Community Land Act
CPO	Compulsory Purchase Order
DAC	Diocesan Advisory Committee
DNH	Department of National Heritage
DOE	Department of the Environment
GDO	General Development Order
GPDO	General Permitted Development Order
H.P.A.	Housing and Planning Act
ICOMOS	International Council on Monuments and Sites
ICUN	World Conservation Union
LBA	Planning (Listed Buildings and Conservation Areas) Act
LBC	Listed Building Consent
LCA	Land Compensation Act
LGA	Local Government Act
LGPLA	Local Government, Planning and Land Act
LPA	Local Planning Authority
NALGO	National Association of Local Government Officers
NHMF	National Heritage Memorial Fund
PCA	Planning and Compensation Act
PCC	Parochial Church Council
PPG	Planning Policy Guidance Note
RCHME	Royal Commission on the Historical Monuments of England
RFAC	Royal Fine Art Commission
RTPI	Royal Town Planning Institute
SPZ	Simplified Planning Zone
T.C.A.A.	Town and Country Amenities Act
T.C.P.A.	Town and Country Planning Act
T.C.P.(A.)A.	Town and Country Planning (Amendment) Act
UDC	Urban Development Corporation
UDP	Unitary Development Plans
UNESCO	United Nations Educational, Scientific and Cultural Organisation
VAT	Value Added Tax
V.A.T.A.	Value Added Tax Act
WHS	World Heritage Site

Planning Policy Guidance Notes

1. Introduction

This book is still concerned with two closely interrelated subjects: the **1.01** statutory basis for the protection and preservation of what is generally termed our "built heritage"; and the practical consequences and effects of the application of those statutory provisions. But first, however, we must set the scene. What, in terms of statute, is our "built heritage"?

On the basis of the King's grave exhortation to the White Rabbit to "begin at the beginning . . . and go on till you come to the end, then stop",[1] we may best attempt to answer this question by examining briefly the chronological development of statutory protection for "heritage conservation" in the United Kingdom. We start with ancient monuments.

It was not until the latter part of the last century that the desirability of protecting and preserving ancient buildings and structures, or their remains, was generally recognised. William Morris took the first really positive steps in this direction by founding the Society for the Protection of Ancient Buildings in 1877, but it was not until 1882 that the first measure of statutory protection was afforded. The Ancient Monument Protection Act of that year marked the start of such protective measures, even though the immediate effects of that Act were only to give the protection of law to 29 such monuments in England and Wales, and 21 in Scotland.[2] Others were added later, as the Schedule which the Act provided for was gradually compiled.

One hundred and thirteen years, nine Acts of Parliament on ancient monuments, and some 13,000 scheduled ancient monuments later, section 61 of the Ancient Monuments and Archaeological Areas Act 1979 provides us with the current definition of what constitutes a monument, and may therefore qualify as an ancient monument:

   (a) any building, structure or work, whether above or below the surface of the land, and any cave or excavation;

   (b) any site comprising the remains of any such building, structure or work or any cave or excavation; and

   (c) any site comprising or comprising the remains of any vehicle, vessel, aircraft or other moveable structure or part thereof which neither constitutes nor forms part of any work which is a monument within paragraph (a) above;

and any machinery attached to a monument shall be regarded as part of a monument if it could not be detached without being dismantled.[3]

---

[1] *Alice's Adventures in Wonderland:* The Trial—"Alice's Evidence".
[2] Sched. to the 1882 Act.
[3] AMAAA 1979, s.61(7).

1.02   A monument may include the site of a monument, or a group of monuments or any part of a monument or group of monuments.[4]

Thus, virtually any edifice may be a monument, although the protection of the law is only actually afforded to those monuments which professional—and, theoretically, public—opinion regards as in some way important to the understanding of our historical, architectural, cultural and, more recently, technological heritage.

The concept of protecting buildings in more or less daily use for essentially historic or aesthetic reasons is of more recent origin. The 1882 Act, and its successors in 1931, 1953 and 1979[5] were mainly concerned with "unoccupied" buildings and structures: henges, castles, bridges, ruins and like structures of essentially antique and historical importance. It was not until 1932 that the desirability of statutory protection for buildings which were, generally, in use, and of architectural or historic interest, found currency in law, and even then, as demonstrated in Chapter 2, powers were discretionary rather than mandatory. As we will see, it has taken subsequent Acts to bring the art of historic building conservation to its present all-embracing level, in which we have approaching 500,000 assorted buildings subject to various measures of statutory protection under the listed buildings legislation.

The definition of what constitutes a building suitable for listing is as broad as that for a monument: a building may be anything from a street lamp to a railway viaduct, a horse trough to a textile mill; what may be a listed building depends on criteria (considered in detail in Chapter 2) which cover almost any "building" at least 10 years old and which is for the identification and protection of historic buildings, conservation areas, and other elements of the historic environment.[6]

1.03   It will be apparent from the foregoing that the statutory provisions for the protection of "buildings of special architectural or historic interest" find their ancestry in the statutory provisions for "ancient monuments", and it is not therefore surprising that it is possible for a building or structure to be both a "scheduled monument" and a "listed building", a potentially confusing situation bearing in mind the complexities of both statutory codes. The Secretary of State for the Environment, however, does not regard it as a significant problem and has indeed seen fit to give guidance on the subject, in Circular 8/87, which, although largely out of date, still has the essential messages:

> **"Overlap between listing of historic buildings and scheduling of ancient monuments**
>
> 49.   Section 1 of the Ancient Monuments and Archaeological Areas Act 1979, as amended by the National Heritage Act 1983, gives to the Secretary of State the duty of compiling a Schedule of Ancient Monuments of National Importance by virtue of their historic, architectural, traditional or archaeological interest. The Secretary of State must consult with the [English Heritage] before adding or removing any monu-

---

[4] *Ibid.* s.61(10). There are also exceptions: s.61(8) (referred to also at para. 8.03) and additional provisions regarding land required for the support and preservation of a monument s.61(9).

[5] See Chap. 8.

[6] PPG 15 (September 1994), para. 1.

ment to or from the Schedule. The great majority of scheduled ancient monuments are archaeological sites or monuments, whose importance resides in their buried archaeological deposits as well as any standing remains and they are located frequently in agricultural land in the countryside. A further large category within the Schedule are ruins or buildings for which there is often no present-day, readily-apparent economic use.

50. Some buildings are both scheduled and listed. However, section 56(1)(b) of the 1971 Act[7] provides that the legislative controls relating to listed buildings do not apply to buildings which are 'for the time being included in the Schedule of Monuments compiled under section 1 of the Ancient Monuments and Archaeological Areas Act 1979.' Buildings in ecclesiastical use and occupied dwelling houses cannot be scheduled, but some agricultural buildings, such as medieval barns or dovecotes, are both scheduled and listed, as are some bridges, urban buildings (e.g. market halls or guildhalls) and, to an increasing extent, industrial monuments, where close control of work is necessary. The selection of monuments for scheduling is based upon a concept of national importance, and in 1983 the Secretary of State published non-statutory criteria to guide selection. Within the framework of this guide the 'Commission' is now committed to a continuous review and expansion of the Schedule, but even an enlarged Schedule is likely to include but a small proportion of the currently known archaeological sites and monuments".

The most recent concept in heritage conservation takes the process **1.04** started in 1882 to what may reasonably be assumed to be a logical conclusion: the recognition of the aesthetic and historic value of whole areas of buildings and the spaces which they enclose or which provide their setting. From 1963 it has been accepted within listed building law that buildings could be listed because of their "group value", rather than on the basis of solely individual architectural or historic merit. As we will see in Chapter 3, this practice remained unchallenged in the courts until 1964, when the Earl of Iveagh questioned the legal validity of group listing, and the Court of Appeal ultimately held that such listing was valid, even though expressing doubt as to whether the Town and Country Planning Act 1947 provisions were adequate for their purpose.[8]

A direct consequence was Duncan-Sandys'—later Lord Duncan-Sandys—Civic Amenities Act 1967, which brought into the statutes the concept of conservation areas, in which whole groups of buildings and their immediate environment could be "designated" and afforded protection similar to that covering listed buildings. In the same way that subsequent amendments to the provisions of the 1947 Act have refined the measures of protection afforded to individual listed buildings, the Civic Amenities Act 1967 was quite speedily updated—and indeed replaced—by subsequent Planning Acts which tied conservation area practice even more closely to listing and listed buildings practice.

Paragraph 2.1 of Planning Policy Guidance Note 15 ("PPG 15") referred to

[7] Superseded by Section 18 of the LBA 1990.
[8] *Iveagh (Earl of) v. Minister of Housing and Local Government* [1964] 1 Q.B. 395; [1963] 3 All E.R. 817.

the fact that "The protection of the historic environment, whether individual listed buildings, conservation areas, parks and gardens, battlefields or the wider historic landscape, is a key aspect of these wider environmental responsibilities, and will need to be taken fully into account both in the formulation of authorities' planning policies and its development control."

The criteria by which any area may be judged worthy of designation as a conservation area are in a sense more simple than those by which ancient monuments are scheduled or buildings listed. They are, however, equally broad in their scope, a further indication of the inter-relationship and common ancestry of the three codes. Conservation areas may be any:

> "areas of special architectural or historic interest, the character or appearance of which it is desirable to preserve or enhance."[9]

Such areas may or may not contain listed buildings or scheduled monuments; if they do, then the codes concerning such buildings and monuments continue to operate in respect of the structures concerned. Here at least there is no potential for conflict, and the various powers effectively complement one another.

1.05   There is, however, one significant difference. Whereas the scheduling of monuments and the listing of buildings is a function which may only be exercised by the Secretary of State, the designation of conservation areas is essentially a local authority function, with the Secretary of State having solely reserve powers, and only requiring to be notified of designations.

Every local authority shall from time to time determine which parts of its area are areas of special architectural or historic interest, the character or appearance of which it is desirable to preserve or enhance, and shall designate those areas as conservation areas. The provisions of section 69 of the Listed Buildings Act 1990 follows from such determination.

Perhaps the major event of the early 1980s in the management of our architectural heritage has been the formation of the Historic Buildings and Monuments Commission for England.[10] Known popularly as English Heritage, this body was set up by the National Heritage Act 1983 and its general duties are to secure and promote the preservation and enhancement of ancient monuments, historic buildings and conservation areas in England; also to promote the public's enjoyment and awareness of such. [Throughout this book the Historic Buildings and Monuments Commission is referred to as "English Heritage", except where the distinction needs to be clearly drawn between it and other bodies, e.g. the Royal Commission on Historical Monuments (England).[11]]

Most of the English Heritage's specific functions were taken over from the Secretary of State for the Environment (but later certain functions were transferred to the Secretary of State for National Heritage) and include the management and preservation of many buildings and monuments, making grants for their upkeep and repair, acquiring or assuming guardianship of certain sites, advising the Secretary of State on listing and on applications made or referred to the Secretary of State to carry out certain works, carrying out and recording the results of research and archaeological investigation, and providing educational facilities.

---

[9] Listed Buildings Act 1990 (s.69(1)).
[10] See also para. 8.33 which also indicates the position in Scotland and Wales.
[11] See e.g. para. 8.33.

It is essential to remember that the Secretaries of State retain overall **1.06** financial control, responsibility for broad policy matters, and his quasi-judicial function. Many of the functions of the Secretary of State may now only be carried out after advice from or on the recommendation of English Heritage. We note throughout the book where such advice must be sought.

Since the start of English Heritage in 1984, various new projects have come into being under its auspices, *e.g.* the power to compile a register of historic gardens. The decisions of English Heritage are made and its activities carried on in consultation with the Ancient Monuments Advisory Committee and the Historic Buildings Advisory Committee.

English Heritage superseded the Historic Buildings Council for England and the Ancient Monuments Board for England, although the corresponding bodies for Wales and for Scotland remain in being.

In January 1995 there were in England a total number of 447,043 listed buildings (of which 11,600 were Grade I), 15,427 scheduled ancient monuments and 8,315 designated conservation areas.

Since the last edition of this book we have the benefit of a new set of Acts of Parliament, which largely restated the provisions of the Government in listed buildings legislation. The Town and Country Planning Act 1990 sets out the principal provisions of the legislation dealing with the planning authorities, the creation and evaluation of development plans—with structure and local plans for non-metropolitan areas, control over development, compensation for the effects of certain orders, notices, etc., rights of owners to require purchase of interests, interests affected by planning proposals, blight, enforcement and special controls such as trees, amenity, and advertisements.

The final chapters of the Act deal with advertisements, acquisition and **1.07** appropriation of land for planning purposes, highways, statutory undertakers, validity, and the application of the Act to Crown Land.

The Planning (Listed Buildings and Conservation Areas) Act 1990 deals with listing, authorisation of works affecting listed buildings, rights of owners, enforcement, prevention of deterioration and damage, conservation areas, and many incidental matters such as the rights of authorities exercising functions under the Act.

Included in the Listed Buildings and Conservation Areas Act were provisions for rights of entry, financial provisions and legislation as to buildings formerly subject to building preservation orders, lapse of building preservation notices, determination of appeals, and the Conservation Area code. The Planning (Hazardous Substances) Act 1990 gave a complete code in respect of hazardous substances. The Planning (Consequential Provisions) Act 1990 provide the substance of the consolidated law dealing with *e.g.* repeals, consequential amendments, and so on relating to the consolidation. It also deals with consequential amendments to the principal Acts.

The Planning and Compensation Act 1991 is a major Act giving new enforcement powers, changes relating to enforcement, control over development, and particular matters such as mines and waste, old planning permissions, trees, listed buildings, conservation areas and hazardous substances. It also deals with development plans and simplified planning zones, and land compensation provisions. It has a major tidying up provision in respect of the previous legislation.

A brief comment should perhaps be made as to the differences in historic building control procedure followed in England, Wales and Scotland. It has already been mentioned[12] that the jurisdiction of English Heritage does not extend to Scotland or Wales, but that these two countries have their own corresponding bodies (as indeed they always had) carrying out similar and co-ordinating functions. The law and practice relating to historic buildings is the same in England and Wales for all practical purposes; and in Scotland too, although, as regards the legislation, variations in detail will be found set out in the statutes, to which reference should be made as necessary.

1.08 The previous DOE Circular 14 of 1985 (paragraph 3.3) mentioned the need for:

" . . . a planning system that works efficiently and effectively, and strikes the right balance between the needs of development and the interests of conservation. It is not to be regarded simply as a means of preventing change."

It is probable that many people do regard historic building controls in this very light, described by Lady Birk as a "pickling policy."[13] Paragraph 3.4 of the circular continues:

"If the planning authority considers it necessary to refuse permission, the onus is on them to demonstrate clearly why the development cannot be permitted and the reasons must be precise, specific and relevant to the application,"

which as a principle applies as much to consents for historic buildings as to general planning permissions.

Are we going too far? A cautionary note was sounded by the former Secretary of State for the Environment, the late Nicholas Ridley, in January 1988, when he said in a speech to the National Association of Conservation Graduates[14]:

"I have a recurring nightmare, that sometime in the next century the entire country will be designated under some conservation order or other. The people actually living there will be smothered with bureaucratic instructions limiting their freedom. We will have created a sanitised, bureaucratised and ossified countryside out of something which has always been, and should always be, a product of the interaction of man and his environment as time goes by."

We are a far cry from the 50 scheduled monuments in 1882. The process of arriving, however, has been, and is, complex, as we will see.

---

[12] See para. 1.06.
[13] Baroness Birk, Parliamentary Under-Secretary of State at the Department of the Environment, opening address at the Oxford Conference 1976, in *Journal of Planning and Environment Law (J.P.L.)*, Occasional Papers (1977), p. 5.
[14] Reported in *Planning Bulletin*, January 8, 1988.

2. Listing

1. GENERAL SUMMARY

Central to planning is a plan; central to listing is the list. The crux is section 1(1) of the LBA 1990 which provides: **2.01**

> "For the purposes of this Act and with a view to the guidance of local planning authorities in the performance of their functions under this Act and the principal Act[1] in relation to buildings of special architectural or historic interest, the Secretary of State shall compile lists of such buildings, or approve, with or without modifications, such lists compiled by the Historic Buildings and Monuments Commission for England (in this Act referred to as "the Commission") or by other persons or bodies of persons, and may amend any list so compiled or approved."

There are no lists compiled by other bodies which have been approved by the Secretary of State: thus the list with which we are presently concerned is the list compiled by the Secretary of State. It is central government (*i.e.*

---

[1] The Town and Country Planning Act 1990.

7

the Department of National Heritage),[2] and not local government, which has the responsibility of listing, although in practice many local authorities encourage central government to place on the list buildings with which they are particularly concerned. Some local authorities and private consultant firms have helped to revise existing lists at the request of and under the supervision of officers of the Department of National Heritage.

The list is not one long document, but a series of lists based on towns or counties. Each list refers to a particular local authority area and is often broken down into parishes, and each list is divided normally in street alphabetical order, although sometimes (but not often) in grade order. Buildings included in the list are divided according to their status. Grade I relates to buildings of outstanding architectural or historic interest (although this grade is sometimes referred to being of particularly great importance to the nation's built heritage, or containing buildings of exceptional interest or outstanding interest or outstanding quality); Grade I contains 11,600 buildings; Grade II contains buildings of "special architectural or historic interest which warrant every effort being made to save them", but many Grade II buildings are of humble and once common building types and have been listed precisely because they are relatively unaltered examples of a particular building type.[3] Particularly important buildings in this section are classified as Grade II*. The grading of a building will affect the grants available to it.

2.02   The procedure for listing a building is described in detail later, but listing is an order made by the Secretary of State and when the civil service head of the branch concerned (being duly authorised to sign on behalf of the Secretary of State) signs and dates the list that, in effect, constitutes the listing.

Buildings appear on the list by one of three methods; first as a result of normal procedures following the methodical re-survey of the country by English Heritage investigators. The second is an expedited procedure: spot listing. Spot listing is in particular used for buildings which appear to be in immediate danger of being demolished. The DOE (and now the DNH) claim that it can spot list a building in less than 24 hours if it is satisfied that it falls into the category of being of "special architectural or historic interest". The third method is as a result of the service by a local planning authority of a building preservation notice in respect of a building which is subsequently added to the list; as to which see paragraph 2.04 below.

The Secretary of State has outlined his policy on conservation to be one of preserving buildings and areas of architectural or historic interest as a fundamental aspect of the Government's commitment to environmental stewardship.[4]

Spot listing is not always thought to be fast enough. This was demon-

---

[2] The Department of National Heritage (DNH) was created in April 1992. The responsibility for the listing of historic buildings passed from the DOE to the DNH in July 1992. (The Transfer of Functions (National Heritage) Order 1992)—with details of working arrangements contained in DOE Circular 10/92. Controls over works to historic buildings (listed buildings consents) and over the demolition of unlisted buildings in conservation areas (conservation area consent) remains the responsibility of the Secretary of State for the Environment. There is close co-operation between the DNH and DOE English Heritage acts as adviser to both departments. *DOE News Release* 294, May 1, 1992.

[3] PPG 15, p. 3.10.

[4] See generally PPG 15, para. 1.1.

strated by the demolition, before the DOE had a chance to protect it through spot listing, of the 1930s Firestone factory in Brentford. The demolition occurred over the August Bank Holiday weekend in 1980, and the mechanics of spot listing could not be brought into action because of the holiday.[5] A spokesman for the DOE criticised Hounslow Borough Council for not issuing a building preservation notice in respect of the building.[6] Sometimes spot listing can be too fast and there is evidence of a building being spot listed following local public pressure which it was subsequently felt did not pass the basic test and was then almost immediately deleted from the list.[7]

As a result of the Brentford case, the then Secretary of State for the Environment announced that he was determined to review the listing procedure to see where improvement might be made: "I have no intention of standing by while buildings of the inter-war period are destroyed without very careful consideration being given to the possibility of preserving them."[8] As a result specific provisions relating to twentieth-century buildings are included in PPG 15 and subsequent advice[9]; paragraph 6.11 of PPG 15 deals with selectivity for the listing of buildings of the post-war period. Already the Secretary of State has listed a number of important twentieth century buildings, including Battersea Power Station, the Stratford upon Avon Memorial Theatre, the Roman Catholic Cathedral in Liverpool, the Hoover factory in West London[10] and the Craven Cottage stands at Fulham Football Club.[11]

In 1993 English Heritage launched a new initiative of surveying post- **2.03** 1939 buildings, type by type.[12] The first group was based on schools and universities and 47 buildings were accepted by the DNH as being candidates for listing. In March 1993 the total number of post-war listed buildings (and groups) of all types in England had reached 79. Among the educational buildings included in the list were the Engineering building at Leicester University 1961–63 (Grade II*) and the Smithdon Secondary School, Hunstanton 1950–54 (Grade II*); both controversial buildings in their time. Some of the buildings in this post-war collection of additions to the list received Grade I status, namely St Catherine's College, Oxford (1960–61) and Falmar House, Sussex University (1960–62).

English Heritage next looked at buildings in the commercial/industrial categories, and is proceeding to examine public and private housing, health care and churches, entertainment and culture, transport and communications, public buildings, military and naval buildings and planned towns.

The methodical re-survey of the country by English Heritage as the Government's statutory advisers has been carried out over 10 years and is largely completed. The number of buildings now on the list is nearing 500,000. Although the re-survey is completed, that is not to say that all buildings of a listable quality are included. Not only are there omissions of

---

[5] (1980) 255 E.G. 851.
[6] *The Sunday Telegraph*, August 31, 1980.
[7] Cottages at White Row, Acomb, York.
[8] Quotation from the Secretary of State, Michael Heseltine (1980).
[9] See paras. 2.37, 2.42 and 2.43 for discussion on listed modern buildings.
[10] *The Times*, October 15, 1980.
[11] *The Times*, March 25, 1987.
[12] *Conservation Bulletin*, July 1993, English Heritage.

buildings not brought to the attention of English Heritage or the Department of National Heritage, but fashions change: buildings at one time not thought to be of listable quality will be discovered. In part this may be as a result of the thematic surveys of post-war buildings (being carried out by English Heritage) partly as a result of spot listing and possibly by the use of the local authorities of the building preservation notices.

History of listing

2.04   The inter-relationship of the various codes has been dealt with in the previous chapter. It is essential to see in some detail the history of the list in order to be able to assess its correct status. The 1932 Planning Act gave local authorities power to make preservation orders for buildings of special architectural or historic interest, but each order had to be approved by the Minister, who had to consider representations of those involved. There were provisions for compensation for those affected by a preservation order. The 1944 Planning Act empowered the new Minister of Town and Country Planning to prepare lists of buildings of special architectural or historic interest, which lists were for the guidance of local authorities. These powers were strengthened in the 1947 Planning Act, when the Minister was placed under a duty to make lists, and the owners of property had merely to be notified of the inclusion of their buildings in such a list. There was no appeal against such listing, and no compensation if a building was listed. Demolition or works on a listed building could not be carried out without two months' notice to the local planning authority, and during that period the authority could serve a building preservation order. Such an order had to be confirmed by the Minister, and normally provided for the consent of the local planning authority to be obtained for the execution of any work specified in the order. The order also gave power to the authority to require the restoration of the building to its former state and created a criminal penalty for contravention of the order. Ecclesiastical buildings and ancient monuments were given special treatment.

As a result of the Town and Country Planning Act 1968 the procedure was again changed. The statutory list became in itself a building preservation order in respect of the buildings on it.[13] There was no need thereafter to have a building preservation order made by the local authority. There was introduced a provision whereby listed building consent (LBC) had to be applied for from a local planning authority in respect of works of demolition, alteration, or extension to a building on the list.[14] In respect of buildings which were not listed, there was a speedy procedure whereby a local planning authority could serve a building preservation notice which would have the effect of temporarily putting the building on the list and giving the local authority all the powers of the list in relation to that building until the issue was resolved.[15]

Those provisions were substantially re-enacted in the Town and Country Planning Act 1971 and again in the LBA 1990. They express in general terms the powers and consequences which we shall deal with later. There are the

---

[13] T.C.P.A. 1968, s.48.
[14] T.C.P.A. 1968, s.40(4)(a).
[15] T.C.P.A. 1968, s.48(1).

obvious corollaries of criminal offences[16] and powers of the local planning authority to require work to reinstate a building by the service of a document called a listed building enforcement notice.[17] These powers are exercised by the local planning authority (except where it, as a local authority, owns a building so affected) even though the list is in the control of the DNH.

In trying to ascertain what is the status of the list, one must remember **2.05** that there is no formal appeal against listing. There is power to amend the list,[18] and PPG 15[19] states that the Department will consider requests to remove buildings from the statutory list where new evidence can be produced to show that they do not possess the special architectural or historic interest ascribed to them. Whilst grounds for listing are given which will show broadly whether the reason for listing is architectural or historic, not all factors which lead the Department to list a building are specified.[20] It thus might be difficult to show that a building should be taken off the list. In February 1978 the Secretary of State, whilst conceding that to list a building "merely on the grounds that [it] was threatened" would be an excessive use of his powers, rejected an allegation that a bus garage in Norbiton had not been properly listed.[21] However, there are cases where the list has been amended by striking off entries where either there was a mistake of description, e.g. the wrong number of house, or where there has been a genuine misjudgment at listing stage. An example of such a misjudgment occurred in 1991 when the DOE accepted a request by English Heritage to spot list a redundant 1920s telephone exchange in Wood Street, London. The building had been listed in February 1991 as "the most outstanding example of an inter-war telephone exchange" [sic], but the owners' expert adviser was able to point to other examples which could be considered more important. English Heritage carried out a reassessment, and in July 1991 advised the Secretary of State that the building did not possess the special architectural or historic interest attributed to it at the time of listing.[22] The DOE admitted that a mistake had been made. The Wood Street exchange was de-listed and another exchange, Faraday House, designed by the same architect, A. W. Myers, in nearby Queen Victoria Street, was listed.[23]

The Odeon Cinema, Shepherd's Bush, was listed because of a clerical error, instead of the Liberty Cinema, Southall, the only art deco Chinese cinema in England.[24] In March 1980 Greater London Council wrote to the DOE about a building in Park Street, part of which had been listed, part of which had not. The DOE did not review the listing, but said that the original listing had been an administrative mistake and wrote to the Council

---

[16] LBA 1990, ss.7 and 9.
[17] LBA 1990, s.38.
[18] LBA 1990, s.1(1).
[19] Requests to de-list should be sent to the Listing Branch, the Department of National Heritage, 2–4 Cockspur Street, London SW1Y 5DH and requests to de-list should now be sent to that department, accompanied by photographs and a location plan.
[20] [1980] J.P.L. 715–719. See *Listed Buildings – Planning Law and Planning Realty* by DH Morgan and S.M. Nett.
[21] [1978] 245 E.G. 860.
[22] *Planning Law Practice*—Monthly Bulletin 1991.
[23] *The Independent*, July 3, 1991.
[24] *The Guardian*, September 3, 1980.

saying "the Department concludes that the building is not of special architectural or historic interest and should not have been included in the statutory list".[25] In 1988 the DOE listed as Grade II a "16th century house" at
Sea Palling in Norfolk. The DOE admitted later that this was a mistake as
the house had been built between 1983 and 1988, the roof having come from
a barn, lintels and doors from demolition sites and the bressumers over two
inglenook fireplaces retrieved from a scrapyard. Settlement had been "built
in". The inspector asserted that the building deserved its Grade II listing
"on the grounds of rarity and eccentricity, if not antiquity" but it ceased to
be listed.[26]

2.06   Where the Department accept a mistake or misjudgment has occurred, an
order will be made in similar form to an order listing a building, but deleting
the entry by amendment.

The "workable non-statutory right" of appeal against listing was referred
to in the House of Lords debate on the Bill which became the Housing and
Planning Act 1986.[27]

Lord Skelmersdale, on behalf of the Government, stated[28]:

> "The grounds of appeal are very limited. It is not a question of judgment
> or interpretation of a structure or local plan. It is a question of fact that
> has to be decided and can be decided without recourse to a full-blown
> appeals mechanism. I accept that there must always be an element of
> subjective judgment in the selection of buildings: but in practice, we
> find that appeals against listing are mostly based on matters of fact
> rather than interpretation."

In reviewing a listing the Department will ask an expert different from
the one who saw the property before listing to visit the property "in the
light of what the owner says about it. The Inspector will, if you wish, make
an appointment to see you when reviewing the case."

In answer to a Parliamentary question on March 16, 1984, it was revealed
that 392 listed buildings had had their status withdrawn in the five years to
December 1983 because either they had lost their qualifying features
through alteration, fire, etc., or their architectural or historic merits had
proved to have been misjudged, or they had been listed in error. These
figures have been updated and are annually as follows: 805 (1985), 451
(1986), 702 (1987), 318 (1988), 216 (1989), 188 (1990), 277 (1991), 213 (1992),
438 (1993) and 561 (1994).[29]

In some people's eyes there has developed, in effect, a *presumption* that
because a building is on the list it has a certain permanent quality of being
of "special architectural or historic interest". The use of the "presumption"
concept in departmental circulars has generated a considerable body of case
law and academic interest.[30] The concept is perhaps best understood as
defining the starting point from which consideration will be given to a
matter which requires a decision, rather than determining upon whom the
onus of proof shall fall.

[25] *Private Eye*, May 23, 1980.
[26] *The Times*, April 11, 1988.
[27] Lord Skelmersdale *Hansard*, Lords October 13, 1986, cols. 599 and 406 and Lord
Swinfen, *ibid.* col. 596.
[28] *Hansard*: House of Lords—October 13, 1986, cols. 406 and 599.
[29] *English Heritage Monitor* 1995.
[30] [1991] J.P.L. 175; [1991] J.P.L. 1014; [1992] J.P.L. 110; [1992] J.P.L. 121.

In recent years "listing" has been emphasised by estate agents as a desirable quality in certain houses, as opposed to its true function, which is a control mechanism. It is this approach to listing which guides members of the public into thinking that the list has a greater significance than it has. Looking at the threads of legislation from 1932 until the present date, it is clear that Parliament considers the list as a control mechanism and not as a definitive assessment of a quality judgment. Many conservationists believe that it should have this latter status, and indeed a SAVE report of December 1975 suggested that listed buildings should be presumed "innocent", and condemned only if an overwhelming case against them has been proved: "otherwise they should be discharged unconditionally". The burden of proof, they say, should rest with the applicant, who should be required to give reasons for demolition—the test should be "Why demolish?" not "Why save?" But the true position we believe was expressed by Lady Birk (sometime Under-Secretary of State for the DOE with a particular concern for listed buildings) who described the listing procedure as "not a pickling policy".[31]

The essential, although not the only, difference between the listing of a **2.07** building and the granting of LBC is the fact that financial considerations are not (nor in practice could they be) taken into account in listing; but these considerations should properly be taken into account in deciding whether or not to grant LBC.

The LBA does not provide a presumption to preserve a listed building, but the Department of the Environment (and now the DNH) has always maintained that there is such a presumption, which has had tacit assent by the House of Lords in the *Number 1 Poultry* case.[32] The House of Lords held that the policy set out in Circular 8/87 that listed building consent for demolition was not to be granted where a building was still capable of economic use, was not an absolute rule and could be overridden in special circumstances. The point about listing buildings was made forcibly in the Court of Appeal in the *John Walker and Sons Limited*[33] case, when Buckley L.J. said:

> "It seems to me that the risk of property being listed as property of architectural or historic interest is a risk which inheres in all ownership of buildings. In many cases it may be an extremely remote risk. In many cases it may be a marginal risk. In some cases it may be a substantial risk. But it is a risk I think which attaches to all buildings, and it is a risk that every owner and every purchaser of property must recognise that he is subject to."

The PPG 15 on Planning and the Historic Environment[34] reiterates the view that demolition of any listed building could not be expected to be granted consent without clear and convincing evidence that all reasonable efforts have been made to sustain existing uses or find viable new uses and these efforts have failed; or that redevelopment would produce substantial

---

[31] Baroness Birk, Parliamentary Under-Secretary of State at the Department of the Environment, Opening Address at the Oxford Conference 1976, in *Journal of Planning and Environment Law*, Occasional Papers (1977), p. 5.

[32] *Save Britain's Heritage v. No. 1 Poultry Ltd and Others.*

[33] *Amalgamated Investment and Property Co. v. Walker (John) and Sons* [1976] 2 All E.R. 509; 120 S.J. 252; [1976] E.G. 277, C.A.

[34] PPG 15, para. 3.13.

planning benefits for the community which would decisively outweigh the loss resulting from demolition.

Certain buildings are "deemed" to be listed. They fall into two categories, which can broadly be described as those buildings which were subject to an extant building preservation order under the earlier Planning Acts, unless and until the Secretary of State revokes that order,[35] and secondly those which are the subject of a building preservation notice served under the LBA 1990.[36]

There are now no buildings which cannot be listed,[37] but different consequences flow in respect of the listing of churches in ecclesiastical use, ancient monuments, and Crown property. Church buildings in use as such have their own code in respect of alteration and extension (but not total demolition)[38]; the ancient monument code overlaps to some extent in practice with the listed buildings code,[39] and there are special consequences for Crown property.[40]

Buildings cease to be listed when LBC to demolish has been granted, and fully implemented. However total demolition of a listed building of itself does not automatically cause the building to be removed from the statutory list. Where the parts still exist in a "reconstructible" state the building continues to be listed.[41] There is no authority for determining the exact moment at which the listing ceases to be of effect, but it is presumably the time when the last of conditions to be implemented has been fulfilled. There is no reason why buildings which have been moved successfully should not be re-listed, even though the building is not on the original site. Different issues may arise in a proposal to re-list a building which is listed for historic interest only.

2. ALTERNATIVE LEGISLATIVE PROCEDURES

2.08   In November 1988 the Kings Cross Railway Bill was published as a private parliamentary bill by the promoters, British Rail, and included within it clause 19: *viz*:

> "The provisions of this Act authorising the carrying out of the works ('works powers') shall have effect notwithstanding the provisions of:
> (a) the Town and Country Planning Act 1971 relating to listed buildings or conservation areas (within the meaning of that Act): and
> (b) the provisions of the enactments relating to historic buildings and ancient monuments;
> and section 42 of the Local Government (Miscellaneous Provisions) Act

---

[35] LBA 1990, s.1(6) and Sched. 1, para. 2.
[36] LBA 1990, s.3.
[37] See "10 year rule" in paras. 2.03 and 2.41–2.43.
[38] See —Chap. 10. on Churches.
[39] See Chap. 8: *Ancient Monuments*.
[40] See para. 5.29 below.
[41] See para. 5.38 below.

1976 . . . shall not apply to the extent that it would make the works powers subject to those provisions."

This clause sought to remove all listed buildings, conservation areas and ancient monuments control from a large site (97 acres) in the vicinity of St Pancras and Kings Cross railway stations, both of which are Grade I listed buildings, and affecting seven other listed buildings, all of which were included within a conservation area.

English Heritage has, since April 1986, taken over the conservation func- **2.09** tions of the former Greater London Council. It therefore has the responsibility of directing the various local planning authorities in London on how they should determine applications for listed building consent unless the authority has determined to refuse it.[42]

Clause 19 of the Kings Cross Railway Bill would have removed the powers of English Heritage in relation to this important site, and English Heritage took the view that it was wrong in principle for powers granted to statutory bodies by public legislation to be removed by subsequent private legislation. English Heritage therefore petitioned against the clause in two respects:

(i) to prevent a precedent being established, and
(ii) to offer as much conservation expertise as possible to the Parliamentary Committees (who would assess whether the works should be authorised), bearing in mind their time constraints.

Private parliamentary bills are governed by a tight timetable under the Standing Orders of the House of Commons (Private Business) which in turn sets out a restricted period within which petitions may be lodged. Such petitions are heard by the Court of Referees of the House of Commons. The procedures for lodging an opposing petition are explained in greater detail in an article on this particular subject in [1990] J.P.L. 633, by Margaret G. Scott.

The outcome of a long hearing of the Select Committee was contained in a Supplementary Report of the Secretary of State for the Environment on the Bill dated February 1, 1990. He saw merit in the promoters of the Bill not having to apply separately for listed building consent to demolish the buildings required, especially if it had been demonstrated to the Committee's satisfaction that their total demolition was essential to meet the operational requirements of the Bill. He was less happy with the possibility of alterations or partial demolition of listed buildings (especially the Grade I station buildings) without their detailed consideration by the local planning authority and English Heritage, with their expertise in conservation work.

The Secretary of State therefore asked the Select Committee to amend Clause 19 to reinstate listed building and conservation area controls to all works other than total demolition of buildings specifically authorised by the Bill, or, if the Committee did not consider this appropriate, to seek an undertaking from the promoters that they would consult the appropriate local planning authority and English Heritage on alterations, extensions, or partial demolition of listed buildings and partial demolition of buildings in conservation areas, and that the Secretary of State would arbitrate on any unresolved cases, after a public inquiry, if that proved necessary.

[42] s.14(1)(a) of LBA 1990.

2.10   In the event, on July 10, 1990, the Select Committee announced that Clause 19 was to be deleted from the Bill.[43]

The reasons for the deletion of the clause by the Select Committee were twofold:

(1) "the exemption from normal planning procedures conferred by the clause would have resulted in the function of [the] planning authority devolving upon Parliament, and in practice upon this Committee." The Committee did not consider that any committee of the House of Commons was likely to have the expertise to carry out such a task. It went on to say "a more unsatisfactory method of taking sensitive decisions on the architectural and historic merits of a large number of buildings cannot easily be imagined";

(2) "it would set a deplorable precedent". The promoters had argued that the need for the clause was necessary because of the sheer scale of the proposed demolition, which the Committee felt was an excellent reason for *retaining* the safeguards contained in the normal planning procedures. The Committee saw no justification in conferring by this means blanket powers to demolish a whole swathe of urban landscape, and considered that the enactment of Clause 19 would have placed in jeopardy the whole existing system of safeguards for listed buildings under the general law. It was further noted that whilst the promoters had given assurances that Clause 19 would not set a precedent, several similar clauses had already been included in private Bills deposited in that present parliamentary Session, and the Committee urged that these subsequent clauses which were open to the criticisms of Clause 19 should be deleted.

This is not a completely new innovation in planning terms, because planning development authorised by private Acts of Parliament had been granted permission by various General Development Orders since 1963, the latest of which is the Town and Country Planning (General Permitted Development) Order 1995—Article 3 and Schedule 2, Part II. Class A(a) and (b) of this Order grants permission, *inter alia*, for development authorised by: (a) a local or private Act of Parliament, and (b) an Order approved by both Houses of Parliament. The permission granted by this Development Order is conditional upon the prior approval of the local planning authority of detailed plans and specifications of the appropriate authority, where the development includes (a) the erection, construction, alteration or extension of any building, bridge, aquaduct, pier or dam, or (b) the formation, laying out or alteration of a means of access to any highway used by vehicular traffic.[44]

There has been concern, both inside and outside Parliament, that the private parliamentary Bill system might be open to abuse, and that promoters of such Bills might see the use of a private Bill as a speedier route to gaining planning permission, or listed building consent, than the normal route, which can involve a public inquiry. The Kings Cross Railway Bill was

---

[43] *Special Report on the Kings Cross Railways Bill*—Session 1989–90, paper 511—House of Commons, June 26, 1990.
[44] T.C.P. (General Permitted Development) Order 1995, Sch. 2, Part 11, Class A(a) and (b).

clearly an important case which caused the creation of a Joint Committee on Private Bill Procedure to examine this matter.[45]

The Joint Committee rejected the arguments to repeal this part of the **2.11** GDO, but recommended fundamental changes in the function of private legislation. These include a new order making procedure to be substituted to authorise railway and train works Bills which would involve a public inquiry with rules similar to those under other procedures where objectors have a right to be heard.

The Committee also considered the subject of precedent and concluded: "We cannot bind any future Committee on any Bill in this House, although no doubt careful note will be taken of everything which is and has been said and due notice will be given to promoters who may be bold enough to attempt to insert such a clause in future Bills." In rejecting the arguments put forward for Clause 19 of the Kings Cross Railways Bill because of the "sheer scale of demolition proposed", the Committee stated that "it may be that from time to time it will be expedient to authorise the demolition of particular listed buildings by means of private legislation . . . ."

The prediction of 1988 that Clause 19 would spawn other private Bills containing similar provisions was soon to be realised. Mainly, the private Bills to emerge following the "Kings Cross" case were related to London Underground.

In 1991 the Government set out criteria for a clause which would be acceptable to both Departments of the Environment and Transport, and which would be supported only in relation to schemes of national or strategic importance and in furtherance of government policies. These criteria were:

    (i) the Bill should contain details of the buildings which would be affected and in that way; blanket clauses would not be acceptable and the Committee should be satisfied that

    (ii) the specific proposals for identified buildings were essential to operational requirements and

    (iii) the views of English Heritage had been respected in so far as was reasonably practicable.[46]

English Heritage decided to maintain its opposition to a compromise **2.12** clause contained in the London Underground Bill in April 1991, on the grounds that the contents of the clause did not remove the original objections nor conform to the Government criteria.

In March 1992 the Transport and Works Bill received the Royal Assent and acknowledged the separate nature of listed building controls from the normal planning procedures. This Bill reached the statute book in 1992 and came into force on different days according to different purposes in 1992 and 1993. Under section 6 of the Act, rules made for the purposes of this section are supplemented, *inter alia*, by the Transport and Works Applications (Listed Buildings, Conservation Areas and Ancient Monuments Procedures) Regulations 1992[47] which specify the procedures to be followed where listed building consent or conservation area consent is required, and has been the subject of a separate application to the local planning authority; or

---

[45] *Session 1987–88*, House of Lords, Paper 97; House of Commons paper 625.
[46] Scott, "Article 2" (1992) J.P.L. p. 899.
[47] S.I., 1992, 3138.

scheduled monument consent is required and there has been no separate application to the Secretary of State.[48]

These regulations came into force on January 1, 1993 and make provision for the assimilation of the procedures and for making applications and holding inquiries where proposals contained in an application made under section 6 of the Transport and Works Act 1992 give rise to a requirement for one or more of the following consents:

(a) listed building consent or conservation area consent under the LBA 1990;

(b) scheduled monument consent under the Ancient Monuments and Archaeological Areas Act 1979.

These regulations modify the requirements of the LBA 1990 and the Ancient Monuments (Applications for Scheduled Monument Consent) Regulations 1981 as regards the documentation to be submitted with an application for the relevant consent and the publishing of notices in the local newspapers. They also make consequential amendments to the 1979 and 1990 Acts.[49]

3. WHAT MAY BE LISTED?

(a) The building

2.13   The answer to this question is set out in the LBA 1990, namely "a building which is of special architectural or historic interest", but we must first decide what is a building.

A building is not defined positively either in the LBA or in the principal Act, but negatively, by showing what is "included" in the definition of building, and not what is, in fact, "a building". It includes "any structure or erection and any part of a building as so defined but does not include any plant or machinery comprised in a building".[50] The Town and Country Planning (General Permitted Development) Order 1995, Article 1(2) gives no positive guidance and merely follows the Act. Section 121(1) of the Building Act 1984 defines "building" for the purposes of Building Regulations as any permanent or temporary building, which includes any other structure or erection of whatever kind or nature; "structure or erection" including a vehicle, vessel, hovercraft, aircraft or other moveable object in certain prescribed circumstances, and "building" includes part of a building.

There are two statutory provisions dealing with the extent of a listed building. The first and most obvious is that laid down in section 1(5) of the LBA 1990:

---

[48] *The Times*, November 19, 1994, published notice of the Channel Tunnel Rail Link Bill. Clause 6 deals with LBA 1990 and Ancient Monuments and Archaeological Areas Act 1979 and NHA 1983; another example of the use of the Private Bill procedure.

[49] *The Transport and Works Applications* (Listed Buildings, Conservation Areas and Ancient Monuments Procedure) Regulations 1992 (S.I. 1992 no. 3138) [J.P.L. 1993, p. 214].

[50] T.C.P.A. 1990, s.336.

18

"In this Act 'listed building' means a building which is for the time being included in a list compiled or approved by the Secretary of State under this section; and for the purpose of this Act—

(a) any object or structure fixed to the building;

(b) any object or structure within the curtilage of the building which, although not fixed to the building, forms part of the land and has done so since before 1 July, 1948,

shall be treated as part of the building."

This is the statutory definition which must be followed in deciding whether a particular item is part of a listed building.

It is, however, worth emphasising that whilst a post 1948 addition to a building is regarded as part of the listing, it is only post 1948 structures within the curtilage of the building and not fixed to it that were excluded from the listing by Schedule 9, paragraph 1, of the Housing and Planning Act 1986 and now re-enacted under section 1(5)(b) of the LBA 1990.

In defining the term "building" section 91(2) of the LBA refers to section **2.14** 336(1) of the principal Act:

" 'building' includes any structure or erection, and any part of a building, as so defined, but does not include plant or machinery comprised in a building."

The *Oxford English Dictionary* defines "building" as "that which is built, a structure, edifice".

What is or is not within the definition of a "building" has been a matter concerning the judges for well over a century. Byles J. in 1859 asked:

"What is 'a building'? Now the verb 'to build' is often used in a wider sense than the substantive 'building' . . . The imperfection of human language renders it not only difficult, but absolutely impossible, to define the word 'building' with any approach to accuracy . . . I may venture to suggest, that, by a 'building' is usually understood a structure of considerable size, and intended to be permanent, or at least to endure for a considerable time."[51]

The judges have determined from time to time what is or is not a building in interpreting various statutes, and they have given *obiter* opinions on the subject. A summary of some of these decisions in section 2.15 below gives some further illustration to the suggestion of Byles J., but these lists are not intended to be comprehensive. It should also be remembered that if the edifice is not a building as such, it might fall within the definition of a structure or erection.

The identity of a listed building may be established by looking at the list **2.15** description. It is important to note that the brief description of a listed building given in the statutory list will *not* contain an exhaustive reference to all features of architectural or historic interest which form part of the listed building. The whole building, whatever its grade, is listed, including the interior. Sometimes curtilage buildings or objects (for example stables or garden features) are listed in their own right, but the fact that, for example, the description does not refer to features such as statuary, must not be taken as indication that such features are not protected by the listing. We suggest that it might be helpful for readers to approach the interpret-

---

[51] *Stevens v. Gourley* [1859] 7 CB (NS) 99 at 112 per Byles J.

ation of section 1(5) of the LBA in a logical fashion by answering the following questions:

(i) Is the edifice an "object or structure?". If it is not, then that is conclusive.

(ii) If the edifice is an "object or structure", is it fixed to the listed building?

(iii) If the edifice is an "object or structure" but is not fixed to the listed building, has it been within the curtilage of the listed building from before July 1, 1948?

Examples of edifices (to use a neutral word) thought to be a building have included a church, a cowhouse; a structure nine feet long, seven feet high, three feet wide, erected some 30 feet in front of the line of street roofed in and fastened securely to the ground; a wooden screen of open trellis work, a hoarding of a permanent nature 156 feet long and 15 feet high for bill posting, statues and monuments, farm walls not appurtenant to farm buildings or used in connection with them; a bandstand where variety entertainments were provided, a model village, a viaduct, and a temporary building.

Edifices thought not to be a building have included a bird cage, a dog-kennel, a hen-coop, a fence or barrier to prevent the acquisition of prescriptive rights to light, a canal, a bank composed of consolidated earth and covered with grass which has kept out the sea for 2,000 years, four walls erected one foot high, and an incomplete structure.

Whilst the principal Act and LBA do not provide a positive definition, a combination of the definitions found in those Acts, the above interpretations by the Courts, and the commentary in PPG 15 give a clearer idea certainly of what the Department regards as a "building" which may be helpful until the matter is authoritatively decided by the Courts.

2.16   If we can define what is a building, we then need to turn our attention to what buildings can be listed:

(a) In the definitions section, section 336 of the principal Act, "building" includes any structure or erection, and any part of a building, as so defined, but does not include plant or machinery comprised in a building.

(b) There is an interesting argument that a "listed building" is a generic term, unrelated to the definition of "a building" as such. Whilst there may be some merit in this argument, we do not consider that it is persuasive. A listed building must first be "a building".

(c) Circular 8/87 gave a list in paragraph VII:2 of items which might be listed, such as:

"Gazebos, temples, follies, grottoes, obelisks, park bridges, statues, urns, vases, ice houses, terraces, ha-ha's, crinkle-crankle walls and boundary walls and gates and gate piers all contribute to the planned landscape and setting." This collection is not repeated in PPG 15.

(d) In PPG 15, advice is given in Annex C on the type of free standing objects which may be regarded as fixtures if they were put in place as part of an overall architectural design. Some indication may be gleaned from this advice as to what may be capable of being listed in its own right. Conservatories, porches, balconies, verandas, door dressings, bargeboards or chimneys, are not only part of the overall design as part of its organic history and, generally, good later features should not therefore be removed in order to restore a building to its earlier form.[51a]

(e) In *Corthorn Land and Timber Co v. Minister of Housing and Local Government*[52] the Divisional Court held that any chattel "definitely" affixed to the building was part of the building. **2.17**

(f) The question of chattels and their fixing is difficult. Two ornamental urns on pedestals in the garden of a listed building were said to have been correctly listed by the DOE, but the Parliamentary Commissioner invited the owner to seek a court ruling to the contrary.[53] The difficulties of interpretation in the context of chattels is well illustrated by the *Three Graces* case. In December 1989 the Secretary of State for the Environment announced that it appeared to him that the Three Graces, a marble sculpture by Canova standing in the sculpture gallery (specifically created to house the statue) at Woburn Abbey was considered to be fixed to a listed building within the meaning of the Planning Acts[54]. However in March 1991[55] the Secretary of State decided, on the basis of further information and legal advice, that the statue was a chattel, not a fixture, and was consequently not part of the listed building.

Tombstones and village pumps are generally accepted not as chattels but structures or erections falling within the definition. Roadways, pavements and horizontal surfaces generally present greater difficulty: although interest in floorscape is growing. Where a pavement is flush with the ground, it is not thought it can be a "structure" and therefore is not normally listable. The cobbles in Richmond market place (North Yorkshire) have however been listed Grade II since 1971. The nearest we can get to reconciling these issues is to adopt the test as to whether an object is a fixture suggested by Scarman L.J. (as he then was) in *Berkley v. Poulett*.[56]

" . . . an object, resting on the ground by its own weight alone, can be a fixture, if it be so heavy that there is no need to tie it into a foundation and if it were put in place to improve the reality. *Prima facie*, however, an object resting on the ground by its own weight alone is not a fixture."

(g) Objects and structures in the curtilage of a listed building. A listed building is defined to include objects and structures fixed to the building; they are obviously part of the building. Listing also extends to any object or structure within the curtilage of the build-

---

[51a] An appellant who wished to apply plastic solar film to the interior of windows in a listed building in a conservation area had this dicussion —[1995] J.P.L. 447.

[52] *Corthorn Land and Timber Co v. Minster of Housing and Local Government* [1965] 63 LGR 490; [1966] 17 P. & C.R. 210; [1965] CLY 3778.

[53] [1980] J.P.L. 715. *Listed Buildings—Planning Law and Planning Reality*, by P. H. Morgan and S. M. Nott, at p. 720. Case reference: fourth Report of the Parliamentary Commissioner for Administration. Session 1975–75, pp. 68–70. Case no. C/278/V/430/J.

[54] 1989 *DOE Press Notice* no. 682.

[55] 1991 *DOE Press Notice* no. 212.

[56] [1976] *E. C. Digest* 754 at 763.

ing which, although not fixed to the building, forms part of the land and had done so since before July 1, 1948. (LBA 1990, s. 1(5)(b)).

Tests: does it form part of the land?

— greenhouses not secured to the ground but standing on their own weight or concrete dollies were held not to be part of the land – *Dibble v. Moore H.E.* [1970] 2 Q.B. 181, C.A.;
— a dry stone wall was clearly a fixture;
— a notable "borderline case" involved carved figures on the stairs, sculptured marble vases in the hall, a pair of marble lions and the head of a flight of garden steps and 16 stone seats—all merely rested on their own weight and were held to be fixtures—the test was whether they were "part of the architectural design". (*D'Eyncourt v. Gregory* [1866] 3 L.R. Eq. 382 per Lord Romilly, MR, page 396).

2.18   It is not always easy to determine whether or not a particular building, object or structure, is within the scope of listing. There is no formal procedure to enable an owner to obtain a definitive answer. An officer's view cannot be legally binding on the authority (*Western Fish Products v. Penwith DC* [1981] 2 All E.R. 204).

To get round this problem one could seek a certificate of lawfulness of proposed use or development (T.C.P. A 1990, section 192) for the carrying out of works which are automatically permitted by the G.D.O. except where they are in the curtilage of a listed building.

The advantage of such an approach is not only that it forces the local planning authority to make a decision that binds it, but it also provides a right of appeal to the Secretary of State (T.C.P. A 1990, section 195) if it appears that the authority has taken a wrong decision.

Every part of a listed building is in law equally "listed". The interior is just as much listed as the exterior, whether or not it is in itself of any interest.

All features on the exterior of the building are equally listed, including any unattractive later additions to an old building and modern replacement windows and doors.

2.19   (h) In December 1993, the Secretary of State for National Heritage announced that as a first step towards creating a heritage management database, the statutory lists of historic buildings were to be computerised. This followed a feasibility study commissioned by the Department of National Heritage which concluded that compiling a database for almost 2,000 bound "green back" volumes comprising some 440,000 entries, would be a viable project. The project was to be undertaken jointly by English Heritage and the RCMH for England. In addition to the lists of historic buildings, the database was to include the list of scheduled ancient monuments, and it would be extended at a later stage to include other heritage information, *e.g.* historic parks and gardens.[57]
       (i) When does a building cease to be a building? If neglect has reduced

---

[57] *DNH News Release* 129/93. [J.P.L. December 1993, p. 1120.]

the architectural interest of a building until it is no more than a mere relic of what it was, it probably has ceased to be a building. But a timber framed building can be listable when the frame is complete but the cladding or even the roof covering is largely destroyed. For practical purposes, however, if the roof and most of the walls have disappeared (say, if less than 50 per cent of the original cubic content is left) it would be difficult to justify listing; however, if that shell had been listed (or was non-listed and in a conservation area) and had been deliberately put into this condition, there is little doubt that a listed building enforcement notice would lie and a prosecution be justified: it would be no answer to say: "it is no longer a listed building". If a listed building is partially destroyed by, say, fire, and approximately 75 per cent of the building remains, it seems reasonable to assume that the local planning authority would maintain that the building was still a listed building and could therefore require restoration in total, using records to ensure that appropriate materials were used in the restoration. If 50 per cent of a listed building was destroyed then the authority might be inclined to press for restoration of the exterior but might allow the owner of the building to do what he liked with the interior. If more than 75 per cent is destroyed then the relevant planning authority might not oppose an application to the DNH to de-list the building.

The 50 per cent rule referred to above is a rule of thumb and although 50 per cent of the building might be destroyed, the above principles do not necessarily apply since that part of the building which has been destroyed might be the most or alternatively the least significant. Thus a qualitative and quantitative judgment must be made in each case.

(j) Thus a wide variety of "buildings, structures or erections" can be listed provided that:
   (i) they are of suitable quality, and
   (ii) they are not chattels as such but pass the test of "definite" affixion or the object and purpose test in *Berkley v. Poulett*, and
   (iii) they have not deteriorated to such an extent that they could not be said to be a building, or structure.

(b) The exterior and the features

We deal in detail with the listable qualities under the section on selection **2.20** and grading[58] and merely observe here the statutory requirements:

(1) A building must be of special architectural or historic interest.
(2) The Secretary of State may take into account not only the building itself, but:

   "(a) any respect which its exterior contributes to the architectural or historic interest of any group of buildings of which it forms part; and

[58] See paras. 2.37–2.44.

23

      (b) the desirability of preserving . . . any feature of the building consisting of a man-made object or structure . . . "[59]

These are perhaps self evident, but the qualification as to the object or structure being "man-made" is interesting and perhaps worth remembering. One could get involved in esoteric debates about what is man-made or made by God. So far no one seems to have challenged a listing on the grounds that the Secretary of State, in his discretion, took into account a feature which was other than man-made.

(c) The structure and the curtilage

2.21   The definition of a "listed building" in section 1(5) of the LBA treats as part of the building:

    "(a) any object or structure fixed to the building;
    (b) any object or structure within the curtilage of the building which, although not fixed to the building, forms part of the land and has done so since before July 1, 1948"

We have so far considered structures when they are either "parts" of the building but freestanding, or freestanding structures which would not ordinarily be thought of as a building: stocks, whipping posts, stiles and pumps.

For the most part it is relatively straightforward to define objects or structures which are physically attached to a listed building whether or not they are actually fixtures in the legal sense.

The wording of section 1(5)(a) LBA appears to be clear. It includes as part of a listed building "any object or structure fixed to the building". Most people reading that would conclude that "fixed" meant physically attached to the wall, floor or ceiling by means of plaster, nails, cement, battens, rivets, brackets, dowels, screws, glues or other fixatives. If it could be said that removal requires a chisel or screwdriver then it is fixed. Thus all panelling, chimney-pieces, staircases, overmantels, windows and door surrounds, door pelmets, dadoes, cornices, fireplaces, windows, balustrades, windvanes, sundials integrated into the fabric of a building, chimneys, floors, wrought iron, stone or wooden balconies are covered by virtue of being physically attached to the building. This category will also include paintings on panels, wood, walls, ceilings, plaster or canvas which are *integrated into the structure itself*, plasterwork, plaques, wood, plaster or stone reliefs, swags, screens, shutters and stained glass which are physically fixed, and in some instances, bookcases, sconces, pierglasses, busts, light fittings and fenders.

These may sometimes lead to uncertainty; tapestries fixed to the wall were considered fixtures in one case (*Re Whaley* [1908] 1 Ch 615) but not in another (*Leigh v. Taylor* [1902] AC 157).

The notable recent case on this subject includes *The Three Graces at Woburn Abbey*. The Secretary of State initially considered that the *Three Graces* statue was a fixture, but stated he did not propose to take listed building enforcement action. SAVE Britain's Heritage then applied to the High Court for judicial review of that decision, which caused the Secretary

---

[59] LBA 1990, s.1(3).

of State to take further advice and he reached the view that the statue was not part of the building within the meaning of section 1(5) and therefore the question of taking enforcement action did not arise.

In some cases objects have at some period been moved or refixed in a different position. Strictly speaking, the removal of any object fixed to the building requires LBC whenever its removal would affect the architectural or historic interest of the building. The fact that any object has been removed or repositioned at some time in the past does not in itself exempt the owner from applying for retrospective LBC to carry out works in relation to it.[60]

But how far does the listing embrace other buildings or structures which may be physically attached to the building named on the list but which themselves are not separately listed and sometimes may not be of listable quality? The answer may be in two directions; whether the other structure is fixed to the building or whether it is within the curtilage of the named listed building. Further examples to assist in this matter appear in paragraph 5.25.

A definitive answer to the "fixed" point derives from an examination of **2.22** the majority decision of the House of Lords in *Debenhams plc v. Westminster City Council*.[61] This was a rating case where rates would not be chargeable if the rating hereditament was included in the list compiled under section 54 of the Town and Country Planning Act 1971 (now section 1(1) LBA). Debenhams were the owners of a rating hereditament which comprised two separate buildings, one in Regent Street and one in Kingly Street. They were opposite each other with the back of the Regent Street premises facing the front of Kingly Street, with Kingly Street between them. They were joined by a footbridge over and a tunnel under the street. The Regent Street building was listed but the Kingly Street building was not. Debenhams used the two buildings as a single commercial unit ("Hamleys" the toy shop). In October 1981 Debenhams vacated the hereditament (*i.e.* both units) and it remained unoccupied for the relevant rating year. Debenhams claimed the exemption for both units but the City Council refused to accede to this argument as only the Regent Street building was listed. The issue was: could the Kingly Street building be a "structure fixed to a (listed) building"?

The House of Lords[62] held that the "object or structure" referred to in section 1(5) LBA referred only to structures ancillary to the listed building itself and not to structures constituting some other complete building. The Kingly Street building did not form part of the listed building as it did not comprise an object or structure fixed to the listed building or within its curtilage.

Lord Mackay observed:

> "Since it is obviously necessary that the list should identify the buildings contained in it, the question whether a particular physical entity is listed or not listed depends on whether on reading the list and taking

---

[60] Paper given by Gill Kerr of English Heritage at the "Planning and the Historic Environment" conference held at the University of Oxford in May 1992.

[61] *Debenhams plc v. Westminster City Council* (1987) A.C. 396; [1987] 1 All E.R. 51; (1987) J.P.L. 344.

[62] *Debenhams plc v. Westminster City Council* (1987) A.C. 396; (1987) J.P.L. 344.

25

account of the statutory provisions that entity is to be regarded as a building or part of a building included in the list."

2.23   Lord Keith observed, having detected an ambiguity between section 54(2) of the T.C.P.A. 1971 (now section 1(3)(b) LBA) where the words "object or structure" were prefaced by the words "man-made" and section 54(9) of the T.C.P.A. 1971 (now section 1(5) LBA) where they were not:

> "in resolving a statutory ambiguity, that meaning which produces an unreasonable result is to be rejected in favour of that which does not, it being presumed that Parliament did not intend to produce such a result. In my opinion to construe the words 'structure' here as embracing a complete building not subordinate to the building of which it is to be treated as forming part, would, in the light of the considerations I have mentioned, indeed produce an unreasonable result . . . the general tenor of the second sentence of section 54(9) satisfies me that the word 'structure' is intended to convey a limitation to such structures as are ancillary to the listed building itself, for example, the stable block of the mansion house, or the steading of a farm house, either fixed to the main building or within its curtilage. In my opinion, the concept envisaged is that of principal and accessory."

Lord Mackay said:

> " . . . section 54(9) is dealing with the question of whether certain things, namely objects or structures, are to be treated as part of a building, not whether what is undoubtedly a building or part of a building is to be regarded as part of another building . . . I think it is not a natural use of language to describe two adjoining houses in a terrace by saying that one is an object or a structure fixed to the other. It would, I think, be a perfectly appropriate provision in a contract for the sale of a house that there was included in the sale any object or structure fixed to the house but I think it is highly unlikely that the purchaser would expect under the terms of such contract to become the owner of the house next door. . . . The respondent's contention involves reading the word 'structure' in its context as including a completely distinct building which is connected structurally to the first building. This reading seriously restricts the power of the Secretary of State in relation to listed buildings since on this interpretation he could not select one out of a terrace of houses . . . to be listed."

2.24   The question of what is the curtilage is a difficult (and still unsettled) issue. But preceding that debate it is necessary to reflect that if the object or structure is to be treated as part of the listed building, it must form part of "the land". Land is defined in section 336 of the T.C.P.A. 1990 as "any corporeal hereditament including a building . . . " Broadly, this is a freehold or leasehold, but the definition does not specify the extent of the land.[63]

How far across the curtilage of land or garden can the listing extend? We have seen that the setting of a building can be significant, so that in considering whether or not to grant planning permission for development affecting "a listed building or its setting" or LBC for any works "the local planning authority or, as the case may be, the Secretary of State, shall have

---

[63] This compares with the definition contained in s.32(3) LBA which is for compulsory purchase reasons.

special regard to the desirability of preserving the building or its setting or any features of special architectural or historic interest which it possesses".[64]

The matter is further complicated by this concept of the "curtilage". It will be remembered that section 1(3)(b) of the LBA (which section determines whether a building should be listed) provides that the Secretary of State may take into account not only the building itself but also "the desirability of preserving, on the ground of its architectural or historic interest, any feature of the building consisting of a man-made object or structure fixed to the building or forming part of the land and comprised with the curtilage of the building".

Section 1(5)(b) LBA treats as part of the definition of a listed building "any object or structure within the curtilage of the building which, although not fixed to the building, forms part of the land and has done so since before 1, July 1948".

What, therefore, is the curtilage? This phrase, hallowed by conveyancers from time immemorial, so far as it can be seen has never been definitively interpreted in the English courts, however the following cases are helpful in tracing what is presently understood by the term. The first of these cases came before the Court of Session in 1950 where the phrase was in issue. The Court of Session held that:

> "the ground which is used for the comfortable enjoyment of a house or other building may be regarded in law as being within the curtilage of that house or building and thereby as an integral part of the same although it has not been marked off or enclosed in any way. It is enough that it serves the purpose of the house or building in some necessary or reasonably useful way".[65]

The dictum of Lord Mackintosh (quoted above) in the *Sinclair-Lockharts Trustees* case was approved by the Lord Justice Clerk in 1964 in the *Scottish Lands Tribunal* case of *Paul v. Ayrshire County Council*.[66]

The problem about the concept of the curtilage is that this definition depends on the need for the curtilage to be an integral part of or at least ancillary to the listed building, and for the curtilage to serve a useful purpose associated with the listed building. This implies congruity of occupation or at least control if not outright ownership. A test can be taken at the time of listing as set out above, *e.g.* does the ice house or the gardener's lodge serve the purpose of the house or building? Yes, it does at the time of listing, but suppose that the lodge is sold off to someone with no connection with the house: it might be assumed no longer to be part of the curtilage. We shall return to such difficulties of interpretation later in this chapter.

In 1979 Lord Justice Buckley in the Court of Appeal in *Methuen–Campbell v. Walters*[67] provided some helpful observations regarding what could be included as part of the curtilage and developed the "integrality" test which had been adopted in the *Sinclair-Lockharts Trustees* case.

The *Methuen-Campbell* case involved the exercise by a tenant of her

[64] LBA 1990, s.66(1).
[65] *Sinclair-Lockharts Trustees v. Central Land Board* [1949–1951] 1 P & CR 195; aff *ibid* 320.
[66] *ibid*.
[67] [1979] 1 All E.R. 606.

"right to buy" under the Leasehold Reform Act 1967. The issue concerned whether a paddock at the bottom of, and fenced off from, a garden was to be enfranchised with the house and garden. Lord Justice Buckley stated the issue in the following way:

> "What then is meant by the curtilage of a property? In my judgment it is not sufficient to constitute two pieces of land as part of one and the same curtilage that they should have been conveyed or demised together, for a single conveyance or lease can comprise more than one parcel of land . . . Nor is it sufficient that they have been occupied together.
> "The test [is not] whether the enjoyment of one [piece of land] is advantageous or convenient or necessary for the full enjoyment of the other. A piece of land may fall clearly within the curtilage of a parcel conveyed without its contributing in any significant way to the convenience or value of the rest of the parcel. On the other hand it may be very advantageous or convenient to the owner of one parcel of land also to own an adjoining parcel, although it may be clear from the facts that the two parcels are entirely distinct pieces of property. In my judgment, for one corporeal hereditament to fall within the curtilage of another, the former must be so intimately associated with the latter as to lead to the conclusion that the former in truth forms part and parcel of the latter.
> "This may extend to ancillary buildings, structures or areas such as outhouses, a garage, a driveway, a garden and so forth. How far it is appropriate to regard this identity as part of one messuage or parcel of land as extending must depend on the characteristics and circumstances of the items under consideration."

The final paragraph of the three extracts quoted from the judgment is significant in that it reflects the need to view the concept of curtilage as one of considerable flexibility which adapts to the characteristics of the principal building under consideration. An interesting discussion on the meaning of the concept of curtilage and the concept, bears its restricted and established meaning connoting a small area forming part or parcel whether the house or building which is contained or to which is attached is part of a judgment of the DOE in relation to *Kentwell Hall Long Melford* [1993] 2 JPL 987 (described in paragraph 2.34.)

2.25   Difficult though the curtilage concept is, a Parliamentary draftsman was not required to seek to define the word in the LBA. Reference will however now be made to the *Debenhams* case above and the *Calderdale* case.[68] In the latter case, three local residents wished to preserve a terrace of 15 four-storey cottages, known as 3–31 Nutclough, Hebden Bridge, from demolition by the local council which owned the houses. The terraced cottages were constructed as mill workers' dwellings. The mill was erected in 1820 and was listed. The terrace was erected in about 1870 and was not listed. Part of the terrace was also used for industrial purposes. There was a stone bridge linking the mill to no. 1 Nutclough and giving direct access to nos. 3 and 5. Until 1973 the land on which the mill and terrace stood were in common ownership. In 1973 the council became the owner of the terrace. Neither the mill nor the bridge nor the terrace were in use. The question for the

[68] *Attorney-General, ex rel Sutcliffe v. Calderdale Borough Council* [1987] J.P.L. 310.

Court of Appeal was whether or not the terrace was "a structure . . . forming part of the land and comprised within the curtilage of the building" (*i.e.* the mill which was listed).

Lord Justice Stephenson concluded that the court should take into **2.26** account the following factors in determining whether a "structure" was within the curtilage whatever might be the conveyancing interpretation. They were:

(1) the physical "layout" of the listed building and the structure;
(2) their ownership, past and present;
(3) their use or function, past and present.

Where they were in common ownership and one was used in connection with the other, there was little difficulty in classifying a structure near a building or even some distance from it, as within its curtilage.

In the *Calderdale* case the court held that the terrace was within the curtilage. Lord Justice Stephenson defined the curtilage of a listed building as:

"an area of land which includes any related objects or structures which naturally form, or formed, with the listed building an integral whole".

The *Calderdale* case appeared therefore to extend the concept of the curtilage to include buildings which had served the principal building in the recent past provided the physical layout indicated that both buildings met the integrality test discussed above.

The view of Stephenson LJ and his tests have to be looked at with some caution because of the comments of the House of Lords in the *Debenhams* case. The *Debenhams* case, it is true, was concerned primarily with structure and affixation rather than curtilage, but it is significant that Lord Mackay opined that *Calderdale* was "a very special case on its facts"[69] and doubted the reasoning of the Court of Appeal in *Calderdale*. Further, Lord Keith in *Debenhams* observed in connection with what constituted a curtilage building, that: "the matter of listing or not listing cannot turn on the business purposes or manner of use of adjoining properties of a particular user".[70] The House of Lords in the *Debenhams* case did not however dissent from the criteria laid down by Lord Justice Stephenson in the *Calderdale* case, merely the interpretation of those criteria.

The owner of North Aston Hall,[71] a Grade II listed building, began exten- **2.27** sive works of restoration to the hall and grounds. There was a ha-ha in front of the hall, a significant part of which had been filled in. The applicant wished to build a dry-stone wall in part, using the stone from the ha-ha. He made an application for listed building consent in 1986 to fill in the ha-ha, which was refused by the Cherwell District Council, and was later dismissed on appeal. In March 1989 a listed building enforcement notice was issued requiring the re-instatement of the ha-ha. The Secretary of State's decision of July 1990 accepted the Inspector's opinion that infilling of the ha-ha had pre-dated listing and granted listed building consent for those parts where the driveway was crossed, but upheld the remainder of the

---

[69] *Debenhams plc v. Westminster City Council* [1987] 1 All E.R. 51 at 60j.
[70] *Ibid.* at p. 55j.
[71] *Watson-Smyth v. Secretary of State for the Environment and Cherwell District Council* (QB Division. Sir Frank Layfield Q.C. as Deputy Judge, October 1, 1994)— J.P.L. 1992, p. 451.

notice. The applicant appealed to the High Court, and alleged errors of law in the form of four questions. These were:

(i) had the first respondent directed himself properly or at all as to the meaning of "curtilage";

(ii) if not, could he have reached a current finding on whether or not the ha-ha had lain within it;

(iii) if the ha-ha marked the boundary to the curtilage, could the ha-ha, as a matter of law, be said to lie within it;

(iv) was a ditch, a structure or an object?

The ha-ha was described as having two elements, a ditch and a wall, and the Inspector dealing with the listed building consent appeal had felt they were integral parts of one structure within the meaning of section 54(9)(b) of the 1971 Act. The Secretary of State had agreed with this view. The Deputy Judge considered the words "object" or "structure" as were used in section 54(9) and applied the ordinary sense of the word "structure" to mean an edifice of framework put together by erection or building. He concurred with both the Inspector and the Secretary of State that the ha-ha was a structure.

It appeared that the ha-ha had been constructed as part of the 18th-century landscape in the immediate area of the Hall and for a purpose directly related to it. The Secretary of State had considered the case of *Debenhams plc v. Westminster City Council* [1987] 1 A.C. 403 in which the concept of "principal and accessory" was established in relation to the subject of "curtilage". Other cases concerning an interpretation of the word "curtilage" were referred to by Counsel for the applicant, including *Methuen-Campbell v. Walters* [1979] 1 Q.B. 525 (CA), *Dyer v. The Dorset County Council* [1988] 3 W.L.R. 213 and *Att. Gen., ex rel. Sutcliff, Rouse and Hughes v. Calderdale Borough Council* [1983] J.P.L. 310.

If the *Calderdale* tests were applied there was ample evidence of the close material and intimate relationship between the hall and the ha-ha as part of a single physical layout and as part of its setting. The hall and ha-ha were in one ownership and had an historic continuity.

The Deputy Judge considered the Secretary of State was entitled in law to decide for the purposes of section 54 (1971 Act) that the ha-ha was within the curtilage of the Hall. The application was dismissed.

2.28   The nature of a "curtilage" was further revisited in 1994 by the High Court (Mr Nigel Macleod Q.C. sitting as a deputy judge) in *McAlpine v. Secretary of State for the Environment*,[72] where the court upheld an enforcement notice requiring the removal of a swimming pool which had been constructed without express planning permission in the grounds of a substantial listed building. There was a formal garden at the rear of the house, and beyond that an extensive open grassed area which had been used by the appellant, as well as by his predecessors, for recreation as part of the garden since the 1960s. From a study of the authorities, the court identified three relevant characteristics of a curtilage: (a) it was confined to a small area about a building; (b) an intimate association with land which was undoubtedly within the curtilage was required in order to make the land under consideration part and parcel of that undoubted curtilage land; and (c) it was not necessary for there to be physical enclosure of that land which was within the curtilage, but the land in question at least needed to be regarded in law

[72] [1994] EGCS 189.

as part of one enclosure with the house. The Inspector had properly applied these tests, and had not confined himself by looking at physical enclosures. The Judge considered that he had not taken into account any irrelevant facts or drawn unreasonable conclusions.

Perhaps, however, we are nearer an answer to the difficult question of **2.29** what happens when the ownership, or indeed perhaps merely the occupation, of an "integral whole" is fragmented. If there is no longer any connection between the fragmented part which contains a structure which might have been considered part of the curtilage and the named listed building, it may be a candidate for de-listing. An application could be made to remove it from the list as it now does not possess the special listable quality which had been ascribed to it when it formed part of the curtilage of the named building.[73] The attitude of the courts to the fragmentation of an "integral whole" is illustrated by reference to the following cases:

(i) In *Dyer v. Dorset County Council*[74] the local authority acquired a large listed Georgian property on the edge of the one hundred acre Kingston Maurwood Park. The property was converted to use as an agricultural college and modern college buildings were erected within the park.

A lecturer at the college occupied a house let to him by the County Council which was situated within, but on the edge of the college grounds. The house lay some distance away from the college buildings, fenced off from the rest of the grounds but with pedestrian access to them. The lecturer exercised his right to buy the property under the Housing Act 1980 as amended. The County Council resisted the claim on the basis of an exception to the right to buy provisions where the house "was within the curtilage of a building used for purposes other than housing".

The matter came before the Court of Appeal in May 1988. Lord Justice Mann said of the term "curtilage" that it "is a term of art, and in employing it, the draftsman and Parliament must have had regard to its meaning as such a term. Its meaning as a term was discussed in *Methuen-Campbell v. Walters*.[75] It appears from that decision that the meaning of the word 'curtilage' is constrained to a small area about a building. The size of the area appears to be a question of fact and degree".

Lord Justice Nourse observed that, while making every allowance for the fact that the size of a curtilage may vary with the size of the house or building, he was in no doubt that the one hundred acre park could not possibly be said to be part and parcel of Kingston Maurwood House, far less any of the college buildings. The lecturer's house could not properly be described as being within the curtilage of the college building. It was entirely separate. In reaching this conclusion Lord Justice Nourse relied on the derivation of the word "curtilage" to support his opinion that the term only referred to a small area of ground.

---

[73] Above at para. 2.05 and see PPG 15, paras. 6.26 and 6.27.
[74] [1989] 1 Q.B. 34, [1988] 3 W.L.R. 213.
[75] [1979] 1 All E.R. 606.

2.30   (ii) *Watts v. Secretary of State for the Environment and another.*[76] Bix
Manor and its associated buildings formed an integral whole until
1981 when the owner sold off most of her landholding but retained
a barn and some outbuildings. The Manor was listed Grade II in
1985. The listing statement did not refer to the Manor's associated
buildings nor to the Manor's brick and flint boundary wall.

Mrs Watts proceeded to demolish part of the boundary wall to
create a vehicular access. An enforcement notice was served by the
local authority.

The matter came before the High Court in October 1990 when
Mrs Watts sought to quash the Secretary of State's decisions to
uphold a deemed refusal of an application for planning permission
for the barn's conversion and to dismiss an appeal against the
listed building enforcement notice.

It was clear from the Inspector's report that he had formed an
opinion, with which the Secretary of State agreed, that the wall
which had been partially demolished was subject to the requirement for listed building consent by virtue of the fact that it was
attached to Bix Manor and fell within the ambit of section 54(9) of
the T.C.P.A. 1971 (now section 1(5) of the LBA).

2.31   Sir Graham Eyre Q.C., sitting as a Deputy Judge of the High
Court, considered at length the *Calderdale* and *Debenhams* cases
before he held—applying Lord Keith's "ancillary concept" in
Debenhams to structures—that to be protected, the wall must be a
structure ancillary to the listed building and in deciding whether
the wall was such an ancillary structure, regard must be had to
both the physical relationship and functional relationship of the
ancillary structure to the listed building. As there was not a functional relationship at the time of listing it was not open to the Secretary of State for the Environment to treat the wall as a structure
ancillary to a listed building. At the time of listing the wall formed
part of the curtilage of a property separate from the listed building
in terms of ownership and physical occupation. The wall was
being put to a wholly independent use disassociated with Bix
Manor.

Sir Graham Eyre Q.C. based his decision not on circumstances
relevant to the original curtilage, nor the physical connection or
layout of the buildings and walls but upon the issue of ownership,
occupation and listing occurring after the subdivision of the
integral whole. The wall in question became ancillary to the converted barn and not Bix Manor.

The question arises (which was not directly addressed in the Bix
Manor case) . . . when a structure becomes protected at the date of
listing by virtue of its status as ancillary to a listed building, does
that protection immediately cease once there is a change in ownership and occupation?[77]

2.32   It would seem that the answer to this question may be "no", if
the contents follow the reasoning in another appeal decision

[76] [1991] 1 PLR 61, J.P.L. (1991) at 718.
[77] Appeal reference T/APP/F/91/Z3825/607134/p6—October 8, 1991 [J.P.L. 1992,
p. 1084].

which relates to this point in respect of a listed building enforcement notice issued by Horsham District Council concerning the contravention of section 7 of the LBA 1990 involving the removal of a brick wall without listed building consent.

The adjoining property was an early 19th-century Grade II listed building which had been divided into two dwellings. At the time when the 19th-century house was listed in May 1980 it was a single dwelling with a garden which included the land covered by the enforcement notice.

After the sub-division of the house it was sold to new owners, but the garden area with the wall fronting the "notice land" was retained by the previous owner of the listed building. In 1989 the Council became aware that the wall had been demolished: the question was raised as to whether the wall, which by then lay on land in separate ownership to that of the listed building, could be treated as being listed as part of the curtilage of the nearby listed building.

The Inspector reiterated the definition of a listed building and at section 1(5)(b) that "any structure within the curtilage of the building which, although not fixed to the building, forms part of the land and has done so since before July 1, 1948, shall be treated as part of the building". The wall in question was not built after July 1, 1948. When the main house was listed in 1980 its garden and boundaries (including the wall) were within its curtilage and formed part of the land.

The Inspector considered that the relevant date for the consideration of whether a structure falls within the meaning of a listed building in section 1(5)(a) is when the building was listed. He looked at the functional connection between the structure and the principal listed building and, in this case, he found that the southern boundary wall (the "notice" wall) formed part of the curtilage of the listed building; it also functioned as a boundary to the property and was therefore a structure to be treated as part of the listed building. He did not feel that the changes in tenure and ownership since 1980 had disconnected each parcel from the operation of listed building control over the listed building and its curtilage at the time of listing.[78]

(iii) *James v. Secretary of State for the Environment & Chichester District Council.*[79] The issue in this case was whether a tennis court which Mr James had constructed some 100 metres from his house was within the curtilage of the house and was thus permitted development within Class E of the General Development Order. The tennis court was situated in an open field and was separated from the house by an area of undergrowth and rough grassland and a partial and indistinct line of trees and shrubs.

Mr James' appeal against the decision of Chichester District Council to refuse to allow him to retain the tennis court was dismissed on the basis that the field was separate and distinct from

[78] Appeal decision T/APP/F/91/Z3825/607134/p6—October 8, 1991 [J.P.L. 1992, p. 1084].
[79] [1991] J.P.L. 550.

the cultivated garden attached to the house and did not have the appearance of being within the same enclosure. Mr James applied to the High Court to quash the decision contending that proper regard had not been paid to the authorities on the meaning of curtilage.

Sir Graham Eyre Q.C. sitting as a Deputy Judge of the High Court, dismissed the application. He observed that "whether development is within the curtilage of a dwelling house is quintessentially a matter of fact. Provided an Inspector adopts the proper approach and applies the proper test, it is a matter for him as to whether development is within a curtilage."

2.33
The Deputy Judge referred to the *Calderdale* and *Methuen-Campbell* cases before drawing attention to the fact that the Inspector clearly recognised that the field on which the tennis court had been constructed was within the same ownership as the dwelling house. There was also recognition of a functional association between them and the Inspector had considered the physical circumstances. The Deputy Judge found that the Inspector's approach was impeccable.

(iv) *Watson-Smith v. Secretary of State for the Environment.*[80] In 1986 Mr Watson-Smyth purchased the derelict Grade II North Aston Hall. During restoration Mr Watson-Smyth constructed a dry stone wall using the material from the "ha-ha" wall. A "ha-ha" consists of a ditch and a retaining wall forming the boundary of a garden but constructed in such a way as to provide a barrier to contain stock but in such a manner that views are not obstructed.

The ha-ha at North Aston Hall was infilled in 1988. In 1989 the local authority served an enforcement notice requiring reinstatement. The Secretary of State accepted his Inspector's recommendation that the enforcement notice be upheld. The ha-ha was part of the 18th-century layout of the landscape of the Hall, on land connected to it, so that it was within the curtilage of the listed building. The two main elements of the ha-ha, the ditch and wall, were an integral part of the structure and so were within the ambit of section 54(9) of the T.C.P.A. 1971 [now section 1(5) of the LBA]. The Secretary of State said that the retention of the ha-ha was desirable even though it no longer fulfilled its original function.

Mr Watson-Smyth applied to the High Court to quash the decision and the matter came before Sir Frank Layfield Q.C., sitting as a Deputy Judge, in October 1991. The Deputy Judge dismissed the application. Although section 54(9) of the T.C.P.A. 1971 [now section 1(5) LBA] had been regarded as ambiguous in the *Debenhams* case, in the present case there was sufficient evidence which enabled the Secretary of State to regard the ha-ha as part of the curtilage and therefore part of the listed building.[80a] The Deputy Judge referred to the meaning of curtilage in the *Dyer* case ("a small area forming part or parcel with the house to which it was attached") and indicated that in each case it was a question of fact and degree as to whether or not a particular area lay within the curtilage of

[80] [1991] EGCS 97.
[80a] [1992] J.P.L. 451.

another, referring to the *Methuen-Campbell* case. "It could not be accepted, therefore, that the Secretary of State had erred in law in holding in the present case that the ha-ha was within the curtilage."

In a case at *Long Melford* (February 1993),[81] which arose from **2.34** the service of a listed building enforcement notice, under section 38 of the LBA the subject of "curtilage" was again rehearsed. Kentwell Hall, Long Melford is a 16th-century moated building with an imposing approach leading from the south and lined by an avenue of lime trees. The approach is terminated by a gateway with surrounding ironwork supported by brick piers. The substance of the appeal against the enforcement notice was that, having been granted listed building consent in July 1985 to remove the main front gates of the Hall, it was a condition of that consent that within two years, replacement gates for those removed, should be re-erected in accordance with an approved scheme.

The appeal centred around whether listed building consent had been required for the removal of the gates and, in particular, whether they were within the curtilage of the Hall, a Grade I listed building. The distance between the Hall and the gateway was about 2 kilometres and the two were linked by the formal avenue and driveway.

The Secretary of State considered his Inspector's report and his recommendation that the appeal should be dismissed and the notice upheld, but asked for a further site visit and fuller report by the Inspector on the issue of the curtilage of the listed building. A second report was produced by the Inspector. The main issue was whether the grant of listed building consent in 1985 (for the removal of the gateway) was in fact required, and whether the gateway was a listed building under section 1(5)(b) by virtue of being a structure within the curtilage of the listed Kentwell Hall.

The *Att-Gen. Sutcliffe-Rouse and Hughes v. Calderdale BC* case (1983) [J.P.L. 310] was quoted, as was the *Debenhams plc v. Westminster CC* [1987] A.C. 396.

The Secretary of State for the Environment concluded that there was a strong functional and geographical relationship between the Hall and its gateway, albeit that they were not constructed at the same time and were a considerable distance apart. He regarded the other judgments as leading to the conclusions that the gateway was within the curtilage of the listed building, and therefore that the gateway was a listed building by virtue of being within the curtilage of Kentwell Hall under the provisions of section 1(5)(b) and that listed building consent had been necessary for the removal of the gates. This case has an interesting discussion of the current meaning of "curtilage". It was also discussed in *Dyer v. Dorset CC* [1988] 3 W.L.R. 213.

These cases perhaps illustrate a different approach to the application of the concept of curtilage than was adopted by the Court of Appeal in the

---

[81] J.P.L. October 1993, p. 987.

Calderdale case. We are reminded of the observation of Lord Justice Buckley in the *Methuen-Campbell* case "How far it is appropriate to regard this identity as parts of one messuage or parcel of land as extending must depend on the characteristics and circumstances of the items under consideration."

When Lord Montagu (formerly Chairman of English Heritage) rejected in the House of Lords the idea of a definition of curtilage, he referred to significant improvements in listing practices which have been made in the light of the *Calderdale* case. He said[82]:

> "The practice of the department now and of my officers is to consider individually all the structures and buildings on a site which can be construed as separate buildings and to list those, and only those, which qualify. The new lists therefore will leave little room for doubt as to whether a building is listed or not . . . ".

2.35 This latest listing practice of English Heritage was used by an Inspector when dealing with two concurrent appeals affecting a site in the London Borough of Richmond on Thames in December 1992.[83] The site straddled the Castlerau conservation area and adjoined a Grade II listed building (Riverside building) and the proposals included applications for (a) conservation area consent for the complete demolition and clearance of all buildings on the site, and (b) listed building consent for complete demolition and clearance of the site, as land at Harrods Depository, Barnes.

The uncertainty over the status of the buildings on the appeal site had caused the two applications to be made. The local planning authority and English Heritage argued that the buildings were listed by virtue of their physical attachment to the Riverside building which was listed in May 1990, or were within its curtilage as defined by section 1(5) of LBA 1990. The appellants disagreed with that interpretation but accepted the need for consent for those structures which fell within the conservation area.

Both the *Debenhams v. Westminster City Council* (1987) judgment and the Court of Appeal decision on the *Calderdale Borough Council* case (1983) were referred to in the submissions. The Inspector concluded that the buildings were not listed and he reasoned that these leading judgments predated the listing of the Riverside building.

Following the difficulties in deciding the extent of listing arising from the Calderdale case, Lord Montagu, the then Chairman of English Heritage, had advised the House of Lords in October 1986 that their practice was then "to consider individually all structures and buildings on a site and to list those, and only those, which qualify". The Inspector applied that practice to the Depository site and concluded that only the Riverside building was worthy of listing and the other historic buildings on the site were excluded from the listing. Other aspects of the physical relationship of the buildings and the concept of "principal and accessory" in assessing whether the appeal site buildings were within the curtilage of the Riverside building did not convince the Inspector that they were listed buildings.

The LBA has been drafted so that section 1(5) reads as indicated at paragraph 2.13 above, thus protecting "any object or structure which although

---

[82] *Hansard*: House of Lords, October 13, 1986, Col. 626.
[83] J.P.L. June 1993, p. 602/3.

not fixed to the building, forms part of the land and has done so since before July 1, 1948".

This does not, of course, remove the result, regarded by many as a strange anomaly, that LBC is not required to erect a building or structure within the curtilage of a listed building[84]; although since the H.P.A. 1986 (consolidated into the LBA) any building or structure so erected will not itself be listable unless it has formed part of the land since before July 1, 1948.[85] Planning permission is however required for the erection of a new building within the curtilage of a listed building. If the structure falls within the limits in the General Permitted Development Order (i.e. it is "permitted development") planning permission is not required unless the relevant class of permitted development has been removed by an Article 4 direction. However the local planning authority must take into account "the setting" of the listed building in considering the grant of planning permission. Permission may of course be granted by the General Permitted Development Order 1995 for minor works of development (which will not require consideration of the setting) unless an Article 4 direction has been made restricting the operation of the Order. Although section 16(2) of the LBA requires the local planning authority to take into account the "setting" of a listed building in considering whether to grant LBC, that requirement cannot make a building into a listed building nor force an unlisted building not within the curtilage into the curtilage.

Conclusions

(1) The building must be a building within the legal definition **2.36** (e.g. not a hen-coop) or a structure or erection (e.g. a lamp-post or pillar box). Of course, something which may not fall within a lawyer's definition of a "building" (e.g. a dog kennel) could be listed because it is a "structure or erection".

(2) The building must be of the appropriate quality (i.e. of special architectural or historic interest).

(3) The building will include an "object or structure fixed to the building". This will often be a subsidiary building to the main building.

(4) The listing of a building will not embrace within its listing a separate "object or structure" which is not listed unless that separate structure is within the curtilage of the listed building, forms part of the land and has done so since before July 1, 1948.

(5) A separate structure will be within the curtilage if it is in common ownership and used in connection with the other even if the separate structure is some distance from the listed building. The separate structure must be on "the land".

(6) A separate structure which is not in common ownership with the listed building may be within its curtilage if the three tests

---

[84] *Cotswold District Council v. Secretary of State for the Environment and Pearson* [1985] J.P.L. 407 (David Widdicombe Q.C. sitting as a deputy High Court judge).

[85] T.C.P.A. 1971 s.54(9)(a) now consolidated in LBA 1990 s.1(5).

in *Calderdale* are satisfied, although some doubt must be cast on the use or function test in view of Lord Keith's comments in the *Debenhams* case. If there is an absence of common ownership (particularly if separated at the time of listing) and the structure is not near the listed building, there seems to be a strongly arguable case that the separate structure is not listed as being not worthy itself, now being within the curtilage and an application could be made for its removal from the list.

(7) It is certainly arguable that the concept of a "moving" curtilage is with us, as opposed to the traditional conveyancers' idea. It could well be argued that as estates are divided up the curtilage becomes smaller—indeed, the definition in the *Oxford English Dictionary* of "curtilage" as "a small court, yard, or piece of ground attached to a dwellinghouse and forming one enclosure with it" could apply and was considered to be significant in the *Dyer* case. The practical difficulty of this is to know the facts on which it is relied to determine the extent of the curtilage, and to determine the material date on which the curtilage is to be defined.

(8) A building cannot be a listable building if it is almost derelict or a shell unless the main structure is complete even without roof covering or cladding (*e.g.* a timber frame).

(9) Otherwise the erection of a separate structure or erection does not require listed building consent. If it forms part of the land it will only be listed if it falls within the curtilage definition.

(10) A chattel cannot be listed unless it:
    (a) is "definitely" affixed to a building, or
    (b) is an object resting on the ground by its own weight alone put in place "to improve the reality". Caution should be exercised here in view of the circumstances of the *Three Graces* case.[86]

(11) The new listings (probably from 1986 onwards) should clearly indicate which buildings within the curtilage are specifically listed.

Finally, there is some doubt as to who interprets the extent of the listing. The Department takes the view that what is covered by the curtilage provisions in any given case is ultimately a matter for the courts, although the relevant local planning authority may be prepared to express its own view in the matter. Although at first sight this may seem unhelpful, it is a correct interpretation of the procedure. The Department lists but it is up to the local planning authority to interpret and act, *e.g.* by a prosecution or listed building enforcement notice. If the owners do not agree, then they have to resort to an argument in the magistrates' court, or an appeal to the Department, which if not satisfactory, will lead to testing in the courts.[87] This however may well be most unsatisfactory for the owners of a listed building who may have to expend considerable expense to mount a challenge to the local authority's decision.

[86] *The Three Graces—1994.*
[87] SE2/5277/270/68 as reported in the *Estates Times*, January 23, 1987.

4. SELECTION AND GRADING

There are two stages in considering a building for the purposes of inclu- **2.37**
sion in the list:

(a) should the building be *selected* for listing? If so:
(b) in what *grade* should it be placed?

(a) Selection

In considering the answer to the question of selection, it is important to
remember the provisions of section 1(3) of the LBA which provide that the
Secretary of State may take into account not only the building itself, but
also:

(1) any respect in which its exterior contributes to the architectural or
historic interest of any group of buildings of which it forms part;
and

(2) the desirability of preserving, on the ground of its architectural or
historic interest, any feature of the building consisting of a man-
made object or structure fixed to the building or forming part of the
land and comprised within the curtilage of the building.

Furthermore the case of *Iveagh v. the Minister of Housing and Local
Government*[88] decided that it was proper to consider the interest of the
whole group in deciding whether to list a building forming part of a terrace.

In considering what constitutes "architectural" interest, a view must be
taken as to whether the term embraces the art and technique of building in
its widest sense, or the design and appearance of a building in a more
limited context. The assessment of what constitutes good architectural
design will be largely subjective and will inevitably stem from a particular
listing Inspector's specialist knowledge and aesthetic judgement, whereas
an assessment of vernacular buildings in a particular locality could have
been made against an objective points system, in which pre-determined
intrinsic features are awarded a certain score.

The development of modern building techniques has created a number of
potentially interesting situations. Could a building which is of great interest structurally be neither of historic nor of architectural interest? Would a
novel technological development which was part of an ugly and modern
building merit the listing of the building which reflected that technology?
Some might aver that certain "point blocks" which were built in the
1960–70 period in the United Kingdom were of significance in the history of
the development of concrete as a building material, and indeed, several residential tower blocks of this period have been listed in Tower Hamlets and
Camden.[89] Would the scarcity value of a particular type of concrete or the
fact that the point blocks are no longer being built today justify the preservation of a last surviving example? Should such a building properly be
listed? It may be neither beautiful nor old, and could not be regarded as "his-

[88] [1964] 1 Q.B. 395; [1963] 3 W.L.R. 974; 3 All E.R. 817; 128 JP 70; 107 SJ 490–851.
[89] Article in *The Times* by Clive Aslet—June 28, 1994.

toric", but we believe it could be properly listed as the word "architectural" has the widest meaning and will embrace types of materials, methods of building expression and form, space, mass, light, scale, colour and the like, so long as that which is to be listed is in fact a building.

2.38   The DOE Guidance Notes[90] advise that in selecting a building for its association with technological innovation or virtuosity, it is essential that the information is absolutely accurate and dependable, as most of the buildings in this category are selected on the basis of historical fact, *e.g.* the first example of its type or the first use of a material rather than on aesthetic qualities.

If it cannot claim any architectural interest, then it may qualify if it is of historic interest. The determination of what constitutes historic interest is eminently debatable and raises many issues. The DOE Guidance Notes 1993 suggest that an assessment of historic interest should deal with:

(i) the importance of the person or event, and

(ii) the importance of the building in relation to that person's life and work or that event. (The transient association of lodgers or tenants, however eminent, should be looked at critically.)

In paragraph 6.15 to the PPG 15 there are interesting views as to how the DOE and DNH consider historical associations in the listing process:

> Well-documented historical associations of national importance will increase the case for the inclusion of a building in the statutory list. They may justify a higher grading than would otherwise be appropriate, and may occasionally be the deciding factor. But in the Secretary of State's view there should normally be some quality or interest in the physical fabric of the building itself to justify the statutory protection afforded by listing. Either the building should be of some architectural merit in itself, or it should be well preserved in a form which directly illustrates and confirms its historical associations (*e.g.* because of the survival of internal features). Where otherwise unremarkable buildings have historical associations, the Secretary of State's view is that they are normally best commemorated by other means (*e.g.* by a plaque), and that listing will be appropriate only in exceptional cases.

Whilst these guidelines are helpful to a degree, they still nevertheless leave considerable scope for individual interpretation. There is no judicial interpretation of what constitutes "architectural" or "historic" interest in this context.

2.39   A building might have one of the following historic characteristics which may justify its listing:

(1) It might be a building which is historic in the sense that an event occurred which affected the nation's social or economic history. An example would be The Citadel in the Mall built in 1939, which was of great significance in the Second World War but is of no architectural significance. Birch Grove House in Horstead Keynes, Sussex,

---

[90] "Guidance Notes to those concerned in the survey for listing" issued by the DOE in 1985 but revised in 1993 referred to throughout as "the DOE Guidance Notes". The DOE Guidelines Notes include titles, *e.g. What listing means; A Guide to the Legislation; A note about Certificates of Immunity from Listing and How to appeal against Listing.*

the home for 60 years of Harold MacMillan qualifies on the same basis.

(2) It might be a building which has significant historical associations, *e.g.* associations with a person of historic significance—*e.g.* 25 Brook Street, Westminster (a c1725 terrace house where Handel lived) or 48 Doughty Street, WC1 (where Dickens lived). However, it should be a building which has a significant national historical association and not merely a local association. According to paragraph 6.15 of PPG 15, such building may justify a higher grading than would otherwise be appropriate, and may occasionally be the deciding factor. The Secretary of State would normally expect some quality or interest in the physical fabric of the building itself to justify the statutory protection afforded by listing.

(3) It might be a building in which some activity of historic interest occurred; an example might be the Minton Hollins factory at Stoke-on-Trent in which large quantities of the tiles were made which decorated so many of the Victorian houses, churches and public buildings.

(4) It might be a building which is primarily of special architectural interest but which is also of historic interest because of the methods of construction or because of the form, style, details or materials used. Almost any building of architectural interest could contain such an historic interest. An example might be The Wakefield Arms in Wakefield, which is listed because it is the only surviving example of a building covered with Joseph Aspdin's patent Portland cement.

(5) It might be a building which combined a number of these virtues, for example Underhill, Gateshead, an ordinary house but which was the residence of Sir Joseph Swan and which is considered in some detail at paragraph 2.41 below.

How then are these historic buildings reconciled and dealt with in the list? The principles seem to be:

(a) The building itself must first pass the statutory test, of being of special architectural or historic interest. If the building itself cannot as such qualify, then it will not be listed. Centre Point, one of London's landmark buildings, was first refused listing because it was said that it was not yet of sufficient architectural or historic significance.

(b) The building must be historic, and not historical. The significance is fine: "historic" suggests perhaps a building which is significant in its own right, "historical" perhaps suggests a vaguer link with history.

(c) Sometimes a building will only get on to the list because of its historic significance, *e.g.* 1a Cato Street, Westminster, which is a hum-drum stable but "the stable loft was the scene of the Cato Street conspiracy of 1820" and the building is included for this reason. In the Millicent Fawcett Hall, Westminster, which was listed in 1992, great strides in the feminist movement were planned in an entirely undistinguished building architecturally.

(d) The building may rank only as Grade II, but its association or activity may upgrade it, *e.g.* the Handel house quoted above is

41

Grade I, similar houses are Grade II; the Dickens house is Grade I, but other similar houses are Grade II. 180 Ebury Street, SW1 is Grade I because Mozart composed his first symphony there in 1764.

(e) A building can be listed partly for each reason, *e.g.* Enderby House, Christchurch Way, SE10, which is a building of "nondescript external appearance but contains a handsome octagonal first floor room giving on to a diagonal bay from whence the ship owner saw his vessels approach". However, Enderby House belonged to the firm of Samuel Enderby, the largest whalers and sealers in Britain and pioneers of Antarctic exploration. Herman Melville describes their flagship and crew in "Moby Dick". The list observes "listed partly for historical (*sic*) reasons".

2.40   One of the problems associated with listing is selectivity. It will be seen that as we look at buildings nearer in age to our time, selectivity is essential: we cannot list all the examples. The Secretary of State's aim is to list the best examples of the type. This may be difficult to determine and may result in unfairness in what is being selected as a best example compared to what is left.

There is always an element of chance. Chance has been one of the principal factors in selecting historic buildings which have survived. It is unreasonable to expect how a totally foolproof system can be devised for modern buildings. One might think that chance should play its part until such time has elapsed for a more rational decision to be made.

Caution should be exercised where an architecturally undistinguished building is considered for listing because of its alleged historic interest. It might be more appropriate to affix a "blue plaque" to the property instead of adding the building to the list, as indeed the Secretary of State advocates in paragraph 6.15 of PPG 15, when he takes the view that listing (for historic associations) will be appropriate only in exceptional cases.

English Heritage is responsible for selecting people to commemorate and organise the erection of a plaque in London in memory of such a person known as a "blue plaque". This can often remind us of the connection with a building which may itself be otherwise undistinguished. The building will be chosen because the distinguished person "lived here", "lived and worked here" or "began her work here".

Well documented historical associations of national importance will increase the case for listing and may be the deciding factor where the case for listing on other grounds is finely balanced. Usually there must be some quality or interest in the physical fabric of the building itself to justify the statutory protection afforded by listing. Either the building must be of architectural merit in itself, or it must be exceptionally well preserved in a form which directly illustrates and confirms its historical associations. For example, it has been decided not to list the Alexandra Palace as no original TV studio or TV broadcasting artefacts remain connected to the building with its use by the BBC for broadcasting purposes shortly after the BBC was created.

2.41   A particularly useful illustration of a building being listed almost entirely for its historic association is found in an article by Paul Bristow[91] in his des-

[91] *Period Home* (January 1985), p. 15.

cription of Underhill at Gateshead, which is listed Grade II*. Although it is considered to be largely an unprepossessing Victorian house typical of many in the north east, its particular importance lies in an early occupant, Sir Joseph Swan FRS, who lived there from 1869–83. During that time he invented the incandescent electric light bulb and the house was the first in England to be wired for domestic electric lighting. Its importance is thus threefold, it was the home for a considerable period of an important inventor and is the place both of the invention and of the first application of the light bulb on which his fame rests. Paul Bristow considers that whereas one of these associations would have made it listable, the three together give it the high grading.

A further example of a listing for historic interest is St Mark's Railway Station, Lincoln. The Inspector in an LBC case, recommending refusal to demolish, noted that the buildings "are of historic interest because they form part of Lincoln's first railway station".[92] Presumably this was thought (as the Secretary of State agreed with his Inspector and refused LBC) to be enough, *i.e.* of local historic interest. It could be argued that if the interest was to be local only, any building of a minute local interest would be adequate to satisfy the test—what about *The Little Puddlecombe Police Cell*? Paragraph 6.16 of PPG 15 suggests such buildings may not merit listing but could be included in a conservation area or the local planning authority could draw up a list of locally important buildings. These could be referred to in local plan policies, but the policies should make clear that such buildings do not enjoy the full protection of statutory listing. But we have no defined criterion as to whether the historic interest is local, regional, or national. A challenge in the courts would, however, be helpful. There may well be found a practical distinction between "architectural" and "historic" citations when the possibility of a demolition and building of a pastiche occurs. Further examples of "historic interest" are to be found in Chapter 4.

How are the buildings chosen? PPG 15 has replaced the old criteria for choosing buildings for listing with new and rather less precise advice. The two relevant paragraphs are as follows:

"6.10 The following are the main criteria which the Secretary of State applies as appropriate in deciding which buildings to include in the statutory lists:

— **architectural interest:** the lists are meant to include all buildings which are of importance to the nation for the interest of their architectural design, decoration and craftsmanship; also important examples of particular building types and techniques (*e.g.* buildings displaying technological innovation or virtuosity) and significant plan forms;

— **historic interest:** this includes buildings which illustrate important aspects of the nation's social, economic, cultural or military history;

— **close historical associations:** with nationally important people or events;

— **group value:** especially where buildings comprise together an

---

[92] DOE reference EMP/5311/270/G5 (reported in *The Estates Times*, July 3, 1981).

important architectural or historical unity or a fine example of planning (*e.g.* squares, terraces or model villages).

Not all these criteria will be relevant to every case, but a particular building may qualify for listing under more than one of them (6.12 of PPG 15).

Age and rarity are relevant considerations, particularly where buildings are proposed for listing on the strength of their historic interest. The older a building is, and the fewer the surviving examples of its kind, the more likely it is to have historic importance. Thus, all buildings built before 1700 which survive in anything like their original condition are listed; and most buildings of about 1700 to 1840 are listed, though some selection is necessary. After about 1840, because of the greatly increased number of buildings erected and the much larger numbers that have survived, greater selection is necessary to identify the best examples of particular building types, and only buildings of definite quality and character are listed. For the same reasons, only selected buildings from the period after 1914 are normally listed. Buildings which are less than 30 years old are normally listed only if they are of outstanding quality and under threat. Buildings which are less than ten years old are not listed."

2.42 The approach adopted for twentieth-century listing is to identify key exemplars for each of a range of building types, industrial, educational, residential, etc., and to treat these exemplars as broadly defining a standard against which to judge proposals for further additions to the list. This approach has already been successfully applied to the inter-war period, and English Heritage is now engaged on a three year research programme to extend it to the post-war period (subject to the "30 year rule" just mentioned). Proposals for listings in each building type will be made as each stage of the research is completed.

On deciding which buildings to include in the list, the Secretary of State is advised by English Heritage; the provision of such advice being one of English Heritage's specific functions under the terms of the National Heritage Act 1983. The DNH keep the listing standards under review and they are revised from time to time. Indeed, Paul Bristow, a former Head of Listing, acknowledges that the selection process has evolved over a considerable period of time, usually just a little ahead of public opinion, but in some fields, particularly Victorian, industrial and modern buildings, some distance behind. The process of revision was also ignited in response to a *cause célèbre* such as the demolition of the Euston Arch (1961) which was listed, and the Firestone factory (1980)[93] which was not.

Post War listing. In launching a national competition in 1987 to identify the first 50 post-war buildings to be listed, Mr William Waldegrave, then Environment Minister, identified guidelines for selection:

"Buildings selected will be of strictly national or international importance. In this context the selection will be made on grounds of architectural quality or historic importance. Buildings selected will *either* be of very high architectural quality *or* reflect innovation in technology, planning or style, *or* will be associated with persons or events of exceptional national significance.

[93] 1980 – 255 E.G. 851.

Competitors were asked to note that *architectural quality* is often apparent in a building (whether innovatory in 'style' or not) in the choice and use of materials, in its detailing, in its proportions or in its planning and general design. It may also be revealed in its originality or ingenuity of treatment, or in the building's contribution to its setting or the townscape. Competitors were encouraged to consider how far the architect has realised his intentions in a building and how these relate to other work of the period.

Buildings may alternatively be listable for their historic importance. This could include major stylistic innovations, pioneering technological or structural techniques and major innovations in planning or within a building type (for example, housing, education, offices, or industrial buildings). It could also include associations with significant person or events."

In very exceptional circumstances, buildings of outstanding quality (*i.e.* Grade I or II*) which are under threat will be listed provided they are 10 years old. The then Environment Minister, William Waldegrave, announced the 10 year rule at a meeting of the Joint Committee of the National Amenity Societies:

"Because of the rapid rate at which redevelopment is going in some places, I think it is necessary to have the capacity to safeguard even quite new buildings. In addition to the 30 year rule, we are therefore now prepared to consider listing any building over 10 years old, provided that it is of outstanding quality and there is an imminent threat to it. We would not expect to list more than a few such buildings each year."[94]

The first listing made under the 30 year rule was Bracken House, situated **2.43** opposite St Paul's Cathedral, which was at the time of its listing in imminent danger of demolition.[95] On April 25, 1991[96] the then Heritage Minister, Lady Blatch, announced the Grade I listing of the Willis Faber Office building, Ipswich, completed in 1975. This was the first 1970s building to be listed under the 30 year rule. As at February 1992 there were 26 buildings listed within the 30 year and 10 year rules.[97] In 1992 English Heritage embarked upon a three year research programme to identify the main post-1939 building types, to identify key examples of such types and to provide guidelines for future listings.[98] An exhibition entitled "A time for change" was opened by Mr Jocelyn Stevens, the Chairman of English Heritage, in July 1992, demonstrating types of post-war buildings which might be considered for listing.

This was followed in March 1995 by an invitation by the then National Heritage Secretary, Stephen Dorrell, for the public to give their views on the 40 modern buildings which had been recommended to him for listing. This was the first time the views of the members of the public as well as the professional and amenity societies were being sought on listing recommendations. Amongst the 40 modern buildings recommended for listing was

---

[94] *DOE News Release*, no. 167, April 2, 1987.

[95] *English Heritage Conservation Bulletin*, February 1992, p. 2.

[96] *DOE News Release* no. 256, April 25, 1991.

[97] *English Heritage Conservation Bulletin*, February 1992.

[98] *English Heritage Conservation Bulletin*, February 1992.

Centre Point in Central London which had previously been regarded as being unworthy of listing.

A building in respect of which the list refers to as having "group value" means that the building is not itself of special architectural or historic interest (otherwise it would be listed) but it may also has merit as part of a group. The building may have achieved a higher grading as a result. A similar effect might have been achieved by the building being part of a conservation area: however, such a designation is not within the power of the Department of National Heritage (which lists buildings) but can only be achieved by the local planning authority (which designates conservation areas). The reference to group value however directs the reader of the list to look about him and consider contributions which the building makes to the group.

Regarding the "group value" of buildings the DOE Guidance Notes of 1993 advise:

> "The replacement factor must also be kept in mind when selecting buildings in the group category. A building must not be chosen merely because its neighbours are good and one is afraid that if it were demolished it would be replaced by an incongruous monstrosity. The design of a new building can and should be controlled under general planning powers and it is not permissible therefore to place a building on the statutory list simply to ensure a congruity of neighbourhood which could as well be achieved in a new building. It must be possible to say that the existing building has some quality in relation to the context which no new building could have."

2.44   This leaves, therefore, buildings which may be significant but which do not fall within any of the above gradings. A building which is of ordinary architectural or historic interest should not be listed. The three tests must be passed, namely that the building must be of interest, the interest must be architectural or historic, and the building must be of "special" architectural or historic interest. An interesting example of the difference in this terminology is to be found in a ministerial planning decision on an appeal by National Westminster Bank Ltd against the refusal of LBC to demolish 10 and 12 St Peter's Street, St Albans, which had been referred to the Secretary of State.[99] The Secretary of State refused LBC and dismissed the appeal, agreeing with his Inspector. The Inspector's report was carefully worded and opened with his description of the building as follows:

> "I am of the opinion in respect of the application for LBC that while the building is not of historical interest or of great architectural merit, its facade makes an important contribution to the attractiveness and interest of the street scene on this side of St Peter's Street, and to the particular character of the group of buildings of which it forms part, and that it merits retention on that account . . . ."

The emphasis in the listing criteria is on national significance. The best examples of local vernacular buildings will normally be listed but many buildings which are valued for their contribution to the local scene or for their local historic associations will not.

[99] [1974] J.P.L. 552 Ref. SE6 1582/270/17; APP/1582/N/63586, December 10, 1973.

(b) Grading

If a building falls within the above principles of selection, then if it is **2.45**
listed, it is graded. English Heritage recommend a grade when recommending listing. However, the final decision on both the listing itself and the
grade rests with the Secretary of State for National Heritage. There is no
reference in the LBA 1990 to grading. There has, however, developed over
the years a system of grading of buildings included in the list which, whilst
it may have no statutory significance as such, has an administrative importance in relation to grants and LBC. The Department gives guidance as to
how it approaches the problem in PPG 15, paragraph 3.6. It is there said that
"the grading of a building in the statutory lists is clearly a material consideration for the exercise of listed building control".

The first division in grading is an historic one between secular and
ecclesiastical buildings. Secular buildings are divided into Grades I, II* and
II and these grades also apply to redundant Anglican churches, proprietory
buildings such as college chapels, and churches of other denominations.
Anglican churches in use were originally graded A, B or C, but since 1977
the Department has graded churches by reference to the secular notation.

Dealing firstly with the secular buildings: Paragraph 3.6 of PPG 15 shows
the present departmental approach to grading: "Grades I and II* identify the
outstanding architectural or historic interest of a small proportion (about
six per cent) of all listed buildings. These buildings are of particularly great
importance to the nation's built heritage: their significance will generally
be beyond dispute"[1].

The PPG 15 emphasises, however, that the statutory controls apply
equally to all listed buildings, irrespective of grade, and since Grade II
includes almost 95 per cent of all listed buildings, representing the major
element in the historic quality of our villages, towns and cities, failure to
give careful scrutiny to proposals for their alteration or demolition could
lead to widespread damage to the historic environment.

The buildings were classified in grades to show their relative importance, **2.46**
and in Circular 8/87 were described as follows, although this description is
not followed through in PPG 15:

Grade I	These are buildings of exceptional interest (only about 1.4 per cent of listed buildings so far are in this grade).
*Grade II**	These are particularly important buildings of more than special interest (some 4.1 per cent of listed buildings).
Grade II	These are buildings of special interest, which warrant every effort being made to preserve them.
Grade III	A non-statutory and now obsolete grade. Grade III buildings were those which, whilst not qualifying for the statutory list, were considered neverthe-less to be of some importance. Many of these buildings are now considered to be of special inter-

---

[1] An interesting breakdown of the various building types contained within the
Grade I category is set out in *Conservation Bulletin* November 1994 in an article
by Sally Embree entitled "Grade 1 buildings at risk survey".

est by current standards, particularly where they possess "group value", and are being added to the statutory lists as these are revised.

The following summary of re-survey grading practice reflects current English Heritage practice and is reproduced with their kind permission:

"Grade I buildings must be of the very highest quality by virtue of their aesthetic, innovative, or other design attributes. Many are likely to be of international significance and they will be largely complete inside and out, as a coherent design, a balance of consecutive designs, or as a discrete and distinctive fragment.

Grade II* buildings will inevitably include buildings which would be of Grade I quality except for unfortunate alterations, demolitions and mutilations. More likely, they will be buildings which retain note-worthy features, internal and external, but are not complete. They may also be absolutely intact examples of modest building, or intact examples of a definable, local, type. Buildings possessing particular his-toric interest, by association with important people or events, are also put into this grade.

As a thematic approach to listing is developed, it will be possible to refine our criteria for judging which buildings fall within Grades I and II* for those classes of buildings identified as currently undervalued or undergraded."

Prior to 1992 there was no definite correlation between grading for listing purposes and grading applicable to grant provision.

However in 1992 in relation to grants administered by English Heritage the former arrangement, which required an assessment of "outstanding-ness" for grants given under section 3A of the Historic Buildings and Ancient Monuments Act 1953 as amended by Schedule 4 of the National Heritage Act 1983, was discontinued and a building to qualify as outstand-ing and receive grant aid must now be Grade I or Grade II*.

2.47 Although there is now no Grade III listing, however, some local planning authorities effectively have a Grade III listing for buildings which do not qualify as buildings of special architectural or historic interest. The local planning authority puts them on a "local list", which "list" may or may not be formally established: what often happens is that the Local Plan indicates that the local planning authority will not in normal circumstances give LBC for the demolition of a building on the "local list". Paragraph 6.16 of PPG 15 points out that it is open to planning authorities to draw up lists of locally important buildings and to formulate local plan policies for their protection through the normal development control procedures. It advises that policies should make it clear that such buildings do not enjoy the full protection of statutory listing. Sometimes the statement in a Local Plan is rather more strongly worded than this and invests these local lists with a greater weight than they are given by statute deserve. It may also seek to impose certain standards on the alteration or extension of buildings on the "local lists". There is no statutory backing for such lists, except in so far as the statute authorises the principle of approval of a Local Plan.

There is therefore a somewhat confusing gradation of protection of a building.

Listed Grade I and II*   On the statutory list with the control exercised by

	the LPA but with the benefit of advice of English Heritage.
Listed Grade II	On the statutory list with the control exercised by the LPA who have the benefit of advice (if they seek to obtain it) of English Heritage.
Conservation Area	A building which is in an area designated by the LPA which controls demolition of most buildings by CAC and which regulates demolition and alteration and extension by normal planning controls, subject to certain exceptions.
"Local list"	A building which has been indicated (either individually or as a building in an area designated in the Plan) as one in relation to which a Local Plan policy will be operated by the LPA. The policy might seek to impose a presumption against demolition or impose general or specific controls on alteration or extensions, but such a policy has no statutory authority under LBA.
"An area which is subject to an Article 4 direction" (under the T.C.P. General Permitted Development Order 1995)	An article 4 direction will take away a building owner's rights to carry out "permitted development". This is to be used only in exceptional circumstances. Either in conjunction with conservation area status or independently, the direction is a form of control which results in an owner having to obtain specific planning permission for various works.

About two per cent of listed buildings are in Grade I; but as the listing **2.48** progresses the percentage of Grade I buildings in relation to the total will no doubt fall—as it is unlikely that many buildings new to the list will be of Grade I standard. The Department elsewhere[2] defines the "Upper Category", *i.e.* Grades I and II*, as of "paramount" or exceptional interest in a national context. For the meaning of "paramount" we might follow the *Oxford English Dictionary's* definition as "above all other in rank, order or jurisdiction"; "exceptional" means, generally, rare or unusual. It is worth noting of the almost 16,303 listed Anglican churches, nearly 3,000 were of the Grade I category and 50 per cent of churches are placed in this "Upper Category".[3]

The fact that grading is a non-statutory process is further confused by a variety of criteria expressed to differentiate buildings in the most important grade. As we have seen, Circular 8/87 defined Grade I buildings as "of exceptional interest", as does the *English Heritage Monitor (1993)* published by English Tourist Board; John Ayers describes a Grade I building as of "outstanding national interest",[4] as does the *Essex County Council Guide to Historic Buildings*.[5] The phrase "exceptional" is a relative term, but the definition of "outstanding national interest", is perhaps a better guide, as

---

[2] DOE "Guidance Notes" 1993.

[3] *English Heritage Monitor*, 1995.

[4] John Ayers, *The Historical and Architectural Criteria*: Address to the Oxford Conference 1976 in *Journal of Planning and Environment Law*, Occasional Papers (1977), p. 53.

[5] *Conservation in Essex no. 4*: "Historic Buildings", Essex CC (undated).

the use of a qualification such as "exceptional" must postulate the question: "exceptional" to whom? to what? The very phrase "outstanding national interest" on the contrary can be quite legitimately read to mean "that which the public will regard as of outstanding interest nationally". With this variety of phraseology we are probably left with the test of "exceptional interest", with all the problems of such a definition, as this is the DOE's own phrase and it is they who invented the process anyway!

2.49   The next problem which arises is trying to determine what buildings should or should not be included in the Grade II* category. How does a building qualify for being "a particularly important building"? Presumably it is less than a building of exceptional interest or of outstanding national interest, but it is more important than being merely of "special architectural or historic interest". One interpretation which appears to be adopted by the Department for administrative purposes is to suggest that not only is the exterior "special", but the interior as well. An alternative interpretation is illustrated in the Underhill, Gateshead case referred to at paragraph 2.41 above, where a multiple historic association justified a higher grading. The majority of buildings are listed solely on their external virtue, and this is right. One of the main purposes of listing is to protect buildings from too hasty demolition. Paragraph 3.17 of PPG 15 states "that there are many outstanding buildings for which it is in practice almost inconceivable that consent for demolition would ever be granted. The demolition of any Grade I or II* building should be wholly exceptional and should require the strongest justification." It continues by saying "the Secretaries of State would not expect consent to be given for the total or substantial demolition of any listed building without clear and convincing evidence that reasonable efforts have been made to sustain existing uses or find viable new uses and those efforts have failed; . . . or that redevelopment would produce substantial benefits for the community which would decisively outweigh the loss resulting from demolition. The Secretaries of State would not expect consent to demolition to be given simply because redevelopment is economically more attractive to the developer than repair and re-use of a historic building, or because the developer acquired the building at a price that reflected the potential for redevelopment rather than the conditions and constraints of the existing historic building."

There emerges from these considerations a hierarchy of buildings which we categorise as follows:

Grade I—	Buildings of exceptional interest: although most of these may have interiors of considerable significance, this is not necessary in order to qualify for this grading. In 1994 in England there were 11,600 listed.
Grade II*—	Buildings which fall into the category of being of exceptional interest but are more worthy than the average building of "special architectural or historic interest". The presence of a fine interior would seem to justify a building being placed in this category as would a strong historical association. In 1994 there were about 23,000 of Grade II* buildings.
Grade II—	Buildings of "special architectural or historic

interest" which warrant every effort being made to preserve them. In 1994 there were 412,443 (representing approximately 94 per cent) of Grade II buildings.

In this latter connection it is important to emphasise that the qualification of warranting every effort being made to preserve the building is not a statutory qualification, nor indeed is the whole of the grading process. All that is required under the LBA is that a building falls within the category of "special architectural or historic interest".

In so far as ecclesiastical buildings are concerned, there was for some time **2.50** (until 1977) a different system of grading for such buildings. The three grades for Anglican churches (including cathedrals) were as follows:

Grade A (i) Medieval—Exceptional and retaining pristine character.
  (ii) Reformation to 1840—Exceptional.
  (iii) Victorian to 1914—Exceptional.
Grade B (i) Medieval—More modest buildings than A(i) or those overlaid by subsequent reconstruction.
  (ii) Reformation to 1840—Of particular importance but not exceptional.
  (iii) Victorian to 1914—Of particular importance but not exceptional.
Grade C (i) Reformation to 1840—Minor or plain buildings, just of statutory quality.
  (ii) 1830 Gothic and standard Victorian—Just of statutory quality.

The Historic Buildings Council (as it then was) advised in August 1977 **2.51** that the use of A, B and C grades for Anglican churches in use to be discontinued, that the Grade I, II* and II be introduced and that the grading of Anglican churches be fully equivalent to that of secular buildings. For listing purposes, the following four categories are recognised[6]:

(i) Churches which are recognisably of pre-Reformation date.
(ii) Churches of post-Reformation date which were built before the 1818 Act though selection is necessary.
(iii) Between 1818 and 1914 churches of definite quality and character apart from those that form part of a group. The selection should include the important works of major architects.
(iv) A selection of churches of 1914 to 1939.

In selecting churches for listing, particular attention should be paid to:

(a) Churches which are important examples of regional church types.
(b) Churches which contain major paintings, glass, sculpture, monuments and fittings. The DOE Guidance Notes comment that there will be few churches which are listable solely for such features and it will be rare that churches in this category do not already qualify for listing under (i), (ii) or (iii) above.
(c) Churches which are materially associated with historic events or persons of national importance. Again the DOE Guidance Notes observe that there will be few churches which do not already qualify under (i), (ii) or (iii) above, and only rarely will a person or event

---

[6] These "Lettered" grades still remain in the older lists.

be of such importance as to transcend all other considerations. This category may well be an important one for non-conformist churches.

(d) Churches having group value especially as an integral part of a planned scheme.

See Chapter 10 for more detail concerning churches.

5. DEEMED LISTING

2.52   Deemed listing is a process by which a building is not treated either as part of the overall survey by the Department, nor spot listed, but is deemed to be included in the list and in respect of which all the listed building provisions will apply.

There are two categories of buildings which are deemed to have been listed, namely those which were specifically covered by building preservation orders[7] and those which are the subject of building preservation notices.[8]

(a) Building preservation order

The building preservation order (see paragraph 2.04 above) was an order which was made by a local authority (subject to Ministerial approval) under the pre-1968 legislation. The purpose of the relevant section of the Town and Country Planning Act 1968 was to give the same protection as a listed building to each building included in the pre–1968 list as compared to those buildings which had been the subject of a specific building preservation order.

The powers in relation to buildings formerly subject to building preservation orders are preserved by section 1(6) and Schedule 1 of the LBA 1990.

2.53   Schedule 1 of the LBA provides that:

"1 Subject to paragraph 2, every building which immediately before 1st January 1969 was subject to a building preservation order under Part III of the 1962 Act, but was not then included in a list compiled or approved under section 32 of that Act, shall be deemed to be a listed building.

2 (1) The Secretary of State may at any time direct, in the case of any building, that paragraph 1 shall no longer apply to it.

(2) The local planning authority in whose area a building in respect of which such a direction is given is situated shall, on being notified of the direction, give notice of it to the owner and occupier of the building.

(3) Before giving such a direction in relation to a building situated in England, the Secretary of State shall consult with the Commission who shall in turn consult with the local planning authority and the owner and occupier of the building.

---

[7] LBA 1990, Sched 1, para. 1.
[8] LBA 1990, s.3(5).

(4) Before giving such a direction in relation to a building not situated in England, the Secretary of State shall consult with the local planning authority and the owner and occupier of the building.

3   In the case of a building to which paragraph 1 applies:

(a) a notice of appeal under section 20 may include a claim that the Secretary of State should give a direction under paragraph 2 with respect to the building and on such an appeal the Secretary of State may give such a direction; and

(b) such a direction may also be given on an appeal under section 39."

The Secretary of State has an obligation under paragraph 2(3) of the Schedule to consult with English Heritage, who in turn is required to consult the local planning authority and the owner or occupier of the building before a direction is given.

Following the re-survey completed during 1987 (see paragraph 2.42 above) there are unlikely to be any buildings now subject to building preservation orders which have not now been incorporated into the list.

(b) Building preservation notice

The building preservation notice is the "emergency" procedure which is **2.54** applicable under sections 3(1) and (2) of the LBA 1990 and which provides that:

"3 (1) If it appears to a local planning authority, other than a county planning authority, that a building in their area which is not a listed building:

(a) is of special architectural or historic interest; and

(b) is in danger of demolition or of alteration in such a way as to affect its character as a building of such interest.

they may serve on the owner and occupier of the building a notice (in this Act referred to as a "building preservation notice").

(2) A building preservation notice served by a local planning authority shall:

(a) state that the building appears to them to be of special architectural or historic interest and that they have requested the Secretary of State to consider including it in a list compiled or approved under section 1; and

(b) explain the effect of subsections (3) to (5) and Schedule 2."

Under section 60(2) of the LBA, a building preservation notice cannot be served in some circumstances including in respect of an ecclesiastical building which is for the time being used for ecclesiastical purposes or a building which is a scheduled monument.

The building preservation notice comes into force as soon as it has been served on both the owner and the occupier of the building to which it relates and remains in force for six months from the date when it is served, or as the case may be, last served; but it ceases to be in force if, before the expiration of that period, the Secretary of State either lists the building or notifies the local planning authority in writing that he does not intend to do so.[9] During the period that a building preservation notice is in force, the provisions of the LBA (other than section 59 of the LBA: damage to listed buildings) shall have effect as if the building were a listed building.[10] If, following the service of a building preservation notice, the Secretary of State notifies the local planning authority that he does not propose to include the building in the list, then the authority must immediately give notice of the Secretary of State's decision to the owner and occupier of the building and may not within 12 months beginning from the date of the notification serve another notice in respect of the building.[11] If it appears to the local planning authority to be urgent that a building preservation notice should come into force, it may instead of serving the notice on the owner and occupier of the building to which it relates, affix the notice conspicuously to some object on the building and this will be treated for all the purposes of section 3 of the LBA and other sections as service of the notice.[12]

2.55   Section 29 of the LBA contains provisions relating to compensation for loss or damage where a building preservation notice is served. It provides that:

> "29 (1) This section applies where a building preservation notice ceases to have effect without the building having been included in a list compiled or approved by the Secretary of State under section 1.
>
> (2) Any person who at the time when the notice was served had an interest in the building shall, on making a claim to the authority within the prescribed time and in the prescribed manner, be entitled to be paid compensation by the local planning authority in respect of any loss or damage directly attributable to the effect of the notice.
>
> (3) The loss or damage in respect of which compensation is payable under subsection (2) shall include a sum payable in respect of any breach of contract caused by the necessity of discontinuing or countermanding any works to the building on account of the building preservation notice being in force with respect to it."

6. THE MECHANICS OF LISTING

2.56   In addition to listing as part of a general re-survey and the methods of deemed listing buildings may be added to the list where they appear on a draft re-survey list and there is an actual or apprehended threat to them. We set out below the mechanics of listing as part of a re-survey[13]:

---

[9] LBA 1990, s.3(3) and (4).
[10] LBA 1990, s.3(5).
[11] LBA 1990, s.3(6) and (7).
[12] LBA 1990, s.4 and T.C.P.A. 1990, s.329 as to service of notice.
[13] [1990] J.P.L. 551: an article by Michael Ross, formerly of the Listing Department of the DOE.

(i) Re-survey fieldwork is the responsibility of the Secretary of State's statutory advisors (English Heritage). A supervising area Inspector prepares a schedule for use by fieldworkers which is divided into target area allocations which take approximately three months to complete. Each allocation is normally processed into one volume of the proposed statutory list, but if more than one volume is required the list will be divided alphabetically by street name.

(ii) Prior to going into the field the fieldworker studies the department's files to ascertain what buildings and structures have previously been assessed. The existing list for the relevant area is perused as well as *Pevsner's Buildings of England*, the *Victoria County Histories* and other published material. Local authorities will be consulted, especially regarding archival material which may be in their possession. Fieldworkers are also urged to consult local history and amenity groups.

(iii) The fieldworker takes to the field armed with a 1:25,000 scale of the Ordnance Survey map, a manual issued by English Heritage and an identity card. The fieldworker consults his colleagues and the area inspector when the need arises. The area supervisor visits each fieldworker from time to time to carry out a quality control check to ensure that the special interest of local styles of building are judged in a national context. Each fieldworker is bound by a code of conduct which gives advice and guidance in a number of areas, including contacting and co-operating with owners, the avoidance of trespass, and the notification to the police and parish councils that fieldworkers are active in an area.

(iv) The exterior of a building is inspected with a view to establishing **2.57** its approximate date, form, and function. Internal inspection of the building, where this can be arranged, will assist the fieldworker to reach a conclusion on whether the property is of listable quality. This is particularly important where internal features survive but external features have been obscured by later alterations.

(v) Each draft recommendation for listing accompanied by a photograph is submitted to a supervising inspector. Each entry is given a serial number, grid reference, address, proposed grading and a note of any group value. The list description details the most important features of the building but the listing covers the entire building. The list description may indicate what is not considered to be of special interest, such as a twentieth century extension.

(vi) The completed draft list goes forward to the Secretary of State for signature. In the majority of cases the decision to list is taken by a senior executive officer in the Department's Listing Branch, although controversial cases will be referred to the Minister responsible for heritage matters. In a few cases the Secretary of State will make the decision whether to list but these usually relate to spot listing cases. In most cases the Secretary of State accepts English Heritage's advice whether to add a property to the statutory list but he is not bound to accept such advice. Once the Secretary of State is satisfied that a building has special architectural or historic interest he is under a duty to list (section 1(1) of the LBA).

(vii) The list takes effect once it is typed and signed. The DOE and now

55

the DNH immediately informs by first class post the relevant local authority which advises the owner or occupier of the building that listing has taken place. The letter to the owner or occupier informs them that henceforth LBC will be required for any alterations to the building. The letter is an informal, non-statutory document and with it the owner or occupier will receive a guidance leaflet.

(viii) The local authority is required formally to serve a statutory notice upon each owner and occupier of a building in a list in compliance with section 2(3) of the LBA informing them of the listing.

(ix) The listing must then be registered as a local land charge by the local authority in accordance with section 2(2) of the LBA.

(x) The DNH has put out for the first time a list of 40 recently built buildings which the DNH proposes to list, but has first invited the public to consider the list.

2.58 Applications for "spot listing" can be made to the Secretary of State for the Department of National Heritage by any person. Paragraph 6.21 of PPG 15 refers to the difficulties that can arise where proposals for spot listing are made at a very late stage of a redevelopment proposal, when buildings are under imminent threat of demolition. Spot listing in such cases can often mean delay, sometimes with serious practical and financial consequences to the developer. It is preferable that buildings should be assessed for possible listing before planning permission has been granted for redevelopment. Requests to list are sent to the listing branch of the DNH or its equivalents in Scotland and Wales and should include an address, location plan, recent photograph and information relevant to the age and history of the building. The department assesses the urgency of the request, usually in conjunction with the local authority. The DNH carry out checks on the documentation that they or English Heritage may hold, for example, details of any previous assessment. If the property has been assessed for listing before and there is no new evidence produced to the DNH, then rejection is likely. If there is new evidence then the DNH request advice from English Heritage. English Heritage are normally given eight weeks in which to respond to the DNH's request for advice. English Heritage then decides whether to make a visit or rely on photographs before reporting to the DNH. If English Heritage report that the building is not listable, then invariably the matter will be dealt with at officer level within the DNH. If English Heritage report that the building is listable, then the Principal Inspector of English Heritage will consider the file before it is passed on to the DNH. Ministers in the DNH see and decide all certificates of immunity and potentially controversial cases. The final decision in the majority of listing cases is taken by a senior executive officer in the DNH and thereafter the procedure is identical to that described above relating to listings resulting from re-surveys.

Spot listing will take place if there is a real risk to the future of the property, *e.g.* if it is up for sale by auction or private treaty; but not where the threat is only a vague one, particularly if there are strong signs that the building will in due course be listed anyway. Spot listings are now personally approved by a Minister. The Department may spot list to enable an owner to obtain the benefit of the VAT exemption if the usual criteria are satisfied.

2.59 We set out below statistics relating to spot listings in the period 1984–1994:

Year	Buildings Listed	Spot Listings	Building Preservation Notices
1984	29,222	744	137
1985	30,211	1,254	295
1986	27,657	1,645	218
1987	32,603	1,789	75
1988	21,460	1,854	113
1989	7,024	1,579	76
1990	2,285		
1991	1,840	1,120	42
1992		814	45
1993		1,052	41
1994		852	39

7. THE LISTED BUILDING AND THE GENERAL PERMITTED DEVELOPMENT ORDER

The Town and Country Planning (General Permitted Development) Order) **2.60**
1995[14] is a general order, applicable to all land in England and Wales, providing for the grant of permission for the development of land pursuant to the provisions of sections 59 to 61 of the T.C.P.A. 1990 is amended by the Planning and Compensations Act 1991. The Order sets out in detail the classes of development ("permitted development") for which planning permission is granted. Most are relatively minor permissions, *e.g.* house extensions, walls and fences, but some have considerable effect. No application for planning permission is required so long as the conditions in the order are adhered to.

The uncertainty created by the case of *Cambridge City Council v. Secretary of State for the Environment and Milton Park Investment Limited*[15–18] relating to the requirement for planning permission in respect of demolition works led the government to introduce selective control of demolition. Section 13 of the Planning and Compensation Act 1991 introduced new provisions into section 55 of the T.C.P. Act 1990 (T.C.P.A.). These new subsections 1A and 2(g) are discussed at 3.15. The effect of these changes is to extend the definition of "building operations" in section 55 of the T.C.P.A. 1990 to include demolition of buildings. But the Secretary of State is empowered to exclude any description of building from the scope of the section. The new controls were brought into force on July 27, 1992 and were designed to confine the control of demolition to a narrow range of property: the power is to be used to exclude from control all demolitions except dwelling houses and adjoining buildings.

In the General Permitted Development Order there appears in Article 4 a provision whereby permitted development can be restricted by a direction (usually no doubt will continue to be known as an "Article 4 direction") made by the Secretary of State or the local planning authority. Generally an Article 4 direction made by a local planning authority has to be approved by the Secretary of State.

Schedule 2 of the Town & Country Planning (General Permitted Develop-

[14] S.I. 1995 — 418.
[15–18] [1991] J.P.L. 428.

ment) Order 1995 makes four main changes and a number of minor changes to the GDO provision. The subjects relate to environmental assessment, closed circuit television cameras, dwelling houses in conservation areas and demolition in conservation areas. For instance part 33 of Schedule 2 relates to Closed Circuit Television Cameras and directs the number of cameras and their position on any building but it differentiates between a non-listed and a listed building, or a scheduled monument.

2.61   Directions under Article 4(2) of the 1995 Order may be used to withdraw permitted development rights for the a series of categories of development as are set out in sub-paragraph(s) of the order. To enable these permitted development rights to be given for such demolition, a new Direction – the Town and Country Planning (Demolition – Descriptions of Buildings) Direction 1994 came into force on June 3, 1995 bringing the demolition of a whole or part of any gate, fence, wall or other means of enclosure in a conservation area within the statutory definition of "development". There is a list of Article 4(2) directions *not* requiring the Secretary of State's approval and a list of procedural points to obtain Article 4(2) directions. Details are provided in connection with development within the curtilage of a dwelling house tidying up a number of useful amendments. Details of changes of use and caravan sites are detailed as are agricultural buildings, forestry buildings industrial and warehouse development, coal mining, waste tipping and mineral exploration. Erection or placing of tents on land by a member of a recreational organisation outwith the curtilage of a dwelling house giving the names of the certificated organisations (*e.g.* The Boys Brigade). Schools, colleges, universities and hospitals are given special provisions.[19]

2.62   A useful Appendix on the best practice in handling planning applications is provided with clear advice on how planning applications may best be approached. Further advice on Consultations before the grant of planning permission is given with very useful advice and a list of useful addresses.[20]

8. THE CONSEQUENCES OF LISTING

2.63   The following are the consequences of a building being included in the statutory list:

(a) The copy of the list relating to a London borough or a district is deposited with the borough or district, and outside Greater London, with the country planning authority whose area includes the district or any part of it (or the relevant district in a metropolitan authority), and where the district is not the district planning authority, *e.g.* in a New Town area, with the proper officer of that area:

(b) The DNH informs the relevant local authority and the owner or occupier of the building that listing has taken place;

(c) A copy is registered in the register of local land charges by the local planning authority;

(d) A notice is served by the local planning authority in the prescribed form on every owner and occupier of the building by the London borough or district stating that the building has been included in the list. The prescribed form is in Town and Country Planning

[19–20] T.C.P. (GPD) Order 1995

(Listed Buildings and Conservation Areas) Regulations 1990 (Schedule 4); s. 1 1990, no. 1519;

(e) A copy of the list is made available by the Secretary of State for public inspection free of charge at reasonable times and in a convenient place [It is also available at the Royal Commission of Historic Monuments' office at 23 Savile Row, London W1X 1AB];

(f) The listing takes effect on the date of the signing of the list, and not on the service of the notice;

(g) If permitted development is being carried out and the building is listed, the owner must stop. However, he must then consider whether the work he is carrying out would affect the character as a building of special architectural or historic interest: it may be a fine judgment to make;

(h) If any person executes or causes to be executed works for demolition, alteration or extension of a building in any manner which would affect its character as a building of special architectural or historic interest (thus it is not all work which offends—only work affecting the character of the building) without the works having been authorised under the LBA, he is guilty of an offence.[21] Under section 8(3) of the LBA he may obtain permission *ex post facto*. However, he is still liable in respect of his original offence and the penalties are on summary conviction imprisonment of up to three months or a fine not exceeding the statutory maximum (at present £20,000)[22] or both; on indictment: imprisonment of up to 12 months or a fine, or both; **2.64**

(i) The fixing or display of almost all advertisements on listed buildings will constitute an "alteration" and LBC will be required in addition to any advertisement consent under the Town and Country Planning (Control of Advertisements) Regulation 1992.[23] The DNH issued a Planning Policy Guidance no. 19 in March 1992 on the subject of Outdoor Advertisement Control;

(j) Where a local planning authority is of the opinion that works are being undertaken in contravention of section 7 of the LBA, it has the power to serve a listed building enforcement notice under section 38 of the LBA; **2.65**

(k) The *ex post facto* authorisation of works under section 8(3) of the LBA may only be excluded from the need to obtain the grant of LBC in the case of a proposal to demolish, or to alter or extend a listed building.[24]

(l) Permitted development under Article 3 of the Town and Country Planning (General Permitted Development) Order 1995 may be curtailed by an Article 4 direction[25];

(m) The local authority has power to carry out works to unoccupied listed buildings and to recharge the owner[26];

---

[21] LBA 1990, ss.7 and 9.

[22] LBA 1990, s.9(4) and PCA 1991 increasing penalty on summary conviction to £20,000.

[23] See also chap. 4.

[24] LBA 1990, s.8(3).

[25] See para. 2.61 above.

[26] See also chap. 5.

(n) The local authority has power to acquire compulsorily listed buildings and in the case of a deliberately neglected building with provision for a direction for "minimum compensation"[27];

(o) If a building has been incorrectly listed, the Secretary of State may amend the list.[28]

9. THE EFFECT OF LISTING ON PLANNING DECISIONS

2.66 This section deals with issues which arise from the relationship between the grant of planning permission for development on listed buildings and the effect of listing on planning decisions generally.

Section 66(1) of the LBA makes specific reference to the relation as follows:

"In considering whether to grant planning permission for development which affects a listed building or its setting, the local planning authority or, as the case may be, the Secretary of State shall have special regard to the desirability of preserving the building or its setting or any features of special architectural or historic interest which it possesses."

The effect of this subsection has been to encourage a degree of flexibility in planning decisions in respect of development affecting a listed building. This is clearly illustrated in the case of an application for the use of a listed residence for office purposes at The Grange, Codicote Road, Welwyn[29] where an Inspector allowed an appeal against a refusal of planning permission. He concluded that although the amount of floorspace to be used for office purposes exceeded the council's policies, he took the view that policies were not inflexible particularly in the case of listed buildings.

The principle of flexibility has even been extended to assist development proposals for a group of unlisted buildings at Jeningsbury Farm near Hertford. A proposal to convert the buildings in question to residential purposes was allowed on appeal[30] because the Inspector regarded the buildings as good examples of vernacular architecture and worth retaining, which outweighed the presumption against development in the Green Belt. Such an approach is not unusual and indeed is embodied in many formal policies of local planning authorities where they are seeking to retain good examples of vernacular architecture, such as the oast-houses found in the Weald of Kent.

2.67 The setting of a listed building raises a further consideration in the determination of development proposals. However, this presupposes that the setting of a listed building is easily defined and that is most certainly not the case. Certainly it cannot be held to be merely contiguous with its curtilage and the general extent of the setting is usually a matter of judgment for the local planning authority, a Department of the Environment Inspector or the Secretary of State. In a case at 44 West Street, Gravesend[31] the Inspector was

[27] See chap. 5.
[28] See para. [2.05] above.
[29] APP/C1950/A/84/010803/P7.
[30] T/APP/J1915/A/84/016386/P2.
[31] APP/K2230/E/85/801205.

clearly of the view that "its setting is rather more extensive than its relatively small curtilage". This case also demonstrates the weight attached to listed building and setting considerations in determining a development proposal which "might otherwise be held to be in broad conformity with the provisions of the emergent local plan". The Inspector concluded that:

" . . . the presumption in favour of granting planning permission, contained in Circulars 22/80 and 14/85, ought to be weighed against the equally relevant policy content of Circulars 23/77 and 12/81 as regards the need to preserve both listed buildings and the setting of listed buildings . . . the merits of the otherwise broadly acceptable retail warehouse proposals . . . would appear to be of comparatively far less importance than the retention of the listed building on the site and its immediate setting."

The appeal was dismissed.

The setting of a listed building in Selby was held to be the principal issue in an appeal[32] against a refusal of permission for the conversion of a house to four dwellings and the erection of three mews houses in the garden land to the rear. The LPA was satisfied with the proposed conversion but the Inspector was concerned at the effect of the sub-division on "the expansive quality befitting a grand domestic house" and that the development to the rear would impinge on the setting of the building.[32a]

The case of The Trustees of the *Bristol Meeting Room Trust v. Secretary* **2.68** *of State for the Environment and Bristol City Council*[33] [34] dealt with a proposal by the applicants to demolish a building adjacent to their meeting room in Bristol. The building, Lynwood House, had been purchased in 1985 with the purpose of demolishing it and using the cleared site as a car park for the adjoining meeting room. In March 1986 Lynwood House was listed. It was accepted that, although neglected, the building was capable of restoration, although no financial appraisal had been carried out. No investigation had been made of alternative uses, since that was not the objective of the applicants in their purchase of the building. The Inspector had identified the relevant issue in the following terms: "A balance has to be struck between the appellants' proven need to solve their own and the local community's traffic problems, and the possible effects that the proposed solution would have upon these other conservation and environmental interests of acknowledged importance". He concluded that the historical (sic) and architectural interest of the building was relatively high and that the listing was fully justified. He also examined whether the poor condition of the building's fabric made its preservation uneconomical and took into account the proposed alternative use and its benefit to the public and the congregation. He concluded that the presumption in favour of preserving the listed building remained important and was not overridden by the highway and traffic benefits of the proposals although in the absence of evidence he was not satisfied that the building was incapable of economic restoration. The

---

[32] APP/B2735/E/800378 as reported in *Planning Appeals Monthly* (February 1985).

[32a] A new opera house at Compton Verney was allowed on an appeal by the Secretary of State against an Inspector's recommendation: Compton Verney Opera Project — Secretary of State decision, March 16, 1995, E.H. Legal Bulletin, No. 5, June, 1995.

[33] QB Division—Sir Graham Eyre Q.C.—Deputy Judge, December 13, 1989—J.P.L. February 1991, pp. 152–159.

[34] J.P.L. February 1991, pp. 152–159.

Secretary of State agreed with the conclusion and, in June 1989, dismissed the appeal; but his view was underpinned by his acceptance of the alleged opinion by the Inspector that although the building was in a poor condition, it was nevertheless capable of economic restoration. No such opinion had been expressed in the Inspector's report. The applicants challenged the decision in the High Court under section 245 of the T.C.P. Act 1971 (now section 63 of the LBA 1990). The Deputy Judge stated that the underlying objective of the scheme of legislation relating to listing was to secure the preservation of buildings so listed and paramount consideration had to be given to that objective. His decision was significant in that it established that the duty "to have special regard to the desirability of preserving the building or its setting or any features of special architectural or historic interest" now set in section 16(2) of the LBA does mean that paramount consideration must be given to such considerations when determining a listed building application. It also upheld the Government's policy towards listed buildings as set out in Circular 8/87 (now revised by PPG 15). The crucial sentence in this particular case was that "The Secretary of State would not expect consent to be given for the total or substantial demolition of any listed building unless without clear and convincing evidence that all reasonable efforts have been made to sustain existing uses or find viable new uses and these efforts have failed." (paragraph 89 of Circular 8/87, later modified by paragraph 3.17 of PPG 15). This judgment makes it a precondition of listed building consent being granted that such an investigation should have been carried out by the applicant. The Trustees won their challenge.

2.69   A further example of a local planning authority acting unreasonably is illustrated by the case of *R v. South Hereford District Council ex parte Felton*.[35] Mr Felton purchased Bollitree Castle near Ross-on-Wye in April 1988. The castle was listed and comprised a number of parts which were listed Grade I, II* and II respectively. In May 1988 he discovered that the local planning authority had granted planning permission for the erection of a potato store on an adjacent farm. Mr Felton commenced an action for judicial review to quash the decision in respect of the grant of planning permission on a number of grounds including the failure of the local authority to have proper regard to the setting of the listed building. The application was granted. The planning officer who dealt with the planning application appeared not to have considered the castle and store from various viewpoints when gauging the effect of the store upon the setting of the listed building. "The decision was unreasonable verging on the absurd." A subsequent appeal to the Court of Appeal by the local authority failed.

On a more light-hearted note, it was interesting to note that an Inspector considered that the erection of a Herbie Tree in the beer garden of the Squirrel Public House at Alveley in Shropshire constituted development requiring planning permission but that it had "none of the attributes of a natural tree, and by its size, colour and general configuration, is visually discordant when seen in the context and as part of the setting of the listed building".[36] The appeal was dismissed.

Although not a planning decision, the Ministry of Agriculture, Fisheries and Food appointed an Inspector to conduct a public inquiry into the St Ives

[35] [1990] J.P.L. 515 and (1991) J.P.L. 633.
[36] APP/J3205/A/85/33569/P2.

Harbour Revisions Order to authorise the construction of a new RNLI boathouse, launchway and ancillary works at West Pier, St Ives.[37] The Inspector was assisted by an architectural assessor and English Heritage was represented at the inquiry. The issue was centred on the effect of the proposals on the setting of the Grade A 15th-century church of St Ives, the Grade II* West Pier and harbour walls and the St Ives Conservation area. The Inspector judged that the character and appearance of the conservation area would not be harmed and that the church tower, West Pier and sea wall would likewise not be adversely harmed.

The provisions of the Town and Country Planning (Control of Advertisements) Regulations 1992 (S.I. 1992 no. 666) define areas of special control. **2.70** PPG 19 "Outdoor Advertisement Control" advises that the Secretary of State has taken the view that a degree of special protection, on grounds of amenity, must be justified before he approves an order (for an area of special control). He cites examples of areas which might be appropriate as candidates for "special control" status, and includes areas where there are important architectural, archaeological, historical or visual characteristics.[38]

Regulation 19 of the Control of Advertising Regulations effectively enables local planning authorities to remove the rights for express consent to display advertisements where they might affect the setting of listed buildings. PPG 19 (paragraph 24) states that "almost all advertisements on listed buildings or scheduled monuments will constitute an "alteration" to the building or the monument's site, and therefore require listed building or scheduled monument consent in addition to any advertisement consent. Special care is essential to ensure that any advertisement displayed on, or close to, a listed building or scheduled monument, does not detract from the integrity of the building's design, historical character or structure and does not spoil or compromise its setting".

It is regrettable that the same provisions do not apply to enable local planning authorities to restrict permitted development rights where they might affect the setting of a listed building, a matter which has concerned English Heritage for some time.

10. THE PROGRESS OF LISTING

Although the statutory provisions may have changed, and the procedure **2.71** varied over the years, it may be of interest to consider the progress as opposed to the process of listing buildings. It is as follows:

1946-early 1950s: the first Provisional Lists were produced.

1950s-1969: statutory lists were complied from the Provisional Lists for all the former district and county borough authorities.

1969-1982: revision of existing lists and issue in the revised formats (*i.e.*

---

[37] *Legal Bulletin*, April 1993.
[38] PPG 19, para. 27.

instead of the former practice of mere details of address and grade of the building, the new lists including descriptive notes, grade and address, are included in one cumulative statutory list).

The lists are good candidates for computerisation, and the possibility has been the subject of six studies since 1986. In fact we are now reasonably clear as to the way ahead: an R.C.H.M.E. study of the Durham lists (June 1991) has shown that it is technically feasible to computerise the existing lists, and English Heritage's review lists (140 in total) are being computerised as they are being compiled. A further (DNH funded) study is, however, underway because DNH is now thinking in terms of a much more ambitious project than simply computerising the statutory lists, *i.e.* a "heritage database". This will comprise a wide range of data on the built heritage, including scheduled ancient monuments, historic parks and gardens and the R.C.H.M.E.'s National Monuments Records. The purpose of this database study is to validate the project.

11. IMMUNITY FROM LISTING

2.72   Schedule 15(5) to the Local Government, Planning and Land Act 1980 sought to alleviate the risk of listing by enabling a person to apply to the Department for a certificate stating that it does not intend to list the building within the ensuing five years provided an application has been made for planning permission or permission given. The provisions in the 1980 Act have been re-enacted as section 6 of the LBA 1990 which provides that if such a certificate is applied for and obtained, the Secretary of State is precluded from exercising his powers under section 1 of the LBA to list the building in question, and under section 6(2)(b) of the LBA a local planning authority is precluded from serving a building preservation notice, for five years from the date of issue of the certificate. Under section 6(3) of the LBA, notice of any application for a certificate must be given to the relevant planning authority at the same time as to the Secretary of State.

Recent figures show that approximately 50 per cent of applications have resulted in immunity certificates being granted, though the numbers of such applications remains fairly low. In 1991, from 30 applications, 21 certificates of immunity were issued, the respective figures for 1992 were 31 and 25. Of those applications, over 70 per cent were decided within 12 weeks.

Heritage Minister, Lady Blatch, announced on March 3, 1992 that The South Bank Centre, including The Hayward Gallery, The Queen Elizabeth Hall, The Purcell Room and associated walkways, were not to be listed as buildings of special architectural or historic interest. The Minister also announced that a certificate of immunity from listing had been issued in respect of these and other buildings on the site.[39]

2.73   The following points should be noted:

(1) The immunity certificate procedure should, if used, avoid the cir-

---

[39] *DOE News Release*, March 3, 1992.

cumstances which arose in the *John Walker*[40] case, where listing took place (unknown to vendor or purchaser) at the same time as exchange of contracts for the sale of the listed property. If the provisions of applying for an immunity certificate had been available in 1976, the proposed vendor or purchaser could have been cleared of the potential listing prior to the exchange of contracts.

(2) Anyone applying for a certificate runs the risk that his application will bring to the notice of the DNH or the local planning authority the existence of a building which might merit listing.

(3) A danger for an owner is that anyone may apply for an immunity certificate so long as the conditions are satisfied—thus a preservation group can apply. Large numbers of buildings have been listed because of the direct intervention of preservation groups. Section 6 of the LBA 1990 therefore does not materially change the former situation: it does however provide for the owner a protection (which he had not had hitherto) from further pressure for five years if the listing is declined and the immunity certificate issued.

(4) An immunity certificate application (for which there is no application form or charge) should be made to the DNH and should be accompanied by a plan showing the position of the building, photographs of each elevation of the building and of any notable interior features, together with the details of the date of construction, the architect and information about the architectural or historic interest. Applicants should also supply a copy of the planning application or planning permission.

(5) There is no time limit to respond imposed on the Secretary of State. Indications from the experience on the early applications are that the turn around of applications for certificates is quite speedy.

(6) There is no obligation on the Department or the local authorities to notify the owner of the application (if not made by the owner), but the existence of a certificate and its expiry date should be disclosed in response to enquiries by prospective purchasers of the building or land, together with other information relating to planning matters. (PPG 15, paragraph 6.28–6.33).

(7) Even if an immunity certificate is granted it does not prevent the building from being included in a conservation area with the need for consent for demolition imposed by that code.

(8) Section 6(4) of the LBA provides that for the purposes of this section, the words "local planning authority", in relation to a building in Greater London, shall include English Heritage.

(9) Where a certificate is issued, the Department will notify English Heritage and both the district and county councils.

12. PROBLEM LISTINGS

If all the listing processes proceed as set out above there might be no problems. But from time to time there have been difficulties and it is worth recording the details of the following three cases as cautionary tales. **2.74**

[40] *Amalgamated Investment and Property Co v. Walker (John) and Sons* [1976] 3 All E.R. 509; [1976] E.G. 277 C.A.

(a) Carlton Cinema, Swansea

The proposed redevelopment of the Carlton Cinema in Swansea[41] resulted in a complex decision-making process, with the public inquiry being held in three different stages under three different inspectors. The first Inspector's report recommended that the cinema was not of sufficient merit to justify its retention. However, the building was listed some three months after the date of the public inquiry and the inquiry was reopened under a different inspector. This inspector considered that "the rarity of listed buildings and other buildings of distinction in the centre of Swansea serves to reinforce the presumption in favour of the preservation of at least the facade", which he had described as "a flamboyant Edwardian Baroque essay" built of Doulton carraware in 1914. The Secretary of State adjourned the inquiry to allow the appellants time to prepare detailed proposals allowing for the retention of the facade. The inquiry was reopened for a third time under a third inspector, who heard conflicting evidence from the appellants on the one hand and from the city council on the other hand. His conclusions were accepted by the Secretary of State, who was not satisfied that it would be impracticable to retain the facade and he therefore refused listed building consent for its demolition.

(b) Upper House Barns, Bronylls Village, Near Brecon, Powys

2.75   The practical problems raised by the time-scales involved in the processing of listed building consent applications is clearly illustrated in a case concerning a range of eighteenth-century Grade II listed buildings at Bronylls near Brecon in Powys.[42] Following the grant of outline planning permission for residential use of a parcel of land in September 1984 on which the "Upper House Barns" were located the owner applied for consent to demolish them in May 1985 to allow the development to proceed unhindered. In view of the apparent advanced state of decay of the building, a structural survey was commissioned by the council to assist their deliberation. The report was completed in August 1985, although by July it was apparent that certain elements of the building were extremely unstable and would be very costly to remedy. In September 1985 the LPA recommended that LBC be granted and notified the Welsh Historic Monuments body (CADW) with a copy of the structural report. In January 1986 the authority was advised that the application would be determined by an inspector appointed by the Secretary of State for Wales. The inquiry was held in June 1986—the Inspector's report was received on September 1, 1986 and concluded that "the condition of the west range of buildings is very dangerous . . . and should be demolished with the minimum of delay". The particular concern raised by this case is that the application remained undetermined for 12 months, albeit not an unusually long time for applications following this procedure, whilst it had already been acknowledged at the outset that parts of the

---

[41] P84/583 Swansea City Council, Welsh Office, August 28, 1985.
[42] Case report courtesy of the Borough of Brecknock.

building were in an extremely dangerous condition and throughout that period constituted a possible danger to the public.

(c) Gas-holder—Carlisle[43]

British Gas sought consent to demolish a listed gas holder on the basis that it was not of such interest as to warrant expenditure simply to preserve it as a monument, but listed building consent was refused by Carlisle City Council. In dismissing the appeal against Carlise City's decision, it was held that the gas holder continued to be of visual special architectural and historic interest and was worthwhile preserving; the approximate cost estimates for restoration and maintenance without a proper survey were not to be relied upon; to give too great an emphasis to the absence of an effective use might be premature and would discount its value as a monument, and the case for demolition was not so convincing as to override the presumption in favour of its preservation.

13. HISTORIC GARDENS

Section 8 of the Historic Buildings and Ancient Monuments Act 1953 (as **2.76** amended by the National Heritage Act 1983[44]) enables English Heritage to "compile a register of gardens and other land situated in England which appears to it to be of special historic interest". The register, for which there is no statutory obligation to require it to be kept nor does it entail any additional statutory controls, lists and grades gardens created before 1939 which still retain their special historic interest. Its purpose, as set out in paragraph 2.24 of PPG 15, is to record their existence so that highway and planning authorities and developers know that they should try to safeguard them when considering new road schemes and new redevelopment generally. The Town and Country Planning (General Development Procedure) Order 1995 S.I. 1995 No 419, introduced changes in the consultation procedures by local planning authorities in relation to Grade I and II* gardens or parks of special historic interest. Development likely to affect these categories of gardens or parks of special interest must be notified to English Heritage as from June 3, 1995.

The Register includes any designed ornamental landscapes, such as private gardens, town walks, squares, public parks and landscape parks. Evidence of meritorious design is the key consideration. The importance of the site in garden history and the extent of survival are also material considerations.

The responsibility for registration rests with the Historic Parks and Gardens team of English Heritage, which from April 1993 was devolved into Regional teams of Conservation groups which deal with planning and grant work with historical and practical expertise developed by the Gardens team.

---

[43] *Carlisle CC v. British Gas (Northern) plc.* Ref T/APP/EC915/E/80791/p7 1992. 7 pad 377 (quoted in *Current Law 1992*, p. 1187).

[44] This section was brought into force on April 1, 1984 by S.I. 1984 No. 208. The detail will be found in Sched. 4 to the 1983 Act, para. 10.

The Register is limited to sites of special interest and is arranged by county volumes which contain a total of 1246 sites. The sites are graded I (10 per cent), II* (29 per cent) and II (61 per cent) with regard to their national importance.[45]

2.77   A comprehensive review of the Register (recorded on a computer database) was commenced in 1990 and at present priority is being given to adding at least 100 municipal parks to the 54 already on the register. Local plan policies increasingly include references to the conservation of historic parks and gardens.

The intrinsic interest of such parks and gardens may be eroded by incremental changes occurring over a long period of time. Such changes include the construction of tennis courts, the removal of paths and hedges, none of which require planning permission, but may need listed building consent.

English Heritage provides an advisory service to owners, developers and local authorities, and advice may also be sought from the Garden History Society.

By January 1988 English Heritage recorded that the last of the 46 county volumes of the *Register of Historic Parks and Gardens* had been published. The total number of registered sites in England in 1995 was 1246. These registered sites range from major man-made landscapes like Blenheim to quite small gardens such as the one hectare garden at Marsh Court in Hampshire. In format, register entries closely resemble statutory historic building lists and the grading is similar.

Notwithstanding the attention being focused on historic gardens as a result of the compilation of the register, they remain a particular problem, principally because they have no statutory protection. Whilst normal planning controls will be sufficient to prevent the development of an historic garden for new dwellings, such as that proposed at the Lutyens house called "The Salutation" in Sandwich, Kent,[46] there is no statutory control over the despoilation of layout, design or form, because they can be neither listed nor be subject to a tree preservation order.

2.78   With the rapid growth of public appreciation of gardens there is now a sizeable body of public opinion in favour of some form of statutory control over historic gardens in particular and special landscapes in general. Indeed, one might rightfully suggest that a Capability Brown landscaped park or a Gertrude Jekyll garden deserves just as much protection as a listed house from the same period, not only because such landscapes or gardens offer to provide a unique setting for a listed building but because they are intrinsically worth preserving in their own right.

The response of English Heritage to proposals by the Department of Transport to route a section of the A34 trunk road through Highclere Park, Hampshire, illustrates three important points. Firstly, it demonstrates the inadequacy of existing controls to protect these important environmental assets. Secondly, it highlights the lack of funds available to tackle not only the threat of major development proposals, but also the long term maintenance problems of gardens. Thirdly, in focusing attention on such an important historic garden or landscape, it serves to illustrate the magnitude of the problem which exists in respect of less well known gardens which nevertheless remain an important part of our heritage.

[45] *English Heritage Monitor* 1995.
[46] *Period Home* (October 1985), p. 9.

Clearly the mobilisation of resources required to save Highclere Park is unlikely to be repeated in respect of all historic gardens and it begs the question as to when action will be taken to provide not only a statutory form of control, but also the necessary resources to ensure that historic gardens can be maintained for the benefit of the community and future generations. George Allen suggests that "if the history of listed building controls repeats itself, it will only be after a series of scandalous and tragic losses that any action will be taken".[47]

Grants are available from English Heritage for the repair of gardens and other land of "outstanding" historic interest.[48] Whether this criterion is satisfied is determined by the Historic Buildings Advisory Committee which is advised by the Historic Landscapes Panel.

2.79 English Heritage was provided with funds by the DOE to fund the repair of storm damage which occurred in 1987 and 1990 respectively. Those registered sites which are not found to be "outstanding" may be eligible for grant assistance from TaskForce Trees, a unit of the Countryside Commission. A pilot scheme regarding more general restoration was launched by English Heritage in 1991.

There are 1246 sites currently on English Heritage's register of historic parks and gardens, and of these those contained in the Grade I and II* categories stands at nearly 500. Many of these are attached to listed buildings and are therefore covered by the existing requirement for local planning authorities to consult English Heritage.[49]

14. HISTORIC LANDSCAPES

2.80 The DOE White Paper "This Common Inheritance" (Cmnd 1200) published in 1990 included an invitation to English Heritage to prepare a list of landscapes of historic importance.

Prior to embarking upon the compilation of the register, English Heritage published a statement setting out their objectives and philosophy regarding the protection of historic landscapes. English Heritage have a statutory duty to promote the understanding and conservation of the whole historic environment.

The proposed register is to be a non-statutory guide identifying nationally important historic landscapes and is to be broadly based upon the following principles:

> "(i) it will need to cover all historical elements of the countryside, and not just those individual features traditionally classified as historic buildings or ancient monuments;
>
> (ii) it will need to provide relative weighting of landscapes of greater or lesser historic importance in order to aid planning and resource allocation;
>
> (iii) it will need to provide a methodology for defining and evaluating man-made features of the countryside which can be used by land-

---

[47] *Ibid.* p. 9—*Period Home.*
[48] *English Heritage Conservation Bulletin*, February 1991, pp. 12–13.
[49] J.P.L. January 1995, p. 17.

owners, local authorities, and English Heritage or the local
identification and grading of historic landscapes;
(iv) it will need to be able to inform and assist local management conservation decision at all levels, from the strategic and national to
the most important day-to-day work of landowners and others
who live on the land".[50]

15. WORLD HERITAGE SITES

2.81   The status of a World Heritage site is referred to in paragraphs 2.22 and
2.23 of PPG 15, where it highlights the outstanding international importance of a site as a "key material" consideration to be taken into account by
local planning authorities in determining planning and listed building consent applications, and by the Secretary of State in determining cases on
appeal or following "call-in".

There are now 300 heritage or man-made sites registered as World Heritage sites arising from the UNESCO World Heritage Convention 1972.
There are also almost 100 entries in the category of "natural" sites which
conform to the concept contained in the Convention of 1991 "An idea in
action" which was designed to protect "the most precious treasures of man-
kind's cultural and "natural heritage".

The United Kingdom became a signatory to the World Heritage Convention in 1984 and has the following sites under the designation:

> Avebury and associated site
> Blenheim Palace and Park
> Canterbury Cathedral with St Augustine's Abbey and St Martin's
>   Church, Canterbury
> Castle and town walls of King Edward in Gwynedd
> City of Bath
> Durham—Cathedral and Castle
> Hadrian's Wall
> Ironbridge Gorge
> Palace of Westminster
> Stonehenge
> Studley Royal Park—including the ruins of Fountains Abbey, St Mary's
>   Church, Studley Royal Park
> The Tower of London[50a]
> Westminster Abbey and St Margaret's Church

The boundaries of many of these sites are inconsistent and are generally
acknowledged to need reviewing.

2.82   The status of the designation within the planning system also leaves
many unanswered questions. In answer to one Parliamentary question by

---

[50] Work is also in hand by English Heritage for including in the register of landscapes,
the feasibility of récording historic battle fields—PPG 15, paras. 2.25 and 6.39.

[50a] A case involving—60 feet high sculpture within the recently created "outstanding
views of the Tower of London" was the subject of a decision by the Secretary of State
— E.H. Legal Bulletin No. 5, June 1959, [1995] 10 PAD 201, September 27, 1994.

Lord Kennet,[51] which related particularly to Stonehenge, Avebury and associated sites, Baroness Trumpington, speaking for the Government, explained that "inclusion of a site in the World Heritage list is not therefore, by itself, a direct instrument of planning control, but it does signal the importance of the site as a material factor to be taken into account by a local planning authority or by the Secretary of State for the Environment on appeal or . . . following call-in".[52]

There have been several planning decisions affecting designated World Heritage sites, but there is, as yet, no clear direction from Government. In his report on the *West Kennet Farm* case[53] affecting the Stonehenge and Avebury sites, the Inspector stated: "the designation draws attention to particular interests of acknowledged importance within the area but it does not impose any further layer of control. There can be no rigid ban on development. The normal flexible approach, with particular attention being paid to the relevant interests of acknowledged importance, should be adopted."

This comment reflects the advice contained in PPG 15 that "policies should reflect the fact that all these sites have been designated for their outstanding universal value, and they should place great weight on the need to protect them for the benefit of future generations as well as our own".

In a case affecting *the setting* of Hadrian's Wall, it was proposed to drill for hydrocarbons, and the likely effects on the World Heritage site was the principal reason for refusal.[54]

PPG 15 has suggested (paragraph 2.22) that "significant development proposals affecting World Heritage sites will generally require formal environmental assessment"[55] to ensure that their immediate impact and their implications for the longer term are fully implemented.

2.83 The former Circular 15/88 suggested that the inclusion of a site in the World Heritage List is not intended to be a direct instrument of planning control in the same way as listing. It is intended to signal the importance of the site as a material consideration to be taken into account by the appropriate decision-maker be it the LPA or the Secretary of State. This is illustrated by the proposal to erect a new bridge at Ironbridge. The application was called in by the Secretary of State for the Environment because of the importance of the site. He agreed with his Inspector's recommendation that planning permission be refused whilst indicating that any future proposal to meet the traffic needs of the area would have to be compatible with Ironbridge's status as a World Heritage Site and Conservation Area.

The DNH advises that no national planning restrictions flow from the inclusion of a site in the World Heritage List. Inclusion does, however, highlight the outstanding national and international importance of the site as a material consideration to be taken into account by local planning authorities as a material consideration in determining planning and listed building consent applications, and by the Secretary of State for the Environment in determining cases on appeal or following call-in.[56] Word Heritage status does not directly affect the availability of grant aid.

[51] *Hansard*, October 21, 1993, pp. 690–694.
[52] *Hansard*, October 21, 1993, p. 702.
[53] SW/P5407/21/74 and 270/199 and HSD/9/2/1517–2004.
[54] APP/R2900/A/91/1905/5.
[55] Circular 15/88.
[56] PPG 15, paras. 3.34 and 3.35.

In March 1994[57] the Secretary of State for the Environment dismissed appeals following a series of inquiries stretching back over two years, for several supermarket proposals near to the World Heritage City of Bath. There were three applications for sites within the conservation area, and in his decisions the Secretary of State regarded the conservation status of Bath as an important factor. It is the only complete city in England to have been designated as a World Heritage site, and the need for new development to be fully integrated within its surroundings and to make a positive contribution to the townscape greatly influenced his decision.

2.84 In December 1993 the High Court held that a local planning authority had a duty to take account of important archaeological considerations and the impact on tourism when deciding development proposals. The case was concerned with open-cast coal extraction from a site in the shadow of Hadrian's Wall in Northumberland, a World Heritage site.

The local planning authority had refused planning permission in order to protect the setting of the Wall. The Inspector, dealing with the subsequent appeal, identified the main issues as the implications for the setting of Hadrian's Wall, the proposed development and the effect of the scheme on tourism in the area. He felt satisfied that the developers had complied with the need to mitigate adverse impact on the Wall, and he recommended that the appeal should be allowed subject to conditions.

The Secretary of State took a contrary view and was concerned at the potential effects of the development on the World Heritage site. The High Court noted that the Wall was an internationally renowned monument, and that although World Heritage sites were not specifically referred to in circulars or planning guidance notes, they had been recognised by the appropriate Minister, in a statement in the House of Lords, as being a material factor in planning decisions. The developer's application to quash the Secretary of State's decision to refuse planning permission was itself quashed.[58]

The PPG 15 advises each local authority to take account of World Heritage site designation in formulating planning policies for inclusion in their development plans, and that these policies should reflect their "outstanding universal value".

---

[57] Appeal decisions SW/P/5116220/3 and 4—and APP/P0105/A/92/211437—March 11, 1994.

[58] *Coal Contractors Ltd v. Secretary of State for the Environment 1993* (EGCS 218) reported in *Planning* March 1994.

3. Conservation Areas

1. GENERAL SUMMARY

Until the middle of this century, measures for the protection of the built **3.01**
environment had largely concentrated on the protection of individual buildings against the possibility of demolition. Subsequent to the 1947 Act, these
limited measures were extended to afford (still limited) control over the
alteration or extension of "buildings of architectural or historic interest"
but "the building" remained the basic unit of conservation interest. It was
not until 1967 that the concept of "area" conservation found statutory
acceptance.

It was perhaps the case of *Iveagh (Earl of) v. Ministry of Housing and
Local Government*[1] which reached the Court of Appeal in 1964, which
marked a turn of the tide. The Earl of Iveagh owned two adjoining houses in
St James' Square, London, providing an unbroken facade in one corner of the
Square. In 1959 the local planning authority made a building preservation
order under the 1947 Act on the ground that alteration or demolition would
be detrimental to the preservation of the character of the Square. The applicant objected and a public inquiry was held. The applicant contended that
to fall within the protection given by the 1947 Act a building must have of
itself special architectural or historic interest and not derive such interest as
part of a group of buildings. The Minister's inspector found that the buildings were not of sufficient quality for the order. The Minister differed from
his inspector and confirmed the order. The applicant moved to quash the
order. Megaw J. (as he then was) dismissed the application. The applicants

[1] [1964] 1 Q.B. 395; [1963] 3 W.L.R. 974; 128 JP 70; 107 SJ 90, 851; [1963] 3 All E.R.
817.

appealed to the Court of Appeal, which held that a building might be of special architectural or historic interest by reason of its setting as one of a group.

The Court of Appeal hearing made it clear that there was a divided view as to whether the preservation order protection given in the 1947 Act (and subsequently re-enacted) was adequate where "the group value" was under consideration, and it was apparent that a more general power was required. As a result there was introduced (at the instance primarily of Mr Duncan-Sandys—later Lord Duncan-Sandys—and the Civic Trust) a Bill which became the Civic Amenities Act 1967. The preamble to that Act made it clear that it was an Act "to make further provision for the protection and improvement of buildings of architectural or historic interest and of the character of areas of such interest." The Act required that:

"every local planning authority shall from time to time determine which parts of their area . . . are areas of special architectural or historic interest the character or appearance of which it is desirable to preserve or enhance and shall designate such areas."

They were referred to as "conservation areas." The Act also strengthened the law with regard to listed buildings.

3.02   The Civic Amenities Act 1967 was repealed and re-enacted in relation to conservation areas as section 277 of the 1971 Act, with certain provisions of the Town and Country Planning Act 1968 in relation to consultations and provision for the display of site notices also being incorporated.

The legislation was further altered by the Town and Country Planning (Amendment) Act 1972, which gave powers to control the demolition of unlisted buildings in conservation areas[2] and for the making of grants or loans for work in conservation areas of "outstanding interest."[3] [4] [5]

The Town and Country Amenities Act 1974 consolidated the legislation and re-enacted with certain amendments section 277 of the 1971 Act, added sections 277A, which enlarged the demolition control provisions, and 277B which required preservation and enhancement proposals to be prepared by local planning authorities. Additionally the protection of trees was provided for through a new section 61A inserted into the 1971 Act.[6]

Town and Country Planning legislation underwent a process of consolidation during the latter end of the 1980s and the relevant legislation relating to conservation areas is now to be found in Part II of the Planning (Listed Buildings and Conservation Areas) Act 1990.

It should be noted that the control afforded by special legislation such as the Planning (Listed Buildings and Conservation Areas) Act 1990 does not

---

[2] T.C.P.(A). A 1972, s.8 (repealed by the T.C.A.A. 1974, which inserted similar provisions as an amendment to T.C.P.A. 1971, s.277).

[3] T.C.P.(A). A 1972, s.10. The term "outstanding" has little practical reference after L.G.P.L.A. 1980 (Sched. 15, para. 27): this swept away the difference which was originally only introduced for grant purposes.

[4] s.277 became ss.69–70 of the 1990 Act; s.277A became ss.74 and 75, and s.277B became s.71 of the 1990 Act.

[5] s.77 of LBA 1990.

[6] The section was further added to by the L.G.A. 1985 and the H.P.A. 1986 and became s.211 of the T.C.P.A. 1990.

preclude or limit a local planning authority from exercising legislation in relation to the particular circumstances of a specific site or building.[7]

2. WHAT IS A CONSERVATION AREA?

Section 69(1)(a) LBA describes a conservation area as "an area of special **3.03** architectural or historic interest the character or appearance of which it is desirable to preserve or enhance." The size and nature of conservation areas vary considerably from small groups of buildings in both urban and rural settings to whole town centres. Many nationally well known areas have been designated as conservation areas, such as the Royal Hospital Chelsea, Cheyne Walk, The Boltons Holland Park, Brompton Square, Bayswater, Millbank, St James's, St John's Wood, and Westminster Cathedral, all in London as well as provincial conservation areas such as Saltaire in Yorkshire.

In 1989 the Yorkshire Dales National Park Authority designated a rural conservation area in Swaledale with the principal objective of protecting the pattern of barns and walls which are so characteristic of the Upper Dales. The conservation area is substantial extending to over 70 square kilometres of farmland and takes in almost 800 barns.[8]

The diversity of subjects considered suitable for conservation area designation is highlighted by a site known as Holt's Field, Marton, near Swansea. It consisted of a chalet settlement originally built for holiday use, but, with the passage of time, occupied permanently by their owners. This settlement was typical of many in coastal locations and was described by the council as a "settlement of self-built dwellings" and an example of "plot land development, a unique part of the nation's built legacy".

Elitestone Ltd[9] applied for a judicial review on several grounds; one was a technical point relating to the failure of the Council to provide at least three days between publishing the agenda and holding the meeting (Local Government Act 1972 (section 100B(3))) at which the sub-committee considered the recommendation that Holt's Field should be designated as a conservation area. MacPherson J. did not accept this argument. The second part of the application was the nature of the chalets themselves. It was submitted that they were not "buildings" within the meaning of section 74 of the LBA 1990, but again MacPherson J. rejected that argument on the grounds that they came within the definition of "buildings" as set out in section 366 of the T.C.P. Act 1990 which states: " 'Building', includes any structure or erection, and any part of the building, as so defined, but does not include plant or machinery comprised in a building."

The next point was to challenge the alleged confusion in the Council's mind between the desire to preserve the community at Holt's Field rather than the area itself. It was claimed that there were neither architectural nor

---

[7] *Hoveringham Gravels Ltd v. Secretary of State for the Environment* [1975] Q.B. 754; [1975] 2 W.L.R. 897; 119 SJ 335; 2 All E.R. 931.
[8] *English Heritage Conservation Bulletin* (June 1989), p. 14.
[9] *R v. Swansea City Council, ex parte Elitestone Ltd*, and *Elitestone Ltd v. Secretary of State for Wales and Swansea City Council* (Q.B. MacPherson J May 12, 1992). J.P.L., p. 1143.

historical reasons for which the Council could or should be entitled to designate this as a conservation area.

Mr Justice Macpherson considered that the Council's discretion in this part of the law was wide. Section 69 of the LBA 1990 allowed the Council to reach its own conclusion in order to "determine which parts of their area are areas of special architectural or historical interest, the character or appearance of which it is desirable to preserve or enhance." In his judgment the Council was fully entitled to take the view that Holt's Field was of historic interest, the character of which it is desirable to preserve or enhance. He concluded that the site as it was could be said to be an interesting part of the social and development history of the area. The judicial review application was accordingly dismissed.

In a commentary on this case in J.P.L. 1992, page 1150, it was said that "such a settlement was the first case in the commentator's knowledge where a conservation area had been designated as an interesting part of the social and development history of the area."

From the definition given above, it is clear that the most important constituent parts of a conservation area will be those parts which contribute most towards the "character or appearance" of the area. A planning appeal decision in Ripon, North Yorkshire, in November 1991 shed light upon the distinction between the word "character" and the word "appearance" when they are applied to the general duty of decision makers contained in section 72 LBA 1990. The Inspector stated "The phraseology of section 72 implies . . . a distinction between 'character' and 'appearance' in a Conservation Area. The meaning of the latter term is obvious, and if 'character' is to be distinguished then it must derive from the remaining, non-visual attributes of the area—its social qualities or ambience."[10]

Buildings which can contribute towards the character or appearance of the area need not themselves necessarily be buildings of special architectural or historic interest. Consequently it is not necessary for the conservation area to be centred on listed buildings, although it may well be, and very often is. PPG 15[11] emphasises that "it is the quality and interest of areas, rather than that of individual buildings, which should be the prime consideration in identifying conservation areas". It continues by providing a list of factors which will be important in conservation area designation and by ensuring that "conservation area designation policy should be seen as the means of recognising the importance of all these factors and of ensuring that conservation policy addresses the quality of townscape in its broadest sense as well as the protection of individual buildings".

The PPG (paragraph 4.2) draws attention to an increasing recognition in recent years that our experience of an historic area depends on much more than the quality of individual buildings. It refers to the historic layout of property boundaries and thoroughfares; on a particular "mix" of uses; on characteristic materials; on appropriate scaling and detailing of contemporary buildings; on the quality of advertisements; shop fronts, street furniture and hard and soft surfaces; on vistas along streets and between buildings; and on the extent to which traffic intrudes and limits pedestrian use of spaces between buildings.

[10] Appeal decisions: T/APP/A2715/A90/167493/P7 and T/APP/A2715/E90/806983/P7 dated November 7, 1991.
[11] PPG 15 (para 4.2), dated September 1994.

The criterion for deciding whether a building contributes to the conservation area is different from the criterion for deciding whether to list it; indeed, the character of the conservation area may derive from features other than buildings and which themselves are incapable of being listed. However, it remains necessary for the area to be of special architectural or historic interest, and the character or appearance of that area to be one which it is desirable to preserve or enhance.

There is a statutory definition of the word "building" for the purposes of **3.04** listing, namely "any structure or erection, and any part of a building, as so defined, but [not including] plant or machinery comprised in a building."[12] There is no definition of what is sufficient to constitute a conservation area[13] nor is there anything in the statutes to define what features may make that area special.

The definition is a double definition, *i.e.* to be capable of being a conservation area, an area must pass two tests; it must be (a) an area of special architectural or historic interest, and (b) an area, the character or appearance of which it is desirable to preserve or enhance.

Although (b) would normally apply to an area which qualified under (a), presumably it is theoretically possible for an area to be of special interest under (a) but not to qualify under (b) because, for instance, the buildings might be substantially unused or derelict or subject to confirmed proposals for demolition, so that any realistic possibility of the preservation or enhancement of the area is unlikely. The correct approach to be adopted by decision makers when considering an application for planning permission in a conservation area was the subject of much judicial activity during the period 1988–1992. The significant decisions are discussed in paragraph 3.11 below. However the question still remains, what, if anything, is the difference between the meaning of the words "special architectural or historic interest" in the context of specific buildings, *i.e.* for listing, and the same words when applied to an "area"? There are no published guidelines as to what makes an area of special interest, to compare with the detailed guidelines which exist for the listing of buildings. PPG 15, paragraph 4.4, assists in what may be included in a conservation area and a Policy Note entitled *Conservation Area Practice.*[14] gives useful guidance in the selection of conservation areas. Paragraph 4.4 emphasises that it is the character of areas, rather than individual buildings, which section 69 LBA seeks to preserve or enhance. Ultimately the point may have to be tested in the courts to determine whether there is or is not any distinction. There is no guidance given as to what types of appearance or character it is desirable to preserve. Is it desirable to preserve or enhance every kind of character or appearance? One would not think of listing a building built five years ago. On the other hand, assuming that there was a remarkably fine group of buildings—perhaps which had been award winning—would one feel justified in making that group a conservation area even though some, or indeed all, of the buildings might have been completed only in the last decade? It seems clear from the High Court decision of Mr R Vandermeer Q.C., sitting as a Deputy Judge in the case of *Archer and Thompson v. Secretary of State for the Environment*

---

[12] T.C.P.A. 1990, s.336(1).
[13] LBA 1990, ss.69 and 91.
[14] Produced by English Heritage.

and *Penwith District Council*[15] that in considering the character of a conservation area a decision maker must take into account considerations such as noise and not just matters which effect the physical structure of an area.[15a]

The first four conservation areas were designated in 1967; by December 1994 there were 8,315.[16] In addition to the large number of designations, existing conservation areas are frequently subject to variation, usually in the form of extension to the core area. A register of all designated conservation areas is published by English Heritage.[17] The register catalogues each conservation area by reference to the relevant county and district but excludes identification by way of maps. A more detailed four-volume register has also been prepared covering the South-East, the Eastern Counties, the North and the West Midlands and the South West. The national picture which has emerged is said, in an issue of *English Heritage's Conservation Bulletin*, to suggest, "a need for consolidation with respect to village designation and indicates a lack of consistency in the designation of industrial towns. Some initiatives which could set a new pattern are revealed: for instance, the inclusion of tiny isolated rural communities and farmsteads within new and extensive conservation areas".[18]

3. THE MECHANICS OF MAKING A CONSERVATION AREA

(a) The duty to determine

3.05   Each local authority has a duty to determine which parts of its area are areas of special architectural or historic interest, the character or appearance of which it is desirable to preserve or enhance and to designate such areas as conservation areas.[19]

The Secretary of State and English Heritage also have power (after consultation with the local planning authority) to designate areas as conservation areas[20]—English Heritage's powers relate to London only, when they are required to consult the London borough council and to obtain the consent of the Secretary of State to the designation.[21] PPG 15 says that these powers are intended to be used only exceptionally[22] and have at the date of writing not yet been exercised. Local planning authorities have a duty to formulate and publish proposals for the preservation and enhancement of conser-

[15] 1991 J.P.L. 1027.
[15a] An unusual case about a United Synagogue Eruv concerning the effect of the poles and wires on the character or appearance of conservation areas—E.H. Legal Bulletin No. 5, June 1995, [1995] 10 PAD 209, September 20, 1994.
[16] *English Heritage Monitor 1995.*
[17] *English Heritage Conservation Bulletin* (June 1990).
[18] *English Heritage Conservation Bulletin* (June 1990).
[19] LBA 1990, s.69(1).
[20] LBA 1990, s.69(3) and s.70(1).
[21] LBA 1990, s.70.
[22] PPG No 15, paras. 4.8 and 4.10.

vation areas from time to time.[23] Such proposals should be discussed at local public meetings, and comments made at such meetings taken into account by the local planning authority.[24]

This appears only rarely to have happened despite the fact that paragraph 4.10 of PPG 15 and its predecessor Circular 8/87 stresses the importance of securing public support and harnessing public enthusiasm for questions of conservation. Local authorities are also advised to set up advisory committees for conservation areas consisting mainly of people who are not members of the local authority; local residential and business interest should be fully represented. In addition to local historical, civic and amenity societies, the authority may, for example, where there is thriving commerce in a conservation area, wish to include representatives of the local Chamber of Trade and, depending on the character of the area, of representatives for national amenity societies and other bodies such as the Civic Trust.[25] The function of such a committee is both to assist in formulating policies for the conservation area, and to advise the local authority on the applications that would affect the character or appearance of a conservation area.[26] The committee would, however, have no statutory function.

There has been an increasing concern that many of the early designated conservation area boundaries were too narrowly drawn and sometimes omitted the full extent of rear plots which are often of archaeological importance and form the historical framework of the town or village. Many areas were, and continue to be, designated without a full appraisal which defines the *special* architectural or historic qualities which warrant designation. There would be greater public acceptance and recognition of conservation areas if these matters were fully explained in a character assessment, and could be linked with the development plan process. PPG 15, paragraph 4.9, advised that "clear assessment and definition of an area's special interest and the action needed to protect it, will help to generate awareness and encourage local property owners to take the right sort of action for themselves."

Adequate policies to protect the special interest of the conservation area are advocated by English Heritage and by the Royal Town Planning Institute[27] for inclusion in the statutory local plan, because this provides the primary means for controlling erosion and for guiding the form of new development in such areas. Moreover, the link with development plans provides an opportunity for regular assessment and provides the designation process with a formal consultation procedure. The PPG advocates a detailed assessment and definition of boundaries of conservation areas are to be tackled separately from the local plan preparation, but authorities will see the local plan as the vehicle for setting out the authority's general strategy for designations and to indicate which new areas are to be appraised during the plan period.

Local Plans and Part I of unitary development plans provide the opportunities for setting out more detailed development control policies for an

[23] LBA 1990, s.71(1).
[24] LBA 1990, s.71(3).
[25] PPG no. 15, para. 4.13.
[26] *Ibid.*
[27] *"The Character of Conservation Areas"*, RTPI October 1993.

authority's area, including the factors to be taken into account in assessing proposals for the change of use of historic buildings and a strategy for the economic regeneration of run down areas will help to identify the opportunities which historic buildings or groups of buildings can offer as a focus of regeneration.

These local plans should also set out the broad criteria for the designation of new conservation areas and the review of existing conservation area boundaries, providing a policy framework of how the more detailed assessment documents relate to the local plan and what weight these documents will be given in making decisions on applications for planning permission and conservation area consent.

Local planning authorities are required from time to time to make a review of their conservation areas, to determine whether any additional areas should be designated, and to designate such areas.[28] Concern has been expressed[29] that extensions of conservation areas have been made by local planning authorities in some cases primarily as a means to bring demolition within the control of the authority, and in recent years there has been a tendency to apply a blanket policy in some Local Plans which seeks to adopt a presumption in favour of retaining all buildings. An example of such a policy was contained in the East Hertfordshire Local Plan and caused the Inspector to require a modification of the policy "to avoid the statement of a presumption in favour of retention of all buildings" (in a conservation area). He concluded with the comment that the statement was a distortion of the emphasis in Circular 8/87 of "control" rather than "prevention" in conservation areas, and said "there could be no objection to the demolition of a building which made no contribution to the character of the conservation area." These principles were confirmed in paragraphs 4.26 and 4.27 of the PPG 15.

There appears to have been no judicial consideration of the section 69 duty in this context until the High Court decision in *R v. Canterbury City Council ex parte Halford*.[30] The case concerned an application under section 63 LBA to quash the designation by Canterbury City Council of an extension to the Barham Conservation Area. A proposal to develop a site on the edge of the conservation area and erect 30 houses and a school was refused planning permission. The developer lodged an appeal but before this could be heard the local planning authority passed a resolution to extend the conservation area to include the appeal site and other land. The planning appeal was then adjourned pending the outcome of the developers' application for judicial review because there was no other statutory remedy open to a person who wished to challenge the legality of the designation of a conservation area. The decision to extend the conservation area was said to be based upon the contribution which the land made to the setting of Barham village and the need to conserve that setting, the trees on the site and views to the conservation area. Mr Justice McCullough quashed the designation because there was no evidence that the local planning committee had considered that the trees on the site were already protected by a tree

---

[28] LBA 1990, s.69(2).
[29] David Morton, *"Conservation Areas—has saturation point been reached?" The Planner*, May 17, 1991, p. 5.
[30] *R v. Canterbury City Council ex parte Halford* [1992], J.P.L. 851.

preservation order nor that the site lay within an *Area of Outstanding Natural Beauty*, and was also within one of the *Special Landscape Areas of the Kent Structure Plan*. These factors were relevant in considering whether the designation was necessary to achieve the objectives of the local authority.

In non-metropolitan areas the district council is not required to consult the county council prior to the designating of a conservation area (although they have concurrent powers). The county is however required to consult the district before making a designation.[31] Structure, local and unitary development plans are the main vehicle for ensuring that conservation policies are co-ordinated and integrated with other planning policies affecting the historic environment.[32] Local plans and the second part of unitary development plans should set out detailed development control policies for an authority's area, but it will be desirable for the process of assessment and detailed definition or revision of boundaries to be tackled separately from the local plan process. It is desirable in the local plan to indicate the authority's broad criteria for designation and of new conservation areas and for the review of existing conservation area boundaries. The advantages of this method of approach are, firstly, that the public would have the fullest opportunity to comment on the proposal. Secondly, it would provide the local planning authority with an opportunity to produce a full appraisal of, and justification for, the area to be designated. Thirdly, conservation area policies would be linked with the overall planning strategies of the authority thereby ensuring that conservation areas were given proper weight and consideration in the overall formulation of district wide policies.

(b) Designation by map

It is recommended that the conservation area designation should contain **3.06** sufficient particulars to identify the area,[33] and nearly all conservation areas so far designated have been by reference to a map, which is often published as part of the publicity procedure.

(c) Notices

Notice of a designation (and indeed of a variation or cancellation) with **3.07** particulars of its effect must be published in the *London Gazette* and at least in one newspaper circulating in the area.[34] The local planning authority must also notify the Secretary of State and (if the area is in England)

---

[31] LBA 1990, Sched. 4, paras. 4(1)–(2).
[32] PPG 15, para. 2.2.
[33] LBA 1990, s.70(7).
[34] LBA 1990, s.70(8).

English Heritage of the designation.[35] Owners and occupiers of individual buildings in the conservation area do not have to be notified and have no right to object. Many authorities have sought to involve the public and the owners and occupiers of properties in the making of the conservation area, particularly where it is intended to improve and enhance the areas. Good practice might also include further publicity than that required by statutory notices prior to designation by the local planning authority and this is advocated in paragraph 4.7 of PPG 15. An objection can only seek to dissuade an authority from designating a conservation area, but once designated it will be very much more difficult to persuade an authority to revoke, cancel or limit that area.

3.08   There is no specific form of notice for publication—the original Circular 53/67[36] merely provided that "the published notices should describe the areas as clearly as possible, with maps where necessary" and Circular 147/74[37] provided that "the notice . . . must [now] give particulars of the effect of the designation . . . and . . . include information about the control of demolition . . . ." No further guidance is to be found in Circular 8/87, PPG 15, or in the LBA. Many authorities seek to go beyond a statutory type of notice and make it clear what is intended, *e.g.*:

> "The effect of designation is that special attention should be paid to the desirability of preserving or enhancing the character or appearance of the area designated. In particular, controls are applied regarding the demolition of buildings (owners are required to apply to the Council for conservation area consent before carrying out works of demolition to any building or part of a building within the areas); control is also imposed in respect of the display of advertisements and the felling, topping and lopping, etc, of trees within the areas. Penalties apply in the event of violations against this control."[38]

Notification must be given to the Secretary of State and (if in England) to English Heritage of the designation of a conservation area, but their consent is not necessary.[39]

3.09   A designation as a conservation area is registrable as a local land charge and must be registered as such by the local planning authority.[40] Indeed, to many owners on a sale of their property, this may be the first knowledge of the existence of the conservation area; on the other hand, estate agents are increasingly using the "conservation area status" as a sale advantage.

3.10   Prior to the LGPLA 1980 local planning authorities were under a duty to review their past exercise of functions relating to the designation of conservation areas "within such period as the Secretary of State might from time to time direct": this has now been changed by section 69(2) LBA requiring a review "from time to time."

---

[35] LBA 1990, s.70(5).

[36] The parts of Circulars 53/67 and 147/74 dealing with conservation areas and listed buildings were cancelled by Circular 23/77, which broadly reiterates the advice and comments given in the circulars referred to, but which itself was cancelled by Circular 8/87 and now superseded by PPG 15.

[37] As above.

[38] Adapted from an advertisement of *Leeds City Council*, April 3, 1975.

[39] LBA 1990, s.70(5).

[40] LBA 1990, s.69(4).

4. THE CONSEQUENCES OF A CONSERVATION AREA DESIGNATION

(a) General policy

The relevant legislative provision is set out in section 72(1) of the LBA, as **3.11** follows:

> "In the exercise, with respect to any buildings or other land in a conservation area, of any powers under any of the provisions mentioned in subsection (2), special attention shall be paid to the desirability of preserving or enhancing the character or appearance of that area."

The provisions mentioned in subsection (2) are the Planning Acts and Part I of the Historic Buildings and Ancient Monuments Act 1953.

Section 72(1) of the LBA is derived from and replaces section 277(8) of the T.C.P.A. 1971. It was not until 1988 that judicial attention became focused upon the correct interpretation of this subsection. In *Steinberg and Sykes v. Secretary of State for the Environment and Camden London Borough Council*,[41] Mr. Lionel Read Q.C., sitting as a Deputy Judge in the High Court, dealt with an application by neighbours of a property in relation to which there was an application to quash a decision of an Inspector, who had allowed an appeal by a property company against a refusal of planning permission by Camden London Borough Council.

The case involved an unused derelict and overgrown site lying between the applicants' properties in the recently designated conservation area. At the planning inquiry the Inspector had approached the issue before him in terms of "whether the proposed development would harm the conservation area." Mr Read stated the statutory duty imposed upon the inspector by section 277(8) of the T.C.P.A. 1971 in the following terms . . . "The obligation imposed by the statute was to pay special attention to the desirability of preserving or enhancing the character of the conservation area in exercising the power to determine the developer's appeal."

Mr Read drew attention to the approach which the duty required an Inspector to take in the following terms:

> "There was a world of difference between the issue which the inspector had defined for himself—whether the proposed development would 'harm' the character of the conservation area—and the need to pay special attention to the desirability of preserving or enhancing the character or appearance of the conservation area. In short, harm was one thing; preservation or enhancement was another. No doubt the inspector had demonstrated his concern that the character of the conservation area should not be harmed. That was not the same thing as paying special attention to the desirability or preserving or enhancing that character as well as its appearance. The concept of avoiding harm was essentially negative. The underlying purpose of section 277(8) seemed to be essentially positive."

The application was allowed and the decision of the Inspector was quashed.

[41] [1989] J.P.L. 258.

The *Steinberg* decision, in its reference to the underlying purpose of section 277(8) of the 1971 Act as "essentially positive", created anxiety as to whether planning permission could only be granted in respect of proposals which improved or enhanced conservation areas.[42] Such confusion has now been dispelled by decisions of the Court of Appeal and the House of Lords in 1991 and 1992 respectively.

On February 6, 1991 in the Court of Appeal Lord Justice Glidewell gave the leading judgment in the case of *The Bath Society v. Secretary of State for the Environment and Hammercrest Developments Ltd.*[43] The chronology of the events of the litigation commenced in September 1987 when Bath City Council, the local planning authority, refused to grant an application submitted by Hammercrest Developments Ltd for permission to erect a block of flats on land adjoining the site of Cavendish Lodge, Bath. Hammercrest appealed and the Secretary of State for the Environment allowed the appeal and granted planning permission in November 1988. The Bath Society, an amenity society, sought to challenge and quash the Secretary of State's decision by way of an application under section 245 of the 1971 Act. The High Court dismissed the application and the Bath Society appealed to the Court of Appeal.

Lord Justice Glidewell summarised the proper approach to be taken by decision makers when considering an application for planning permission for development in conservation areas in the following way:

"(i) If permission be sought for development on a site not within a conservation area, the person or body charged with deciding the matter—the local planning authority, the Secretary of State or his inspector on an appeal—was normally subject to one statutory duty, that imposed by section 29(1) and, in the case of an appeal, section 36 of the 1971 Act.[44] The departmental policy embodied in paragraph 15 of PPG 1[45] was in such circumstances a perfectly proper approach to the carrying out of that statutory duty.

(ii) If however, the site of proposed development was in a conservation area, then the decision-maker had two statutory duties to perform—those imposed by section 277(8) as well as section 29(1) of the Act. The question was how are these duties to be performed in reconciliation with each other, and how do they relate to the policy in paragraph 15 of PPG 1?

(iii) In [his] opinion, in a conservation area the requirement under section 277(8) to pay 'special attention' should be the first consideration for the decision-maker. It was true that the desirability of preserving or enhancing the character or appearance of the conservation area was, in formal terms, a 'material consideration', within section 29(1). Since, however, it was a consideration to which special attention was to be paid as a matter of statutory duty, it must be regarded as having considerable importance and weight.

(iv) If, therefore, the decision-maker decided that the development

[42] M Stubbs and A Lavers *"Steinberg and After: Decision Making and Development Control in Conservation Areas"* (1991) J.P.L., p. 9.
[43] [1991] 1 W.L.R. 1303 and 1991 J.P.L. 663.
[44] See ss.70, 78 and 79 T.C.P.A. 1990.
[45] Planning Policy Guidance 1 "General Policy and Principles".

would either enhance or preserve the character or appearance of the conservation area, this must be a major point in favour of allowing the development.

(v) Nevertheless, there will be some cases in which a development can simultaneously enhance the character or appearance of a conservation area but nevertheless cause some detriment. That detrimental effect was a material consideration. The Harrow case,[46] in which the inspector concluded that the quality of design of the proposed theatre would enhance the area, but that the additional traffic was a detriment, and that these two factors had to be weighed, the one against the other, was a good example of this. This seems to be a perfectly proper approach.

(vi) If, however, the decision-maker decided that the proposed development will neither preserve nor enhance the character or appearance of the conservation area, then it was almost inevitable that the development will have some detrimental, i.e. harmful, effect on that character or appearance. In lawyers' terms, the presumption derived from the policy in paragraph 15 is then rebutted. As he had said, the conclusion that the development would neither enhance nor preserve will be a consideration of considerable importance and weight. This does not necessarily mean that the application for permission must be refused, but it does in [his] view mean that the development should only be permitted if the decision-maker concluded that it carried some advantage or benefit which outweighed the failure to satisfy the section 277(8) test and such detriment as may inevitably follow from that."

The decision in the *Bath Society* case was followed by the deliberations of the House of Lords in January 1992 in the case of *South Lakeland District Council v. Secretary of State for the Environment and Carlisle Diocesan Parsonages Board.*[47] The issue in this case was what did the desirability of preserving or enhancing the character or appearance of a conservation area involve? Did it erect a barrier against *any* building development which did not either enhance or "positively preserve" the character or the appearance of the area? Or did it only inhibit development which would in some degree adversely affect the character or appearance of the area?

The leading opinion was given by Lord Bridge, who referred to the object of section 277(8) of the 1971 Act in terms that:

"There is no dispute that the intention of section 277(8) is that planning decisions in respect of development proposed to be carried out in a conservation area must give a high priority to the objective of preserving or enhancing the character or appearance of the area. If any proposed development would conflict with that objective, there will be a strong presumption against the grant of planning permission, though, no doubt, in exceptional cases the presumption may be overridden in favour of development which is desirable on the ground of some other public interest. But if a development would not conflict with that objective, the special attention required to be paid to that objective will

---

[46] *The Mayor and Burgesses of the London Borough of Harrow v. Secretary of State for the Environment* [1991] J.P.L. p. 137.
[47] [1992] 2 W.L.R. 204 HL.

no longer stand in its way and the development will be permitted or refused in the application of ordinary planning criteria. The issue raised in this appeal is as to the scope of the objective itself."

Lord Bridge had no hesitation in adopting the construction of section 277(8) of the 1971 Act appearing in the judgment of Lord Justice Mann in the Court of Appeal, here quoted:

> "In seeking to resolve the issue I start with the obvious. First, that which is desirable is the preservation or enhancement of the character or appearance of the conservation area. Second, the statute does not in terms require that a development must perform a preserving or enhancing function. Such a requirement would have been a stringent one which many an inoffensive proposal would have been inherently incapable of satisfying. Neither 'preserving' nor 'enhancing' is used in any meaning other than its ordinary English meaning. The Court was not here concerned with enhancement, but the ordinary meaning of 'preserve' as a transitive verb was 'to keep safe from harm or injury; to keep in safety, save, take care of, guard': Oxford English Dictionary, 2nd ed (1989), vol XII, p 404. In my judgment, character or appearance can be said to be preserved where they are not harmed. Cases may be envisaged where development would itself make a positive contribution to preservation of character or appearance. A work of reinstatement might be such. The Parsonage Board never advocated the new vicarage on that basis. It was not a basis which the inspector was invited to address but importantly he did not have to address it because the statute does not require him so to do. The statutorily desirable object of preserving the character or appearance of an area is achieved either by a positive contribution to preservation or by development which left character or appearance unharmed, that was to say, preserved."[48]

When read together, the *Bath Society* and *South Lakeland* cases represent the definitive view in relation to the application of section 72 of the LBA. Our conclusion is that the first five principles expressed in the *Bath* case by Glidewell L.J. still stand but that the sixth is now subject to the view of the House of Lords in the *South Lakeland* case. It is no longer correct to assume that if the proposed development will neither preserve nor enhance, it is "almost inevitable that the development will have some detrimental, ie harmful, effect on the character or appearance." The view expressed by Mann L.J. in the *South Lakeland* case and approved by the House of Lords in that case is summed up by saying (as did Mann L.J.) that "character or appearance can be said to be preserved where they are not harmed."

(b) Development control in conservation areas

3.12 Section 73 of the LBA provides that where a planning application is made for development which would in the opinion of the local planning authority effect the character or appearance of a conservation area, the provisions of section 67 LBA apply and a notice must be published in a local paper (by the

---

[48] *South Lakeland District Council v. Secretary of State for the Environment and Carlisle Diocesan Parsonages Board* [1991] J.P.L. 654.

authority, not by the applicant) indicating the nature of the application and stating the place where a copy of the application is open for inspection for a period of 21 days. Such a notice must be displayed on or near the site for seven days (again, by the authority and not by the applicant) and the application cannot be determined until 21 days have elapsed after the later of the date of publication of the press notice, and the date the site notice was first displayed. There is no statutory form of notice for display to be found in the Planning (Listed Buildings and Conservation Areas) Regulations 1990.[49] These regulations do however prescribe the form of certificate and notice to be given by an applicant in relation to ownership. These notices can be adapted as site notices. Section 73 (incorporating provisions of section 67(2)) requires the local planning authority to state in the press notice what is the proposal, and where and when the plans can be inspected. The form of notice prescribed additionally provides for an invitation to make representations. Local planning authorities almost invariably follow this form.

The local planning authority must take into account any representations as a result of these notices in determining the application.[50] Emphasis was laid in Circular 8/87 and is repeated in PPG 15, paragraph 4.19, that the policy in relation to planning decisions in respect of development in conservation areas must give a high priority to the objective of preserving or enhancing the character or appearance of the area. "If any proposed development would conflict with that objective, there will be a strong presumption against the grant of planning permission, though in exceptional cases the presumption may be overridden in favour of development which is desirable on the ground of some other public interest". The following case may serve to illustrate the issues here.

A proposal to carry out alterations to the front elevation of the Grade II former inn The Old White Hart at Odiham[51] to provide additional office accommodation was approved on appeal in 1990 in spite of the Inspector's conclusion that the development would not serve directly to preserve or enhance the listed building or conservation area since "the development could make a small but nevertheless valuable contribution to the continuing viability of the building and vitality of the area". Permission was granted on appeal.

Paragraph 4.20 of PPG 15 refers to the decision of the Court in *South Lakeland DC v. Secretary of State for the Environment and Halpin* [1993] J.P.L. 644. The PPG observes from the judgment that there is no requirement in the legislation that conservation areas should be protected from all development which does not enhance or positively preserve. The paragraph continues "whilst the character and appearance of conservation areas should always be given full weight in planning decisions, the objective of preservation can be achieved either by development which makes a positive contribution to an area's character or appearance, or by development which leaves character and appearance unharmed".[52]

Paragraph 4.17 of PPG 15 points out that when considering consent for

---

[49] Planning (Listed Buildings and Conservation Areas) Regulations 1990 (S.I. 1990 No 1519).

[50] LBA 1990, ss.73 and 67(7).

[51] T/APP/N1730/A/89/141018 and E/89/805385/P8 (1990) J.P.L. 700.

[52] There is a useful commentary on the case in [1993] J.P.L. 650 which has useful references to further cases.

new buildings in a conservation area the design should be of "high quality" and should be designed with respect for its context as part of a larger whole which has a well-established character in and appearance of its own. To this extent detailed rather than outline plans may be called for showing the new development in its setting[53]; Conservation Areas, however, will sometimes be drawn widely and it will probably not be necessary to insist on detailed applications throughout the area.

If the local planning authority requires plans and drawings to be made available illustrating the proposed development in its setting, it must, in accordance with Article 3(2) of the General Development Procedure Order 1995 request additional information not provided with the outline application within one month of the date of receipt of the application.

3.13   The importance of illustrative material and design considerations may be noted from the following cases. An application was made in Camden for an infill in a late eighteenth/early nineteenth-century street,[54] This application was refused on design grounds. The street was partly in a conservation area. The part under consideration was not, but the council proposed to extend the designation. They argued that the proposal was, by reason of its height and alignment with the neighbouring houses, out of sympathy with the street scene. The Inspector said that by reason of the diversity which existed in the street, he could see little virtue in requiring the building should conform to the outlines of its neighbours (two original estate buildings). The design would, in fact, due to its complete variance with its immediate neighbours, add interest to the street scene. He allowed the appeal.

In June 1988 an Inspector granted planning permission, listed building consent, and conservation area consent for a major office, shopping and restaurant development on a site in Poultry near the Mansion House in the heart of the City of London.[55] The Inspector was of the opinion that there was a sufficient number of correspondences between the design and important architectural and visual characteristics of surrounding buildings in the conservation area to enable him to draw a conclusion that the scheme would conform to, and preserve, the character of the area as a whole. In his decision letter he stated that it was his assessment "that the appeal proposals, by their dignified order, their imaginative ingenuity and pervading overall consistency would contribute more both to the immediate environment and to the architectural heritage than the retention of the existing buildings."[56]

In Barking, the Inspector decided that a proposed petrol station and car wash in a conservation area would not be unduly intrusive, particularly as the tranquillity of the area was already disturbed by sustained traffic[57]; and in Gloucester it was thought that the removal of a former postal sorting office, which in itself did not have any particular visual significance, would open up views of a nearby church, and demolition was therefore allowed.[58]

---

[53] PPG 15, para. 4.18.
[54] *Planning Appeals Vol. 1*, p. 28, T/APP/5008/A/75/2800/G9.
[55] APP/K5030/A/88/809225, APP/K5030/E/88/803073 June 1988.
[56] *Save Britain's Heritage v. SoS for the Environment and No. 1 Poultry and City Index Property* [1991] 1 W.L.R. 153 HL.
[57] APP/Z5060/A/85/2743
[58] APP/U1620/A85/35495.

In a case in Bishop's Stortford, the applicant, Peter Dominic, appealed **3.14**
against a decision of the local planning authority to refuse planning permission for the demolition of existing buildings and the erection of three
shops with two offices over. The inspector concluded that the existing Peter
Dominic building dominated the south east corner of Market Square, "and
was essential to the character of the conservation area," and furthermore
that the application to demolish the building arose from the "failure of the
appellants to appreciate its inherent qualities and its outstanding contribution to the street scene" which was enhanced by the reticence of the adjacent building. The inspector concluded that the appellants' proposed
building would by reason of its "unsympathetic form, ungainly proportions
and plain fenestration adversely affect the character of the conservation area
by replacing a fine Victorian building by an ugly modern one." The appeal
was dismissed on the basis of the architectural merits of the existing buildings and the unsympathetic nature of the design of the proposed replacement building.[59]

The question of the economics of a building or development in a conservation area is clearly as acute, if not more acute, than the issue in a listed
building consent case. The law on this subject is far from certain, but the
subject is dealt with generally in section 4 of PPG 15—see in particular paragraph 4.16.

(c) Conservation area consent required

For almost 40 years demolition was not regarded as "development" **3.15**
within the meaning of the various town planning statutes and a recommendation to include this in the Dobry report of 1974[60] was not implemented.
However in January 1991 Mr David Widdicombe Q.C., sitting as a Deputy
Judge of the High Court in the case of *Cambridge City Council v. Secretary
of State for the Environment and Milton Park Investment Ltd*,[61] held that
demolition was an operation normally undertaken by a builder and consequently planning permission was required before demolition works could
proceed. The Court of Appeal later overturned the decision[62] but the uncertainty which the case created led to the introduction by the Government of
selective demolition controls. Section 13 of the Planning and Compensation Act 1991 introduced new sub-sections 1A and 2(g) into section 55 of the
1990 T.C.P.A., accepting that demolition was a "building operation" normally undertaken by a person carrying on business as a builder. Section
55(1A) extends the definition of "building operations" to include demolition of buildings; rebuilding; structural alterations of or additions to buildings; and other operations normally undertaken by a person carrying on
business as a builder. Subsection 2(g) empowers the Secretary of State to
exclude any description of building from the scope of the section. The provisions are now in force, and exclude from control from July 27, 1992, all
demolitions except demolitions of dwelling-houses. Additionally if a local
planning authority wished to prevent demolition in a specific case or in an

---

[59] *Planning Appeals Vol. 1*, p. 49, APP/5253/A/6394.
[60] *Review of the Development Control System—the Dobry report.*
[61] [1991] J.P.L. 428.
[62] [1992] J.P.L. 644.

area it considered to be vulnerable, the Secretary of State could use his power to give a direction requiring applicants to seek planning permission before proceeding with demolition. The control of demolition in conservation areas has clearly been a factor in some designations[63] but it remains to be seen whether the new legislative provisions will have any discernible effect.

Ancient monuments and listed buildings are specifically dealt with under their respective legislative provisions so that demolition cannot proceed without specific authority. The critical factor so far as conservation areas are concerned and which gave "teeth" to the conservation area principle is the requirement that a building in a conservation area is subject to similar limitations as apply to demolition as a listed building and that conservation area consent must be obtained for its demolition.[64]

The criterion which the local planning authority must apply is the desirability of preserving or enhancing the character or appearance of the conservation area in which the building is situated.[65]

These general principles are subject to two major comments. First, the control is a control against demolition—the LBA does not seek in any special way to prevent extension or alteration of a building in a conservation area, except in so far as planning permission is required or in so far as an Article 4 direction has been made withdrawing the planning permission granted by the General Permitted Development Order. Secondly, there are a number of permissions to demolish granted by the Secretary of State in circular 9/95 which came into operation on June 3, 1995.

3.16   The general rule, however, is incorporated in section 74 LBA and applies the control of demolition to a building in a conservation area as if it were a listed building, with the exception of buildings within the provisions of section 75:

> (a) buildings which are themselves listed;
> (b) ecclesiastical buildings which are for the time being used for ecclesiastical purposes;
> (c) buildings for the time being included in the Schedule of Ancient Monuments; or
> (d) buildings in relation to which a direction has been made by the Secretary of State under section 75(2) LBA which enables the Secretary of State to exempt an individual building or types of building. Such a direction may be given to a local planning authority or to local planning authorities generally.

The Secretary of State has made a direction taking certain classes of buildings outside the ambit of section 75 LBA (namely that these buildings which are not subject to the control) and this is set out in the Town and Country Planning (Listed Buildings and Conservation Areas) Regulations 1990. The broad categories taken outside the ambit of section 75 LBA for which consent is thereby given:

> (a) any building (but not a part of a building) with a total cubic content not exceeding 115 cubic metres;

---

[63] *Roger W Suddards and David M Morton, "The Character of Conservation Areas"* (1991) J.P.L. 1011.

[64] LBA 1990, s.74.

[65] LBA 1990, s.72.

(b) a gate, wall, etc., under certain heights;

(c) a building erected since 1914 and used for agriculture or forestry;

(d) an industrial building subject to cubic content restrictions;

(e) a building subject to a discontinuance order or an enforcement notice;

(f) a building agreed to be demolished under a section 106 agreement;

(g) a building where the provisions of an enforcement notice require demolition;

(h) a building which is required to be demolished as a condition of a planning permission;

(i) a building which is the subject of a demolition order under the Housing Act 1985;

(j) a building included in a compulsory purchase order made under the Housing Act 1985;

(k) buildings to be demolished as a result of orders under the Pastoral Measure 1983.

5. DEMOLITION OF UNLISTED BUILDINGS IN A CONSERVATION AREA

3.17 Unless consent is not required by virtue of section 75 or by the provisions of the direction under sub-section 2 of that section, or is contained in the direction in paragraph 97 of Circular 8/87, an application to demolish must be made for "conservation area consent" (specifically so called in the Listed Buildings and Conservation Areas Regulations 1990).[66] Applications for consent to demolish must be made to the local planning authority; except where a local authority is itself making such an application when it is then made to the Secretary of State.[67] There is no general form of application prescribed in the regulations, but all planning authorities have their own standard application forms. Sufficient identification (including a plan) and such other plans and drawings as are necessary to describe the works will be required with copies.[68] The local planning authority must advertise the application unless the application falls within the exceptions relating to the interior of a Grade II (unstarred) building.[69]

Until the coming into force of the Local Government, Planning and Land Act 1980, a planning permission could in certain circumstances be deemed to grant consent to demolish. By virtue of the 1980 Act, Schedule 15, paragraph 26, this ceased to be the case, and so, with effect from November 13, 1980, two separate decisions are necessary, when the site falls within a conservation area. Although certain authorities will continue to accept both applications on one form, it is perhaps less likely to cause confusion if two separate applications are made.

3.18 It is recommended in the PPG 15, paragraph 4.27, that demolition consent for an unlisted building in a conservation area, where it is clear that redevelopment of the site will follow, should only be given where the redevelopment proposals are acceptable and detailed plans for the redevel-

---

[66] *Ibid.*

[67] PPG 15, para. 4.25.

[68] Regulation 10, Planning (LB & CA) Regulations, 1990.

[69] Regulation 5(3)(a) Planning (LB & CA) Regulations 1990.

opment are seen. The Courts have held that the function of giving consent to demolish an unlisted building in a conservation area cannot be performed without seeing what is to be substituted and how it would fit into the area.[70] Further, to avoid the possibility of the building being demolished but the development plans not being carried through, the proposed redevelopment could be the subject to an enforceable agreement under what is now section 106 of the T.C.P.A. 1990.[71] This advice is perhaps strengthened by section 17(3) of the LBA 1990 whereby consent for the demolition of a listed building may be granted subject to a condition that the building shall not be demolished before a contract for redevelopment of the site has been made and planning permission for these works has been granted and is advocated in paragraph 4.29 of PPG 15. This provision is applied by section 74(3) of the LBA in relation to buildings in a conservation area. However, the difficulties of this provision and its enforcement as well as current problems of recession will no doubt cause planning authorities to look much more to a section 106 agreement than merely relying on the fact that a contract for the redevelopment of the site has been made.

Many conservation areas are also areas of archaeological interest, and in such areas developers are expected to provide, with their planning applications, an archaeological evaluation of the development site so that the implications of the proposed scheme can be assessed. The advice on this subject is contained in PPG 16 "Archaeology and Planning" issued by the DOE in November 1990, and the subject is covered in more detail in Chapter 8.

An option recommended in PPG 16 is the preservation of any archaeological remains *in situ*, but where this is not feasible an archaeological excavation may be required for the purposes of "preservation by record". There can be a conflict between the desirability of a planning authority requiring the demolition of a building in a conservation area to be delayed until a contract for redevelopment of the site has been made, and the need for a realistic time for any archaeological excavation.

This calls for co-operation and a well balanced approach to be taken by both developer and archaeologist (and ultimately the local planning authority) and to this end the British Archaeologists' and Developers' Liaison Group has formulated a Code of Practice with the objective of reducing any conflict between the relevant parties.

In relation to demolition generally it has been pointed out that, because the operation of section 59 LBA (acts causing or likely to result in damage to listed buildings) does not extend to unlisted buildings in conservation areas, it seems quite possible that small but significant acts of demolition, *e.g.* the removal of a cornice, will be beyond the control of the local planning authority.[72] It is often difficult to draw the line between demolition (which does require conservation area consent) and some limited forms of alteration

---

[70] *Richmond-upon-Thames LBC v. Secretary of State for the Environment* [1979] J.P.L. 175.

[71] The provisions of which were extended by s.126 of the Housing Act 1974 which in turn was replaced by s.33 of the Local Government Miscellaneous Provisions) Act 1982. The PPG 15 (4.29) advises the imposition on the grant of consent for demolition a condition under s.17(3) of the Act, as applied by s.74(3) to cover this type of situation.

[72] *"Townscape in Trouble"*, The English Historic Towns Forum (1992).

(which may not require conservation area consent for an unlisted building in a conservation area): this matter is discussed in full at paragraphs 5.20 below.

Paragraph 4.28 of PPG 15 discusses the interpretation of the meaning of demolition. Section 336 of the principal Act states that a building includes "any part of a building". The demolition of part of a building should therefore be regarded as falling within the scope of conservation area control. Each case must be a matter of fact and degree, to be decided in the particular case. The PPG 15, paragraph 4.28 advises that it will be for the Courts to give an authoritative interpretation of the meaning of demolition, but the Secretary of State considers that it would be proper to have regard to the scale and nature of the works involved, and whether they would result in the removal of a significant part of the building in question. Routine works of repair, maintenance or replacement involving such items as doors or windows, seems not in the Secretary of State's view normally constitute a demolition. Likewise, the removal of internal features, whether replaced or not, would not usually constitute a demolition and for the purposes of conservation area consent, would not, in any event, have a material impact on the building's appearance or the character or appearance of the area.

The principles applicable to the consent to demolish a listed building do not apply to an unlisted building in a conservation area. The test as to whether or not consent should be granted in respect of a listed building is that regard should be had to the character of the building itself as one of special architectural or historic interest. The test in relation to a non-listed building in a conservation area is the effect on "the character or appearance of the conservation area in which the building is situated". This was given recognition in Planning (Listed Buildings and Buildings in Conservation Areas) Regulations 1990, Schedule 3 under reference to section 38. Thus, in enforcement notice proceedings,[73] the test is not the building itself but the effect of the loss of the building on the character and appearance of the conservation area.

6. THE GENERAL PERMITTED DEVELOPMENT ORDER AND ARTICLE 4 DIRECTIONS IN CONSERVATION AREAS

Article 4. Article 4 of the Town and Country Planning (General Permitted **3.19** Development) Order 1995[74] provides that:

In June 1995 two new statutory instruments (S.I. 1995 No. 418 and S.I. 1995 No. 419) came into effect. The Town and Country Planning (General Permitted Development) Order 1995 consolidates the permitted development provisions contained in the 1988 General Development Order, and its subsequent amendments, and the Town and Country Planning (General Development Procedure) Order 1995 consolidates the procedure provisions of the 1988 Order.

The General Permitted Development Order 1995 follows the pattern

[73] Para. 4.25 of PPG 15.
[74] Town and Country Planning (General Permitted Development) Order 1995 (S.I. 1995 No. 418).

established by the 1988 Order, by setting out the categories of "permitted development" in Schedule 2 for which Article 3 grants permission. The General Development Procedure Order sets out the procedures to be followed by both applicants for planning permission and local planning authorities, including a table of categories of application on which a local planning authority must consult (with names of consultees), before granting planning permission.

The General Permitted Development Order repeats the provisions in Article 4 where if the Secretary of State or the appropriate local planning authority is satisfied that it is expedient that certain specified Part, Class or paragraph in Schedule 2, should not be carried out under the "permitted development" provisions, he or they may give a direction under Article 4 that the permission granted by Article 3 shall not apply. The Order gives to local planning authorities the power to issue Article 4 directions withdrawing certain permitted development rights in conservation areas without requiring the approval of the Secretary of State:

(i) all or any development of the Part, Class or paragraph in question in an area specified in the direction, or

(ii) any particular development, falling within that Part, Class or paragraph which is specified in the direction, and the direction shall specify that it is made under this paragraph."

Consent. A LPA may now,[75] without the consent of the Secretary of State give a direction under Article 4 in respect of any particular development described in Article 4(5)—being mainly development associated with dwellinghouses and features within their curtilage—where this proposal is in the whole or part of a conservation area, and when the LPA is satisfied that it is expedient that the development should not be carried out unless permission is granted for it on an application.[76]

3.20 *Departmental advice.* Advice to local planning authorities on the use of Article 4 directions is given in paragraph 4.23 of PPG 15. Basically the advice is that a local planning authority should gauge the attitude of the local population in a conservation area. The Secretary of State takes the view that permitted development rights should not be withdrawn without clear justification and that residents in conservation areas should continue to enjoy the same freedom to undertake development as residents elsewhere. The mere existence of a conservation area is not sufficient justification for making a blanket Article 4 direction in relation to it. Broadly, a local planning authority should make directions where these are backed by a clear assessment of an area's special architectural or historic interest, when the importance to that special interest of the features in question is established,

[75] The Town and Country Planning (General Permitted Development Order) 1995— which came into effect in June 1995.
[76] Article 4(2) of the above Order.

when the local planning authority can demonstrate local support for the direction, and where the direction involves the minimum withdrawal of permitted development rights (in terms of both area and types of development) necessary to achieve its objective.[77]

A deterioration in the character and appearance of conservation areas by reason of alterations to buildings which are "permitted development" has generated public concern in recent years. The particular areas of concern are those where relatively small changes have occurred in terms of individual properties, but which incrementally can have a defacing effect upon the character or appearance of the conservation area.[78] The use of UPVC windows in some unlisted dwelling-houses, coloured concrete tiles replacing natural slates, plate glass windows or "off-the-peg" bow windows replacing Victorian bays, are just some of the elements which can erode the homogeneous quality of areas which have been selected for their special character. In October 1990, English Heritage's London Division convened a major conference[79] to consider "Conservation Areas—problems, policies and opportunities". There was unanimous agreement that the greatest single problem facing conservation areas in London was the damage caused by permitted development rights. The architectural integrity of whole areas was said to be undermined by the cumulative impact of unsympathetic alterations, and some London Boroughs were even contemplating de-designation of their most damaged conservation areas. Efforts were made in the early stages of the Planning and Compensation Bill in the House of Lords in February 1991 which would have resulted in a curtailment of the scope of permitted development rights within conservation areas, but this was opposed by the Government. The contention was that such a change would be far-reaching in its effects and would give rise to an unacceptable administrative burden for local authorities. However, an outcome of this debate was for the Secretary of State to announce, in March 1994, that there will be new proposals to permit local planning authorities to bring certain types of alterations to single dwelling-houses within planning control, by the making of directions which will not require the Secretary of State's approval.[80] The Town and Country Planning (General Permitted Development) Order 1995 brought these proposals into effect.

There was, prior to 1991, a high rejection rate of requests for Article 4 directions by the Department of the Environment, and this led to English Heritage seeking endorsement by the Department of an Advice Note on the subject of "Article 4 directions in conservation areas". This Advice Note sets out guidance on the scope of controls and the need for precise definition of the area to which the direction applies, with emphasis being given to showing how the direction would provide a positive policy for preserving and enhancing the character or appearance of the conservation area. The Government has commented by stating that the existing Article 4 direction

---

[77] PPG 15, para. 4.23.
[78] *English Heritage Conservation Bulletin*, June 1989 and *"Townscape in Trouble"*, *English Historic Towns Forum*, March 1992.
[79] *English Heritage Conservation Bulletin*, February 1991.
[80] Para. 4.22 of PPG 15.

route provides the best means of achieving the common goals of conservation area preservation and enhancement.[81]

3.21 *Departmental approval.* There now appears to be a greater readiness in the Department to approve Article 4 directions and to extend the range of them, particularly if there is an active conservation scheme in progress and grant aid is provided. East Lindsay D C had an Article 4 direction approved for Horncastle which extended to include external painting schemes; though that council's attempt to have an Article 4 direction approved to prevent stone cladding, roof and window alterations in a Louth conservation area was unsuccessful in respect of the windows.[82]

At Tixall Gatehouse, Stafford, where there was felt to be an urgent need to provide control over the setting of this Grade I listed building, an Article 4 direction was made, approved and served in the record time of one week.[83] This was at a time when consent from the Secretary of State was required for an Article 4 direction even in respect of a listed building.

Compensation. The local planning authority, of course, will be concerned as to the financial consequences of making an Article 4 direction. An Article 4 direction withdraws the permission granted by the General Permitted Development Order and makes it necessary to apply to the local planning authority for a specific permission. If that is refused, or granted subject to conditions, the owner is entitled to compensation on the footing that permission already granted (by the General Permitted Development Order) has been revoked or modified. Article 4 directions do not enable the Secretary of State or the local planning authority to withdraw a permission which has been given and acted upon.

7. TREES IN A CONSERVATION AREA

3.22 Trees which are not subject to a tree preservation order but which are in a conservation area, are given protection by section 211 of the Town and Country Planning Act 1990. The LBA contains no definition of a "tree" but Lord Denning M R in *Kent CC v. Batchelor*[84] suggested that a distinction might be drawn between mature trees and saplings, with only trees having a diameter greater than seven inches or eight inches being protected. Broadly, the protection given is the same as for a tree outside a conservation area which is subject to a tree preservation order. The purpose of the requirement is to give the authority a final opportunity to make a tree preservation order, if appropriate.

---

[81] *English Heritage Commission Bulletin*, June 1991, but see Mr David Curry's statement in March 1994.
[82] Both cases courtesy of East Lindsay D.C.
[83] Coutesy of Stafford B.C.
[84] *The Times*, October 7, 1976, (CA); [1976] J.P.L. 754, CA.

The difference is one of mechanics, namely that by section 211, anyone intending to do any act which would be prohibited under section 198, i.e. if the tree was protected by a tree preservation order, must give six weeks notice of such intention to the local planning authority. If after six weeks of such notice being given the local planning authority has not responded, or if it grants consent, work may proceed. It seems that in giving consent, conditions cannot be imposed. If the local planning authority is not willing to grant consent, or if it felt it appropriate to attach conditions, it may make a tree preservation order.

The six week interim protection lapses after a period of two years from the date of the notice. This does not however preclude the local planning authority from making a tree preservation order outside the six week period.

Penalties for contravening the requirements given in the notice are similar to penalties for breach of a tree preservation order (including a duty to replant).[85]

The local planning authority must keep a register of applications available for public inspection.[86] The Secretary of State may by regulations exempt certain classes of tree from the operation of section 211 by reference to their location, size, species or other designation.[87]

The significance of the visual contribution which the presence of trees may make to the character or appearance of a conservation area is amply illustrated in an appeal against Bournemouth Borough Council's refusal to grant outline planning permission for the erection of 90 flats on a site containing over 400 trees in September 1990.[88] In considering the visual impact of the proposal, the inspector considered that the effect on the trees, the likely impact of the new buildings, and the consequences of the loss of the existing buildings, were the issues of primary importance. The trees, especially those on the periphery of the site, made a valuable contribution to the amenity of the area. Although the inspector was seriously concerned by the amount of tree loss which the proposal would entail, he decided that the tree loss of itself would not have been a reason to reject the proposal provided "any detailed scheme was accompanied by a comprehensive landscape scheme providing not only for new planting but also for the proper maintenance and management of the existing trees . . . so that the attractive grounds continued to make a significant contribution to the character and appearance of the conservation area".[89]

3.23 Town and Country Planning (Tree Preservation Order) (Amendment) and (Trees in Conservation Areas) (Exempted Cases) Regulations 1975 were made on March 12, 1975 and provide in Regulation 3 that section 61A of the Town and Country Planning Act 1971 now re-enacted as section 211 of the T.C.P.A. 1990 shall not apply where the act is:

(i) the cutting down, uprooting, topping or lopping of a tree in the circumstances mentioned in section 198(6) of the T.C.P.A. 1990 (i.e. the cutting down, topping or lopping of trees which are dying or

---

[85] s.210, T.C.P.A. 1990.
[86] s.214, T.C.P.A. 1990.
[87] s.212, T.C.P.A. 1990.
[88] 1991, 6 PAD 160.
[89] T/APP/A1205/A/89/140495/P2, A/88/2557/0.

dead or have become dangerous, or the cutting down, topping or lopping of any trees in compliance with any obligations imposed by or under an Act of Parliament or so far as may be necessary for the prevention or abatement of a nuisance);

(ii) the cutting down of a tree in the circumstances mentioned in paragraph (1) or (2), or the cutting down, uprooting, topping or lopping of a tree in the circumstances mentioned in paragraph (3), of the Second Schedule to the form of Tree Preservation Order contained in the Schedule to the Town and Country Planning (Tree Preservation Order) Regulations 1969 (SI 1969 no. 17) (as amended by the 1975 Regulations) (which broadly relate to woodlands schemes approved by the Forestry Commission);

(iii) the cutting down of a tree in accordance with a felling licence granted by the Forestry Commissioners;

(iv) the cutting down, uprooting, topping or lopping of a tree on land in the occupation of a local planning authority and the act is done by or with the consent of that authority;

(v) the cutting down, uprooting, topping or lopping of a tree having a diameter not exceeding 75 millimetres or the cutting down or uprooting of a tree having a diameter not exceeding 100 millimetres where the act is carried out to improve the growth of other trees.

[N.B. the reference to "diameter" is construed as measured over the bark at a point 1.5 metres above ground level.]

3.24   Section 203 of the T.C.P.A. 1990 is an enabling provision as to compensation payable in respect of loss or damage caused or incurred in consequence of the refusal of any consent required under a section 198 Tree Preservation Order. The provision is nowhere expressed to apply to trees protected under section 211, but it is worthwhile to note that the measure of such compensation, following the decision of the Court of Appeal in *Bell v. Canterbury City Council*[90] is the diminution in the value of the land resulting from the refusal, and not merely the commercial value of the timber which the owner cannot realise.

3.25   If a tree which is located in a conservation area (and is not covered by the exceptions referred to above) is removed, uprooted or destroyed in contravention of section 211 T.C.P.A. 1990, or dies at a time when its cutting down or uprooting is authorised, there is an automatic replanting obligation. The effect of these requirements contained in section 213 of T.C.P.A. 1990 is more stringent than is applicable to a tree covered by a tree preservation order, wherein the requirement to replant only applies where a tree has had to be removed because it was dying, dead or dangerous (section 198(6) T.C.P.A. 1990) or because of the prevention or abatement of a nuisance (section 198(6)(b) T.C.P.A. 1990).

The Planning and Compensation Act 1991 inserted section 23(7) into the T.C.P.A. 1990 resulting in a new section 214A. This conferred power on a local planning authority to seek an injunction in support of its functions in relation to tree preservation. This new provision became effective from January 1992.

[90] [1988] 56 P & CR 211; [1989] J.P.L. 536.

8. PAINTING, STONE-CLEANING AND REPLACEMENT MATERIALS IN CONSERVATION AREAS

The control over the painting of the exterior of a building was unclear for **3.26** many years, but the subject was considered by the Queen's Bench Division of the High Court in December 1987 in the case of *Royal Borough of Windsor and Maidenhead v. Secretary of State for the Environment and others.*[91] The court held that the painting or re-painting of a building was capable of amounting to a building operation (as defined in section 55(1A) of the Town and Country Planning Act 1990) as "operations normally undertaken by a person carrying out a business as a builder". Painting or re-painting can thus be "development" requiring planning permission. Under Class C of Part 2, Schedule 2, of the General Permitted Development Order 1995 "the painting of the exterior of any building or work" is permitted development. In this context 'painting' includes any application of colour. It does not however extend to painting for the purpose of advertisement, announcement or direction. As with most other categories of permitted development these rights may be withdrawn by the use of an Article 4 direction.

Listed building consent is required under the LBA 1990 in the case of painting or re-painting of a *listed building* in cases where such works constitute an "alteration" affecting the character of a building as one of special architectural or historic interest.

If a local planning authority wished to exercise control over external painting in order to preserve or enhance the character or appearance of a *conservation area*, it is open to them to apply for an Article 4 direction (see paragraph 3.19).

Guidance on external painting of listed buildings is included in Annex C17 of PPG 15.

If painting or re-painting is to be included in an Article 4 direction it is **3.27** suggested that the local planning authority should publish a colour code of acceptable colours, and this has been done frequently and to good effect.

In the case of *Royal Crescent at Bath,*[92] the problem was tested in connection with the painting of a front door of a listed building situated in a conservation area. The owner wished to paint the door a canary yellow and did so but was then subject to an enforcement notice requiring the painting to be altered. The enforcement notice was not upheld (on other grounds) but the ability of the local planning authority to make an enforcement order in these circumstances was not challenged.

Listed building consent may be required for painting or repainting a listed building if this would affect its character as a building of special architectural or historic interest, whether the building is in a conservation area or not. However two listed stone properties in Sleaford (which were in a conservation area) had been painted. The result was described by the Inspector as follows: "I am satisfied that the painting of the stonework of the facade, by obscuring the colour, texture and scale of the stonework, has inevitably had a very detrimental effect on the appearance and character of this listed building, of the group of listed buildings of which it forms part, of the gener-

---

[91] [1988] J.P.L. 410.
[92] [1972] J.P.L. 650.

ally attractive street scene, and of the surrounding conservation area." The Secretary of State dismissed the enforcement notice appeal and refused to grant LBC for the works enforced against.[93]

An appeal was heard in November 1989[94] against a listed building enforcement notice served by Rugby Borough Council where it was alleged that re-painting, in black, of the woodwork of the ground floor windows, door frame, fanlight and hood on the front elevation at 16 Church Street, Rugby (a Grade II* building in a conservation area) had amounted to an alteration of the building. The Inspector took into account the amended advice introduced to Circular 8/87 (contained in Circular 18/88) following the judgment in the *Windsor and Maidenhead* case, where it recognised that re-painting was capable of being an "alteration". He applied the test of whether the re-painting had affected the special architectural character of the listed building, and concluded that it had. He felt the black paint on the ground floor windows and other elements had seriously compromised the subtle definition of the timber detailing of this early nineteenth-century building. The inspector also considered the implications of the property being located within a conservation area, and decided that although the black paintwork had only a minimal impact on the overall character and appearance of that area, the immediate vicinity of the conservation area suffered due to the impoverishment of the listed building. The appeals were dismissed and the enforcement notices upheld.

3.28   Stone cleaning[95] is a subject which involves basic town planning questions such as whether it requires planning permission at all, and whether or not it requires listed building consent. It certainly would not require conservation area consent for an unlisted building within a conservation area. Annex C of PPG 15, paragraph C18, deals with external cleaning of buildings and states that cleaning a building usually requires listed building consent. Cleaning a listed building using water and bristle brushes is the simplest method, although this can lead to saturation of walls and outbreak of rot in timbers. Other methods of cleaning stone or brickwork can have a marked effect on the character of the building by destroying detail and will certainly require listed building consent. Strangely there appear to be no cases in the courts and no reported ministerial decisions in England. However the matter has been considered carefully in Scotland, where the legislation is expressed in similar terms to that in England, and the following conclusions seem to emerge[96]:

> (a)   The first question is whether stone-cleaning is development. The Reporter (the equivalent of an English inspector) held in a case relating to a building in Downaside Road, Glasgow[97] that whilst a colour change on stone-cleaning and affected the building's external appearance, he did not consider the change to be "material"— so escaping the provisions of the legislation defining "develop-

---

[93] 1972 J.P.L. 782: (APP/5312/F/77/26); see also [1981] J.P.L. 607 considered at para. 4.46 below.

[94] [1990] J.P.L. 223.

[95] See para. C18 of Annex C to PPG 15 in relation to listed buildings.

[96] We are indebted to Eric Young and his article in *Estates Gazette* (August 1, 1987), Vol. 283, p. 540.

[97] P/ENA/SL/199, October 3, 1985.

ment" by virtue of (the English section 22(2)(a) of the 1971 Act). Equally in a further appeal[98] relating to a building in Clarence Drive, Glasgow, the Reporter took the view that the effect of stone-cleaning had been to restore the building to a condition closely resembling that which it must have possessed when originally built. He regarded the cleaning as "maintenance"—and as such not involving development.

(b) But even if the stone-cleaning does not require planning permission, it may still require listed building consent as section 55 LBA does not refer to "development" in relation to a listed building, but "works"—of which term there is no definition. The George Hotel in George Street, Edinburgh was proposed to be stone-cleaned.[99] The local planning authority's policy on the cleaning of listed buildings was to weigh the visual desirability of clean buildings against the adverse effects which some methods of stone-cleaning can have. The Secretary of State accepted that the determining issue was whether the risk of damage could be regarded as justifiable. He stated that in general, he accepted the planning authority's policy of seeking to protect sandstone buildings from the severe damage which could be caused by abrasives or acid used in stone-cleaning. "Had the listed building had a begrimed or shabby appearance, cleaning might have been justified, but here the building had a well-maintained appearance and a pleasant patina which blended well with the stonework of most of the buildings in the vicinity." He therefore dismissed the appeal.

The effect of roof works upon the character and appearance of a conservation area in Stockport was a central issue in an appeal by Wren Properties Ltd against an enforcement notice issued by Stockport Metropolitan Borough Council in June of 1990.[1] The appeal property was a large semi-detached dwelling in an established suburb of Stockport. It was one of eight properties which had many decorative features, including finial tiles and decorative ridge tiles. Protection of the Victorian and Edwardian character of the area had been the specific reason for the original conservation area designation. All the properties were roofed with Welsh slates save for the appeal property, whose slates had been replaced by red concrete tiles. The Council issued an enforcement notice requiring replacement of the tiles. **3.29**

The Inspector dismissed the appeal partly on the basis that the replacement tiles were inappropriate. He stated "These tiles, because of their colour, design and total lack of embellishment, were prominent in comparison to the weathered roofs of neighbouring properties. The other roofs complemented the Edwardian and Victorian architecture. The stark, modern appearance of the new tiles spoilt the whole balance and rhythm of the terrace, and produced a market diminution in the appearance of the street. The roof did not preserve or enhance the character or appearance of the conservation area." The Inspector also dismissed the appellants submission that the tiles might be painted a sympathetic colour.

[98] P/ENA/SL/201, November 25, 1985.
[99] HGJ/2/LA/50, December 19, 1984.
[1] 1990 5 PAD 542, Appeal reference T/APP/C/89/C4235/000009/P6.

9. CONTROL OF ADVERTISEMENTS

3.30   Circular 5/92 and PPG 19 (repeated in PPG 15, paragraphs 4.31–4.37) expect local planning authorities to pay special attention to the desirability of preserving or enhancing the appearance of conservation areas, and to apply more exacting standards when considering whether to grant consent for an advertisement in a conservation area. Local planning authorities are recommended to be sensitive in the use of their powers and to take account of the fact that the conservation area may well include areas of thriving commerce. Section 220 of the TCPA 1990, however, requires the Secretary of State to make regulations to control the display of advertisements in the interest of amenity or public safety and enable such regulations to provide for regulating the dimensions, appearance or position, and requiring planning consent for the display of advertisements; also for the constitution of advisory committees. Currently operative regulations under the LBA are, in fact, general advertisement control regulations made in 1992 and include specific advice as to conservation areas. The Town and Country Planning (Control of Advertisements) Regulations 1992 Circular No 5/92 advise that advertisement controls are exercisable only in the interests of amenity, and public safety, taking account of any material factors and in particular, in the case of amenity, the general characteristics of the locality, including the presence of any feature of historic, architectural, cultural or similar interest, disregarding if they (the local planning authority) think fit, any advertisements being displayed there.

Circular 5/92 and PPG 19 (Outdoor Advertisement Control) incorporates advice[2] on the making of applications for the display of outdoor advertisements and the general procedures to be adopted by the local planning authority. PPG 19 provides advice relating to the display of advertisements and, in paragraph 24, refers to the additional controls which may apply to advertisements for display on listed buildings, because almost all such advertisements will constitute an "alteration" to the building and will therefore require listed building consent as well as any advertisement consent. The test of whether the proposed advertisement would affect the character of the building as one of special architectural or historic interest would seem to apply, and not a general requirement for all advertisements on listed buildings to be the subject of applications for consent.

There are several categories of advertisements which may be displayed under the terms of the Town and Country Planning (Control of Advertisements) Regulations 1992 with "deemed consent"—that is without the express consent of the local planning authority—but this discretion is not absolute.

Schedule 2 of the 1992 Regulations introduces 10 excepted classes of advertisement which do not normally require the express consent of the local planning authority. Some of these classes of advertisements are specifically excluded from, *inter alia*, conservation areas.

It is suggested in Annex to PPG 19 that smaller sized poster panels could be acceptable if they are in scale with other street furniture and related to the scale of surrounding buildings and have regard to the symmetry or architectural features of their location.

---

[2] Published in March 1992.

Provision is made in section 221(1) of the Town and Country Planning Act 1990 for Regulations enabling the Secretary of State to make different provisions with respect to controlling advertisements in different areas, including conservation areas (section 221(1)(a)), experimental areas (section 221(b)) and "areas of special control" (section 221(1)(c)). An "area of special control" can include rural areas or an area which appears to the Secretary of State to require special protection on grounds of amenity (section 221(3)(a) & (b)). PPG 19, paragraph 27 describes the circumstances which would lead to the Secretary of State being satisfied that there were relevant planning considerations justifying the views of the local planning authority that a proposed area required "special protection on grounds of amenity". Examples of such candidates for this special protection are "a small enclave in an otherwise mainly commercial city centre where there are important architectural, archaeological, historical or visual characteristics, e.g. the precincts of a cathedral and neighbouring ecclesiastical buildings, or a historic market place". The designation of such an area requires the Secretary of State's approval, and the Circular makes it clear that because it involves stricter control over outdoor advertising, the local planning authority submitting the Order must be able to show that there are compelling and relevant planning considerations to justify their view will be expected to have consulted local trade and amenity organisations about the proposal. Following the approval of an "area of special control" order by the Secretary of State it must be reviewed at intervals of not more than five years. It is perhaps surprising to learn, from the Circular, that rather more than 45 per cent of the total area of England and Wales has been designated by local planning authorities as areas of special control in relation to advertisements. The explanation for this large geographical area lies in the fact that National Parks are automatically given the "area of special control" status.

10. URGENT REPAIRS TO A BUILDING IN A CONSERVATION AREA

Section 76 of the LBA 1990 is concerned with urgent works to certain **3.31** unoccupied buildings in a conservation area and provides that the Secretary of State may make a direction that the section 54 provisions (urgent works to preserve buildings) should apply if it is important for maintaining the character or appearance of the area. The subject is considered in Chapter 7 in relation to listed buildings but there are some differences which should be noted:

   (a) The section only relates to those unoccupied unlisted buildings in a conservation area for which the Secretary of State has made a direction if it appears to him that the preservation of the building is important for maintaining the character or appearance of the conservation area.[3] The Secretary of State must consult English Heritage before giving such a direction.[4]

   (b) Either the Secretary of State or the local planning authority may, if of opinion that works are urgently necessary for the preservation of

---

[3] LBA 1990, s.76(1).
[4] LBA 1990, s.76(2).

the building, execute the works. English Heritage, if authorised by the Secretary of State, may carry out the works but the Secretary of State has indicated that he will only do so where the conservation area is of national rather than of local significance and the building in question is so important that failure to carry out emergency repairs to it may affect the character of the area.[5]

In other respects, the rules in respect of a notice under this section in relation to a building in a conservation area follow those in relation to listed buildings, details of which will be found at paragraphs 7.10–7.13 below. The provisions of sections 47 and 48 LBA relating to non-urgent repairs to a listed building are now repealed and substituted by the Planning and Compensation Act 1991, Schedule 4, paragraph 22, with effect from February 10, 1992.

11. FINANCIAL ASSISTANCE

3.32   There are a number of provisions by which the Secretary of State, English Heritage, or the local planning authority (frequently as agent of the Secretary of State), may provide conservation moneys to the owners of properties in conservation areas by way of grant or loan, and they are dealt with more particularly in Chapter 12.

12. CONSERVATION AREA PARTNERSHIPS

3.33   In May 1993 English Heritage published a consultation paper outlining proposals for a refocusing of the existing methods of funding the conservation areas. The paper referred to the valuable part which "conservation area grants" had made over the past 25 years to improving the quality of the selected areas in which they operate, and the key component created by the partnerships between English Heritage and local authorities—both at County and District level—in strengthening local commitment to conservation.

The main objectives of these grants had been to ensure that the quality of England's historic townscapes was recognised and protected, to encourage those repairs or other changes, often on a small scale or incremental basis, which made a contribution to the historic identity of an area, and to help foster a positive attitude to conservation within those local authorities in whose areas grants had been made available. Due to limited resources and the current recession, the grant aid had been available only to a small fraction of the country's 7,500 conservation areas. It was therefore decided that grant schemes should be re-targeted to ensure that assistance was directed to those authorities most in need of help.

The main proposal to arise from this review was that of forming a Conservation Area partnership which would be entered into with the participating local authority. The powers available under sections 79–80 of the LBA 1990 would be used for the repair of buildings in conservation areas with joint

---

[5] Circular 8/87, para. 126.

schemes, known as "Town Schemes" using English Heritage together with local authority funding or resources from elsewhere, in such a way that these schemes would be as flexible and responsive as possible to real needs. The grants available under section 77 of the LBA 1990 for enhancement work in conservation areas would continue to be available "when they make a significant contribution" to the proposed programme.

In selecting new conservation area grant schemes, English Heritage would need to be satisfied that the special architectural or historic interest of the conservation area must be of demonstrable quality; that there is a need for urgent action to protect specific elements in the proposed action area (where possible using the "buildings at risk" survey); that any structural repairs are based on an assessment of economic need, which will take into account patterns of property ownership and typical property values, together with the rate of grant matching the perceived need for financial support. Notwithstanding the assessment of the area's economic need, an individual financial assessment will still be necessary for the more substantial grants, although the aim will be to provide an incentive necessary to help owners carry out repairs or enhancements which will be to public as well as to their own private benefit, and that will contribute to the uplift of an area that already requires attention.

The commitment to conservation standards by local authorities would be examined by English Heritage in order to safeguard the financial investment to be made through partnership funding, and this would include reviewing the conservation issues set out in local plans and supplementary guidance as well as being satisfied with the authority's effective development control on planning and listed building matters. The need for appropriately qualified conservation staff, the treatment of the authority's own listed buildings, and its own financial contribution towards the Conservation Area partnership would all be significant factors.

As, at the time of publication of the consultation document, there were almost 400 existing schemes with local authorities, it was decided that a number of pilot schemes would be set up in 1994 in order to refine the approach to these partnerships for a further launch based on a more general invitation to all authorities to put forward applications in the new format with the aim that the first tranche of schemes would be in train in April 1995. The full translation of those existing schemes which will qualify for partnership status is expected to be implemented by 1996/97.[6]

---

[6] *Conservation Area Partnerships—Conservation Bulletin*, Nov. 1993.

4. Listed Building Consent—The Criteria for Consent to Demolish, Alter and Extend

1. GENERAL SUMMARY

4.01   Listing is too often considered to be a permanent freezing of a building. This was never the intention nor in practice should it be the way in which listing should operate. Sir Hugh Casson, in giving evidence for Barclays Bank in connection with a building at 39/40 Lombard Street, London summarised, in our view quite correctly, the relationship between listing and the granting of LBC. He said:

> "While the facade is not distinguished, in my view the Inspectorate was correct in listing the building as Grade II. Listing, however, means no more than it says. It permits time for study and for second thoughts.

Such study should properly balance the practicabilities of preservation with the visual loss to the street of demolition."[1]

Similarly Lady Birk denied that listing was "a pickling policy" (1977).[2]

Planning Policy Guidance Note 15, hereinafter called PPG 15, gives the most up to date thinking on the subject of listed buildings and conservation areas, and sets out the criteria expected to be taken into account by local planning authorities or the Secretary of State when considering LBC applications. Paragraph 3.16 of the PPG states that it is an objective of Government policy to secure the preservation of historic buildings, but acknowledges that there will very occasionally be cases where demolition is unavoidable. Listed building controls ensure that proposals for demolition are fully scrutinised before any decision is reached.

The listing of a building should not—according to paragraph 3.3 of the PPG—be seen as a bar to all future change, but rather as a means of ensuring that its special architectural or historic interest is fully taken into account. The PPG further advises that the "starting point" for the exercise of listed building control must be the statutory requirement to "have special regard to the desirability of preserving the building or its setting or any features of special architectural or historic interest which it possesses" (section 16 of the LBA). This reflects the very great importance to society of protecting listed buildings from unnecessary demolition and from inappropriate and insensitive alterations. The general issues to be taken into account in considering all listed building consent applications are set out in paragraph 3.5 of the PPG 15 and are as follows:

(i) the importance of the building, its intrinsic architectural and his- **4.02** toric interest and rarity, in both national and local terms;

(ii) the particular physical features of the building (which may include its design, plan, materials or location) which justify its inclusion in the list: list descriptions may draw attention to features of particular interest or value, but they are not exhaustive and other features of importance (e.g. interiors) may come to light after the building's inclusion in the list;

(iii) the building's setting and its contribution to the local scene, which may be very important, e.g. where it forms an element in a group, park, garden or other townscape or landscape, or where it shares particular architectural forms or details with other buildings nearby;

(iv) the extent to which the proposed works would bring substantial benefits for the community, in particular by contributing to the economic regeneration of the area or the enhancement of its environment (including other listed buildings).

There are two problems in ascertaining the practical consequences of policies expressed in PPG 15 and its predecessor Circular 8/87. Firstly, obtaining details of ministerial decisions on LBC appeals and call-ins, which might be expected to reveal the Secretary of State's interpretation of stated policies. Secondly, the relatively limited number of LBC appeals and

---

[1] [1976] JPL 445; Ref. B/5002/270/14 April 9, 1976.
[2] Opening address to Oxford Conference in 1976, reported in [1977] J.P.L.5.

call-ins.[3] Access to data on relevant cases is complicated by the fact that the DOE does not maintain any central, publicly accessible "register" of such cases. Appeal and call-in case records are kept at individual DOE regional offices,[4] and copies of inspectors' reports and Secretary of State's decision letters are available on payment of copying charges. The publication of details of decisions thus depends largely on the goodwill of those parties, the vigilance of the press and publishers, and in some respects, the notoriety and/or publicity value of the cases themselves.

4.03   It should be remembered that the number of buildings of special architectural or historic interest is limited. Accordingly, the PPG recommends that there should be a general presumption in favour of the preservation of listed buildings, except where a convincing case can be made out against the criteria set out above. Formerly, following guidance given in Circular 8/87, there was said to be a Government policy which amounted to a "presumption" against the demolition of a listed building.

An example of the former policy occurred in a case in August 1987: the Secretary of State refused an application by Freemans plc to demolish two Grade II properties at 127 and 129 Clapham Road, London.[5] These properties formed part of Freemans existing premises which was the subject of the redevelopment application. The Secretary of State said:

> "Numbers 127 and 129 Clapham Road are Grade II listed buildings and are considered to be capable of being renovated and refurbished to bring them back into beneficial use. Given the general presumption in favour of preservation except where a strong case can be made out for granting consent the Secretary of State is not satisfied that your clients have made every possible effort to retain these listed buildings; the commercial expediency and financial arguments are not of themselves considered sufficient justification for their demolition."

The Department of the Environment has always made its attitude clear, but is its attitude correct? There is no statutory basis for a presumption in favour of preserving listed buildings to be found—only the requirement to have "special regard to the desirability of preserving the building . . . ." Nonetheless, the Department has consistently referred to presumption, and that presumption has been noted by the Courts.

4.04   In *Save Britain's Heritage v. No. 1 Poultry Ltd* and others[6] the House of Lords considered the decision of the Secretary of State in relation to the group of buildings in the City of London for which there had been an application to demolish eight Grade II listed buildings and other buildings which

---

[3] Midgeley, *Restoration and Renewal*, Leeds Polytechnic, August 1980.

[4] Although listing is done centrally by the DNH, LBC appeals and call-ins are processed, and decisions and recommendations made at the DOE's regional offices unless the case is of particular national significance or of such importance that either the Secretary of State of his own volition, or at the request of a Member wishes to look at it, or the regional controller refers it to the Minister. In every LBC appeal or call-in case, however, the actual decision is that of the Secretary of State for the Environment.

[5] APP/N5660/E/86/801378)
APP/N5660/E/87/802072) August 1987
APP/N5660/A/87/062514)

[6] *Save Britain's Heritage v. SoS for the Environment and Number 1 Poultry and City Index Property* (1991) 1 WLR 153.

were unlisted but in a conservation area and their replacement by a single modern building.

The main issue in the hearing was the adequacy of reasons given for a planning decision and consideration of the burden of proof lying on the applicant to show that he was substantially prejudiced by the deficiency in the reasons.

Although, in the words of Lord Bridge, the public controversy about traditional and contemporary architectural styles are of "no concern whatever of the Courts", the question of the presumption recited above was discussed in the case.

Lord Bridge quoted from paragraph 91 of Circular 8/87 and also the Inspector's report which contained the phrase: "A new scheme must have outstanding qualities if it is to overcome the strong presumption in favour of the retention of the listed buildings and the attractive opportunities that conservation can offer." The Secretary of State's decision letter in the *No. 1 Poultry* case contained his view of the situation:

"There is a general presumption in favour of the preservation of listed buildings as stated in Circular 8/87. There are many listed buildings in respect of which it would be inconceivable that listed building consent to demolish would ever be granted whatever the merits of any replacement building proposed to be erected on the site."

Although the issue in the case was decided on the wording of the Secretary of State's decision letter, it was clear from the opinion of Lord Bridge that there was then a presumption in favour of the retention of listed buildings with the exception therein referred to. As a general principle, the House of Lords supported the presumption. PPG 15 alludes to this situation in paragraph 3.16 where it states: "Whilst it is an objective of Government policy to secure the preservation of historic buildings, there will very occasionally be cases when demolition is unavoidable"; it continues in paragraph 3.17 by saying "the Secretaries of State would not expect consent to be given for the total or substantial demolition of any listed building without clear and convincing evidence that all reasonable efforts have been made to sustain existing uses or find viable new ones, and that these efforts have failed; . . . or that redevelopment would produce substantial benefits for the community which would decisively outweigh the loss resulting from demolition. The Secretaries of State would not expect consent to demolition to be given simply because redevelopment is economically more attractive to the developer than repair and re-use of an historic building, or because the developer acquired the building at a price that reflected the potential for redevelopment rather than the condition and constraints of the existing historic building".

In paragraph 3.19(iii) the PPG deals with the merits of alternative proposals for the site, and states that "whilst these are a material consideration, the Secretaries of State take the view that subjective claims for the architectural merits of proposed replacement buildings should not in themselves be held to justify the demolition of any listed building. There may very exceptionally be cases where the proposed works would bring substantial benefits for the community which have to be weighed against arguments in favour of preservation." It continues by suggesting that even in these circumstances it will often be feasible to incorporate listed buildings within new development.

4.05   Section 54A of the T.C.P.A. 1990[7] introduces a new status for development plans:

> "Where in making any determination under the planning Acts, regard is to be had to the development plan, the determination shall be made in accordance with the development plan unless material considerations indicate otherwise."

The apparent result seems to be that section 54A elevates the development plan to the starting point for the consideration of all planning applications, and in the absence of other material considerations (including the age of the plan and the status of the plan *vis-à-vis* its progress in the policy formulation procedure) applications will be decided in accordance with the development plan (provided the plan contains considerations which are relevant to the specific application).

We do not believe that this apparent result is the final answer. The presumption in favour of the applicant was embedded in the philosophy behind the 1947 Act. If this is so, how then does it square with the new section 54A? Perhaps the answer is that the presumption in favour of development expressed in paragraph 15 of PPG 1 is a material consideration which may thus "indicate otherwise."[8]

Section 54A requires the application to be determined in accordance with the plan, unless material considerations indicate otherwise .... An applicant who proposes a development which is clearly in conflict with the development plan would need to produce convincing reasons to demonstrate why the plan should not prevail.[9]

The PPG 15 refers to the role of section 54A and the need for development plans to set out clearly all conservation policies relevant to the exercise of an authority's development control functions, but it also states, in paragraph 2.4, that "the Courts have accepted that section 54A does not apply to decisions on applications for listed building consent or conservation area consent, since in those cases there is no statutory requirement to have regard to the provisions of the development plan." It does nevertheless advise authorities to include policies for alterations, extensions, or for works of demolition to listed buildings in their development plans to which section 54A will directly apply.

This can result in different decisions being made on an application or applications for listed building consent and for planning permission. Such a case arose with a proposal which gave rise to appeals and was for the erection of a three-storey rear extension for office purposes on land at Winckley Square, Preston. The planning decision concerned the principle of additional office development on the appeal site, having regard to the provisions of the development plan and the effect of a sizeable extension on the working conditions of neighbouring offices. The conservation issues were centred on the duty of the local planning authority to have special regard to the desirability of preserving the appeal building and its northerly neighbour, or their settings, or any features of special architectural or historic

---

[7] Introduced by s.26 PCA 1991.
[8] See the judgment of Mr. David Widdicombe Q.C. (sitting as a Deputy Judge) in *St. Alban's District Council v. Secretary of State* [1993] 1 PLR 88 and 1993 J.P.L. 374.
[9] PPG 1, para. 25.

interest which they possess and to the desirability of preserving or enhancing the character or appearance of the Winckley Square conservation area.

On the contents of the Local Plan, new office development of the size proposed was excluded, and for that reason, coupled with the significant loss of privacy to adjoining properties, the Inspector recommended that the planning appeal be dismissed.

On the impact of the proposal on the listed buildings and conservation area, the Inspector felt the character and appearance of the conservation area as a whole would not be harmed by the proposed extension, and that the impact on the historic integrity of the Square would be acceptable. He therefore allowed in 1993 the second appeal subject to conditions.[10]

Another case which illustrates the importance of the development plan **4.06** when assessing a proposal was that of St. Mary's Church, Tintern, which is a listed building and had been severely damaged by fire in 1977, following which neither the church authorities nor the planning authority had made any effort to ensure that the qualities of the building were restored. The planning authority had tended towards the belief that the destruction of the listed building had enhanced the conservation area and turned it into a "romantic ruin".

The Inspector felt that the application to convert the church into "holiday lets" would go a long way towards reversing the neglect and would restore much of the building's special architectural and historic interest, and the restored building would enhance the character and appearance of the conservation area, and the Area of Outstanding Natural Beauty.

Although it was accepted that the vehicular access would be poor, the Inspector felt that the desirability of restoring the listed building outweighed the appellant's "loose arrangement" for car parking. The appellant company had received support from CADW's Historic Buildings Architect, their Conservation Architect, the Royal Commission on Ancient and Historic Monuments in Wales, and the Glamorgan-Gwent Archaeological Trust.

The Secretary of State agreed with the Inspector's assessment that the proposal would restore much of the church's special architectural and historic interest and he accepted the recommendation that listed building consent be granted.

As to the planning appeal, the Secretary of State considered the development plan proposals and noted that its policies supported re-use of redundant buildings for self-catering tourist accommodation, subject to certain criteria. When these criteria were applied individually to the proposal they failed to meet the requirement that the building should be capable of conversion without major external alterations or reconstruction, and the parking and access arrangements had been recognised by the Inspector to be not entirely appropriate. The Secretary of State applied the element of flexibility, as recommended in Circular 8/87, in relation to the provision of parking spaces, but in all the circumstances concluded that the arrangements were not acceptable. Accordingly, the proposal did not fully conform to the provisions of the Structure Plan. There were also drainage difficulties

---

[10] Appeal ref. APP/N2345/A/92/203945 and APP/N/2345/E/92/808911—January 21, 1993 [J.P.L. 1993, p. 600].

which could not be resolved within the land owned by the appellant and with expressed opposition to the use of adjoining land, and therefore there was no reasonable prospect of being able to provide a septic tank by the use of a "Grampian-type" condition.

The Secretary of State therefore allowed the appeal against the refusal of listed building consent and granted such consent for the conversion of the redundant church into two holiday lets, but dismissed the planning appeal and refused to grant planning permission for the proposed conversion.[11]

2. STATUTORY PROVISIONS

4.07 There is very little statutory guidance as to what criteria are to be used when considering applications for LBC. Section 16(2) of the LBA provides that:

> "In considering whether to grant listed building consent for any works the local planning authority or the Secretary of State shall have special regard to the desirability of preserving the building or its setting or any features of special architectural or historic interest which it possesses."

Section 66(1) of the LBA outlines the general duty as regards listed buildings in exercise of planning functions:

> "In considering whether to grant planning permission for development which affects a listed building or its setting, the local planning authority or, as the case may be, the Secretary of State, shall have special regard to the desirability of preserving the building or its setting or any features of special architectural or historic interest which it possesses."

Section 17(1) of the LBA refers to the conditions which may be attached to a grant of LBC including "the preservation of particular features of the building", making good any damage caused to the building by the works, and reconstruction of the building with the use of original materials, where practicable, after the works have been carried out. Section 17(2) of the LBA provides that a condition may be attached to an LBC requiring specified details of the works for subsequent approval by the local planning authority or by the Secretary of State. Section 17(3) of the LBA provides that:

> "Listed building consent for the demolition of a listed building may be granted subject to a condition that the building shall not be demolished before–
> (a) a contract for the carrying out of works of redevelopment of the site has been made; and
> (b) planning permission has been granted for the redevelopment for which the contract provides."

---

[11] *Monumental Corporation Ltd appeal*, J.P.L., April 1994, p. 388. APP/33/11, and 33/27, August 25, 1993.

3. DEPARTMENTAL CRITERIA FOR CONSENT

The guidance provided by the Secretary of State on criteria which should **4.08** be employed by local authorities when considering all listed building consent applications is now set out in PPG 15. This guidance is accepted as a basis for consideration, but it should be remembered that it is not statutory. Other factors may thus also be relevant.

Paragraph 3.17 of PPG 15 adds that the Secretary of State would not expect consent to be given for the total or substantial demolition of any listed building without clear and convincing evidence that all reasonable efforts have been made to sustain existing uses or find viable new uses and these efforts have failed; or that redevelopment would produce substantial benefits for the community which would decisively outweigh the loss resulting from demolition.

Paragraph 3.19 of the PPG sets out the general considerations which the **4.09** Secretaries of State would expect authorities to address in considering applications for consent to demolition:

"(i) the condition of the building, the cost of repairing and maintaining it in relation to its importance and to the value derived from its continued use. Any such assessment should be based on consistent and long-term assumptions. Less favourable levels of rents and yields cannot automatically be assumed for historic buildings. Also, they may offer proven technical performance, physical attractiveness and functional spaces that, in an age of rapid change, may outlast the short-lived and inflexible technical specifications that have sometimes shaped new developments. Any assessment should also take into account of the possibility of tax allowances and exemptions and of grants from public or charitable sources. In the rare cases where it is clear that a building has been deliberately neglected in the hope of obtaining consent for demolition, less weight should be given to costs of repair;

(ii) the adequacy of efforts made to retain the building in use. The Secretaries of State would not expect listed building consent to be granted for demolition unless the authority (or where appropriate the Secretary of State himself) is satisfied that real efforts have been made without success to continue the present use or to find compatible alternative uses for the building. This should include the offer of the unrestricted freehold of the building on the open market at a realistic price reflecting the building's condition (the offer of a lease only, or the imposition of restrictive covenants, would normally reduce the chances of finding a new use for the building);

(iii) the merits of alternative proposals for the site. Whilst these are a material consideration, the Secretaries of State take the view that subjective claims for the architectural merits of proposed replacement buildings should not in themselves be held to justify the demolition of any listed building. There may very exceptionally be cases where the proposed works would bring substantial benefits for the community which have to be weighed against the arguments in favour of preservation. Even here, it will often be feasible to incorporate listed buildings within new development, and this option should be carefully considered: the challenge presented by retaining listed buildings can be a stimulus to imaginative new design to accommodate them".

Local authorities are required to deal with their own buildings in ways which will provide examples of good practice to other owners (paragraph 3.37 of the PPG).

4. THE IMPORTANCE OF THE BUILDING

4.10   The criteria stated in paragraph 3.5 of PPG 15 which are regarded as relevant to consideration of all applications for listed building consent are:

"the importance of the building, its intrinsic architectural and historic interest and rarity, in both national and local terms" is the first criterion in paragraph 3.5.

The "principles of selection" are set out in paragraph 6.10 of the PPG 15 and are as follows:

— **architectural interest:** the lists are meant to include all buildings which are of importance to the nation for the interest of their architectural design, decoration and craftsmanship; also important examples of particular building types and techniques, (e.g. buildings displaying technological innovation or virtuosity) and significant plan forms;
— **historic interest:** this includes buildings which illustrate important aspects of the nation's social, economic, cultural or military history;
— **close historical association:** with nationally important people or events;
— **group value,** especially where buildings comprise an important architectural or historical unity or a fine example of planning (e.g. squares, terraces or model villages).

4.11   A particular building may qualify for listing under more than one of these criteria.

The problem is one of differing subjective judgments, even among experts on aesthetics. As was said by Forbes J. (as he then was): "experts do tend to differ and for every expert that one could find who said, looking at pure aesthetics, that something was exceptionally fine, one might quite easily find another expert who took exactly the opposite view."[12] The Inspector in his report in the Mansion House Square planning appeal[13] said of aesthetic judgment:

"It is I believe well said that there should be no disputation over matters of taste, since each person's view is highly personal and affected by a whole variety of influences and impressions, likes and dislikes,

---

[12] *Winchester City Council v. Secretary of State for the Environment* [1978] 3 P & C R 455 at 473.
[13] APP/K5030/A/88/089225
APP/K5030/E/88/803073

114

accumulated over a long period. To attempt to search for a consensus of rightness or wrongness in aesthetic matters is accordingly likely to be a fruitless task. It is not perhaps surprising that those continuously engaged in making decisions on the appearance of things, and trained particularly for that purpose, should have different perceptions from those of others. Similarly it is not surprising that those who are mainly concerned with the preservation of what already exists should have different perceptions from those more involved with the making of new things."

On September 16, 1990 during the Joint Planning Law Conference held at New College, Oxford, Mr Richard Saxon gave a paper entitled "Architecture and Design—Material Considerations" in which he stated: "Prominent, ambitious design is . . . castrated whilst the mediocre slides through . . . St. Paul's, Somerset House and the Houses of Parliament were all railed against in their day as the greatest horrors, paying no respect to their surroundings. They would never have got planning permission today . . . "

Mr. Saxon also said of aesthetics and visual perspective in his paper: "Professors of perception like Richard Gregory make it quite clear that people do not see like cameras, they recognise things based on their memories and education. So you see what you know. People like things based on their culture, accepting things which are approved by their peer group; you like what you know you should. Original vision is the mark of the artist and is often recognised and liked initially only by the unusually perceptive. Public acclaim may follow after the culture is re-educated by critics."[14]

In some cases a building may be important because there are only a few of its type in the neighbourhood or because it has a fine interior, while in other cases its importance may be enhanced because it forms part of a group or series. Attention should also be paid to the contribution to the local scene made by a building, particularly if it is in a conservation area; but the absence of such a contribution is not a reason for demolition or alteration.

The listing grade is a material consideration to the importance of the building, but it is not of itself a reliable guide to the sensitivity of a building to alteration.

4.12 With these considerations in mind we turn our attention to PPG 15, paragraph 6.14: the importance of the building where the subject of aesthetic merits is discussed: "The external appearance of a building—both its intrinsic architectural merit and any group value—is a key consideration in judging listing proposals, but the special interest of a building will not always be reflected in obvious visual quality. Buildings which are important for reasons of technological innovation or as illustrating particular aspects of social or economic history, may well have little external visual quality."

We look at the question of whether the building justified the listing. We turn to the question of the rarity value of the building. We consider finally the contribution which the building makes to the local scene—most often the street scene.

Should the building have been listed in the first place? It is always open to the applicant to claim that the building should not have been listed.[15] This is simply an assertion that the building should not have been regarded

[14] 1990 Joint Planning Law Conference, Oxford.
[15] See para. 2.05 above.

as of special architectural or historic interest. An application by Bradford and Bingley Building Society for listed building consent to demolish number 71 Highgate, Kendal[16] was refused by the South Lakeland District Council. An appeal ensued. In his report the Inspector commented upon the application property that:

> "Sufficient work still stands, in my estimation, for the listing of the building to be justified. Beyond this, however, the appeal premises are part of an extensive range of old buildings lining Highgate, similarly listed, so that number 71 also makes a contribution to the attractive historic character of the streetscene. It must follow, to my mind, that there is a presumption in favour of preservation, so that demolition ought to be permitted only if a strong case he made in its favour."

Later in the appeal decision the Inspector said, "It is the interests of the building, not those occupying it, which are of principal concern."

4.13   *The relative number and "rarity" of listed buildings and the contribution which the building makes to the local scene* in an area may be a material consideration in any decision related to the grant or refusal of listed building consent. In 1989, Cabra Ltd, the freehold owners of Fulham Football Ground, submitted applications to Hammersmith and Fulham London Borough Council to carry out development which entailed the demolition of the Stevenage Road stand.[17] The Inspector appointed to deal with the inquiry into the non-determination of the applications by the local planning authority said, of the Stevenage Road stand, that its architectural interest was enhanced by being part of a group which included the original turnstiles and Craven Cottage (football ground). He stated, refusing LBC, that:

"The comparative rarity of listed buildings adds to the significance of the stadium group for this area, which is further enhanced by its proximity to two conservation areas."

The second general issue expressed in paragraph 3.5 of PPG 15 is *"the particular physical features of the building* (which may include its design, plan, materials or location) which justify its inclusion in the list: list descriptions may draw attention to features of particular interest or value, but they are not exhaustive and other features of importance (*e.g.* interiors) may come to light after the building's inclusion in the list."

The subject of physical features of a listed building was raised when an appeal was lodged against the refusal of listed building consent to renew the thatched roof of The Old Post House at Stansfield, in the district of St Edmundsbury Borough Council.[18]

The roof timbers of this listed building had been attacked by insects and needed to be replaced. The owners felt it presented an opportunity to replace the thatch with another traditional local material, namely reclaimed red/brown plain clay tiles. Arguments were advanced in support of the proposal relating to the difficulties in obtaining a specialist thatcher, the length of time it would take to re-thatch the whole roof and the costs

---

[16] APP/5166/A/82/12104)
   APP/5166/A/83/369) January 9, 1984.
   APP/5166/E/82/350.
[17] 6 Planning Appeal Decisions 1991, p. 121.
[18] APP/E3525/E/86/801302, August 19, 1986, J.P.L. 1987, p. 50.

involved. Additionally, the use of clay tiles would substantially reduce the household insurance costs. The Council took the view that thatched buildings were an important survival of a craft and a very early vernacular type, and were prepared to offer a grant towards the replacement of the thatch.

The Inspector felt that the substitution of tiles for thatch would fundamentally affect the external appearance of the listed building and detract from its essential character. The Secretary of State accepted that advice and dismissed the appeal.

Physical features of a building can be wide ranging, as indicated in paren- **4.14** thesis in this paragraph: "design, plan, materials or location."

Materials is one aspect which has caused many local planning authorities to take action, and in particular when an owner of a listed building has, sometimes unwittingly, sought "to improve or repair" the building.

Such a case came before the Queen's Bench Division in March 1992 in response to the owner of a listed building having replaced some rear facing windows with modern windows which, in the opinion of the local planning authority, detracted from the appearance and historical interest of the building. A listed building enforcement notice was issued requiring the replacement of the modern windows within 28 days. This proved impossible for the builders and a summons was issued alleging failure to take the required steps (at that time covered by section 98(1) of the 1971 Act). The magistrates considered the owner had taken all reasonable steps and had discharged his responsibility.[19] Since this case, the PCA 1991 introduced a replacement section 43, which gives the defendant a defence to show that "he did everything he could be expected to do to secure that all the steps required by the notice were taken".[20]

A listed building enforcement notice was issued by the Chesterfield Borough Council concerning works undertaken to Somersall Hall,[21] a Grade II building, without listed building consent. The Hall was also in a Conservation Area and formed one of a group of listed buildings on the fringe of the built-up area of Chesterfield. The works against which enforcement action was taken involved the removal and replacement of windows by UPVC double glazed windows and the introduction of concrete slates to the central valley roof pitches of that Hall.

The Inspector decided that the UPVC windows and the artificial slates were significantly different, in materials and appearance, from the windows and the roof covering that were previously there, and he concluded that the alterations enforced against had affected the character of the building as a building of special architectural or historic interest.

Furthermore, no evidence had been submitted to demonstrate that the alleged works were urgently necessary in the interests of safety, health or for the preservation of the building. The design of the replacement windows was found to be significantly different from the former timber sashes or side-hung casements, and the new windows looked ungainly and incongruous when seen from both outside and inside the building and were therefore out of character with this, otherwise, fine building.

The use of concrete slates of a relatively uniform colour, size and texture

---

[19] *Mid-Devon Council v. Avery* (65 P CR 47) 1992 (the Court of Appeal overturned the magistrate's decision, dismissing the "reasonable steps" argument).

[20] Schedule 3.(6) of the PCA 1991 creating a new s.43 of the LBA 1990.

[21] APP/F/89/A/1015/1–2/PG, July 12, 1990 (J.P.L. 1991, p. 287)

was also considered to detract significantly from the special architectural character of the building.

The works enforced against devalued the architectural quality of the group of listed buildings as a whole, and therefore constituted a contravention of section 55 of the 1971 Act and the appeals failed.

In July 1984 the Secretary of State on a "called in" planning application refused listed building consent for the carrying out of alterations and extensions in connection with a proposed change of use of Fawsley Hall to form 22 flats at Fawsley, Northamptonshire.[22]

The Inspector found that it was unlikely that the application proposals would have any material effect on the exterior character of the buildings, and with regard to the interiors of the application buildings he said:

> "they are in my opinion bound to be affected to some extent from almost any form of conversion for acceptable present day uses. The integrity of the existing spaces, particularly those of the Great Hall and the large room of the Salvin wings, already seemed to have suffered considerably from years of neglect, decay and vandalism. In the absence of any practical use for those rooms in their original form and extent restoration would not appear to be a worthwhile proposition."

The Secretary of State did not consider that the building was in such significant risk of deterioration that further time could not be given to seeking other ways of restoring it and listed building consent was refused.

4.15 The third general issue expressed in paragraph 3.5 of the PPG 15 is "the building's setting and its contribution to the local scene".

Given that it is agreed that a building is properly listed, sometimes the importance in a larger group—the street scene—plays a part in the decision making. There have been cases where the strict criterion as to listing the individual building has been put aside in favour of "group value" which is surely a matter for a conservation area rather than a listing. In an application to Runnymede Borough Council for listed building consent to demolish 68–76 (evens) London Street, Chertsey, Surrey,[23] the Secretary of State for the Environment drew attention to the conclusions of the Inspector which referred in particular to the contribution of the existing properties to the street scene. The Inspector said:

> "This listed row of cottages forms an integral and attractive part of a larger group of listed buildings, extending to the east and west, within the Chertsey Conservation Area, near to its east boundary. It makes a very important contribution to the streetscene not only in its own right, but as part of the group, and in its relationship with a group of listed buildings on the opposite north side of London Street."

The Secretary of State accepted the Inspector's recommendation to refuse listed building consent to demolish the cottages since every possible effort had not been made to preserve the important row of listed cottages.

An application by the National Westminster Bank Ltd for LBC to demolish 10/12 St Peter's Street, St Albans, was refused by the local planning authority. An appeal ensued[24] and in his report the Inspector said: "I am of

[22] EMP/5324/270/29, July 4, 1984.
[23] SE2/5389/411/1, December 7, 1984.
[24] [1974] J.P.L. 552 Ref. SE/6/1582/270/17; APP/1582/A/63583, December 10, 1973.

the opinion in respect of the application for LBC that while the building is not of historic interest or of great architectural merit, its facade makes an important contribution to the attractiveness and interest of the street scene on this side of St. Peter's Street, and to the particular character of the group of buildings of which it forms part and that it merits retention on that account." For that and other reasons the Inspector recommended that LBC should not be granted, which view was shared by the Secretary of State. It is perhaps a pity that this case was not taken to the High Court, bearing in mind that the test adopted by the Inspector and the Secretary of State appears not to be the test as set out in the statute, but more a conservation area test.

The importance of the building in the local—or street—scene has often **4.16** been emphasised in Secretary of State decisions.

The street scene was important in a case concerning Barclays Bank Ltd, whose application to demolish the facade of 39/40 Lombard Street, London, was refused.[25] The Inspector in that case observed: "No 39/40 Lombard Street is a massive four-storey stone building situated on the south side of the street at its eastern end and forming the corner of Gracechurch Street. It is constructed in the full Victorian classical 'palazzo' style, with profuse ornamentation and a crowning heavy cornice and balustrade. No. 39/40, situated as it is at the curved end of Lombard Street, plays an important role in the street scene." The Secretary of State granted LBC for the demolition of the building with the exception of the facades facing Lombard Street and Gracechurch Street, together with sufficient depth of the existing building to ensure their stability.

In an application by Nottinghamshire County Council for consent to demolish three listed buildings in Castle Hill, Worksop (in a conservation area), the Secretary of State agreed with the Inspector's report that although it was desirable to keep the buildings which contributed to the appearance and character of the street containing many similar old buildings, in this particular case the cost of repair and rehabilitation was not economically viable because the buildings were in such poor condition, LBC was granted.[26]

In May 1988, South Hertfordshire District Council granted planning permission for the erection of a potato store at Bolltree Farm, adjacent to Bolltree Castle, a complex of listed buildings.[27] The owner of the Castle, who had acquired it shortly before the granting of permission for the potato store, applied for judicial review on June 30, 1988. The farmer and the owner of the Castle subsequently tried to arrive at an amicable agreement which would have involved resiting the potato store; an alternative site was chosen and an application submitted for it, but the Parish Council objected on grounds of amenity. The delayed application for leave was heard on January 23, 1989, and on May 18, 1989 the original planning permission was quashed. The Council appealed to the Court of Appeal.

The two issues which arose on this appeal were (a) to ask if the decision of the judge was unreasonable (see *Associated Provincial Picture Houses v.*

[25] [1976] J.P.L. 445 Ref. 8–3/5002/270/14, April 14, 1976.
[26] [1979] 250 EG 48. Ref. EMP/1935/270/5, February 1, 1979. See also APP/5034/80/08935 (*Estates Times*, December 4, 1981).
[27] *R. v. South Hertfordshire District Council, ex. p. Felton.* (Court of Appeal—9 March 1990, J.P.L. July 1991, p. 633.

119

Wednesbury Corporation 1948 1KB 223 [1947] All E.R. 680) for the Council's planning officers to form the opinion that the construction of the potato store, in the position where it had been constructed, would not affect the setting of the listed building at Bolltree Castle?

Secondly, was it wrong for the judge to grant relief by way of a judicial review on the substantive hearing, despite the delay there had been on the part of the applicant in proceeding with the application for leave to move?

Dillon L.J. felt that it was impossible to say that the erection of the potato store did not affect the setting of the listed buildings, since it was visible from the approaches to and around the main house, and as it was the largest building in the vicinity it overpowered the listed buildings round the castle from across the lane. He therefore agreed that in this case it had been made out that the action of the planning authority in forming the opinion that the setting of the listed buildings would not be effective was "unreasonable".

This Court of Appeal decision was described in the J.P.L. 1991, page 633, as being a fairly rare example both of what may be termed "pure" Wednesbury unreasonableness and of a grant of planning permission being quashed on an application for judicial review by a neighbour.

4.17   Consent to demolish may be given in circumstances where the "street scene" around a listed building has deteriorated. The demolition of two listed school cottages in Colchester was allowed because their surroundings had been demolished and redeveloped.[28] The cottages themselves were capable of restoration, yet the Inspector advocated demolition, quoting Development Control Policy Note 7: "An old building can be destroyed, as surely by changes in its surroundings as by direct assault . . . " A similar case involving an appeal against the refusal by Richmond-upon-Thames London Borough Council to allow listed building consent (now conservation area consent) of two unlisted buildings in a conservation area was heard in 1984.[29] The Inspector's recommendation to the Secretary of State to allow the appeal was confirmed by the Secretary of State who drew attention to the Inspector's finding that:

> "With the disappearance of all the more distinguished old buildings, mostly in the years since the war, the original character which old Bridge Street at the approach to the bridge head must once have had, has largely been lost. Numbers 9 and 11 are no longer part of a regular development or a built up frontage which it would be desirable to keep intact."

Still on the subject of "setting of a listed building", an appeal arose from an enforcement notice issued by Colchester Borough Council and against refusals of planning permission and listed building consent in relation to the erection of children's play equipment on land in front of a Grade II listed public house.[30]

The appeal under section 20 of the LBA 1990 relating to works for which listed building consent was refused was ruled by the Inspector not to have

---

[28] [1979] 250 E.G. 993. Refs. APP/5214/E/78/116; and APP/5214/A/78/08348 May 9, 1979.

[29] APP/L5810/E/83/004045)
APP/L5810/A/83/003070) June 14, 1984.

[30] APP/C/93/A1530/629449 and APP/A/1530/A/93/225837, May 12, 1994 [J.P.L. 1994, p. 867].

required listed building consent by reason of the equipment being "separate structures in the curtilage of a listed building which had been erected after 1 July, 1948" and therefore the play equipment was not treated as part of the listed building. On that aspect of the appeal the Inspector took no further action.

On the refusal of planning permission and the enforcement notice he decided that the brightly coloured play equipment was damaging to the setting of the Rovers Tye, a late 17th/early 18th-century building now used as a public house, and that it stood out in such a prominent and obtrusive way that it constituted a strongly inappropriate intrusion into the building's setting.

He dismissed the appeal and, with the variations, upheld the enforcement notice.

The fourth general issue expressed in paragraph 3.5 of PPG 15 is: **4.18**

"*the extent to which the proposed works would bring substantial benefits for the community*, in particular by contributing to the economic regeneration of the area or the enhancement of its environment (including other listed buildings)".

Appeals were lodged against the refusal of Cotswold District Council to permit the change of use and conversion of the New Inn and its outbuildings at Coln, St. Aldwyns, to form seven dwellings[31] and a scheme for retention of a smaller public house, with conversion of the existing dwellings into six dwellings plus two houses at the rear.

The appeals were dismissed by the Secretary of State, on the recommendation of the Inspector, who considered the proposals would harm the social and economic life of this isolated village and of local tourism.

The public house was a listed building and the Secretary of State saw no reason why it could not, if re-opened, be run successfully as a public house and/or restaurant. He also felt that the proposal to convert the interior of the New Inn to seven dwellings would effectively destroy the interior's architectural and historic interest. The alternative scheme would have constituted an over-development of a cramped site. The appeals against refusal of planning permission and of listed building consent were dismissed.

In another appeals case[32] planning permission and listed building consent had been refused by Norwich City Council for the change of use of the Jolly Butchers public house, Norwich, to offices.

The Inspector considered the effect of the proposed change of use and consequent alterations on the character and integrity of this listed building. He also considered the effects of the proposed development on the character or appearance of the conservation area; whether there were any special circumstances to justify permitting the loss of existing residential accommodation as an exception to the Local Plan policy which was to encourage the retention and to re-introduce residential uses in the central area, and whether the proposed use would affect the free flow of pedestrian and vehicular traffic in the street.

The Inspector felt the building would require considerable investment to bring the public house and residential accommodation to acceptable

---

[31] APP/F/1610/E/88/803778, December 14, 1989, J.P.L. 1990, p. 377.
[32] T/APP/G/2625/A/89/132810, January J.P.L. 1990, p. 460.

modern standards. He felt that "the very particular character of this public house" would result in the proposed office use being an appropriate alternative use.

The exterior of the building required no alteration and the interior features could be preserved by applying some flexibility to the Building and Fire Regulations. The contribution of the Jolly Butcher's public house to the Conservation Area would be preserved under the scheme. Even the substandard existing access to the rear of the site was not seen as a problem, since it was an "integral part of the listed building and has therefore been used for many years". The appeal was allowed and planning permission for offices was granted, subject to conditions.

The Secretary of State called in an application to demolish a seafront cafe in Beach Street, Folkestone and refused to permit its demolition. The building was said to have little architectural merit but was of historic interest, as it was the sole survivor of buildings which had formed part of the original fishing village. The appeal by the original applicant to the High Court was on three main grounds. The first was that the Secretary of State should have looked only at the surrounding area as it existed, and not at some hypothetical future development of the area. The second ground was related to the economic value of the building, and it was claimed that he should have confined himself to the building alone and not the site on which it stood. Finally, he was said to have failed to make the necessary findings of fact and therefore his reasons were flawed. Stuart-Smith J. considered that a wide spectrum of considerations might be relevant in a matter of this sort, and he held that the Secretary of State had not erred when taking the potential development in the area into consideration.

The Judge also felt the Inspector was entitled to look at the whole site, of which the listed building formed a proportion, and especially as the appellant had sought to obtain planning permission subject to obtaining listed building consent for the whole site. It therefore seemed reasonable to take into account the alternative proposals for the site involving the retention of the listed building and to weigh the rival proposals as a whole. The third ground was found to be unfounded, but the appeal was dismissed.[33]

5. THE ARCHITECTURAL MERIT AND HISTORIC INTEREST OF A BUILDING

4.19 The PPG 15 separates the intrinsic architectural interest and the historic interest in relation to the importance of the building (see paragraph 3.5).

In assessing the architectural interest, the main criteria which the Secretary of State applies as set out in paragraph 6.10 of PPG 15 and includes all buildings which are of importance to the nation for the interest of their architectural design, decoration and craftsmanship; also important examples of particular building types and techniques, *e.g.* buildings displaying technological innovation or virtuosity, and significant plan forms; in addition are included:

— historic interest includes buildings which illustrate important

[33] *Godden v. Secretary of State for the Environment* (Q.B. Division July 31, 1987, J.P.L. 1988, p. 99).

122

aspects of the nation's social, economic, cultural or military history;
— close historic associations with nationally important people or events;
— group value applies especially where buildings comprise together an important architectural or historic unity or a fine example of planning, *e.g.* squares, terraces or model villages.

A particular building may qualify for listing under more than one of these various criteria.

We divide our consideration of the cases into broad sections; the architectural interest and historic interest. Most of the cases relate to architectural issues—a case on historic interest alone is rare. These are quite different issues. Admittedly both pose fundamental questions—What is architecture? What is history? Over the last 20 or so years there have developed some answers to the former question. It is more difficult to answer the question as to what is history and demonstrate the qualities which might be seen in a building with special historic interest. But what is "special" and what is "of special historic interest"?

Looking at special architectural interest, we have the example of the redundant Rehoboth Chapel, [34] the more modern pithead baths in Northumberland[35] and the Georgian wing at High Head Castle, Carlisle.[36] The four cases: Stott's Motors,[37] Fulham football ground stand,[38] Dee House,[39] the bottle kiln at Woodville[40] and the watermill at Stotford Mill[41] are good examples of what is of special historic interest.

The proposed conversion of the redundant Rehoboth Chapel, Wadhurst, **4.20** East Sussex, to a residential studio entailing partial demolition of the property failed to obtain listed building consent from the Secretary of State in late 1987.[42] The Inspector's report referred to the national importance of the chapel and its inclusion in the Royal Commission on Historic Monuments' list of the 300 chapels most worthy of preservation. It was an austere but attractive building, the structural condition of which was reasonable although some maintenance was urgently required. The Inspector felt that the demolition and alteration works were architecturally acceptable and would create an interesting dwelling. However they would result in the loss of many of the features which made the chapel worthy of listing. The Secretary of State accepted the Inspector's recommendation and listed building consent was refused.[42a]

The National Coal Board's application to Morpeth Borough Council for listed building consent to demolish the Grade II* old pithead baths at Lyne-

---

[34] SE2/5208/270/123 and 411/3—November 17, 1987.
[35] N/533/270 p. 50, July 22, 1987.
[36] PNW/5164/270/20, October 23, 1985.
[37] PNW/5085/344/3, July 31, 1986.
[38] Planning Appeal Decisions (1991), p. 121.
[39] PNW/5143/344/4, May 1988.
[40] EMP/5174/270/19, July 26, 1984.
[41] E1/5124/270/71 and E1/5124/411/4, May 6, 1987.
[42] SE2/5208/270/123 and 411/3, November 17, 1987.
[42a] To distinguish between "demolition" and "alteration" see *Shimuzu (UK) Ltd. v. Westminster City Council* [1995] E.G.C.S. 205.

mouth, Northumberland was called in by the Secretary of State in 1987[43] under powers now contained in section 12 of the LBA 1990. The Inspector's report drew attention to the fact that the building was designed in 1938 by F. J. Frizzell and exhibited features which were characteristic of the modern movement in English architecture and which gave the building "considerable strength contributing to a particularly interesting character". The baths were important both intrinsically and bearing in mind the limited number of similar buildings of its period and of its type. The building, which had been recently listed, combined considerable architectural, historic and social interest and had survived virtually intact. There was no evidence of the need for any major repairs to the building and it was possible for the National Coal Board to modify their proposed landscaping scheme in order to retain the building. The Inspector concluded that no strong case had been made to dislodge the presumption in favour of preservation. His recommendation that listed building consent be refused was accepted by the Secretary of State.

An application by Mr. W. Dickman to demolish the Georgian wing of High Head Castle, Ivegill, Carlisle was called in by the Secretary of State in mid 1985.[44]

The Inspector reported that the Georgian wing had "a particular quality" and its siting on the edge of a deep ravine was dramatic. The quality of the detailing and external decoration gave the property an intrinsic value and its Grade II* listing was entirely justified, " . . . even in its empty and derelict state the Georgian wing has a quality and splendour".

The danger from falling masonry was found to be insufficient to outweigh the presumption in favour of preservation. During the period between the application for listed building consent and the inquiry, the applicant had made no attempt to secure the future of the building. In recommending refusal of the application the Inspector noted:

> "Listed buildings are part of the heritage of the nation; they are limited in number and irreplaceable. Individuals who own them have special obligations."

4.21 There are a small number of cases which appear to rely primarily on the historic criteria. An application by Stotts Motors Limited of Manchester for listed building consent to demolish a former tram depot was called in by the Secretary of State in 1986.[45] The Secretary of State accepted the Inspector's recommendation that listed building consent be refused and drew attention to the section of the Inspector's report which dealt with the historic importance of the application depot:

> "Manchester as a city seems to be most important for its expansion in Victorian times as a great centre for the industrial conurbation which was founded on cotton and engineering. A building which still survives dating from this era and which represents a particular facet of the expansion must be historically important. The development of the carriage of the ordinary working population to and from work and for pleasure was a very important step in enabling the area to develop and the enterprises which created this facility were clearly important to the

[43] N/5333/270p/50, July 22, 1987.
[44] PNW/5164/270/20, October 23, 1985.
[45] PNW/5085/344/3, July 31, 1986.

social history. The horse-drawn tram and later the electric tram were the fore-runners of the current urban bus services. Except for a much altered smaller tram depot at Great Western Street, Manchester, the application building seems to be the only surviving example of the network in the area, or possibly in the country. The presumption for its retention on historical grounds must therefore be strong."

At the inquiry relating to the application by Cabra Ltd in 1991 to redevelop part of Fulham Football ground, the Inspector referred to the historic interest of the stadium in the following way:

"No less significant is the historic interest of the whole stadium, marking the association of the club with this part of Fulham and serving as an early example of its type. No other stadium buildings in England are listed."[46]

In May 1988 the Secretary of State for the Environment disagreed with the recommendation of his Inspector and granted listed building consent for the demolition of Dee House, St John's Street, Chester, a Grade II listed building.[47] The application property had been erected over part of a Roman amphitheatre. The Secretary of State recognised the "considerable historic rarity" of the amphitheatre by virtue of its being part of one of only three legionary fortresses in Britain. There were other good examples of eighteenth-century town houses in Chester which appeared to have undergone less alteration than Dee House. In order to emphasise the unique nature of the proposed development demolition of Dee House was necessary. The excavation of the amphitheatre was of outstanding importance in terms of the national heritage.

An application to South Derbyshire District Council by Donald Ward **4.22** Limited for listed building consent to demolish a bottle kiln at the Rawdon Works, Woodville[48] was unsuccessful on several grounds but especially due to the special historic interest of the bottle kiln. The Secretary of State agreed with the Inspector's conclusions and accepted his recommendation that the listed building consent be refused. In his decision letter the Secretary of State stated that:

"Having regard . . . especially to the special historic interest of the kiln as a surviving example of a bottle kiln and also as a reminder of the local pottery industry which resulted in the development of Woodville, and for the lack of any conclusive evidence that the building is in a dangerous structural state as claimed by the applicants, I can see no overriding reason for the grant of listed building consent for the demolition of the kiln as an exception to the general presumption against the demolition of a building of special architectural or historic interest."

In May 1987 the Secretary of State for the Environment accepted his Inspector's recommendation to refuse listed building consent for the conversion of the Grade II Stotford Mill, Bedfordshire[49] into a dwelling but allowed listed building consent for conversion of two other buildings on the

---

[46] 1991, 6 Planning Appeal Decisions at p. 121.
[47] PNW/5143/344/4, May 1988.
[48] EMP/5174/270/19, July 26, 1984.
[49] E1/5124/270/71
E1/5124/411/4, May 6, 1987.

site for residential use. In his report to the Secretary of State the Inspector referred to the mill as being of importance because it showed the development of a particular skill and technology. The Inspector said:

"Only seven watermills remain in Bedfordshire which are capable of being worked again; three of these mills are statutory listed buildings. In my judgment Stotford Mill is important because it shows the development of a particular skill and technology. The machinery shows how the watermill was modernised and steam power added. It is the complete story of this development of the mill machinery which in my opinion is important; even unique. . . . I consider the mill and its machinery to be of national importance."

The balancing of the issues

In so many cases when assessing the architectural or historic interest, the fundamental issue is one of balance, a point made in paragraph 1.3 of the PPG 15, where it is said that " . . . the historic environment of England is all-pervasive, but it cannot in practice be preserved unchanged". Two cases demonstrate this:

An application by the Parochial Church Council of St Peter's, Redcar for demolition of St Peter's Church[50] was called in by the Secretary of State for the Environment in 1987. The report of the Inspector referred to the importance of the building in terms of it being one of the few buildings of architectural or historic interest in the centre of Redcar. The part of the exterior of the church designed by Ignatius Bonomi had a refined and elegant appearance. The church had significant architectural merit and was of importance to the history of the Gothick Revival movement in both Cleveland and the north of England. Structurally the building was in reasonable condition but in need of considerable repair. Despite the applicants having no intention to restore the building for use as a church and it having no feasible alternative use the Inspector recommended that listed building consent for demolition be refused principally because he was not convinced that all the possibilities for saving the building had been fully explored. In reaching this conclusion the Inspector paid regard to the economic value of the building when repaired and to any saving obtained through not having to provide alternative accommodation in a new building. The cost of erecting a new church could well approach the cost of putting the existing building in a structurally sound condition, although the maintenance costs of a new building would be lower. The financial benefits which would arise from the construction of a replacement building did not outweigh the loss of the important listed church. The Secretary of State agreed with his Inspector's recommendation and listed building consent was consequently refused.

4.23   In February 1987 appeals by Tilcon Limited were heard against the decision by Macclesfield Borough Council to refuse listed building consent for the demolition of the stable block and icehouse at Eaton Hall Works, Congleton.[51] The case was an interesting one in that it concerned the com-

[50] N/5152/270p/31(2), June 17, 1987.
[51] APP/C0630/E/85/800906) October 30, 1987.
  APP/C0630/E/86/801585) October 30, 1987.
  APP/C0630/E/86/801586) October 30, 1987.

peting interests of preservation and the right of the landowner to extract a £50 million mineral deposit.

The Grade II listed buildings were designed by Louis Wyatt. The Inspector found that the stable block was well worth preserving. It had intrinsic visual merit and was one of the limited number of examples of the surviving works of a significant 19th-century architect. Although not approaching the stable block in architectural significance, the icehouse was nevertheless worthy of preservation because of the historic interest of its function, construction and excellent condition:

The possibility that the listed buildings be left *in situ* whilst sand was extracted around them did not find favour with the Inspector, who said:

"If listed building consent for the demolition of the stable block and icehouse were not granted, the continued presence of the buildings would prevent the excavation of a quantity of silica sand worth almost £50 million. Given this loss and the planning permission that exists, it is almost inconceivable that the appellant, instead of exercising the legitimate right to excavate all the remaining sand, would leave a significant volume untouched to form a causeway connecting the listed buildings to the shore of the lake. It is therefore almost certain that the buildings would be left on an island, access to which would need to be by either a bridge or a specially constructed causeway. The cost of both the bridge and the causeway would far exceed the capital value of the stable block even when converted to its most commercially advantageous form. When taken into account, this cost would destroy the feasibility of such a conversion. The likelihood of a connecting causeway or bridge being built seems therefore remote and the possibility that the building would be left isolated on an island unconnected to the lake's shore is overwhelming. Without a connection to the island the stable block would probably be seldom visited; in its isolation the building might well become a rather sad and meaningless relic, stripped of any relevant context and incapable of serving a useful purpose."

The Inspector considered the commercial position of Tilcon Limited which had made a massive investment in the Eaton Hall site with a view to extracting the high quality mineral deposit. The retention of the listed buildings and consequent loss to Tilcon Limited would have serious commercial consequences. Not only would Tilcon Limited lose sand with a market value of £50 million but the company would be liable for the cost of bringing the stable block into a reasonable state of repair plus the annual costs of maintenance which were estimated by Tilcon Limited to be £390,000 and £2,000 per annum, respectively. The Inspector set out a possible solution to the problem in the following way:

"In the conflicting circumstances surrounding this appeal in which, with the buildings retained in position, there is no room for any compromise, it seems to me that serious consideration should be directed towards the possibilities of dismantling the stable block and icehouse, of removing them from the site and of rebuilding them elsewhere."

The Secretary of State allowed the appeal for listed building consent to demolish the listed buildings, however he did not impose conditions relating to their re-erection, as the Inspector had recommended, since such a requirement would have been very onerous. The Secretary of State said:

127

"Such measures may be justified in relation to a unique or outstanding building but the stable block, although worthy of its Grade II listing, is not considered to be either. The Inspector records that 30 examples of Louis Wyatt's work survive, and the statutory list shows that there are some 50 listed stable blocks in the Macclesfield and Congleton districts of Cheshire."

Enabling development

4.24   The case of *Westminster City Council, ex parte Monahan*, involved the Royal Opera House, Covent Garden, and has—since it was decided in the Court of Appeal in October 1988[52]—been known as "the Covent Garden case".

The Court of Appeal unanimously upheld the judgment of the High Court on February 5, 1988, whereby the Court refused to quash a planning decision made by the Westminster City Council in June–July 1987, which involved the granting of outline planning permission to the Royal Opera House to carry out a mixed development scheme. The purpose behind the scheme was to effect much-needed improvements to the theatre and its ancillary facilities in order that it could maintain its national and international status as an Opera House. To provide the financial resources to pay for these improvements, the development scheme was devised as a means of generating income. The proposed offices were a subsidiary part of the application to redevelop part of the Opera House, and the continued existence and expansion of the Opera House was in accord with the Local Plan for the Covent Garden area, although the office aspect of the scheme was not. The Westminster City Council had resolved to contemplate a departure from the development plan, since it was convinced that the commercial development was the only means of financing the Opera House improvements.

The City Council therefore paid attention to the provisions of the development plan, and also to "other material considerations", which included the financial aspects of improving the Opera House. The planning permission granted by the City Council was challenged by the Covent Garden Association by way of a judicial review on two grounds: the first being that the inclusion of offices in the scheme purely for financial reasons was not a "material consideration" (under what was then section 29(1) of the 1971 Act), and secondly, that the City Council had failed to investigate all the financial aspects in order to be satisfied that a departure from the development plan by providing offices was necessary to secure the future of the Opera House.

Webster J. rejected both these grounds, and the Court of Appeal confirmed that judgment.[52a]

In an article[53] on this case, Sir Desmond Heap commented thus:

"All the Royal Opera House case does is to make it clear that financial matters touching the viability of a thoroughly welcome scheme of

---

[52] J.P.L. 1989, pp. 107 and 1 PLR 36.

[52a] On the subject of materiality the House of Lords dismissed an appeal in *Tesco Stores Ltd v. Secretary of State for the Environment* in May 1995, [1995] E.G.C.S. 82.

[53] J.P.L. January 1989, pp. 3–8.

development are material considerations which may lawfully be taken into consideration by the local planning authority having the duty to grant or refuse planning permission for the aforesaid 'thoroughly welcome scheme of development'."[54]

Three decisions were to follow where the "Covent Garden" influence can **4.25** be seen. The first was against a decision by the Malvern Hills District Council to refuse planning permission to erect eight houses in the kitchen garden of Croome Court, Worcestershire.[55]

Croome Court is a Grade I listed building, and, at the time of the appeal, was unoccupied. It was started by Lancelot (Capability) Brown for the 6th Earl of Coventry in 1751, and the interiors were by Robert Adam. It was described as "the finest house in Worcestershire, and one of the finest in the country".

There were other buildings associated with the house, many of which were listed Grade I, and a Rotunda c.1760—possibly by Robert Adam—which was listed Grade I.

The walled garden is some 6.75 acres in size and is one of the largest in Europe. In addition to the listing of its walls and other features, it is included in the Grade I listing of the Croome Court parkland, and in the non-statutory register of gardens and parks of special historic interest compiled by English Heritage. The main garden walls are some 16 feet high and in parts were, at the time of the appeal, in a state of severe disrepair or collapse.

Since the Second World War the house had been occupied by a variety of users. The appeal proposed was to erect eight houses in part of the walled garden and to form an opening in the western wall of the garden to give access to these dwellings.

The Inspector identified the main issues as being:

(1) Would the appeal proposals constitute dwellings in the open countryside and, if so, could they be considered to fall within one of the categories of such development permitted in the Structure Plan?

(2) Would the appeal proposals have a detrimental effect on the character of the walled garden and the setting of a group of listed buildings, and, if so, to what extent?

(3) If the appeal proposals were judged to be unsatisfactory in terms of the first two issues, should the need to ensure the preservation of listed buildings over-ride all other considerations in this case?

He concluded that the appeal proposals would constitute dwellings in open countryside and would therefore be contrary to the approved Structure Plan. Notwithstanding the fact that a location within the walled garden was probably the least visible for any new dwellings, the Inspector felt the dwellings would constitute a new and incongruous element in an historic setting which would diminish the importance of the walled garden. He then turned to the question of whether there were special circumstances that would over-ride the other considerations. Having heard of the costs involved of restoring three Grade I listed buildings and the other Grade II buildings, the Inspector decided that the appellant's proposals would generate enough cash to enable restoration of Croome Court to proceed. He

---

[54] J.P.L. January 1989, pp. 3–8.
[55] T/APP/G1820/A/88/103529/p3, November 28, 1989, J.P.L. 1990, p. 623.

allowed the appeals and granted planning permission subject to conditions which attempted to relate the implementation of the enabling development to a programme of restoration of the various listed buildings.

4.26 The second case involved a proposal for a superstore at Broadlands, Hampshire.[56] The applicants argued that by permitting the development the financial benefits which accrued from the superstore would enable Broadlands House to be maintained, together with its immediate surroundings. Broadlands House is a building of national importance as reflected in its Grade I status. There are 51 other listed buildings on the Estate.

The Inspector in this case felt there were sound reasons why this appeal should be dismissed in terms of its effect on the countryside and conflict with countryside policies, although he could find no reason to refuse permission on shopping policy grounds. He believed that Broadlands House was of such significance that the benefits of securing its future in such a way to maintain public access to it must carry considerable weight in this appeal, and he decided those benefits were sufficient to outweigh the countryside objections. He recommended that the appeal be allowed. The Secretary of State was however unable to agree with his Inspector's judgment that the needs of this historic house could justify the introduction of this inappropriate and intensive form of development. The Secretary of State did not accept the Inspector's recommendation, and dismissed the appeal.

The third case is another example of *enabling development*—this time for a golf course which would generate sufficient endowment funds for a 20 year programme of repairs of some nationally important listed buildings—Mapledurham, near Reading (South Oxfordshire District Council) in January 1994.

The appellants in this case were owners of Mapledurham House and estate, and much of the village had been owned and managed by the same family for some 500 years. There were 40 listed buildings on the estate and 18 within the village. When the present owner took over the administration of the estate in 1960 the house was in a dilapidated condition, but due to his efforts, Mapledurham House and Watermill had been saved and are now open to the public. The village had, through his efforts, been designated as a conservation area and English Heritage had identified the historic core of the estate as being of national importance. The upkeep of the listed buildings had placed a great financial burden upon the estate which the declining income from agriculture had proved insufficient to meet. An "Estate Plan" had been produced following discussions with English Heritage and South Oxfordshire District Council in an attempt to quantify the scale of the problem and to identify uses which would supplant the declining agricultural income and provide the necessary finance to restore and repair the listed buildings. These costs were estimated to be some £1.7 million, and the works of repair were urgently needed.

The solution to the problem was submitted to the Council in August 1993 in the form of a planning application for two 18-hole golf courses, a club-house with associated car parking. The site of the proposal was within an area designated as an Area of Outstanding Natural Beauty, known as "The Chilterns Landscape" in a publication by the Countryside Commission. The pros and cons of changing the rural landscape by introducing greens, tees, bunkers, fairways and a lake, plus a large club-house, were

[56] APP/C1760/A/89/113112, September 27, 1989, J.P.L. 1990, p. 453.

rehearsed at the public inquiry, and the Inspector had the task of considering whether these proposals would harm the character and appearance of the area bearing in mind the Council's policies, and then, if they were harmful, whether there were other material considerations which would outweigh any objections there may be.

The Inspector decided the character and appearance of the site would be radically altered by the proposed golf course, and to that extent the rural character of the site would be harmed. He took account of the desirability of preserving the various listed buildings or other settings or any other features of special architectural or historic interest which they possessed. He concluded that the three listed buildings on the application site would not be harmed, but that the essential character of the area would be altered and harmed by the scale of the development proposed and would be contrary to the Rural Areas Local Plan.

Turning to "the other material considerations", he noted the national importance of Mapledurham Village, and the programme of diverting the income from the golf course to the repairs to the various listed buildings over a 20 year period. He noted also the work already undertaken by the estate owner since 1960 in saving the buildings and encouraging the designation of the conservation area. Having taken all the issues into consideration, he decided that although the golf course proposed would harm the Area of Outstanding Natural Beauty, that harm would not be excessive and the advantages of the proposal, in particular the resultant repair of nationally important listed buildings, would outweigh the disadvantages. The endowment proposed to be created by the section 106 obligation in this case was said to be very similar to that practised by such trustees as the National Trust and the National Heritage Memorial Fund.[57]

Following the decision of the Inspector in relation to the application to develop the golf course with ancillary facilities at Mapledurham, near Reading, there was an application under T.C.P.A. 1990, section 288 for an order to quash that decision.

Sir Graham Eyre Q.C., sitting as Deputy Judge, held on April 22, 1994 that the Inspector was manifestly seized of the relevant facts and made the judgment that the marketing would ensure that the income derived from the proposal was used mainly for securing the listed buildings on the Mapledurham estate, and he so expressly found. The issue of enforceability is disposed of by the provisions of section 106, wherein there is a planning obligation for the purpose of the section. None of the grounds of challenge was made out, and consequently the application to quash the Inspector's decision failed.[58]

As an example of a failed attempt to achieve permission based on **4.27** "enabling development", there was an appeal in 1992 lodged by Worsted Investments Ltd against the refusal by Uttlesford District Council for a sizeable amount of new buildings for business use, with associated parking and access roads, and restoration of the former moat at Thremhall Priory, Stansted, a Grade II listed building.

The Priory had a planning history of hotel use, with extensions and conference facilities approved, and, in 1991, a change of use to offices which

[57] T/APP/Q3115/A/93/221244/P7, January 24, 1994, J.P.L. 1994, p. 479.
[58] *South Oxfordshire District Council v. Secretary of State for the Environment and others.* Q.B. Division. April 1994—J.P.L. October 1994, p. B113.

included the restoration of the listed house. Amongst the issues to be determined by the Inspector were the harm on the character of the area, and the harm to the setting of the listed building. He took into account the well-screened nature of the site and the new planting proposals, but felt that however well designed, detailed and landscaped, the character of the area would be harmed by such aspects as "considerable activity, substantial car parking and driveways". The Secretary of State agreed with the Inspector's recommendation that the appeal be dismissed.[59]

6. THE CONDITION OF THE BUILDING

4.28   In paragraph 3.19 of PPG 15, the main considerations which the Secretary of State would expect authorities to address in considering applications for consent either to total or substantial demolition: these include the condition of the building:

"(i) the condition of the building, the cost of repairing and maintaining it in relation to its importance and to the value derived from its continued use. Any such assessment should be based on consistent and long-term assumptions. Less favourable levels of rents and yields cannot automatically be assumed for historic buildings. Also, they may offer proven technical performance, physical attractiveness and functional spaces that, in an age of rapid change, may outlast the short-lived and inflexible technical specifications that have sometimes shaped new developments. Any assessment should also take account of the possibility of tax allowances and exemptions and of grants from public or charitable sources. In the rare cases where it is clear that a building has been deliberately neglected in the hope of obtaining consent for demolition, less weight should be given to the costs of repair."

Historic buildings have often been changed over the centuries and their exterior appearance can belie their true age and character. An examination of the rear elevation or the roofspan can often reveal more of the age of the building than appears from the front elevation. This does not always prove to be true. In a case involving an application to demolish a listed building at "The Greyhound" Fordingbridge[60] the building had been upgraded "because the essential structure should make a careful restoration possible". There was some evidence of c.17 and c.18 work, but mainly this was hidden by an unremarkable c.19 building with later additions. The Inspector saw the building following the stripping of plaster and found nothing of special architectural or historic interest behind the facade, and only a few turned balusters on the staircase. This lack of special interest, coupled with its bad state of repair and poor structural condition and a generally poor appearance, led the Inspector to conclude that it was incapable of being restored and he recommended demolition, subject to the building not being demolished before a contract for the works of redevelopment of the site had been made.

[59] Planning Appeal Decision, April 1993, p. 176.
    APP/F/1230/E/92/808961.
[60] SE 2/5235/270/87/411/1, December 18, 1986.

The condition of a listed building perhaps raises the most difficult issues, **4.29** both for the applicant for LBC and for the local planning authority or Secretary of State. It is obvious that a route to demolition lies by way of neglect. The owner of a listed building may well allow the building to deteriorate to such an extent that it might fall down of its own accord; or hope that if it gets into a condition whereby an economic restoration is impossible, he will be able to persuade the local planning authority or the Secretary of State that he should be granted consent to demolish it. Obviously we have moved on from the stage when that simple proposition was accepted. Local planning authorities up and down the country are generally watchful, and mindful of people who deliberately let buildings decline so that those arguments can be put forward.

English Heritage has carried out studies into buildings at risk and produced a report on the subject of emphasising that the time to get to work on a building in decline is before it descends to an impossibly expensive ruin.[61]

But should an owner be penalised by his being required to spend money to maintain a building he does not want, for the good of future generations? Put another way, should the owner be able to obtain the advantage of release from his obligations as "a trustee for the future" and so be enabled to achieve a cleared site? The solution to the problem tends to mix facts with morality. Whether this should or should not be is a matter for individual judgment, but the following cases demonstrate the problems which the Secretary of State and the local planning authorities have in this connection.

The cases on the condition of the building encompass a wide range of circumstances. Deterioration through disuse and neglect did not justify a consent,[62] nor did "deliberate neglect",[63] nor did long delay.[64] Old age,[65] particularly where no grant for restoration would be available[66] has justified a consent, but some buildings are quite inappropriate for modern use.[67] Buildings which are unsafe and unusable are candidates for listed building consent to demolish.[68] But if a building is in good condition though not in demand it might be maintained for an improved climate when it may have a very considerable future life.[69] Local authorities have a particular duty to set a good example in maintaining listed buildings and LBC was refused where a local authority building was not in a serious condition.[70]

Financial balancing is, as always, an important matter: merely wanting to demolish a building as a result of commercial expediency is generally not on its own an adequate reason for granting LBC.[71] Exceptionally there have been cases where to retain a building would hold up a major scheme of

[61] Report on *Buildings at Risk*, English Heritage 1991.
[62] Bristol Meeting Room Trust, 1991 J.P.L. 152–159, and also in Denzil Millichap's article in 1993 2 J.P.L. 1111.
[63] *Hendford Manor*: SW/P/5367/270/15, Planning Appeals Vol. 3, p. 258—1978.
[64] *High Head Castle*: PNW/5165/270/20, October 23, 1985.
[65] APP/N1920/E/83/000607, May 19, 1986.
[66] E1/5320/411/2, May 14, 1986.
[67] APP/5316/E/81/139, June 10, 1982 and
[1977] 242 E.G. 304, quoted at [1980] J.P.L. 722.
[68] APP/5098/A/75/3580 and E75/65
YH/1869/270/58P.
[69] APP/5098/A/75/3580 and E75/65.
[70] EMP/5303/270/45.
[71] [1979] 252 E.G. 76, EMP/5303/270/45, June 26, 1979.

redevelopment.[72] Access can play an important part.[73] A view has to be taken as to whether a building is worth reinstating.[74]

We have divided our discussion of the cases concerning the condition of the building under the following headings:

(a) Disuse and neglect;
(b) Old age;
(c) Old age and no grant;
(d) Building fallen out of use;
(e) Unsafe and unusable;
(f) Good condition and usable;
(g) Poor condition but not serious;
(h) Economic conditions;
(i) Relationship to planning and redevelopment decisions.

(a) Disuse and neglect

4.30   The trustees of the Bristol Meeting Room Trust applied to Bristol City Council for listed building consent to demolish a Grade II Victorian house in Brislington, in Bristol. The applicants purchased the property in 1985 with the express purpose of demolishing the property in order to provide additional parking for their meeting room. The property was added to the statutory list in March 1986. In the planning inquiry which followed the refusal of LBC, the Inspector referred to the deterioration in the condition of the listed building in the following terms:

> "The Trustees indicate that, as it stands, the house would have a value of £100,000 to £120,000 but no attempt has been made since it became a listed building to put it for sale on the open market. Instead it has undoubtedly deteriorated through disuse and neglect, and it is apparent to me that rather than fulfil their duties as owners of a listed building to preserve it through its use and maintenance, or to find a suitable alternative use for the building, or to offer to sell the freehold as they had no further use for it, the Trustees have retained the deteriorating building for a further three years in the hope of obtaining permission eventually to demolish. In these circumstances, I do not accept that the evidence concerning the condition of the building is conclusive proof of the need or the justification for granting listed building consent for the total demolition of this building."[75]

The Deputy Judge quashed the decision of the Secretary of State. However, perhaps an interesting example of "deliberate neglect" is a case in Yeo-

---

[72] YH/5114/270/2P.
[73] SW(P)5191/270/23.
[74] APP/C0630/E/85/800906
    APP/C0630/E/86/801585
    APP/C0630/E/86/801586
[75] [1991] J.P.L. pp. 152–9.

vil, where the Yeovil District Council had applied for consent to demolish Hendford Manor, Yeovil. The Secretary of State ordered an inquiry, and in his report,[76] the Inspector commented: "Despite the advice contained in Circular 61/68, repeated in Circular 23/77 and in paragraph 91 of Circular 8/87, the council, as a matter of policy, has not properly maintained Hendford Manor even though it was listed as long ago as 1970 [the decision was in 1978] and its present sad condition is a direct result of this action." It is understood that only approximate estimates of the cost of rehabilitation had been put forward and the market for sale had not been properly tested. The Inspector's opinion was that it had not been established that the expenditure of public funds need be so great as to warrant the loss of an exceptionally rare, valuable and important building in a town notably lacking in properties of similar calibre. The Inspector concluded: "The council should accept the consequences of their previous policy (however well-intentioned) and, by repairing the building in the same manner as would be expected by a private owner, set an example to others." The Secretary of State agreed with the Inspector's recommendation of refusal of consent to demolish.

He also refused consent for the demolition of Baynard's Park, Cromleigh, which, it was claimed, was being deliberately allowed to deteriorate by its owner, who wished to obtain LBC to demolish and replace it with a modern bungalow. Private Eye[77] observed:

"if the four applications to demolish have had little effect, [the owner's] policy of deliberate neglect certainly has. The once grand mansion is now in a parlous state of repair."

Soon afterwards, as a result of most of the building being destroyed by a fire, LBC for demolition was granted.[78]

In the *High Heads Castle, Carlisle* case[79] the Inspector commented upon the application in the following terms:

"I note that the applicant was unaware until 1982 that the building is listed. However, approximately two years elapsed between that time and the application which is the subject of this inquiry. Council officers were available to advise yet no attempt was made by Mr Dickman [the owner and applicant] to secure the future of the building. Listed buildings are part of the heritage of the nation; they are limited in number and irreplaceable. Individuals who own them have special obligations. I do not regard Mr Dickman's ignorance of the position prior to 1982 as in any way justifying consent now for demolition. Furthermore, I cannot agree with the applicant that the demolition of the building and the reuse of salvaged stone on other unspecified sites for purposes unknown is a valid approach to conservation here."

The Inspector recommended that LBC for demolition of the Georgian wing of High Heads Castle be refused, which recommendation the Secretary of State accepted.

---

[76] *Planning Appeals*, Vol. 3, p. 258. (Ambit 1979)
 Ref. SW/P/5367/270/15 South West Region 1978.
[77] *Private Eye*, August 17, 1979.
[78] [1980] J.P.L. 485 Ref. SE2/5393/411/1, November 14, 1979.
[79] PNW/5165/270/20, October 23, 1985.

(b) Old age

Following consideration of his Inspector's report in May 1986 the Secretary of State for the Environment allowed an appeal by *Howard v. Leach Limited* against the refusal of Hartsmere Borough Council to grant listed building consent for the demolition of The Cloisters, High Street, Bushey, Hertfordshire.[80] The Inspector reported that the premises were in need of repair but were not neglected. Their poor condition had arisen in part from the lack of weather resistance of the fabric of the property. The Inspector found that:

> "The structure is poorly founded and constructed and with age has reached the point where it is so far defective as to be incapable of satisfactory repair and refurbishment. In my opinion the building has outlived its useful life and renovation is not justified."

There was no prospect of preservation and demolition was therefore allowed.

(c) Old age and no grant

4.31   In a case concerning Burgh Hall, Melton Constable, the evidence showed that the North wing was in a poor state of repair, that rehabilitation would be expensive, that no grants were available, and the local authority were not prepared to press for repairs. In these circumstances the Secretary of State granted consent to demolish the wing.[81]

(d) Building fallen out of use

In June 1982 the Burton Group Limited successfully appealed against the refusal by Breckland District Council to grant listed building consent for the demolition of the old maltings at Thetford.[82] In his report to the Secretary of State for the Environment the Inspector found that there was nothing in the building's structural condition, save for the reinstatement of some fire damage, which would justify its demolition. However due to the building's design problems, for example low ceiling heights and closely spaced columns, the Inspector found that reinstatement would be a wasted exercise. Any conversion scheme would be likely to destroy much of the character of the building. With some regret regarding the circumstances of the case, the Secretary of State decided that he would not be justified in withholding listed building consent for demolition.

Another case where neglect had not been deliberate and LBC was granted was that of an application to demolish a row of 19th-century weavers cottages, where it was concluded that any attempt at restoration would "pre-

---

[80] APP/N1920/E/83/000607, May 19, 1986.
[81] E1/5320/411/2, May 14, 1986.
[82] APP/5316/E/81/139, June 10, 1982.

serve a shell, but not the outward appearance, ambience or atmosphere of the original dwellings."[83]

(e) Unsafe and unusable

In February 1989, following a local inquiry, the Secretary of State for the **4.32** Environment accepted his Inspector's recommendation and granted listed building consent to G. Holden (Caravans) Ltd to demolish the Grade II* Carter Place Hall, Haslingden.[84] In his report the Inspector referred to the strong presumption in favour of preserving the Hall, however increasing concern regarding the stability of the outer walls and the proximity of other occupied buildings and mobile homes led the Inspector to recommend the grant of listed building consent for demolition "in the absence of any real tangible prospect that the building will be made safe in the fairly near future."

Where the structural condition of the building is virtually beyond recall and is potentially dangerous, as in the Haslingden case, this is clearly an important factor which is taken into account. This was significant in connection with the application for LBC to demolish nos 3 and 5 and the buildings known as Queen's Hotel, Micklegate, York.[85] The Secretary of State, having called in the application because of the Grade II* grading of the buildings and a great deal of public concern over the proposals, was also "concerned at the danger to the public and the owner's contractors, the risk to the buildings themselves, and also to the internal features, many of which are no less important than the exterior." The Secretary of State continued:

"The reports of surveys commissioned by the owners and by the various societies have been considered. A common element in all the reports was fear about the structural condition of the buildings. It is clear that differential settlement has taken place and is continuing; that the timbers have been attacked by beetle; and that the outer skin of the front wall of the hotel is inadequately bonded to the supporting piers; and that the brickwork has been the subject of serious and progressive decay. He is also advised that deep piling would be required to support the buildings or any that replaced them.

Although it is accepted that there are techniques which might be used to arrest the deterioration of the buildings and prepare them for the difficult task of restoration, the Secretary of State is not persuaded that any of the schemes put forward offers reasonable hope of preservation. There are strong grounds for believing that the structural condition of the group is worse than was at first realised, and that the works necessary to effect restoration are so extensive that they could result in premature collapse. Also the evidence suggests that the end result of restoration, even if it were technically successful, would be unacceptable on aesthetic grounds.

The Secretary of State is of the opinion that these buildings are out-

[83] [1977] 242 E.G. 304, quoted at 1980 J.P.L. 722.
[84] PNW/5296/344/4 February 1989.
[85] [1974] J.P.L. 493 Ref. YH/1869/270/58P May 8, 1974.

standingly important not only individually but also as a group and for
the contribution they make to the townscape of Micklegate, and agrees
with objectors that demolition should only be permitted on condition
that they are replaced in replica. He also considers that he himself
should approve the details of the replacement buildings before they are
erected."

In April 1987, the Secretary of State for the Environment allowed an appeal
by Northfield Developments Limited for LBC for the demolition of 11–13
Market Place, Newbury, Berkshire.[86] Listed building consent for demolition
was given primarily because of the poor structural condition of the application properties. In his report to the Secretary of State the Inspector said:

"The structural condition, especially of the offshoots, is extremely
poor. The conditions . . . also stem in my opinion from a measure of
neglect, but most importantly from the alterations of the 19th century,
when two quite different forms of construction, i.e. frame and load
bearing, were inadvisedly intermingled. To my mind, with the efflux-
ion of time, the weaknesses inherent in the combined structure have
come to the fore and the building is so far defective and unsound that
removal is justified."

(f) Good condition and usable

4.33   On an appeal by the British Gas Corporation for consent to demolish a
listed building within the Sheffield Metropolitan District Council area,
being the former Gas Offices, Commercial Street, Sheffield,[87] the Inspector
concluded that:

"the original Gas Office building has architectural merit, both from an
external design and workmanship point of view, and also having regard
to some internal features relating to the Board Room and Cash Hall.
The classical style design of the Victorian era could contribute to the
evolving character of this part of the town centre of Sheffield, assuming
that adjacent redevelopment is suitably designed. For these reasons I
am of the view that the former Gas Offices are properly listed as a
Grade II building of special architectural or historic interest and that
these premises should, if possible, be preserved. I note the various
schemes, and related valuations submitted by the appellants, indicating
that the refurbishing of this listed building and redevelopment of the
remainder of the site would result in a financial loss. In addition, there
is now a surfeit of office space in Sheffield and no prospective occupant
for the building has been found. However, there are other considerations that in my view outweigh the above factors. The structural condition of this listed building is good generally, and these premises could
be so maintained pending an improved climate, economically and from
the urban redevelopment point of view, which could favour rehabili-

---

[86] SE2/5127/270/114
    SE2/5127/411/6, April 14, 1987.
[87] *Appeal by British Gas Corporation.* Planning Appeals, Vol. 3, p. 119—Ref. APP/
    5098/A/75/3580 and E75/65.

tation. The nature of the buildings is such that, if rehabilitated, the premises will have a very considerable future life."

The Inspector recommended that the appeal against LBC refusal be dismissed and the Secretary of State agreed.

(g) Poor condition but not serious

A case where the cost of restoration was not allowed to outweigh the **4.34** advantage of conservation of a building not in a serious condition was that of Lutterworth Hall, Leicestershire.[88] The hall was a good example of an early nineteenth century villa possessing a facade with characteristics of the Greek Revival style. The Inspector felt that the condition of the building was not serious and that demolition ought not to be allowed, especially since an industrial company was prepared to buy the hall for offices. The Secretary of State agreed and refused LBC, criticising the applicants, Harborough District Council, for allowing the building to fall into disrepair through neglect, contrary to the advice contained in what later became paragraph 91 of Circular 8/87 and is now paragraph 3.37 of PPG 15: where the local authority themselves owned a listed building, they should be careful to set a good example to others.[89]

The interesting question is whether or not the kind of case in Micklegate, York involving dubious ground conditions and structural defects, can be distinguished from the sort of case where neglect has obviously been permitted. Morally one can take a view about this kind of case, but at the end of the day when the Secretary of State is presented with the problem of whether or not to grant LBC, does it matter? Should the owner be castigated because he has apparently permitted the building to decay? The moral argument is an interesting one, but what should be the relevant question for the Secretary of State? This is not an easy question to answer, but the views of the Secretary of State appear to be reflected in the Bristol Meeting Room Trust and High Head Castle cases already discussed above.

(h) Economic considerations

The fact that the preservation of a listed building would hinder or restrict **4.35** a redevelopment scheme which is otherwise acceptable and for which planning permission has already been given does not prevent refusal of listed building consent to demolish, particularly if the building is of good quality and the retention only causes inconvenience to the redevelopment proposal rather than insuperable obstacles. In the Freemans plc decision referred to in paragraph 4.03 the Secretary of State for the Environment ordered an inquiry to be held regarding Freemans application to demolish two listed

---

[88] [1979] 252 E.G. 76 DOE Ref. EMP/5303/270/45, June 26, 1979; see also DOE Ref. E1/5382/270/96 where the demolition of a 16th-century farmhouse was refused LBC as it was not beyond repair, though empty for 17 years (see *Planning Appeals Monthly*, May 1981).

[89] See paras. 4.36–4.39.

buildings in Clapham Road, London as part of its redevelopment scheme. The Inspector reported that:

"As a starting point in relation to any development of a site containing listed buildings there has to be a presumption in favour of preserving those buildings. In my view, no clearly substantiated case other than commercial expediency and that the inclusion of the buildings would give rise to higher construction costs, has been put forward to justify the demolition of the listed buildings. The appellants clearly do not want to retain the listed buildings. The original design concept should have taken into account the constraints imposed by the presence of the listed buildings on the site rather than by the late exercise of "fitting in" the listed buildings into an indicative scheme. In my view some additional costs would be incurred by the inclusion of the listed buildings but I am not convinced that the costs would be prohibitive as to jeopardise the whole of the redevelopment proposal. In my opinion the demolition of numbers 127/129 should be resisted."

The Secretary of State for the Environment in withholding listed building consent for the demolition of 127 and 129 Clapham Road, London stated:

"Numbers 127 and 129 Clapham Road are Grade II listed buildings and, as already stated, are considered to be capable of being renovated and refurbished to bring them back into beneficial use. Given the general presumption in favour of preservation except where a strong case can be made out for granting consent the Secretary of State is not satisfied that your clients have made every possible effort to retain these listed buildings; the commercial expediency and financial arguments are not of themselves considered sufficient justification for their demolition."[90]

4.36   Oldham MBC applied for LBC to demolish a former railway goods warehouse to enable a proposed retail park scheme to go ahead. Oldham Metropolitan Borough Council[91] was found by the Inspector to have made significant efforts to sell the property and to find suitable alternative uses for the building. After the council had purchased the warehouse they had attempted to persuade four developers who were shortlisted to develop the site to incorporate the listed building into their proposals. However those efforts were unsuccessful. The building had local historic importance as a vestige of Oldham's past supremacy in the cotton industry. The quality and design of the building was high and it had an unusual curved design. The Inspector found that:

" . . . when these are considered together with the likelihood that the development of the retail warehouse park will considerably increase the chances of an economic use being found for the building and that this development can be carried out without the space occupied by the listed building, then the argument for demolition cannot be sustained."

The Secretary of State agreed with the Inspector's conclusions and accepted his recommendation that listed building consent for demolition be refused. In reaching his decision the Secretary of State referred to the importance of development to the area which could create new job oppor-

[90] PNW/5083/344/1, August 20, 1987.
[91] PNW/5083/344/1, June 12, 1986.

tunities and the Inspector's conclusions that the proposed retail warehouse park could proceed without requiring the demolition of the listed building.

Balancing the case

The views on the economic problems of listed buildings are expressed in **4.37** decisions of the Secretary of State as we have seen from the foregoing examples in this chapter dealing with architectural or historic interest and the condition of the building. In this section we try to bring together cases where the Secretary of State or his Inspectors have tried to balance the competing factors in determining whether to grant or refuse listed building consent.

We start with buildings which are now physically useless for any purpose[92] or incapable of repair, moving on to buildings which had deteriorated to such an extent that restoration was not viable,[93] or where the building was in such a poor condition that the work which would be needed to repair would be so extensive that much of value would be lost.[94] There are cases where the retention and repair of buildings would be economic.[95] Consent in such cases would normally be granted.

Certain buildings do not lend themselves to alternative uses.[96] Some buildings do not have a sensible alternative use and would have excessive conversion costs.[97] In the latter case LBC for demolition was refused. Consent has been given where a conversion was unlikely to have financed a development and in a case where a shop could be converted to a residential use.[98]

A refusal of LBC resulted from an application where a building was reasonably sound so as to justify repair.[99] However in a case of a building which was not unsound but in need of repair where the costs were likely to be high, with little likelihood of the conversion being warranted LBC was granted.[1] Similarly a combination of a mediocre building, in an inappropriate setting and an unhappy location within a development site justified LBC for demolition.[2]

In all the cases it is essential to look to the future. Where, for the existing listed building, there is a reasonable commercial future for the existing listed building, LBC for demolition will normally be refused.[3] Refusal was ordered where alternative answers to demolition might be found for a fine

---

[92] *Broomhall Place:* Ref. YH/5098/270/89; The Old Maltings: APP/H5960/E/86/ 801432, September 3, 1984.

[93] *East Lodge, Broxborne:* APP/W1905/E/88/803960; 3/89.

[94] *The Old Maltings, Thetford.* APP/5316/E/81/139, June 10, 1982.

[95] *Kent Messenger v. SOSE* [1976] J.P.L. 372.

[96] *Cemetery Chapel:* SE2/5128/270/67 and *Estates Gazette* July 25, 1981.

[97] *Glemsford:* APP/2239/A/74/2967, 2761, APP/2239/E/74/32.

[98] *Daventry:* APP/Y2810/A/85/039335) August 13, 1986
APP/Y2810/E/85/801180)
Fowlmere: SE6/5142/411/1 and *Planning Appeals Volume 1*, p. 143.

[99] *Retford:* APP/A3010/E/84/800454, April 30, 1985.

[1] *Sunderland:* N/5103/270P/25, February 19, 1987.

[2] *Crockford Farm, Basingstoke:* APP/H1705/E/86/801934, October 21, 1989.

[3] *Berwick Grammar School* (1981) 253 E.G. 436.
Stotford Mill: E1/5124/270/71).
E1/5124/411/4) 20/87

structure.[4] Sometimes the type of conversion may save a building: consent for conversion was given for office use as opposed to residential.[5] An interesting consent was given for a part demolition of a 16th-century farmhouse where the part demolished would reveal the original gable of the farmhouse.[6] Alteration cases are difficult to decide—even where in one case there would be little effect on the exterior there would be a greater effect on the interior, consent was refused.[7] The inadequacy of grants to bring a building into repair justified an Inspector granting listed building consent for demolition.[8]

In September 1984 the Secretary of State, following an inquiry into Sheffield City Council's application for listed building consent to demolish 23–29 and 35–41 Broomhall Place, accepted his Inspector's findings of fact and agreed with his conclusions. He confirmed that he was satisfied that all reasonable avenues for the restoration or conversion of Broomhall Place had been explored and that the fabric of the terrace was in too poor a condition to be reasonably capable of repair. In particular the Secretary of State referred to the following extract from his Inspector's report:

> "The houses in the order (a compulsory purchase order under Part III of the Housing Act 1957) are irremediably unfit by reason of their advanced decay, progressive instability and endemic dampness. They cannot be made satisfactory for residential or any other beneficial use and are coming to the end of their useful life. The Council have considered all reasonable alternatives to demolition. By reason of the age and inherent defects of the buildings the most satisfactory method of dealing with the conditions in the area is the demolition of all the buildings in the area."[9]

In May 1989, an inquiry was held regarding an appeal by Gunn Developments Limited against the decision of Broxborne Borough Council to refuse listed building consent for the demolition of East Lodge, Broxborne, Hertfordshire.[10] In his report the Inspector found that the condition of the building had deteriorated to such an extent that restoration was not viable. There were severe structural problems mainly arising from the effects of water in the building and the estimated costs of retaining the building varied from £68,250 to £96,000. The freehold value of the building was placed at £40,000 and the value of the renovated building at between £60–70,000. The Inspector was of the opinion that even on the basis of the lower figure, when VAT and professional fees had been allowed for, the estimate would be likely to rise to over £80,000. Taking account of acquisition costs and the fact that no significant grant aid would be likely to be available, restoration would not be viable. The Secretary of State considered that in the circumstances a strong case had been made for demolition and LBC was granted.

4.38   This also was the substance of the decision which later reached the courts, in the case of *Kent Messenger Ltd v. Secretary of State for the*

---

[4] *Smardale Gill Viaduct, Cumbria:* APP/T0925/E/85/801046, June 6, 1986.
[5] *Cheltenham:* T/APP/B1605/A/84/14004/P7 reported in EG, March 2, 1984.
[6] *Burgh Hall:* E1/5320/411/2, May 14, 1985.
[7] *Fawsley Hall:* EMP/5324/270/29, July 4, 1984.
[8] *Bath Road, Worcester:* WMR/P/5248/270/94, June 30, 1988.
[9] *Sheffield CC, Broomhall Place,* September 3, 1984.
[10] *Broxborne BC, East Lodge,* APP/W1905/E/88/803960. 3/89.

Environment[11] where the Inspector recommended that LBC should be granted, summarising the economic arguments by reporting: "It seems to me therefore, that there is some substance in the applicants' submission that the retention and repair of the building would be uneconomic."

Typical of these examples where the economic argument is used was an application by Reading Borough Council for LBC to demolish a disused cemetery chapel. The structural condition was poor and possibly dangerous. The cost of reinstatement would have been (at 1981 prices) £93,700; even to retain the roofless shell of the building as a landscape feature was likely to cost £24,000. The Inspector reported that the building was properly listed. The surrounding cemetery was still in use. The council was not prepared to spend a large sum of public money on a building which was no longer required for its original purpose, had been unused for many years and for which there seemed no prospect of funding an appropriate alternative and economically viable use. There were, it was said, more deserving cases on which the limited funds available for restoration work should be spent. The Inspector recommended the grant of LBC and the Secretary of State agreed.[12]

Not always, however, is the economic argument the determinant factor. Often the economic argument appears to be referred to as the "beneficial use" of the property. Perhaps the phrase "beneficial use" can be interpreted in this context to mean that there is a sensible economic use. The former West Suffolk County Council refused LBC for the demolition of the Silk Mill at Glemsford and planning permission for residential development of the site.[13] The mill was situated in a conservation area and was recognised by the Inspector as being of industrial and sociological historic interest, but because of widespread structural failures, subsidence, and inadequate foundations, he was satisfied that it was of no beneficial use, requiring an unrealistic expenditure to convert it to a suitable use. He therefore recommended consent for demolition of the mill be granted and that planning permission be given for the residential development. The Secretary of State did not agree, and commented on his Inspector's report that: "He appears to have relied too heavily on the lack of the mill's beneficial use and the cost of conversion which it is thought should not be overriding factors in deciding whether to give consent to the demolition of a listed building." The Secretary of State felt that investigation should be made as speedily as possible into the financial and practical aspects of converting it into some other use and dismissed the appeal.

An appeal against the decisions of Daventry District Council to refuse planning permission and listed building consent for the conversion of Oak Tree Hill Barn, Church Stowe, Northamptonshire to a dwelling was heard in 1986.[14] The Inspector concluded that the alternative use proposed by Daventry District Council would be unlikely to provide sufficient income

[11] [1976] J.P.L. 372.
[12] DOE reference SE2/5128/270/67 reported in Estates Gazette, July 25, 1981. See also N/5102/270(P)/9 *Planning Appeals Monthly* June 1981 (demolition of a hospital).
[13] *Planning Appeals*, Vol. 1 p. 142. Ref. APP/2239/A/74/2967, 2761, APP/2239/E/74/32.
[14] APP/Y2810/A/85/039335), August 13, 1986.
APP/Y2810/E/85/801180)

to finance a satisfactory standard of refurbishment. The Inspector concluded that the most favourable means of securing the future of the little used agricultural building was by allowing its conversion to a dwelling. The Secretary of State accepted the Inspector's recommendations and allowed the appeals subject to conditions.

4.39   Another case concerned a shop in Fowlmere, a suburb of Cambridge.[15] The Inspector considered that the building had been altered so much that it possessed little intrinsic merit, and its importance lay chiefly in the contribution which it made to the village scene on account of its materials, siting, and mass form. He said: "To repair and convert the building to residential use would in my opinion be unlikely to prove economically viable, and the objections to restoring it to a shopping use are soundly based." He was confident that an appropriate replacement building could be secured by negotiation and the Secretary of State agreed with his recommendation that LBC be granted for demolition.

The availability of grant aid towards the cost of necessary repairs was a factor in the decision by the Secretary of State to dismiss an appeal by A.H. Turner Group Ltd against refusal of listed building consent to demolish 27 Grove Street, Retford by Bassetlaw District Council. Evidence was given during the inquiry that Nottinghamshire County Council had grants available for the financial year 1985/86 to assist with the cost of repair of listed buildings. In addition the Nottinghamshire Buildings Preservation Trust Limited was interested in acquiring the building for repair and refurbishment. The Inspector concluded that the building had sufficient merit both architecturally and in its townscape setting with other buildings within the conservation area to justify its repair. Much of the present state of disrepair of the building was due to the neglect of the appellant. However the fabric of the building was in reasonably sound condition and the Inspector concluded that with sufficient interest and investment the building could be restored to a beneficial use.[16]

Another case concerned an application by Sunderland Borough Council for listed building consent to demolish number 1 and 2 Grain Warehouses, Hudson Dock, Sunderland. The Inspector was of the opinion that the application buildings made a significant contribution to the dock landscape and that demolition would cause a marked change in the dock and its townscape. The buildings were not unsound, although in need of repair, but the likely costs of bringing them into a reasonable state of repair was likely to be high. The buildings were obsolete and required new uses. However, apart from the dock or dock-related uses there was no parking or direct access. The Inspector noted that the buildings were in an area of heavy industry and their situation within the port weighed heavily against alternative uses. With regard to the costs of renovation in the context of preservation the Inspector said:

> "The costings put forward are not tested on the market but their drift is not doubted and neither is the conclusion that conversion would result in substantial losses. The buildings have been tested for sale or lease on the market by both owner and tenants and they have proved unattractive. In my opinion there is little likelihood of another use or owner

[15] *Planning Appeals*, Vol. 1, p. 143. Ref. SE6/5142/411/1.
[16] APP/A3010/E/84/800454, April 30, 1985.

emerging in the foreseeable future or of the conversion being warranted. My conclusion is that the inherent difficulties outweigh the presumption that there is for retention."

The Secretary of State accepted the Inspector's conclusions and recommendations that LBC be given for demolition.[17]

At an appeal by Louisville Investments Limited against a decision by Basingstoke and Deane Borough Council to refuse listed building consent for the demolition of Crockford Farm farmhouse, Basingstoke.[18] The Inspector concluded that he was satisfied that the costs of conversion of the Grade II farmhouse would "be too high in relation to expected returns, taking account of the size and physical constraints of the building and its location remote from a commercial centre, to make conversion an economically viable proposition". The Inspector was of the opinion that the merits of the building were not so great, nor the building so unique or important, that its preservation became a matter of overriding concern. In addition the Inspector was of the opinion that finding an alternative use for the property could not be accommodated without major physical alterations which would alter the character of the building adversely", and thus concluded:

"The case for granting consent for demolition, while not wholly convincing in respect of the particular proposal used to demonstrate it, did nevertheless in its generality convince (the Inspector) that demolition was necessary to allow development to follow, given the inappropriate setting of the building, its unhappy location within a development site and the problems inherent in conversion."

The Secretary of State accepted the Inspector's recommendation and granted LBC for the demolition of Crockford Farm farmhouse.

In the Grade II Stotford Mill case referred to at paragraph 4.22 above, the **4.40** reasonably sound structural condition of the mill was a relevant factor in the decision of the Secretary of State to refuse listed building consent for the conversion of the mill to a residential unit. Although the structural condition of the mill was reasonably sound, its general state of repair caused the Inspector some concern. The decision turned upon the historic importance of the mill and the commercial viability of using the application building for its original purpose or combined with museum use.

An appeal by the British Railways Board against the decision of Eden District Council to refuse listed building consent to demolish the Smardale Gill viaduct, Cumbria, was dismissed in June 1986.[19] The Inspector found that the viaduct was clearly in need of repair. Eden District Council estimated the cost of the repair at £125,000 whereas the cost of blowing up the viaduct would be at least £66,000. On the evidence before the Inspector there was no certainty that the demolition costs would be lower than £175,000 and therefore the demolition of the viaduct would be dearer than repair and retention. The Inspector stated in his report:

"Looked at in financial terms alone, there is no clear advantage in demolishing the viaduct rather than restoring it except perhaps the long term advantage to British Railways Board that they would not have to

[17] N/5103/270P/25, February 19, 1987.
[18] APP/H1705/E/86/801934, October 21, 1987.
[19] APP/T0925/E/85/801046, June 6, 1986.

inspect and be responsible for maintaining it. However owners of listed buildings have a duty to maintain them. The viaduct is not in a dangerous condition and the Board have stated that it would be practicable to repair it. Smardale Gill Viaduct is a fine building which makes a valuable contribution to the local scene and which should be preserved . . . Listed building consent is normally only given where there is no reasonable alternative to demolition. In this case there are alternatives which include the British Railways Board repairing the viaduct themselves at costs which compare favourably with the likely costs of demolition; or handing over the ownership of the viaduct to a body which would have adequate resources and which would take over responsibility for repairing and preserving the viaduct."

The Secretary of State agreed with the Inspector's conclusions and accepted his recommendation that the appeal be dismissed.

In the case of a listed Regency property in Cheltenham, conversion to office use was allowed by the Inspector on appeal. It was felt that the proposed office use was a better economic proposition than the building's conversion to flats, and that this was a factor to take into account in maintaining the character of a listed building.[20] The following cases also illustrate the relative importance of the condition of a listed building in the context of an LBC application.

4.41   In May 1986 the Secretary of State granted listed building consent for the demolition of the north wing of Burgh Hall, Melton Constable, Norfolk.[21] Burgh Hall itself originated with a 16th-century farmhouse which was historically of considerable importance as it dated from a period when little was built in the district and from which there were few survivors. In contrast the north wing was not especially rare and dated from a period of substantial building activity. The demolition of the north wing would reveal the original gable of the farm house amongst other potential benefits.

The structural condition of the north wing was reasonably satisfactory but the building itself was in a poor state of maintenance due to damp penetration and roofing defects. Despite those defects, the Inspector was of the opinion that the north wing was far from being beyond reasonable repair. The Inspector also found that the north wing was not in urgent need of demolition but there was sufficient evidence to suggest that even if the wing were rehabilitated it would not be marketable. The Inspector said in his report:

"There is a strong presumption in favour of preserving listed buildings . . . but I conclude that the possibility of the north wing being rehabilitated is remote. There are some historical and architectural benefits if the north wing is not retained to set against its loss and I am satisfied that the circumstances in this case are such that they overcome the presumption of preservation."

The Secretary of State agreed with his Inspector and Listed Building Consent was approved.

[20] T/APP/B1605/A/84/14004/P7, reported in E.G. March 2, 1984. Similar considerations influenced the decision in relation to *Robinwood Mill, Todmorden* (YH/5112/270/141) reported in *Estates Times*, March 20, 1987.

[21] E1/5350/411/2, May 14, 1986.

(i) Relationship to planning and redevelopment decisions

However, redevelopment proposals which have been approved may some- **4.42** times be sufficient to justify LBC to demolish. One large redevelopment scheme had been approved before the listing but the merits of the building were not great enough "to justify abandoning the basic planning objective". This view was taken by the Secretary of State in connection with an application by MEPC to demolish a group of buildings in Boar Lane, New Station Street, Alfred Street and Briggate, Leeds, which was called in.[22] The demolition was needed to create a pedestrian deck linking a pedestrianised area to the north of Boar Lane with a proposed redevelopment to the south.

The Inspector felt that the architectural importance of the buildings was not so great as to justify abandoning the basic planning objective of developing the area to the south of Boar Lane as an extension of the pedestrianised area to the north. He felt that without the pedestrian deck, while continuity could be provided with other pedestrian links, it was doubtful whether they would provide a link of adequate width and attraction to ensure the success of the area to the south. The Secretary of State said that he accepted these conclusions "with the greatest reluctance". He said that had the scheme been a new development scheme he would have had no hesitation in refusing LBC, but noted that the principle of the pedestrian deck which must involve the demolition of some of the listed buildings was part of the Comprehensive Development Area proposals first put forward in 1966. He felt he would not be justified in requiring the scheme to be completely recast and he had been guided principally by the view that the local authority and the developer "could reasonably have thought that the ministerial decision of 1968 (when the properties were included in a Comprehensive Development Area approved by the Secretary of State) justified them in preparing a scheme on the lines they did". LBC to demolish the buildings was granted.

Consent to demolish has been granted where demolition was essential for access to a new development for which planning permission had already been given. Such a decision arose in Bridport, where West Dorset District Council sought LBC (now CAC) for the demolition of several unlisted buildings in a Conservation Area in St Mary's Place and South Street, Bridport.[23] The buildings were in a conservation area, but planning permission had already been given for a new development at the rear of the buildings. It was essential that access to the development be provided through South Street. An alternative to demolition of the buildings was to provide the access to the south of the buildings, but this would "add to the cost of the scheme to an unacceptable degree". However, one of the revised plans for the access enabled some of the affected buildings to be saved. It was this plan which was accepted by the Secretary of State, who refused LBC for the buildings which would not be affected by it, eight in total, and granted LBC for the remaining eight, all in South Street.

The importance of an integrated approach towards the demolition of a listed building and redevelopment of the site is illustrated by the case of the

[22] *Planning Appeals*, Vol. 1, p. 141. Ref. YH/5114/270/2P.
[23] *Planning Appeals*, Vol. 1, p. 141. Ref. SW(P)5191/270/23.

Blyth Central Methodist Church, 21 Bridge Street, Blyth.[24] The Secretary of State for the Environment issued his decision letter on October 6, 1988 in respect of an application by Huntingate Developments Limited for listed building consent for the demolition of Blyth Central Methodist Church which the Secretary of State had called in. In his report the Inspector concluded that the church was a building of outstanding architectural interest which it was desirable to preserve if possible. The structural condition of the church, though needing substantial remedial action, was basically sound. The Inspector was not convinced that the value of the listed building was such that it should be preserved at all costs bearing in mind the degree of functional obsolescence of the building for church use, the effect of its retention on the viability of the proposed redevelopment scheme and costs of renovation. The Inspector recommended that listed building consent for demolition be granted subject to a condition to ensure that demolition was only undertaken when a comprehensive scheme of redevelopment was commenced. The Secretary of State accepted the Inspector's recommendations and granted listed building consent for demolition.

4.43   Thus the present approach to the importance of the state of repair of a listed building in relation to LBC to demolish appears to be:

(1) a state of good repair is a strong factor against granting LBC;

(2) a state of bad repair resulting from natural causes is a strong factor in favour of granting LBC;

(3) a state of bad repair brought about through neglect may well give rise to a presumption against granting LBC; and

(4) local authorities ought to take a lead in keeping listed buildings in good repair.

7. ECONOMIC FACTORS—THE VIEW OF THE COURTS AND THE DEPARTMENT: ANY SUBSTANTIAL BENEFITS FOR THE COMMUNITY?

4.44   The question of how far economic factors, especially cost, are relevant in determining planning applications has received judicial consideration notably in the High Court in the *Sovmots Investments Ltd*[25] case and the later decision of the Court of Appeal in *R. v. Westminster City Council v. ex parte Monahan* [1989]. Whether, in any given case, a financial consideration will be material will depend on whether the financial matter is a valid planning consideration. It seems from the Court of Appeal's decision in the Westminster City Council case that the financial constraints on the economic viability of a desirable planning development are "unavoidable facts of life in an imperfect world".[26] Although in some cases the decisions referred to below were decided before the views of the courts were expressed on economic considerations, nevertheless there appears to be a consistent approach in the departmental decisions which mirrors to a large extent the views of the Courts.

---

[24] N/5332/270p/3, October 6, 1988.
[25] [1977] 2 All E.R. 385.
[26] [1989] 2 All E.R. 91 at 96.

(a) The attitude of the courts

In so far as the courts are concerned, a start is made with *J. Murphy and Sons v. Secretary of State for the Environment*,[27] where the Secretary of State's decision granting the London Borough of Camden planning permission was challenged *inter alia* on the ground that he had failed to have regard to a material consideration (the high cost of developing the site). The application was dismissed. Ackner J. (as he then was) said:

"The planning authority exercises no paternalistic or avuncular jurisdiction over would-be developers to safeguard them from their financial follies. If it had such jurisdiction, planning inquiries would last even longer than they do now, and the problems of establishing whether or not a particular development was or was not economically justifiable would be countless."

In *Sovmots Investments Limited v. The Secretary of State for the Environment*[28] (the *Centre Point* case) Forbes J. (as he then was), after summarising the *Murphy* case, stated:

"If Mr. Justice Ackner was intending to say that cost can never be a relevant consideration either in a planning appeal or on a compulsory purchase order (and that I am told is how this decision is interpreted in Whitehall), then I find myself unable to agree with him. Of course planning is concerned with land use, but the Minister charged with the overall duty of considering applications for planning permission and the confirmation of planning proposals for particular areas must, it seems to me, be entitled to bear in mind the likelihood of the proposed development being carried into effect."

The decision of Forbes J. was reversed in the Court of Appeal,[29] but the point mentioned above was not discussed nor was it in the House of Lords,[30] which reversed the decision of the Court of Appeal on other grounds.

However, in the case of *Hambledon and Chiddingfold Parish Councils v.* **4.45** *Secretary of State for the Environment*[31] Ackner J. qualified his statement in the *Murphy* case. He said:

"Notwithstanding my own natural affection for consistency, and while I still think the decision was correct, I might have stated a general proposition too widely. Nevertheless, it was clear from the Secretary of State's decision letter that he had considered the question of costs and so the point was not relevant."

This leaves the view of the courts in the uncertain position that economic factors probably can be a relevant factor in making a planning decision.

---

[27] [1973] 2 All E.R. 26; [1973] 1 W.L.R. 560; 117 S.J. 304; [1973] 71 L.G.R. 273; [1973] J.P.L. 362.
[28] [1977] 2 All E.R. 385, [1979] A.C. 144, [1977] 2 W.L.R. 951, 121 SOL JO 336, 75 L.G.R. 510, 35 P. & C.R. 350, [1977] RVR 200, H.L.
[29] [1976] 3 All E.R. 720; [1976] 3 W.L.R. 597.
[30] *Sovmots Investments Ltd. v. Secretary of State for the Environment* [1977] 2 All E.R. p. 385 H.L.
[31] [1976] J.P.L. 502.

The materiality of financial considerations to planning decisions rests upon whether the financial matter is a planning consideration.[32] A financial matter has been held to be a planning consideration where a refusal of planning permission would have resulted in a building being left derelict and unoccupied. This was the situation in the case of *Sosmo Trust Limited v. Secretary of State for the Environment* in which the judge stated "what could be significant was not the lack of financial viability but the consequences of that financial viability or the lack of financial viability".[33]

The whole area of dispute was laid to rest in the Court of Appeal in the *R. v. Westminster City Council ex parte Monahan* case, known generally as the "Covent Garden" case.[34] In that case the question was posed "whether, as a matter of common sense, there could be any reason why the financial viability of the desirable development and the means of achieving it, must necessarily be immaterial considerations". Kerr L.J. concluded that there was not. He held that "financial constraints on the economic viability of a desirable planning development are unavoidable facts of life in an imperfect world. It would be unreal and contrary to common sense to insist that they must be excluded from the range of considerations as material in determining planning applications". He added that the local planning authorities must be careful not to give weight too readily to assertions of financial constraints as a ground for relaxing policies which have been formulated in the public interest. It should be noted that the proceedings related to the financial considerations arising from a single application relating to a single site and a single proposal.

The statement by Kerr L.J. quoted above relating to general planning matters must apply to listed building and conservation area issues.

(b) The attitude of the Department

4.46   The PPG 15, paragraph 3.8 covers the subject of efforts being made to retain the listed building in use, and, in paragraph 3.17, confirms that the Secretary of State would not expect listed building consent to be granted for the total or substantial demolition of any listed building unless the authority (or the Secretary of State himself) is satisfied that, without clear and convincing evidence, all reasonable efforts have been made to sustain existing uses or find viable new uses and these efforts have failed; or that redevelopment would produce substantial benefits for the community which would decisively outweigh the loss resulting from demolition.

PPG 1 stressed the importance of three objectives of the planning process; the one being an instrument for protecting and enhancing the environment in towns and country, and the other in preserving the historic buildings and rural landscape and the maintenance of green belts. PPG 15 advised that it be seen as essential that the planning processes should take full account of both the need for economic growth and the need to protect historic build-

---

[32] *See Niarchos (London) Ltd. v. Secretary of State for the Environment* [1977] 35 P. & C.R. 259 and *Brighton Borough Council v. Secretary of State for the Environment* [1978] 1979 J.P.L. 173.

[33] *Sosmo Trust Ltd. v. Secretary of State for the Environment and Camden London Borough Council* [1983] J.P.L.806.

[34] [1989] 2 All E.R. 91.

ings and areas. These objectives should not be seen as necessarily in opposition; on the one hand conservation can play a key part in promoting economic prosperity, and environmental quality is increasingly seen as a key factor in many economic decisions. PPG 15, paragraph 1.3, states that it is part of the planning system to define through development plans the capacity for change, and when proposals for new development come forward, to assess their impact on the historic environment and give it full weight, alongside other considerations.[34a]

Grant assistance

The inter-relationship between the criteria set out in paragraph 3.19 of **4.47** PPG 15 (which superseded paragraph 90 of Circular 8/87) and grant assistance is illustrated in the following cases:

Following a public local inquiry into an application for listed building consent to demolish 12/14 Bath Road, Worcester,[35] the Secretary of State for the Environment considered his Inspector's report on this called in application and granted listed building consent for the application subject to conditions. The Inspector found that the buildings which were the subject of the application were worthy of listing but they were in an advanced state of disrepair with evidence of serious structural faults. Renovation of the listed buildings would have cost approximately £340,000, and in view of this the rehabilitation would fall far short of viability.

The Inspector said in relation to the possibility of grant assistance for the project:

"While grant assistance from a number of possible sources would help to reduce any financial shortfall, there is no evidence to show that the shortfall identified would be offset by any grant or grants, even if they were more than a qualified recommendation to the grant making authority. Having regard to the applicant's difficulty in establishing any level of grant assistance available; the need for substantial grant aid to meet the identified shortfall; the possible need to meet stringent grant conditions; and the experience of having to repay Housing Acts grants awarded in respect of 16 and 18 Bath Road, I understand the reluctance to seek grant assistance, notwithstanding the invitation from English Heritage. Despite this conclusion, the principle of offering a considerable grant from public funds, to render this otherwise non-viable proposal to substantially rebuild the listed building an attractive proposition to a building contractor, is a matter that I hold in question at this time when monies are not unlimited . . . On the evidence before me I consider the case for demolition, hinging on the structural condition of the properties and the cost of renovation, has been adequately made out in the face of the usual presumption favouring preservation."
Listed building consent for demolition was granted

Trustees of a night refuge in Crispin Street, London E1, appealed against **4.48** decisions of Tower Hamlets to refuse LBC (now conservation area consent) to demolish a 95 year old unlisted building within a conservation area and

---

[34a] An example of the economics of preserving a listed building when other uses had failed is at Leigh near Wigan—Secretary of State; decision in September 1994, E.H. Legal Bulletin No. 5: June 1995, [1995] 10 PAD 46.
[35] WMR/P/5248/270/94, June 30, 1988.

redevelop the site with six-storey offices. The appeal premises had been empty for two years but were in reasonable structural condition.

The Inspector agreed that the estimated £350,000 for repairs and refurbishment could not be justified on the basis of a capital value of the property of £257,000, but "a lot of work specified—though desirable—was not essential". The appellants were looking for a 12 per cent. return which the Inspector (in February 1987) considered high. In the end, however, the appeal failed because of design characteristics.[36]

Where the cost of reinstatement is similar to that of erection of the new building, the presumption[37] against demolition appears in most cases to operate if there are sound commercial prospects for restoring the premises, and LBC will be refused.[38]

On a called in application for listed building consent for demolition of a barn at Shillingham Manor Farm, Saltash, Cornwall[39] in September 1985, the Secretary of State agreed with the conclusions of his Inspector and accepted his recommendation that LBC for the demolition of the barn be granted. The barn, which was the subject of the application, was an attractive vernacular barn which was part of Shillingham Manor Farm, a farm of considerable architectural, historical and archaeological interest. The barn was in poor structural condition and extensive repair work was required. The building was of very limited use for modern farming purposes, and even if full repair work were to be completed there did not appear to be a suitable alternative use either in whole or in part for the property. The Inspector had found that the expensive repair work necessary to ensure the preservation of the building would need to be so extensive that much of the original workmanship and character of the rubble walling would be lost and the historic and architectural value of the building would be considerably diminished. There appears to be no use for the building even if repaired or converted.

In the *High Head Castle, Ivegill* case,[40] referred to above, the cost of consolidating the shell of the Georgian wing of the building was estimated to be approximately £100,000 by English Heritage. In addition, English Heritage also agreed in principle to grant aiding an approved programme of repairs. The Inspector found the Georgian wing of High Head Castle had a "particular quality" and the Secretary of State accepted the Inspector's conclusions and recommendations that listed building consent for the demolition of the Georgian wing of the castle be refused.

(c) Evidential considerations

4.49   Consideration should also be given to what in fact constitutes admissible evidence of cost and economic value.

In the case at Bridport[41] it was said that the alternative to the demolition of the buildings was to provide the access to the south of the buildings,

[36] APP/E5900/E/86/801505—1987.
[37] Note the discussion at 4.03 regarding the use of presumptions.
[38] See the reference to the Mansion House Square case at 4.53.
[39] SW/P/5155/270/9, September 9, 1985.
[40] PNW/51/65/270/20, October 23, 1985. See also para. 4.30.
[41] *Planning Appeals*, Vol. 1, p. 141. Ref. SW(P) 5191/270/23.

although this would "add to the cost of the scheme to an unacceptable degree". What is an acceptable and what is an unacceptable degree?

Some guidance is available on how evidence as to cost and the economic value should be presented. Consent was sought for the demolition of the Royal Oak Public House, Biggleswade.[42] The estimated cost of repair and adaptation put forward were not related to specific proposals but were based on an estimated cost per square metre and differed widely. The Inspector doubted the use of estimates on that basis for the sort of work required. There were obvious difficulties of comparability where the rate per square metre was based on what had been the rate elsewhere. Consent was granted.

Similarly, in an appeal against the refusal of the Borough of Hove to give consent to demolish 1–6 Victoria Terrace, Hove,[43] the Inspector, after considering the merits of the buildings, turned his attention to financial matters. Whilst he did not disagree with the manner in which estimated costs for rendering the buildings sound for their previous uses had been deduced, he did not fully accept the financial implications drawn on behalf of the appellants. He identified the estimated costs for normal refurbishment as consisting of maintenance work to keep any such accommodation in a reasonable condition and improvement works which would enhance the property beyond its former standards. He considered that most of the items of expenditure ought to be disregarded in assessing any additional costs necessarily incurred due to the age and type of construction of the buildings. In addition, the costs included items extending beyond what he considered necessary to preserve the most important historic visual qualities of the buildings. The costs of refurbishment directly attributable to the retention of historic features were thus likely to be considerably less than those proposed on behalf of the appellants, so much so that he was not convinced that alternative accommodation in a new structure of a similar scale and standard would be appreciably different in cost. He concluded that the possibilities of retaining the buildings had not been fully explored and was unconvinced that their demolition ought, out of economic necessity, to be permitted. He therefore recommended refusal of consent and the Secretary of State agreed.

An appeal against the decision of Erewash Borough Council to refuse **4.50** listed building consent for the demolition of the Elim Pentecostal Church, Ilkeston, Derbyshire[44] was heard in 1986. The Inspector concluded that despite the deterioration in the condition of the church it was nevertheless a building of some importance worthy of efforts to preserve. Complete refurbishment would be costly. A figure for refurbishment costs of between £80,000 and £90,000 was dismissed by the Inspector as unreasonable since immediate and complete refurbishment was not essential and it was likely that the building could be safely occupied and brought into use for significantly less expenditure. The recent structural survey and planning application to convert the church to craft workshop/retail use with an offer of £25,000 for the building (at 1986 prices) supported the Inspector's view. Even modest repairs were beyond the means of the applicants but that was not sufficient in itself to justify demolition. Erewash Borough Council indicated that they would be flexible in considering alternative uses for the

---

[42] *Planning Appeals*, Vol. 3, p. 257. Ref. APP/5214/E/76/120.
[43] *Planning Appeals*, Vol. 3, p. 256. Ref. APP/5205/E/76/138, SE/1239/270/49.
[44] APP/N1025/E/85/801031, August 1, 1986.

building. In the circumstances the Secretary of State accepted the Inspector's conclusions and the appeal against the refusal of listed building consent for demolition was dismissed.

It is submitted that if these are the conclusions which were to be drawn from these cases, then they depart from reality. An owner of a listed building cannot say to his contractor: "Ignore the costs necessarily incurred due to the age and type of construction of the buildings; only present me with an estimate which will keep the accommodation in reasonable condition." Indeed, PPG 15 does not say this. It says that the Secretary of State would expect authorities to address the following when considering applications for consent to demolition: "the condition of the building, the cost of repairing and maintaining it in relation to its importance and to the value derived from its continued use".[45]

8. ECONOMIC FACTORS—CONCLUSIONS

4.51   It is not easy to draw conclusions, but it is suggested that the following is the present interpretation of the law in relation to the application of economic factors to the determination of a LBC application:

(1) Economic factors are relevant in making a planning decision.

(2) Economic factors have always been considered as relevant in determining LBC applications (by both the Secretary of State and the Courts).

(3) The lack of financial viability on conversion for re-use of a listed building is a criterion which might lead to a consent.

(4) One test of financial viability after conversion for re-use is whether there will be an economically beneficial use—if there will not be this would be a criterion which might lead to consent.

(5) The arguments for demolition are reinforced if the replacement building proposed will be appropriate in the street scene.

(6) Lack of financial viability is, on its own, not necessarily a reason for consent, nor is it an overriding factor.

(7) The financial benefit likely to accrue from development may be taken into account.

(8) If the cost of reinstatement is similar to that of erection of a new building, it seems that LBC will not normally be granted if there are sound commercial prospects for the restored premises.

(9) No consent is likely to be forthcoming unless:

  (a) every effort has been made to continue the existing or to find a suitable alternative use, and;

  (b) usually evidence is forthcoming that the freehold has been offered for sale on the open market—without success, *i.e.* no sale, or offers, at very low prices—well below the market value had the property not been listed.

(10) On the admissibility of evidence of cost and economic value, the following conclusions emerge from an analysis of the cases discussed above:

  (a) The estimated costs of refurbishing the building in issue are

---

[45] PPG 15, para. 3.19(i).

relevant but a global estimate based on a per square metre cost is not acceptable.

(b) The additional costs incurred due to the age and type of construction of the building are material but may be ignored dependant upon the circumstances of the case.

(c) Only the cost of maintenance work to keep accommodation in a reasonable condition should be considered (and not the desirable extras).

(d) Improvement works which would enhance the property beyond its standard at the time of the application should be ignored.

9. ALTERNATIVE USES FOR THE SITE

"New uses may often be the key to a building's or an area's preservation, **4.52** and control over land use, density, plot ratio, daylighting and other planning matters should be exercisable sympathetically where this would enable a historic building or area to be given a new lease of life. The Secretary of State is not generally in favour of tightening development controls or changes of use as a specific instrument of conservation policy. He considers that in general the same provision on change of use should apply to historic buildings as to all others. Patterns of economic activity inevitably change over time, and it would be unrealistic to seek to prevent such change by the use of planning controls."[46]

There had been some uncertainty prior to PPG 15 as to whether or not this is a valid criterion, but it was accepted by the Secretary of State in dealing with an application for demolition of a listed building in the Banbury Town Centre Conservation Area. Planning permission had been given by the former Oxfordshire County Council in January 1974 for redevelopment of the site containing a Victorian building with a new terraced office building. This building was subsequently listed along with many others in the conservation area. The appeal related to the demolition of the listed building. The Inspector felt the proposal should be considered in the light of the criteria set out in Circular 61/68 (later 8/87). In this respect he noted that the building was listed not because of special architectural importance, but because of its group value. Concerning the proposed replacement building, the Inspector thought that this would "be in harmony with its setting and would form an unobtrusive unit within the row of old buildings . . . unlike the existing one . . . it would occupy the full width of its curtilage, and by closing the only gap in the row of buildings would turn this into an uninterrupted terrace. Whilst the existing house is obtrusive and disrupts the continuity of the row, the proposal would be of a design and materials in sympathy with those of the adjacent buildings". He recommended that LBC for demolition be granted, and the Secretary of State agreed with him.[47]

The Inspector's decision letter in the *Mansion House Square* case[48] and **4.53** the later opinions of the House of Lords clearly established that a replacement building may be a material consideration when the merits of alterna-

[46] PPG 15, para. 2.18.
[47] Ref. APP/5352/E/76/1.
[48] 1990 J.P.L., p. 831.

tive proposals for a site are considered; a subject which now falls within sub-paragraph (iii) of paragraph 3.19 of PPG 15. The Inspector in the *Mansion House Square* case noted that the Secretary of State had advised in Circular 8/87 that any alternative use for a site was one of the criteria which may have proved helpful when applications for listed building consent to demolish or alter listed buildings were considered. He said:

> "When as here the particular use proposed is closely expressed in architectural form I do not see that it is practicable to give full attention to that criterion without considering the qualities of the building in which the use is to be carried on. The criterion goes on to refer to the question of whether the use of the site for some public purpose would make it possible to enhance the environment, so introducing a further consideration of the effects of what is proposed to replace the listed building. I see no particular reason why that consideration should be limited to proposed uses for some public purpose or why it should not be extended in appropriate circumstances, so as to include the effects on the environment of other kinds of uses.
>
> A consequence of the line of reasoning which I have set out may well be that if it can be shown that the proposed replacement is likely to be of higher quality than what exists, even though what exists may well be recognised statutorily as having special architectural or historic interest, it may nevertheless be right for consent for demolition to be granted."

The House of Lords approved this statement.[49]

The PPG 15 deals with the subject of the merits of alternative proposals for a site (where demolition of listed buildings is proposed). It accepts that these are a material consideration, but explains in paragraph 3.19(iii) that the "subjective claims for the architectural merits of proposed replacement buildings should not in themselves be held to justify the demolition of any listed building".

This statement has been widely interpreted as being evidence that the *Mansion House Square* case should be seen as a unique exception rather than a precedent.

The alternative uses for the building

4.54   The importance of any alternative use for the building is clearly a significant criterion in decision making. Norfolk County Council wanted to extend their law courts, by a partial demolition of one building and complete demolition of granaries at the rear of the court complex.[50] The Inspector considered these granaries outdated. He said: "I cannot see them serving any future useful purpose. With the small openings, low ceiling heights, great depth of structure, there is little prospect of conversion to domestic or office use."He accepted that the present courts were inadequate and that new ones should be built, and LBC for demolition of the granaries was

---

[49] *Mansion House Square* case, *Save Britain's Heritage v. Number 1 Poultry Ltd and others* (1991) 1 W.L.R. 153, 1990, 2 All E.R. 10 (House of Lords).
[50] *Planning Appeals*, Vol. 1, p. 143. Ref. SE6/1278/411/1.

granted. However, this principle cannot successfully be invoked unless it can be shown that all possibilities of disposal have been fully explored.

Eastleigh Borough Council wanted to demolish a house and outbuildings in Leigh Row, Eastleigh.[51] The Inspector concluded that although there were no clearly agreed alternative uses for the buildings apart from rehabilitation of the farm house for some form of residential accommodation and the continuation of storage use of the barn, it was impossible to believe that alternative uses would not readily emerge in the future. In his opinion, retention of the buildings would not frustrate possible future plans for the extension of the civic centre and the buildings could, if restored, provide a valuable adjunct to it. He recommended that consent should not be given, and the Secretary of State agreed.

In December 1990, the Secretary of State accepted the recommendations of his Inspector that an appeal should be allowed against the refusal of Thamesdown Borough Council to grant planning permission in a Conservation Area for the rebuilding with extensions of the Mechanics Institute, Emlyn Square, Swindon,[52] for use as a hotel, and listed building consent for the partial demolition and the rebuilding with extensions of the Institute. The Secretary of State accepted that the continuation of the original use of the Mechanics Institute was no longer a practicable option and that the use of the Institute as a hotel was appropriate. Given the poor state of the repair of the building and the lack of positive alternative proposals which would be sufficiently effective in securing the restoration, refurbishment and future maintenance of the building, the Secretary of State accepted that the proposed scheme would be the best means of securing the long term future of the listed building and granted permission and listed building consent.

It should be remembered that there are a number of commercial publi- **4.55** cations offering a service for those endeavouring to dispose of historic buildings. These are in place of the quarterly list formerly produced by the Historic Buildings Bureau. Such information exchanges are important and were significant in a case in Scotland where the congregational board of the Allan Park South Church was refused LBC for the demolition of the church in Stirling.[53] The board appealed and served a listed buildings purchase notice on the local planning authority, Stirling District Council. The grounds of the appeal were that since the amalgamation of the congregations of South and Allan Park Churches in 1970, the South Church building had become surplus to requirements. Up to that time the appellants held that the church had been maintained, and had been widely advertised for sale. Several enquiries were received which were referred to the then planning authority, Stirling Town Council, which informed them that it would probably require any prospective developer to make provision for vehicle parking, loading and unloading. At no time were enquirers informed by the local planning authority that the building was listed, and the appellants were also oblivious of this fact. However, dry rot was detected in the upper hall of the church, so an application for consent to demolish was made, and only then did the Church Board discover the property was listed. The local planning authority submitted that they considered the church to

---

[51] *Planning Appeals*, Vol. 3, p. 254. Ref. SE2/1070/270/2.
[52] 1991 J.P.L. p. 997.
[53] *Planning Appeals*, Vol. 2, pp. 260/261. Ref. HB/PN/CC/1. *Scottish Development Department.*

be a good example of Gothick Revival architecture, and their main reason for refusal was that they thought the church to be of considerable architectural merit and high townscape value. While accepting that the church had been advertised for sale, they pointed out that the services of the Historic Buildings Bureau, despite being brought to the attention of the Church Board, had not been utilised. The building had been listed in 1965 and notification to the owners had been carried out by the Scottish Development Department. The Reporter recognised the architectural qualities of the Church, which he considered to be a good but not outstanding example of its category. Together with its townscape value, this made him feel that further efforts should be made to secure its preservation, and he did not consider that the owners had been deprived of reasonably beneficial use of land without a further round of advertisements being undertaken and the services of the Historic Buildings Bureau being enlisted. He therefore recommended that the appeal be dismissed and that the listed building purchase notice be not confirmed, with which view the Secretary of State concurred.

4.56   An application by Oyston Limited of Blackpool for listed building consent to demolish Ilex Mill, Bacup Road, Rawtenstall[54] was called in by the Secretary of State for the Environment following an inquiry into the application.

In his report to the Secretary of State the Inspector found that although the mill had suffered long periods without adequate maintenance, the mill, despite its defects, was not unsafe or unstable and that it could be refurbished given adequate finance. Although the cost of repairing and maintaining the building could be high, the Inspector was not satisfied that sufficient investigation of possible alternative uses had been carried out. In addition the property had not been adequately marketed. In the circumstances the Inspector recommended that listed building consent be refused and the Secretary of State accepted the Inspector's recommendation.

In March 1987, the Secretary of State for the Environment accepted the recommendation of his Inspector who had reported on an application by Wood Mac Limited for listed building consent for the demolition of Robinwood Mill, Burnley Road, Todmorden.[55] The Inspector recommended that listed building consent for demolition be refused. The mill was in reasonably sound structural condition as reflected in the high quality of the architectural and engineering design, the high standard of workmanship achieved in its construction and selection of building materials. The mill itself had an elegant and outstanding architectural distinction. It had historical associations with figures of local importance and offered scope for either full or partial conversion. In refusing listed building consent for the demolition of the mill, the Secretary of State stressed that he would not be prepared to grant consent for the demolition of the listed building unless he was satisfied that every possible effort had been made to continue the present use or to find a suitable alternative use. On the evidence which had been presented at the inquiry, the Secretary of State was satisfied that there was still a reasonable possibility that the building could be preserved and an alternative use found which would not spoil the mill's historic integrity.

4.57   Although the importance of alternative use is a criterion) it is not (in the same way that the economic aspect is not the overriding criterion) the only

---

[54] PNW/5296/344/2, March 31, 1987.
[55] YH/5112/270/141, March 2, 1987.

158

criterion, nor an overwhelming consideration. Finding an alternative use does not automatically mean that preservation will follow. With regard to barns, for example, Essex County Council, in 1985, went so far as to advise that it would no longer be permissible to convert historic barns for housing in that county.[56] We should be wary of "adapting unsuitable buildings for unnecessary uses". These were the words of the Inspector in a case where the Secretary of State was considering applications by the City of Kingston upon Hull for consent to demolish a listed building and 18 unlisted buildings within the Old Town Conservation Area, Hull.[57] The Inspector held that whilst it would be physically possible to build a court complex (which was the purpose of the planning application) and retain the application buildings, he was of the opinion that decayed and derelict buildings of uncertain life could hardly be retained in close proximity to a major prestige project and would prejudice the courts in carrying out their function with dignity in their proper setting. Chapel Lane, he said, presented itself as a narrow back lane, lined with decaying, inferior, industrial premises of unattractive appearance and lacking any form of appeal. Had it not been in a conservation area he considered that it was most unlikely that anyone would have taken notice of it. After considering the views of objectors the Inspector concluded that adapting unsuitable buildings for unnecessary uses instead of providing modern purpose-built accommodation was not likely to encourage organic growth and would not serve the true aims of conservation. The Secretary of State agreed with the Inspector's recommendation that consent be granted for the demolition of the majority of the unlisted buildings.

10. CHURCHES

Churches represent a particularly interesting and perhaps difficult prob- **4.58** lem and are dealt with in more detail in Chapter 10. Because a church is such a purpose-built structure it may well be that the finest features, those most worthy of preservation, are those which would conflict directly with secular use, and this may justify consent to demolish. In September 1988 the Secretary of State for the Environment, on a called in application, granted LBC for the partial demolition of the Baptist Church and other buildings on South Street, Yeovil. The case for the preservation of the entire church rested upon the quality of and possibilities for preserving its interior. However, whilst the interior was good, it was not remarkable, unusual or exceptional. The Secretary of State accepted that there was no alternative use which could be found which would preserve the church's interior intact. There were problems in identifying an alternative use which would retain the church in good order and problems associated with the treatment of dry rot. In the circumstances, the Secretary of State concluded that exceptional circumstances existed which would warrant a departure from his normal policy and LBC was granted.[58]

An application was made to demolish St. Cuthbert's Church and Presby-

---

[56] *English Heritage Monitor* (1986), p. 8.
[57] *Planning Appeals*, Vol. 3, p. 256. Ref. YH/5267/270/17P.
[58] SW/P/5367/270/358 [Sept. 1988].

tery and an adjacent house in Bedford Street, North Shields.[59] The Inspector considered that the arched sanctuary, lancet windows and a cornice, would conflict with any secular use, and yet if they were covered up or removed the objective of preservation would be defeated. With its strong ecclesiastical character the building would be unacceptable and incongruous as premises for a social club. The Inspector found it difficult to justify the estimated expenditure to reinstate the church which he did not think of sufficient architectural or historic character to warrant retention at any cost. In addition, there appeared to have been no interest shown in the church from any religious organisation since religious services ceased, and there were other disused churches in the area. He recommended the grant of LBC to demolish and the Secretary of State agreed.

There also seems to be a feeling of the need to retain the dignity of a church building, and the suggestion that demolition may be preferable to the indignity of the proposed alternative. North East Derbyshire District Council had applied to the Secretary of State for consent to demolish the former Methodist Church on land at High Street, Eckington.[60] The former chapel in its present condition was considered by the Inspector to be of limited interest with the proposed inner relief road alignment detracting from its setting. Putting aside the question of the road proposals, he was not convinced that, on balance, the expenditure of substantial public funds was justified to restore the building externally and to convert it internally for any foreseeable use. The uses suggested were, in most cases, incompatible with the residential nature of the area and would cause problems with regard to vehicular access and parking. In addition, many uses he considered to be incompatible with the dignity that a preserved chapel and family monument should warrant. In his opinion, a major change in the road alignment to preserve some setting for the building was unwarranted and he therefore recommended grant of consent, with which view the Secretary of State agreed.

11. REPLACEMENT, REPLICA AND PASTICHE

4.59   LBC may, as we have seen, be granted subject to conditions, one of which may be in respect of the reconstruction of the building or any part of it following the execution of any works, with the use of original materials so far as practicable, and with such alterations of the interior of the building as may be specified in conditions.[61] The growth in interest in buildings of special architectural or historic interest has led to intense debates on questions of replacements and replicas and whether they should be encouraged or discouraged following the grant of listed building consent for demolition.

Indeed, such interest has even resulted in a philosophical debate being aired in an appeal decision in respect of students' accommodation at an Oxford College. This particular case raised the issue of whether a replica facade to replace a demolished building in the sensitive St. Aldate's area in

[59] *Planning Appeals*, Vol. 3, p. 254. Ref. EMP/5173/270/4.
[60] *Planning Appeals*, Vol. 3, p. 254. Ref. EMP/5173/270/4.
[61] LBA 1990, s.17(1)(c).

Oxford[62] was desirable. On balance, it was decided that the best solution was for a well designed modern building to act as a replacement.

However, there are a number of points arising from consideration of these issues which merit further investigation and discussion.

(a) Rehabilitation versus replacement

The first and basic issue arises with the consideration of whether a listed **4.60** building should be retained and rehabilitated or replaced. Naturally, such decisions are not reached without considerable detailed argument about the architectural or historic interest of the building in question and whether its replacement is justified for a multiplicity of planning, land use, amenity or design reasons.

However, such decisions are becoming increasingly difficult to reach because the choice is not often so simple, given the weight attached to the arguments of facadism, replica and pastiche which are increasingly introduced into the debate.

The comparable economic cost of reinstatement of an existing listed building and a replacement building arose in 1987 relating to an application by the parochial church council of St. Peter's Church, Redcar, for listed building consent for the demolition of the church.[63] The Inspector concluded that it would be feasible for the building to be restored and used again as a church subject to the funds being available to carry out the necessary works including future maintenance. The Inspector indicated that due regard should be paid to the economic value of the building when repaired and to any saving through not having to provide alternative accommodation in a new building. The overall cost of £250,000 at 1986 prices would provide only a very basic church and more money would be required to provide an adequate standard of building. The cost of erecting a new church could well approach the cost of carrying out works which were initially necessary to put the existing church into a sound structural condition. Despite the fact that the maintenance costs of a new church were likely to be considerably lower than for the existing church the Inspector concluded that:

> "I do not consider that the financial benefits that seem likely to arise from the rebuilding of the church would outweigh the loss of the church as an important listed building and as a building of townscape interest in Redcar."

The Secretary of State accepted the Inspector's recommendations that LBC for demolition be refused.

An application for LBC to demolish 7 London Road, Kimbolton, Huntingdon was called in by the Secretary of State in 1984.[64] The Inspector who held a local inquiry into the application concluded that the cottage was an important element in the street scene which merited its listing and if possible ought to be preserved. The Inspector was satisfied that the building's

---

[62] APP/5363/e/82/260 SE.
[63] N/5152/270p/31(2), June 17, 1987.
[64] E1/5140/411/10, December 18, 1984.

structure could be repaired, stabilised and preserved at a reasonable cost which would be substantially less than the cost of a replacement building.

"Allowing for only the mandatory grant aid which would be available, I consider that renovation along the lines suggested . . . would be an economically viable proposition."

The Secretary of State for the Environment agreed with the Inspector's conclusions, accepted his recommendation and refused LBC for the demolition.

(b) Facades

4.61   At first blush, the retention of a facade of a listed building, which is often the most visible and therefore arguably the most important element of the building, represents an attractive solution. Its retention would often result in minimal disruption to the street scene and the townscape would therefore remain largely unaltered. However, notwithstanding the technical difficulties which often arise with solutions designed to retain facades, it raises a number of fundamental issues. Should the facade remain listed or does the loss of the original building devalue it to such an extent that it should no longer be worthy of listing? Does the new building attached to the facade automatically become listed because of its attachment? Does a single wall facade constitute a sufficiently significant element of the original building or should a greater proportion of the building be retained, e.g. facade and one room depth? In September 1984, the Secretary of State for the Environment allowed the appeals by J. Smith and Sons (Clerkenwell) Limited against the decision of the London Borough of Islington to refuse listed building consent for the partial demolition of 49–52 St John's Square and 8 Jerusalem Passage, London.[65] The Secretary of State took account of his Inspector's comments that it was inconceivable that the buildings would be of any use to any one in their present form and that to continue in any kind of way they must be altered once again. Major alterations were necessary to the internal layout of the application properties. The Secretary of State concluded that while the financial value of the buildings and their potential for future use may not have been tested on the open market, the valuation must reflect the considerable cost to any prospective buyer of the need to carry out extensive works to provide an adequate internal layout. The Secretary of State was prepared to allow the applicant's appeals and granted LBC and planning permission for the demolition of the properties behind their facades.

If facades are considered an acceptable solution or compromise, it begs the question as to whether the facade is preserved throughout the construction period of the new building behind or whether it should be dismantled and re-erected at the end of the construction taking place so as to ensure that it is not damaged by repair. This may of course raise the question as to whether any part of the building would then be listed. We believe that if the facade of the building has remained "the building" could remain listed

[65] APP/V5570/A/83/009474
APP/V5570/E/83/8000, September 28, 1984.

which will include its extension, but this would depend both on the quantity which remains and its quality.

(c) Replicas

If it is not possible or desirable to retain the original facade or building, it **4.62** may be possible to propose a replica of the original, which for the purposes of the continuity of the street scene or the retention of an important landmark, may merit some consideration. An application by National Provident Institution for listed building consent to demolish and reconstruct numbers 12 and 10 Garden Street, Tunbridge Wells was called in by the Secretary of State in 1987.[66] The Inspector appointed to hold an inquiry into the application stated:

> "The properties had very serious structural defects. . . . There was unlikely to be any financial advantage . . . in the proposal to demolish and reconstruct the application building compared to any attempt to renovate it."

The Inspector felt that the proposal to demolish and reconstruct was not an indication of a casual attitude on the part of the applicants to the value of listed buildings but was the only practicable means of preserving the appearance of the building and its contribution to the street scene. The likely cost of preservation without recourse to demolition would be in the order of £90,000 (at 1987 prices). This would be of the same order as the figure for demolition and reconstruction. The Secretary of State accepted the Inspector's recommendation that listed building consent be granted for the demolition of the application properties.

However, for many reasons the introduction of a replica does not always find support. In the eyes of some, there are no sound or logical reasons why a new building should be a replica of an original. The proposed new building has often been designed to perform a different function from the building which it is to replace and is very likely to benefit from modern design and construction techniques which bear no relation to those used on the original building. More important is the relationship of a replica elevation to the internal layout, floor levels, etc. The integrity of a building is lost if the two do not work together. For all these reasons a replica is often regarded as merely a pastiche and undesirable.

These issues were carefully considered in an appeal decision involving the erection of replacement flats at Haverstock Hill in the London Borough of Camden. The Inspector concluded that the rehabilitation of the buildings to be demolished which dated from 1820 and were in a conservation area would be too expensive due to the condition and layout of the buildings. He was of the opinion that the replacement building was satisfactory and he rejected contentions that the existing structure was a "local landmark building" and that the proposals were a pastiche. He considered that the design proposed, which was clearly 20th-century, satisfactorily respected the scale and proportions of the surroundings.[67]

---

[66] SE2/5285/270/130
  SE2/5285/411/4, June 22, 1987.
[67] APP/X5210/A/84/021565.

4.63   In another case affecting former terrace houses in Lombard Street, Birmingham, an appeal was lodged against the refusal of listed building consent to demolish these Grade II listed buildings. The Inspector identified the issue to be determined as whether the condition of the properties, their setting and the possible value and use of the buildings, would justify the works necessary for their preservation. There was said to be an extensive amount of rebuilding involved if these former cottages were to be renovated. The area in which these buildings were located was mainly devoted to industrial uses, and the intention by the appellants was to clear the buildings and create an area for off-street car-parking.

The Inspector received evidence of the costs involved in the restoration and the amount of reconstruction and repair which would be required to bring these buildings back to a useable condition. He concluded that the preservation of these buildings would result in general with a copy only, not serving any useful purpose, and standing out as a sham frontage in alien surroundings. He believed the dilapidated buildings had reached that state through their basic weakness of construction rather than deliberate neglect of their owners, and that these structures had reached the end of their reasonable life.

He allowed the appeal and granted listed building consent for the demolition of the building and clearance of the area for off-street car-parking.[68]

However, in a case where the owners of the Hackney Empire had demolished the hall's ornate twin domes without consent, but had offered to replace them with glass fibre substitutes, they were ordered to restore them as closely as possible to the originals at a likely cost (at 1984 prices) in excess of £200,000. Clearly the importance of the materials used and the method of construction was a major consideration in this decision even though it is feasible that the glass fibre substitutes could have been designed to have an almost identical appearance to the originals. Thus it appears that the integrity of the original building in this case was of an overriding importance.[69]

In these instances the introduction of a replica would have been likely to maintain the architectural interest, but it is doubtful whether the "historic interest" would have been maintained to the same degree in a replica building for the simple reason that such interest largely disappears if the original building is changed. The only common factor which remains is the geographical location and this is much less interesting than the actual house where the great man lived or worked or where the treaty was signed. In any event in London the point could be made by a blue plaque.

(d) Dismantling buildings

4.64   On the other hand, it would be possible to dismantle an "historic" listed building and re-erect it elsewhere, but the loss of its true geographic location would also devalue it in no small measure. The same objections could be raised about re-erecting a building which is listed for its "architectural" interest, although this is not likely to diminish to the same degree if

[68] T/APP/P4605/E/91/807757/p. 8, September 17, 1991. 1992, J.P.L. p. 492.
[69] Reported in the *Evening Standard*, July 31, 1984.

such a building was relocated. The careful demolition of the building would not necessarily result in it being delisted.[70]

Undoubtedly the biggest and most important loss involved with dismantling and re-erecting listed buildings is the original "setting" of the building in question,[71] which is often almost impossible to recreate.

Nevertheless, the dismantling of a listed building for re-erection elsewhere does constitute a more acceptable solution than the loss of the building altogether, but it is not our role to adjudicate between the relative merits of replacement, replica or relocation.[72] The proposed demolition of the stable block and icehouse at Eaton Hall Works, Eaton, near Congleton is illustrative of the relevance of an existing planning permission affecting the site upon which listed buildings are situated and their settings. In that case the Grade II listed buildings were situated on a site which effectively prevented the excavation by Tilcon Limited of sand with a value on the open market of £50 million. In his report to the Secretary of State, the Inspector made particular reference to the fact that there were compelling reasons for the removal of the listed buildings from their site and not only because of the incompatibility of their continued presence with the legitimate commercial activity of Tilcon Limited for which planning permission existed. The fact that the stables continued to exist *in situ* after the planning permission had been granted was largely due to Tilcon's compliance with the local authority's request to delay demolition. The Inspector thought that Tilcon's actions in this respect were a matter to which some weight should be attached.[72a]

(e) Reinstatement of parts

An example of this was put forward in respect of Queen's Hotel, Micklegate, York,[73] where an application for LBC to demolish Nos. 3 to 5 Micklegate, York, was granted subject to conditions which in effect provided for the replacement of the original interior fittings and a replica elevation. **4.65**

In another case a condition was imposed that certain specific features should be salvaged. Medway Ports Authority applied for consent to demolish the early nineteenth century Quadrangle Storehouse, Sheerness Dockyard, to allow construction of a container terminal.[74] The Inspector was convinced that the continued prosperity of the Port and the Isle of Sheppey would be best served by allowing the redevelopment. The Secretary of State agreed, subject to the building's clock tower being carefully dismantled and re-erected on a site to be agreed with the Swale District Council. He

---

[70] R. v. Leominster D C, ex p. Antique Country Buildings Ltd et al (1988), J.P.L., p. 554.

[71] LBA 1990, s.16(2).

[72] It is worth noting that the late Lord Clark in his autobiography: The Other Half (John Murray (1977), p. 171) notes of Japanese buildings in Nara: "many of these buildings are extremely ancient, eighth or ninth century, but as the Japanese very sensibly remake their old buildings every fifty years or so, imitating exactly the originals, they look quite new."

[72A] APP/CO630/E/85/800906, October 30, 1987.

[73] APP/5353/E/82/260(SE).

[74] Planning Appeals, Vol. 3, p. 259. Ref. SE2/1527/270/5 and SE2/1527/422/1.

requested that consideration be given to the careful salvage and safekeeping of any materials such as doors, window frames, Yorkshire floor slabs, cast iron beams, etc., which might be capable of use in the area for display in a maritime museum or other suitable location.

The National Trust has recently been engaged in restoring Uppark House, Sussex as closely as possible to its former condition prior to the disastrous fire in August 1989. The work involved the complete reconstruction of the gutted upper part of the house, including the recreation in replica of the first floor rooms. As much of the original fabric at ground floor level as possible has been retained, particularly the old floor beams in the principal rooms. The aim of the National Trust has been to use traditional materials and methods as far as reasonably possible.

When the house was first built it was likely to have had a roof tiled in red tiles. However, the outer roof surfaces had over time been renewed at different times and with different slates. The roof will henceforth be clad completely with Delabole slates.[75]

12. CONCLUSIONS

4.66   It is suggested that the following may reflect recent trends in the law and practice in relation to replacements, replicas and pastiches:

(1) As a first assumption, it should be established that the building was at the time of the listing properly listed and remains properly listed.

(2) What is the result of the proposed work; does it amount to an application for demolition, alteration or extension or materially to affect the building?

(3) Probably in all cases mentioned above, it will amount to a demolition of part in view of the present state of the cases on demolition.

(4) Thus LBC will be required.

(5) It is proper for the LPA to impose conditions on the LBC: the broad provisions in section 17(1) LBA 1990 will be applicable as to preservation of particular features, the making good of any damage caused to the building by the works, and the reconstruction of the building or any part of it with the use of original materials and with such alterations to the interior of the building as may be specified.

(6) Thus all the works specified in paragraphs 4.30–4.38 above could be, and often are, incorporated as conditions to an LBC.

(7) It must follow that the building remains a listed building following the works.

(8) The question then will arise as to whether, after the works have been carried out, the building remains of listable quality. There could be serious arguments as to whether it does.

(9) To do the work in the absence of an LBC could well be a criminal offence, as well as potentially giving rise to an enforcement notice; so the moral must be to obtain the LBC first. There is no provision in the LBA to enable an applicant to obtain a view of the local planning authority as to whether LBC is required.

(10) Thereafter there is no reason why the application to de-list should

[75] *Country Life*, February 20, 1992.

not be made, on the ground that there is new evidence that the building is not (now) of listable quality.

(11) A prudent landowner who sees no advantage in his reconstructed building being listed might well be advised to apply quickly for a certificate of immunity after reconstruction.

13. LOCAL AUTHORITIES

The principle that local authorities have special responsibility to take a **4.67** lead in historic building conservation is carried through into practice. In the case of the Town Hall of Buckingham which the owner, Aylesbury Vale District Council, wished to demolish, consent was refused by the Secretary of State.[76] Here local authority ownership was a significant factor in the refusal. Having commented on the architectural townscape qualities of the building, its role in the social life of the area, the fact that there were no proposals to replace the building, the Inspector expressed the view that the county council's and objectors' repair estimates were more realistic than those of the applicants. The Inspector commented:

"Whilst the obligations of owners of listed buildings are clear and planning authorities are given sanctions to enforce them, local authorities who are themselves owners of listed buildings have been given advice on their special responsibilities in the example which they set to other owners. It was pointed out that there had been some flagrant cases of demolition of buildings in local authority ownership."

Consent to demolish was refused.

An example of a case of wilful or deliberate neglect which was called in by the Secretary of State for the Environment in August 1985 related to an application by Toddington Parish Council for listed building consent for the demolition of the Toddington Town Hall,[77] Bedfordshire. In his report to the Secretary of State the Inspector referred to both the architectural and historic qualities of the Town Hall and noted that:

" . . . a considerable amount of the original medieval timber-framed building remains intact. The ancient fabric is not so far defective that it could not be repaired, and if such repairs were undertaken the opportunity would present itself to restore traditional features lost during earlier works."

The Inspector found that the Town Hall made a vital contribution to the groupings of historic buildings enclosing the village green. The Inspector commented upon the neglected condition of the listed building:

"The Parish Council have spent little money on the building of late, thereby contributing to its rate of deterioration and ensuring no great prospect of reoccupation. Such continued neglect must surely advance the demise of the Town Hall if it is not halted. The Town Hall is a

[76] *Planning Appeals*, Vol. 2, pp. 258/259. Ref. E1/5132/270/41/Pt II
[77] E1/5125/411/2, August 21, 1985.

listed building prominently positioned in a conservation area, and as such is part of the nation's heritage. For a publicly elected body to neglect this asset, and seek to secure its demolition, when alternative courses of action are open is reprehensible."

The Town Hall was not structurally unsafe and the Secretary of State accepted his Inspector's recommendation that listed building consent for demolition be refused.

A similar case, which has already been discussed at paragraph 4.34 above, is that of Lutterworth Hall, Leicestershire, where the local authority, as owner of the building, was criticised for setting a bad example by allowing the building to deteriorate. This view was also followed in the earlier case of Yeovil District Council (mentioned at paragraph 4.30 above) when the Inspector (supported by the Secretary of State) commented: "The council should accept the consequences of their previous policy (however well-intentioned) and, by repairing the building in the same manner as would be expected by a private owner, set an example to others."

4.68   Paragraph 3.37 of PPG 15 deals with the listed buildings in the ownership of local authorities, and the Secretary of State asks authorities to deal with their own buildings in ways which will provide examples of good practice to other owners. It concludes in 3.38 by stating that the Secretary of State will not be disposed to grant consent for the demolition of listed buildings in authorities' ownership unless there is clear and convincing evidence that alternative possibilities for new ownership and new uses have been thoroughly explored.

That advice extends to alterations to listed buildings owned by local authorities. The Town Hall in Pontypool was listed for its special architectural or historic interest, and without prior consent the Council—as owners—replaced the former timber-framed windows by UPVC framed windows. The Inspector who conducted a public inquiry, in October 1982, described the building before it had undergone the alterations as "an outstandingly handsome building". The style and materials of the replacement windows was said to be "so unacceptable that they have seriously harmed the character and appearance of the listed building". The Inspector considered the works were in conflict with national and Structure and Local Plan policies and were alien to the building's character. He recommended listed building consent be refused and the Secretary of State agreed.

Apart from the architectural merits of the case, the Inspector refused to be drawn into a comparative cost exercise, but restated the duty (which he believed to be widely understood) of owners of listed buildings to preserve the special character of such buildings, even though repair and restoration works might be more expensive than would be the case if the building were not listed. He felt it particularly important that local planning authorities take this attitude themselves and set an example to others. He observed that the CADW guidance letter pointed out that UPVC windows in listed buildings "are almost always unacceptable" and recommended that listed building consent be refused.[78]

The previous advice contained in Circular 8/87 reminded local authorities of the advice given in paragraph 24 of Circular 23/77, concerning

---

[78] APP/35/12, January 18, 1993. J.P.L. June 1993, p. 604–605.

"New Uses for Old Buildings": planning authorities were encouraged to consider relaxation of land use, density and daylighting standards, and other controls where such action would secure a new and viable use for a redundant building; as a starting point to preserve wherever possible the original use, but otherwise promote new uses for redundant buildings, both within their own ownership and those of others; and to make use of, and advise other owners to make use of, the services of the Department's Historic Buildings Bureau (now, the Buildings at Risk Unit of English Heritage) in disposing of such buildings.

The need to apply flexibility when operating the Building Regulations and Fire Regulations in connection with the repair or conversion of historic buildings is repeated in paragraph 3.26 of PPG 15.

The duty of care on the part of a local planning authority in considering an LBC application was interestingly demonstrated in a case considered by the Ombudsman.[79] The Feering and Kelvedon Preservation Society successfully brought an *Ombudsman* case against the Braintree District Council for allowing the demolition of a massive six-octagon shafted 17th-century chimney stack at the White Hart Public House in Kelvedon, Essex, which was listed Grade II. The Ombudsman found maladministration, in that the planning officer accepted the brewery surveyor's opinion of unsafeness without consulting the county council's specialist advice team. The Ombudsman suggested that the council should have obtained it and not merely relied upon the view of the building owner or his professional adviser, however competent.

Local authorities have a duty to facilitate easy and dignified access to all **4.69** buildings, and this applies to historic buildings. Paragraph 3.28 of PPG 15 suggests that if it is treated as part of an integrated review of the access requirements for all visitors or users, and a flexible and pragmatic approach is taken, it should normally be possible to plan suitable access for disabled people without compromising a building's special interest. Alternative routes or re-organising the use of spaces may achieve the desired results without the need for damaging alterations.

This was the subject of an appeal in 1992 when the West Dorset District Council refused listed building consent for a new ramp to be cut into the front steps of a Grade II* listed post office at Bridport in Dorset. The Inspector who considered the appeal had no doubts that the effect of the proposal on the listed building would be unacceptable from an historic buildings point of view. It would destroy the integrity of a complete and particularly fine classical entrance portico by removing central steps which were architecturally and historically vital elements of the building. He addressed the fact that the building was used as a post office to which disabled people would normally expect to have access, but considered these special needs were not such as to override the need to preserve the architectural integrity of the Grade II* listed building.[80] The Secretary of State dismissed this appeal.

---

[79] *Commission for Local Administration in England*, report by the local ombudsman (investigation into Complaint no. INV/262/A/86, Braintree DC). Courtesy of Essex CC Planning Dept.

[80] *Planning Appeal Decisions*, April 1993. APP/F/1230/E/92/808961, November 1992.

14. BALANCING THE FACTORS AND THE PUBLIC INTEREST

4.70   In balancing the factors as to whether or not LBC should be granted, the public interest is relevant.

In 1985, the Secretary of State for the Environment called in an application by Dean Clough Industrial Park Limited for listed building consent to demolish "C" mill on the Dean Clough Industrial Park, Halifax.[81] The Inspector concluded that the application mill was a plain and commonplace mid 19th-century utilitarian industrial building having little intrinsic architectural merit or special historical significance. It was obsolete and was not suitable as it stood for renewed industrial use. The Inspector found that:

> "The cost of upgrading to current standards is well beyond current justification by prospective rental income even if the hurdle of substantial existing surplus of more convenient and better serviced space is discounted. Office use in the face of known surplus of better located spaces is an unrealistic expectation. Residential use of the building in the centre of a low lying historically industrial site, overlooked on all sides, overlooking factory roofs and without private land around it would be contrary to all generally accepted land use principles and housing standards. Viable conversion for squash courts or any other indoor sport of 74,000 square feet of narrow building space fragmented by closely spaced internal columns is beyond the bounds of serious consideration . . . restoration through beneficial use of any sort is not foreseeable."

Later in his report the Inspector said that:

> "The greater weight and clearer public benefit lie with the aims of foreseeable enhancement and improvement of the viability of the complex and generation of new business and job opportunities in the town where the council is convincingly aware of local needs and clearly active in pursuit of ways and means to help satisfy them. Neither aim should be prevented by lack of consent."

The Secretary of State agreed with the Inspector's findings of fact and agreed with his conclusions that LBC to demolish be granted. The Secretary of State said that he was satisfied that no reasonable possibilities for any future use of the "C" mill remained. He took the view that the costs of refurbishment which would be necessary to bring the building up to current industrial standards to enable it to be returned to productive use would not be economically viable and in view of the limited internal space it would be unrealistic to expect that another use would be found for the building.

4.71   In January 1988 the Secretary of State for the Environment was not inclined to accept his Inspector's recommendation that listed building consent for the conversion of the Grade II* St. Wilfrid's Church, Brighton to 24 flats be refused.[82] The Inspector concluded in his report to the Secretary of State that:

[81] YH/5112/270/91P, April 25, 1985.
[82] SE2/5202/270/195
    SE2/5202/411/5 January 1988.

" . . . the external appearance of the church would be significantly changed by the insertion of additional windows, especially those in the roof. . . . The more damaging effect of the scheme would be the extensive sub-division of the main interior space by inserting floors, partitions, stairs and lifts."

The fact that the building was not superficially attractive or immediately appealing did not override the importance of the building as a major work of Goodhart Rendel.

The Secretary of State considered that there were special factors in the case which went further than purely architectural considerations. The building was a striking and dominant feature and any proposal to demolish would not receive the Secretary of State's support. He therefore decided that it would not be desirable to leave the church as it stood without a positive function in the community. Conversion to residential use would provide such a function and much needed housing units. The conversion scheme provided an acceptable compromise between the architectural standing of the church and its potential as a community asset. Listed building consent for conversion was therefore granted.

The Secretary of State's decision to allow Deva Roman Centre Limited to demolish Dee House and other buildings at Little St. John's Street, Chester, was largely due to the importance of the alternative use of the site.[83] The Grade II Dee House was erected partly above the site of a Roman Amphitheatre. The Secretary of State was of the opinion that in order to emphasise the uniqueness of the proposed development the demolition of Dee House would be required. Given the importance of the alternative use of the site the Secretary of State was of the opinion that there were justifiable reasons to override the normal presumption in favour of preservation. Excavation of the amphitheatre which was of outstanding importance in terms of the national heritage would promote the public's enjoyment and advancement of their knowledge of Roman life in Britain.

An application was made for the erection of a vicarage in a conservation area on land adjoining a listed building. The Inspector said that the main issues raised at the inquiry related to the effect of the proposed development on Manor House, a Grade II listed building in the Ringwood Conservation Area, the effect on other neighbouring properties and the adequacy of the site. The Inspector had reservations about the neighbourliness of a large house on the appeal site, but against these reservations considered the arguments relating to the need for a new vicarage. He said: "I am therefore driven, despite my reservations and with some reluctance but with little doubt to the conclusion, that on balance the public interest would be best served by permitting the erection of the parsonage house as proposed on this site."[84]

Similarly, this factor was taken into account when Carlsberg Brewery Ltd. applied for LBC to demolish a warehouse in Northampton.[85] This application was called in by the Secretary of State and the Inspector felt that the building was "of some historic interest, but its architectural merits are at the best dubious." He found that it was a prominent edifice which from most viewpoints was in a deplorable state and would remain so unless

---

[83] PNW/5143/344/4, May 1988.
[84] [1981] J.P.L. 614.
[85] *Planning Appeals*, Vol. 2, p. 260. Ref. EMP/1458/270/39.

extensive and costly works of reinstatement were carried out. The appellants were not able readily to find a use for the building, as it had low floor heights and poor daylighting, but the Inspector considered this to be partly because they had designed the new brewery complex on the assumption that the warehouse would be demolished. Notwithstanding this, he felt that the public interest would now best be served by its demolition providing it was replaced by a new building. However, until such a building had received planning approval, and the appellants were ready to start it, he recommended that LBC should be refused for the time being, with which view the Secretary of State agreed and LBC was refused.

This decision accords with section 17(3) of the LBA 1990, wherein "listed building consent for the demolition of a listed building may be granted subject to a condition that the building shall not be demolished before (a) a contract for the carrying out of works of redevelopment of the site has been made, and (b) planning permission has been granted for the redevelopment for which the contract provides".

4.72   At Shillingham Manor Farm, Saltash, Cornwall, an application to demolish a listed barn was approved. The balancing of the different criteria is summarised in the Secretary of State's decision:

> "The expensive repair work necessary to ensure the preservation of the building would need to be so extensive that much of the original workmanship and character of the rubble walling would be lost and the historical and architectural value of the building would be considerably diminished. There appears to be no use for the building even if repaired or converted."[86]

Louisville Investments Limited lodged an appeal against the decision of Basingstoke and Deane Borough Council to refuse listed building consent for the conversion of Crockford Farm, Basingstoke in 1987.[87] In his report to the Secretary of State, the Inspector considered the cost of the proposed conversion scheme and the anticipated cost of putting the building back into reasonable condition. The Inspector said that the proposed scheme:

> " . . . was costly and well in excess of the cost of straightforward restoration as a farmhouse dwelling or of new office construction. Unless the building was to be restored as a prestige commercial project where cost was not the governing factor such outlay would not ordinarily be feasible. The cost of repairing the roof in order to arrest further dilapidation of the building was shown to be modest, but served only to restore the roof and not address the problem of adapting the building to a new use."

Later in the decision letter the Inspector concluded:

> "I am satisfied that the costs of conversion would be too high in relation to expected returns, taking account of the size and physical constraints of the building and its location remote from a commercial centre, to make conversion an economically viable proposition. In my opinion therefore the merits are not so great, nor the building so unique

---

[86] SW/P/5155/270/9, October 21, 1987.
[87] APP/H1705/E/86/801934, October 21, 1987.

or important, that its preservation becomes a matter of overriding concern."

The Inspector recommended that the appeal be allowed subject to conditions and the Secretary of State concurred with that view.

15. TESTING THE MARKET

A sensitive and sensible application of the Building Act 1984 and the fire **4.73** safety legislation is also extremely important. This advice is particularly important at the present time when the future of so many old buildings is threatened by neglect and decay if not by wanton destruction or redevelopment proposals. Local authorities are asked to help owners find ways of keeping their buildings in economic use and thus in repair.

We believe that there is much sound advice offered in PPG 15 and in particular in section 7. In addition to dealing with the general statement on the upkeep and repair of historic buildings, owners will find that the good advice on urgent works, repairs notices, compulsory acquisitions of listed buildings in need of repair, is helpful.

There are many decisions emerging which emphasise the importance of **4.74** testing the market and finding alternative uses. Indeed, it is apparent that many appeals are still lost simply because the applicants have failed to demonstrate that they have undertaken a thorough marketing exercise. One example is a "called-in" case in Edgbaston,[88] which concerned an application for LBC to demolish a substantial Victorian property in large grounds. The physical viability of the building and successful rehabilitation of the house was unquestioned. But the Secretary of State agreed with his Inspector that a case for demolition had not been established, particularly in view of the complete absence of serious attempts to find alternative uses for the building by the simple expedient of offering it for sale in the open market. He said: "Until the market value of the house or its site (or both) are tested, I would regard consent for its demolition as premature." Similarly, the Secretary of State agreed with his Inspector in respect of St. Mark's Railway Station, Lincoln, where the Inspector said that British Rail had not made a sufficiently strong case to justify demolition. He said he was not satisfied that all the possibilities for use of the buildings, after they became surplus to railway requirements, had been fully explored.[89] A more recent example is provided by the Bristol Meeting Room Trust case discussed at paragraph 4.30.

In a case at Godmanchester[90] an appeal was dismissed because the Secretary of State concurred with his Inspector's conclusions that "although its repair and rehabilitation would not be economically viable for the appellant, there is now a strong possibility of the property being purchased and

---

[88] [1981] 253 E.G. 744 and see DOE Reference APP/5226/E/80/52 where an appeal against the refusal of LBC for demolition of a listed warehouse at Gloucester Docks was refused as the Secretary of State was "not convinced that every effort had been made to find an alternative use, where necessary taking steps to dispose of the building in order to achieve this"—reported in Estates Gazette, June 27, 1981.

[89] [1981] 253 EG 852. (See also *Estates Times*, June 12, 1981, reference YH/5111/270/31P) and *Estates Times*, July 3, 1981.

[90] APP/5140/E/83/052.

repaired in an acceptable manner by the Civic Society." The same emphasis is reflected in a case at Crawley[91] where consent to demolish two listed buildings was refused because "they were capable of being repaired at reasonable cost and could be sold at a price that reflected the land's potential value", even though it was acknowledged that "neither had any real architectural or historic merit". The demolition of the Old Grammar School in Berwick[92] was refused consent because the Secretary of State said that it "was difficult to accept that an alternative use could not be found for the building". A proposal to demolish a cottage in Kimbolton, near Huntingdon[93] failed because the Inspector accepted evidence that a financially viable scheme of renovation could be achieved, whilst a further proposal to demolish a row of cottages in Chertsey[94] was rejected because of the lack of a detailed survey and economic assessment of the potential of the structure and any effort to sell the premises for renovation.

16. OTHER BUILDING REQUIREMENTS

4.75   It should not be forgotten that compliance with Building Regulations and Fire Regulations is as necessary in dealing with the preservation of a listed building as with any other building.[95] PPG 15 (paragraph 3.26) reminds local authorities that in exercising their responsibilities for the safety of buildings under the Building Regulations and Fire Regulations, they should deal sympathetically with proposals for the repair or conversion of historic buildings. There are powers available to relax or dispense with some of the mandatory requirements where authorities feel that their strict application would present an unreasonable obstacle to the repair of a historic building.

The Alliance Building Society applied for consent to demolish 30 Westgate Street, Gloucester.[96] This was refused, and on appeal the Inspector considered the premises to form part of a fine group of buildings within an attractive conservation area, the character of which should be preserved or enhanced. He considered the appellant's costs of rehabilitation to be too high, possibly reflecting an unduly pessimistic assessment of the work necessary. He not only considered the cost of rehabilitation to be broadly comparable with the cost of redevelopment, but criticised the appearance of the proposed new building.

With regard to the rehabilitation scheme put forward at the inquiry, he was of the opinion that the listed building status of the existing premises warranted a relaxation of some aspects of the normal building bye-laws and fire regulations and that relaxation would probably be forthcoming. The Secretary of State agreed with the Inspector's recommendation that the appeal be dismissed and permission refused. (It is understood that a modified refurbishment scheme was subsequently put forward which found

---

[91] SE2/5403/270/14 reported in *Estates Gazette Planning Appeals*, May 26, 1984.

[92] APP/E2910/E/84/800362 reported in *Planning Appeals Monthly*, May 1985.

[93] E1/5140/411/10 reported in *Planning Appeals Monthly* December 1984.

[94] SE2/5389/411/1 reported in *Planning Appeals Monthly* December 1984.

[95] An excellent paper on Fire safety in historic buildings by Alan Parnell and David H. Ashford, has been published by the Society for the Protection of Ancient Buildings and the Fire Protection Assocation (obtainable from SPAB).

[96] Ref. SW/APP/5226/E/76/140.

acceptance, and the building was rehabilitated, being subsequently occupied by the applicants.)

17. ALTERATIONS AND EXTENSIONS

LBC is required for any works for the alteration or extension of a listed **4.76** building "in any manner which would affect its character as a building of special architectural or historic interest".

Potentially, any alteration to a listed building may require consent, internal alterations included. This applies regardless of the grade of the building. It is sometimes said that the difference between Grade II and Grade II* buildings is that the latter contain particularly fine interiors. This supposition has no statutory basis to it; buildings in Grade II* are merely particularly important examples of Grade II buildings. It is therefore wrong to assume that unstarred Grade II buildings do not require consent for internal alterations: grading is only a quasi-statutory designation for administrative purposes.[97] There is, however, a difference drawn between the requirement to notify the Secretary of State of an application for demolition extension or alteration in respect of Grade II* and Grade II (unstarred) buildings.

What matters for the purposes of LBC is the effect of the works on the character of the building.

As a broad principle, it is stated in the PPG 15, paragraph 3.2, that controls apply to all works, both external and internal, which would affect the character of a building as one of special architectural or historic interest. Consent is not normally required for repairs, but where these involve alterations which affect the building's character, consent may be required. It may be that the sensible answer to the problem on alterations to listed buildings which offers a "foremost principle" of works to historic buildings is "conserve as found", with the principle of successful conservation being to repair the existing fabric on a "like for like" basis.

South Hams District Council refused a planning application and listed **4,77** building consent for retention of an air conditioning unit at no. 50 Fore Street, Totnes, Devon. The owner of the Grade II* listed Elizabethan building appealed by way of written representations. The appeal property had a modern shop front but was listed Grade II* for its interior and group value. The air conditioning unit was not visible from the public highway but was attached to a wall overlooking a rear yard. The Inspector concluded that no damage of any significance was occasioned to the fabric of any part of the building from the installation of the unit which was supported on brackets attached to a modern extension to the building. The Inspector could see little real benefit in insisting on the unit's removal. The Secretary of State agreed with his Inspector's appraisal. In view of the unit's installation on a modern extension of the rear of a listed building and facing on to a service yard of unprepossessing appearance, the Secretary of State considered that the unit's visual impact on the listed building and its setting was minimal and insufficient to warrant refusing LBC. The Secretary of State allowed the LBC appeal and granted LBC for the retention of the air conditioning unit.[98]

---

[97] See also paras 2.45 and 2.46.
[98] 1991 6 Planning Appeal Decisions 586.

In assessing the difference between "repairs" and "alteration" there is a fine line to be drawn, and this calls for careful judgment. The following case illustrates this point. Nalgo House, The Crescent, Taunton, is a listed building. The National Association of Local Government Officers which occupied Nalgo House removed the weathered clay tiles and replaced them with modern machine-made concrete tiles without consent. This resulted in an LB enforcement notice. On an appeal by NALGO, the Secretary of State concluded that he was "satisfied that the works carried out to the building constitute a contravention of section 7 of the TCP Act 1971 in that they affect its character as a building of special architectural or historic interest, but LBC was not obtained; that the works have seriously harmed the character of the listed building and therefore LBC should not be granted".[99]

The owner of a property in Eaton Terrace, London, appealed against the decision of Westminster City Council to refuse planning permission and listed building consent for the erection of two additional storeys and alterations to the rear of 77 Eaton Terrace, London.[1] The local planning authority did not dispute the proposed rear alterations and it indicated that a degree of change might be acceptable but that an alternative solution was the erection of a new mansard roof. The Inspector concluded that the retention of number 77 Eaton Terrace in its present form was important from a historical point of view. The addition of a complete new floor would detrimentally alter the architectural integrity of the building. The four three-storey houses of which the application property was part were important in their contribution to the transition from two-storey terraces to the more dominant four-storey buildings in Eaton Terrace. The proposed additional two floors would create an imbalance which would seriously harm the important character and appearance of the listed building and the terrace itself and in the Inspector's view the scheme would not conform either with the council's policies for the protection of listed buildings nor the advice contained in 90(a) and 90(b) of Circular 8/87. The appeals were therefore dismissed.

4.78   Appeals were lodged against the non-determination of Lambeth London Borough Council to deal with applications for planning permission and listed building consent for alterations and extensions to 150 Waterloo Road, a Grade II listed building in connection with its proposed use or offices. The building had been built as a fire station in 1910 in what was described as a "free classical style". The main facade had retained its large openings to the appliance room, all of which retained their original partially glazed doors. After various intervening uses, the building had been empty for several years and was showing signs of vandalism and neglect.

Waterloo Station lies to the north of the appeal site, from which the building is visible from the first floor covered concourse. The site is within a conservation area.

There were two schemes submitted, but their differences were in design rather than substance. Both schemes involved the refurbishment of the main building for use as offices, and both involved extensions to provide additional office space. The main issues of these cases were identified as whether the scale of development was excessive for the site and whether

---

[99] DOE reference SW/APP/5365/F/80/55, 68 and 69, reported in *Estates Times* July 10, 1981.
[1] 1990 5 Planning Appeal Decisions 314.

the proposals may be said to preserve or enhance the character or appearance of the conservation area, and in respect of the listed building appeals, whether the proposed rear extension would be detrimental to the appearance and integrity of the listed building by reason of its over-dominance.

The Council raised no objection to the use of the site for offices, and the Inspector considered the plot ratio standards and felt that the specific proposals, although exceeding the plot ratios in the local plan, would not be enough in itself to reject the proposal.

In any case, such instruments of planning control, including plot ratios, were recommended in Circular 8/87 as aspects to be relaxed where this would enable a listed building to be restored and re-used and given a new lease of life. These factors had to be weighed against that benefit and assessed against the objection put forward by the Council based on the cumulative impact on overcrowding at Waterloo Station.

Since 1982 there had been a substantial increase in the morning peak-hour passengers entering Central London and this had caused congestion at stations, including Waterloo. The appeal proposals were however in general conformity with the office location criteria set out in the Greater London Development Plan, wherein the conservation of buildings of historic or architectural interest was specifically identified as a planning advantage.

The Inspector considered the "conservation aspects" of the proposals and concluded that the appeal building had a dignified appearance and was a prominent landmark in the Waterloo Road street scene, even though its impact was marred by it being empty and neglected. To bring the building back to use would contribute to the character of the appearance of the area.

The Inspector then considered the "listed building aspects" of both schemes and concluded that the original proposal would be too assertive in character and would result in the rear addition being too dominant, and compromising the integrity and setting of the listed building and its role within the conservation area. The revised scheme was more modest and appropriate in its design and respected the listed building.

The decision taken by the Inspector was that the first appeal scheme should fail on both listed buildings and conservation area grounds, and the second scheme should succeed. He accordingly refused planning permission and listed building consent for the first scheme and allowed the appeals for the revised proposal.[2]

The meaning of alteration has been taken to include the removal of a **4.79** painting from a Hall of Woodperry House, a Grade II* listed building in Oxfordshire; the details of this case are set out at paragraph 5.25 below in the section dealing with interiors. On the other hand, it was held in a case concerning the laying of two strips of York stone paving in the garden of a listed residential property at The Boltons, London SW10 that the placing of additional objects or structures on land within the curtilage of a listed building is not the carrying out of works for the demolition, alteration or extension of any of the existing structures and accordingly is not within section 7 of the LBA.[3]

---

[2] J.P.L. June 1991, p. 600.
  T/APP/N5660/A/89/140556 and E/89/805404 and
  T/APP/N5660/A/90/161656 and E/90/806463) September 24, 1990.
[3] APP/5021/F/74/7. For a full discussion of the curtilage problem, see paras. 2.17–2.20.

4.80   Alterations can arise from the new functional requirements of a listed building as illustrated in the case of Clarence House, North Street, Brighton. Clarence House is a large c.18 building, listed Grade II, formerly a coaching inn, and situated in the main shopping area of Brighton. It remained in use as a hotel until the last war, and although it had undergone a number of alterations, it had retained the access for coaches through an opening in the front of the building to the land behind. The building had been converted to offices and substantial efforts had been made to return the facade to its original state. As a result of the Fire Officer's requirement, one area of the ground floor which adjoined the coach access had to be isolated from the remainder of the accommodation, and the owners decided it would be appropriate for it to be used as a shop. Existing windows would light the shop from the North Street side, but a conventional shop front was proposed to be inserted facing the coach access. The appeals were against the refusal of listed building consent for the insertion of a window and door into the side passageway, and the alteration of the interior in connection with the small retail unit.

The building was the only listed building in North Street, and the last surviving example of the coaching inns, which were once a feature of the area. As one of the few surviving c.18 buildings in Brighton, it now made a major contribution to the conservation area.

The Inspector did not consider that the new fenestration within the coach access would have any harmful effect upon the character of the conservation area, and he even felt the new shop front would be a distinct addition to the appearance of the area as a whole. He then considered the effect of the proposals on the historic integrity of Clarence House but accepted the view that "changes made to an historic building which arise out of functional requirements form part of a natural progression". He felt the proposed alterations had been handled skilfully and would not affect the unity of the main North Street elevation, and concluded that there would be an enhancement of the character and the appearance of the building. The office use had already affected the character of the building while preserving its original appearance, and the Inspector considered the introduction of a further alien use in a position which would not impinge upon the main facade and would not adversely affect the historic importance of the building. He concluded by stating that the proposal would enliven the plain or dull alleyway (the coach access) and he allowed the appeals on April 23, 1991.[4]

An appeal by M. Camps and Son Limited against the refusal of St Edmundsbury Borough Council to grant listed building consent for the erection of a non-illuminated hanging sign at 9b The Traverse, Bury St Edmunds, Suffolk, was considered in 1990.[5] The application building was listed Grade II and was within the Bury St Edmunds Conservation Area. The Inspector concluded that the centre of Bury St Edmunds was very attractive and comprised mainly 18th and 19th-century buildings lining a medieval pattern of a narrow street round the focal points of Corn Hill and the Butter Market. The Traverse contained a fascinating variety of buildings and had a lively and attractive character. It was the sort of street scene to which hanging signs might contribute without causing clutter, provided that their size, location and design were in keeping with the building on

[4] J.P.L. December 1991, p. 1169. T/APP/N1405/90/A/163842/p. 7, 23 April 1991.
[5] 1990 5 Planning Appeal Decisions 99.

which they were displayed. The Secretary of State agreed with the Inspector's appraisal and recommendation that the LBC appeal should be allowed. He agreed that the architectural interest of a number of the listed buildings had been compromised by the insertion of modern shop fronts and accepted that provided the details of size, location and design were in keeping with the building on which they were to be displayed the principle of a hanging sign at facia level was acceptable. The appeals were allowed subject to conditions relating to the size of the hanging sign, the materials to be used in its construction, painting and type of brackets used.

Whilst most of the cases of painting buildings[6] seem to have related to buildings in conservation areas, an appeal was heard in 1980 relating to an enforcement notice served by Dover District Council alleging that the painting of the brickwork front elevation, the erection of shutters to the windows and the erection of a vertical fillet to the party wall line of the front elevation of 15 New Street, Sandwich, had been executed without authorisation in contravention of section 7 of the T.C.P. Act 1971. The district council's view that the appeal works had harmed the appearance and character of the listed building, the streetscape and the outstanding conservation area was accepted by the Inspector and the Secretary of State.[7] **4.81**

Painting the exterior of a listed building in such a manner that its character as a building of special architectural or historic interest was affected might well require LBC since repainting is capable of being an alteration.[8]

There is no reason why the criteria applicable on applications for consent to demolish should not also be applied to alterations, except that the difference in scale may make them inappropriate. For example, if it could be shown that certain alterations were necessary if a use were to be found for a listed building, that would be a relevant consideration just as it would on an application to demolish. The criteria for consent to demolish relate broadly to the building as a whole, and are therefore unlikely to be appropriate except for very major alterations; the detailed guidelines on alteration in PPG 15 are more likely to be relevant. **4.82**

The provisions of section 21(3) of the LBA 1990 should be remembered, whereby an appeal against refusal of consent or grant subject to conditions may include a claim that the building is not of special architectural or historic interest and should be removed from any list, apply to applications for alteration just as for demolition.

The effect of alterations to a listed building are sometimes difficult to quantify, particularly where such buildings have been subject to numerous accretions over a long period of time. This particular issue was highlighted by the problems encountered by the Borough of Watford in dealing with an application for LBC for the improvement and refurbishment of a range of

---

[6] See also para. 3.26 above and para. 6.06 below.

[7] [1981] J.P.L. 607. See also a case relating to conversion of a window in a Grade II building to a door (APP/5091/A/80/05323) reported in the *Estates Times*, October 16, 1981.

[8] *Windsor and Maidenhead Borough Council v. Secretary of State for the Environment: The Times* January 6, 1988. Where Mann J. (as he then was) held that having regard to the possible meaning in ordinary language of the word "alteration" and having regard to the purpose of s.55(1) of the TCP Act 1971, he was justified in concluding that repainting was capable of being an alteration; and that in any case the critical question would be whether the repainting affected the character of the building as a building of special architectural or historic interest.

buildings and the removal of rear sections at 129–151 High Street and 1A Carey Place, Watford.[9] The group of timber framed listed buildings had been altered over a considerable period of time and the local planning authority took the view that until "opening up" works had been undertaken it was not possible to provide the detailed plans and elevations showing the building in its finished form with its timber frame exposed. In effect, the local planning authority resorted to dealing with the application almost in "outline" form, but by requiring the applicants to enter into a section 52 [now s.106 of the TCPA 1990] agreement to provide a controlled and staged "opening up" process, with the subsequent submission of detailed drawings at each stage of the process, the local planning authority adopted an unusually novel but pragmatic method of dealing with a problem which must often face many local planning authorities.

4.83   Whilst this approach may not be that which was strictly intended by section 7 of the LBA, it nevertheless demonstrates a practical approach to and an understanding of the problems of dealing with alterations to listed buildings. An appeal was allowed in October 1990 against the decision of York City Council to refuse planning permission and listed building consent for the construction of two dormer windows, removal of chimney stack and internal alterations at St Andrew's Church, St Andrewgate, York[10]—a Grade II* listed building lying within the central historic core conservation area of York. The council objected to the removal of the chimney breast and stack because it was anxious to retain the fabric of a listed building and referred to the guidelines laid down in Circular 8/87. The Inspector considered that the proposed works would represent an enhancement of the Grade II* listed building to the benefit of the character of the conservation area and thus planning permission and LBC were granted.

We started this chapter with a comment from what we consider is a frequent consideration; that listing is too often considered to be a permanent freezing of a building. We set out to show that this was not the correct view of the situation—we hope that the detail in this chapter has shown that listing is not a permanent freezing: may be a frequent occasion, but not a universal one!

---

[9] Application Ref. 9/385/86LB, by courtesy of the Director of Technical Services, Borough of Watford.
[10] 1991 6 Planning Appeal Decisions 99.

5. Listed Buildings— The Mechanics of Control

1. GENERAL SUMMARY

This chapter deals with the mechanics of the application for LBC to **5.01** demolish, to alter, or extend. Whilst most of the chapter is devoted to demolition (which in practice causes many of the contentious problems) a note is added at the end of the chapter as to the differences in relation to applications for alterations and extensions. Such applications can create very difficult problems, but the procedure is now almost identical to that in relation to demolition.

It is not intended to undertake a full discussion of what can or cannot be done without planning permission under the ordinary planning law. However, a brief summary of the position helps to show precisely the extent of additional control in the case of listed buildings.

Planning permission is required for development, other than permitted development which is granted by a General Permitted Development Order. Development is defined by section 55 T.C.P.A. 1990 as:

> "the carrying out of building, engineering, mining or other operations in, on, over, or under land, or the making of any material change in the use of any buildings or other land."[1]

Whether or not demolition is development is a vexed question.[2] In *Coleshill and District Investment Co Ltd v. Minister of Housing and Local Government*[3] the House of Lords was faced with the question of whether the removal of protective soil embankments and blast walls from around a disused explosive store constituted development within the meaning of section 12(1) of the Town and Country Planning Act 1962. Section 12(1) of the T.C.P.A. 1962 provided that:

> "(1) In this Act . . . 'development', subject to the following provisions of this section, means the carrying out of building, engineering, mining or other operations in, on, over or under land, or the making of any material change in the use of any buildings or other land."

The Court held that on the true construction of section 12(1) T.C.P.A. 1962, it depended on the facts of the particular case whether demolition or removal operations constituted development. Lord Morris drew attention to the question of whether demolition constituted development in the following passage of his opinion:

> "My Lords, one question that was persistently raised in this appeal was formulated as being whether demolition constitutes development for the purposes of the Town and Country Planning Act 1962. Neat and arresting as the question so expressed may seem to be, it is not in fact the direct question which calls for our decision. If someone propounded a question of comparable generality such as whether modernisation constitutes development someone else might ask for a ruling whether renovation constitutes development. Not one of these enquiries has precision. If development needs permission, which in most cases it

---

[1] Section 55 T.C.P.A. 1990 has now been amended by s.13 P.C.A. 1991. The definition of mining operations for the purposes of the Act includes at s.55(4): "the removal of material of any description from a mineral working deposit, from a deposit of pulverised fuel ash or other furnace ash or clinker or from a deposit of iron, steel or other metallic slags and the extraction of minerals from a disused railway embankment".

[2] See also para. 3.17 and 5.21 above.

[3] [1969] 2 All E.R. 525, HL For a full discussion on this point, see the paper by Sir Iain Glidewell who considered the relationship between Coleshill and Iddenden [1972] 3 All E.R. 882—"Development—some current legal problems" contained in *Development Control—Thirty Years On* J.P.L. Occasional Papers, [1979].

does, and if development is defined, as in the Act it is, the true path of enquiry first involves ascertaining exactly what it is that it is desired to do or exactly what it is that has been done and then to see whether that comes within the statutory definition of development. Once some completed or projected work or operation is fully and clearly described then the words of definition can be applied. It is unnecessary and may be misleading to give the work or operation some single labelling word and then to try to apply the definition to that word. We are here concerned with actual operations and not with possible operations or with those which can for the future be imagined. Why, then, introduce and interpose some general word of description when precise words of description are at hand? Why gaze into the crystal when one can read the book?"

The House of Lords upheld the Minister's decision that the removal of **5.02** the embankments and walls were integral parts of each building and that their removal constituted development requiring planning permission. The removal of the embankments was an "engineering operation", and the removal of the walls was a "building operation", namely the structural alteration of a building which materially affected their external appearance, within the definition of "development" in what are now sections 55(1) and 336 of the T.C.P.A. 1990. Planning permission was therefore required.

The House of Lords was unanimous in upholding the Minister's decision on the enforcement notice appeal. It was notable that all the Law Lords rejected the suggestion that the issue to be determined was whether demolition by itself was development.

In a later case of *Iddenden and others v. Secretary of State for the Environment and another*,[4] the Court of Appeal had to determine whether an enforcement notice was invalid which required the removal of buildings which Mr Iddenden had erected without planning permission and the reinstatement of the original buildings which had been demolished.

The Court held that the steps which had to be specified by the enforcement notice were those required to remedy the breach of planning control. The demolition of the old buildings was not a breach of planning control; the only breach was the erection of the new buildings and their unauthorised use.

In his judgment Lord Denning MR stated that he "did not think their (*i.e.* the original old buildings on the site) demolition was a breach of planning control. Whilst some demolition operations may be development (he then referred to the Coleshill case), the demolition of buildings such as these was not development. Mr Iddenden did not need planning permission so as to pull them down".

In the High Court in January of 1991, Mr David Widdicombe Q.C. sitting as a Deputy Judge in the case of *Cambridge City Council v. Secretary of State for the Environment and Milton Park Investment Ltd*[5] held that the demolition of part of two semi-detached houses adjoining a recently constructed office block for the purpose of providing additional car parking, was a "building operation", and that it was an "other operation normally under-

[4] [1972] 3 All E.R. 883; [1972] 1 W.L.R. 1433.
[5] 1991 J.P.L. 428, *The Times* February 27, 1992 [1991] P.L.R. 109.

taken by a person carrying on business as a builder" (words used since the T.C.P.A. 1947).

The Deputy Judge reviewed the authorities, including the Coleshill and Iddenden cases before reaching his conclusion upon whether demolition of the houses was development within the terms of section 22(1) T.C.P.A. 1971 (now section 55 T.C.P.A. 1990). "This was a question which like a ghost has haunted planning law for many years. The time has come when the ghost has to be laid to rest." There had been no decision that total demolition of a building could not be development. He decided that the demolition of the houses was a "building operation", that was an "other operation normally undertaken by a person carrying on business as a builder". There were many demolitions which would normally be the business of a builder but the pulling down of ordinary dwelling-houses like these in Cambridge seemed unquestionably within the scope of a builder's business, whether he went on to develop the site or not.

In the *Cambridge* case the Deputy Judge did not state that the demolition of houses such as these is capable of being considered as "other operations normally undertaken by a person carrying on business as a builder" but rather that the demolition was development.[6] This contrasts with the approach of Lord Morris in the Coleshill case.

The Cambridge decision was later overturned on appeal but the uncertainty generated by the decision led to the introduction of selective controls upon demolition. Section 13 PCA 1991 introduced sub-sections 1A and 2(g) into Section 55 of the T.C.P.A. 1990.

5.03   Section 55(1A) now extends the definition of "building operations" to include demolition of buildings, rebuilding, structural alterations of or additions to buildings, and other operations normally undertaken by a person carrying on business as a builder. Sub-section 2(g) empowers the Secretary of State to exclude any description of building from the scope of the section. Control of all demolitions is now excluded from control except dwelling-houses as provided by Circular 26/92 entitled "Planning Controls over Demolition" June 4, 1992.[7]

The fact that it is a "building" which is being demolished is not conclusive. This is more important in the context of listed buildings than it is in the course of the ordinary planning law, because many listed buildings are not buildings in the normal sense of the word; there are, *e.g.* lamp-posts and bird baths which are listed buildings, and it is easier to imagine the demolition of these without involving building or engineering operations than it is the demolition of a house. Only in exceptional circumstances does demolition of itself amount to development; the Coleshill decision is based on its own unusual facts. No reported case has yet tested the particular circumstances of the demolition of a listed structure, but we would adopt a cautious view that the demolition at all events of lamp-posts and bird baths might be "other operations".

Demolition works are only authorised if:

(a) the local planning authority or the Secretary of State has granted written consent (LBC) for the execution of the works and the works are executed in accordance within the terms of the consent, and

[6] 1992 J.P.L. 644.
[7] T.C.P. (Demolition, Description of Buildings) Direction, Annex to Circular 26/92, *Planning controls over demolition.*

(b) notice of the proposal has been given to the Royal Commission on the Historical Monuments of England,[8] and either:
   (i) for at least one month following the grant of consent and before commencement of the works reasonable access has been made available to the Commission for the purpose of recording the building; or
   (ii) the Commission have by their Secretary or other authorised officer stated in writing that they have completed their recording of the building or that they do not wish to record it.[9]

Where the demolition or the alteration or extension requires a specific grant of LBC to authorise it, the procedure for obtaining this is dealt with in paragraphs 2.12, 3.1 and 3.2 of PPG 15. It is necessary for the local planning authority to examine applications for planning permission and LBC separately and it is usual for the authority to give separate decisions. It should be noted that the setting of a listed building is a criterion which must be taken into account in the consideration of both an application for LBC and an application for planning permission. Sections 16(2) and 66(1) respectively of the LBA 1990 are the operative provisions.

LBC normally is granted for the continuing benefit of the building, and although the local planning authority has power to impose a condition to limit the benefit of the consent to a specified person or persons, this rarely happens.[10]

Personal planning permissions are granted very rarely. Indeed, the theory must be that the legislation is more concerned with the building than with the individual owner. Perhaps the spirit of William Morris' dictum is to be borne in mind: " . . . these old buildings do not belong to us only . . . they belong to our forefathers and they will belong to our descendants unless we play them false . . . We are only trustees for those that come after us."

The buildings owned by local planning authorities are dealt with by the Town and Country Planning General Regulations 1992 (no. 1492), Regulation 11, where the authority is required to make application to the Secretary of State.

There are certain special cases when dealing with the need for LBC which will be treated separately. They are:

(a) Ancient monuments—dealt with at paragraph 5.27 below and in Chapter 8;
(b) Ecclesiastical buildings—dealt with at paragraph 5.28 below; and below in Chapter 10.
(c) Listed buildings and non-listed buildings in conservation areas within a compulsory purchase area—dealt with at paragraphs 5.31 and 5.32 below;
(d) Buildings which have become dangerous structures—dealt with at paragraph 5.42 below.

---

[8] See para. 13.03 below. LBA 1990, s.8(2)(b) & (4). Royal Commission, in this context, means: The Royal Commission on the Historical Monuments of England; and The Royal Commission on Ancient and Historical Monuments in Wales, s.8(4)(b).
[9] LBA 1990 s.8(2)(c).
[10] LBA, 1990, s.16(3).

2. PROCEDURE

5.04   The procedure for obtaining LBC is to be found in sections 10 and 11 LBA 1990 and in the Town and Country Planning (Listed Buildings and Buildings in Conservation Areas) Regulations 1990,[11] which also provide for the form of an application for LBC, how it should be made, the advertising of it by the LPA, and the time for dealing with it.

Transport and Works Applications (Listed Buildings, Conservation Areas and Ancient Monuments Procedures) Regulations 1992 came into force on January 1, 1993 and give provision for the making of applications and holding inquiries when proposals covered by section 6 of the Transport and Works Act 1992 give rise to a requirement for the following consents:

(a) listed building consent or conservation area consent under the LBA 1990; or

(b) scheduled monument consent under the Ancient Monument and Archaeological Areas Act 1979.

Applications for LBC should be made to the district planning authority, the City of London Common Council or the London Docklands Development Corporation, for which special provisions are applicable and are dealt with at paragraph 5.08 below. Urban Development Corporations (UDC's) act as the planning authority for the relevant area and hence an application for LBC should be made to the appropriate UDC.

The application should be accompanied by plans and drawings illustrating the proposal.[12] Perhaps it should be emphasised how important it is to ensure a good quality of drawings and plans. We believe that many LBC cases are lost or delayed because of inadequate presentation; and this is not necessarily always the fault of the application. It will be safest to err on the side of too much detail, although this may prove to be an expensive use of resources for an applicant, if the application is ultimately unsuccessful. Paragraph 3.4 of PPG 15 advises applicants to provide the local planning authority with full information to enable them to assess the likely impact of their proposals on the special architectural or historic interest of the building and on its setting. It does not follow that all applications in conservation areas must be accompanied by fully detailed drawings; there will be occasions where the context of the site is peripheral to the conservation area and an outline application will be acceptable.

5.05   A certificate must also be provided stating that the applicant is the owner, or has notified the owner of the application site[13]; i.e. equivalent to a certificate under section 66 T.C.P.A. 1990 for an ordinary planning application. The prescribed form of notices and certificates as to ownership, etc., are contained in Schedule 2 of the 1990 Regulations. "Owner" includes the owner of the freehold, or of a lease with at least seven years unexpired at the

---

[11] As modified by the Transport and Works (Listed Buildings, Conservation Areas and Ancient Monuments Procedure) Regulations 1992 (S.I. 1992 No. 3138) and see J.P.L. March 1993, p. 214.

[12] 1990 LBA s.10(2) and Town and Country Planning (Listed Buildings and Buildings in Conservation Areas) Regulations 1990, regulation 3(1) and Annex B (B3) of PPG 15.

[13] Town and Country Planning (Listed Buildings and Buildings in Conservation Areas) Regulations 1990, regulation 6(1).

relevant time.[14] Under regulation 5 of the 1990 Regulations, local authorities are required to advertise in a local newspaper applications for LBC made to them; to display a notice on or near the site the subject of the application; and to take into account any representations received. The requirements for such publicity do not apply to applications for LBC for works affecting only the interior of a Grade II unstarred building (see below).

Retrospective consent is possible, as provided for by section 8(3) LBA 1990 which enables a LPA or the Secretary of State to give written consent for the retention of works for the demolition, extension or alteration of a listed building, where those works have already been executed without such consent.

Section 15(5) LBA gives the Secretary of State power to direct that local planning authorities should notify bodies of persons specified by him of any applications they receive for LBC and of their decision. Such a direction is given in paragraph 81 of the Circular 8/87 which requires that notice of all applications for consent to demolish a listed building, and the decisions taken thereon, should be given to the following bodies:

The Ancient Monuments Society,
The Council for British Archaeology,
The Society for the Protection of Ancient Buildings,
The Georgian Group,
The Victorian Society,
The appropriate Royal Commission on Historical Monuments.

Except in the case of *The Royal Commissions on Historical Monuments* (who are notified because of the possible need to record the building, should consent to demolish be granted), the notifications of the applications are required to be accompanied by the relevant extract from the list describing the building. Any representations received in response to these notifications must be taken into account when the application is being considered by the local planning authority. There is a formal requirement upon a local planning authority to take into account representations following the notification as contained in Circular 8/87, paragraph 81 stating that "any representation received in response to these notifications should be taken into account when the application is considered". The question of whether the decision makers have a duty to take account of any representations received from the notification or consultation procedure, was considered in *R v. Secretary of State for the Environment ex parte Kent* (1988),[15] when it was held, by the Court of Appeal, that there was no general requirement and that neither the letter, nor the general informal practice of discretionary notification, created such a duty. There is, however, a non-statutory Code of Practice which was devised through the National Development Control Forum in 1980 in relation to consultation in development control. The national amenity societies required to be consulted under the direction, as required under paragraph 81 of Circular 8/87, are amongst the bodies cited in the code with whom local planning authorities must by law consult in appropriate cases.

The code was designed to refine and improve the consultation procedures

[14] *Ibid* regulation 6(5) and CLA 1975, s.6(1) and (2).
[15] J.P.L. 1988 706.

and is non-statutory and therefore does not override the provision of the Town and Country Planning (General Development Procedure) Order 1995. The code specifically applies to "all authorities and bodies consulted on application", amongst which is the requirement to consult on listed building demolition applications; it does not apply,—*inter alia*,—to "occasional notification and consultation on planning applications carried out on a voluntary basis by local authorities".[16]

A local planning authority *will* take into account any representations received from a consultee in determining an application, except where those representations are received outside the period laid down (normally 28 days) or outside an agreed extended period.

5.06   In the case of consultations on listed building demolition applications, the local authority is required to provide a copy of the application form within seven days of receipt of a complete application, plus an extract from the "list" entry describing the building and any other supporting information as it deems appropriate.

It is noteworthy that there is no statutory provision whereby the local planning authority is required to wait for a specific period after notifications to the six bodies, although the Code of Practice recommends 28 days, following the despatch of the application. The consultees may request an extension of that period and shall notify the local planning authority within 21 days of the application being despatched with details as to why an extended period is required. Presumably it is expected that the six bodies will respond in adequate time for the decision to be given in eight weeks. The application may not be determined by the local planning authority until the 28 day period has elapsed and after both the date of the expiry of the press advertisement and the seven day period from the date on which the site notice was first displayed have passed.

In the case of development proposals by local planning authorities, the obligation to give publicity extends not only to development proposed by the local authority, but also where the authority seeks deemed permission for development. In *R v. Lambeth London BC ex p. Sharp* (1987) J.P.L. 440, the Court of Appeal held that the requirement of the Town & Country Planning Regulations 1976 were mandatory and strict compliance was required. The Court quashed a deemed grant of planning permission for an application for planning permission affecting a conservation area which referred to representations rather than objections and failed to specify a period within which an objection should be made.[17]

Annex B of PPG 15, paragraph B17, extended the earlier requirement contained in the direction of Circular 8/87 by stating that local planning authorities shall notify English Heritage[18] of all applications for listed building consent affecting any Grade I or II* building outside Greater

---

[16] Para. E of preamble to the Code of Practice – National Development Control Forum 1980.

[17] *R v. Lambeth London BC ex p. Sharp* (1987) J.P.L. 440.

[18] English Heritage performs an advisory role in relation to cases which are notified to them by local planning authorities. English Heritage's views are therefore available to be taken into consideration by the planning committee of the local planning authority, when it reaches a decision upon an application for LBC for full or partial demolition. English Heritage's intervention at this stage is as adviser to the local planning authority. However, negotiation between officers of English Heritage and the owner of a listed building is common.

London and any grade of listed building in Greater London would be notifiable to the regional office if the local authority were minded to grant consent, and on which English Heritage could subsequently advise the D.O.E. on the case for calling-in. This means that all applications involving the total demolition of a Grade II building or the substantial demolition of any external elevation including the roof or the demolition of substantially most of its interior, must be notified to the Secretary of State, along with works to Grade I and II*, for which the local planning authority is minded to grant consent. There are supplementary directions relating to the London Docklands.

The decision on a listed building application must be given within eight weeks, although the period can be extended with the consent of the applicant. The Secretary of State may direct that applications be referred to him,[19] and he must in any case be notified of the application in accordance with section 13 LBA, before LBC is granted, so that he can decide whether to call in the application for his own decision. A local planning authority on an application covered by any direction made under section 12 of the LBA 1990 cannot grant LBC for demolition unless it has notified the Secretary of State of the application and given details of the works for which consent is required.[20] Such notification is made to the DOE regional office, and in so doing local authorities are asked to send copies of any representations received, particularly from the amenity societies named above, and to send recent photographs of the building.[21] The Secretary of State has directed that, with the exception of various specified types of demolition work, the need to notify him shall not apply to applications for consent to demolish, alter or extend certain minor Grade II (unstarred) buildings, other than a building in respect of which a grant has been made under section 4 of the Historic Building and Ancient Monuments Act 1953, or a building in respect of which such a grant has been applied for but the application has not been decided.[22]

Section 62 of the Town and Country Planning Act 1990 provides that any **5.07** application to a local planning authority for planning permission shall be made in such manner as may be prescribed by regulation under the Act.

There is provision that where an application for development of any land would, in the opinion of the local planning authority, affect the character or appearance of a conservation area or the setting of a listed building, they are obliged to publish notice of it in a local newspaper and to post on or near the site, a notice, under section 73 of the Listed Building Act. Consultation provisions are also made by the Town and Country Planning (General Development Procedure) Order 1995, as to demolition or alteration of a listed building in Greater London and development likely to affect the site of a scheduled monument in England and Wales.

Once a local planning authority refers a case for possible "call-in" by the Secretary of State, he will invite English Heritage to advise whether he

---

[19] LBA s.12(1).
[20] LBA s.13(1) and (2).
[21] Para. B3 of Annex B, PPG 15.
[22] Circular 8/87, para. 86.

should determine the case himself. English Heritage acts in an advisory capacity and the ultimate decision on an application will be that of the Secretary of State if the case is called-in and by the local planning authority if it is not. At this stage, English Heritage is acting in its capacity as advisor to the Secretary of State so that negotiation with the local planning authority and the owner of the listed building is not possible. Once the DOE has considered English Heritage's advice and has reached a decision on whether to call in the application, English Heritage is again free to negotiate.

The following table illustrates the increase in both notifications and referrals handled by English Heritage.

TABLE 1

LISTED BUILDING CONSENT STATISTICS (OUTSIDE LONDON)

Year from April–March	84/85	85/86	86/87	87/88	88/89	89/90	90/91
Number of List entries	333079	367395	395377	405386	420310	435000	438230
LBC notifications, LPAs to EH	558	1113	2110	3026	1954	2441	2763
LBC referrals from DOE to EH	2648	3294	3607	2454	2289	2033	2030

TABLE 2

CALL-IN RECOMMENDATIONS AND PUBLIC INQUIRIES

Year from April–March	84/85	85/86	86/87	87/88	88/89	89/90	90/91
Call-in recommended by EH	47	63	60	42	37	26	25
Call-in agreed by DOE	41	53	46	36	30	23	20
Withdrawn after call-in agreed	4	25	15	19	20	13	8
LBC refused after PI	19	9	21	9.5*	8	7	1
LBC granted after PI	18	19	10	7.5*	2	2	0
Awaiting PI result	0	0	0	0	0	1	11

LBC   Listed Building Consent
DOE   Department of Environment
LPA   Local Planning Authorities
PI   Public Inquiry

* Case where part-demolition and part-retention recommended as result of PI.

If the Secretary of State calls in an application he must, before determining the application, afford either the applicant or the authority an opportunity of appearing before and being heard by a person appointed by him. The local planning authority may not determine the application until 28 days after notifying the Secretary of State, unless before the expiration of 28 days from notification, the Secretary of State has advised the authority that he does not intend to call in the application. If the Secretary of State considers that he needs more than 28 days to make up his mind, he may so notify the authority, who must not determine the application before the Secretary of State advises the authority of his decision whether or not to call in the application. There is no time limit on the Secretary of State for this further consideration.[24]

The decision of the Secretary of State on a called-in application is final, save of course on an appeal to the High Court by a person aggrieved under the provisions of sections 63 and 65 LBA.[25]

Notice of the decision (whether of a local planning authority or one called in by the Secretary of State) must be given in writing, and if the decision is a refusal of LBC or a grant of consent subject to conditions, the reasons for the refusal or the conditions must be stated.[26] The local planning authority must, when it gives such a decision, point out to the applicant:

(i) that he has a right of appeal to the Secretary of State;
(ii) the possibility of serving a purchase notice if the building is incapable of reasonably beneficial use;
(iii) that in certain circumstances there is a right to claim compensation (but not on refusal of demolition consent).[27]

3. LONDON PROVISIONS

Prior to the abolition of the Greater London Council, all the London **5.08** borough councils had to notify the Greater London Council of all the London borough council applications for listed building consent, other than those they intended to refuse, and could not grant until authorised to do so by the Greater London Council as to how the application should be determined.

[23] See also s.67 of the Listed Building Act.
[24] In 1986 Lord Elton reported in the House of Lords that out of 2,057 applications for LBC which came in for consideration, only 34 proved substantial enough to call in (HL *Hansard* (July 30, 1986) Co. 856).
[25] For an authoritative discussion on the role of the Courts in development control see the paper by Mr Peter Boydell, Q.C. in *Development Control—Thirty Years on* published as J.P.L. Occasional Papers 1979.
[26] Town and Country Planning (Listed Buildings and Buildings in Conservation Areas) Regulations 1990, regulation 3(5). Reasons have acquired a particular significance since Simon Brown J. found that a decision of the Secretary of State in connection with property used by the Inner London Education Authority was invalid because of the absence of reasons, see *The Times*, March 30, 1988. Note also the decision of the House of Lords in the Mansion House Square case (J.P.L. 1990, p. 83; *The Times*, April 4, 1990).
[27] Town and Country Planning (Listed Building and Buildings in Conservation Areas) Regulations 1990, regulation 3(5) and Sched. 1, Pt II.

The functions of the Greater London Council, with some modifications, were transferred from April 1, 1986 under section 6 of, and Schedule 2 to, the Local Government Act 1985, from the Greater London Council to English Heritage.

In Greater London, section 14 LBA, requires London borough councils to notify English Heritage of any application for listed building consent which they do not intend to refuse, and provides that they shall not grant consent until English Heritage either authorises them to do so or directs them how to determine it.[28]

The other principal difference for notification procedures in Greater London is that which requires all local planning authorities in London to notify English Heritage of all applications for listed building consent to alter, extend or demolish any grade of listed buildings or of planning applications affecting the fabric as well as the setting of all Grade I, and Grade II* buildings. Outside Greater London, local planning authorities are only required to notify English Heritage of applications in respect of Grade I or Grade II* buildings. (These arrangements do not apply to the London Docklands Development Corporation which follows the procedure for authorities outside Greater London).[29]

Where the English Heritage has given a London borough council a direction to refuse consent which the authority is unwilling to accept, the council may within 28 days from the date of the direction being made, notify the Secretary of State of the application for him either to call in or to give notice that he does not intend to do so.

It is, however, expected that the English Heritage and the local planning authority will have made every attempt to reconcile differences of opinion in order to reach a solution before any application is referred to the Secretary of State. Where the Secretary of State decides not to require reference of the application to him, the direction of English Heritage will stand.[30]

4. CONDITIONS IN A LISTED BUILDING CONSENT

5.09   LBC may be granted unconditionally, or subject to conditions.[31] Under section 17(1) LBA conditions may in particular include:

"(a) the preservation of particular features of the building, either as part of it or after severance from it;

(b) the making good, after the works are completed, of any damage caused to the building by the works;

(c) the reconstruction of the building or any part of it following the execution of any works, with the use of original materials so far as practicable and with such alterations of the interior of the building as may be specified in the conditions."

Section 17(2) of the LBA provides that:

"A condition may also be imposed requiring specified details of the works (whether or not set out in the application) to be approved sub-

[28] LBA 1990, s.14(1) and (2).
[29] LBA 1990, s.14(1).
[30] LBA 1990, s.14.
[31] LBA 1990, s.16(1).

192

sequently by the local planning authority or, in the case of consent granted by the Secretary of State, specifying whether such details are to be approved by the local planning authority or by him."

There is provision under section 19 of LBA 1990 for an application to vary or discharge conditions attached to a listed building consent. This may be made by "any person interested" in a listed building (section 19(1) of the LBA 1990). The word "interested" has been held to mean holding a proprietary interest in the land (*Jones v. Secretary of State for Wales* (1974) 28 P. & C.R. 280) though a wider view was mooted by Eveleigh L.J. in *Pennine Raceway Ltd v. Kirklees MDC* [1982] 3 All E.R. 628.

In 1988 the Secretary of State granted LBC for the partial demolition of the Baptist Church, hall and school, Yeovil subject to the following conditions:

"(i) the demolitions hereby permitted shall be begun not later than five years from the date of this consent;

(ii) the South Street facades of the Baptist Church, the Baptist Hall and the Baptist School (Newnam Memorial Block) and no's. 75 and 76 South Street shall be retained and incorporated in the new structure;

(iii) the developer shall afford access at all reasonable times to any archaeologist nominated by the local planning authority, and shall allow him to observe the demolition works and record items of interest and finds;

(iv) for a period of six weeks before the commencement of the works reasonable access to the buildings shall be given to members or officers of the Royal Commission on the Historical Monuments of England, for the purposes of recording them; and

(v) the internal fittings which are removed in accordance with this consent shall, wherever practicable, be preserved for re-use or incorporation in the new buildings.[32]"

In the *St. Aldates, Oxford* case[33] the Secretary of State allowed LBC to demolish on condition that various historic interior fittings be carefully dismantled and stored so that they could be refitted in the replacement building.

An application for the demolition of a barn in Aylesbury Vale invited a **5.10** condition requiring its re-erection met with a suggestion by the Inspector that the consent should be delayed until expert advice could confirm the possibility of removal of the timber framed structure. The Secretary of State disagreed and allowed the appeal, as he was convinced that its removal was practicable.[34] In a case involving buildings containing cruck frames at Tring, Hertfordshire, the Secretary of State, whilst not imposing a condition requiring retention of the frames for possible future use, expressed the hope that the buildings concerned would be carefully demolished with a view to the crucks being preserved for eventual re-erection elsewhere. In deciding, following an inquiry, to grant LBC for the demolition, the Secretary of State accepted that the cost of repairs was substantial, that the remains of the crucks were in poor condition, that demolition would not preclude investi-

[32] Baptist Church, Yeovil – 1988.
[33] See para. 5.11 below.
[34] APP/5132/E/79/128 reported in *Planning Appeals Monthly*, 1981.

gation of the history of the timber frame construction of the buildings, and that the dilapidated appearance of the property detracted from the conservation area in which it was located. The local authority (Dacorum District Council) supported the proposal to demolish.[35]

In 1987, Tilcon Ltd successfully appealed to the Secretary of State for LBC to demolish the stable block and ice house at Eaton Hall Works, Congleton. The Secretary of State did not impose a condition upon the LBC which was recommended by his Inspector that the listed buildings be dismantled and re-erected on another site. Such a condition was considered to be very onerous and was not justified in relation to buildings which were neither unique nor outstanding.[36]

An unusual listed building was the former North East Marine hammerhead crane situated at Willington Quay, Wallsend. The application to demolish the crane in 1991 was referred to the Secretary of State for the Environment under section 12 of the LBA 1990.

The Tyne and Wear Development Corporation had argued that in their capacity as local planning authority and in the event of conflict, their duty to secure regeneration of the area under section 136(1) of the Local Government, Planning and Land Act 1980 must prevail over the duty to preserve listed buildings. The Secretary of State did not accept that the object of the Corporation to secure regeneration would automatically override the need to have special regard to the desirability of preserving a listed building or its setting. These were all matters to be taken carefully into account and balanced in making any decision on an application for listed building consent.

On the merits of the case, the Inspector acknowledged that the crane would stand in the way of the full, safe, efficient and flexible use of the site. Its possible re-location to a proposed museum was explored, but was not seen as a practical proposition in the foreseeable future. The benefits of the new construction complex, which affected the site of the crane, were said to bring benefits to the economy of Tyneside, and these benefits outweighed the desirability of preserving the crane. The Inspector recommended that consent be granted and the Secretary of State concurred by granting listed building consent subject to conditions, amongst which was one requiring the dismantling of the crane by a "contractor specialising in this work" and the storage of the parts for a period of three years during which period they should be offered to a museum or similar preservation body nominated by the Development Corporation. An interesting side aspect to this decision was the offer by the Development Corporation to produce a video film showing the details of the crane and a working model of it, which the Secretary of State felt would be "highly appropriate" although not suitable for imposition as a condition.[37]

Under section 17(3) LBA there is a provision that listed building consent for the demolition of a listed building may be granted subject to a condition that the building shall not be demolished before a contract for the carrying out of works of redevelopment of the site has been made, and planning per-

---

[35] DOE reference E1/5252/270/17, Eastern Charles House. Additional information supplied by Dacorum District Council.

[36] See a fuller discussion of this case in Chap. 4 (APP/C0630/E/85/800906), October 30, 1987.

[37] Appeal Ref: N/5038/270P/35, August 28, 1991 [J.P.L. 1992, p. 695].

mission has been granted for the redevelopment for which the contract provides. An example of this being imposed can be found in the decision of the Secretary of State in relation to the demolition of a Baptist Chapel and Manse at Husbands Bosworth, Leicestershire.[38]

Although it may be considered reasonable as a question of principle that **5.11** the architectural and other merits of the proposed new development should be taken into account in considering whether to grant LBC to demolish, the problem is always that demolition might not be followed by the proposed development. Paragraph B5 of Annex B of PPG 15 suggests that local authorities should avoid authorising demolition to make way for new development unless it is certain that the new development will proceed. It continues by reiterating that it may be appropriate to impose on the grant of consent for demolition, as a condition under section 17(3) of the Act, as a prelude to redevelopment to the effect that demolition shall not take place before a contract for carrying out the works of redevelopment on the site has been made and planning permission has been granted for the redevelopment for which the contract provides. It is further suggested that the question of enforceability of the redevelopment might be resolved by concluding the parallel agreement under section 33 of the Local Government (Miscellaneous Provisions) Act 1982.[39] This may be particularly appropriate in the case of demolition within a conservation area, where the subsequent development and the risks of unsightly gaps may be more important than in the case of an isolated listed building. It will be interesting to see how section 17(3) LBA helps with this problem. The intention is obviously excellent, but the bald words of section 17(3) leave a lot of questions unanswered. The whole of the site? How is the contract to be approved? What if the contract is rescinded? So far, however, the subsection, it appears, has not met with any pitfalls in its application; again, the *St. Aldates, Oxford* decision[40] is a case in point.

Local planning authorities, and the Secretary of State, try from time to time to impose conditions which will have the effect of preserving parts of the building. An interesting example is one arising from an application by the Medway Ports Authority to demolish the early nineteenth century Quadrangle Storehouse at Sheerness Dockyard to allow construction of a container terminal.[41] The Inspector was convinced that the continued prosperity of the port would best be served by allowing the redevelopment. The Secretary of State agreed, subject to the building's clock tower being carefully dismantled and re-erected on a site to be agreed with the Swale District Council. He requested that consideration be given to the careful salvage and safe keeping of any materials such as doors, window frames, Yorkshire floor slabs, cast iron beams, etc., which might be capable of use in the area for display in a maritime museum or other suitable location. Obviously the intentions behind such conditions are worthy, but are conditions framed in this way really enforceable? Was the alternative site "under the control" of the applicants? No doubt the owners were happy to get their consent and comply with the conditions, but it is submitted that conditions on these lines are suspect. Did they in fact comply with the cri-

---

[38] [1981] 257 E.G. 436.
[39] ie. one specifically enforceable.
[40] See para. 5.09 above.
[41] *Plannning Appeals*, Vol. 3, p. 259. Ref: SE2/1527/270/5 SE2/1527/422/1.

teria set out in paragraph 24 if PPG 1[42]; namely that conditions should be necessary, relevant to planning, relevant to the development to be permitted, enforceable, precise and reasonable?

Perhaps when suspect conditions such as these are in contemplation, the use of a formal agreement under section 106 T.C.P.A. 1990, as amended by section 12 of the Planning and Compensation Act 1991, might be considered, but there are presently practical and legal difficulties in the Secretary of State imposing such an agreement upon an appellant.

Mention should also be made of the time limits for listed building consents under section 18 LBA. The normal time limit by which the approved works must be begun is set at five years from the date of consent, but the period can be determined to be longer or shorter. The Act offers no guidance as to what constitutes the "beginning" of the works. If consent is allowed to lapse, an application for further consent may be made; although this carries danger for the applicant that the LPA's policy may have changed since the original consent was issued.

Section 19 LBA provides that any interested person may apply to the LPA for the variation or discharge of conditions attached to an LBC. On such an application, the local planning authority, or Secretary of State, may vary or discharge the conditions attached to the consent and may add new conditions upon the variation of discharge. The important aspect is that the consent itself is still valid.

5. PRESUMPTION AS TO REFUSAL

5.12   Unless the local planning authority give notice of their decision, or the applicant agrees to an extension of the decision period, or the application has been referred to the Secretary of State within the eight week period or any agreed extension thereof, LBC is treated as having been refused,[43] which would enable the applicant to appeal to the Secretary of State. This provision includes applications for approval of details of works required under a condition of an LBC already granted, or of requests to vary or discharge a condition of LBC.

6. RIGHTS OF APPEAL[44]

5.13   The applicant has a right to appeal to the Secretary of State where the local planning authority refuses LBC or grants it subject to conditions, or if no decision is given within the prescribed eight weeks or any such extended

[42] PPG 1. General Policy Principles (1992).
[43] LBA 1990, s.20(2).
[44] Procedure on listed building appeals is governed by the Town and Country Planning (Inquiries Procedure) Rules 1988 (as amended by revised Rules S.I. 1992 No. 2039) where the final decision is to be taken by the Secretary of State, and by the Town and Country Planning Appeals (Determination by Appointed Persons) (Inquiries Procedure) Rules 1988 (as amended by revised Rules S.I. 1992 2038) where jurisdiction is transferred to an Inspector. See also the Town and Country Planning (Enforcement Notices and Appeals) Regulations 1981.

period as the applicant may have agreed to. The applicant may appeal within six months of the receipt of the decision, or such longer time as the Secretary of State may allow.[45]

The notice of appeal may include a claim that the building is not of special architectural or historic interest and ought to be removed from any list.[46]

Unless the appeal relates to an application to demolish any listed building, to alter or extend a Grade I or Grade II* listed building, or to an enforcement notice in connection with either case, the Secretary of State may appoint someone to determine the appeal instead of doing so himself.[47] Before determining the appeal, the Secretary of State or his Inspector must, if either party so desires, afford both the appellant and the local planning authority the opportunity of appearing before and being heard by a person appointed by him.[48] There is no reason why the written representation procedure should not be used for an LBC case on the usual conditions.[49]

The appeal procedure corresponds with the planning appeal procedure under section 78 of the T.C.P.A. 1990, except that the appellant may include in his appeal the ground that the building is not of special architectural or historic interest, and should not have been listed. The Secretary of State may, in determining the appeal, remove the building from the list.[50] His decision is final, save of course on an appeal to the High Court by a person aggrieved under the provisions of sections 63 and 65 of the LBA 1990.

It should be noted that where an appeal is lodged against a condition the whole consent is at risk, and the Secretary of State can treat the matter as if the application had been referred to him in the first place.

Circular 2/87 (Awards of Costs Incurred in Planning and CPO Proceedings) governs the costs aspect of appeals relating to listed buildings as well as general planning appeals. The Circular reiterates the principle that there is always a presumption in favour of allowing planning applications, and that an LPA may lay itself open to an award of costs against itself where, by its refusal, it is shown to have acted unreasonably in any way, causing the applicant to incur unnecessary expense. Equally, where it is shown that for any reason it was unreasonable for an appeal to have been brought, the appellant may become liable for costs. Experience following the publication of Circular 2/87 suggests that costs are being taken much more seriously in decision making on listed building appeals, both by the appellants and the local planning authorities.

In a planning appeal in 1988, the costs of the third parties were awarded against the local planning authority.[51] Cost applications should be made at the inquiry before the proceedings are over, and as from March 2, 1987 all

---

[45] Town and Country Planning (Listed Buildings and Buildings in Conservation Areas) Regulations 1990, regulation 8(1).

[46] LBA 1990 s.21(3).

[47] Sched. 3 LBA 1990 and the T. & C.P. (Determination of Appeals by Appointed Perons) (Prescribed Classes) Regulations 1981 as amended by S.I. 1986 (No. 623) and S.I. 1989 (No. 1087).

[48] LBA 1990 s.22(2) and Sched. 3 para. 3(4).

[49] See Town and Country Planning (Appeals) (Written Representations) Procedure Regulations 1987, 1987 S.I. 701.

[50] LBA 1990, s.22(1)(b).

[51] APP/G4240/A/87/65338 reported in Chartered Surveyor Weekly, January 28, 1988.

applications for costs are determined by the Inspector unless the appeal itself is to be decided by the Secretary of State.

The High Court[52] quashed a planning decision by a local planning authority which had been granted without having been properly advertised or notified to English Heritage. Although it was a matter for the local planning authority, the Act did not require that the proposed redevelopment would "substantially" affect the setting of a listed building. The decision was upheld by the Court of Appeal.[53]

7. NOTIFICATION TO OTHERS OF DECISION

5.14   Where LBC to demolish is granted, local planning authorities are required by sections 8(1) and (2) of the LBA to allow the Royal Commission (RCHME) at least one month to record the building. Paragraph B4 (Annex B) of the PPG 15 suggests that it would be helpful if authorities would draw attention in their decision notice to indicate that the applicant must permit the Royal Commission on Historical Monuments to record the building before demolition. The following wording is recommended:

> "Attention is drawn to section 8(2) LBA, the effect of which is that demolition may not be undertaken (despite the terms of the consent granted by the local planning authority) until notice of the proposal has been given to the Royal Commission on Historical Monuments,[54] and the Commission subsequently have either been given reasonable access to the building for at least one month following the grant of consent, or have stated that they have completed their record of their building or that they do not wish to record it";

The authority is recommended to send the applicant a form on which he can notify the Royal Commission of the proposal to demolish the building; and to give the Royal Commission advance warning by immediately sending them a copy of the decision notice.

However, the above three requirements do not apply to demolition of unlisted buildings in conservation areas.

8. REVOCATION OF LISTED BUILDING CONSENT

5.15   The local planning authority may, if it appears expedient to them having regard to the development plan and other material considerations, make an order revoking or modifying LBC.[55] Such an order revoking or modifying the consent does not take effect unless it is confirmed by the Secretary of State, except under the procedure specified below.

Where the owner and the occupier (and all persons who in the opinion of the local planning authority will be affected) have notified the authority

---

[52] *R v. South Hereford DC ex p. Felton* (1989) 3 PCR 81.
[53] (1990), EGCS 34.
[54] LBA 1990 s.8(2)(c).
[55] LBA 1990, s.23.

that they do not object, the authority must advertise the fact that the order has been made. The authority must also specify a period during which persons affected by the order should give notice to the Secretary of State if they want an opportunity to be heard, and also specifying a period at the expiration of which the order will take effect without confirmation if no notice has been given.[56] A copy of the advertisement must be sent to the Secretary of State within three days of publication.[57] If any person claiming to be affected by the order gives notice to the Secretary of State in writing, and if the Secretary of State has not directed that the order be submitted to him for confirmation, the order takes effect accordingly and compensation will be payable.[58] This procedure does not apply to an order which revokes or modifies consent granted by the Secretary of State.

Where an order is submitted to the Secretary of State for confirmation, notice must be served on the owner, the occupier, and any other person who in the authority's opinion will be affected by the order, and, at the request of any such person, an opportunity to be heard by a person appointed by the Secretary of State must be given both to that person and to the local authority.[59] The Secretary of State may himself make an order revoking or modifying consent. Except where an order takes effect without compensation,[60] compensation must be paid to a person who has incurred expenditure or abortive works or has otherwise sustained loss or damage and the preparation of plans for the purposes of any works or other matters preparatory to such works may be included in the compensation claims.[61]

9. COMPENSATION WHERE LISTED BUILDING CONSENT IS REVOKED OR MODIFIED

A local planning authority is liable to pay compensation under section 28 **5.16** T.C.P.A. 1990 in certain limited circumstances on the revocation or modification of a LBC. A provision for compensation for refusal of consent to alteration, etc., of a listed building (formerly in section 27 of the 1990 Act) was repealed by the Planning and Compensation Act 1991, Schedule 19 Pt II. The principal points under section 28 are:

(a) Section 28 has effect where listed building consent is revoked or modified by an order under section 23, *i.e.* if it appears to the local planning authority that it is expedient to revoke or modify any LBC, then they may do so (having regard to the development plan and to any other material considerations). The revocation or modification must be exercised at any time before the works have been carried out.[62]

---

[56] LBA 1990, s.25.
[57] LBA 1990, s.25(2)(c).
[58] LBA 1990, s.23; s.24; s.25 and s.28.
[59] LBA 1990, s.24(4).
[60] LBA 1990, s.23 and s.24.
[61] LBA 1990, s.28.
[62] LBA 1990, s.23.

5.17   (b) Under section 28 LBA 1990, if, on a claim made to the local planning authority within the prescribed time and in the prescribed manner, it is shown that the person interested in the building has incurred expenditure in carrying out works which are rendered abortive by the revocation or modification under section 23, or has otherwise sustained loss or damage which is directly attributable to the revocation or modification, the authority shall pay that person compensation in respect of that expenditure, loss or damage. There is a provision about any works carried out before the grant of the listed building consent which is revoked or modified or any other loss or damage before the grant of the consent for which no compensation shall be paid.[63]

The rules set out in section 5 of the LCA 1961 govern the assessment of compensation.

10. LISTED BUILDING PURCHASE NOTICES

5.18   Where LBC is refused or granted subject to conditions, or where consent is revoked or modified after being granted, any owner of the building may in certain circumstances serve a notice on the council of the borough or county district or London borough in which the land is situated, requiring the council to purchase his interest in the land ("listed building purchase notice").[64]

To justify the service of a listed building purchase notice, the owner of the land must claim and be able to show the following criteria:

(a) that the buildings and land have become incapable of reasonably beneficial use in their existing state; and

(b) in a case where consent was granted subject to conditions with respect to the execution of works, or has been modified by the imposition of such conditions that the land cannot be rendered capable of such use by the carrying out of the works in accordance with those conditions; and

(c) in any case, that the land cannot be rendered capable of such use by the carrying out of any other works for which listed building con-

---

[63] LBA 1990, s.28(3).
[64] LBA 1990, s.32.

sent has been granted or for which the local planning authority or the Secretary of State has undertaken to grant such consent.[65]

"The land" means the building in respect of which consent has been refused, or granted subject to conditions, or is revoked or modified by the imposition of conditions, and in respect of which a notice under sections 23, 26 or 32 LBA has been served, together with any land comprising the building, or contiguous or adjacent to it, and owned with it, being land as to which the owner claims that its use is substantially inseparable from that of the building, and that it ought to be treated, together with the building, as a single holding.[66]

Where a question arises as to what is or would in any particular circumstances be a reasonably beneficial use of land, no account is to be taken of any prospective use of that land which would involve the carrying out of any new development or of any works requiring LBC which might be executed to the building, other than works for which the local planning authority or the Secretary of State have undertaken to grant consent.[67] Excluded from this description of "development" is the rebuilding of any building which was in existence on July 1, 1948 or any building which was in existence before that date but was destroyed or demolished after January 7, 1937, including the making good of war damage; the rebuilding of any building created after July 1, 1948, so long as the cubic capacity of the original building is not substantially exceeded. Also the carrying out of maintenance, improvement or other alterations to any building where the works affect only the interior of the building or do not materially affect its external appearance. Additionally, the description does not apply to the use, as two or more separate dwellinghouses of any building which at a material date was used as a single dwellinghouse.[68] In confirming a listed building purchase notice the Secretary of State need not have regard to any history of neglect or decay of the building (*Leominster Borough Council v. Minister of Housing and Local Government*).[69]

Within three months of the service of a listed building purchase notice on **5.19** the appropriate council, the council must serve notice on the owner stating either:

(1) that they are willing to comply; or
(2) that another local authority or statutory undertaker specified in the notice has agreed to comply in their place; or
(3) that for reasons specified they are not willing to comply and have not found any other local authority or statutory undertakers who will agree to comply in their place, and that they have transmitted to the Secretary of State a copy of the purchase notice and of the council's notice in reply.[70]

In the first two cases above, *i.e.* the council is willing to comply, or others are willing to comply in their place, the council or other statutory authority are deemed to be authorised compulsorily to acquire the owner's interest

[65] LBA 1990, s.32(2).
[66] LBA 1990, s.32(3).
[67] LBA 1990, s.32(4).
[68] T.C.P.A. 1990, Sched. 3, Parts (1) and (2).
[69] (1971) 218 E.G. 1419.
[70] LBA 1990, s.33(1) and (2).

and are deemed to have served a notice to treat at the date of service of the council's notice.[71] In the third case above, *i.e.* where neither the council nor others are willing to comply, the council must transmit to the Secretary of State a copy of the purchase notice, together with a copy of their notice in reply.[72] The procedure thereafter is the same as for a purchase notice on refusal of planning permission (for which see sections 137–144 T.C.P.A. 1990). Indeed, where both planning permission and listed building consent have been refused or conditionally granted, a purchase notice and a listed building purchase notice may be served in respect of the same building. A model purchase notice appears in Appendix 1 of DOE Circular 13/83 and can be adapted for listed buildings. If the Secretary of State is satisfied that the conditions in section 32 (set out as conditions (1) to (3), above) are fulfilled, he has the power to confirm the notice. His power in respect of part only of the land, if he is only satisfied that the conditions are fulfilled in respect of part of the land remains the same.[73] But before confirming a notice he must be satisfied that the land is contiguous or adjacent to the building as is required for preserving the building or its amenities, or for affording access to it, or for its proper control or management.[74]

Where the notice was served because LBC was refused or granted subject to conditions, the Secretary of State may if it appears to him expedient, grant LBC for the works, or revoke or amend the conditions imposed on the consent, instead of confirming the listed building purchase notice.[75] Similarly, where the purchase notice was served because LBC had been revoked or modified, the Secretary of State may cancel the order that revoked the consent, or revoke or amend conditions imposed by an order that modified LBC, instead of confirming the purchase notice.[76]

If the land could be rendered capable of reasonably beneficial use within a reasonable time by carrying out other works for which LBC ought to be granted or by the carrying out of development for which planning permission ought to be granted, the Secretary of State may direct that such consent or planning permission shall be granted within a reasonable time if an application is made, instead of confirming the purchase notice.[77]

Where a notice is confirmed by the Secretary of State, the council or other authority are deemed to be authorised to acquire compulsorily the owner's interest, and are deemed to have served a notice to treat on such date as the Secretary of State may direct.[78]

If, before the end of a certain period of time which is either nine months from the service of the purchase notice, or six months from the transmission of the notice to the Secretary of State, whichever is the earlier, the Secretary of State has neither confirmed the notice, nor taken any other action as indicated above, and has not notified the owner that he does not propose to confirm the notice, it is deemed to be confirmed at the end of the period.[79]

---

[71] LBA 1990, s.33(3)(a) and (b).
[72] LBA 1990, s.33(1)(c).
[73] LBA 1990, s.35(2).
[74] LBA 1990, s.35(3).
[75] LBA 1990, s.35(4).
[76] LBA 1990, s.35(4).
[77] LBA 1990, s.35(5).
[78] LBA 1990, s.36(1).
[79] LBA 1990, s.36(2).

11. ACQUISITION OF LISTED BUILDINGS IN NEED OF REPAIR

5.20 Vale Farmhouse at Broad Oak Canterbury,[80] was a mid-eighteenth-century Grade II listed building and was owned by the Mid-Kent Water Company. The owners had been served with a compulsory purchase order following the service of a repairs notice in June 1988. The Water Company had owned the building since 1974, and at the inquiry into the appeal against the order, the Inspector found that the company had consistently failed to take reasonable steps to ensure the preservation of the farmhouse. The Water Company foresaw the need for a reservoir by the year 2000 and felt that Broad Oak was the only geological site for it. They had applied unsuccessfully to the local planning authority to relocate the farmhouse to a nearby location, and had concluded that the market value of the resulting dwelling (had it been approved) would have covered the cost of dismantling and re-erection, whereas the cost of carrying out repairs to the farmhouse *in situ* would be £150,000 and would be lost if the land was subsequently submerged by the reservoir.

The Secretary of State confirmed the order and agreed with his Inspector that reasonable steps were not being taken for properly preserving the building, and he was satisfied that it was expedient to make provision for its compulsory acquisition. The Inspector had also concluded that the minimum compensation direction in the order was justified, but the Secretary of State considered it was not a matter on which he could adjudicate. Any person having an interest in the building was entitled to apply within a period of 28 days after the making of the Order to a Magistrates' Court for an Order that the direction be not included in the compulsory purchase order under the provisions of section 50(6) of the LBA 1990.

12. DEMOLITION, ALTERATIONS AND EXTENSIONS: THE GENERAL PRINCIPLES

5.21 Reference is made earlier to the problem of whether demolition is development,[81] and the difficulty of drawing the line between what is demolition (which, *e.g.* requires conservation area consent in the case of unlisted buildings in conservation areas) and alteration (which does not).[82]

We now seek to set out the principles on which these problems are to be determined:

    (a) Demolition may amount to development,[83] but it does not generally require planning permission.[84]

    (b) Demolition of a listed building requires listed building consent,[85]

---

[80] [1991] J.P.L., SE3/5273/362/1.
[81] See also paras. 5.01–5.02 above.
[82] See also paras. 3.15–3.16 above.
[83] See para. 5.01 above.
[84] See Circular 16/92.
[85] LBA 1990 ss.7 and 8.

and demolition of a scheduled ancient monument requires scheduled monument consent.[86]

(c) Demolition of an unlisted building in a conservation area generally requires conservation area consent,[87] whereas an alteration or extension to an unlisted building in a conservation area does not require such consent.

(d) Demolition is not a term which is defined in the LBA, nor is there a definition or guidance in the regulations nor in PPG 15; however Circular 26/92 now addresses the issue of planning controls over demolition.

(e) The problem arises in determining the line between demolition and partial demolition (a phrase not used in the LBA) and the line between demolition and the removal of materials which is required for the purpose of an alteration or addition to a listed building.

(f) If demolition only is concerned, i.e. there is no extension or alteration involved, then listed building consent or conservation area consent may be required, however small the extent of the demolition. "Building" includes in its definition "part of a building."[88] Partial demolition cannot be justified as avoiding the need for LBC or CAC on the grounds that only a few stones are removed: they might be the vital ones. But this will not apply to free standing structures built after 1948 within the curtilage nor to the other exemptions in the Direction in Circular 8/87.

(g) Mr Justice Comyn in considering this question of demolition or alteration/extension in relation to addition to an old farm house, involving "keying-in" or marrying the extension to the existing building, concluded that not every piece of work by way of alteration or extension necessarily amounted to demolition.[89] He thought any court would be prepared to overlook and be prepared to treat as an alteration rather than demolition "something small by way of interference with a listed building." In the event he found that what had been proposed did amount to demolition and quashed, on the application by a neighbour for judicial review, decisions of the local planning authority granting planning permission and listed building consent. The decisions of the authority would have been in order if the words stood simply as stated in section 55 of the T.C.P.A. 1971: "demolition of a [listed] building or [for its] alteration or extension" (now found in section 8 LBA) but the decisions were bad because the interpretation section of the Act defined "building" as including "a part of a building."

(h) To adopt the criterion of Comyn J. we must then determine what is "something small." There is no authority on this subject, but we suggest two tests: a qualitative and a quantitative test.

(i) Applying a qualitative test we would expect the DNH to view as alterations and not as demolition: the replacement of one type of roofing material with another, e.g. asbestos tiles for slate, the removal of part of the fabric of a building purely to facilitate the

---

[86] See paras. 8.16–8.17 below.
[87] For exceptions to the general rule, see paras. 3.13–3.14 above.
[88] s.366 T.C.P.A. 1990.
[89] R v. North Hertfordshire DC ex p. Lorana Olcott Sullivan (1981) J.P.L. 752.

carrying out of alterations or extensions (particularly the removal of part of the roof or wall to enable an extension to be constructed), new windows in enlarged openings or new doors, always on the assumption that such alterations or extensions would affect the character as a building of special architectural or historic interest and therefore require LBC.

(j) To apply a quantitative test, it might be helpful to consider a 10 per cent of the cubic content basis; 10 per cent or under might not be considered demolition. The genesis of this (perhaps not unreasonable) basis is that 10 per cent is that element of the cubic content of a Grade II (unstarred) listed building which does not require listed building consent.[90] A further example of the use of 10 per cent as a *de minimis* criterion is the direction which exempts the necessity for a conservation area consent in relation to the demolition of 10 per cent of a building used for an industrial process.[91]

(k) The former section 55(1) of the T.C.P.A. 1971 provided that "if a person executes or causes to be executed any works for the demolition of a listed building . . . and the works are not authorised . . . he shall be guilty of an offence." This section is re-enacted in section 9 of the LBA 1990, and sub-section (5) provides that where a person is guilty of an offence, the court shall in particular "have regard to any financial benefit which has accrued or appears likely to accrue to him in consequence of the offence."

Offences

In October 1988 at Cambridge Crown Court (case: *R v. Chambers and others*), J T Chambers (Chartcris) Ltd were convicted of two charges of demolishing a listed building without consent. They were ordered to pay a fine of £1,000 on each count, plus £1,000 prosecution costs to the Fenland District Council. Two directors of the company were similarly and separately convicted of two charges of unlawfully demolishing a listed building and both were ordered to pay a fine of £17,000 on each count, *i.e.* £34,000, plus £1,100 prosecution costs, or in default a 12 months' imprisonment. The buildings were listed Grade II and were a pair of mid-19th-century cottages. Previous applications to demolish them had been refused and they were demolished the day before a letter was received by the Council from the Planning Inspectorate, refusing an application by the company for listed building consent to demolish the cottages.

The judge took account of the financial benefits received by the company and decided the penalty should be by way of a fine rather than imprisonment.[92]

5.22

---

[90] Direction contained in para. 86 of Circular 8/87.
[91] Direction contained in para. 97 to Circular 8/87.
[92] J.P.L. 1989, p. 299.

13. ALTERATIONS AND EXTENSIONS: THE MECHANICS OF CONSENT

5.23   Alterations and extensions are little different from demolition in relation to the mechanics of obtaining consent. Publicity need not be given to an application for the alteration of the interior of a Grade II unstarred listed building. Conservation area consent is not required for an alteration or an extension to an unlisted building in a conservation area. Otherwise the procedure for obtaining consent to alter or extend a listed building is the same as for a demolition.[93] There is a fine line to be drawn between "demolition" and "repair". In a prosecution brought before the Magistrates in September 1994 it was alleged by the local planning authority that part of a listed building had been demolished in breach of sections 7 and 9 of the LBA 1990. The District Council focused on two issues: the one being that no listed building consent had been granted for the demolition, and secondly, the words of the Act are "any work of demolition . . . ". The works in question involved taking down a wall and rebuilding it using the same bricks. The Magistrates took the view that the taking down involved demolition and that the intention to rebuild like-for-like did not affect the preceding demolition. We have some doubt as to the validity of this decision.[94]

Listed building consent is required if the proposed works would affect the building's character, and the local planning authority is expected to judge carefully in respect of each application they receive as to the impact of the proposed works on the building's character.

Where these works would *not* affect the character of the building as one of special architectural or historic interest, listed building consent is not required.

This raises the subject of listed building control over repairs; paragraph 3.2 of PPG 15 specifically states that "consent is not normally required for repairs but, where repairs involve alterations which would affect the character of the listed building, consent is required."

It is clear that there is often a fine line between repairs which constitute alterations and those which do not. Routine repairs would not normally affect the character of the building, and especially if undertaken by craftsmen experienced in working on historic buildings where attention to detail is important. Annex C of PPG 15 gives guidance on the general principles to be adopted when altering listed buildings, and much of this advice applies equally to repairs. In paragraph C40 of this Annex to the PPG, it advises that the rule to be adopted in dealing with such items as windows in historic buildings—if they are beyond repair—is that they should be replaced on a "like-for-like" basis. If this advice is followed, the works would not normally constitute demolition.

The philosophy when undertaking repairs is that they should be "low-key" and the finished appearance should not reveal evidence of the work, if listed building consent is to be avoided.

---

[93] The question of what is or is not an alteration as regards listed buildings has been discussed in various cases concerning VAT liability. See Chap. 9.

[94] Denison Till, York. October, 1994.

14. EXTERIORS AND INTERIORS: THE PRINCIPLES

Alterations or extensions in many cases will be permitted development, **5.24** which do not require planning permission. However such changes may still require LBC, for consent must be obtained for any works for the alteration or extension of a listed building in any manner which would affect its character as a building of special architectural or historic interest. It follows that works for the alteration or extension of a listed building in a manner which would not affect its character as a building of special architectural or historic interest will not require LBC (indeed if such works are not develop-ment or are permitted development they might not require any specific per-mission or consent whatsoever).

Clearly it is important to know what is meant by the phrase "in any man-ner which would affect its character as a building of special architectural or historic interest." The LBA offers no guidance on the point, but Annex C of PPG 15 offers guidance. Nevertheless, the question is one of subjective judgment whether particular works affect the architectural or historic inter-est of the building. The LBA does not specifically make the local planning authority nor the Secretary of State the arbiter on this point. However where there is a dispute as to what lays within the ambit of section 8 LBA the local planning authority and ultimately the Secretary of State (or the Court on a point of law) will be the arbiter. As regards listed buildings, there is no provision equivalent to section 64 T.C.P.A. 1990 whereby an inter-ested person may apply to have the question determined whether proposed operations would or would not constitute or involve development and thereby require planning permission. The Government's view on this matter was that a formal certificate procedure would be "unnecessarily complex" and "confusing".[95] It is therefore perhaps of interest to note that in Northern Ireland there is provision for an owner to establish whether or not listed building consent is required in the Planning (Northern Ireland) Order 1991.

The important point is that it is not the works themselves that must be considered, but the manner in which they affect the building. Hence an Inspector in determining an appeal against a refusal of listed building con-sent for the conversion of a stable block to a dwelling at Milwich Hall near Stafford, concluded that "the conversion to residential accommodation in the manner proposed would secure preservation of and improvement to the structure of the stable block without harm to its appearance or to the character of Milwich Hall. For these reasons, it is considered that there are no grounds on which listed building consent for the proposed works should be withheld".[96] The appellant in that case however failed to convince the Inspector that there were any circumstances to justify the grant of planning permission for the proposed use in that particular area, and he dismissed the planning appeal.

The manner in which works affect the building is an issue which has been **5.25** particularly important in respect of the interiors of buildings. This is evi-

[95] *Hansard* (H.L.) Deb. January 29, 1991.
[96] APP/5373/A/79/11330 and 5373/E/80/37 dated January 21, 1981 (courtesy of Staf-ford Borough Council).

denced by the growth in interest in the details of interiors of buildings, and this in turn is reflected in decisions emanating from the DOE or DNH. The following illustrates the point in question. The first example concerned an application to remove a mural sculpture created by Eric Gill which was originally in the centre lounge of the Midland Hotel, Morecambe, a Grade II* listed building. Permission had been given in 1977 for the sculpture to be removed to another room. At the time of the appeal, it was stored in pieces. The Secretary of State ruled that in spite of alterations to the hotel, the remaining interior features were an integral part of the design (by Oliver Hill) and it should be reinstated *in situ*.[97]

In another case, an application for consent to remove a painting of Westminster Abbey from the hall at Woodperry House, a Grade II* listed building at Woodperry, Stanton St John, Oxfordshire, was refused by South Oxfordshire District Council with support being lent by the Georgian Group. The Secretary of State supported his Inspector's appraisal and concluded that "the Westminster painting is important architecturally and historically and it is a good and unspoilt example of an 18th-century decorative scheme with a local connection. It forms an extremely attractive centrepiece to the overmantel and serves as a splendid focal point to the hall and is entirely appropriate to its setting . . . its removal would be seriously detrimental to the character of Woodperry House as a building of special architectural or historic interest."[98]

Although this example is concerned with a particular painting, it raises many issues of wider concern, not least of which is that it draws a useful distinction between a painting which is merely hanging on a wall and a painting which occupies an integral part of the design of the room in which it is located. It appears that such a distinction proved in this case to be the determining issue as to whether it constituted a fixture as specified in section 1(5) of the LBA.

Paragraphs 3.31 and 3.32 of the PPG 15 explain that the tests to be applied in determining whether an object or structure forms part of a listed building or not, is the same as that used in common law to decide whether an article is a fixture. It is relevant to consider both the degree of attachment or physical annexation and also the nature and purpose of annexation. Generally, it would be reasonable to expect some degree of physical annexation, together with indications that the annexation was carried out with the intention of making the object an integral part of the land or building. In the light of this test, it is likely that items such as chimney-pieces, wall panelling and painted or plastered ceilings, will be found to be part of the building.

It may be difficult in some individual cases to decide whether a particular object or structure is a fixture or not. Free-standing objects, *e.g.* statues, may still be fixtures if they were put in place as part of an overall architectural design. But works of art which were placed in a building primarily to be enjoyed as objects in their own right, rather than forming part of the land or of the building, are not likely to be properly considered as fixtures (this is clearly a reference to The Three Graces at Woburn Abbey).

---

[97] DOE reference APP/5292/E/80/187 reported in *Planning Appeals Monthly*, May 1981. See also a case on the removal of a picture forming part of a chimney piece APP/5355/E/80/155 reported in *Planning Appeals Monthly* June, 1981.

[98] APP/Q3115/E/84/800390 dated May 23, 1985 (courtesy of South Oxfordshire District Council).

The uncertainty arising from the decisions on *The Three Graces* and *Orchardleigh* cases was assisted in a decision of November 1994 concerning internal items at Leighton Hall in Welshpool, Mid-Wales.[98a]

The appeals were against two enforcement notices which alleged the removal of a carillon clock, along with its mechanism, and the removal of three ormola bronze chandeliers from the Great Hall of Leighton Hall, without submitting an application for listed building consent.

The Inspector identified the tests to be applied, which were: firstly, the degree to which the objects were fixed to the building, including the ease with which they were removed and any damage caused to the structure by their removal; and secondly, the object or purpose of their annexation to the building, whether for the improvement of the property or for ornamentation and the enjoyment of the objects themselves.

Leighton Hall is a neo-Gothic Grade II* listed building and once formed the centrepiece of a model Victorian agricultural estate. The appeal decisions concentrated on the importance of the twin tests, as contained in section 1(5) of the 1990 Act, of whether or not a fixture comprises part of a listed building by being an "object or structure fixed to the building".

The Great Hall of this "Puginesque" building was lit by three massive ormola bronze chandeliers, all of which hung on bronze coloured metal rods cast to resemble ropes. The entrance tower of this building contained a carillon turret clock which, according to an expert in horology, was a mechanical marvel of its time. It rested on its own weight but was connected to weight shutes in each corner of the tower. In 1991, the absentee owner of the Hall sold these items to a dealer.

The local council issued listed building enforcement notices and a public inquiry ensued. The Secretary of State, in reaching his decision, applied the twin tests; he considered the degree of annexation to the chandeliers and decided that their means of being fixed to the main roof trusses was important. He then considered the object of annexation, and concluded that despite their classical design, which would have been despised by followers of Pugin, they were nevertheless chosen to illuminate and decorate the Great Hall. He therefore considered them to be fixtures of Leighton Hall, and listed building consent was required for their removal.

The Secretary of State then turned his attention to the carillon clock and considered that it was connected to the building to a significant degree by reason of its fixings to the entrance tower and the manner in which the clock was designed as an elaborate piece of furniture, specifically to accommodate it. The entrance tower itself had been adapted to accommodate the workings of the clock. He concluded that the clock was an integral part of the listed building in terms of its fixings, connections to the tower, and the specially designed furniture and decoration to accommodate it; it was therefore part of the listed building.

On the merits of the case the Inspector felt the Great Hall without the chandeliers, when compared with photographs of them *in situ*, illustrated the visual impact of their removal, which detracted from the special character of the building. The void left in the tower since the removal of the clock had resulted in a series of meaningless adapted rooms and mechanisms in this important listed building. The Secretary of State accepted these opinions and refused to grant listed building consent on the application

---

[98a] [1995] J.P.L., March, p. 256.

deemed to have been made. He also upheld the listed buildings enforcement notices and dismissed the appeals.

In contrast to the *Leighton Hall* case are cases involving the buildings in New Bond Street, London, owned by Time/Life International and concerning a bronze sculpture by Henry Moore, a painting by Ben Nicholson, an heraldic clock by Christopher Ironside and an iron sculpture by Geoffrey Clarke.

Listed buildings enforcement notices were issued in July 1993 and December 1993 requiring the return and reinstatement of these works of art to their respective places within the building, a 1950s Grade II listed building.

It has been an objective of the Time/Life organisation to ensure that the building represented in every detail the highest standards of contemporary British skill and imagination in painting, sculpture, fabric and furniture design, etc.

Time/Life had, by the time of the enforcement notice, vacated the building and it was being gutted and refurbished.

The Moore sculpture rested on its own weight on a bronze base which had no fixings. It had been designed for one end of the first floor terrace, but in the 1970s had been relocated. At both times the terrace paving was designed to fit the plinth. The Nicholson painting was on to battened hardboard and was located on the stairway, with a surround of Derbydene marble. Its removal had exposed the bare brick wall behind.

The Ironside clock was hung on Paroba wood cladding on a wall in the reception area, but had been removed to a conference room.

The Clarke iron sculpture originally stood on a column in the reception area and was fixed by hooks and eyes against a white marble backing. It was later moved to the stairway.

The two tests of (i) degree of annexation and (ii) purpose of annexation, were applied to each subject.

There was no physical annexation by weight or any other method of the Moore sculpture, and that conclusively determined it was not a "fixture". On the second test, it was chosen for the building from a number of similar reclining-figures, but was not done specially for the building.

The Nicholson painting was heavy, but its degree of annexation was no greater than was necessary to securely display the painting. The damage caused by its removal was regarded as slight and could easily be restored. Nicholson had been commissioned on behalf of Time/Life to produce a painting for the building, and had chosen an existing one for which a battened board and sample of the marble were supplied. There was contemporary evidence of the mural having been applied to this panel so that it could be moved elsewhere.

The Clarke sculpture was moved by simply lifting it off the wall and so there was no degree of physical annexation. The evidence suggested that although commissioned by Time/Life, it had been considered as a chattel.

The Ironside clock was entirely portable and therefore had no degree of annexation. Again, it was commissioned and paid for by Time/Life but was an ornament without architectural significance and nothing in the purpose of annexation suggested any intention to make the clock part of the reality.

The Inspector considered all the facts and conclusions and felt that, when the building was listed (1988), all the work of art which were enforced against were chattels, and not fixtures, under the common law relating to fixtures. Consequently they were not "fixed" to the listed building within the meaning of s.1(5) of the 1990 Act. They were not part of the listed building and their removal did not constitute a breach of listed building control. The Secretary of State allowed these appeals and directed that the listed building enforcement notices be quashed.[98b]

Each of these two cases must be treated in the light of its own facts, and owners who are contemplating works are advised to contact their local planning authority first.

Another means of drawing a distinction between objects and structures attached to a listed building are covered in an article by Charles Mynors, entitled "The Extent of Listing".[99] He describes the critical test to determine whether or not an object is included would be whether it is a "fixture", *e.g.* carved wood panelling, or a "fitting" (furniture or paintings). Even then there are areas of uncertainty with, for example, tapestries which are fixed to the wall. In two cases: re Whaley [1908] 1 CH 615 tapestries were considered fixtures, and *Leigh v. Taylor* [1902] AC 157 they were not.

The key lesson to be drawn from these examples and advice is that the **5.26** evidence adduced from exacting historical research proved to be critical in determining the association of the fixtures in question with the listed building. Thus where it is known what features of a building were regarded as important on the listing of the building, it is logical to assume that alterations or extensions affecting those features would affect the character of the building as one of special architectural or historic interest and would therefore require LBC. This principle can only be treated as a guideline for a number of reasons:

(1) the building may not yet have been listed; it may be the subject of a building preservation notice which will rarely contain any descriptive material;

(2) the factors which were considered important in deciding to list may not be known—in the case of those buildings which were listed prior to the DOE's 1982–87 survey the Inspector's notes on "list description" may not necessarily have been incorporated into the list;

(3) there may have been subsequent changes to the building or its site, or its setting (whether or not such changes required LBC themselves) which may mean that the factors decisive on listing have been reduced in importance or that new factors should now be taken into account;

(4) the listing inspector may have failed to appreciate certain features of the building, or may have been mistaken as to certain features;

(5) in many cases the listing fieldworker will not have had access to the interior of the building which would have enabled him to make a record of significant internal features;

(6) the list description is not intended to be a justification or explanation for listing; its purpose is partly to serve as a record of features

---

[98b] T/APP/F/93/X5900/630150–1 and T/APP/F/94/X5900/632377–8 [1995] J.P.L., March.

[99] Charles Mynors, *The Extent of Listing*, J.P.L., February 1993.

existing at that date, and partly as an aid to identifying the building in question, but the DNH certainly does not regard it as exhaustive;

(7) Most local authorities do not have a detailed record of interiors and until proposals are submitted their officers may not be aware of any special features.

(8) The two tests which appear now to be applied when assessing the question of fittings and fixtures are i) the degree to which the objects are fixed to a building and ii) the object or purpose of their annexation.

Guidance Notes on Alterations to Listed Buildings set out in Annex C, C58 of PPG 15 gives specific advice on interiors.

Regardless of what features were considered important by the Department on listing, it is thought that the question of whether an alteration or extension would affect the character of a building as one of special architectural or historic interest falls to be determined according to the criteria generally applicable on listing, and that the criteria to be applied should be those applicable as at the date of the proposed alteration or extension.

PPG 15 sets out detailed guidelines on the technical aspects of alterations to listed buildings[1] and summarises "the characteristics and features which make up the special interest of most listed buildings." They should not be regarded as doing more than that. In particular the guidelines are not an attempt to define what alterations require LBC; only after it has been decided that LBC is needed for certain alterations should these guidelines be considered. Logical though this may be, the distinction may not always be obvious. On the subject of doors, for example, the guidelines say: "Original doorways or any surviving original doors should be retained". This does not mean that the alteration or original doorways or doors will always require LBC. Consent will obviously be required where doors or doorways are of such significance in the first place that their alteration must affect the character of the building as one of special architectural or historic interest. There will be cases, however, where the door is so insignificant, its alteration or substitution would not possibly affect the character of the building as being of special architectural or historic interest. These comments apply to many of the other features discussed in the guidelines.

15. ANCIENT MONUMENTS

5.27   The provisions of sections 7–9 LBA 1990 do not apply to "a building for the time being included in the schedule of monuments compiled and maintained under section 1 of the Ancient Monuments and Archaeological Areas Act 1979."[2]

The provisions for the authorisation of works affecting ancient monuments (it is an offence to effect certain specified works without such authorisation) are contained in section 2 of the Ancient Monuments and Archaeological Areas Act 1979. These are considered in Chapter 8.

---

[1] PPG 15, Annex C.
[2] LBA 1990 ss.60(1) and (2) and 61(1) and (2).

16. ECCLESIASTICAL BUILDINGS

Ecclesiastical buildings have always presented particular problems in **5.28**
planning terms. There are three main aspects to this issue. The first is that
no one is sure what the term "ecclesiastical" covers. Whilst one would
expect that all Christian denominations of all kinds might fall within this
definition, what about buildings of non-Christian religions? The second is
that churches in the Anglican community have, since 1913, been treated in
a special way. The third aspect is that churches are so essential a part of our
rich architectural heritage. There are probably 20,000 or so churches belonging to Anglicans, Non Conformists and Roman Catholics alone. Of these,
over 12,000 are listed and 4,500 or so are listed Grade I (or A—a category of
listing once used most such former gradings having now been replaced by
the Grade I category).

The current position regarding ecclesiastical buildings is discussed in
Chapter 10.

17. CROWN LAND

Although section 83(1)(a) LBA [formerly section 266(1) of the Town and **5.29**
Country Planning Act 1971] did not preclude a "building which for the time
being is Crown land" being listed, it was not until 1984 that formal provision was made by which the Crown in respect of Crown land could seek
LBC. This was introduced by the Town and Country Planning Act 1984,
which came into force on August 12, 1984 and is re-enacted in section 84 of
the LBA 1990. In particular, it renders redundant the procedure by which
disposing departments sought an informal opinion from local planning
authorities about appropriate uses of surplus Crown land. The detailed provisions of the Act are fully explained in Circular 18/84—Crown Land and
Crown Development and by the Town and Country Planning (Crown Land
Applications) Regulations 1984. Section 84(1) of the LBA 1990 enables the
Crown to dispose of Crown land or an interest in such land with the benefit
of, *inter alia*, listed building consent or conservation area consent. Corresponding provision is made in the T.C.P.A. 1990 for obtaining planning permission and tree preservation order consent prior to disposal of any interest
in the land.

It is known that planning permission and possibly listed building consents and conservation area consents have been granted in the past in
respect of Crown land in which there was no other interest and that their
validity may be thought to be in doubt. Subsection (8) of s.84 of the LBA
1990 removes this doubt by providing that such permissions and consents
shall be deemed to be valid.

An application for LBC on behalf of the Crown, prior to the disposal of
Crown land, is made to the local planning authority but is required to be
accompanied by a statement confirming there is no private interest held in
the land, and a copy of the consent of the appropriate authority. This latter
requirement was added to Regulation 15(1)(c) of the Planning (Listed Buildings and Conservation Areas) Regulations 1990. The appropriate authority

shall, as soon as may be, after disposing of the listed building in respect of which an application has been made under section 84(2) of the LBA, give notice in writing to the local planning authority on such disposal.

Any consent granted under section 84 applies only to works carried out after the land has ceased to be Crown land, and so long as it continues to be Crown land, to works carried out by virtue of a private interest in the land. Any refusal of consent, or conditions, may be appealed against to the Secretary of State.

(a) Buildings of special architectural or historic interest

5.30   Whilst these "enabling" provisions are intended to assist the Crown, there are no provisions introduced to require a Crown developer to seek listed building consent to demolish, alter or extend a listed building. However, Circular 18/84, Part IV, paragraph 31 provides that departments must consult the local planning authority in a manner prescribed in Part IV, paragraph 9 of the Circular about any proposal to demolish a listed building (rather than one scheduled as an ancient monument or held in departmental care under the provision of the Ancient Monuments and Archaeological Areas Act 1979—for which different procedures apply (see below) or to alter or extend a building in a way which would affect its character as a building of special architectural or historic interest. The local planning authority is asked to advertise such proposals and to notify those bodies listed in Annex A to PPG 15 and local amenity societies, in the same way as they would if application had been made for listed building consent.

If the local planning authority do not themselves wish to make representations, but where, following advertisement and notification, objections are received, the objections should be passed on to the developing department. The department in question then has discretion to decide whether to proceed in the light of the objections or alternatively to consider whether "the substance of the objections is such that it would be appropriate for the Secretary of State to decide whether the proposal should proceed."[3] If they so decide, the developing department then forwards the objections to the Department of the Environment for consideration. In that case and in cases where the Department of the Environment has been notified by the developing department of unresolved disagreement between themselves and the local planning authority, the method of dealing with them is set out in Part IV, paragraph 25 of the Circular. The procedures identified involve either written representations exchanged between all bodies expressing views; or a meeting between representatives of the developing department and the local planning authority, chaired by an officer of the Department of the Environment (this would only be appropriate if there were no other interested bodies); or finally a non-statutory public inquiry may be held and determined by the Secretary of State.

If the proposal involves the demolition of a listed building, government departments are required to give at least one month's notice before commencing demolition to the Royal Commission on Historical Monuments or, in Wales, to the Royal Commission on Ancient and Historical Monu-

---

[3] Circular 18/84, Part IV, para. 32.

ments to enable the respective Commission to consider whether to make a record of the building.

Special consideration needs to be given to listed buildings which are used as hospitals in the green belt. Guidelines for the future use of redundant hospital sites in the green belt are contained in PPG 2 on Green Belts.[4]

(b) Unlisted buildings in conservation areas

Developing departments are required to consult the local planning auth- **5.31** ority, in the manner prescribed in paragraph 9 of Circular 18/84, about any proposals to demolish a building in a conservation area, except where the building is included in one of the descriptions of buildings set out in paragraph 97 of Circular 8/87, when the Secretary of State has directed that control should not apply to the following descriptions of buildings:

(a) buildings with a total cubic content not exceeding 115 cubic metres;
(b) gates, walls, fences, etc., which are less than 1 metre high when abutting a highway or 2 metres in other cases;
(c) buildings erected since January 1914 and used for agriculture or forestry;
(d) buildings used for an industrial process providing that part to be demolished does not exceed 10 per cent of cubic content of original building, or 500 square metres of floor space;
(e) buildings to be demolished under s.102 of the T.C.P. Act;
(f) buildings to be demolished under s.106 of the T.C.P. Act;
(g) buildings required to be demolished as a result of an enforcement notice;
(h) buildings required to be demolished as a condition of planning permission;
(i) buildings to which a demolition order under the Housing Act 1985 applies;
(j) buildings included in a compulsory purchase order made under the Housing Act 1985;
(k) a redundant building covered by the Pastoral Measure 1983.[5]

Where the local planning authority object to the proposed demolition and the matter cannot be resolved to the satisfaction of both parties, the department is required to advise the Department of the Environment and the procedures for resolving the disagreement are substantially the same as those set out above.

(c) The consultation process

This is described in Circular 18/84 on Crown Land and Crown Develop- **5.32** ment (Part IV):

"9 When the formal stage of consultation is reached, the developing

---

[4] PPG 2 "Green Belts" – January 1995.
[5] See Chap. 10.

Department will send to the local planning authority four copies of a statement of their proposal marked 'Notice of Proposed Development by (Department)' sufficient to enable the authority to appreciate its nature and extent.

They will also supply four copies of a location plan showing the relationship of the proposed development to adjoining property and, except where the proposal involves only a material change of use, four copies of plans of the proposed development.

10 The Notice will make it clear whether the proposal is submitted with all relevant details, or in outline only to be followed by the submission of details. If it is in outline, the Notice will specify which, if any, of the reserved matters as defined in the General Development Order, *i.e.* siting, design, external appearance, means of access and landscaping of the site, are included. The local planning authority will not be expected to ask at this stage for further details except where this is essential to enable them to form a view on the proposed development.

11 When the Crown does not hold all the interests in the land, the developing Department will advise the owner, any agricultural tenant and any other tenant with seven or more years of his tenancy to run of the submission and contents of the Notice of Proposed Development.

12 The local planning authority will treat the Notice in the same way as they would a statutory planning application but are recommended to keep a non-statutory addendum to Part II of the register in respect of Notices of Proposed Development."

(d) Crown lands and section 106 agreements

5.33 In view of the increasing use of section 106 agreements (T.C.P.A. 1990) in the planning process, a cautionary note in relation to Crown lands may be thought worthwhile. The essential feature of a section 106 agreement, which is intended to regulate or restrict (either permanently or temporarily) the use of land, is that it is directly enforceable by the local planning authority against the owner for the time being when the LPA wishes to enforce a breach—without the necessity of bringing into an action any intervening owners. But this advantage can only be obtained if the agreement is registered as a local land charge.

Although the Town and Country Planning Act 1984 widened the provisions relating to Crown land as described in the preceding paragraphs, it is to be noted that the 1984 Act specifically did not make reference to what was, at that time, section 52 of the 1971 Act. The basic legal principle is that a statute does not apply to the Crown unless it specifically so states.

5.34 The consequences of this must be that whilst a Crown department may enter into an agreement with a local planning authority, it cannot have the same effect as a section 106 agreement indeed it is strictly not registrable as a local land charge.

There are two solutions to this problem. One is for the Crown land department to enter into a "section 106 type" agreement with the local planning authority—and this agreement would, for enforceability reasons, have to be under seal—whereby the appropriate Secretary of State would agree to procure that on any subsequent disposal of the land the purchaser would enter into a new agreement under seal with the local planning authority in similar terms. The other possibility might be to deal with it by condition on the listed building consent or the conservation area consent. The latter solution might be rather more risky than the first in view of the remaining doubt about positive conditions.

Although the Grampian case[6] suggested that a planning condition might be drawn so that the planning permission did not have effect until work carried out by some third party was effected, that principle has not been tested specifically in the listed buildings area. The former solution would in our view be preferable.

18. PUBLIC HEALTH ACT AND HOUSING ACT CASES

If a building is subject to an order under sections 77 or 78 of the Building **5.35** Act 1984 or under section 52 of the London Building Acts (Amendment) Act 1939 the owner of the building has the choice of demolishing it instead of carrying out works to remedy the danger. It is contended by the Secretary of State that this does not release the owner from the obligation of obtaining LBC if the dangerous structure is listed. Similarly, if a listed building is subject to a notice served by the local authority under section 79 of the 1984 Act because it is a ruinous or dilapidated building which is seriously detrimental to amenity, then LBC is still needed for its demolition. PPG 15 suggests that owners should be reminded of the need for LBC under these circumstances, and the local planning authority must consider whether or not they should use their powers under sections 47, 58 and 54 LBA.[7]

Under the Housing Act 1985 there is no power to make a demolition order in respect of a listed building or one subject to a building preservation notice. The local authority is limited to make a closing order under section 304 of the Housing Act 1935. If the listed building is in a slum clearance area and the local planning authority has purchased it by agreement, they can apply within three months to the Secretary of State for his consent to demolition, or if the authority has made a compulsory purchase order in respect of it, they may, within three months of the listing, apply to the Secretary of State for listed building consent. If the application is refused, the compulsory purchase order ceases to have effect in relation to the building and it ceases to be part of the clearance area.

19. LISTED BUILDINGS ENFORCEMENT NOTICE

Carrying out works without LBC (in breach of section 7 LBA) or in contra- **5.36** vention of a condition attached to a consent (in breach of section 9(2) LBA) can lead either to prosecution or the issuing of an enforcement notice or

---

[6] *Grampian Regional Council v. City of Aberdeen DC* [1984] J.P.L. 590.
[7] PPG 15, Annex B B16 and s.56, LBA 1990.

both. However, in relation to an enforcement notice, the Secretary of State considers it beyond the powers provided in the LBA to require reinstatement of property damaged or destroyed by accident. There is no time limitation provision which restricts the service of an enforcement notice.

Section 38 LBA provides for listed building enforcement notices (together with section 39 LBA relating to appeals against such notices), and has been amended, particularly in relation to the penalties for breach of the provisions of the LBA, the withdrawal of listed building enforcement notices, appeals, variation and enforcement provisions relating to such notices.[8]

Section 38(2) of the LBA provides that:

> (2) A listed building enforcement notice shall specify the alleged contravention and require such steps as may be specified in the notice to be taken within such period as may be so specified:
>
> (a) for restoring the building to its former state; or
>
> (b) if the authority consider that such restoration would not be reasonably practicable or would be undesirable, for executing such further works specified in the notice as they consider necessary to alleviate the effect of the works which were carried out without listed building consent; or
>
> (c) for bringing the building to the state in which it would have been if the terms and conditions of any listed building consent which has been granted for the works had been complied with.

The section provides a local authority with a wide range of powers and flexibility where it is not possible or desirable to undertake a faithful restoration. The *Stagbatch Farm* case referred to below is a case in point.[9]

An interesting point arose with the view expressed by the Secretary of State in a listed building enforcement notice in respect of 6 Mark Square, Stafford. In that case, the Secretary of State said that he considered it beyond the powers provided in the Act under the enforcement procedures to require the reinstatement of property damaged or destroyed by accident. The essence of an enforcement notice is that it is triggered by a breach of planning control which may itself, particularly in relation to a listed building, constitute a criminal offence.[10]

Where a requirement is imposed in the terms stated in section 38(2)(b) above, section 38(7) LBA provides that LBC shall be deemed to be granted for any works of demolition, alteration or extension of the building executed as a result of compliance with the notice.

5.37 Copies of the notice must be served on the owner/occupier of the building and on any other person whose interest in the building is, in the opinion of the authority, materially affected by the notice, the service of which is to take place not later than 28 days after the date of issue of the notice, and not later than 28 days before the date specified in the notice as the date on which it is to take effect.[11] The local planning authority may withdraw a listed building enforcement notice (without prejudice to their power to issue another one) at any time before it takes effect, and if they do withdraw

[8] PCA 1991 s.25 and Sched. 3.
[9] APP/C1815/F/86/162, July 13, 1987.
[10] [1981] J.P.L. 443 APP/5373/F/79/33.
[11] LBA 1990, s.38(4).

such a notice, every person on whom the notice has been served must be notified of the fact.[12]

Section 38 LBA confers no power on a local planning authority to require the improvement of a building to restore an historic appearance. In *Bath City Council v. Secretary of State*[13] the roof of an hotel was composed of two-thirds Welsh slate and one third asbestos cement slates. The owners decided to re-cover the whole roof entirely with asbestos slates, and an enforcement notice was served requiring all the asbestos slates to be replaced by Welsh slates. Woolf J. (as he then was) quashed the enforcement notice. He concluded that this provision could not be used to secure an improvement to a listed building compared to its state before the unauthorised works were carried out.

A further point has been found to arise in practice related to the content and wording of the notice. It would seem that the DOE encourage a local planning authority as a general rule to be somewhat more specific than to require restoration in a manner or with materials "to be agreed by the local planning authority". Does this mean that the authority is to specify materials by name, or even the manufacturer?

Of course it is often the case that a number of enforcement notices are served. The demolition and storage of materials pending sale in America of the listed barn at Stagbatch Farm, near Leominster[14] gave rise to enforcement notices being served on the site owners, the contractors and an "antique company" responsible for the re-sale. The barn was dated about 1620 and was found to have been properly listed. About 75 per cent of the structural frame had been safely recovered and it was accepted that the only way to satisfy the requirements of the notice was to re-erect it on the original site. At 1985 prices, £3750 had been paid for the salvageable fabric and a contract had been entered into to sell the same at a profit; this justified the dealer being brought into the enforcement proceedings as a person with an "interest". The appellant argued that rebuilding of the barn would have resulted in a replacement of better quality, thus going beyond the requirements of what was to become section 38 LBA. The Secretary of State determined that there might be some improvement, but concluded that the antique company was in the best position to restore the barn as they had made a photographic survey of it during its dismantling, upheld the enforcement notice and allowed six months to rebuild.[15] The case was subsequently heard by Mr Justice Mann in the High Court. The issues before the Court were:

(a) Did a local planning authority have power to serve a listed building enforcement notice despite the fact that the building to which it related had been demolished?

(b) Is a person capable of being regarded as the owner of a listed building when he is the owner of (1) all of the extant parts of the building which have been demolished, or (2) some of the extant parts of the building which had been demolished?

[12] LBA 1990, s.38(5) and (6) and PCA 1991 s.25 and Sched. 3 para. 2.
[13] *The Times*, March 25, 1983; [1983] J.P.L. 737.
[14] See *R. v. Scominster DC ex p. Antique Country Buildings Ltd* [1988] J.P.L. 554.
[15] APP/C1815/F86/162, July 13, 1987—reported in *Planning* (July 31, 1987) and *Chartered Surveyor Weekly* (August 6, 1987).

Mann J said, referring to the Act: "restoring the building to its former state", does that exclude cases in which the demolition has been so complete that there is nothing left which, in other contexts, one might ordinarily describe as a building? Mr Justice Mann did not accept that he should make semantic distinctions as to whether or not what was left could be described contextually as a building or not. He concluded that in the context of section 96 T.C.P.A. 1971 the word "building" is perfectly capable of meaning something which had been a listed building but which had since been demolished. He did point out however that an enforcement notice can only require "restoration", and therefore the extent of the demolition may be important. If there is only rubble or ash remaining, e.g. if the timbers had been burned, then mere replication would be possible, and he considered that a requirement to "restore" could not extend to the construction of a replica.[16]

Some authorities, faced with a situation which would justify both the service of an enforcement notice and the institution of a prosecution might be tempted to back the situation both ways. The South Lakeland District Council did this in relation to the Crown Inn at Flookburgh, near Grange-over-Sands.[17] The prosecution was dealt with first; the enforcement proceedings thereafter. The Secretary of State in dealing with the listed building enforcement notice stated:

> "The Secretary of State notes the Inspector's conclusion and recommendation. However, in view of the judgment given in the Crown Court at Barrow, on appeal against the conviction in the Magistrates Court, and in that it was found that the alteration was to a very nominal extent and did not justify a conviction, the present appeal must, in the Secretary of State's opinion, succeed on ground (b) of Section 97(1) of the Act. Accordingly, the Secretary of State allows your client's appeal and hereby directs that the listed building enforcement notice issued on December 21, 1984 be quashed".

5.38   If the whole of a building is demolished and the materials which formed part of the building are destroyed, thus distinguishing the situation from the facts of the *Stagbatch Farm* case referred to above, then there is a question as to whether or not an enforcement notice would lie at all on the grounds that there is no building left to be the subject of an enforcement notice. It is understood that the view of the DOE is that if there is a substantial part of the building left, then this can be the subject of a valid enforcement notice. There is no clear authority on where the dividing line (if there be a dividing line) comes between what can be the subject of an enforcement notice and what cannot, but the opinion of Mr Justice Mann in the *Stagbatch Farm* case it should be borne in mind.

Much will depend on the intent of the owners. An accident is one thing; a deliberate act is another. In the middle of all this comes a mistake such as the *Monkspath Hall, Solihull*, case,[18] where the defendant company's bull-

---

[16] *R v. Leominster DC ex p. Antique Country Buildings Ltd* [1988] J.P.L. 554.

[17] APP/X0990/F/85/19.

[18] *Solihull BC v. D. Doyle Contractors (Birmingham) Ltd*, reported in *The Times*, November 7, 1985, and also *The Times*, May 19, 1981.

dozer driver mistakenly demolished an eighteenth-century Grade II listed farmhouse instead of farm buildings across the road. Driver and company were successfully prosecuted and there was an order in the High Court for the company to pay for the costs of rebuilding and preservation of still-intact parts of the farmhouse (estimated in 1985 at £200,000), and also the costs of the hearing and the professional fees involved, but this was a result of a breach of the contractual relationship between the council (which commissioned the demolition of the (other) building) and the contractors.

In the end there are two factors which are taken into account in practical terms in relation to listed buildings enforcement notices. They are "wilfulness" and "the 50 per cent. rule". Neither has statutory effect and neither can be relied on as constituting a defence to a listed building enforcement notice. But in practice local planning authorities rarely serve enforcement notices unless those responsible for the building have wilfully damaged it. If there is less than 50 per cent of the building left, a broad test, (but thought to be 50 per cent of the cubic content), the Department will rarely, it seems, uphold a listed building enforcement notice.

With those two, albeit unofficial, criteria in mind, the result seems to be: **5.39**

- (a) if all that is left is a heap of assorted rubble, a listed building enforcement notice will not lie or is unlikely to be upheld;
- (b) if all the basic structural parts of the building are there but not in place, it seems now more likely that an enforcement notice will lie (see the *Stagbatch Farm, Leominster* decision above).
- (c) if the "building" on site is less than 50 per cent by cubic content is in place, it seems unlikely that, particularly in the absence of a wilful act, a local planning authority would serve a listed building enforcement notice or that the Department would uphold it;
- (d) if the roof was off but otherwise the "building" was substantially in place, an enforcement notice would probably lie and be upheld;
- (e) if there were parts of the building missing—perhaps because of a fire or other accidental damage, then it is unlikely—particularly in the absence of wilfulness and if there was difficulty in reproducing the craftsmanship—that an enforcement notice would lie or be enforced (see the *Stafford* case below at paragraph 5.42);
- (f) there is no limitation period within which an enforcement notice must be issued;
- (g) if the owner of land on whom a listed building enforcement notice is served, parts with the ownership of land before the end of the compliance period, he may attempt to have liability apportioned between himself and the new owner. The listed building enforcement notice is registered as a local land charge and therefore the new owner should have been aware of the notice when he acquired the land. The original owner is entitled to lay information to state that he has ceased to own the land and to have the subsequent owner brought before the court by giving the prosecution three clear days notice. The original owner may pass the responsibility for taking any steps required by the notice to the subsequent owner, who may then be convicted of the offence. If the original owner is able to prove that he took all responsible steps to comply with the notice, he must be acquitted.

20. APPEAL AGAINST ENFORCEMENT NOTICE

5.40   Under section 39(1) LBA a person on whom a listed building enforcement notice is served, or any other person with an interest in the building (which includes a person who, at the date of issue of the notice, occupies the land or building by virtue of a licence in writing and continues so to occupy when the appeal is brought),[19] may appeal to the Secretary of State against the notice on any of the following grounds:

(a) that the building is not of special architectural or historic interest;

(b) that the matters alleged to constitute a contravention of section 9(1) or (2) LBA do not involve such a contravention;

(c) that the contravention of that section alleged in the notice has not taken place;

(d) that the works were urgently necessary in the interests of safety or health or for the preservation of the building, that it was not practicable to secure safety or health or, as the case may be, the preservation of the building by works of repair or works for affording temporary support or shelter, and that the works carried out were limited to the minimum measures immediately necessary;

(e) that listed building consent ought to be granted for the works, or that any relevant condition of such consent which has been granted ought to be discharged or different conditions substituted;

(f) that copies of the notice were not served as required by section 38(4) (of the LBA);

(g) except in relation to such a requirement as is mentioned in section 38(2)(b) or (c) LBA, the requirements of the notice exceed what is necessary for restoring the building to its condition before the works were carried out;

(h) that the period specified in the notice as the period within which any step required by the notice is to be taken falls short of what should reasonably be allowed;

(i) that the steps required by the notice for the purpose of restoring the character of the building to its former state would not serve that purpose;

(j) that the steps required to be taken by virtue of section 38(2)(b) LBA exceed what is necessary to alleviate the effect of the works executed to the building;

(k) that the steps required to be taken by virtue of section 38(2)(c) LBA exceed what is necessary to bring the building to the state in which it would have been if the terms and conditions of the listed building consent had been complied with;

(l) a local planning authority may apply to the Court for an injunction under the provisions of section 222 of the Local Government Act 1973 where they consider it expedient for the promotion or protection of the interests of the inhabitants of their area. The appropriate court is the High Court or County Court.[20] English Heritage

---

[19] LBA 1990, s.39(7).
[20] LBA 1990, s.44A.

has similar powers to institute proceedings to restrain contraventions[21];

(m) if it appears to the Secretary of State to be expedient that a listed building enforcement notice should be issued in respect of any land, he may issue such a notice after consulting the local planning authority and, if the land is situated in England, the Commission.[22]

On an appeal against an enforcement notice served by Lincoln City Council in respect of the erection of external shutters to the sash windows of a house, the Inspector concluded that although the house would look marginally better without the shutters, the appellant, who had restored the previously dilapidated building, should be given the benefit of the doubt and allowed to retain the shutters; the Secretary of State allowed the appeal.[23] **5.41**

Change of materials or use of inappropriate materials is often the subject of listed building enforcement action by local planning authorities. At Buckingham, an enforcement notice was served in respect of works which replaced the rendering on the front of a building with a "Mock Tudor" finish which, in the words of the Inspector, "produced a facade which is not even an hybrid of good architectural styles and which is unacceptable." The appeal against the enforcement notice was dismissed, although the period for compliance was extended.[24] By contrast, an enforcement notice served by Shepway District Council in relation to roofing alterations at The Barn, Home Farm, Newington, was quashed on the Inspector's recommendation. The notice required that Kent peg roofing tiles be replaced by the available original tiles and additional matching tiles; however, three-quarters of the original tiles had been removed from the roof before service of a building preservation notice, which made the building subject to the listed building controls. Consequently it was only the removal of the remaining 25 per cent against which the local planning authority could enforce, and the Inspector considered that such enforcement would serve no useful purpose and would be absurd.[25] There have been a number of cases involving telephone kiosks, the most significant of which occurred in 1989. Listed building enforcement notices were issued in respect of alterations to telephone kiosks by the introduction of coloured "Payphone" panels in The Promenade, Cheltenham.[26] This location was described as one of fine townscape quality, much of it laid out and developed in the Regency period. The appellants, British Telecommunications plc had agreed to the listing of a K6 telephone box on The Promenade. Appeals on the ground that these kiosks were not of listable quality were rejected because the appellants' witnesses conceded that works carried out to kiosks contravened section 7 and that replacement panels could be improved.

A similar case arose in Stafford where an enforcement notice was served alleging that the pilaster mouldings, console brackets and flat cornice hood had been removed from the doorway of a Grade II listed building. The local **5.42**

---

[21] National Heritage Act 1985, s.33, as amended by Planning and Compensation Act 1991, s.29.
[22] LBA 1990, s.46.
[23] *Planning Appeals*, Vol. 2, p. 262 Ref: APP/5311/F/76/4.
[24] *Planning Appeals*, Vol. 2, p. 262 Ref: APP/918/F/74/3.
[25] *Planning Appeals*, Vol. 3, p. 259 Ref: APP/5281/F/77/34.
[26] T/APP/F/88/B1605/1/P6.

planning authority did not dispute that the original cornice hood projected into the inside of a bend in the highway and had been damaged on occasions by vehicles and had deteriorated to a point beyond which it was impossible to repair or replace it. The Secretary of State considered that in view of the extent of the damage already caused by vehicular impact, the eventual removal of the cornice, console brackets and pilasters, could not reasonably be regarded as an alteration affecting the character of the listed building and that therefore the action is unlikely to have constituted a contravention of section 7 LBA. He also considered it beyond the powers provided in the Act under the enforcement procedures to require the reinstatement of property damaged or destroyed by accident. Accordingly, he allowed the appeal and quashed the enforcement notice. He also awarded costs to the appellant, as he felt that the council ought to have realised in the particular circumstances of the case that the removal of the cornice, console brackets and pilasters could not reasonably be regarded as an alteration affecting the character of the building.[27]

5.43 The Planning and Compensation Act 1991 substituted new provisions in section 41 of the LBA 1990 which gave the Secretary of State power on an appeal under section 39 of the LBA 1990 to correct any defect error or misdescription in a listed building enforcement notice or vary the terms of a listed building enforcement notice if he is satisfied that the correction or variation will not cause injustice to the appellant or local planning authority. It also gave the Secretary of State power to quash the notice where he determines to allow the appeal.

The Secretary of State's powers under sections 40 and 41 LBA relating to appeals against listed building enforcement notices (under section 39 LBA) include power to make regulations prescribing time limits for the making of an appeal, and for dismissing an appeal if it is made outside that time limit, or for allowing it if the local planning authority fails to comply with any requirements and regulations. The detailed provisions for appeals against listed building enforcement notices are contained in the Town and Country Planning (Enforcement) Notices and Appeals (Amendment) Regulations 1992 and The Town and Country Planning (Inquiries Procedure) Rules 1992 which apply the same procedure to these appeals as to ordinary enforcement notice appeals. The Secretary of State may also correct immaterial defects in the notice, quash the notice, grant LBC for the works to which the notice relates, discharge or substitute conditions, grant planning permission, or remove the building from the list.[28]

If an appeal is made before the date specified in the listed building enforcement notice, it does not take effect until the withdrawal or final determination of the appeal (section 39(3)). An appeal is not finally determined until the Secretary of State has given his decision and time has been allowed for appealing to the High Court or from them to the Court of Appeal or the House of Lords has expired. An appeal cannot be regarded as having been finally determined until there is no longer the possibility of it being remitted by a court under section 65 for determination or re-determination by the Secretary of State.[29]

There is a right of appeal from a decision of the Secretary of State to the

[27] [1981] J.P.L. 443, APP/5373/F/79/33.
[28] LBA 1990, s.41.
[29] *R v. Kuxhaus* [1988] J.P.L. 545 (1988) 2 PLR 59.

High Court on a question of law[30] but in relation to the merits of the grant of planning permission or LBC his decision is final.[31]

Appeals are determined on the basis of the T.C.P. (Determination of appeals by Appointed Persons) (Prescribed Classes) Regulations 1981 (S.I. 1981 No. 804) (as amended by S.I. 1986 No. 623(c)(d) and further substituted by S.I. 1989 No. 1087).[32]

Inspectors are enabled to determine listed building consent (section 20 of LBA 1990) and listed building enforcement notice (section 39 of LBA 1990) appeals relating to the demolition of Grade II listed buildings as well as those appeals relating to their alteration and extension. The Secretary of State for the Environment continues to determine appeals relating to Grade I and II* listed buildings; and appeals relating to buildings for which grants have been made under section 3A or 4 of the Historic Buildings and Ancient Monuments Act 1953. Appeals relating to listed building consent, listed building enforcement notices, and control of demolition in conservation areas affecting buildings in Wales, will continue to be dealt with by the Secretary of State.

21. CRIMINAL MATTERS

There are five principal sanctions by way of criminal prosecutions in relation to listed buildings, and unlisted buildings in conservation areas. There are also specific criminal penalties in relation to ancient monuments but these are dealt with separately in Chapter 8. **5.44**

(a) Section 7 LBA—unauthorised work to a listed building

Under section 7 of the LBA 1990:

" . . . no person shall execute or cause to be executed any works for the demolition of a listed building or for its alteration or extension in any manner which would affect its character as a building of special architectural or historic interest, unless the works are authorised."

In March 1990 Beverley Borough Council successfully prosecuted the owner of a listed building who had removed C18 walling from the ground floor of 20 North Bar Beverley, without obtaining LBC. The matter was heard before a jury in the Crown Court. The jury was unanimous in finding the owner guilty of carrying out works which had affected the character of the building as a listed building. The owner was fined £5,000 plus costs.[33]

If section 7 is contravened then an offence is committed under section 9.

---

[30] LBA 1990, s.65.
[31] LBA 1990.
[32] [1989] J.P.L. 662—Encyclopedia of Planning Law.
[33] Article by T. G. Atkinson in Association of Conservation Officer's Journal, CONTEXT, September, 1990.

9(3) "In proceedings for an offence under this section it shall be a defence to prove the following matters—

(a) that works to the building were urgently necessary in the interest of safety or health or for the preservation of the building;

(b) that it was not practicable to secure safety or health or, as the case may be, the preservation of the building by works of repair or works for affording temporary support or shelter;

(c) that the works carried out were limited to the minimum measures immediately necessary; and

(d) that notice in writing justifying in detail the carrying out of the works was given to the local planning authority as soon as reasonably practicable."

[amendments introduced by Planning and Compensation Act 1991]:

9(4) "A person guilty of an offence under this section shall be liable

(a) on summary conviction to imprisonment for a term not exceeding six months or a fine not exceeding the statutory maximum,[34] or both; or

(b) on conviction on indictment to imprisonment for a term not exceeding two years or a fine, or both.

9(5) In determining the amount of any fine to be imposed on a person convicted of an offence under this section, the court shall in particular have regard to any financial benefit which has accrued or appears likely to accrue to him in consequence of the offence."

These provisions also apply to the demolition of unlisted buildings in conservation areas (section 74(3) LBA 1990).

(b) Section 59(1) LBA—acts causing or likely to result in damage to listed buildings

5.45 59(1) If, with the intention of causing damage to a listed building, any relevant person does or permits the doing of any act which causes or is likely to result in damage to the building, he shall be guilty of an offence and liable on summary conviction to a fine not exceeding level 3 on the standard scale.

(2) A person is a relevant person for the purpose of subsection (1) if apart from that subsection he would be entitled to do or permit the act in question.

(3) Subsection (1) does not apply to an act for the execution:

(a) of works authorised by planning permission granted or deemed to be granted in pursuance of an application under the principal Act; or

(b) of works for which listed building consent has been given under this Act.

[34] Presently £20,000, s.25 and Sched. 3 PCA 1991.

(4) If a person convicted of an offence under this section fails to take such reasonable steps as may be necessary to prevent any damage or further damage resulting from the offence, he shall be guilty of a further offence and liable on summary conviction to a fine not exceeding one tenth of level 3 on the standard scale for each day on which the failure continues.

(c) Section 43 LBA—non-compliance with a listed building enforcement notice

Section 43 has been completely amended by a revision introduced by the **5.46** Planning and Compensation Act 1991, Schedule 3, paragraph 6.[35] The former section was entitled "Penalties for non compliance with listed building notice"; the current section 43 is headed: "Offence where listed building enforcement notice not complied with".

The present section 43 provides that where, at any time after the end of the period for compliance with the notice any step required by a listed building enforcement notice to be taken has not been taken, the person who is the owner of the land is in breach of the notice.

Any person who is guilty of an offence under the section shall be liable, on summary conviction, to a fine not exceeding £20,000, and on conviction on indictment, to a fine.

The section provides:

(1) Where, at any time after the end of the period for compliance with the notice, any step required by a listed building enforcement notice to be taken has not been taken, the person who is then owner of the land is in breach of the notice.

(2) If at any time the owner of the land is in breach of a listed building enforcement notice, he shall be guilty of an offence.

(3) An offence under this section may be charged by reference to any day or longer period of time, and a person may be convicted of a second or subsequent offence under this section by reference to any period of time following the preceding conviction for such an offence.

(4) In proceedings against any person for an offence under this section, it shall be a defence for him to show:
  (a) that he did everything he could be expected to do to secure that all the steps required by the notice were taken; or
  (b) that he was not served with a copy of the listed building enforcement notice and was not aware of its existence.

(5) A person guilty of an offence under this section shall be liable:
  (a) to a summary conviction, to a fine not exceeding £20,000, and
  (b) on conviction on indictment, to a fine.

(6) In determining the amount of fine to be imposed on a person convicted of an offence under this section, the court shall in particular

---

[35] S.I. 1991, No. 2905, commenced January 2, 1992.

have regard to any financial benefit which has accrued or appears likely to accrue to him in consequence of the offence.

In a case *Mid-Devon District Council v. Avery*[36] the LPA had issued a listed building enforcement notice requiring the respondent to replace modern window frames that had been put into a listed building without consent. The respondent instructed his builder to make up the replacement frames, but he failed to do so within the time allowed by the notices. When the summons was issued by the LPA, the magistrates dismissed the proceedings on the ground that the appellant had taken all reasonable steps to comply with the notice and thereby discharged his statutory duty. The Court of Appeal overturned that decision. The offence was an absolute offence and it was no defence to show that all reasonable steps had been taken to comply with the notice.

This case occurred before the introduction of a new section 43 by the PCA 1991, Schedule 3, paragraph 6 (which took effect in January 1992) and the new section introduces a defence but in narrower terms. It is now a defence for the defendant to show "that he did everything he could be expected to do to secure that all the steps required by the notice were taken". (Section 43(4)(a)).

(d) Section 58—Non compliance with a building preservation notice

5.47   If a building preservation notice is served[37] and, whilst it is in force, an act is done which would be an offence if it was a listed building, the criminal provisions of section 7 LBA (see paragraph 5.44 above) will be applicable. The provisions of section 59 (paragraph 5.45 above) do not however apply to an "act causing or likely to cause damage" in relation to an unlisted building which is the subject of a building preservation notice.

(e) Non-compliance with a dangerous structures notice

5.48   A local authority must consider the provisions contained in sections 47, 48 and 55 of the LBA 1990 before making a dangerous structures notice under the Buildings Act 1984 and the London Building (Amendment) Act 1939. If LBC is not obtained before the works are carried out then a prosecution may be commenced under section 7 LBA 1990 (see paragraph 5.44 above). Of course the defences in section 9 will be available to the defendant that the works were urgently necessary in the interests of safety or health. These provisions apply to listed buildings, unlisted buildings in conser-

---

[36] 1992 P. & C.R. 47.
[37] See para. 2.54 above and LBA 1990 s.3.

vation areas (where demolition is the act complained of) and where buildings are the subject of a building preservation notice. Prosecutions under section 59 LBA 1990 prosecutions could also be brought except in relation to damage to listed buildings subject only to a number of exemptions, namely: Crown land, ecclesiastical buildings; scheduled monuments; unlisted buildings in conservation areas or works authorised by planning permission.

(f) Criminal sanctions generally

In an answer to a Parliamentary Question in the House of Lords, 16 April **5.49** 1991,[38] Baroness Blatch (then Under-Secretary of State at the Department of the Environment) referred to the Planning and Compensation Bill, which was at that time at the "Committee stage" in the Commons and which contained three amendments to the LBA 1990 which would enable increased fines to be imposed by the courts for breaches of listed building controls. The maximum fine on summary conviction for unauthorised works to a listed building was increased from £2,000 to £20,000, and similar increases were made for the offence of not complying with a listed building enforcement notice, again to a maximum of £20,000. For conviction on indictment of either of these offences, the existing penalty is an unlimited fine.

The schedule extends to the Magistrates' Court the existing Crown Court power (section 9(5) of the LBA 1990) which provides that, in determining the amount of any fine to be imposed on a person convicted on indictment of an offence under section 9, the court shall in particular have regard to any financial benefit which has accrued or appears likely to accrue to him in consequence of the offence.

Following the implementation of the Planning and Compensation Act 1991 criminal sanctions for breach of listed building controls are now more likely to be an effective deterrent. Schedule 3 of the PCA 1991 increases the maximum fine in section 9 LBA on summary conviction for unauthorised works to a listed building from £2,000 to £20,000. A similar increase applies in respect of summary conviction for an offence under section 43 LBA (failure to comply with a listed building enforcement notice). On conviction on indictment the penalty is an unlimited fine.

There are other criminal sanctions in relation to listed buildings but **5.50** these, *e.g.* failure to permit entry, are only an application of the criminal offences relating to planning law generally.

There are a number of points which relate to this aspect of listed building legislation, many of them arising from the experience of prosecutions:

(a) Where there is a choice of prosecuting before the Magistrates or before a Crown Court (which is the meaning of the phrase "on indictment") it is up to the prosecution so to elect. It would be expected that the more serious the case, the more likely it would be that it will be dealt with at the Crown Court. In certain circumstances the defendant may, if prosecuted in the Magistrates Court,

[38] [1991] J.P.L., June, p. 518.

opt for trial at the Crown Court. This he must do on the opening of the case. He will usually do it if he feels he will fare better with a jury which will be involved in a trial in the Crown Court.

(b) The prosecution may also opt between a section 7 LBA and a section 59 LBA prosecution. In a section 7 prosecution it must be shown that the act complained of would "affect" the character of the building. There is no such requirement on section 59—only damage need be shown. But section 59 prosecutions may only go to the Magistrates and the penalties are lower than on section 7 prosecution.

(c) A prosecution may be commenced by anyone so long as he can persuade a Magistrate to issue a summons. This requires him to show a *prima facie* cause. Most prosecutions will be by the local authority which is also the local planning authority. But some of the most successful prosecutions have been initiated by the Society for the Protection of Ancient Buildings.

(d) Magistrates are limited to the maximum fine (and in the case of imprisonment to maximum period). Level 3 (mentioned in section 59) is now the standard scale of maximum fine for summary offences, *i.e.* those triable by the Magistrates. This idea was introduced by the Criminal Justice Act 1982, so as to enable the levels to be increased by order of the Secretary of State. Level 3 is presently (in January 1995) a maximum of £400.[39] The Crown Courts however have no limit and it will be seen that the Crown Court in relation to a prosecution under section 7 may fine a defendant to reflect the financial benefit accrued or likely to accrue to him. Although there is no mention in the Act, any court may order the defendant to pay the costs of the prosecution, but this is discretionary.

(e) Section 7 creates an absolute offence, *i.e.* it is not necessary for it to be shown that the defendant knew that the building was a listed building. The Divisional Court, in a 1986 case, pointed out that intent need not be proved — there was a discretion whether to prosecute or not and to refrain from punishment by either fine or imprisonment in appropriate cases.[40]

(f) It was held in *Maltglade v. St Albans*[41] which concerned the service of a building preservation notice, that actual service of the notice must be proved where it was important to establish the date from which the notice took effect, service through the ordinary course of post could not be presumed.

(g) Sometimes the circumstances would justify both enforcement proceedings and a criminal prosecution. But this may not be wise as the criminal prosecution might deter the Secretary of State from confirming a listed building enforcement notice.

(h) Some examples of prosecutions (including prosecutions relating to ancient monuments) which have all led to convictions are:

---

[39] Criminal Penalties etc (Increase) Order 1984 (S.I. 1984 No. 447).

[40] *R v. Wells Streets Stipendiary Magistrate, ex parte Westminster CC* [1986] 3 All E.R. 4.

[41] [1972] 3 All E.R. 129.

Date of Conviction	Nature of Offence	Penalty imposed
1975	Demolition of listed building	Crown Court fine £10,000 and £1,000 costs[42]
1980	Removal of pantiles from roof of Clock Tower, Walton	Fine £50 and £40 costs[43]
1981	Demolition of a C18 listed cottage, Portsmouth, defendant claimed he was ignorant of listing	Fine £500[44]
1981	Demolition of listed almshouses at Welby	Fine £1,000 and £2,000 costs[45]
1985	Demolition of listed Monkspath Hall, Solihull Defence of mistake did not succeed	Bulldozer driver. Fine £1,500; Company (of which he was a director) £2,000 (see Note at end of table)[46]
1985	Demolition of a listed house in Royston. Defence of urgent necessity did not succeed	Fine £5,000 on one defendant. £1000 on another. Both to pay costs[47]
1986	Removal of shop front from an unlisted building in a Conservation Area	Fine £1,500 and £500 costs[48]
1986	Removal of chimney pieces, doors and staircases from listed building	Divisional court held panalled doors and lack of knowledge that it was a listed building no defence. Case sent back to magistrate to complete[49]
1986	Removal of windows in a listed building by a window replacement company	Fine £500 and ordered to pay costs[50]

[42] *R v. Endersley Properties Ltd* (1975) 32 P. & C.R. 399.
[43] Courtesy of Elmbridge Borough Council.
[44] *The Times*, September 25, 1981.
[45] Private prosecution brought by the Society for the Protection of Ancient Buildings in respect of the demolition of Welby Almshouses, Grantham, Lincolnshire.
[46] *The Times*, May 19, 1981.
[47] Reported in *The Planner*, August 1986, p. 4.
[48] T/APP/A5270/C/85/1185/86.
[49] *R v. Wells St stipendiary Magistrate* [1986] 3 All E.R. 4.
[50] Courtesy of Hove Borough Council, October 22, 1986.

231

March 1990	Demolition of C18 ground floor internal wall in listed shop at Beverley North Humberside	£5,000 fine and costs
April 1990	Unauthorised excavation at Legbourne Priory near Lincoln (a scheduled ancient monument)	£15,000 fine, and £1,400 costs
April 1990	Unauthorised cement rendering applied to Grade II Palace House Mansion Newmarket Suffolk	Injunction £25,000 fine for contempt and costs
June 1991	Excavation of material from basement of warehouse erected on site of Winchester Palace, Southwark, South London (a scheduled ancient monument)	£75,000 fine and £1,000 costs
Oct 1991	Serious damage to Roman archaeological remains caused by tipping at Binchester Hall	£30,000 fine and £10,000 costs
Apr 1992	Deliberate destruction (with explosives) of Wesleyan Chapel, Dartmouth, Devon	4 month term of imprisonment

22. ALTERNATIVE ENFORCEMENT PROCEDURES

5.52   Additional to criminal proceedings and the enforcement provisions under the Listed Buildings and Ancient Monuments legislation, is the possibility of injunction proceedings. At *Stagbatch Farm, Leominster* an interim injunction was granted in the High Court to restrain a dismantled 500 year old cruck-framed barn from being exported to the United States, pending a High Court action to determine the future of the building.[51]

In the subsequent High Court hearing, Mr Justice Mann held that the local planning authority did have power to serve a listed building enforcement notice even though the listed building was a demolished listed building. 70–80 per cent of the building's timbers were in a condition which made re-erection possible. The building was capable of restoration and the local planning authority could legitimately issue an enforcement notice.

[51] *The Times*, August 12, 1986.

There is no equivalent provision in the listed building legislation to a "stop notice" under sections 183, 184 and 187 of the T.C.P.A. 1990, whereby a local planning authority may follow up a planning enforcement notice with a notice compelling the person on whom it is served forthwith to suspend the operation complained of. Clearly, however, it is always open to the local planning authority to apply to the High Court for an injunction having the same effect, as we have just seen. Useful references to the use of injunctions in listed building enforcement are to be found in *Runnymede BC v. Ball* [1986] 1 W.L.R. 853, J.P.L. 1986, p. 288 and *City of London v. Bovis Construction Ltd* [1989], J.P.L. 1989, p. 263 in which Bingham L.J. sets out "guiding principles".

This aspect of the law is in a state of development. There seems more and more enthusiasm to establish civil rights—with civil remedies which can be much more direct and speedy.

In ecclesiastical cases, where work has been carried out without a faculty, it is possible for a parishioner or any interested party to petition for a faculty authorising the restoration of the building to its previous state; or to oppose a retrospective confirmatory faculty sought by the church authorities. Moreover, orders for costs in this connection are enforceable through the county court.

23. ARCHITECTURAL THEFT

Of increasing concern is the incidence of theft of artefacts and architec- **5.53** tural features from historic buildings. London is an area where properties arc particularly at risk especially Mayfair, Bloomsbury and Marylebone. Thefts have included an entire street of York stone paving in Islington and a listed police call post in Piccadilly Circus. English Heritage recommends that in addition to keeping a photographic record, vulnerable features should be marked to aid identification and recovery.

24. GENERAL INFORMATION ON OFFENCES

Section 1 of the PCA 1991 introduced new sections 171C and 171D into **5.54** the T.C.P.A. 1990. The effect of section 1 is to introduce a new procedure in circumstances where the local planning authority has reason to believe that there has been a breach of planning control, but the authority does not have sufficient evidence to establish the breach. The notice which it can serve may require information regarding the operations carried out on the land. Failure to comply within 21 days is an offence under section 171 A of the T.C.P.A. 1990.

6. Problem Operations and Features—The Nuts and Bolts of Listed Building and Conservation Area Control

1. GENERAL SUMMARY

6.01   Case studies can often be of considerable help to the practitioner. This chapter, which was introduced into the second edition of this book, has been considerably expanded. It includes cases of interest to owners of both listed buildings and unlisted buildings within a conservation area and their professional advisers as well as local planning authority officers and other interest and amenity groups. The cases quoted serve to demonstrate, if nothing else, that no hard and fast rules can be applied, even in the interpretation of the legislative framework and supporting guidance which surround listed buildings and conservation areas. As with all planning decisions, the merits of the case must be considered and there will always be decisions which, to one interested party or another, could be said to defy explanation!

2. CANOPIES

The addition of canopies to listed buildings continues to cause problems **6.02** for local planning authorities, particularly as they are often erected without consent in the first place. North West Leicestershire District Council successfully served listed building enforcement notices to secure the removal of advertisement canopies at a property in Ashby-de-la-Zouch.[1] The Inspector's analysis of the issues involved is very thorough and raises some interesting points about the method of fixing canopies to the building. His conclusions read as follows:

"The canopies attached to this Grade II listed building obscure the incised lintels over the windows and cover part of the windows. The effect of this is to alter the visual proportion of the windows which are a specific feature of a Georgian window. While the method of fixing, by two clips and two screws to each canopy, does not constitute any structural alteration to the fabric of the building, the creation of the canopies does materially affect the appearance of the building and the terrace in which it is situated.

The structural connections to the building do not in themselves alter the character of the building, for if the canopies were removed the fixing clips or holes would not alter the character of the building; the obscuring effect of the canopies does however materially affect the appearance of the building. By the obscuring of detail and visually altering the proportion of the windows, we consider that the canopies do constitute an alteration to the building and as such contravene section 55(1) of the 1971 Act and as such ground (b) fails.

As we conclude that the erection of canopies would contravene section 55 of the 1971 Act then, as the canopies have already been erected, it follows that a contravention has taken place, as such therefore ground (c) must fail.

Dutch style canopies are not a traditional Georgian feature and their introduction, which obscures detail and the proportions of the building, is detrimental to the character of the building and to the facade of the terrace in which they are situated.

Whilst we appreciate that some of the detailing obscured by the canopies can be seen from the pavement directly below the canopies, it is from the longer range that the architectural value of the appeal premises and the terrace can be appreciated. From such viewpoint the character of the appeal premises and the terrace are adversely affected by the canopies which introduce a non-traditional feature at first floor level as well as obscuring some of the detailing of the facade; for such reasons we consider ground (e) fails.

Restoration of the building to its original appearance could be achieved by the simple expedient of removing the canopies, a matter of removing two screws per canopy and lifting the canopies off their retaining clips. Whilst it is accepted that the fixings do not in themselves affect the structural condition of the building, the removal of the canopies is a necessary operation to restore the building to its former condition; accordingly ground (g) fails.

[1] APP/G2435/F/84/68.

To say that the removal of the canopies would not serve the purpose of restoring the building to its former state is not valid. While the fixing of the canopies does not affect the structural integrity of the building, the visual appearance of the building has to be taken into account. As such the removal of the canopies must serve to restore the building to its former appearance and for that reason ground (i) must fail.

The use of the first floor windows of the appeal premises for display purposes, besides having limited visual impact, does not in our opinion warrant or justify the installation of the canopies. Whilst accepting that confectionery products would require protection from sunlight, in our opinion this unusual form of display at first floor level, behind barred windows containing some bulls-eyed glass panes, is of doubtful commercial or visual merit.

In view of the ease by which the canopies could be removed, we consider that the period for the compliance with the notice is more than sufficient."

In a further case involving first floor canopies on a listed Georgian building in Newbury,[2] the appellant's argument that the canopies were required to advertise the business premises was set aside by the Secretary of State, who did not consider the business interest of the appellant to be relevant to the effect the proposal would have on the listed building. He was concerned that the canopies would detract from the appearance of the listed building and have a harmful effect on the Newbury Town Centre Conservation area, whose character was largely dependent on the unchanged and uncluttered appearance of the period buildings within it.

A contrast is offered by a decision relating to an application for listed building consent for an illuminated box sign and a canopy in respect of a terraced property near Paddington station in West London.[3] Westminster City Council had refused consent, and also refused a parallel application for express consent under the Control of Advertisement regulations in respect of the sign. The Inspector reported to the Secretary of State that:

"The proliferation of blinds within the locality suggests that some, at least, must be there with the approval of the Council. Whatever the merits of such features it cannot reasonably be held otherwise but that in this particular section of the street they combine, with shop signs and heavy pedestrian and vehicular traffic, to give a busy and colourful street scene at ground level. Although this gallimaufry lacks any real aesthetic merit it provides an interesting and not unattractive contrast with the restrained, sober facades at first floor level and above. In this respect therefore the terrace in question provides a microcosm of the shopping area in which it is situated. Although most of this shopping section of the street lies outside the Conservation Area the terrace is still seen as forming part of it. The abundance of blinds within the terrace therefore cannot reasonably be held to noticeably, or unacceptably, detract from the appearance of their surroundings.

In such circumstances I find it difficult to see what seriously detrimental effect the proposed blind would have—especially as, to misuse a phrase, it would merely "fill a small gap in an otherwise fully developed

[2] APP/G0310/E/85/801164.
[3] APP/X5990/E/91/807460, October 1991.

236

frontage". Given that its use would enable the blind above the sandwich bar to be seen at one with its neighbours I find its provision could well enhance the appearance of both the listed buildings and the surrounding area."

The Secretary of State concluded that the canopy blind enhanced the appearance of the conservation area and he allowed that element of the appeal.

3. SIGNS[4]

The fixing of signs to listed buildings or unlisted buildings in a conser- **6.03**
vation area often involves commercial considerations and public houses are at the forefront of this contentious activity.

It is not therefore surprising to learn that Trafford Metropolitan Borough Council refused permission for the retention of five red plastic canopies, 20 brass wall lights and a total of 15 illuminated and non-illuminated board and canopy signs at a public house in Altringham.[5] The pub was large and occupied a very prominent position in a conservation area. The Secretary of State was concerned that the materials used in the door and window canopies contrasted sharply with the colours of the appeal building. Furthermore, the combination of signs and wall lights gave the building a cluttered appearance which was detrimental to the visual amenity and character of the conservation area. The signs at the upper level were considered to be unduly prominent and unrelated to the main fenestration of the building. The appeal was dismissed.

Notwithstanding this resounding defeat for the brewing industry, it was successful in winning an appeal against the London Borough of Harrow which had refused listed building consent for a hanging sign and the erection of illuminated and non-illuminated signs on a listed pub. The Council's contention, that the modern signs introduced an obtrusive commercial element into a predominantly residential street and that they were not in keeping with the listed building, was not accepted by the Secretary of State.[6] He took the view that the signs, although not traditional in style or construction, did not have an unduly harmful effect on the appearance of the building. He was of the opinion that the hanging sign was sufficiently distant from the building to have little effect and he allowed the appeal with the exception of two black swan-necked lamps which illuminated the name sign on the front elevation of the public house.

The Secretary of State reached a different conclusion in relation to a sign in a shopping street. While allowing a canopy over a ground floor doorway of a terraced property in a street near Paddington Station in West London,[7] the Secretary of State concluded that a first floor illuminated box sign would unacceptably detract from the appearance both of the listed building and the conservation area, notwithstanding the existence of a similar sign on

---

[4] Signs are subject to a double form of control in that they are also governed by Regulations as to control of advertisements, see para. 3.30 above.
[5] PLUP/5088/175/132.
[6] APP/M5450/E/84/800605.
[7] See para. 6.02; APP/X5990/E/91/807460.

another property in the same terrace. This was considered by the Inspector to "detract greatly from the appearance of a unified whole", namely the upper facade of the terrace. The appeal was dismissed.

4. CLADDING AND RENDERING

6.04   The application of new materials to the external elevations of properties constructed in traditional materials is a cause of great concern to local planning authorities and conservationists alike. The desire of the householder to lend his property individuality often runs into conflict with the principles of conservation and two particular cases illustrate the wide gulf which exists between conservationists and the householder in some instances.

In a case within the Kirklees area of West Yorkshire[8] the owner of an end-of-terrace stone listed building had not only replaced the windows with small paned windows with top opening lights, but had covered the external elevations with swirl textured white render, which was also interspersed with randomly placed projected stones. The Secretary of State concluded that these works were inappropriate and detracted from the character of the listed building.

In a second case, the owner of a small terraced brick built property in the South Highfields Conservation Area in Leicester[9] had applied imitation stone cladding to the front elevation of this property without planning permission. The conservation area was also subject to an Article 4 direction[10] and the Inspector concluded as follows:

> "The work which has been carried out on the appeal property has retained the string course, lintels and cills. The appearance of the house has, however, been fundamentally changed as a result of the obliteration of the characteristic red brickwork. The cladding used has a predominantly light colour which emphasises the difference in appearance between the appeal property and the adjoining premises. I therefore consider that the cladding has had an unacceptable effect on the appearance of Churchill Street and if retained would damage the efforts the authority is making to retain and enhance the character of the South Highfields Conservation Area.
>
> Although I accept that the appellant did not understand the need to obtain planning permission for this work when it was begun, I consider that in this case the authority has given widespread publicity to its policies and proposals. I also note that the appellant was advised to stop the work before its completion and to apply for a grant towards the costs of reinstatement, brick cleaning and repointing. Since this advice was not followed, I do not consider that the cost and inconvenience involved in the removal of the stone cladding can be sufficient reason to set aside the clear policies which apply in this case."

The Inspector dismissed the appeal despite the fact that the appellant was supported by many of the local residents.

[8] APP/J4715/E/85/800678.
[9] T/APP/U2425/A/84/021265/P3.
[10] See para. 3.19 above.

5. CLEANING OF LISTED BUILDINGS[11]

The cleaning of listed buildings is an issue which has caused concern to **6.05** some local planning authorities especially in regard to whether the act of cleaning requires listed building consent. The practice among local planning authorities has varied with Bath City Council not requiring applications for consent to clean listed buildings, but Edinburgh City Council taking the opposing view.

Annex C to PPG 15 (Guidance on Alterations to Listed Buildings) gives detailed advice on cleaning, at paragraph C18 and goes a long way towards clarifying the issue:

> "Cleaning a building usually requires listed building consent. This is not only because cleaning can have a marked effect on the character of buildings, but also because cleaning processes can affect the historic fabric. The cleaning of a building within a homogeneous terrace would obviously affect the appearance of the terrace as a whole. All cleaning methods can cause damage if carelessly handled. Cleaning with water and bristle brushes is the simplest method, although water cleaning can lead to saturation of the walls and outbreaks of rot in timbers. Other methods including abrasive and chemical cleaning can damage wall surfaces and destroy detail. Local planning authorities should satisfy themselves that such cleaning is both necessary and worthwhile to remove corrosive dirt or to bring a major improvement in appearance, and should ensure that cleaning is carried out by specialist firms and under close supervision. Areas not being cleaned should be protected".

While this guidance is helpful in clarifying the position regarding the cleaning of listed buildings, it remains the case that the question of whether the cleaning of a listed building requires LBC will depend upon two factors:

    (i) the materials to be cleaned;
    (ii) the cleaning process to be used.

It is therefore essential that there is a dialogue between the owners of listed buildings, cleaning contractors and the local planning authority before cleaning works commence. In particular, owners of listed buildings should be encouraged to discuss proposals for cleaning before they undertake such work so that a considered assessment can be made of the likely effects of the work proposed on the character of the listed building, and thus the need for listed building consent.

6. PAINTING OF LISTED BUILDINGS[12]

The painting of a building does not amount to development within the **6.06** meaning of section 55 of the Town and Country Planning Act 1990, unless it can be said "materially to affect the external appearance of the building." Furthermore, if painting is deemed to constitute development, it would nor-

[11] See also para. 3.26 above.
[12] See also para. 3.26.

mally constitute permitted development by virtue of the provisions of Article 3 and Class C of Part 2 of Schedule 2 of the Town and Country Planning (General Permitted Development) Order 1995.

It is arguable as to whether the application of paint in itself could be said inevitably to affect the character of a building as one of special architectural or historic interest. Notwithstanding the esoteric arguments which might be advanced in this direction, experience generally supports the view that painting of a listed building would usually require consent, and that is reflected in the advice contained in Annex C to PPG 15 (paragraph C17):

> "Painting—or repainting such as a change of colour—requires listed building consent when it could affect the character of a listed building. Previously unpainted surfaces should not normally be painted over. (An exception to this rule can be made for the sheltercoating of decayed stonework with a lime-based mixture). In many cases the colour of the paint may be less important than the first application of an unsuitable covering which could be damaging to remove. Cement based or other waterproof and hard gloss paints should not be used on surfaces covered with traditional render. The correct finish for traditional renders and plasters is limewash (although much 19th century stucco has traditionally been coated in oil paint). When inappropriate paint has been applied, expert advice should be obtained on suitable methods of removal".

In a case at *Hexham in County Durham*,[13] Tynedale District Council refused listed building consent for the painting of the front stonework of a shop in white and the woodwork in signal red. The property was located in a conservation area and the council argued that the colour scheme was out of keeping with neighbouring properties and had destroyed the architectural quality of the building. The Secretary of State concurred with the council, stating that the paintwork gave the appeal building an unbalanced appearance and that it had a harmful effect on the conservation area. The matter seems to have been settled by the Divisional Court, which further considered the matter in *Windsor and Maidenhead Borough Council v. Secretary of State for the Environment*,[14] a case in which the Secretary of State had said that because the facade of the building in question was already painted, the action of repainting could not therefore be said to have constituted works of alteration. Mann J. disagreed, holding that having regard to the possible meaning in ordinary language of the word "alteration" in section 55 of the 1971 Act[15] and having regard to the purpose of that section, repainting was capable of being an alteration.

6.07   In a subsequent enforcement appeal the effect of repainting woodwork is discussed.[16] Rugby Borough Council had served a listed building enforcement notice following the repainting in black of the ground floor windows, door frame, fanlight and hood of a grade II* listed building. The Inspector found that the repainting had led to the ground floor becoming visually divorced from the upper floors. More importantly, the balance and contrast between the brickwork and the woodwork had changed. He continued:

[13] APP/B2925/E/85/801501.
[14] *The Times*, January 6, 1988.
[15] Now section 7 of the Planning (Listed Buildings and Conservation Areas) Act 1990.
[16] APP/F/88/E3715/2–6, November 1989.

240

"The essential question concerns the effect of the repainting in black on the architectural character of the listed building. My site inspection revealed that from the opposite side of Church Street much of the contrast between the window glazing and surrounding joinery can be lost. This results in the ground floor window and door surrounding reading as large holes in the wall, which could not have been intended when the building was designed. Although the brickwork is particularly attractive, my opinion is that the change in balance between wall and openings detract from the special qualities of the building.

At close range, the details of the joinery become more obvious. However, at the present time the black repainting on the ground floor and the white joinery above can be usefully compared. On the white woodwork the shadows are more pronounced. This had the beneficial effect of contributing to the modelling of the facade and its architectural interest. My opinion is that the black paint seriously compromises the subtle definition of the timber detailing. This adverse effect would not be satisfactorily overcome, although it would be partially mitigated, by removing all old paint and repainting again in black, as the appellants suggest."

The Inspector also concluded that the painting adversely affected the conservation area because of the "impoverishment" of the listed building. The Secretary of State agreed with his Inspector's conclusions, dismissed the appeal and upheld the notice.

7. REINSTATEMENT OF ORIGINAL FEATURES

The architectural or historic integrity of listed buildings is regarded by **6.08** many conservationists to be of paramount importance and it is therefore interesting to compare some appeal decisions in respect of the reinstatement of original features on listed buildings.

In a case at Bridlington in East Yorkshire[17] the removal of a Victorian shop front in a Georgian building brought an opinion from the Georgian Society to the effect that upon removal of the shop front the elevation should be restored to its original condition. The Inspector disagreed with this view and saw the determining issue as to whether the proposals put forward were sympathetic to the character of the listed building, having regard to the fact that it had previously been altered. He concluded that the scheme of refurbishment was beneficial and he allowed the appeal.

The use of plastic gutters and downpipes on a restaurant conversion of a listed building in Allerdale, Cumbria[18] was in breach of a condition requiring that the rainwater goods should be in cast iron of similar design to the existing. The council was concerned about the unsympathetic qualities of plastic goods, but the appellant had used them because the requirements of the condition were unduly onerous and costly. The Secretary of State noted that the plastic gutters and downpipes which had already been placed on the building were not prominent and toned in well with the building's stonework. He allowed the appeal and discharged the condition.

[17] YH/5268/270/36P.
[18] APP/R0905/E/84/800327.

However the removal of castellations and a parapet wall from a listed hydraulic tower in Liverpool[19] were considered by the City Council adversely to affect the architectural integrity and character of the building. The Secretary of State noted the appellants' arguments that these features had been removed for safety reasons following the deterioration of the soft chalky mortar between the stonework and after several stone falls. Indeed, the Secretary of State accepted that the work might have been justified at the time on public safety grounds, but took the view that as a listed building of special interest which was also an important local landmark, the tower should be reinstated as required by the City Council. The appeal was dismissed.

8. ROOF MATERIALS

6.09   "The roof is nearly always a dominant feature of a building and the retention of its original structure, shape, pitch, cladding and ornament is important"

advises Annex C of PPG 15 (paragraph C27).

Reconstituted roof materials. The replacement of roof materials on listed buildings is a recurring problem for owners and local planning authorities alike. The most contentious issue arises through the desire to use machine made or reconstituted roof materials which are often cheaper and more readily available than handmade or secondhand materials. Two specific examples serve to illustrate the view of local planning authorities and DOE inspectors.

In a case where the Cotswold District Council had refused consent for the use of reconstituted stone slates on a house,[20] the Secretary of State concurred with that view and considered that modern slates would not be satisfactory. In particular he was concerned that modern slates would be of "reconstituted, machine made material, mainly regular in size and would be markedly different from the variety of size, thickness, colour and texture of the natural material."

A similar view was taken in a case in Filkins in West Oxfordshire,[21] where a proposal to strip the natural stone slates from the roofs of four cottages owned by the District Council and their replacement by concrete tiles was refused consent and a subsequent appeal was dismissed. The Inspector's observations are particularly valuable and highlight the importance attached to the distinctive qualities of traditional materials.

"I note that a natural material which was the raison d'être behind the building of these houses would be replaced by an artificial product. No matter how cleverly contrived to match the original effect of Cotswold stone roofing, the social, historic and architectural integrity of the initial concept would be impaired. For this reason I consider the proposed use of concrete tiles undesirable. It would greatly detract from the reasons which led to the buildings being listed in the first place. To

---

[19] APP/Z4310/F/84/000087.
[20] SW/APP/F1610/E/84/800142.
[21] SE2/5356/411/2.

this must be added the resulting visual quality. It is clear to me, if only from the many examples of concrete-tile roofs in the village, using the kind of tiles suggested, that they lack the ruggedness of form, surface colour and texture of the original work. The constructional approach is different, whether in relation to the random sizes of stone slates, requiring considerable care in the laying, or the manner of treating the roof valleys. Even allowing for the effects of weathering over the years the appearance would not match the singular qualities of the traditional roofing."

Even the extra cost of re-roofing in natural materials (£6,300 per house as opposed to £4,500 per house at 1985 prices) was not considered sufficient to override the inappropriateness of the proposals.

Thatch. As a traditional roofing material, thatch is often regarded as **6.10** being particularly attractive from an aesthetic point of view and recent appeal decisions appear to support the retention of thatch for aesthetic reasons. The advice of PPG 15 (Annex C, paragraph C29) is unequivocal:

> "Thatched roofs should be preserved, and consent should not be given for their replacement by different roof coverings".

In a case at Daventry[22] a proposal to replace thatch with tiles was held to be unacceptable by the Secretary of State, who considered that the beauty of the group of buildings of which the appeal house formed part would be best preserved by the re-thatching of the roof. He did not accept the appellant's argument that thatch was a fire hazard, provided that all normal safety precautions were taken.

In a second case, the Secretary of State supported Chichester District Council in its refusal of consent for the replacement of straw thatch with hand made clay tiles at a house in the West Burton Conservation Area.[23] The council contended that the architectural character of the listed building depended to a large extent on its thatched roof and was concerned that the re-roofing proposals also involved the loss of "eyebrow" windows, which were an attractive feature of the appeal building and which were to be replaced by ill-proportioned tiled dormers. The Secretary of State concluded that the loss of these features and the thatched roof would be seriously detrimental to the character of the listed building and dismissed the appeal.

Finally, in a case at Stansfield in the Borough of St Edmunsbury[24] the Secretary of State supported the Borough Council's refusal of listed building consent to replace thatch with reclaimed red/brown clay plain tiles. All the arguments put forward by the appellant in respect of problems securing the services of a thatcher within a reasonable period, the length of time it takes to thatch a building, the maintenance problems associated with thatch, the expense and the insurance costs, were not considered sufficiently strong to override the importance attached to the use of thatch in the locality and it was concluded that its replacement would fundamentally affect the external appearance of the listed building and detract from its essential character.

[22] APP/12810/E/84/800127.
[23] APP/L3815/E/85/800962.
[24] APP/E3525/E/86/801302.

9. TECHNOLOGICAL INNOVATION

6.11   Listed buildings are increasingly subjected to pressures for change or alterations as a result of technological innovation. Three particular examples; bank service tills, solar panels and security shutters serve to illustrate the problems of incorporating modern technology into listed buildings constructed in traditional materials. In addition, the particular difficulties experienced by British Telecom in updating its public telephones in response to technological change in listed telephone kiosks are of interest and are of wider application

6.12   *Bank service tills.* Service tills are often a source of concern to local planning authorities, not least because they will normally need to be located on the external elevation of a building if they are to serve the purpose for which they are intended. This creates potential conflict with the need to protect the character of listed buildings. An example of this concern is reflected in the decision of the London Borough of Harrow[25] to refuse LBC for a second service till at a bank, the first having been installed prior to the building having been statutorily listed. The council was concerned that the combined effect of two closely located service tills of matching design would adversely affect the appearance and symmetry of the bank building. In dismissing the subsequent appeal, the Secretary of State accepted the argument that the proposal would disrupt the major architectural elements of the building and so diminish its visual impact and significance.

6.13   *Solar panels.* Although the installation of solar heating panels into the roof of a listed farmhouse was refused by the High Peak Borough Council,[26] the Secretary of State supported the Inspector's view that as the existing roof tiles were almost as dark as the panels would be, and although they would be readily visible, they would not adversely affect the character of the listed building.

It is interesting to speculate how such a proposal might be viewed in an area of the country where the prevailing colour of the roofscape is much lighter than that found in the High Peak. Furthermore, it is evident that this particular Inspector placed considerable emphasis on the colour of the solar panel, but appears to have attached less weight to the texture and form of the panels and their relationship with the traditional roof tiles.

6.14   *Security shutters.* The installation of security shutters is now deemed necessary by many businesses, especially in the retail trade, to protect their property or the stock it contains. They are now widely evident in town and city centres throughout the land and take many different forms. Annex C to PPG 15, however, is quite clear as to the suitability on listed buildings of external steel shutters (Paragraph C55):

> "External steel roller shutters are not suitable for historic shop fronts. Traditional timber shutters give reasonable protection: laminated glass and internal chain-link screens are modern alternatives. Traditional stall-risers are an effective deterrent to 'ram-raiders', as are small shop windows between masonry piers."

[25] APP/M5450/A/85/032896.
[26] APP/T1030/E/84/800618.

244

There can be some doubt that the external application to a shop front of a box to accommodate a roller shutter constitutes development as defined in section 55 of the Town and Country Planning Act 1990 since it is an alteration which materially affects the external appearance of a building. Listed building consent will additionally be required if, as will usually be the case, it affects the character of the listed building.

Richmondshire District Council in North Yorkshire took enforcement action against just such a development comprising external shutters to display windows and an entrance door housed in white painted metal boxing fixed below the fascia within Richmond town centre. In the subsequent appeal decision[27] the Inspector concluded that, notwithstanding numerous "smash and grab" raids, the most important consideration was maintenance of the special character of the area, which was a conservation area. He noted that alternative, less obtrusive, solutions to the problem of security were evident on nearby premises and that the appeal site was in a prominent corner location. He also took into account the Council's efforts to enhance the attractiveness of the town's shopping core and concluded that it would be inappropriate for the present security measures at the appeal premises to remain. The appeal was dismissed.

Telephone kiosks. The listing of selected telephone kiosks was under-   **6.15** taken by the DOE following the privatisation of British Telecom and its subsequent modernisation of public telephones. Two groups of kiosks in central Cheltenham were listed. Subsequently British Telecom replaced the telephone equipment and also replaced the word "TELEPHONE" in maroon letters on a white background with either the word "TELEPHONE" in yellow letters on a black background or the word "PHONECARD", with a logo, in white on a green background. Cheltenham Borough Council served listed building enforcement notices. In the ensuing appeal[28] the Inspector noted that the revised guidelines for listing telephone kiosks published by the DOE in June 1987 included a provision that preference was to be given to kiosks which retained the original glass panels, as was the case here. He also noted that British Telecom had been consulted on, and had agreed to, the listing of these particular kiosks. He concluded that, because the kiosks were mass-produced items, relatively small alterations could significantly change their character. He considered that inadequate care and skill had been taken in the design of the replacement panels for the cardphone units, and that the works did not preserve or enhance the character of the conservation area. Accordingly the appeals were dismissed and the notices upheld.

10. WINDOWS

The installation of new windows into listed buildings or buildings within   **6.16** conservation areas continues to create more conflict between owners and local planning authorities than any other single form of alteration, and the subject is discussed in some detail in Appendix C to PPG 15.

---

[27] T/APP/C/88/E2720/5P6.
[28] T/APP/F/88/B1605/1/P6, August 1989.

Taking a balanced view of the large number of appeals which are determined, it is evident that local planning authorities are experiencing some degree of success in their efforts to control the replacement of traditional sash windows with aluminum framed or UPVC windows in listed buildings. However, such success is often achieved after the service of enforcement notices and in many instances applications are submitted in retrospect after the works have been carried out.

A typical case of the many which have been determined, involve the London Borough of Haringay enforcing against the installation of new double-glazed windows in a dwelling in the Tower Gardens Conservation Area,[29] which was covered by an Article 4 direction removing permitted development rights to make alterations to the appearance of buildings in a conservation area.

The Inspector took the view that the new aluminum framed windows were quite different from those in the rest of the terrace and because of their size and prominence were a visually disturbing feature in the street scene. In dismissing the appeal, the Inspector ruled that the windows should be replaced or permanently altered so as to look like the original wooden sashes, but conceded that the materials and the manner in which that could be achieved should be left to the appellant.

6.17   The requirements of an enforcement notice upheld in respect of a Grade II listed Georgian terrace house were far more stringent. Bath City Council had taken enforcement action against the installation of three UPVC windows on the front elevation of a building.[30] The windows were double-glazed with mock glazing bars between the two panes. The Secretary of State was concerned that the windows seriously detracted from the character of the appeal building and the terrace of which it formed part. Furthermore, he concluded that acceptable standards of security and sound insulation could be achieved by the use of locks and internal secondary glazing. The notice required the reinstatement of vertical sliding timber sash windows each sub-divided into six panes by thin glazing bars, and the appeal was dismissed.

South Hams District Council was also successful in an appeal against an enforcement notice concerning the removal of traditional vertical sliding sashes from the second floor of a listed building in Dartmouth.[31] The appellants argued that severe maintenance problems were experienced with timber windows in exposed coastal locations but these problems were not accepted as being incapable of solution and the Secretary of State dismissed the appeal because he thought that the windows adversely affected the character of the building.

The London Borough of Southwark successfully enforced against the installation of aluminum framed double glazing in a Georgian house in the Holly Grove Conservation Area.[32] Notwithstanding the fact that the new windows were of a similar shape, style and size to the timber framed sliding sashes they replaced, the Secretary of State stated that the alterations detracted from the appearance of the appeal premises despite the effort made to replicate the original windows. He was not satisfied that it was

[29] T/APP/Y5420/C/85/3159/86.
[30] SW/APP/P0105/F/85/9.
[31] SW/APP/V1125/E/84/71–72.
[32] APP/A/5840/F/85/14.

necessary to replace the original windows with double-glazed units in the interests of health, safety or for the preservation of the building. These interests could have been safeguarded by the replacement of decayed window frames by replicas of traditional design and materials. It is possible to produce aluminum frames which are of similar shape, style and size to timber windows it is not possible, so far as we are concerned, to produce exact copies. Glazing bars are often thicker and the mouldings which give timber windows much of their character, cannot be replicated satisfactorily in aluminum. Very slight changes in proportion arising from these shortcomings can have a marked effect on the character of the building.

Even local planning authorities make mistakes. A retrospective application by the London Borough of Bromley for listed building consent for replacement UPVC double glazed windows in the front elevation of a public hall in Beckenham was refused by the Secretary of State.[33] The Council indicated that the failure to obtain listed building consent had been an unfortunate oversight but that the previous timber frames had rotted and needed urgent replacement following complaints from users. Neither this urgency, nor the lack of budgetary provision to rectify this mistake, was sufficient to move the Secretary of State who agreed with his inspecting officer that the special character of the prominent revival style listed building was harmed by the replacement windows, as was the character of the conservation area.

There are instances however where appeals have been allowed, particu- **6.18**
larly if the area in question has already been infiltrated by modern windows. This point is very well illustrated by two cases involving Hove Borough Council. In the first case enforcement action had been taken against replacement windows (UPVC) in a principal elevation of Brunswick Terrace in Hove, a Grade I listed seafront terrace.[33a] The appellants argued that the replacement windows were of greater aesthetic quality than those which they had replaced which in any event were not original. The Council refuted this argument because they did not resemble the traditional timber sliding sashes found elsewhere in the building and therefore detracted from the continuity of the terrace as a whole. The Secretary of State observed that as the windows were only visible from a distance, the materials used in their construction were not readily noticeable. In allowing the appeal, he acknowledged that the appeal windows were not of a type indigenous to the appeal building, but did not regard them as out of keeping when seen against the multiplicity of window types in the terrace.

In the second case, the offending replacement aluminum windows were located on the fourth floor of a listed building in Hove.[34] The council argued that they were highly visible from an adjacent square and significantly different from those prevailing in the area. The Inspector's report concluded that the replacement windows had altered the overall appearance of the appeal building and had not enhanced the character of the conservation area in which the building was located; nevertheless the Secretary of State took the view that although the windows were at variance with the main fenestration in the building, they were no more harmful than those they had replaced. The appeal was allowed.

[33] LRP270/G5180/01, August 1990.
[33a] APP/F1420/F/84/121, February 1986.
[34] APP/F1420/F/85/53.

This is a recurring point. Dover District Council took enforcement action against replacement UPVC double glazed window units on the first and second floors of a listed building within a conservation area close to the White Cliffs and to the docks. The first floor unit replaced a modern timber unit, the original having been removed many years earlier. The Inspector concluded[35] that the first floor alterations did not discernably affect the character of the listed building and as such did not constitute a contravention of section 7 of the LBA. The same did not apply to the second floor window, where a traditional timber vertical sliding sash window had been replaced. The UPVC window, its method of opening and false glazing strips sandwiched between the panes adversely affected the character and unity of the terrace. The Inspector attached little weight to the allegation that other buildings and owners may be in breach of listed building control and considered:

"... that the lack of comment regarding your windows by the 15 million passengers who travel through the nearby docks every year is less telling than the national public support for the protection of old buildings and the best parts of our towns."

The appeal was dismissed, and the notice upheld, in relation to the second floor window.

In an appeal regarding four replacement white aluminum windows in a listed building, now a golf clubhouse but for a time the home of Emperor Napoleon III and his wife the Empress Eugenie, the quality of the relevant section of the building was judged to be the determining issue.[36] The building in Chislehurst had been extended in 1938 and the replacement windows were to be in that extension. The extension, with contemporary steel window frames, was considered by the Inspector to be particularly unfortunate in its relationship with the original building while the existing windows bore no relation in proportion, materials, or opening method, to those of the main building. The Inspector concluded that, exceptionally, the proposed windows could be permitted without establishing a precedent for the installation of such windows in listed buildings elsewhere. The Secretary of State agreed with his Inspector and allowed the appeal.

6.19 The details of a case involving windows in the roof of a listed building in Chorley New Road, Bolton[37] serve to demonstrate the aesthetic problems of incorporating this type of modern window into such buildings, but also show the importance attached to the economic use of listed buildings by the Secretary of State.

The case involved an appeal against an enforcement notice requiring the removal of two Velux roof windows, a section 36 appeal against the refusal of planning permission for their installation and an appeal against the refusal of listed building consent for their installation. In each case the appeals were allowed based upon the following analysis of the merits of the case by the Inspector:

"The planning merits of the development the subject of the enforcement notice are relevant also to consideration of the appeals against refusal of planning permission and listed building consent. I agree with

[35] T/APP/F/89/X2220/3/P6, January 1991.
[36] APP/G5180/E/90/807029, April 1991.
[37] APP/N4205/F/84/23; APP/N4205/N/84/012283; APP/N4205/F/84/800178.

248

the Council's appraisal of the quality of the listed building and the character of its surroundings. The roof lights interrupt the plane of the roof and when seen from the north side of Chorley New Road they disturb the balance of the pair of former dwellings, which is comprised of the appeal premises and the neighbouring property. However, the dominant elements of the facade of the building are the red brick walling and the regularly spaced windows and doors. I consider that in this instance the slated roof is a subordinate element within which the Velux windows, by virtue of the low pitch of the roof, are not particularly conspicuous, even when open. The works of conversion which the appellants have undertaken have served to restore 51 Chorley New Road, to put the listed building to a useful purpose in the furtherance of a commercial business, and seem likely to ensure its future for a number of years to come. I am unable to determine, on the evidence which I heard, the extent to which the viability of the conversion depends upon the retention of the rooflights, but I have no doubt that they enhance the usable office space within the building and thereby contribute to the benefits which have stemmed from the appellants' enterprise. In my opinion, this consideration outweighs the small adverse impact of the roof lights upon the appearance of the listed building and the surrounding area. I find no reason to question the Council's policy to preserve the attractiveness of Chorley New Road, but in the special circumstances of this case I consider that the Velux windows ought to be permitted."

An unusual decision was reached in respect of an appeal following an application made retrospectively to South Lakeland District Council.[38] It related to a Grade II listed terraced house in the conservation area in Burton.

A strong compassionate case was put forward on behalf of the owner who was 84 years old, frail and unable to open and close sash windows. Double glazing was said to be important to reduce noise and also heating bills. The Inspector concluded:

"I am led to the conclusion that the crudity of detailing and modelling of the new windows is to the detriment of the character and historic interest of this listed building, including its neighbours in the same terrace and, as such, conflicts with the aims of listed building policies and the specific intention to preserve and enhance the character and appearance of the conservation area.

On the question of the effects of these changes justifying a refusal of consent I have to consider the balance of interests which would be involved. It appears to me that there is no doubt that, to comply with listed building legislation, an application for consent should have been submitted before works were put in hand. This would have given the opportunity to examine the needs and the options available and to arrive at a solution which could have met the physical needs which I appreciate led you to your decision as well as recognising the value of the present window form and its contribution to the character of the building. I am satisfied that, if the original windows were not capable of adaptation and improvement, a more sympathetic solution could have

---

[38] [1991] J.P.L., 440.

been arrived at which would still have achieved the requirements of sound and heat insulation and draught proofing.

In the circumstances of this case and recognising the costs and disruption which would be caused and the accepted physical benefits which have accrued from the work to the assistance and comfort of an aged resident, I consider that a slight relaxation of the strict application the appropriate policies would be justified in this instance. In taking this view, I am recognising that, whilst the window details are important elements in the composition of the facade of the building, its main contribution to its surroundings is its basic form and texture with the dressed stone quoins, window surrounds and entrance door details. In this broader picture and in its historical perspective, the details of the windows and their irregularity are of interest but not essential when considered against the needs of modern living."

He then went on to say: "Whilst I appreciate and broadly agree with the intentions of the Council when they reached their decision, I am of the view that there is some justification for a more relaxed final decision to be reached in this particular case in the light of the circumstances of the present occupier."

The Council's appeal to the High Court was in vain. The Deputy Judge agreed with the conclusion of counsel for the Secretary of State that the Inspector had considered all the necessary factors and found in favour of the council but had gone on to express the view that the circumstances exceptionally justified a "slight relaxation of the strict policy."

11. DEMOLITION

6.20   Whilst the question of demolition is dealt with in much greater detail elsewhere in this book,[39] the following examples are given to demonstrate some of the arguments which are used to secure or resist total demolition or partial demolition of buildings at appeal.

Total Demolition. It is unusual for the decision on whether to allow the total demolition of listed buildings to hinge on the question of the economic benefits which might not otherwise arise if LBC was refused for their demolition. This is very well illustrated by a widely reported case involving proposals to demolish listed buildings in Ellior Street, Clayton Square and Deane Street in Liverpool[40] for the redevelopment of the site as a shopping centre. The comprehensive redevelopment proposals submitted by Wimpey Property Holdings were the subject of an inquiry to consider both the compulsory purchase order made by the City Council and applications for listed building consent. The Inspector felt that the merits of the proposed retail development in improving the attraction of Liverpool as a regional shopping centre and in providing a greater variety of shops were not sufficiently strong arguments to outweigh the value of the listed buildings. The Secretary of State did not agree with his Inspector and considered that apart from the listed buildings issue, the development of the site in the manner

[39] See above at para. 5.21.
[40] PNW/5091/12/17.

proposed was satisfactory and that the scheme had both interest and merit. The completion of the scheme would bring the City Centre Plan to fruition and would attract investment to the area. He recognised that the development could not proceed without the demolition of the listed buildings and he took the view that the area would continue to decline without the revitalisation offered by the redevelopment scheme. He regretted the loss but considered that the benefits outweighed the loss of the listed buildings; he allowed the appeal and the compulsory purchase order was also confirmed.

The need carefully to balance the conflicting policies aimed at promoting development on the one hand and preserving listed buildings on the other, was clearly recognised in an appeal decision involving retail warehouse proposals on a site at West Street, Gravesend, Kent,[41] which also included a listed building within the appeal site. The Inspector's conclusions are particularly succinct on this important issue:

"I generally conclude that the presumption in favour of granting planning permission, contained in Circulars 22/80 and 14/85, ought to be weighed against the equally relevant policy content of Circular 23/77 and 12/81[42] as regards the need to preserve both listed buildings and the settings of such buildings. In this particular instance, the merits of the otherwise broadly acceptable retail warehousing proposals the subject of the first appeal would appear to be of comparatively far less importance than the retention of the listed buildings on the site and its immediate setting. There would appear to be no immediate prospect of reconciling the retention of the small group of buildings with the use of the land for development which might otherwise be held to be in broad conformity with the provisions of the emergent local plan."

The Secretary of State agreed with his Inspector and dismissed the appeal.

An application for demolition of a Grade II* listed hammerhead crane at **6.21** Wallsend within the area of operations of the Tyne and Wear Development Corporation was decided by the Secretary of State.[43] He considered that while the crane was historically important and structurally sound, it was not unique and the duty placed upon the Development Corporation of securing the regeneration of its area was a material consideration. This did not override the duty to preserve listed buildings, but since alternative uses, and even relocation, had been extensively considered, the importance to the regional economy of the proposed oil industry construction site was so great as to justify the crane's demolition. Listed building consent was therefore granted.

It is also clear that proposals to secure the total demolition of listed buildings have to be supported by unequivocal evidence that no alternative uses can be found. Two cases illustrate the emphasis given by the Secretary of State on fully exploring alternatives before consent is granted.

In a case involving a proposal to demolish a row of cottages in Chertsey[44] in the area of Runnymede District Council, the appeal failed because the appellants had not produced a detailed structural survey, nor had any econ-

[41] SE2/5277/270/68.
[42] Both circulars were consolidated in Circular 8/87 which has in turn been replaced by PPG 15.
[43] N/5038/270P/35, August 1991.
[44] SE2/5389/411/1.

omic assessment of the potential of the structure been undertaken and no effort had been made to sell the premises for renovation. Not even the support of the District Council and the County Council's historic buildings architect were sufficient to support the appellant's contention that the buildings were not capable of repair at reasonable cost.

A similar conclusion was reached by an Inspector determining an appeal against the decision of Mid Suffolk District Council to refuse listed building consent for the demolition of a thatched timber framed cottage.[45] The Inspector took the view that the building was basically sound and that it was an uncommon example of its period. Although no scheme for renovation had been prepared, the Inspector thought that funding would be forthcoming from the local planning authority.

Canterbury City Council refused consent for the demolition of a group of listed buildings and their re-erection nearby.[46] The buildings, at Tyler Hill, would be flooded if a proposed reservoir were to be built. The reservoir proposal had in the past been dismissed at appeal partly on prematurity grounds. The Inspector concluded that while the reservoir might now appear to be inevitable, while there was any prospect of the listed buildings remaining unaffected in their setting, any application was premature.

The Secretary of State agreed and dismissed the appeal.

6.22 In an important case with implications for all highway authorities, Durham County Council sought listed building and conservation area consents for demolition of various buildings to clear the way for the final Stage V of the Darlington Ring Road. The applications were considered at an inquiry where the related draft compulsory purchase orders were also considered.[47] The Inspector found the listed buildings to be visually and historically important. The proposed new road, the gaps created by it and the paraphernalia associated with it would, he concluded, detract in the most profound and serious manner from the quality of the townscape in one of the most sensitive parts of Darlington. The benefits alleged to derive from the road's construction were considered to be overstated and unproven. He concluded that:

> "Taking all these matters into consideration, I come to the conclusion that the benefits that would follow from the completion of the ring road are insufficient to outweigh the extremely serious environmental damage that would be caused by both the loss of the listed buildings and buildings in the conservation areas and by the concomitant effects of routeing a major road through a residential area. I also take the view that alternative means of improving the road network have not been exhausted.
>
> I therefore intend to recommend that the implementation of Stage V of the Darlington Inner Ring Road should not proceed."

In his decision, the Secretary of State accepted that both the inclusion of the road scheme in development plans, and the grant of planning permission for it were cogent arguments in its favour. He agreed with the Inspector's conclusions however and considered it desirable to preserve the

---

[45] APP/W3520/E/84/800425.
[46] APP/J2210/E/89/805177, September 1990.
[47] N/5195/270P/59, 60, 61; N/5195/433P/6 & 7, June 1990.

listed and unlisted buildings concerned. He therefore refused the applications.

Partial demolition. The question of whether minor works to a listed **6.23** building or unlisted building in a conservation area amount to partial demolition often raises many esoteric arguments. This is well illustrated in a case involving the installation of a new shop front in Bridport on an unlisted building in a conservation area.[48] West Dorest District Council claimed that "listed building consent" (now conservation area consent) was required for its demolition or partial demolition, but not for its alteration or extension.

The Secretary of State took the view that any demolition work undertaken during the installation of the shop front was minimal and the works involved did not therefore amount to demolition or partial demolition within the meaning of the 1971 T.C.P.A. He quashed the enforcement notice and allowed the appeal.

12. WORKS HIDDEN FROM VIEW

The fact that proposed alterations to a listed building which are largely **6.24** hidden from view does not in itself constitute sufficient reason to guarantee the grant of listed building consent. The decisions which have emerged from local planning authorities and the Secretary of State are not consistent and appear to depend on the weight attached to the integrity of the building in question.

In a case at Chester,[49] the Secretary of State overruled the City Council which had refused alterations at the rear of a restaurant occupying an 18th-century listed building in Lower Bridge Street. The Secretary of State took the view that the works were largely hidden from view and that as they would enable the restaurant to function more efficiently, drawing on the advice embodied in Circular 23/77,[49a] they were acceptable and he allowed the appeal.

However, the decision of Edinburgh City Council to refuse consent for the erection of a rear staircase to a listed building was fully supported by the Reporter.[50] He was not convinced by the fact that the development could not be seen from the public highway and considered that the quality of the appeal building was worth conserving in its own right and should therefore be altered as little as possible. The strength of this argument was reinforced by the fact that the building was in an outstanding conservation area where policies for rear staircases on listed buildings were consistently applied by the council.

[48] APP/F1230/F/85/46.
[49] APP/X0605/E/84/800546.
[49A] Subsequently replaced by Circular 8/87 which has in turn been replaced by PPG 15.
[50] P/PPA/LA/365 (Scottish Development Department).

7. "Problem Buildings": Redundancy, Neglect and Disrepair

1. GENERAL SUMMARY

7.01   Listing is essentially an action through which society attempts to protect from what it sees as unsympathetic change, that portion of the built environment which it perceives as being an important aesthetic or historic factor in the quality of life which it enjoys. However, the vast majority of buildings which are listed for this reason are also integral parts of an overall economic system upon which much of this quality of life depends, and all such buildings have, to some extent, to be capable of adaptation or role change in order to meet changing economic demands and circumstances.

In listing buildings, the Secretary of State does not concern himself with this latter factor, and consequently he has no regard to the economic consequences of his actions, notwithstanding that implicit in a listing is a restriction on the physical, and therefore in all probability the economic, adaptability of the buildings concerned.

Similarly, in the consideration of applications for LBC there have been obvious presumptions in favour of the intrinsic, architectural and historic and rarity criteria as principal determinant factors.[1] Despite various recom-

[1] PPG 15, para. 3.5(i).

254

mendations of the Secretary of State in respect of the consideration of financial and economic implications and consequences[2] and of alternative use potential,[3] economic factors have been clearly secondary to aesthetic ones.

If to the foregoing considerations is added the fact that society expects the owners of the buildings it seeks to preserve to meet the ongoing costs of their "preservation" (public grants, though they run into millions of pounds a year, represent only a minor contribution to the overall cost of implementing conservation policies), it is inevitable that situations will arise on which buildings cease to be physically, or economically, capable of sustaining the use for which they were originally intended. They become redundant, are neglected, and fall into disrepair. They may even be neglected whilst in use. Whatever the circumstances, they become "problem buildings".

Initially it should be stated that nowhere in the listed buildings legislation is there an obligation cast on an owner or occupier to keep the building in repair. There are sanctions if a building falls into disrepair, but nowhere is there a positive obligation, nor is it primarily a criminal offence to fail to repair unless it is a breach of a specific notice or order served in accordance with the LBA 1990 or the various Public Health Acts.

There are no simple instantaneous remedies for problem buildings. There are, however, a number of options available to both local authorities and to building owners. The principal purpose of this chapter is to consider those options. Additionally, consideration is given to certain options for owners of buildings which they suspect might become subject to the various statutory listing and conservation measures.

We set out the statutory provisions in detail but demonstrate in the tables which appear at the end of this chapter the options which are open, as follows:

(1) to the DNH and to local authorities in respect of a listed building appearing to be in need of repair;
(2) to local authorities in respect of a building which is dangerous, defective, ruinous, dilapidated or unfit;
(3) to the owner of a "redundant" listed building;
(4) to the owner of a non-listed building not in a conservation area, suspecting that it is of a type likely to be listed and wishing to avoid the consequences: building not in beneficial use;
(5) to the owner of a listed building: building in beneficial use but where there is a use change, demolition or major alteration is possible in the future; and
(6) to the owner of a non-listed building which is unlikely to be listed, but which is located in an area likely to be designated as a conservation area.

[2] PPG 15, para. 1.4.
[3] PPG 15, para. 2.18; and PPG 1.

2. COMPULSORY ACQUISITION OF LISTED BUILDINGS IN NEED OF REPAIR

(a) General

7.02 Section 47 of the LBA empowers the Secretary of State, in circumstances where it appears to him that reasonable steps are not being taken for properly preserving a listed building, to authorise the appropriate authority[4] to acquire the building or to do so himself.[5] An order may not be made in respect of an excepted building, *i.e.* ecclesiastical buildings or an ancient monument, compulsorily to acquire such a building.[6]

Additionally, the Secretary of State may either acquire, or authorise any appropriate authority to acquire, any land comprising or contiguous or adjacent to the building which appears to be required for preserving the building or its amenities, or for affording access to it, or for its proper control or management.[7] It is provided that the Secretary of State shall consult with English Heritage before making or confirming a compulsory purchase order in the case of a building situated in England.[8]

In making or confirming an order, the Secretary of State must be satisfied that it is expedient to make provision for the preservation of the building and to authorise its compulsory acquisition for that purpose. He will also need to be satisfied that the means and the resources necessary for securing the building's repair will be available.[9]

It was said in *English Heritage Conservation Bulletin* (June 1991, page 11) that authorities are reluctant to consider compulsory acquisition of listed buildings in need of repair due to the belief that if they acquire and re-sell such listed buildings restrictions on capital finance automatically apply so that an authority may only use 50 per cent of the sale proceeds for other projects. This is an erroneous view, for, provided the building is not retained in local authority ownership, there need be no financial penalty. The relevant rules are detailed in the Local Authorities (Capital Finance) Regulations 1990 [S.I. 1990 No. 432] and the Local Authority (Capital Finance)

---

[4] LBA 1990 s.47(7). The appropriate authority means the county or district council of the area in which the building is situated or in the case of a building situated in Greater London, English Heritage or the council of the London Borough in which the building is situated in the case of a building situated outside Greater London, the joint planning board for the area in which the building is situated or in the case of a building situated within the Broads, the Broads Authority.

[5] LBA 1990, s.47(1)(a) and (b).

[6] LBA 1990, s.60(1) and 61(1).

[7] LBA 1990, s.47(1). For the purposes of this section "relevant land" is described in s.47(7).

[8] PPG 15, para. 7.12.

[9] PPG 15, para. 7.12.

(Amendment) Regulations 1991 [S.I. 1991 No. 500]. Circular 11/90 explains the rules. It should be noted that if the re-sale proceeds are the same or less than the purchase price paid by the local authority then the capital receipt is unrestricted. Any profit which is realised is subject to normal restrictions save for legal costs of acquisition and other similar incidental expenditure.

An authority can either dispose of the building immediately without carrying out works itself or may delay disposal for up to three years provided a contract for disposal has been exchanged within two years of the date of acquisition. The disposal must cover the interest acquired, but the freehold may be retained if a lease of at least 125 years is granted and 90 per cent of the sale proceeds are received within a year from the date of disposal. The regulations[10] allow local authorities to carry out "enhancement" works prior to disposal provided not more than two years elapse before the disposal.

It is open to an authority to acquire a listed building and then enter into a conditional lease with a purchaser, which on the satisfactory completion of the repair works is translated into a freehold sale.[11] These are general guides. Any authority considering acquisition and resale should look carefully at the current regulations to ensure that the criteria are met.

The advice contained in PPG 15 (paragraph 7.13) suggests that the Secretary of State considers that privately owned historic buildings should, wherever possible, remain in the private sector. Local planning authorities are encouraged to identify private individuals or bodies, e.g. Building Preservation Trusts, which have access to funds to enable them to carry out the necessary repairs and to which the building will be sold on as quickly as possible.

(b) Repairs notice as preliminary to section 47 LBA action

A repairs notice made and served under section 48 of the LBA 1990 is a pre- **7.03** requisite to any compulsory acquisition under section 47 of the 1990 Acts. These compulsory purchase powers are unique amongst such powers insofar as they confer power on the magistrates' court to make orders.

(c) Consequences and applications of repairs notice procedure

Although the principal purpose of a repairs notice under section 48 LBA is **7.04** to facilitate the commencement of section 47 LBA compulsory acquisition proceedings, it would however appear that such notices are capable of being

[10] Reg No. 17, see s.40 Local Government & Housing Act 1989.
[11] *Emergency Repairs for Historic Buildings* by Eleanor Michell, published by English Heritage (1988).

used primarily for the purpose of persuading the owners of listed buildings to which they apply to effect requisite repairs—the implied consequences of non-compliance being the probability of compulsory acquisition. In 1987 the Court of Appeal upheld the finding of the High Court in the case of *Rolf v. North Shropshire District Council*[12] that when serving a (Section 48 LBA) repairs notice the local authority need not take into account the means of the owner of the listed building in specifying what works of preservation were required. Any appropriate local authority can serve a repairs notice; only the Secretary of State can undertake, or authorise the undertaking of, compulsory purchase proceedings under section 47 LBA.

It is, however, apparent that the provisions of sections 47 and 48 of the LBA may be used by owners to divest themselves of buildings which have become a liability. An owner may well deliberately neglect his listed building in the hope that either the Secretary of State, or more probably the local authority, will serve a repairs notice, and on his not complying with its requirements, the Secretary of State will start, or authorise, compulsory purchase proceedings. The owner himself may be able to force the pace by serving a listed building purchase notice on the authority which has served the repairs notice, although he cannot do this until the expiration of three months from the service of the repairs notice and is precluded if within that period the authority serving the repairs notice begins the compulsory acquisition procedure.[13]

The Association of Conservation Officers produced a report[14] in 1992 sub-titled "Study of listed building repairs notices used in England—April 1984 to March 1990 under sections 47 to 51 of the Listed Buildings Act 1990". Over 87 per cent of authorities in England responded to the request for information for the survey and the following table summarises the outcome of the repairs notices served in the relevant period.

Total Repairs Notices Served[15]	162
Repair started by the original owner[16]	87
Case went straight to a CPO Inquiry	21
Building transferred to new owner who repaired	9
Building transferred to Council who repaired	6
Case dropped and turned into Urgent Works Notice	2
Building demolished illegally	1
Building demolished after successful LBC on Appeal	1
Cases still in progress	8
Unresolved cases for lack of information from LPA	27
Total	**162**

The report indicates that a total of 287 repair notices were authorised over the 6 year period. Thus in 42 per cent of cases, it seems likely that the auth-

[12] [1988] J.P.L. 103 C.A.
[13] LBA 1990, s.48(5).
[14] *Listed Building Repairs Notices*, Bob Kindred, 1992.
[15] The repairs notice information is reproduced with the kind permission of the Association of Conservation Officers.
[16] Of the 87 cases where the owner started work, 14 got to the CPO inquiry stage before that work started.

orisation of such a notice prompted the relevant listed building owners either to commence repairs or dispose of their interest. The report comments upon the above table as follows:

> "If the unresolved cases and those in progress are excluded, then once a Notice had to be formally served, in 80% of the remaining cases, action was then prompted in the form of repair or sale to a third party. In only 16% of cases did the buildings end up as the subject of a CPO Public Inquiry.
>
> Unfortunately there is no information on the number of Councils who embarked on the Repairs Notice process only to abandon it leaving the building to continue to deteriorate.
>
> The prospect of an owner facing a Public Inquiry and possibly being deprived of his property encouraged further action on some buildings. In only 5 cases out of the 287 originally authorised was a Compulsory Purchase Order eventually confirmed by the Secretary of State.
>
> It must be concluded that on average there is a less than one in fifty chance of a Council ending up with a CPO building. With a sympathetic buyer waiting in support of the Council (either a Building Preservation Trust, sympathetic developer or individual) why should there be so much fear of the consequences of using the legislation?"

Even the provisions of section 50 LBA (whereby minimum compensation **7.05** only may be payable in respect of a listed building deliberately left to fall into disrepair) (see paragraph 7.09 below) may not prompt a reluctant owner to effect requisite repairs, especially when the cost of so doing may produce a lower value than might be obtained with even minimum compensation on compulsory acquisition.

It is also significant to remember that if a repairs notice is served and compulsory acquisition is effected as a result of non-compliance, the responsibility for the subsequent repair and upkeep of the listed building until, and if, it is disposed of by the acquiring authority to another party devolves upon the acquiring authority.

For this reason in particular the incidence of the service of repairs notices is relatively low. Moreover, although there is no statutory obligation for the serving authority (be it the Secretary of State or a local authority) to follow non-compliance with a repairs notice by compulsory acquisition, the authority risks a purchase notice being served on it by the owner under section 48(5) of the LBA 1990. There may be a moral or face-saving obligation; in the emotive circumstances which frequently surround neglected listed buildings, the Secretary of State or a local authority would face much criticism if it "threatened" to acquire a building in order to preserve it, and then failed to do so when the owner ignored the notice. Equally difficult is the situation where a local authority compulsorily acquires a building, the subject of a repairs notice, and then re-sells. If the new purchaser contracts to do the repairs and fails to do so, the authority has a problem and may need to acquire compulsorily again. A better way might be to grant an agreement for a lease and require the proposed lessee to carry out the repairs; on doing so satisfactorily the authority will then dispose of the freehold to him.

In practice, it is unlikely that a repairs notice would be served without any prior consultation with an owner, and thus the service of such a notice must generally be regarded as a last resort when all efforts at informal persuasion have failed.

As there is nothing in the LBA 1990 to the contrary, it would appear that a repairs notice may be served in respect of an unoccupied listed building notwithstanding the probability that action under section 54 LBA[17] may be more appropriate in such circumstances. As we have explained the purpose of a section 54 LBA notice is to effect urgent repairs to prevent further deterioration: tarpaulins and breeze block are the consequences of a section 54 LBA notice, rather than the longer term consequences of a section 48 LBA notice.

The use of temporary repairs and the care of unused buildings is the subject of an interesting study undertaken on behalf of English Heritage by Eleanor Michell in 1988 and entitled *Emergency Repairs for Historic Buildings*. The book contains a number of case instances illustrating the ways in which the future of a building can be secured whilst funds are raised and a scheme is prepared for permanent restoration. These steps often take time to finalise and may coincide with the deterioration of the building arising from lack of weatherproofing and vandalism.

(d) Repairs notice procedure

7.06
(i) A repairs notice must be served at least two months prior to the initiation of compulsory purchase proceedings in respect of a building to which section 48 LBA applies, *i.e.* a listed building which is not an excepted building by virtue of sections 60(1) and 61(1) of the LBA 1990. The notice is to be served on the owner of the building.

(ii) The notice may be served by either the Secretary of State (this would be the procedure in the case of a notice relating to a listed building owned by a local authority; the Act does not preclude such action); or by English Heritage (who would be more likely to serve than the Secretary of State); or by the county or district council in whose area the building is situated; or in Greater London, by English Heritage, by the appropriate London borough, by the joint planning board, or by a Development Corporation.

Whilst a notice under section 48 LBA may be served by any of the above parties, only the Secretary of State may initiate or authorise any subsequent compulsory purchase under section 47 LBA, see paragraph 7.08 below.

(iii) There is no prescribed form of notice. The notice must however specify[18]:

(a) the works which the Secretary of State, English Heritage or the local authority consider "reasonably necessary for the proper preservation of the building" and;

(b) the effect of sections 47–50 of the LBA (see below).

The decision of the House of Lords in *Robbins v. Secretary of State for the Environment*[19] in 1989 concerned the validity of such a repairs notice. Ashford Borough Council accepted that six of the 20

---

[17] See paras. 7.10–7.13 below.
[18] LBA 1990, ss.48(1)(a) and (b).
[19] [1989] 1 W.L.R. 201.

items in the repairs notice went beyond preservation works and involved restoration.

Those six items therefore went beyond the proper scope of a repairs notice. Lord Bridge said that the term "preservation" was to be given its ordinary meaning and this involved an objective limitation on what could properly be included in a repairs notice. The case was also important in that it addressed the issue of at what time should the "preservation" test be made—at the date of listing or when the repairs notice was served? Lord Bridge decided that the works of preservation must relate to the condition of the building at the date of listing. He also concluded that the inclusion of restoration works in the repairs notice did not invalidate the notice and the subsequent compulsory purchase order, provided the amount of "preservation" required was substantial enough to support a conclusion by the Secretary of State that reasonable steps were not being taken for the proper preservation of the listed building.

The specification of works required will result from a survey or investigation of the building by the serving authority. Such a survey may be taken under powers conferred by section 88(2)(a) LBA (rights of entry and supplementary provisions thereto, described in Chapter 11); an owner who wilfully obstructs an authorised entry shall be guilty of an offence.[20]

(iv) The demolition of a building after the service of a repairs notice does not prevent the serving authority from being authorised compulsorily to acquire the site of the building under section 47 LBA powers.[21]

(v) The serving authority may withdraw the notice at any time but must notify any person served with the notice immediately that they have done so.[22] This of course might prompt the owner to serve a purchase notice under and subject to the conditions of sections 137(6) T.C.P.A. 1990 and 48(5) LBA 1990.

(e) The owner's response

(i) On receipt of a repairs notice, it would appear that an owner has **7.07** four options:

    (a) to undertake (or at least commence) the works specified as necessary in the notice, within two months of receipt;

    (b) to undertake works which he considers necessary (but which do not necessarily accord with those specified in the notice);

    (c) to take no action at all and wait for compulsory purchase proceedings to be initiated;

    (d) to consider serving a purchase notice; but which he cannot do until the expiration of three months from the service of the repairs notice.

---

[20] LBA 1990, s.88(3).
[21] LBA 1990, s.48(2).
[22] LBA 1990, s.48(3).

(ii) In the case of option (i)(a), such action should remove the threat of compulsory acquisition under section 47 LBA, as the Secretary of State's authority under that section can only arise "where it appears to him that reasonable steps are not being taken for properly preserving" the building.[23]

(iii) In the case of option (i)(b), which may well arise where the owner considers the works specified in the notice are more than are required for the proper preservation of the building, it would appear that an owner is at liberty to proceed with such works as he considers necessary (subject, of course, to such works not amounting to alterations or extensions requiring LBC).

An owner would be ill-advised so to proceed without first consulting the serving authority—such consultation may well produce a mutually acceptable solution, and the consequent withdrawal of the notice. However, if such a solution were not to be achieved, the owner could still proceed with repairs which he considered necessary and, if compulsory purchase proceedings were still initiated, he could, at the appropriate point therein (see paragraph 7.08(iv) below) apply to a magistrates court for an order staying the proceedings, on the grounds that reasonable steps had been taken for properly preserving the building.[24]

(iv) In the case of option (i)(c), such inaction could be expected to result, at the end of two months, in the commencement of compulsory purchase proceedings. This may well be the option chosen by an owner who wished to divest himself of responsibility for the building.

(v) In the case of option (1)(d) if the compulsory purchase proceedings do not materialise, the owner under section 33(2) may serve a purchase notice after waiting three months.

(vi) Again, if the compulsory purchase proceedings are abandoned, then the owner may serve a purchase notice on the local authority having issued the repairs notice.

(f) Compulsory purchase under section 47 LBA

7.08 (i) In a situation where, two months after the service of a repairs notice under section 48 LBA, it appears that reasonable steps are not being taken for properly preserving the building, and the notice has not been withdrawn, if the Secretary of State is satisfied "that it is expedient to make provision for the preservation of the building and to authorise its compulsory acquisition for that purpose",[25] he may compulsorily acquire the building, or authorise the council of the county or district, English Heritage, the London Borough in which the building is situated, the planning board or development corporation, compulsorily to acquire the building.[26] The procedures for service of a repairs notice under section 48 LBA

[23] LBA 1990, s.47(1).
[24] LBA 1990, s.47(4).
[25] LBA 1990, s.47(3).
[26] LBA 1990, s.47(1).

and subsequent compulsory acquisition under section 47 LBA are perhaps unduly complicated in that they potentially involve three bodies. The repairs notice served under section 48 LBA by a local authority should specify what works the authority consider reasonably necessary; the Secretary of State may authorise a local authority compulsorily to acquire a listed building where it appears to the Secretary of State that reasonable steps are not being taken properly to preserve the building; and the magistrates court may have to deal with an application by the owner of a listed building for an order staying the compulsory acquisition proceedings under section 47(4) LBA. The court will stay such proceedings if it is satisfied that reasonable steps have been taken properly to preserve the listed building.

(ii) The procedure for compulsory acquisition under section 47 LBA is that applicable by virtue of the Acquisition of Land Act 1981.

(iii) Any owner, lessee or occupier (other than a tenant for one month or less) has the right to object to the confirmation of an order made under Acquisition of Land Act 1981, in the manner and during the time prescribed in the notice required to be served on such persons under section 12(1) of that Act, whereupon the Secretary of State must either afford to the objector an opportunity of being heard by a person duly appointed for the purpose, or cause a public local inquiry to be held, where any other objectors have the right to be heard.[27]

Norfolk County Council was in the process of compulsorily acquiring the Grade I listed Waxham Court Barn at Sea Palling to enable the Council to ensure its proper preservation, to afford access to it and to secure its proper control and management. The owners of the barn were unable to fund the necessary repairs from their own resources but were not willing to sell the freehold. The Council had served a repairs notice which had not been complied with. The Secretary of State confirmed with modifications the compulsory purchase order made by the Inspector appointed to hold the public local inquiry.[28]

(iv) Any person having an interest in the building may, under section 47(4) and 47(5) LBA 1990, "within 28 days after the service of the notice . . . apply to a magistrates' court acting for the petty sessions area within which the building is situated for an order staying further proceedings on the compulsory purchase order"; and, if the court is satisfied that reasonable steps have been taken for properly preserving the building, the court shall make an order accordingly. Such an application was made by the owner of Pell Wall Hall in the mid 1980s to the magistrates court, (see the case of *Rolf v. North Shropshire District Council*[29] referred to at 7.04 above) under section 114(1) T.C.P.A. 1971 [now section 47(4) LBA] but the court refused to grant a stay and the owner exercised his right to appeal to the Crown Court under section 144(7) T.C.P.A.

---

[27] *Middlesex County Council v. Minister of Local Government and Planning* (1953) 2 P. & C.R. 227, CA.

[28] Appeal case ref E1/5320/362/2 0026A; [1988] J.P.L. 103.

[29] [1988] J.P.L. 103 C.A.

191 [now section 47(6) LBA] which was also unsuccessful. He also failed in the Court of Appeal.

(v) If a staying order is granted by the Magistrates, then by implication the compulsory purchase order cannot be proceeded with, as the powers under section 47(5) LBA can only be used where reasonable steps have been taken for properly preserving the building.

(vi) If the Magistrates Court does not make an order (because it is satisfied that reasonable steps are being taken) any person aggrieved by the Magistrates' decision may appeal to the Crown Court.[30]

(g) Compensation on compulsory acquisition under section 47 LBA

7.09 If the building sought to be acquired is a "normal", *i.e.* non-listed building to which section 50 LBA will not apply, then the usual rules of compensation flowing from the Acquisition of Land Act 1981 will apply. However, the provisions regarding compensation on the compulsory acquisition of a listed building deliberately left derelict are set out in section 50 LBA.

(i) If an appropriate authority[31] proposing to acquire a building under section 47(1) LBA is satisfied that it has been deliberately allowed to fall into disrepair for the purpose of justifying its demolition and the development or re-development of the site or any site adjoining, it may include in the compulsory purchase order which it submits to the Secretary of State for confirmation a direction for minimum compensation.[32]

Such a minimum compensation order was made in the following case.[33] *North Shropshire District Council* had been involved in a series of litigious proceedings relating to the Grade II* Pell Wall Hall designed by Sir John Soane culminating in the Secretary of State confirming a compulsory purchase order with minimum compensation. The Lands Tribunal set a price for the house and 4.35 acres of land of £1. This underscores the significance of a minimum compensation order.[34]

(ii) The Secretary of State may also include such a direction in a case where he is making a compulsory purchase order under section 50 LBA, and is satisfied that the building has been deliberately allowed to fall into disrepair for the purposes stated in (i) above.[35]

(iii) Notices[36] stating the effect of a compulsory purchase order including a direction under section 50 LBA must specify that such a direction is included in the order, and explain the meaning of

---

[30] LBA 1990, s.47(6).

[31] LBA 1990, s.47(1).

[32] LBA 1990, s.50(1).

[33] *English Heritage Conservation Bulletin*, February 1991, p. 7.

[34] Note also the case of *Vale Farm, Broad Oak, Canterbury*, a c17 farmhouse in respect of which the Secretary of State confirmed a compulsory purchase order with minimum compensation. *English Heritage Conservation Bulletin*, February 1991, p. 7.

[35] LBA 1990, s.50(2).

[36] Acquisition of Land Act 1981, s.12(1).

"direction for minimum compensation".[37] There is no prescribed form of notice.

(iv) Such a direction limits the compensation which would be otherwise payable by assessing it on the assumption that LBC would only be granted for works for the restoration of the building to a proper state of repair and for maintaining it in that state.[38] A form of direction is included in the Encyclopedia L50.05.

(v) Where a direction for minimum compensation is included in a compulsory purchase order under section 47 LBA, any person having an interest in the building may within 28 days of the service of the notice of the order[39] apply to the magistrates' court for the area in which the building is situated, for an order that the direction should not be included. If the court is satisfied that the building has not been deliberately allowed to fall into disrepair for the purposes mentioned in (i) above, the court shall make such an order.[40] If a person applying for such an order from the magistrates' court is aggrieved by the court's decision there is a right of appeal to the Crown Court.[41]

(vi) The first time that the Secretary of State exercised his powers under section 48 LBA 1990 was in St Ann's Hotel, Buxton. The hotel has since been sold voluntarily to the District Council and, with grant aid from English Heritage and the National Heritage Memorial Fund, repair work was started in October 1993.[42]

3. URGENT REPAIR OF UNOCCUPIED LISTED BUILDINGS

Under section 54 LBA, local authorities are empowered to execute any **7.10** works which in the opinion of the authority are urgently needed for the preservation of a listed building,[43] other than an excepted building.[44] In Greater London, English Heritage has concurrent powers with the London boroughs and may carry out such works without the approval of the Secretary of State.[45]

The procedures leading to, and for the undertaking of, action under section 50 LBA are illustrated in Table 1.[46] It should be noted that the Secretary of State also has the power to take such action,[47] and has power to authorise English Heritage so to do, although he has indicated that he will authorise

---

[37] LBA 1990, s.50(3).

[38] LBA 1990, ss.50(4) and (5).

[39] LBA 1990, s.47(4).

[40] LBA 1990, ss.50(6) and (7).

[41] LBA 1990, s.50(8). See also *Cook v. Southend Borough Council*, [1990] 1 All E.R. 243, a case where the local authority exercised its right of appeal as an aggrieved person.

[42] *English Heritage Legal Bulletin*, February 1994.

[43] LBA 1990, s.55(1).

[44] LBA 1990, ss.60(1) and 61(1) (ecclesiastical buildings and ancient monuments).

[45] LBA 1990, s.54(7).

[46] Table 1.

[47] LBA 1990, s.54(2)(a) and (b).

English Heritage only where the building is of exceptional interest.[48] It is believed that the Secretary of State first used his power to serve what is now a section 50 LBA notice in respect of Barlaston Hall, Staffordshire[49]; and in December 1987 English Heritage was authorised for the first time to serve a notice and carry out repairs, at Revesby Abbey, a neglected Grade I listed Victorian mansion near Boston, Lincolnshire.[50] In Greater London, English Heritage may carry out such works without the approval of the Secretary of State.

The works at Revesby Abbey cost £120,000 and under section 55 costs under LBA have been recovered from the owner. In this case, the "recovery notice" was sent to the "tenant for life", who appealed under section 55(4) LBA. The Secretary of State refused the appeal and confirmed the recovery notice in full. The provision in this case allowing works to be paid for out of capital money rather than from income opens up the possibility of utilising the capital rather than income which the tenant for life might be unable to afford.[51]

The Secretary of State may also direct that section 54 LBA should apply to an unlisted building in a conservation area if he is satisfied that the preservation of the building is important to the character or appearance of the area.[52] Local planning authorities or members of the public may ask the Secretary of State to make such a direction.[53] The works may consist of or include works for affording temporary support or shelter for the building.[54]

If the building is occupied, works may be carried out only to those parts which are not in use. This provision will obviate the problem of defining what was occupation. The words "in use" have a clearer perception in rating law and interpretation may no doubt be drawn from them.

The owner must be given at least seven days notice in writing of the intention to carry out the works and the notice must contain a description of the works.[55] The costs of carrying out the works may be recovered from the owner[56] and the owner may appeal against a notice requiring payment of the cost of works, on four grounds:

(a) that some or all of the works were unnecessary for the preservation of the building, or;

(b) in the case of works for affording temporary support of shelter, that the temporary arrangements have continued for an unreasonable length of time, or;

(c) that the amount specified in the notice is unreasonable, or;

(d) that the recovery of that amount would cause him hardship.[57]

Ground (c) may well be of relevance in a period of economic constraint. Whilst undoubtedly intended to provide for cases where some helpless individual owning a crumbling Georgian mansion simply could not afford to

[48] PPG 15, para. 7.6.
[49] J.P.L. August 1982.
[50] Reported in *Planning*, January 8, 1988.
[51] *English Heritage Conservation Bulletin*, October 1991, p. 4.
[52] LBA 1990, s.76(1), and see also s.54 of the Act.
[53] PPG 15, para. 7.5.
[54] LBA 1990, s.54(3).
[55] LBA 1990, s.54(5).
[56] LBA 1990, s.55(4).
[57] LBA 1990, s.55(4).

effect repairs even if willing to do so, it may well be much more relevant to the firm owning two large factories, and having to choose between expensive repairs to one which was listed and redundant, and capital investment in another that was not listed and in full production. The Secretary of State is the final arbiter in such matters.

In respect of works and the costs thereof, PPG 15 paragraph 7.7 gives local **7.11** authorities some indication of the considerations to which the Secretary of State would have regard in the event of an owner making representations on temporary repair.[58]

Any work done on a building under section 54 LBA should be the minimum required for its preservation and be carried out at a reasonable cost; expensive permanent repairs should not be carried out under these powers. It is considered that only emergency repairs, for example to keep a building wind and weatherproof and safe from collapse or action to prevent vandalism or theft. The steps taken should be the minimum consistent with achieving this objective and should not involve an owner in great expense. Inexpensive repairs done in time often arrest the deterioration of a building. English Heritage has published a handbook which gives advice on methods of temporary repair entitled *Emergency Repairs—A Handbook* (1988).

The financial circumstances of the owner should be taken into account at the outset and any sums authorities wish to recover from him should not be unreasonable in relation to his means.

Special care is needed when dealing with large buildings, especially those owned by charities. Even limited repairs to a large building are likely to prove expensive and may be beyond the owner's means. Since local authorities have already been asked not to involve owners in great expense, this is particularly important where a large building like a church is empty and in need of repair.

Churches need special care, not only because they are usually large and the available resources limited, but because of the problem of churches becoming redundant.[59]

In one of the few decisions on this subject, there are some interesting **7.12** comments on how the Secretary of State interprets what is now section 55 LBA. A case for determination by the Secretary of State for the Environment followed representations under the then section 101(7)(a), (b) and (c) of the 1971 Act against a notice served under section 101(6) of that Act by the Hampshire County Council which sought reimbursement of the sum of £1,356 expended by that council in executing works urgently necessary for the preservation of the listed building at 29/31 Bell Street, Romsey, Hants.[60] The Secretary of State said:

"The Secretary of State is anxious that local planning authorities should use the powers given to them by section 101 in cases where prompt and effective action can save the building from further deterioration. In the opinion of the Secretary of State a notice under [section 54 LBA 1990] should describe in as much detail as possible the work which

---

[58] PPG 15, para. 7.7.
[59] See chapter 10 on Churches.
[60] [1978] J.P.L. 637; SE2/5420/480/2 May 10, 1978, and see also *R. v. London Borough of Camden ex p. Comyn China Co.* [1983] 47 P. & C.R. 417.

the authority consider is urgently necessary so that the owner knows what he has to do to comply with its terms or is forewarned of the work which will be done by the council if he fails to do it himself. Such a notice also gives the owner the opportunity to discuss other possible solutions which will achieve the same effect with the council or to dispute that at the time the works are not urgently necessary. It is also important that the works specified should be capable of being completed so that one account for their total cost can be sent to the owner and he is not involved in a continuing liability. For the powers of section 54 LBA to be properly exercised, the work must be urgently necessary at the time the notice is served and it is not considered that the fact that one notice has been served specifying certain work to be done, enables an authority to recover cost of works done to the building which are in addition to those covered by the notice unless a further notice under section 54(5) LBA is served describing the additional work subsequently considered necessary.

It has been considered whether or not the amount referred to by the county council should be recoverable from the owner but it has been concluded that recovery would not be justified and would cause the owner hardship because, at the time of the service of the original notice, there was a conflict of view as to the necessity for the preservation of the building between the district council, the local authority primarily responsible for the control of the demolition of listed buildings, and the county council.

While it is legitimate to take section [54 LBA] action while the future of a building is under discussion so that the question of demolition is not decided by its collapse in the meantime, it is, in the Secretary of State's opinion, unreasonable to carry out work of the type undertaken by the council when it has already been indicated that the building may be demolished when a satisfactory scheme of redevelopment has been approved. The Secretary of State therefore serves no notice for the recovery of costs in this case."

7.13 Hampshire County Council applied to the High Court for an order of *certiorari*, but the application was dismissed by the Court on June 25, 1980. There were a number of grounds, but two comments from the judgment of Donaldson LJ (as he then was) are particularly important:

"We considered the decision letter to be slightly inaccurate in referring to the owner wishing to carry out the works herself and to 'comply with its terms'. It is inaccurate in that the notice does not call upon the owner to do any work. The intention of the seven days notice is to enable the owner to discuss the nature of the works and to be aware of what the county council propose doing. It does therefore serve a purpose. The Secretary of State is right in saying that it is important to go into some detail in describing the works contemplated. It must however be borne in mind that this is an emergency procedure and hence not to be compared with section 115 [of the 1971 TCP] Act. It would have been enough if the estimate had been included with the notice. But the notice did not give a clue and the owner was entitled to some notice of the works contemplated.

We decline to define 'hardship'. It clearly covers the personal circumstances of the owner and it is submitted by the county council that it could include a great disparity between the cost of the works and the resultant value of the building."[61]

4. LOCAL AUTHORITY OPTIONS IN RESPECT OF "DANGEROUS" LISTED BUILDINGS

(a) General powers relating to all buildings (other than buildings in London)

The Building Act 1984 makes certain provisions in respect of buildings or **7.14** structures, or parts of such, which appear to local authorities to be in such a state of repair or are being used to carry such loads, as to be dangerous. It should be noted that local authorities are under a duty, by virtue of section 56 LBA, to consider whether they should exercise their powers under sections 47, 48 or 54 LBA before using the powers in the Building Act 1984. Leaving aside for the present the difficult issue of what constitutes a "dangerous building" (see paragraph 7.17 below) the relevant powers are as follows:

(i) Where the authority considers the danger to be such as to warrant immediate action for its removal, it may take such steps as are necessary to remove the danger by virtue of section 78(1) of the 1984 Act. This power is qualified by requirements for the giving of notice of proposed action under the section to owners and occupiers,[62] power of recovery of the expenses of such action from owners,[63] and a number of provisions regarding any subsequent court proceedings for the recovery of such expenses.[64]

(ii) Where an authority considers the danger to be less than such as to require urgent action, application may be made by the authority to a magistrates' court under the provisions of section 77 of the 1984 Act,[65] for an order requiring the owner:

(a) where danger arises from the condition of the building, to execute any works necessary to obviate the danger, or, if the owner elects, to demolish the building or any dangerous parts of it, and remove the resultant rubbish, or;

(b) where danger arises from overloading, to restrict the use of the building until works (in respect of the danger thus created) have been executed to the satisfaction of the court, and the order has been withdrawn or modified.[66]

Failure to comply with an order under section 77 of the Building Act 1984

---

[61] [1980] J.P.L. 731.
[62] B.A. 1984, s.78(2).
[63] B.A. 1984, s.78(3) and (4).
[64] B.A. 1984, s.78(5), (6) and (7).
[65] This section is now to be read in conjunction with LBA 1990 s.56, see para. 7.19 below.
[66] B.A. 1984, s.77(1), and see para. 7.19 below.

within the time specified in the order (the Act does not stipulate any particular period to be stated in an order) may result in the local authority executing the works. In such circumstances the authority have power to recover expenses reasonably incurred from the owner, who may also be liable to a fine for non-compliance not exceeding £50.

(b) General powers relating to all buildings in London

7.15   Similar powers to those described in paragraph 7.14 above are provided in respect of buildings in London by sections 65 or 69(1) of the London Building Acts (Amendment) Act 1939.[67] The powers are exercisable as appropriate by the councils of the London boroughs, or the common council of the City.[68]

(c) Powers of entry for investigating dangerous buildings

7.16   (i) Outside London, sections 95 and 96 of the Building Act 1984 provide a range of powers of entry for purposes under that Act (in this respect, section 77, is described at paragraph 7.14; (ii) above). Sections 95 and 96 do not, however, extend to entry pursuant to powers under section 78 of the 1984 Act (paragraph 7.14; (i) above). Although it is implicit in section 78 that entry may be effected for the purpose of carrying out works considered necessary by the authority, there does not appear to be any provision in the 1984 Act in respect of entry necessary for ascertaining whether or not the building is dangerous in the first place.

(ii) Within London, section 139 of the London Building Acts (Amendment) Act 1939, as extended by section 9, London County Council (General Powers) Act 1955, provides a range of powers of entry of authorised persons in respect, *inter alia*, of the powers referred to in paragraph 7.15 above.

(d) Definition of a dangerous building

7.17   Neither the Acts referred to, nor, so far as can be ascertained, do any other Acts, provide a statutory definition of what constitutes a dangerous building. Whilst logic might suggest that any building, or part of any building, which is likely to collapse on either its occupants or on passers by, might be considered dangerous, who is to pronounce upon the scale, or the urgency,

---

[67] London Building Acts (Amendment) Act 1939 s.61 (information and survey of dangerous structures); s.62 (certification of dangerous structures); s.63 (arbitration in respect of s.62 certification); s.64 (enforcement proceedings); s.65 (Court orders notwithstanding arbitration); s.66 (expenses of authorities); s.67 (power to remove inmates of dangerous structures).

[68] London County Council (General Powers) Act 1958, s.15(1).

of the (alleged) danger? It is true that structural engineers have sophisticated techniques for measuring movement in buildings, and these might be used as a test as might tests and calculations of floor loadings. One might possibly disagree with G.E. Allan's suggestion that the "assessment of the structural safety of a building is a subjective affair".[69] Reported case law on the subject is sparse and not, apparently, wholly conclusive. In *London County Council v. Herring*[70] it was held that a structure need not be dangerous to the public in order to be considered to be in a dangerous state[71]; in *London County Council v. Jones*[72] a reasonable apprehension of danger was sufficient for such a view to be taken.[73]

(e) Dangerous listed buildings

Whilst the law regarding the options of local authorities in respect of **7.18** dangerous buildings in general is reasonably clear (notwithstanding the absence of any precise criteria for the determination of what constitutes "danger") distinct problems are created when consideration has to be given by a local authority to the possibility of using these powers in respect of a dangerous listed building.

The principal problem arises where an authority considers a listed building to be so dangerous as to warrant its immediate removal. The appropriate power, under circumstances in which a listed building is not involved, would be section 78 of the Building Act 1984 (see paragraph 7.14; (i) above). However, section 83 of the Public Health Act 1961 prohibits the use of any power under the Act where it would be "unlawful under the law relating to ancient monuments or to town and country planning".

Under section 7 LBA it is unlawful to demolish (or alter), with certain exceptions,[74] any listed building without such demolition (or alteration) being "authorised" by the grant of LBC. The procedures for obtaining such consent are described in Chapter 5, and it may be seen from that description that it could take between four and eleven weeks (or possibly more) to obtain such consent and be in a position to commence demolition works.[75] Thus an argument that action under section 78 of the 1984 Act is "urgently necessary" may be negated by a local authority or an owner having first to obtain LBC in order to avoid conflict with section 83 of the 1961 Act.[76]

[69] Allan, G.E., *Conservation of Buildings of Merit*, [1977] J.P.L. 569.
[70] [1948] 2 Q.B. 522.
[71] Noted in the former *Halsbury's Statutes* (3rd ed.), Vol. 20, p. 186 in respect of definition of dangerous structure in London Building Acts (Amendment) Act 1939, s.61.
[72] [1912] 2 K.B. 504.
[73] [1980] J.P.L. 731.
[74] LBA 1990 ss.60 and 61.
[75] An application for LBC must be advertised for 21 days before a decision as to its determination is taken by the local planning authority. The authority must then convey their recommendation and send certain other papers to the Secretary of State, and may not decide the application until either 28 days have expired, or the Secretary of State has indicated that he does not wish to "call in" the application. Once such conditions have been fulfilled, and consent has been granted up to 28 days notice has to be given to the Royal Commission on Historical Monuments before demolition can commence—see para. 5.03 above.
[76] For an extreme example of a protracted application for consent to demolish, see the *Upper House Barns, Brecon* case noted above at para. 2.52.

Section 9(3) of the LBA 1990 provides that:

"In proceedings for an offence under this section it shall be a defence to prove the following matters:

(a) that works to the building were urgently necessary in the interests of safety or health or for the preservation of the building;

(b) that it was not practicable to secure safety or health or, as the case may be, the preservation of the building by works or repair or works for affording temporary support or shelter;

(c) that the works carried out were limited to the minimum measures immediately necessary; and

(d) that notice in writing justifying in detail the carrying out of the works was given to the local planning authority as soon as reasonably practicable."

This provision might appear to give a local authority wishing to pursue its powers under the Public Health and Building Acts a defence in any prosecution under the Planning Acts, arising from its having demolished a listed building without consent. However, this is only a defence; it does not alter the fact that an offence would have been committed by the authority. Section 83 of the Public Health Act 1961 prohibits the use of any power which would be unlawful under planning law, it can only be taken that action by a local authority under section 77 of the 1984 Act, without LBC, would in any event be *ultra vires*. There would also be an additional problem for any authority taking such action and being prosecuted under section 7 LBA as a result; with the building removed, and with it, the physical evidence of the danger which gave rise to its removal, the authority could have difficulty in substantiating a defence of urgent necessity.

7.19   Where the dangerous condition of a listed building is considered by a local authority to be less than warranting urgent action under section 78 of the 1984 Act, action under section 77 may be appropriate. Such action may, however, cause problems for owners as well as for the authority seeking the relevant order from the magistrates' court. To overcome this difficulty, section 56 LBA provides that a LPA must consider whether they should exercise their powers under sections 47, 48 or section 54 LBA before taking any steps with a view to making a dangerous structures order, and a new subsection to section 77 of the Building Act 1984, provides that these sections have effect subject to the relevant provisions of the LBA 1990. This makes it plain that works specified in a dangerous structure order require listed building consent.

Annex B, B16 of PPG 15 suggests that authorities taking action under these dangerous structure provisions should remind owners of the need to obtain LBC or give notice under section 56 LBA 1990. Would the owner have any defence if he merely gave notice to the local planning authority of intent to demolish (because of urgent need) and then proceeded to do so? As the action giving rise to the order under section 77 of the 1984 Act would have been based on the local authority's implied contention that the condition of the building was less serious than to warrant urgent action, could the defence of urgent necessity indicated in section 9(3) LBA be used in any subsequent proceedings? Logically if the section 77 of 1984 procedure is used, the case is unlikely to fall within a defence offered in section 9(3) LBA. But it may not be quite so clear cut, as the words "urgently necessary" in section 9(3)(a) seem to imply a subjective judgment which might make the subsection applicable if the owner thought the demolition was urgently necessary.

With such doubt existing, the owner's only option in such circumstances would be to elect to demolish the building after obtaining LBC. Clearly the court would have to have regard to the probable time needed to obtain such consent in stating the period for compliance, but that is an issue which would be readily resolvable.

More difficult to resolve would be the issue of the owner's position if he were to be refused LBC for demolition. The local authority which, if the owner failed to comply with the order (because of refusal of LBC) could take action under section 77 of the 1984 Act by executing the order themselves and recovering from the owner the costs of so doing.

(f) Dangerous listed buildings in London

7.20 The issues raised in paragraphs 7.18–7.19 above also apply substantially to action taken by local authorities in London under the powers described in paragraph 7.15 above save that the provisions of section 83 of the Public Health Act 1961 do not apply to London. The provision in section 83 prohibits the use of any power under the Act where it would be "unlawful under the law relating to . . . town and country planning". Therefore, whilst demolition pursuant to an order under the London Building Acts (Amendment) Act 1939 might constitute an offence if LBC had not first been obtained, it would not be *ultra vires* if the action were taken by a London borough council or the common council of the City.

5. LOCAL AUTHORITY OPTIONS IN RESPECT OF "DEFECTIVE" PREMISES

(a) Defective premises in general

7.21 Section 76(1) of the Building Act 1984 provides that where it appears to a local authority that any premises are in such a state (in the section referred to as a "defective state") as to be prejudicial to health, or a nuisance[77] and unreasonable delay in remedying the situation, would be occasioned by taking action under sections 93–95 of the Public Health Act 1936 (in respect of statutory nuisances as defined in section 92 of that Act) the local authority may serve on any person upon whom it would have served an abatement notice under section 93, a notice stating that the authority itself intends to remedy the "defective state" of the premises, and specifying the defects which it intends to remedy.

---

[77] Nuisance: see *Halsbury's Laws* (4th ed.), Vol. 34, para. 337. The definitions of public nuisance and private nuisance in respect of buildings revolve very much around the extent to which a building is in a ruinous condition and the extent to which it is considered to represent a danger (to third parties). As noted at para. 7.17 above there is no precise definition of "danger" in respect of buildings.

Nine days after the service of a notice under section 76(1) the local authority may take the action specified in their notice, unless within seven days of the service the person on whom the notice was served issues a counter-notice stating that he intends to remedy the defects specified in the notice. In such a case the local authority can take no action in respect of their notice unless the person serving the counter-notice fails to execute the works within a reasonable time, or fails to make progress to the satisfaction of the local authority.[78]

Section 76 makes provisions for the recovery of expenses of action under the section by the local authority and provides for matters to be considered by the court in such action for recovery of expenses.[79] Section 76 powers are also applicable in Greater London by virtue of the Greater London (General Powers) Act 1967, section 25.

(b) Defective listed premises

7.22 It would appear that the application of section 76 of the Building Act 1984 to listed buildings throws up problems not dissimilar to those produced by the application of section 78 powers, discussed at paragraphs 7.18–7.19 above. Section 76(6) of Building Act 1984 states that a notice may not be served, or works proceeded with, by an authority if the works would contravene a building preservation order under section 29 of the Town and Country Planning Act 1947. Section 29 of the 1947 Act was replaced by section 30 of the Town and Country Planning Act 1962, and this itself was repealed and not replaced in the Town and Country Planning Act 1968. In consequence building preservation orders no longer exist; section 76(6) of the Public Health Act 1961 however has not subsequently been amended or repealed to recognise the fact.

Allan[80] suggests that "since all buildings subject to such orders are now listed buildings or deemed to be listed, the prohibition" [in what is now section 76(6)] "cannot apply and the subsection must be regarded as repealed by implication".

It would, however, seem that a different interpretation is possible. Section 40(10) of the Town and Country Planning Act 1968 provides that all buildings which were subject to building preservation orders immediately before the commencement of that part of the Act would be deemed to be listed, and this provision is repeated in Schedule 1, paragraph 1, LBA 1990.[81] As building preservation orders have been replaced by deemed listing, a problem arises in connection with section 76(6) which would appear still to apply in respect of notices and works under section 76. This might result in there being contravention of a deemed listing, and the powers and restrictions applied thereto by sections 1, 2, 7, 8 and 9 of the LBA.

If this latter supposition is correct (and there are no cases reported to indicate the contrary), then action by a local authority under section 76 in respect of a listed building may well be an offence under the LBA 1990, if

---

[78] B.A. 1984, s.76(3).
[79] B.A. 1984, ss.76(4) and (5).
[80] Allan, G.E., *Conservation of Buildings of Merit* [1977] J.P.L. 569.
[81] Para. 2.52 above.

LBC is not obtained first; and *ultra vires* by virtue of section 83 of the Public Health Act 1961 (considered at paragraphs 7.18–7.19 above).

6. LOCAL AUTHORITY OPTIONS IN RESPECT OF "RUINOUS AND DILAPIDATED" BUILDINGS

(a) Ruinous buildings in general

Section 79(1) of the Building Act 1984 provides that if a local authority **7.23** considers a building to be seriously detrimental to the amenities of the neighbourhood because of its ruinous or dilapidated condition, it may serve notice on the owner requiring him either to undertake such works of repair or restoration as they consider necessary in the interests of amenity, or to demolish the building and remove resultant rubbish in order to achieve this aim.

This section does not apply to inner London, which is covered by the provisions of the London Government Act 1963.[82]

(b) Ruinous listed buildings

So far as a local authority is concerned, because their action under this **7.24** section is only to require an owner to take action, it would appear that when the action concerns a listed building, the authority is not prohibited from acting because of section 83 of the 1961 Act (paragraphs 7.18–7.19 above). It would, however, seem to be fair that an authority serving a notice under section 79 of the 1984 Act in respect of a listed building should make the person served with the notice aware of the possible need to obtain LBC before carrying out any works required by the authority.

7. LOCAL AUTHORITY POWERS UNDER THE HOUSING ACTS

In common with all other buildings which are houses or dwellings, listed **7.25** residential buildings may be subject to powers of local authorities under the Housing Act 1985, where such premises are considered to be either unfit, or require substantial repairs (capable of implementation at reasonable expense).[83] In housing action areas or general improvement areas,[84] authorities may serve improvement notices on the owners of dwellings not having standard amenities and considered capable of improvement at reasonable expense.[85] Alongside these powers, local authorities have cer-

---

[82] s.40(1) and Sched. 2, Part 1, para. 36.
[83] H.A. 1985, ss.189, 190.
[84] H.A. 1985, Part VIII.
[85] H.A. 1985, Part VII.

tain powers and duties to make grants under the Acts to facilitate such works as are necessary. These grants are considered in Chapter 12.

8. BUILDINGS AT RISK

7.26   In 1992 English Heritage published the findings of its sample survey to ascertain the state of repair of listed buildings in England. The survey concludes that most listed buildings are in use and in good repair, but until this survey was undertaken it was difficult to know the scale of buildings which were neglected or in need of repair. It has been calculated that some 7 per cent—or nearly 37,000—listed buildings are in danger of falling into disrepair. The highest percentage of neglected buildings are redundant building types (principally agricultural and storage). English Heritage consider the major role of discovering which buildings are at risk should rest with local authorities who should produce a survey of the listed buildings within their area which will eventually provide a register of buildings at risk. To support the objective of targeting financial assistance in the direction of structures which are most in need of repair, English Heritage has introduced Buildings at Risk grants.

In 1991 a survey of buildings at risk was undertaken in Greater London, when about 950 buildings were identified as being at risk from neglect or dilapidation. These included c19 warehouses, public monuments, redundant chapels, churches and hospitals, and over 70 per cent of the total were c18 terraced houses in run-down inner city areas (of which about 75 were in the Grade I or II* categories). Grants specifically to repair these potentially fine houses have been introduced by English Heritage with encouragement being given to Building Preservation Trusts as well as private, public and voluntary sectors.

9. "PROBLEM BUILDINGS"—OWNERS' OPTIONS

7.27   This concluding section on options and remedies for problem buildings consists of a series of Tables and accompanying notes. Their purpose is to provide owners of listed (or possibly listable) buildings and their professional advisers, with an "instant" basic appraisal of various possible courses of action depending on particular circumstances, and of the implications of the principal stages of options indicated. Where appropriate, the notes to each Table cross-reference to specific chapters, from which additional information may be obtained on the matter referred to. Some cross-references are also included in the Tables themselves.

Attention is in particular drawn to the provisions of Table 5 in respect of "immunity certificates" under section 6 LBA. Owners considering this course of action should have special regard to the implications of the immunity certificate provisions. The matter is dealt with at paragraphs 2.72–2.73 above.

We conclude with Tables 4 and 5 which deal with the situation of the owner of a non-listed building not in a conservation area, who suspects that it is of a type likely to be listed and wishing to avoid the consequences.

Table 6 which follows deals with the situation of a non-listed building in an area likely to be designated as a conservation area.

10. TABLES

These tables set out to illustrate the above problems and some of their solu- **7.28** tions:

1 Options open to the DNH and to local authorities in respect of a listed building appearing to be in need of repair.
2 Options open to local authorities in respect of a building which is dangerous, defective, ruinous, dilapidated or unfit.
3 Options open to owners of "redundant" listed buildings.
4 Options open to the owner of a non-listed building not in a conservation area, suspecting that it is of a type likely to be listed and wishing to avoid the consequences; building not in beneficial use.
5 Options open to the owner of a non-listed building not in a conservation area, suspecting that it is of a type likely to be listed and wishing to avoid the consequences; building in beneficial use but use change/demolition/major alteration possible in future.
6 Options open to the owner of a non-listed building which is unlikely to be listed but which is located in an area likely to be designated as a conservation area.

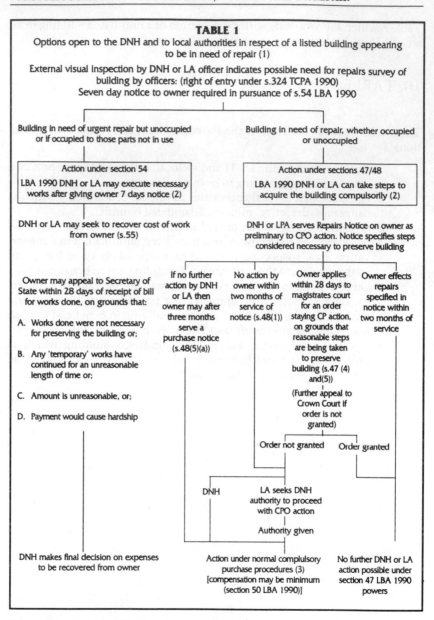

TABLE 1

Options open to the DNH and to local authorities in respect of a listed building appearing to be in need of repair (1)

External visual inspection by DNH or LA officer indicates possible need for repairs survey of building by officers: (right of entry under s.324 TCPA 1990)
Seven day notice to owner required in pursuance of s.54 LBA 1990

Building in need of urgent repair but unoccupied or if occupied to those parts not in use

Action under section 54

LBA 1990 DNH or LA may execute necessary works after giving owner 7 days notice (2)

DNH or LA may seek to recover cost of work from owner (s.55)

Owner may appeal to Secretary of State within 28 days of receipt of bill for works done, on grounds that:

A. Works done were not necessary for preserving the building or;

B. Any 'temporary' works have continued for an unreasonable length of time or;

C. Amount is unreasonable, or;

D. Payment would cause hardship

DNH makes final decision on expenses to be recovered from owner

Building in need of repair, whether occupied or unoccupied

Action under sections 47/48

LBA 1990 DNH or LA can take steps to acquire the building compulsorily (2)

DNH or LPA serves Repairs Notice on owner as preliminary to CPO action. Notice specifies steps considered necessary to preserve building

If no further action by DNH or LA then owner may after three months serve a purchase notice (s.48(5)(a))

No action by owner within two months of service of notice (s.48(1))

Owner applies within 28 days to magistrates court for an order staying CP action, on grounds that reasonable steps are being taken to preserve building (s.47 (4) and(5))

(Further appeal to Crown Court if order is not granted)

Owner effects repairs specified in notice within two months of service

Order not granted   Order granted

DNH   LA seeks DNH authority to proceed with CPO action

Authority given

Action under normal compulsory purchase procedures (3) [compensation may be minimum (section 50 LBA 1990)]

No further DNH or LA action possible under section 47 LBA 1990 powers

(1) Other than listed buildings "excepted" under section 75(1) LBA.
(2) This and subsequent action under the powers referred to is taken by the authority initiating the action. Normally such actions are undertaken by the district planning authority.
(3) If acquiring authority is satisfied that building has been deliberately allowed to fall into disrepair, owner may appeal to courts challenging any "direction for minimum compensation" under section 50 LBA.

©

R W Suddards and June Hargreaves
1995

TABLE 2

Options open to local authorities in respect of a building which is dangerous, defective, ruinous, dilapidated or unfit

Condition of building	Appropriate LA power	Possible problem if listed building (1)	Chapter Section
Dangerous: urgent action needed (all building types)	Outside London: Building Act 1984, s.78(1)	P.H. Act 1961 s.83 and LBA 1990 ss 1, 2, 7, 8, 9 may conflict LA and Owner affected	para. 7.14; (i) and para 7.18
	London: London Building Acts (Amdt) Act 1939	Apparently none	para. 7.15 and para 7.20
Dangerous, but urgent action not needed (all building types)	Outside London: Building Act 1984, s.77 but see s.56 LBA 1990	Poss. conflict as above. LBC may be needed for works. Owner affected	para 7. 14; (ii) and para 7.19
	London: London Building Acts (Amdt) Act 1939	Apparently none	para. 7.15 and para. 7.20
Defective (so as to be prejudicial to health, or a nuisance); and "urgent" (all building types)	All areas incl. London: Building Act 1984, s.76. (Defective Premises Notices)	LBC may be needed for works — interpretation of s.76(6) important	paras. 7.21–7.22
Defective (so as to be prejudicial to health, or a nuisance) but not urgent (all building types)	All areas incl. London. Public Health Act 1936, ss 93 – 95 (Abatement Notices)	LBC may be needed for works	paras 7.21 – 7.22
Ruinous or dilapidated; and detrimental to amenity (all building types)	All areas other than at note (2); Building Act 1984, s.79 but see s.56 LBA 1990	LBC may be needed for works – owner affected	paras 7.23 – 7.24
	Areas as note (2); Powers as note (3)	As above	As above
Unfit or defectice (dwellings only)	All areas. Housing Act 1985 and Local Government and Housing Act 1989.	LBC may be needed for certain works	para. 7.25

(1) or unlisted building in conservation areas.
(2) Inner London Boroughs, the City and the Temples.
(3) London Government Act 1963, Schedule 11, Part II, paragraph 9.

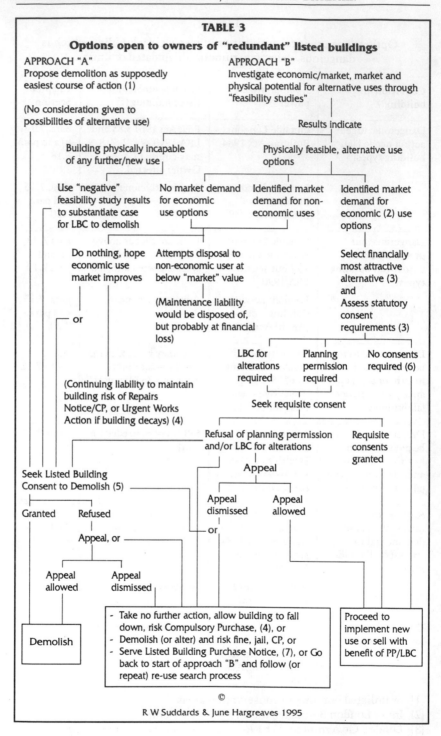

TABLE 3

Options open to owners of "redundant" listed buildings

APPROACH "A"
Propose demolition as supposedly easiest course of action (1)

(No consideration given to possibilities of alternative use)

APPROACH "B"
Investigate economic/market, market and physical potential for alternative uses through "feasibility studies"

Results indicate

Building physically incapable of any further/new use

Physically feasible, alternative use options

Use "negative" feasibility study results to substantiate case for LBC to demolish

No market demand for economic use options

Identified market demand for non-economic uses

Identified market demand for economic (2) use options

Do nothing, hope economic use market improves

Attempts disposal to non-economic user at below "market" value

(Maintenance liability would be disposed of, but probably at financial loss)

Select financially most attractive alternative (3) and Assess statutory consent requirements (3)

or

LBC for alterations required

Planning permission required

No consents required (6)

(Continuing liability to maintain building risk of Repairs Notice/CP, or Urgent Works Action if building decays) (4)

Seek requisite consent

Refusal of planning permission and/or LBC for alterations

Requisite consents granted

Appeal

Seek Listed Building Consent to Demolish (5)

Appeal dismissed

Appeal allowed

or

Granted   Refused

Appeal, or

Appeal allowed

Appeal dismissed

or

Demolish

- Take no further action, allow building to fall down, risk Compulsory Purchase, (4), or
- Demolish (or alter) and risk fine, jail, CP, or
- Serve Listed Building Purchase Notice, (7), or Go back to start of approach "B" and follow (or repeat) re-use search process

Proceed to implement new use or sell with benefit of PP/LBC

©
R W Suddards & June Hargreaves 1995

(1) Approach "A" may appear to be the easiest, quickest and cheapest. However, evidence of DNH and local authority policy of demolition of listed buildings indicates that the only route to LBC for demolition is by way of proving that all alternative use possibilities have been fully explored, and that the results are negative. Thus Approach "B" is effectively the only practical approach. See also Chapter 4.

(2) "Economic" uses in this context are those in which the user pays either market value for the freehold, or a rent which properly reflects the owner's investment in the property. "Non-economic" uses are those in which the user, whilst requiring the type of floorspace available, cannot afford to pay a market price or rent, *e.g.* charities.

(3) Relevant inputs will be produced in the feasibility studies.

(4) Repairs Notice: LBA 1990 s.48. Urgent Works Action: Listed Buildings 1990 s.54. See para 7.01, and Table 1.

(5) LBC procedure: see paras. 5.04–5.06 above.

(6) Situations may arise in which the introduction of a new use involves neither physical alterations requiring LBC, nor any material change of use, or any other works giving rise to the need for planning permission. It should however be noted that Building Regulations approval may be required.

(7) Listed building purchase notice: LBA 1990 s.32. See paras. 5.18–5.19 above.

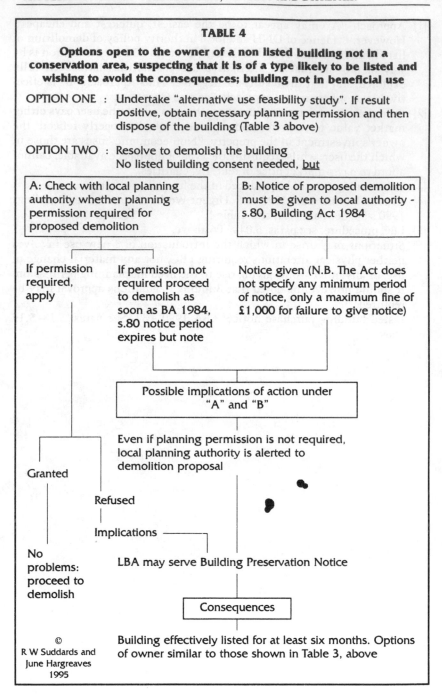

TABLE 4

Options open to the owner of a non listed building not in a conservation area, suspecting that it is of a type likely to be listed and wishing to avoid the consequences; building not in beneficial use

OPTION ONE : Undertake "alternative use feasibility study". If result positive, obtain necessary planning permission and then dispose of the building (Table 3 above)

OPTION TWO : Resolve to demolish the building
No listed building consent needed, <u>but</u>

A: Check with local planning authority whether planning permission required for proposed demolition

B: Notice of proposed demolition must be given to local authority - s.80, Building Act 1984

If permission required, apply

If permission not required proceed to demolish as soon as BA 1984, s.80 notice period expires but note

Notice given (N.B. The Act does not specify any minimum period of notice, only a maximum fine of £1,000 for failure to give notice)

Possible implications of action under "A" and "B"

Even if planning permission is not required, local planning authority is alerted to demolition proposal

Granted

Refused

Implications

No problems: proceed to demolish

LBA may serve Building Preservation Notice

Consequences

©
R W Suddards and June Hargreaves 1995

Building effectively listed for at least six months. Options of owner similar to those shown in Table 3, above

TABLE 5

Options open to the owner of a non listed building not in a conservation area, suspecting that it is of a type likely to be listed and wishing to avoid the consequences; building not in beneficial use but use change/demolition/major alteration possible in the future

OPTION ONE : Do nothing and hope that if building is listed, listing will not adversely affect future use potential/proposals

OPTION TWO : Apply for planning permission for a wholly innocuous alteration, which the planning authority will have no reason to refuse. (No need for any <u>intent</u> to implement proposal. Planning application is solely to enable action for the next step)

Apply to the Secretary of State for a certificate under s.6 LBA confirming that the building will not be listed for at least five years

Certificate not granted	Certificate granted
Take steps as suggested in Table 4 <u>before</u> implied probability of listing becomes a reality	Building is "safe" from listing or Building Preservation Notice for at least five years
or	<u>But note:</u>
Do nothing and hope as in option One above	It is entirely possible that before the Secretary of State responds to the s.6 LBA certificate application (and the LBA does not specify any response period) the local planning authority may still, on the basis of the planning application, conclude that <u>in their opinion</u> the building is of "architectural or historic interest.... and... in danger of demolition or (adverse) alteration," and serve a s.3 Building Preservation Notice <u>before</u> the SoS issues a s.6 LBA
	The Building Preservation Notice will be valid until the SoS notifies the local planning authority (under s.3(3) and (4) LBA) of no intention to list. Until such action the building would effectively be listed

©
R W Suddards and
June Hargreaves
1995

TABLE 6

Options open to an owner of a non listed building which is unlikely to be listed but which is located in an area likely to be designated as a conservation area

POSSIBILITIES RELATIVE TO FUTURE OF BUILD-ING		IMPLICATIONS OF CONSERVATION AREA DESIGNATION
Change of use probable	(i)	No implications if change of use does not adversely affect character of area
	(ii)	Possible difficulties in obtaining planning permission if new use is "bad neighbour" (T.C.P.A. 1990 s.65) or affects character of areas adversely (e.g. by creating increased traffic)
Major alterations likely to be required	(i)	No implications if alterations are sympathetic to character or appearance of the area of special architectural or historic merit, but wise to obtain planning permission before designation
	(ii)	Planning permission problems likely for "non-sympathetic" alterations. Therefore seek planning permission prior to designation, or adapt proposals to gain approval
Major extensions		Implications as for major alterations
Major alterations involving demolition of significant parts of the building		Conservation area consent will be required for demolition aspects of proposals
		[See Chapter 4 (Criteria for Consent to Demolish) and 5 (Mechanics of control)]

©
R W Suddards and June Hargreaves
1995

8. Ancient Monuments And Archaeology

1. GENERAL SUMMARY

The law relating to ancient monuments is largely contained in the **8.01** Ancient Monuments and Archaeological Areas Act 1979 (in this chapter referred to as "the Act"). The Act relates to England and Wales and (with appropriate modifications) to Scotland. Although the Act provides an almost complete code in relation to ancient monuments, it still carries forward some of the provisions of the earlier legislation and enjoys the exceptions contained in section 61 of the LBA 1990. It may therefore be useful to recapitulate on the progress of legislation relating to ancient monuments, which in fact pre-dates the legislation as to listed buildings by some 60 years or so.

The parliamentary campaign for the protection and preservation of the nation's ancient monuments began in the 1870s and was led by Sir John Lubbock, who was a Member of Parliament for Maidstone, a Trustee of the British Museum and a keen antiquarian. He steered on to the statute book

285

the Ancient Monuments Acts of 1882 and 1900, though not without some difficulties—in the House of Lords, despite the pleas for "modest protection", Lord Francis Hervey asked why we should retain anything from our barbarous past. He refused to recognise our ancestors, who "stained themselves blue, ran about naked and practised absurd, perhaps obscene, rites under the mistletoe." The latter Act contained a schedule of ancient monuments. A Royal Commission reported in 1908, there was a further Act in 1910, and the Ancient Monuments Consolidation and Amendment Act 1913 was passed. Amongst other matters, the 1913 Act provided for an Ancient Monuments Board with Inspectors and Commissioners of Works who were required to prepare a list of monuments, the preservation of which was of national importance. The Board was also empowered to prepare a list of other monuments which were of less than national importance but which should be preserved in the public interest, a distinction which might perhaps be helpful in considering the criteria for preservation under the 1979 Act.

By 1931 some 3,000 ancient monuments had been listed, and the number controlled by the Commissioners was then 200. The 1913 Act was found to be inadequate, and strengthening powers were given in the 1931 Act, in particular in relation to schemes for the purpose of preserving the amenities of an ancient monument. The next Act was the Historic Buildings and Ancient Monuments Act 1953, which brought under control not merely the ancient monument, but its owner. The range of ancient monuments was widened to include monuments which had a reference to industrial archaeology by virtue of that Act. Running throughout the legislation from 1900 onwards was the requirement for a list of ancient monuments to be maintained. It is this element which is preserved in the 1979 Act (substantially amended by the National Heritage Act 1983). As at December 1994 there were 15,429 scheduled ancient monuments[1] which have been compiled over a period of a hundred years. In February 1986 English Heritage announced plans to extend the schedule by 47,000 new sites in the following seven to 10 years, thus expecting to bring the total of scheduled ancient monuments up to almost 60,000. This figure was, however, reduced to 45,000 in May 1993, and it is expected that 80 per cent of the programme will be completed by 2003.[2] Previously, scheduling had been carried out on an *ad hoc* basis, whereas under the new system (known as the Monuments Protection Programme) the monuments would be dealt with parish by parish and would include all monuments deemed to be of national importance.

8.02   The purpose behind the Monuments Protection Programme was to review and develop scheduling records and procedures,[3] and especially to assess in a systematic and cost-effective manner over 600,000 recorded archaeological sites. The programme was designed to identify the range of monuments which reflected the history of the country by applying class characterisation criteria such as "period", "rarity" and "diversity" and also by a selection process to identify sites of national importance within categories such as survival, group value, potential (both archaeological and historical), diversity and amenity value.

---

[1] *English Heritage Monitor* 1995.
[2] *English Heritage Monitor* 1995.
[3] *Conservation Bulletin*, October 1988, English Heritage.

The Act introduced a number of new phrases and definitions and it is essential to note the differences between these definitions.

First, a *monument* is defined in section 61(7) as:

"(a) any building, structure or work, whether above or below the surface of the land, and any cave or excavation;

(b) any site comprising the remains of any such building, structure or work or of any cave or excavation; and

(c) any site comprising, or comprising the remains of, any vehicle, vessel, aircraft, or other moveable structure or part thereof which neither constitutes nor forms part of any work which is a monument within paragraph (a) above

and any machinery attached to a monument shall be regarded as part of the monument if it could not be detached without being dismantled."

This section specifically provides that references in the Act to a monument include references to the site of the monument in question and to a group of monuments or any part of a monument or group of monuments.[4] Further, it provides that references in the Act to the site of a monument are references to the monument itself where it consists of a site, and in any other case includes references to the monument itself.[5]

There are, however, exclusions from the definition of a monument, and the exclusions relate to the definition above. There is excluded from subsection (7)(a) any ecclesiastical building for the time being used for ecclesiastical purposes[6]; sub-section (7)(c) does not apply to a site comprising any object or its remains unless the situation of that object or its remains in that particular site is a matter of public interest,[7] nor to a site comprising, or comprising the remains of, any vessel which is protected by an order under the Protection of Wrecks Act 1973.[8]   **8.03**

Thus, the above is the basic definition of a monument, and a monument cannot become either a scheduled monument or an ancient monument, or a protected monument, unless the hurdles of the definition above are overcome.

A *scheduled monument* is defined by section 1 of the Act as "any monument which is for the time being included in the Schedule". The Schedule is the schedule of monuments compiled and maintained for the purposes of the Act by the Secretary of State for National Heritage. The Secretary of State was obliged on first compiling the Schedule to include therein any monument included in the list last published under the 1913 Act[9] and any monument in respect of which the Secretary of State has served notice, in accordance with the 1931 Act, of his intention to include it in a list to be published under that Act, the service of such notice being prior to October 9, 1981 (the commencement date for Part I of the 1979 Act).[10]

---

[4] s.61(10).

[5] s.61(11).

[6] s.61(8).

[7] s.61(8)(a).

[8] s.61(8)(b). An example of the problem under this Act is found in a letter to *The Times*, March 7, 1988.

[9] ss.1(2)(a) and (b).

[10] *Ibid.*

In addition to those monuments which must of necessity be included in the Schedule, the Secretary of State may on first compiling the Schedule or at any time thereafter include therein any monument which appears to him to be of national importance,[11] with the proviso that he shall consult English Heritage before including a monument situated in England. The only exception is that he may not include a structure which is occupied as a dwellinghouse by any person other than a person employed as a caretaker thereof or his family.[12]

8.04   An *"ancient monument"* is wider than the category of scheduled monuments and is defined in section 61(12) as meaning any scheduled monument and any other monument which in the opinion of the Secretary of State is of public interest by reason of the historic, architectural, traditional, artistic or archaeological interest attaching to it. In section 34(3) of the NHA 1983 the phrase is defined more specifically as any structure, work, site, garden or area.

A DOE consultation document of April 1991 recommended the repeal of some sections of the 1979 Act in order to overcome the discrepancy between the definitions of an "ancient monument" in section 61(12) of that Act, as "a scheduled monument or one which in the opinion of the Secretary of State is of public interest by reason of the historic, architectural, traditional, artistic or archaeological interest attaching to it", and the National Heritage Act 1983, section 33(8) where "ancient monument" means "any structure, work, site, garden or area which in the opinion of English Heritage is of historic, architectural, traditional, artistic or archaeological interest". Since the 1979 Act provides for English Heritage to give grants to monuments, it was recommended by the DOE that the definition be extended to enable them to determine which sites should benefit from such grant provisions.[13] No action has been taken on these recommendations.

A *"protected monument"* (the definition for which appears to be included solely to define those monuments in respect of which an offence can occur by damaging them) means any scheduled monument and any monument under the ownership or guardianship of the Secretary of State, English Heritage, or a local authority by virtue of the Act.[14]

To complete the range of definitions, it is as well to remember that *"a protected place"* is defined in section 42(2) (the section dealing with the restrictions on the use of metal detectors) as any place which is either the site of a scheduled monument or of any monument under the ownership or guardianship of the Secretary of State, English Heritage or a local authority or is a place situated in an area of archaeological importance. An *"area of archaeological importance"* is defined in section 33 as an area which the Secretary of State may, having consulted English Heritage, from time to time by order designate as such if "any area which appears to him to merit treatment as such for the purposes of this Act."

8.05   It will be seen that there are a number of different criteria for admission to protection.

---

[11] s.1(3) (as amended by the NHA 1983, Schedule 4).
[12] s.1(4).
[13] DOE Consultation Paper on Ancient Monument legislation, April 1991.
[14] s.28(3).

The criteria for judging monuments worthy of inclusion in the schedule were published in November 1983[15] and are as follows:

(a) *Period*: all types of monuments which characterise a category or period should be considered for preservation.

(b) *Rarity*: there are some monument categories which in certain periods are so scarce that all surviving examples which still retain some archaeological potential should be preserved. In general, however, a selection must be made which portrays the typical and commonplace as well as the rare. This process should take account of all aspects of the distribution of a particular class of monument, both in a national and regional context.

(c) *Documentation*: the significance of a monument may be enhanced by the existence of records of previous investigation, or in the case of more recent monuments, by the supporting evidence of contemporary written records.

(d) *Group Value*: the value of a single monument (such as a field system) may be greatly enhanced by its association with related contemporary monuments (such as a settlement and cemetery) or with monuments of different periods. In some cases, it is preferable to protect the complete group of monuments, including associated and adjacent land, rather than to protect isolated monuments within the group.

(e) *Survival/Condition*: the survival of a monument's archaeological potential both above and below ground is a particularly important consideration and should be assessed in relation to its present condition and surviving features.

(f) *Fragility/Vulnerability*: highly important archaeological evidence from some field monuments can be destroyed by a single ploughing or unsympathetic treatment; vulnerable monuments of this nature would particularly benefit from the statutory protection which scheduling confers. There are also standing structures of particular form or complexity whose value can again be severely reduced by neglect or careless treatment and which are similarly well suited by scheduled monument protection, even if these structures are already listed historic buildings.

(g) *Diversity*: some monuments may be selected for scheduling because they possess a combination of high quality features, others because of a single important attribute.

(h) *Potential*: on occasion, the nature of the evidence cannot be specified precisely but it may still be possible to document reasons anticipating its existence and importance and so to demonstrate the justification for scheduling. This is usually confined to sites rather than upstanding monuments.

Unless the monument is on a list under the 1913 Act or has been subject to a notice under the 1931 Act, the Secretary of State must not include in the schedule any monument until he has consulted English Heritage or unless it "appears to him to be of national importance". Further, if the

[15] Informal criterion first published in Historic Buildings and Ancient Monuments First Report for the Environment Committee 1986/87, reprinted in Annex 4 of PPG 16.

monument is in category (c) of section 61(7), namely a "moveable" monument, it may only by definition be a monument if the site comprising any object or its remains "is a matter of public interest."[16]

The ancient monument definition embraces the scheduled monument and "any other monument which in the opinion of the Secretary of State is of public interest by reason of the historic, architectural, traditional, artistic or archaeological interest attaching to it". This therefore appears to define more closely the definition of "public interest", and it is perhaps worthy of note that the word here used is "historic" and not "historical", a distinction which for practical purposes may be of no significance but which a grammarian might justify. It will be seen that, for instance, in the powers of the entry provisions in section 6 these powers relate to inspecting the land with a view to recording any matters of archaeological or historic interest. Presumably therefore the power of entry would not be available for use if it were sought to record architectural, traditional or artistic interest; whether or not the fine distinction between "historic" and "historical" could be drawn here must await a decision.

The draftsman of the Act must be assumed to have used these differing criteria deliberately. There are no definitions of the phrases such as "public interest", "national importance", "historic, architectural, traditional, artistic or archaeological interest". It would seem that there have been no decided cases on the legislation which would throw any light on these criteria, although it is perhaps of interest to note that a distinction was drawn in section 12 of the 1913 Act between "monuments of national importance" and "other monuments which were of less than national importance but should be preserved in the public interest".

8.06   In practical terms, the distinctions operate in the following way. The Act will not bite on any building which is not a monument. If it is a monument it may, in the manner above indicated, become a scheduled monument. A scheduled monument is protected in Part I of the Act under which it is a criminal offence to do certain works to a scheduled monument without scheduled monument consent[17]; there are limited provisions for compensation for refusal of scheduled monument consent.[18] There is also a provision for the execution of works for preservation of a scheduled monument by the Secretary of State in cases of urgency. An ancient monument (the definition of which is wider than that of a scheduled monument[19]) is subject to a code under Part I which permits compulsory acquisition, or acquisition by agreement or gift.[20] Ancient monuments may be placed under guardianship which has the effect of the Secretary of State, English Heritage or a relevant authority being required to maintain the ancient monument until determination.[21] The criminal offence section[22] in relation to damage to an ancient monument brings in the even wider definition of the protected monument. Finally, the designation of areas of archaeological importance[23] (a code not

[16] s.61(8)(a).
[17] s.2(1) and (2).
[18] s.7.
[19] s.61(12).
[20] ss.10 and 11.
[21] s.12.
[22] s.28.
[23] s.33.

dissimilar to the conservation area code) gives a wider definition, which is also used in relation to the restrictions on the use of metal detectors under section 42 in what is described as a "protected place": see Table 7 below.

It will be seen that the definition of a monument is a wide one. As indi- **8.07** cated above, there would appear to be no logical reason why any building or site should not rank as a monument provided it passes the relevant criteria. Prior to the coming into force of the 1979 Act, the broad definition of an ancient monument was the only one which was applicable.

The English Tourist Board carried out an interesting survey as at December 1985 of categories of objects which constituted ancient monuments. The list was expressed to be non-exhaustive, but the variety and relative range, even within this list, is perhaps of interest. The 11 categories gave rise to 12,875 ancient monuments. Burial mounds and megalithic monuments accounted for 19 per cent; camps and settlements for 15 per cent; Roman remains for 7 per cent; ecclesiastical ruins for 6 per cent; crosses and inscribed stones for 5 per cent; castles and fortifications for 9 per cent; deserted villages and moated sites 8 per cent; linear earthworks 3 per cent; ancient bridges 4 per cent; industrial monuments 2 per cent; and other secular sites and buildings 12 per cent.[24]

In the 542 monuments scheduled during 1992, just over half were burial mounds, 17 per cent were moated sites, and 16 per cent were hut circles.[25]

A few well known examples of ancient monuments are the castles of Edinburgh, Caernarvon and Conway, and the Tower of London, Fountains Abbey and Glastonbury Abbey, Stonehenge and Hadrian's Wall. Other ancient monuments include the Globe Theatre site in Southwark, London, the Cannington Shaw bottle shop, Shadley Works and the shifthead and headgear near Caphouse Colliery, Overton, West Yorkshire. Scheduled monuments may be as old as 500,000 years or as recent as 40 years, for example, World War II military defences. An example of a less famous ancient monument, and perhaps more unexpectedly scheduled as such, is the Anderton Boat Lift connecting the Trent and Mersey Canal to the Weaver Navigation in Cheshire.

2. THE MECHANICS OF SCHEDULING

These are set out in section 1 of the Act. The Secretary of State has, in **8.08** effect, three powers, namely that of including any monument in the Schedule, amending the Schedule in relation to any monument, and excluding any monument from the Schedule. As we have seen, there are certain mandatory monuments to be included in the first listing[26]; thereafter, so long as a monument appears to the Secretary of State to be of national importance, it may be included so long as it is not a structure which is occupied as a dwelling house by any person other than a person employed as a caretaker thereof or his family,[27] nor is an ecclesiastical building used for the time being for ecclesiastical purposes,[28] nor a vessel protected under the Protec-

---

[24] *Conservation Bulletin*, February 1987, *Archaeology and Farming*.
[25] *English Heritage Monitor 1993*.
[26] s.1(2).
[27] s.1(4).
[28] s.61(8).

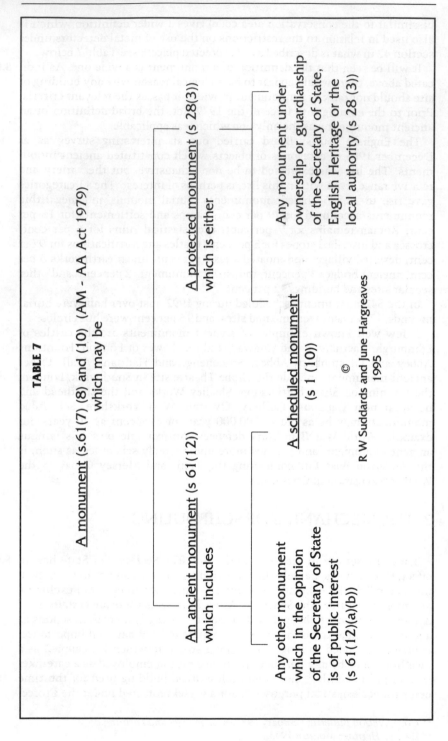

TABLE 7

A monument (s.61(7) (8) and (10) (AM - AA Act 1979)
which may be

An ancient monument (s 61(12))
which includes

Any other monument
which in the opinion
of the Secretary of State
is of public interest
(s 61(12)(a)(b))

A scheduled monument
(s 1 (10))

A protected monument (s 28(3))
which is either

Any monument under
ownership or guardianship
of the Secretary of State,
English Heritage or the
local authority (s 28 (3))

©
R W Suddards and June Hargreaves
1995

tion of Wrecks Act 1973.[29] However, if there is no order made under section 1 of the Protection of Wrecks Act 1973, a monument in territorial waters can be an ancient monument by virtue of section 53 of the 1979 Act which provides that "a monument situated in, on, or under the sea bed within the seaward limits of the United Kingdom territorial waters" may be included in the Schedule.

On including, amending, or excluding any monument, English Heritage is required to inform the owner and (if the owner is not the occupier) the occupier of the monument, and any local authority in whose area the monument is situated, and in the event of an inclusion or an amendment, English Heritage must send to him or them a copy of the entry or of the amended entry in the Schedule.[30]

An entry in the Schedule recording the inclusion therein of a monument **8.09** situated in England and Wales must be entered as a local land charge. Although section 1(9) refers only to the "inclusion" of a monument, it is thought that the effect of this sub-section would be that the provisions of the Local Land Charges Act 1975 will apply to all entries in the Schedule relating to monuments in England and Wales.

Scheduling proposals can originate from almost anyone, but typically they come from local archaeologists and their associations, local authorities and universities. In England, English Heritage inspectors of ancient monuments, who are its professional archaeologists, then review the evidence and probably visit the site (the submitted evidence may include details and photographs which might render a visit superfluous) to assess whether the site or monument appears to be of national importance (which is the sole criterion laid down by statute for inclusion in the Schedule of Ancient Monuments) and put forward a recommendation if they think it qualifies. At this point the owner is notified of the intention to schedule and the details of the proposal are checked. The scheduling recommendation is passed via the Ancient Monuments Advisory Committee of England Heritage to the Secretary of State for National Heritage, who then formally confirms or rejects the proposed scheduling and the owner is finally notified by English Heritage.

In each of the three countries (England, Scotland and Wales) the appropri- **8.10** ate Secretary of State is required from time to time to publish a list of all the monuments which are for the time being included in the Schedule, whether as a single list or in sections containing the monuments situated in particular areas. There is no obligation to publish area lists simultaneously, and the Secretary of State may maintain for the purposes of the Act the Schedule in such form as he thinks fit. It may be helpful to note that while the publication is officially the *List of Ancient Monuments*, it is always referred to as the Schedule, and the process of adding to it is called "scheduling", because the original list was published as the Schedule to the first Ancient Monuments Act 1882, and nowadays because it provides a convenient and very useful distinction from the listing of buildings of special architectural or historic interest under the LBA 1990.

The Secretaries of State have power (but are not obliged) to publish amendments of any list,[31] and there is provision in section 1 that any such

[29] s.61(8)(b).
[30] s.1(6).
[31] s.1(8).

lists (as amended) shall be evidence of the inclusion in the Schedule for the time being.[32] If there is any doubt about the status of a monument, English Heritage obtains a letter signed by the Department confirming that the monument is scheduled.

3. THE CONSEQUENCES OF SCHEDULING

(a) No appeal against scheduling

8.11   The monument remains in the Schedule until it is excluded or amended by order of the Secretary of State for National Heritage. There is no provision for appealing against inclusion in the Schedule, but, as with listed buildings, there is nothing to stop an owner applying to the Secretary of State for exclusion or amendment which the Secretary of State has power to do by section 1. However, there is no appeal against the refusal of the Secretary of State to exclude or amend, and the owner would then only have the power to apply for scheduled monument consent (see paragraphs 8.15–8.17 below), unless the Secretary of State has made a procedural error which would be sufficiently serious to permit a judicial review.

(b) Unauthorised works may be an offence

8.12   Inclusion in the Schedule gives rise to the control of works affecting the scheduled monument. Section 2 provides that if any person executes or causes or permits to be executed any works to which that section applies he shall be guilty of an offence unless the works are authorised, *i.e.* unless he has scheduled monument consent either specifically given in relation to the scheduled monument, or given under section 3 (by which section the Secretary of State has power to make a general order not dissimilar to the General Permitted Development Order under the Town and Country Planning Act 1990).

The Ancient Monuments (Class Consents) Order 1994[33] came into operation on 14 June 1994 and gave scheduled monument consent for the execution of works comprising the following classes:

1 *Permitted works*: Agricultural, horticultural and forestry works of the same kind as works previously carried out lawfully in the same location and on the same spot within that location within the period of six years immediately preceding the date on which the works commence: but excluding the following categories (see *Works not permitted* below).

2 *Permitted works*: Works executed more than 10 metres below ground level by the British Coal Corporation or any person acting pursuant to a licence granted by the Corporation under section 36(2) of the Coal Industry Nationalisation Act 1946.

[32] *Ibid.*
[33] S.I. 1994 No. 1381. For Scotland, a similar order came into operation on November 30, 1981 (S.I. 1981, No. 1468) (as amended by S.I. 1984 No. 222).

3 *Permitted works*: Works executed by the British Waterways Board, in relation to land owned or occupied by them, being works of repair or maintenance not involving a material alteration to a scheduled monument, which are essential for the purpose of ensuring the functioning of a canal.

4 *Permitted works*: Works for the repair or maintenance of machinery, being works which do not involve a material alteration to a scheduled monument.

5 *Permitted works*: Works which are urgently necessary in the interests of safety or health, provided that;
    (a) the works are limited to the minimum measures immediately necessary; and
    (b) notice in writing justifying in detail the need for the works is given to the Secretary of State as soon as reasonably practicable.

6 *Permitted works*: Works executed by English Heritage.

7 *Permitted works*: Works of archaeological evaluation carried out by or on behalf of a person who has applied for consent under section 2 of the Act, being works carried out:
    (a) in order to supply the Secretary of State with information required by him for the determination of that application;
    (b) under the supervision of a person approved for that purpose in writing by the Secretary of State or English Heritage; and
    (c) in accordance with a written specification approved for that purpose by the Secretary of State or English Heritage.

8 *Permitted works*: Works for the maintenance or preservation of a scheduled monument or its amenities being works executed in accordance with the terms of a written agreement between the occupier of the monument and the Secretary of State or English Heritage under section 17 of the Act.

9 *Permitted works*: Works for the preservation, maintenance or management of a scheduled monument, being works executed in accordance with the terms of a written agreement under which the Secretary of State or English Heritage defray, or contribute towards, the cost of those works pursuant to their powers under section 24 of the Act.

10 *Permitted works*: Works consisting of placing of survey markers to a depth not exceeding 300 millimetres for the purpose of measured surveying of visible remains undertaken by the Royal Commission on the Historical Monuments of England or by the Royal Commission on Ancient and Historical Monuments of Wales.

Works not permitted (relating to Agricultural, Horticultural and Forestry Works):
    (a) in the case of ploughed land, any works likely to disturb the soil of any part of that land below the depth at which ploughing of that part has previously been carried out lawfully;
    (b) in the case of land other than ploughed land, any works likely to disturb the soil below the depth of 300 millimetres;
    (c) sub-soiling, drainage works, the planting or uprooting of trees, hedges or shrubs, the stripping of top soil, tipping operations, or the commercial cutting and removal of turf;

295

    (d) the demolition, removal, extension, alteration or disturbance of any building, structure or work or of the remains thereat;

    (e) the erection of any building or structure;

    (f) in the case of works other than domestic gardening works, the laying of paths, hard standings or foundations for buildings or the erection of fences or other barriers.

There are several separate matters which could give rise to an offence, namely works resulting in the demolition or destruction of, or damage to, a scheduled monument; works for the purpose of removing or repairing a scheduled monument, or any part of it, or of making any alterations or additions thereto; and flooding or tipping operations on land in, on or under which there is a scheduled monument.[34] There is no definition of what is demolition, destruction or damage, but presumably the distinction between demolition and damage on the one hand and destruction on the other is that in demolition parts are removed and parts retained; in destruction, the fabric of the monument is physically destroyed. "Flooding or tipping operations" are defined respectively as covering land with water or any other liquid or partially liquid substance, and tipping soil or spoil or depositing building or other materials or matter (including waste materials or refuse) on any land.

8.13   In the year to March 1992 there were 32 reported cases of damage to scheduled monuments and two successful prosecutions. This compares with 72 cases of damage in 1988.[35]

The power to institute proceedings against those who are suspected of causing damage to scheduled archaeological sites is not confined to the Secretary of State[36] nor to English Heritage. English Heritage has adopted a policy of encouraging local authorities to take the initiative in prosecuting those responsible for damage to monuments and officers of English Heritage are prepared to provide evidence.[37] In March 1989 a prosecution case for alleged damage to a scheduled ancient monument at Condicote Henge, Gloucestershire was dismissed by the Crown Court following a technical submission that evidence of the existence of the Schedule of Ancient Monuments was not made available. The public reaction to this dismissal caused both English Heritage and the Department of the Environment to re-affirm their confidence in the legal validity of the Schedule and their intention to instigate prosecutions when wilful damage was caused to scheduled monuments.[38] The number of successful prosecutions has since increased and includes examples such as one under section 42 of the Act for the illegal use of a metal detector on a scheduled ancient monument in Norfolk, when the defendants were fined £110 with costs. A farmer was convicted in June 1989 of causing damage to a scheduled hill fort at Ratlinghope Castle Ring, Shropshire by ploughing and was fined £300 with costs.[39] The Marquess of Hertford was fined £10,000 for unlawful ploughing operations at a Roman settlement at Alcester in December 1985. The fine was reduced to £3,000 by the Court of Appeal, which held that such a large fine would have been

---

[34] s.2(2).
[35] *English Heritage Monitor* 1989 and 1993.
[36] *Damage to Monuments—English Heritage Conservation Bulletin*, October 1988.
[37] [1988] J.P.L. p. 738.
[38] *DOE News Release*, March 7, 1989.
[39] *Conservation Bulletin*, October 1989.

more appropriate to a flagrant disregard of an ancient monument for the purposes of personal gain.[40]

A fine in another scheduled monument damage case was imposed at Lincoln Crown Court in April 1990 on a farming company, when they pleaded guilty to damaging a medieval nunnery at Legbourne Priory near Louth, Lincolnshire, by creating a large lake. The fine of £15,000 was described by the Judge as having "some element of deterrence, otherwise actions like this drive a cart and horses through the framework to protect sites."[41] The largest fine to date was imposed by the Inner London Crown Court on the owner of Winchester Palace, Southwark, for excavating a basement without scheduled monument consent and damaging both Roman and medieval layers. English Heritage referred the matter to the Crown Prosecution Service, and at the trial the defendant pleaded guilty. Judge Prendergast considered this monument to be of national significance (it was the London town house of the Bishops of Winchester) and fined the defendant £15,000 plus £1,000 costs.[42] The powers of the Crown Court are unlimited under section 2 of the Act.

There are four defences to the claim that an offence has been committed.[43] They are:

8.14

(i) that the defendant took all reasonable precautions and exercised all due diligence to avoid contravening the conditions of a scheduled monument consent where failure to comply with any condition attached to such consent is alleged:

(ii) where demolition, destruction, or damage is alleged, the defendant can prove that he took all reasonable precautions and exercised all due diligence to avoid or prevent damage to the monument;

(iii) where demolition, destruction, damage, flooding or tipping is alleged, it is a defence for the accused to prove that he did not know, and had no reason to believe, that the monument was within the area affected by the works, or (as the case may be) that it was a scheduled monument;

(iv) the last defence is for the defendant to prove that the works were urgently necessary in the interest of safety or health, and that notice in writing of the need for the works was given to the Secretary of State as soon as reasonably practicable. The words "need for the works" suggests a prior notice, but nowhere is it specifically stated.

Defence number (iv) above is comparable with the defence available under section 9 of the LBA 1990 relating to listed buildings, though drafted less restrictively. Moreover, the three other defences set out above are not available in relation to listed buildings. Particularly, it should be noted that, unlike the provisions under the LBA 1990, offences with regard to scheduled monuments are not absolute offences.

Indeed, the approach to offences committed against the listed buildings code differs substantially from that related to the scheduled monuments code. Breaches of listed building consent are offences of strict liability,

---

[40] *R v. Seymour* 1988 1 PLR.
[41] *The Planner*, May 11, 1990.
[42] *English Heritage, Consevation Bulletin*, October 1991.
[43] s.2(6)–(9).

hence it is not necessary to prove knowledge of listing or malicious or reckless intent.[44]

In contrast, the 1979 Act provides specifically for a defence of ignorance for each of its offences (sections 2(7) and 2(8) of the Act). The matter is complicated in cases where some buildings are both listed and scheduled ancient monuments. Where this occurs, the ancient monuments code takes precedence. This code has however weaker penalties and repair provisions, and no enforcement procedures.

The Criminal Division of the Court of Appeal[45] held in R. v. J O Sims Ltd that where the company had pleaded guilty to causing or permitting works to be executed which, resulted in damage to a scheduled monument, contrary to section 2(1), on the basis that it had been negligent rather than deliberately flouting the law, the degree of negligence involved is a relevant consideration in sentencing.

A consultation paper[46] proposed a tightening of section 2(9) of the Act, where it is a defence to prove that unauthorised works to a scheduled monument were carried out in the interests of health or safety, and that the Secretary of State was given notice as soon as reasonably practicable. The suggested amendments would provide that such works should be limited to the minimum measures immediately necessary, thus bringing it in line with section 9(3) of the LBA 1990 in respect of listed buildings. As yet, the statutory amendment has not been made.

An amendment was introduced by the National Heritage Act 1983 (section 33(2A)), where, in relation to England, English Heritage's powers were extended to prosecute for offences under both Part I of the 1979 Act and the LBA 1990, and also to seek injunctions to restrain any contraventions of these provisions.[47]

In the DOE's consultation document referred to above, views were invited on the possibility of removing the "ignorance defence" in prosecutions for damage to ancient monuments. As we have seen, under section 2(8) of the Act, it is a defence to prove that unauthorised works on scheduled monuments were carried out in ignorance that the area was scheduled. Owners should however know that a site is scheduled through the Land Charges Register in England (or sasines in Scotland). Ignorance in relation to listed buildings legislation is no defence.[48]

(c) Need to obtain scheduled monument consent for works

8.15 The person executing, causing or permitting to be executed, any works to which section 2 applies, shall not be guilty of an offence if he has a scheduled monument consent (in writing) for the execution of the works and the

---

[44] R v. Wells St Stipendiary Magistrate ex p. Westminster CC [1986] J.P.L. p. 903.
[45] The Independent August 3, 1992.
[46] Urgent Works in the Interest of Health and Safety, DOE Consultation Paper, April 1991.
[47] Planning and Compensation Act 1991.
[48] Ancient Monument Legislation DOE Consultation Paper, April 1991.

works are executed in accordance with the terms of the consent and of any conditions attached to the consent.[49]

Despite the transfer of some of the functions formerly exercised by the Secretary of State to English Heritage, it is the Secretary of State for National Heritage who grants the scheduled monument consent. At present, the Secretary of State must consult with English Heritage before determining applications involving works to scheduled monuments. It is believed that English Heritage feels that this duplication of work, where the advice-giving and decision-taking functions are separated, is cumbersome and adds to delay and misunderstanding; and that a better system would be for the Secretary of State to transfer his responsibilities to English Heritage. English Heritage itself receives advice from its Ancient Monuments Advisory Committee. The procedure might well be reviewed and changed.

The phrase "the terms" of the consent seems to be wider than merely the general provisions of the scheduled monument consent—in section 8(3) there is a provision whereby the Secretary of State for the Environment may grant a scheduled monument consent "on terms" that no works in respect of which compensation (for refusal of scheduled monument consent or a grant subject to conditions) has been paid are to be executed in pursuance of the consent until the recoverable amount has been repaid to the Secretary of State or secured to his satisfaction.

The provision for scheduled monument consent closely follows the principles of LBC on which code it appears to have been modelled. There are two types of scheduled monument consent; the consent relating specifically to a particular monument granted by the Secretary of State on application by a person who has a relevant interest in that monument, and the scheduled monument consent granted by order under section 3—a section which seems to have been modelled on the principles of the General Permitted Development Order. The current order is the Ancient Monuments (Class Consents) Order 1994, as set out in paragraph 8.12 above.[50]

A "specific" scheduled monument consent is applied for under section **8.16** 2(11) which refers to Part I of Schedule I of the Act, which provides for the detailed machinery dealing with applications for scheduled monument consent. The Ancient Monuments (Applications for Scheduled Monument Consent) Regulations 1981[51] prescribes a form of application for scheduled monument consent, requires that the application be accompanied by plans and drawings, and obliges the applicant to supply such further information as the Secretary of State may request. The Regulations provide for the form of certificate which should accompany the application and the form of notice which has to be given to all persons who were owners of the monument 21 days before the submission of the application. The owner is the fee simple owner or is a person entitled to a certain tenancy of which not less than seven years remain unexpired. The procedure is not unlike the procedure for LBC and similarly requires notices to be given to the owners of the monument where the applicant is not the owner, or a certificate as to the inability to issue such a certificate. There is provision for the Secretary of State to cause a public local inquiry to be held or to afford the applicant or

---

[49] s.2(3).
[50] See paragraph 8.12.
[51] S.I. 1981 No. 1301. For Scotland, a similar order came into operation on November 30, 1981 (S.I. 1981 No. 1467).

any other person to whom it appears expedient the opportunity of appearing before and being heard by a person appointed by the Secretary of State for the purpose. There is an obligation on the Secretary of State to consider any representations and the report of any inquiry of hearing[52]; and the Secretary of State's decision may be challenged in the High Court on a point of law.

Scheduled monument consent can be granted subject to conditions. In the case of works at the Roman Governor's Palace by Cannon Street Station[53] the Secretary of State decided that withholding consent would not be justified given the physical condition of that part of the monument the limited extent of the ground works proposed and the arrangements made by the developers for an archaeological record of the site. The condition required that before any ground works were begun, the Museum of London archaeological staff should be afforded reasonable time to observe and record matters of archaeological interest on the site.

Objections have in fact been raised to what appears to be the "secretive" nature of the process, compared to the procedures relating to listed buildings. There is no obligation to advertise the application; the decision is not made public; nor, apparently, may any party other than the owner, English Heritage or the Secretary of State, express a view on an application as a matter of right.[54] Indeed, the local planning authority may be unaware of the proposal, since there is no formal provision for consultation with local authorities on scheduled monument consent applications. English Heritage normally discusses the application with the local planning authority where the application relates to a development proposal.[55]

Public inquiries into applications for scheduled monument consent under section 2 of the Act are rare, but such an inquiry was held when British Telecommunications applied for consent to construct a radio mast on a scheduled monument site at Trundle, near Chichester. The Inspector recommended that consent be refused on grounds that the proposed mast would seriously harm the intrinsic character and archaeological importance of the monument, and that the excavation proposed would detract from the monument's archaeological importance. The Secretary of State declined to accept the Inspector's recommendation and granted scheduled monument consent, taking the view that the proper test to be applied was not limited to the effect the proposed development would have on the monument both visually and physically in terms of its effect on the archaeological remains, but should also include the need to erect the mast and radio station on the application site.[56] This decision followed the publication of PPG 16 but was taken against the background of an earlier decision—in February 1986, when the Secretary of State had granted planning permission for the same development at the same site, again against the Inspector's recommendation.

Another inquiry occurred when a proposal was submitted for a hotel complex, with conference centre, hostel and study centre, at West Kennet Farm, Avebury, Wiltshire. The inquiry was a combined planning/listed building/ and scheduled monument inquiry, and the Inspector recommended that

---

[52] *Archaeology and Planning*, November 1990, PPG 16, Annex 3 (para. 9).
[53] HSD 9/2/1295 Part 2—Decision letter dated 19 November 1987.
[54] Michael Farley, *The Times*, 25 January 1986.
[55] Para. 8, Annex 3 of PPG 16.
[56] [1991] J.P.L. p. 301.

scheduled monument consent be granted, but planning permission and listed building consent be refused. The Secretary of State accepted the recommendation on the refusal of the planning permission and listed building consent, but declined to accept his Inspector's recommendation on scheduled monument consent, on the grounds that in the particular circumstances the preference must be for physical preservation of the monument rather than preservation by record.[57]

(d) Time limits applicable to a scheduled monument consent

Section 4(1) provides that if no works to which a scheduled monument **8.17** consent relates are executed or started within a period of five years, beginning with the date on which the consent was granted or such longer or shorter period as may be specified in the consent for the purposes of section 4(1), the consent shall cease to have effect at the end of that period unless it has been previously revoked. There is also a provision by which the scheduled monument consent may specifically be stated to cease to have effect at the end of a period specified in the consent.[58]

(e) Scheduled monument consent may be modified or revoked

There is a provision for the Secretary of State to modify or revoke a sched- **8.18** uled monument consent to any extent which he considers expedient[59] (which includes specifying or altering any period). Part II of Schedule 1 to the Act has effect with respect to directions under the section for modifying or revoking a scheduled monument consent and a procedure exists which is not unlike the modification or revocation procedures in respect of a planning permission. Where the direction would affect a monument in England, the Secretary of State is required to consult with English Heritage before he gives such a direction. Unlike the procedures relating to listed buildings, there is no provision for compensation if a scheduled monument consent is modified or revoked unless the person having an interest in the monument has incurred "abortive expenditure".[60]

(f) Compensation may be payable on refusal of scheduled monument consent

There is however a provision for compensation for refusal of scheduled **8.19** monument consent. The provisions are fairly restrictive, largely as a result of the decision in *Hoveringham Gravels Ltd v. Secretary of State for the*

[57] [1991] J.P.L. April.
[58] s.4(2).
[59] s.4(3) (as amended by the N.H.A., s.33 and Sched. 4).
[60] s.9(1)(a).

301

Environment[61] where it was held that likely harm to an ancient monument may be a material consideration in refusing planning permission, and that without planning permission there could be no claim for compensation. The fact that the desirability of preserving an ancient monument in its setting is a material consideration in determining planning applications was stated categorically in PPG 16.[62] The upshot of this is that, unless express or implied planning permission is granted before a monument is scheduled, compensation is limited to works which are reasonably necessary for the continuation of any existing use of the monument.

The provision is found in section 7 of the 1979 Act and there are four requirements which must be satisfied before compensation will be awarded. They are:

(1) The claimant must have an interest in the whole or any part of the monument;

(2) The claimant must have incurred expenditure or otherwise sustained loss or damage in consequence of the refusal;

(3) The expenditure or loss or damage must have been incurred or sustained in consequence of the refusal or the granting subject to conditions of the scheduled monument consent; and

(4) The scheduled monument consent must relate to works of a description mentioned in section 7(2), as to which see paragraph 8.20 below.

An interest to qualify for compensation must be in accordance with regulations prescribing interest qualifications as provided for in section 47 of the Act. As yet, no such regulations have been made.[63]

8.20 The works which will qualify for compensation are:

(1) Works which are reasonably necessary for carrying out any development for which planning permission had been granted (otherwise than by a General Development Order) before the time when the monument in question became a scheduled monument and was still effective at the date of the application for scheduled monument consent;

(2) Works which do not constitute development or constitute development such that planning permission is granted therefore by a General Development Order; and

(3) Works which are reasonably necessary for the continuation of any use of the monument for any purpose for which it was in use immediately before the date of the application for scheduled monument consent, save that any use in contravention of any legal restrictions for the time being applying to the use of the monument shall be disregarded.[64]

The distinction between (1) and (2) appears to be that compensation is payable where, at the time of scheduling of a monument, there is a planning permission specifically outstanding but not implemented in respect of the monument so scheduled. Compensation will not be paid in respect of a

[61] [1975] Q.B. 754.

[62] PPG 16, November 1990.

[63] Regulations as to claims for compensation for land in Scotland: See S.I. 1981 No. 1469, operative November 30, 1981.

[64] s.7(2).

planning permission granted after scheduling of the monument, but compensation will always be paid for prevention of the carrying out of General Permitted Development Order permission or for works which do not constitute development. As the General Permitted Development Order permission or the definition of what does not constitute development would be applicable both before or after the scheduling of the monument, the question of time in this respect is irrelevant.

Section 7(3) provides that compensation payable under (1) above shall be limited to loss sustained by virtue of the fact that any development for which the planning permission was granted could not be carried out without contravening section 2(1), in consequence of the Secretary of State's decision.

The applicant is not entitled to compensation under (2) above if the works in question or any of them would or might result in the total or partial demolition or destruction of the monument unless those works consist solely of operations involved in or incidental to the use of the site of the monument for purposes of agriculture or forestry (including afforestation).[65] Presumably the reasoning for this is that at all events total demolition or destruction of the monument would result in a more valuable site than one which is encumbered with a scheduled monument. Similarly, where scheduled monument consent is granted subject to conditions, a person will not be entitled to compensation by virtue of subsection (2)(c) of section 7 unless compliance with those conditions would in effect make it impossible to use the monument for the purpose there mentioned.[66]

There are provisions which build in an assumption to the valuation that any subsequent application for a scheduled monument consent in relation to works of a like description will be determined in the same way (no doubt to defeat the argument that it would be likely that a wider scheduled monument consent would be made available) and a requirement that the valuation reflects any undertaking by the Secretary of State on refusing consent to grant consent for some other works affecting the monument in the event of an application being made in that behalf.[67]

The implications of compensation which might follow from the scheduling of a monument caused much ado when, in 1989, the remains of the Shakespearean Rose Theatre was uncovered at Southwark prior to the development of the site, but after planning permission had been given for the development. This excited the imagination of the theatrical world and calls for the site to be scheduled were voiced.

The Secretary of State decided at that time not to schedule the site as a monument of national importance on the grounds that:

(1) the developer was willing to preserve the remains and modify the development project;
(2) the effect of scheduling would involve a risk of compensation becoming payable to the developer; and
(3) he had to balance the desirability of preserving archaelogical remains against the need for redevelopment in central London to enable the capital to thrive.

---

[65] s.7(4).
[66] s.7(5).
[67] s.7(6).

The Secretary of State's decision was challenged in the High Court in July 1989.[68] The High Court ruled that the use of the word "may" rather than "shall" in section 1(3) of the Act gave the Secretary of State of the Environment a wide discretion to decide whether to schedule the site, and the Secretary was entitled to regard as a relevant factor the risk that compensation might be payable if he were to have scheduled the remains, given that planning permission had already been granted for the proposed development scheme. He could also take into account at the scheduling stage the need to balance the desirability of preserving archaeological remains against the need for redevelopment in central London, and was not obliged first to schedule the monument and then carry out the balancing exercise when application was made to him for scheduled monument consent. The Secretary of State is therefore not obliged to schedule any monument, in comparison to the requirement of the Secretary of State who *must* list a building which qualifies as one of those of special architectural or historic interest. For the record, the Rose Theatre in Southwark was subsequently included amongst the monuments scheduled in 1992.[69]

(g) Compensation may be payable for depreciation

8.21   There are some provisions which apply to compensation for depreciation generally under Part I to be found in section 27, and in particular valuation assumptions in relation to land in respect of depreciation of the value of the interest subject to the mortgage.

(h) Compensation may be recovered on subsequent grant of scheduled monument consent

8.22   There is a provision in section 8 for the recovery of any compensation paid out under section 7 on a subsequent grant of consent. Thus, if compensation was paid on a section 7 claim and there is a subsequent grant of a scheduled monument consent, or a scheduled monument consent is modified so that if the consent was subject to conditions or any of them cease to apply to the execution of all or any of the works in respect of which compensation was paid, then there is a repayment provision. This is on condition that, firstly, the compensation paid exceeded £20 and, secondly, that English Heritage (in Scotland and Wales, the Secretaries of State) have caused notice of the payment of compensation to be deposited with the appropriate local authority.[70] There is a provision for appeal to the Lands Tribunal by a person who has an interest in the whole or any part of the monument where he is aggrieved by the amount recoverable by the Secretary of State.[71] A notice deposited in the case of a monument situated in England and Wales must be entered as a Local Land Charge.[72]

[68] *R v. Secretary of State for the Environment ex parte* Rose Theatre Trust Company, [1990] J.P.L. 360; [1990] 1 All E.R. 754 High Court.
[69] *English Heritage Monitor* 1993.
[70] s.8(2) and (2A).
[71] s.8(4).
[72] s.8(6).

(i) Compensation may be payable for "abortive expenditure"

Where works affecting a scheduled monument have been authorised, *i.e.* **8.23** by a scheduled monument consent, or by a section 3 scheduled monument consent order, and subsequently cease to be authorised, *e.g.* by a modification or revocation, then any person who has an interest in any part of the monument who has incurred expenditure in carrying out works which are rendered abortive by the fact that further works have ceased to be so authorised or has otherwise sustained loss or damage which is directly attributable to that fact, may apply to English Heritage (in Scotland and Wales, to the Secretaries of State) who shall be required to pay that person compensation in respect of that expenditure, loss or damage.[73]

Where under section 9 the work ceases to be authorised by virtue of the fact that a scheduled monument consent granted by order under section 3 ceases to apply to any scheduled monument, the applicant is not entitled to compensation unless he specifically applies for a scheduled monument consent for the works in question and consent is refused, or is granted subject to conditions other than those which previously applied under the order.

(j) Urgent works may be undertaken by the Secretary of State

There is a provision whereby the Secretary of State (or, on his authoris- **8.24** ation, English Heritage) may, if it appears to him that any works are urgently necessary for the preservation of any scheduled monument, enter the site of the monument and execute the works after giving the owners and (if the owner is not the occupier) the occupier of the monument, not less than seven days notice in writing of his intention so to do.[74] These powers were used in the case of *Marrick Smelt Mill, North Yorkshire*, when English Heritage used section 5 to carry out urgent works to prevent imminent collapse of this 18th or 19th-century industrial monument. This was the first major occasion when these powers had been used.[75] There is no recharging provision here. If the Secretary of State (or on his behalf, English Heritage) undertakes this work, they undertake it at their own expense. If however there is any compensation order made in respect of payment of compensation by a convicted person under the Powers of Criminal Courts Act 1973, the order is made in favour of the Secretary of State, which is as far as the Secretary of State appears to want to go in relation to recoupment. The Department of the Environment referred, in its consultation paper of April 1991,[76] to the disparity between listed building and ancient monument legislation, where in sections 54 and 55 of LBA 1990 local authorities or English Heritage (when authorised by the Secretary of State) can carry out

---

[73] s.9.
[74] s.5(1).
[75] *English Heritage Monitor* 1993.
[76] *Recovery of costs for urgent repairs to scheduled monuments*, a consultation paper on Ancient Monuments legislation, Department of Environment, April 1991.

urgent repairs to listed buildings and charge the owner, who has the right of appeal against these charges. No comparable recovery procedure exists in the case of English Heritage carrying out urgent repairs to an ancient monument with the Secretary of State's authorisation.

Under the Act there is no obligation of any sort by an owner of an ancient monument to keep it in a sound state of repair. The Department decided against recommending any recovery of charges because to do so would be tantamount to requiring an owner to carry out repairs to the monument which the Department does not support.

(k) Extensive powers of entry are applicable

8.25   There are substantial powers of entry contained in section 6 for the various stages of ascertaining the condition of a scheduled monument for viewing works to which a scheduled monument consent relates and for recording matters of archaeological or historical interest. These powers of entry and recording are dealt with in Chapter 11.

4. ACQUISITION OF AN ANCIENT MONUMENT

8.26   There are three ways in which an ancient monument can be acquired: the Secretary of State has power to acquire compulsorily or by agreement, or may accept it as a gift.[77] English Heritage (with the consent of the Secretary of State) or a local authority, however, may only acquire by agreement or accept a gift.[78] The gift in either case may be either by deed or by a will.

If the Secretary of State wishes to acquire compulsorily, he must first consult with English Heritage. He may acquire any ancient monument but only for the purposes of securing its preservation, and in practice the Secretary of State will only acquire compulsorily if it is the only way of securing the preservation of the monument. The Acquisition of Land Act 1981 applies, and there is a built-in assumption in respect of the compensation, namely that it is to be assumed that scheduled monument consent would not be granted for any works which would or might result in the demolition, destruction or removal of the monument or any part of it.[79] An undertaking was given by the Secretary of State in the House of Commons on the second reading of the Bill that the compulsory power would only be used when it was the only way of securing the preservation of a monument.[80] In so far as section 11 of the 1979 Act is concerned (acquisition by agreement or gift), the provisions of Part I of the Compulsory Purchase Act 1965 (with some exceptions) are applicable.

8.27   There is a further provision in section 15 of the Act which permits land adjoining or in the vicinity of an ancient monument to be acquired compulsorily if it appears to the Secretary of State or English Heritage to be reason-

---

[77] ss.10 and 11, and see also Chap. 9 as to the taxation consequences.
[78] s.11(2) and (3).
[79] s.10(2) and (4).
[80] *Hansard* (HC Deb. Vol 965, Col 1361, April 4, 1979).

ably required for the purpose of maintenance of the monument or its amenities, providing or facilitating access, the exercise of proper control or management, the storage of equipment or materials, and the provision of facilities and services for the public for or in connection with affording public access to the monument. Wide powers under this section are given to the Secretary of State and English Heritage in respect of this land so acquired.

5. GUARDIANSHIP OF ANCIENT MONUMENTS

As an alternative to acquisition of an ancient monument there is provision for guardianship (the early practice of compulsory guardianship having proved unsuccessful). The broad intention of guardianship is that the legal estate in the land is left with the owner, but that the Secretary of State, English Heritage or the local authority become the guardians of the land (and in particular, the monument). An ancient monument need not be a scheduled monument before it is taken into guardianship. There is a duty on the guardian (be it the Secretary of State, English Heritage or the local authority) to maintain the monument, for which it has full control and management powers.[81] There is an obligation (with some safeguards) to permit the public access to the monument under guardianship.[82] Guardianship orders are not new—indeed, the original guardianship provisions were contained in the 1913 Act and have been effectively used for the last 75 years. There are now over 440 monuments in the care of English Heritage alone.[83] **8.28**

The power is given to a person who has an interest either in the fee simple, in the leasehold estate or an interest in possession (being an estate or interest for a term of which no less than 45 years are unexpired or renewable for a term of not less than 45 years), or an interest in possession for his own life or on the life of another, to constitute the Secretary of State (with his consent) or English Heritage (with its and the Secretary of State's consent) by deed, the guardianship of the monument. With regard to a monument situated in England, the Secretary of State must consult with English Heritage before consenting to guardianship.[84] As an alternative, a person with such an interest in an ancient monument may with the consent of any local authority in or in the vicinity of whose area the monument is situated, by deed constitute that authority guardians of the monument.[85] There is a prohibition against consenting to a guardianship of a structure which is occupied as a dwelling house except by a caretaker or his family occupying it as such.[86]

There is an overriding restriction on both guardianship provisions whereby a person who is not the occupier of the ancient monument may not establish guardianship unless the occupier is also a party to the deed executed with the guardian.[87] Any person who has an interest in an ancient monument may be a party to the deed in addition to the person establishing **8.29**

[81] s.13.
[82] s.19.
[83] *English Heritage Monitor* 1993.
[84] s.12(1).
[85] s.12(2).
[86] s.12(10).
[87] s.12(4).

the guardianship of the monument and the occupier. It may be prudent for such a person so to enter into the arrangements which would give him some (although rather limited) rights if the guardianship is sought to be terminated under the provisions of section 14. The person who has such an interest must at the time of the proposal to terminate, be "immediately affected by the operation of the guardianship deed", it is difficult to see how he could not be, and in practical terms his presence as a party under the deed would no doubt result in his being properly consulted.

The effect of the guardianship is dealt with in section 13 of the Act. The main effect is that the guardian is under a duty to maintain the monument (at its own expense). There is a specific provision defining maintenance as including fencing, repairing and covering in of a monument and the doing of any other act or thing which may be required for the purpose of repairing the monument or protecting it from decay or injury.[88] In return, the guardian has full control and management of the monument and power to do all things as may be necessary for the maintenance of the monument and for the exercise by the guardian of proper control and management with respect to the monument. In particular the guardian may examine, open up, excavate or remove the whole or any part of the monument. Access by the public to the monument must be over and along a defined route indicated on a plan annexed to the guardianship agreement "with or without horses, carts and mechanically propelled vehicles". Little else is included in the standard agreement. All the provisions of section 13 are subject to any provision to the contrary contained in the guardianship deed.

8.30   Having accepted guardianship of an ancient monument, it is less easy for the guardian to get rid of the responsibility. Under section 14, the guardian (if it is a local authority it must consult the Secretary of State before entering into any agreement under this section, but if it is the Secretary of State he must consult with English Heritage) may by agreement with the persons "who are for the time being immediately affected by the operation of the guardianship deed" exclude any part of the monument from guardianship or renounce guardianship of the monument.[89] But it will still remain under guardianship (unless the monument is acquired by its guardian) until the occupier of the monument who is entitled to terminate the guardianship gives notice in writing to that effect to the guardian of the monument.

The occupier is in a stronger position because he is entitled to terminate the guardianship if he has any interest in the monument which would qualify him to establish guardianship under section 13 of the Act, *i.e.* fee simple, leasehold estate for 45 years, interest in possession for life or life of another,[90] and if he is not bound by the guardianship deed. This is the effect of the provisions of section 14(1). It is thought that the word "bound" must mean that he is not bound adversely by any provision in the guardianship deed to the contrary. He will be presumably bound by the deed if under section 12(5) he enters into it, and the provisions of the guardianship deed, being a local land charge, will be binding on a subsequent occupier.

However, the guardian may not enter into any such agreement unless he is satisfied with respect to the part of the monument, or, as the case may be, with respect to the whole of the monument in question, that satisfactory

[88] s.13(7).
[89] s.14(1).
[90] s.12(3).

arrangements have been made for securing its preservation after termination of the guardianship or that it is no longer practicable to preserve it (whether because of the cost of preserving it or otherwise).[91] There is a provision to take into guardianship, by virtue of section 15, land in the vicinity of an ancient monument if it appears to the guardian to be reasonably required for the purpose of maintenance, access, control or management, storage of equipment or materials, or facilities and services to the public for or in connection with affording public access.

In addition, there is a provision for the acquisition of easements or other similar rights over land in the vicinity of an ancient monument whereby the Secretary of State may acquire by agreement or compulsorily any easement "which appears to him to be necessary" for any of the purposes relating to the monument mentioned in section 15(1), *e.g.* maintenance, access, control or management, etc., or for the use of any land associated with that monument for any of those purposes.[92] English Heritage or a local authority may also by agreement acquire easements.[93]

6. AGREEMENTS CONCERNING ANCIENT MONUMENTS AND LAND IN THEIR VICINITY

The Secretary of State and English Heritage have a general power in section 17 to enter into an agreement with the occupier of an ancient monument or of any land adjoining or in the vicinity of an ancient monument. The local authority has a similar power. In 1985–86 English Heritage concluded 44 such management agreements which they regarded as particularly valuable in preserving field monuments. "Limited owners", being persons defined by section 18 as a body corporate or corporation sole and any other persons who have a limited interest such as a tenant for life or a statutory owner or trustees for sale, have power under section 18 to enter into such agreements and guardianship agreements. **8.31**

7. PUBLIC RIGHTS

The public is given rights of access under section 19 to any monument under the ownership or guardianship of the Secretary of State, English Heritage or a local authority by virtue of the Act. Restrictions are imposed so that the Secretary of State, English Heritage or a local authority may nevertheless control the times of the normal public access by regulations made under the section, and the power of a local authority entirely to exclude the public from access to any monument, shall only be exercisable with the consent of the Secretary of State.[94] There is provision also for the Secretary **8.32**

[91] s.14(3).
[92] s.16(1).
[93] s.16(2).
[94] s.19(4).

of State, English Heritage and a local authority to make charges and to refuse admission to any person believed to be likely to do anything which would tend to disfigure or injure the monument or its amenities. There is a penalty provision in section 19(7) in respect of any person contravening or failing to comply with the provisions of section 19. The Act also makes provision for facilities for the public—power is given to the Secretary of State and any local authority to provide facilities to the public and information for or in connection with affording public access to any monument.[95] [See also Chapter 12.]

These statutory public access rights have given rise to well-known difficulties at Stonehenge, which is the most popular of English Heritage's properties, visited by about 700,000 people per year. The days are gone when people could clamber over the stones, and the standing stones are now protected from direct contact with those who visit the monument. The former chairman of English Heritage described Stonehenge as " . . . one of the great European ancient monuments—indeed, it has worldwide significance . . . We must care for it and equally improve the visitor facilities to enable the public to understand it better, to recognise its unique quality and to marvel at its age and beauty."[96]

There is a mystique attached to Stonehenge which brings with it a range of problems. Not only have the coaches and cars to be accommodated, but this number of visitors demand that a refreshment and souvenir building is also provided. There are plans to provide a full scale visitors' centre, but this is fraught with difficulties of land ownership and conflict with the setting of the monument itself. Added to this are the periodic invasions from those who regard the stones of Stonehenge as a magnet at the summer solstice, thus creating an added security problem. Here is an example *par excellence* of the magic of 4,000 years of history and the heritage industry coming together in an uneasy relationship. It is hoped that a new visitors' centre will be built in the next few years.

8. ANCIENT MONUMENTS BOARDS[97]

8.33   There were three Ancient Monuments Boards originally constituted under the 1913 Act: one for England, one for Scotland and one for Wales. Section 39(2) of the National Heritage Act 1983 abolished the Ancient Monuments Board for England, whose functions were taken over by the Historic Buildings and Monuments Commission for England, established by the 1983 Act, and now called "English Heritage". The function of English Heritage and the Ancient Monuments Boards for Scotland and Wales is to advise the Secretaries of State in respect of the exercise of their functions under the Act whether generally or in relation to any particular case or classes of case.[98] The Ancient Monuments Boards for Scotland and Wales are each required by section 23 of the 1979 Act to produce annual reports (as

---

[95] s.20.
[96] Speech by Lord Montagu at Banqueting House, April 2, 1984, *Stonehenge Study Group Report.*
[97] See also para. 8.01.
[98] s.22(6).

does English Heritage), and these are laid before Parliament and published as "House of Commons Papers".

It should be remembered that by section 33 of the National Heritage Act 1983, the general functions of English Heritage are to preserve, and to promote the public enjoyment and awareness of, ancient monuments and historic buildings; to provide educational facilities and give advice; and for the purpose of exercising these functions it is empowered to enter into contracts and to acquire and dispose of land and other property. English Heritage then is very much more than an advisory body, having major executive functions in its own right.

9. THE ORGANISATION OF THE ANCIENT MONUMENTS ADMINISTRATION[99]

In England the work of the Department of National Heritage on ancient **8.34** monuments and the general administration of the service is carried out by English Heritage. Internally, English Heritage has its work organised into two broad groups, one of which deals with properties in its own care, the other dealing with properties in the care of other owners. Both groups have multi-disciplinary teams incorporating inspectors.

English Heritage Inspectors work closely with its architects in preserving and displaying the monuments in its care, and confer with them on the technical measures to be taken. They also give advice to private owners and local authorities when requested. The preparation of lists of monuments worthy of being scheduled for submission to the Ancient Monuments Advisory Committee is another important duty of the Inspectors, and in this they rely substantially on co-operation and information from local archaeologists.

The Inspectors also scrutinise plans for new development such as building, quarrying, roads and pipelines which might interfere with ancient sites and structures. They also arrange, and in some cases personally supervise, the excavation of such sites in order to ensure that the archaeological evidence of monuments which cannot be permanently preserved is properly examined and recorded before destruction.

The Ancient Monuments Laboratory of English Heritage provides the necessary scientific back-up to the work of the Inspectors and other bodies undertaking archaeological excavations on behalf of English Heritage. It also maintains the collections on display at the museums established at certain monuments. Its staff are trained in a variety of scientific disciplines and, under the direction of the head of the Ancient Monuments Laboratory, work in four main subject areas; geophysics, environmental studies, early technology, and conservation. The work of the Inspectors' staff includes preparing the standard guidebooks and also editing for publication the reports of archaeological excavations.

Advice and architectural services related to ancient monuments and historic buildings are given to English Heritage by its own architects, and the

---

[99] We are much indebted to the Ancient Monument section of English Heritage for the information on the administration of the Act.

greater part of the work on the monuments is carried out by a directly employed labour staff. Craftsmen in most of the building trades are employed, some of whom have spent a lifetime in the service of the DOE and now English Heritage.

8.35 English Heritage's architects are responsible for the preparation of reports on monuments prior to being taken into care, in which they assess the condition of the monument, recommend the treatment necessary for its preservation, maintenance and display to the public, and estimate the cost of so doing. However, their primary function is the structural preservation of monuments taken into the care of English Heritage. The techniques used in this work are the result of the experience gained over many years combined with constant research into new methods. It is the policy of English Heritage to treat the ancient monuments for which it is responsible so that they are not only structurally safe for the future but retain unimpaired the historic significance which justifies their preservation.

The architects and craftsmen are additionally responsible for the maintenance, management and custody of the sites, and the ancillary buildings associated with them. The aim is to maintain the condition of the sites to a high standard and provide the service that the visiting public have come to expect. These responsibilities are partly shared with the presentation branch of English Heritage.

Public services in the form of car parks, ticket offices, site museums, toilets and refreshment rooms where these are provided, are planned and designed by English Heritage's architects. With the growth of the tourist trade and greater public appreciation of the heritage, there is an ever increasing commitment to provide more sophisticated public facilities. The interpretation of ancient monuments in an innovative way for an increasing number of visitors has raised problems of visual integration with historic sites and areas of landscape value. Two examples which have brought their problems are Stonehenge and Fountains Abbey, both World Heritage sites, and dealing annually with 700,000 and 300,000 visitors respectively. Fountains Abbey has a new visitors' centre, and Stonehenge should eventually have similarly a new visitors' centre.

Architects and technical staff are also called upon to give advice on monuments not in the care of English Heritage, and, in certain cases, work for private owners of monuments is carried out by English Heritage's direct labour staff, the costs being recovered from the owner. The architectural group includes civil, mechanical and electrical engineers, and quantity surveyors, and is able to call upon other servicing divisions for their assistance when required.

Another department of English Heritage is responsible for publicising monuments in the care of English Heritage, and for making recommendations on the need for the provision of shops and any other services which may be needed at these sites. This publicity work is carried out in liaison with tourist authorities, travel agencies and coach operators and with the National Trust and owners of historic houses. Similar arrangements apply in Scotland and Wales, where the administration is a function of the Scottish and Welsh offices respectively.

In November 1990 the DOE published a Planning Policy Guidance Note (No 16) (in this chapter referred to as "PPG 16") on Archaeology and Planning which is the Department's definitive view on the subject. In December 1991 a joint statement was issued by English Heritage and the Museum of

London on the subject of "Archaeology in London".[1] These bodies shared the objective of seeking the best practicable protection, recording, study and presentation, of London's internationally important archaeological heritage. The statement echoed the important role of the planning process in relation to archaeology as set out in PPG 16.[2]

Following the demise of the Greater London Council in 1983 the statutory duty for securing an adequate archaeological service for the Greater London area was inherited by English Heritage.[3] In April 1990[4] English Heritage undertook to establish a planning advisory service for the London boroughs to assist in the discharge of their responsibilities towards the archaeological heritage through the planning process. This service was intended to be operated in conjunction with the Greater London Sites and Monuments Record and to identify archaeological needs and priorities. In January 1994 it was announced that there would be a review of the archaeological services in London within the existing framework of English Heritage giving planning advice on archaeological matters to most of the boroughs. The continuing role of the Museum of London was also to be assessed. **8.36**

In the case of London, English Heritage holds the Sites and Monuments Record and will be the primary source of archaeological advice to planning authorities in London. In addition to maintenance of the Sites and Monuments Record, English Heritage also undertook to fund the Museum's publication programme based on excavations carried out in the London area.

10. GENERAL POWERS

There are a number of general powers in the 1979 Act. Section 24 provides that English Heritage may defray or contribute towards the cost of the acquisition by any person of any ancient monument. Section 25 provides that English Heritage may give advice with reference to the treatment of any ancient monument and superintend any work in connection with a scheduled monument, if in its opinion it is advisable, and may make a charge for giving that advice and superintendence, or may give it free of charge as it thinks fit. There are a number of powers of entry,[5] all of which are dealt with in Chapter 12. There is a general power for the transfer of ancient monuments between local authorities and English Heritage,[6] and there is a power given to the Secretary of State or a local authority to dispose of land acquired by them under the Act.[7] The Secretary of State or a local authority may receive voluntary contributions under section 31 towards the cost of any expenditure incurred under Part I of the Act. English Heritage may also undertake (section 45) or assist in, or defray, or contribute towards the cost of any archaeological investigation of any land, as may a local authority. There is power for the Secretary of State, English Heritage or a local **8.37**

[1] *Archaeology in London*, Press release, English Heritage 1991.
[2] *Archaeology and Planning*, DOE, November 1990.
[3] National Heritage Act 1983.
[4] *Archaeology and Planning in London*, Paper by English Heritage, April 1990.
[5] s.26.
[6] s.21.
[7] s.30.

authority to publish the results of archaeological investigation undertaken, and there is provision for English Heritage[8] to make grants to the Architectural Heritage Fund.

11. DUTIES IMPOSED IN THE ACT

8.38   There are certain duties imposed in the Act. Under section 46 there is a requirement for the Secretary of State or English Heritage or other authority on whose behalf an archaeological investigation has been carried out, to pay compensation for any damage to land or to chattels on application being made within the time and in the manner prescribed, disputed amounts of compensation being referred to the Lands Tribunal. Under the Common Law in England, objects which are found within the soil become part of the ownership and property of the landowner unless they fall into the category of treasure trove.[9] In the case of objects of archeological or historical interest which are discovered during excavations, observations or examinations and which do not form part of an exercise established under the Act, the authorised person may take "temporary custody" of these finds and remove them from the site for the purpose of examining, testing, treating, recording or preserving them.[10] The objects may not be retained beyond a period which may be reasonably required for these purposes and it is particularly important that, before work begins on an excavation site, the treatment and final custody of these finds is clearly established by all parties.

In a speech in the House of Lords on Museums and Galleries (December 13, 1989) Lord Hesketh (then Parliamentary Under-Secretary at the Department of the Environment) referred to public interest in the knowledge represented by casual finds on archeological sites. Whilst he felt there was a case for strengthening the controls over finds from scheduled sites, he did not think the problem was great enough to warrant a compulsory reporting system.

In the Department of the Environment consultation paper of April 1991[11] it was proposed to make the removal of finds from a scheduled site without consent, an offence. Under section 42 of the Act it is only an offence if such finds were discovered through use of a metal detector (see paragraph 8.76 below). The courts had found difficulty in convicting in cases covered by section 2(2)(a) of the Act, wherein it is an offence to damage a scheduled monument in any way without consent, because it is often difficult to obtain evidence of damage to structures and in order to obtain evidence of damage to buried remains it is necessary to carry out further, and often equally damaging, excavations. The consultation document therefore proposed to specify in addition to section 2(2)(a–c) " . . . any disturbance to land in, on, or under which there is a scheduled monument requires consent."[12] This proposal has not received legislative approval.

---

[8] s.49. In Scotland, this power is exercisable by the Secretary of State.
[9] See para. 8.77.
[10] s.54.
[11] *Portable Antiquities*, DOE consultation paper on Ancient Monument legislation, April 1991.
[12] *Ibid.*

12. ARCHAEOLOGY AND PLANNING

The growing importance of archaeology as a strategic issue in relation to **8.39** town and country planning and as a "material consideration" to be taken into consideration by local planning authorities when dealing with development proposals has been given further recognition by the Department of the Environment through its publication in November 1990, of PPG 16.

There have been several *causes célèbre* in recent years which resulted in public and political pressure for clearer guidance on the subject of archaeology and planning for local planning authorities, property owners, developers, archaeologists, amenity societies and the general public. PPG 16 established clear principles for archaeological conservation within the planning process. These can be summarised as follows:

(1) strong development plan policies, including the recognition of sensitive areas of landscape and based on clear presumptions in favour of preserving the most important archaeological sites, their settings, and the amenity associated with them;

(2) the continuous maintenance of adequate databases in the form of Sites and Monuments Records;

(3) an acceptance of the need for proposal-specific impact assessment and archaeological field evaluations;

(4) an acceptance of the desirability of preserving the archaeology of sites physically intact;

(5) the necessity, when important archaeology cannot be physically preserved, for proper provision to be made by developers and planners for *in situ* preservation below development and for the appropriate recording; unless planning authorities are satisfied on this point it will often be reasonable to withhold permission.[13]

We now divide this expanding subject into a number of headings dealing with the different responsibilities for archaeology in practical terms:

(a) Archaeological Policies

The Department of the Environment advised in Circular 22/84[14] that **8.40** "where appropriate, structure and local plans may include land use policies and proposals dealing with conservation,' for example:

(a) proposals for the enhancement of, or control of, development within conservation areas;

(b) policies for the protection, enhancement and preservation of the setting of buildings of architectural or historic importance, historic gardens, ancient monuments and sites of archaeological importance and their settings;

(c) the designation of special landscape areas, along with the policies to be applied for the protection and enhancement of such areas."

[13] *Archaeological Conservation and Planning*, English Heritage Conservation Bulletin, October 1990.
[14] Circular 22/84, para. 4.36.

The Department of National Heritage to which certain responsibilities for conservation and casework were transferred following the creation of this new Government department, in 1992—regards archaeological remains as a finite and non-renewable resource and considers that "appropriate management" is therefore essential to ensure that they survive in good condition. Where nationally important archaeological remains, whether scheduled or not, and their settings are affected by proposed development, there should be a presumption in favour of their physical preservation.[15] Physical preservation *in situ* of important archaeological remains is nearly always seen as the preferred option,[16] and the justification for this choice is that excavation means the total destruction of evidence (apart from removable artefacts) from which future scientific techniques (which are developing rapidly) could almost certainly extract more information than is currently possible. Excavation costs are also high and time consuming, and therefore from an archaeological point of view are regarded as a second best option.

The proposals maps which accompany development plans should define the areas and sites to which the policies and proposals apply,[17] and these policies will then provide an important framework for the consideration of individual proposals for development which affect archaeological remains. They are intended to help guide developers when preparing planning applications.

Development plans should normally identify archaeological remains which are of national importance and which are earmarked for preservation,[18] and local planning authorities (and others) should bear in mind that not all nationally important remains which merit preservation will necessarily be scheduled. In appropriate circumstances, such remains and other unscheduled remains of more local importance may also be identified in development plans as particularly worthy of preservation.

(b) Sites and monuments records

8.41   These records are maintained by all shire counties mostly under the guidance of a county archaeologist. English Heritage has taken on the role of giving independent advice to the London boroughs[19] and for maintaining their Sites and Monuments Records, and is the primary source of archaeological advice to planning authorities in London.

Prospective developers are advised,[20] when undertaking research into the potential development of a site prior to submitting a planning application, to obtain an initial assessment of whether the site is known to contain or is likely to contain archaeological remains. An examination of the Sites and Monuments Record is recommended as the "first step" and this should provide information about the locations where archaeological remains are

---

[15] PPG 16, para. 8.
[16] PPG 16, para. 27.
[17] PPG 16, para. 15.
[18] PPG 16, para. 16.
[19] *Archaeology in London*, English Heritage, Museum of London statement, December 1991.
[20] PPG 16, para. 19.

known to exist or where the indications are that remains are likely to prove important. This early assessment is strongly recommended in PPG 16 and is described as a "desk-bound evaluation" of existing information making use of historic records.

(c) Site evaluation

The relevance and materiality of ancient monuments in relation to town **8.42** and country planning was recognised by the courts in *Hoveringham Gravels Limited v. Secretary of State for the Environment* in 1975.[21] In this case the argument that ancient monuments legislation constituted a complete and exclusive code was expressly rejected.

In cases where a development proposal submitted to the local planning authority is likely to affect the site of a scheduled ancient monument, the table forming part of Article 10 of the Town and Country Planning (General Development Procedure Order) 1995 requires the authority to consult English Heritage (and in Wales, the Secretary of State).

PPG 16 extends the scope of the desirability of preserving an ancient monument and its setting as a "material consideration" to any monument "whether that monument is scheduled or not",[22] and it urges developers and local planning authorities to take into account archaeological considerations and deal with them from the beginning of the development process. Developers are advised to enter into discussions with planning authorities at an early stage to avoid potential conflict between the needs of archaeology and development, and they arc warned that to do otherwise removes the scope for flexibility which, if required, becomes more difficult and expensive to achieve.[22a]

Prospective developers should in all cases include as part of their research into the potential development of a site and before making a planning application, an initial assessment of whether the site is known or likely to contain archaeological remains. Where these preliminary enquiries indicate that archaeological remains may exist, it may be considered reasonable for the planning authority to request the prospective developer to arrange for an archaeological field evaluation to be carried out before any decision on the planning application is taken. This type of evaluation is intended to help define the character and extent of the archaeological remains which exist in the area of the proposed development, and thus the weight which ought to be attached to their preservation by the local planning authority. English Heritage is willing to be consulted on applications for development of non-scheduled sites.

If evaluation reveals possible conflict between the development proposal and archaeological remains, the local planning authority could request that

---

[21] 1975 Q.B. 754.

[22] PPG 16, para. 18.

[22a] The effect on the archaeology to construct an opera house at Compton Verney was considered by the Secretary of State: Compton Verney Opera Project—Secretary of State decision, March 16, 1995, E.H. Legal Bulletin No. 5, June, 1995.

the scheme be modified, for example by adjusting the design of the foundations, before a favourable recommendation is forthcoming.[23]

(d) Planning conditions

8.43   Conditions may be imposed by a local planning authority in accordance with model conditions set out in Circular 1/85 (paragraphs 37 and 38) which state that: "No development shall take place until fencing has been erected in a manner to be agreed with the local planning authority . . . and no works shall take place within the area inside that fencing without the consent of the local planning authority", and "the developer shall afford access at all reasonable times to any archaeologist nominated by the local planning authority, and shall allow him to observe the excavations and record items of interest and finds". A footnote to these model conditions advises that conditions should not require work to be held up while archaeological investigation takes place, though some developers may be willing to give such facilities.

Where sites are already scheduled as ancient monuments by Part I of the 1979 Act and investigation for archaeological purposes is provided for in the designated areas of archaeological importance under Part II of that Act, these conditions should not be duplicated. Paragraph 30 of PPG 16 also suggests that planning authorities may, when granting planning permission, wish to secure the provision of archaeological excavation and the subsequent recording of remains, by adopting the use of a negative (or *Grampian*) condition[24] which prohibits the carrying out of development until such time as works or other action, *e.g.* in this case, excavation, has been undertaken by a third party. The suggested wording of such a condition is contained in this a paragraph, viz:

> "No development shall take place within the area indicated [this would be the area of archaeological interest] until the applicant has secured the implementation of a programme of archaeological work in accordance with a written scheme of investigation which has been submitted by the applicant and approved by the local planning authority."

A footnote to this condition suggests that developers will wish to ensure that in drawing up a scheme the timetable for the investigation is included within the details of the agreed scheme. Caution is required in relation to the use of a "negative" condition, and is illustrated in a case[25] which came before the Court of Appeal in June 1990, where it was held that unless there was some evidence of a reasonable prospect of the obstacle (giving rise to the "negative condition") being removed, then a *Grampian* type condition should not be applied.

Where planning permission is granted for development which might affect a monument which is not scheduled, or which affects land which is

---

[23] HSD 9/2/473 Part 2. Decision letter dated March 20, 1989 in respect of the Round Burrows south east of Horsell Common, Woking—quoted in Michael Redman's paper to conference on *Planning Gain—archaeological aspects*, October 1990.
[24] *Grampian Regional Council v. City of Aberdeen* [1984] J.P.L. 590.
[25] *Jones v. Secretary of State for Wales*, [1990] J.P.L. p. 907.

not designated as an area of archaeological importance, the local planning authority may wish to impose the above conditions provided that the requirements of the conditions are reasonable in all the circumstances of the case.

PPG 16 does not advocate the use of conditions as a first option, para- **8.44** graphs 25 and 29 make clear the desirability of proceeding with the use of agreements and paragraph 26 refers to the possible types of agreement, including the British Archaeologists' and Developers' Liaison Group model agreement. In the absence of such an agreement, planning authorities can have recourse to the use of conditions. The criteria for planning conditions are set out in Circular 1/85. The circumstances of the individual case will determine whether a particular condition might be regarded as valid. Is it appropriate for a local planning authority to nominate an archaeological contractor for the purposes of carrying out excavation ahead of development? There may be instances when a local planning authority felt that there was only one archaeological body capable of undertaking the work to a required standard, but that would be a decision taken on a case-by-case basis. The view taken by the Department of the Environment in 1991 was that an invariable rule that a particular archaeological body should carry out all excavations within a particular area would not pass the test of "reasonableness" in the Circular 1/85.[26]

In cases where a developer is unwilling voluntarily to provide an assessment and evaluation of a site where there is good reason to believe there are remains of archaeological importance, the local planning authority may wish to consider whether it would be appropriate to direct the applicant to supply further information under the provisions of Regulation 4 of the Town and Country Planning (Applications) Regulations 1988.[27]

There may also be circumstances where a formal environmental assessment is seen as appropriate, under the Town and Country Planning (Assessments of Environmental Effects) Regulations 1988. In paragraph 24 of the Circular 15/88 dealing with environmental assessments it is stated that the relationship between a project and the location proposed for it will often be a crucial consideration. The more environmentally sensitive the location the more likely it is that environmental effects will be significant and will warrant assessment. Amongst the examples quoted in Schedule 2 of Appendix A of the Circular 15/88 are "small urban development schemes in particularly sensitive areas". In cases of doubt regarding the need for an environmental assessment in relation to projects affecting the built heritage, it is suggested that English Heritage be consulted.[28] An area or monument of major archaeological importance is cited (paragraph 24) as one of several projects which are likely to have significant effects on the special character of a protected area or site. The publication of PPG 16 in November 1990 has, to a large extent, overtaken the need for local planning authorities to resort to environmental assessments since it is now accepted practice to require developers to produce archaeological assessments.[28a]

There may be occasions when a local planning authority is aware of a real and specific threat to a known archaeological site as a result of works pro-

[26] Letter from the Head of Heritage Division to the BADL Group, July 1991.
[27] S.I. 1988, No. 1812.
[28] Circular 15/88, Sched. 2, para. 17.
[28a] An Inspector dismissed an appeal which might have adversely affected archaeological remains prior to a full evaluation—E. H. Legal Bulletin No. 5, June 1995.

posed under Schedule 2 of the Town and Country Planning (General Permitted Development) Order 1995, *i.e.* permitted development. PPG 16 advises the local planning authority in those circumstances to consider the use of powers under Article 4 of the GPDO thus withdrawing these permitted development rights and requiring that specific planning permission is obtained before the development can proceed. In an issue of *London Archaeologist* (Volume 6, page 142) it is alleged that the works carried out by statutory undertakers without the need for planning permission are a major threat to archaeology. Only in Areas of Archaeological Importance see paragraph 8.64 below–do these types of works need to be the subject of an operations notice, but subject to certain exemptions, thus enabling the archaeologists in the five designated towns the opportunity to observe trenches and holes created by these statutory undertakers.

8.45   In the General Permitted Development Order 1995, Article 7 includes provisions for restricting permitted development for mineral exploration when it involves drilling boreholes, carrying out seismic surveys or making other excavations, or where it involves the removal of material from a mineral-working deposit other than a stockpile. This empowers the mineral planning authority to make a direction (similar to an Article 4 direction) on land which—*inter alia*—includes a site of archaeological interest and the operation to be carried out is not one described in the Schedule to the Areas of Archaeological Importance (Notification of Operations) (Exemption) Order 1984.

Archaeological issues are however often important in minerals planning, particularly in the extraction of sand and gravel. The contribution made by the mineral's extraction industry to archaeology has been substantial in terms of both historical evidence and financial contributions. In 1993, a 250,000 year old mammoth tusk was found at Stanton Harcourt in Oxfordshire which enabled scientists to identify a hitherto unknown warm interglacial period, and in 1983 the largest rural Roman villa complex in Western Europe was uncovered at a gravel pit at Stanwick near Northampton. The estimated cost to the gravel industry as a whole between 1991 and 1993 in contributing to archaeology was more than £10 million.[29]

The Confederation for British Industry republished, in June 1991, a Code of Practice for Mineral Operators (first issued in 1982) with the intention of eliminating conflict between mineral operators and archaeologists by the use of pre-planning consultation. The updated code continues the aim of balancing the preservation of archaeological sites *in situ* against the needs for exploitation of mineral resources. An appeal involving the balance between the need for mineral extraction and archaeology was decided in February 1991. It involved a 130 acre site at Marston Meysey in Wiltshire and was located in the valley of the River Thames. The application was for the extraction of sand and gravel and the Inspector considered this in relation to the development plan policies, archaeological implications and the impact on the highway network. There was found to be a compelling need

---

[29] Letter to *The Times*, May 23, 1994 by Chairman of ARC Ltd.

to find suitable landbank resources; the site was located in an area of special archaeological significance where the structure plan restricted development if it would damage or destroy important remains. There was disagreement about the extent of the remains which ranged from a Neolithic cause-wayed enclosure to part of a Romano-British settlement. Although the Inspector found it impossible to reach a firm view on the likelihood of finding these remains, he concluded that there was sufficient evidence to indicate their presence and that even the smallest risk of destroying such rare and nationally important monuments should not be taken. He also found the likely increase in vehicles would amount to an overriding objection. The appeal was dismissed.[30]

(e) Variation of planning enforcement notices

Arising from a planning enforcement case (*McKay v. Secretary of State for* **8.46** *the Environment, Cornwall County Council, Penwith District Council*)[31] an appeal was made to the High Court against the terms of the Inspector's decision letter in dismissing an appeal which related to the unauthorised use of land for the deposit of waste materials at St Just, Cornwall.

A substantial part of the site was a Scheduled Ancient Monument, and in his decision letter, the Inspector varied the wording of the Enforcement Notice to require *inter alia* "subject to within six months of the granting of Scheduled Monument Consent . . . " (and proceeded to set out certain physical works required to reinstate the site).

It was argued, on behalf of the appellant, that the decision was a nullity because it required the appellant to carry out works necessarily in breach of section 2 of the Ancient Monuments and Archaeological Areas Act 1979, namely works resulting in the demolition, destruction or damage to a scheduled monument. The decision amounted to a requirement to carry out a criminal offence. There was said to be no guarantee that scheduled monument consent would be forthcoming, and yet failure to comply with the notice within the prescribed period would also amount to an offence under section 179 of the T.C.P. Act 1990. Whichever way the appellant chose to act, or not to act, he would attract criminal liability. The outcome of this case (Q.B. Division, March 12, 1993) before Mr Nigel McLeod Q.C., acting as a Deputy Judge, was to rule that the Enforcement Notice (as amended by the Inspector) was a nullity and was incapable of variation.

There have been several cases in the past where decisions under one piece of legislation have been contrary to the requirements of other legislation. The Building Act 1984 and the Housing and Planning Act 1986 are now amended in section 56 LBA 1990 to make it clear that listed building control takes priority. Unfortunately the status gives no guidance as to whether enforcement notices can require works to listed buildings and ancient monuments without the necessary consents first being obtained.

[30] APP/W3900/A/90/156831/P5. February 1991.
[31] [1994] J.P.L., March 12, 1993, p. 806.

(f) Simplified planning zones

8.47   The introduction of Simplified Planning Zones[32] (SPZs) in 1988 provided for certain areas to be designated and, once adopted, granted planning permission for the type of development specified in the scheme; thereafter, there is no need for developers to submit a planning application. PPG 5 acknowledges the need for some SPZ's to include special sub-zones in which the scheme is tailored to take account of local factors. Examples of the type of sub-zones which may be required included "ancient monument sub-zones around important archaeological sites".[33]

(g) Rescue archaeology

8.48   Where it is not feasible to preserve the remains of an archaeological site, an acceptable solution may be to arrange for the excavation of the site prior to its development during which the archaeological evidence can be recorded.[34] This "second best" option is advocated when preservation is no longer possible because the value of the archaeological resource is outweighed by some other factor. A site or standing structure may be investigated to record as much as possible of its structure and form, thus in effect preserving it on paper. This is known as preservation by record, or is more commonly known as "rescue archaeology". This process of rescue archaeology is expensive, and particularly so in urban areas which are often rich in archaeological deposits.[35] There has been a substantial change of direction since the publication of a discussion paper by the Department of the Environment in 1981.[36] That paper stated that the designation of an archaeological area (embodied in Part II of the Act) was not a preservation or conservation measure, and that "areas so designated were, in effect, archaeologically expendable in that it is only the information held within the site that is extracted while the archaeological content is destroyed". In the report of English Heritage of 1987/88 on Rescue Archaeology Funding (June 1987) it is stated that "the excavation option is now expensive to pursue and can only be followed when all attempts to mitigate the threat through the planning process and to obtain alternative sources of funding should excavation become inevitable, have been made". Furthermore, rescue excavation has shown that it is not always possible to be certain of the quality of the buried deposits.[37]

In June 1991, English Heritage issued a policy statement[38] on the subject of "Rescue Archaeology Funding" re-stating its primary objective of securing the preservation of archaeological remains, and only where that is not

---

[32] Town and Country Planning Act 1990, s.82.

[33] PPG 5, para. 16 to Annex (January 1988).

[34] PPG 16, para. 13.

[35] *Archaeological Review* 1988–89, English Heritage.

[36] [1981] J.P.L., p. 151.

[37] *Protecting the archaeology of historic towns, English Heritage Conservation Bulletin*, February 1991.

[38] *Rescue Archaeology—A policy statement, English Heritage Conservation Bulletin*, June 1991.

feasible, then seeking to ensure that archaeological work is carried out to investigate and record important remains before they are destroyed.

The expensive nature of this form of recording is acknowledged and its **8.49** destructive effect upon archaeological deposits is seen as disadvantageous, leading to the conclusion that "if left in the ground (the deposits) would yield greater information to future generations armed with more developed recording and analytical techniques".[39] This statement represented a very different attitude towards rescue archaeology from the first policy adopted by English Heritage in 1986 which was issued at a time when central government provided the bulk of the funding. The revised statement does however reflect the advice contained in PPG 16 on "Archaeology and Planning" issued in November 1990.

(h) Archaeology in urban areas

Many major historic towns qualify as being of "schedulable" quality but **8.50** in practical terms these are often places containing thriving commercial centres where the best deposits underlie their historic cores. Their standing buildings are mainly "listed" as being of special architectural or historic interest, and they have been designated as conservation areas in order that their character or appearance may be preserved or enhanced. Rescue archaeology in such circumstances is seldom a practicable solution, and many years of rescue excavation have shown that it is not always possible to be certain of the quality of buried deposits without exploration beneath the surface.

Scheduling of individual monuments or buried deposits in such towns may sometimes be appropriate, but it is seldom realistic for the whole of an urban historic centre to be scheduled as an ancient monument. The approach of English Heritage to this subject was illustrated in June 1994, when it was revealed that as part of the redevelopment scheme on the site of 1 Poultry, near the Mansion House in London, the owner had allowed the archaeologists 44 weeks and £2 million to undertake excavations. The site was likely to reveal the richest collection of Roman remains and artifacts yet found in Britain. As the original permission to develop this site pre-dated PPG 16, the local authority did not have a duty to take archaeology into account when determining the planning application. To prevent development, the entire site would have had to be scheduled as an ancient monument, but the chief archaeologist of English Heritage was reported to have said[40] that they would have opposed such a move as "it would be wrong to try to sterilise a site of such commercial importance".

It is estimated that there are some 120 towns emanating from the Roman **8.51** period, 160 from the early medieval period, and there are some 950 towns which date back to the end of the medieval period. The current solution adopted by English Heritage is to produce a strategy document for these nationally important major historic towns, setting out advice to the planning authority, developers and archaeologists. Ideally, a strategic plan is

[39] *Ibid.*
[40] *The Times*, June 14, 1994.

required for each of these 950 towns, but in practice English Heritage[41] is giving priority to 80 or so large towns or seaports. Work has commenced on five reports: London, York, Chester, Cirencester and Durham. With the exception of London these reports will be produced in partnership with the relevant local planning authority.

The key features of these documents will be as follows:

(1) a survey of the survival of archaeological deposits within the study areas;

(2) the provision of an archaeological and historical framework against which the deposit survival survey can be set; and

(3) the formulation of strategies and a statement of the future management of the archaeological resource.

The strategies will be reviewed from time to time and are seen as essential documents to provide a framework in which the legitimate pressures of economic development can be properly reconciled with the need to protect that part of our heritage which such historic towns represent. The first of these policies to emerge was commissioned by York City Council and English Heritage and was published in May 1991 by Ove Arup and Partners in conjunction with the University of York and Bernard Thorp and Partners.[42] The primary purpose of the report was:

"To update knowledge of the City's archaeological resource and to provide a framework for ensuring the development of sites is secured in a way in which can conserve the most outstanding archaeological resources."

8.52 The archaeological research framework recommended in the York statement is expressed as nine projects, which are, in summary:

(1) *Project 1:* site evaluation (low cost desk and field study) of every site in the designated area which is the subject of a planning application;

(2) *Project 2:* formal excavation (where this option has been exercised by developers), with adequate time allowed only for those sites of high current archaeological value where deposit quality matches the research agenda. All other sites to be preserved;

(3) *Project 3–9:* seven non-destructive projects, including studies of historic buildings, documents, finds, the hinterland, the natural environment and preservation strategies for underground deposits.

The York statement makes recommendations on the need to design foundations to suit a variety of types of development, archaeological remains and ground conditions. It also proposes the adoption of an "archaeological mitigation strategy" the components of which are archaeological evaluation, archaeological preservation by record (excavation) and archaeological preservation *in situ* (minimum destruction by development). The developer would be expected to meet the costs of the site evaluation and the implementation of the mitigation strategy, and where this proposed strategy

---

[41] *Protecting the Archaeology of Historic Towns* by Bill Startin; *English Heritage Conservation Bulletin*, February 1991, p. 14.

[42] *York Development and Archaeological Study*, Ove Arup and Partners and others, May 1991.

includes the option of a formal archaeological excavation, this will be treated as a development proposal in its own right, requiring planning permission.

As a consequence of the *York Development and Archaeology Study* prepared by Ove Arup and Partners, the City Council itself produced a draft archaeological policy statement in October 1991[43] as a consultation document. In addition to the area of archaeological importance, whose origins are in section 33 of the Act, the City Council has introduced a new term and supported it with a plan shown an "Area of Archaeological Significance". Any application (for planning permission) which lies within 100 metres of the former and within the latter of these special areas, will normally be expected to be accompanied by supplementary information, which will include an assessment of the archaeological deposits and a statement indicating how disturbance of these deposits will be kept to a minimum, and the specific steps which will be taken to mitigate disturbance of the deposits. Applications which lie within the Area of Archaeological Significance will be required to include this information "at the discretion of the Director of Development Services". The recommendation contained within the Ove Arup report regarding "archaeological excavation projects" which do not form part of a "mitigation strategy" are embodied in the policy of the City Council by its requirement of being the subject of a separate planning application. The recommendation goes further by stating that permission will be refused where excavation proposals do not meet certain criteria (which are set out).

(i) Archaeology in rural areas

Of the 13,000 scheduled ancient monuments, it is estimated that some 70 per cent are field monuments, which means that much of the nation's archaeological heritage lies in the countryside. Changes in agricultural policies and practices in recent years have caused many of the non-scheduled (and frequently unrecorded) sites to be damaged or destroyed. The Sites and Monuments Records should have incorporated many of the burial mounds, hillforts, villa sites, deserted villages, etc, within their database, but the fact remains that landowners are often, and sometimes unwittingly, the custodians or guardians of the nation's rural archaeology.[44] **8.53**

In addition to the ancient monuments legislation, there are several other pieces of legislation[45] which indirectly relate to rural archaeology. Although conservation areas are normally associated with urban areas, they can be applied to rural areas and can be designated in whole or in part because of their archaeological value. Examples where this has occurred are

[43] Draft Conservation Policies for York, *Archaeology*, York City Council, October 1991.
[44] *Ancient Monuments in the Countryside*, T Darvill, published by English Heritage, 1987.
[45] *Countryside Legislation and Statutory Codes of Practice, English Conservation Bulletin*, June 1990.

in Hampshire (the Upper Way Valley) and in village fringes in north Oxfordshire.

The Countryside Act 1968 enables National Parks to provide educational and tourist facilities for "objects of architectural, archaeological or historical interest" within their areas and gives responsibilities to Government, and such other bodies as English Heritage and the private water companies, to take into account countryside matters in all aspects of their works. The Wildlife and Countryside Act 1981 gives protection to historic components of the landscape and provides—in section 39—for management agreements to conserve and enhance landscape amenity.

The Agriculture Act 1986 provides for the establishment of "Environmentally Sensitive Areas" whose objectives include the protection of historic features in traditional landscapes. This aims to integrate conservation with farming practice. Amongst the areas which may be defined within these special areas are those "to protect buildings or other objects of archaeological, architectural or historic interest".

The Protection of Military Remains Act 1986 aims to secure the protection from unauthorised interference of remains of military aircraft and vessels which have crashed, sunk or been stranded and of any associated human remains. In the countryside, the Act mainly applies to military remains under 200 years old which have been designated for protection by the Secretary of State. Once they have been designated, it becomes an offence to disturb them without a licence.

8.54 The Water Act 1989 imposes a duty on privatised water companies, internal drainage boards and the National Rivers Authority "to have regard to the desirability of protecting and conserving buildings, sites and objects of archaeological, architectural or historic interest" and to take these features into account when formulating proposals. These requirements were re-enacted in the section 16 of the Water Resources Act 1991 and section 3 of the Water Industry Act 1991. Provision can therefore be made for management agreements or covenants to cover future land use and public access and to encourage good conservation practice.

The Electricity Act 1989 (Schedule 9(1)(1)(a)) places a duty on persons authorised to generate or supply electricity, but not to transmit electricity, "to have regard to the desirability of preserving . . . features of special interest and of protecting sites, buildings and objects of architectural, historic or archaeological interest" and "to do all that (they) reasonably can to mitigate any effect which (their) proposals would have on the . . . features, sites, buildings and objects". The licence holder is required—under Schedule 9, paragraph 2—within 12 months of obtaining the grant of a licence to prepare a statement setting out *inter alia* the consultation procedures he intends to follow, and this includes consultations with the Countryside Commission, the Nature Conservancy Council and English Heritage. The Schedule 9 statements are non-statutory documents which do not require the Secretary of State's approval.

Another threat to rural archaeology which has emerged in recent years is the creation of golf courses in the countryside. By the end of 1990 it was estimated that over 1000 applications had been received by local planning authorities in England, most of which were for 18 hole courses involving 50 hectares of land per course. Many of these proposals affected historic parkland. There are four documents which need to be consulted by a local planning authority immediately on receipt of an enquiry from a golf course promoter; the County Sites and Monuments Record, the list of buildings of special architectural or historic interest, the local plan for any conservation area designations and the Register of Parks and Gardens of special historic interest in England. Applications affecting any scheduled monuments are required to be referred to English Heritage and special conservation advice can be obtained from them also on the Register of Parks and Gardens (see Chapter [2]).

There will be instances where an environmental assessment of golf course proposals will be required by the local planning authority under the Town and Country Planning (Assessment of Environmental Effects) Regulations 1988 and subsequent amendments, and an assessment will be especially appropriate if the project includes other associated development such as club house, hotel or holiday village, which developers often regard as economically necessary. The level of information required to support an application for this type of development will largely depend upon the quality of the landscape which is to be affected by it. Until the existing value of the landscape has been assessed, it is unwise to embark on producing a layout for the golf course. Draft guidance notes on assessing the impact on golf course construction are available from English Heritage.[46]

A complete list of legislation which has recognised the importance of **8.55** archaeological remains is as follows:

> Electricity Supply Act 1926 (section 44(3))
> Coastal Protection Act 1949 (section 47(d))
> Coal Mining Subsidence Act 1957 (section 9(1))
> Land Powers Defence Act 1958 (section 6(4)(b))
> Mines (Working Facilities and Support) Act 1966 (section 7(8))
> Forestry Act 1967 (section 40(2))
> Land Drainage Act 1976 (section 111)
> Agricultural Holdings Act 1984
> Protection of Military Remains Act 1986
> Water Act 1989
> Electricity Act 1989

In February 1992, Pagoda Associates, a firm of management consultants, published a review[47] of the effectiveness of PPG 16 based on interviews and written submissions from archaeologists working for or advising planning authorities, developers and their archaeological advisers. The consultants found that every local planning authority in England had adopted the advice given in PPG 16 and the archaeological significance of virtually all planning applications was being properly considered and a more consistent approach was being produced to the subject of archaeology in the planning process. The Department of the Environment is undertaking a vetting procedure of all emerging Local Plans and UDP's to assess their respective policies in relation to archaeology.

---

[46] Golf Course proposals in historic landscapes (draft)—*English Heritage*, March 1991 (also *The Times* August 23, 1991).

[47] *An Evaluation of the Impact of PPG 16 on Archaeology and Planning* (Pagoda Associates Ltd, January 31, 1992).

(j) Funding of archaeology in the planning process

8.56   Section 45 of the Act (as amended by the National Heritage Act 1983) empowering English Heritage "to undertake, or assist in, or defray or contribute towards the cost of, an archaeological investigation of any land in England which they consider may contain an ancient monument or anything else of archaeological or historical interest . . . ". These powers relate to ancient monuments in general and not just those which had been scheduled. In the early 1980s central government made block grants[48] for rescue archaeology to archaeological units, but this was later changed to funding by project. With the recognition of the great increase in the number and variety of sites and landscapes as being of archaeological and historical importance it became necessary to pursue a more selective policy so that grants for rescue archaeology were allocated for projects which could be justified within a framework of academic priorities. By April 1986,[49] English Heritage was "welcoming participation by developers and others in the funding of rescue programmes" because its resources were inadequate to carry that burden alone. Local planning authorities were advised that they had a clear role not only to ensure that the archaeological implications of their planning decisions were properly assessed, but also that when destruction of such sites was unavoidable, provision for essential archaeological recording was to be agreed before permission for that development was granted.

In 1986 the British Property Federation (representing most major developers) and the Standing Conference of Archaeological Unit Managers formed the British Archaeologists' and Developers' Liaison Group, with the objective of ensuring long-term understanding, goodwill and co-operation between archaeologists and those involved with development. The Group has both a liaison and an advisory role, providing guidance to those seeking funding for the recovery of archaeological data and assisting developers faced with the need for sites to be excavated in advance of building work.

In April 1986 the Liaison Group published a Code of Practice for Archaeologists and Developers which was widely distributed and adopted by many local planning authorities. The ethos of the code was its voluntary nature, and through its auspices it has underpinned huge expansions in urban archaeology over the past few years. The funding of archaeology by developers and business interests increased by nearly 5,000 per cent in the years between 1980 and 1988[50] and this coincided with a drop in central government funding from one half to one third of the total. A report compiled by the British Archaeological Trust in 1988 from information provided by organisations involved in rescue archaeology revealed that public and private sector developers had contributed £3.37 million in 1986/87, some 17 per cent of the total, and equal to the contribution made by local authorities. In *Archaeology Review*[51] for 1988–89 some of the achievements which had occurred over the previous decade were discussed. These included the acceptance of archaeology as a "material consideration" in the

---

[48] *Rescue Archaeology Funding*, Policy Statement, April 1986 (HBMC).
[49] *Ibid.*
[50] *The Times*, June 21, 1988.
[51] Published by English Heritage, 1989.

planning process, with the result that development schemes were now being designed to minimise damage to archaeological remains or to incorporate them within the building design. Another "achievement" was said to be that "public awareness and inclusion of archaeology in the planning process have combined to persuade developers to commit resources to providing a record of the archaeological remains that are to be affected by their activities". This was said to have "significantly altered the balance of private funding for rescue archaeology".

In a speech to a conference on "Archaeology and Development" in April **8.57** 1989, the Under-Secretary for the Department of the Environment reported that in the previous year the funding of archaeology by English Heritage of £7 million had been supplemented by a further £14 million from developers. "Developer funding" therefore became an accepted part of the archaeology vocabulary by the later 1980s and under the Code of Practice developers agreed to allow both adequate time and financial support to permit worthwhile excavations. This voluntary approach is commended in the PPG 16 and gives scope for developers or their archaeological consultants and local planning authorities to apply flexibility in covering excavation, recording and the publication of the results. The Secretary of State regards the terms and spirit of the Code of Practice as the way forward in securing the continued co-operation of the two interests.

In paragraph 25 of PPG 16, planning authorities are advised not to include in their development plans policies which require developers to finance archaeological works in return for the grant of planning permission, but the PPG also advises that "it would be entirely reasonable for the planning authority to satisfy itself before granting planning permission that the developer had made appropriate and satisfactory provision for the excavation and recording of the remains" in cases where preservation *in situ* is not justified.

Stress is laid in paragraph 26 of PPG 16 on the voluntary nature of the agreements between developers and archaeologists and to their being "likely to provide more flexibility and be of greater mutual benefit to all parties than could be provided by alternative statutory means".

In line with the advice contained in PPG 16, English Heritage adopted a revised policy in June 1991 to allocate the funds at its disposal for recording those archaeological sites which could not be preserved and whose destruction was beyond the control of agencies, with the powers and resources (taken to be central and local government) to deal with the problem. English Heritage takes the view that responsibility for producing a published record of archaeological deposits which are threatened by development and which cannot be preserved *in situ* lies with the developer whether in public or private sectors.

There may be cases where it is not practicable for a developer to fund archaeological work required by a planning authority (for example, a non-profit making body, or even a commercial developer whose scheme is desirable but only marginally profitable), and English Heritage may be prepared to offer some financial support subject to the availability of funds. An example of such a case would be where a proper site evaluation had occurred and then unexpected and important evidence emerged after the granting of planning permission and which was beyond the resources set aside for the archaeological work. A manual has been produced by English Heritage which sets out good practice for the archaeological project management for recipients of its own grants and as an aid to other financial sponsors.[52]

(k) Archaeological agreements

8.58   Apart from the model conditions referred to in paragraph 8.43 above, there are other ways open to local planning authorities to provide for archaeological investigations whilst still conforming to the edict[53] that voluntary agreements are likely to provide more flexibility and would be of greater mutual benefit to all parties. The developer will normally wish to enter into a formal agreement with the appropriate archaeological unit covering the licence for access to the site as well as the terms of funding. Some developers are willing also to include provision for the publication of post-excavation results and see this as the tangible result of their public relations exercise. Others regard this type of publication as the academic record of the work for which they have provided the means, but which goes beyond the scope of their responsibility. PPG 16 advises that agreements covering excavation, recording and publication of the results, may take different forms.

The British Archaeologists' and Developers' Liaison Group has itself published two versions of a model agreement between developers and the appropriate archaeological body for archaeological site investigations. One is a fully detailed agreement and the other a shorter version for small-scale projects.[54] Another set of guidelines for the preparation of contracts for archaeological excavations was drawn up by a Working Party consisting of representatives of the Association of Metropolitan Authorities, the British Property Federation, the Council for British Archaeology, the Department of the Environment, the Royal Institution of Chartered Surveyors and the Standing Conference of Unit Managers.[55]

PPG 16 also suggests that developers or their archaeological consultants and local planning authorities may wish to include a voluntary planning agreement under section 106 of the Town and Country Planning Act 1990. In its previous incarnation this section was more familiarly known as "section 52" and in Circular 28/83 local planning authorities are reminded that developers cannot be required to enter into such agreements by means of a planning condition. The advantage of this type of agreement is that when it is in the nature of a negative covenant,[56] it is enforceable by the local planning authority against successors in title of the person or body which enters into the agreement. Positive covenants can be included in such agreements provided they achieve the purpose of restricting or regulating the use or development of land. Incidental and consequential provisions (including provisions of a financial character) which are considered necessary or expedient for the purposes of the agreement, may also be included.

[52] *The Management of Archaeological Projects, English Heritage*, 2nd Edition, 1991.
[53] PPG 16, para. 26.
[54] Available from the British Property Federation, 35 Catherine Street, London SW1E 6DX.
[55] Published as Appendix 1 to *Site Management, Information Sheet No. 64* by the Chartered Institute of Building in 1981.
[56] *Grampian Regional Council v. City of Aberdeen* [1984] J.P.L., p. 590).

Some types of positive obligations or covenants can be enforced against **8.59** successors in title under section 33 of the Local Government (Miscellaneous Provisions) Act 1982 and are entered into by persons with an interest in land undertaking to carry out work or to do any other thing on or in relation to that land. There are four stipulations relating to this type of agreement made under seal and which:

(a) is made for the purpose of securing the carrying out of works on land in the Council's area in which the person entering into the covenant has an interest; or

(b) is made for the purpose of facilitating the development of land (in or outside the Council's area) in which he has an interest; or

(c) is made for the purpose of regulating the use of land (in or outside the Council's area) in which he has an interest, *e.g.* an agreement to use some of the land as a car park to serve the development on the remainder; or

(d) is otherwise connected with land in which the person entering into the covenant has an interest, *e.g.* an obligation to carry out certain demolition or other works or to pay towards the cost of such works if carried out by the Council.

Advice on the circumstances where it may be possible to grant permission if the matter is the subject of an agreement is contained in PPG 1 (paragraphs 25 and 26). Here again, local planning authorities are advised that they are not entitled to use the agreement mechanism and the applicant's need for planning permission as an opportunity to extract a payment of benefit for the ratepayers at large. Paragraph 26 of that PPG sets out the terms of agreements which are likely to be reasonable depending upon:

(i) whether what is required:
— is needed to enable the development to proceed, for example, alteration to road access or additional sewerage; or
— is a financial payment towards the cost of such works; or
— is otherwise so directly related to the development or its subsequent use that permission should not be given without it, for example, the provision of car parking or open space, or a financial contribution towards its provision by others; or
— is designed to secure an acceptable balance of planning uses on the site;

(ii) whether what is sought is fairly and reasonably related in scale and kind to the proposed development;

(iii) whether what the developer is being asked to provide or help to finance represents in itself a reasonable charge on the developer as distinct from being financed by national or local taxation or other means, for example, by a charge on users of the facilities to be provided or financed by the developer under the terms of the agreement.

There is a cautionary tale for those who, having been advised that planning permission will be forthcoming on the completion of an agreement, allow archaeologists to start excavation work on the site before actually receiving the permission. West Oxford District Council resolved to approve a development scheme and had written to the applicants conveying this resolution. At that time the Council was unaware of the archaeological

331

importance of the site, and it was only when the Oxford Archaeological Unit commenced work that its importance became apparent. Before the agreement had been entered into and the planning permission released, the Council changed its mind and refused to grant planning permission. It was held[57] that the Council had not granted planning permission merely by passing a resolution to do so, nor was the local planning authority estopped from changing its decision.

(l) Unexpected archaeological finds

8.60   Emphasis is laid by PPG 16 on the need for an early assessment of a potential development site, and where appropriate, an evaluation which will help to define the character and extent of the archaeological remains which might exist in the area of the potential development. The funding of rescue archaeology, where this is the only accepted method of recording the archaeology of the site, is clearly now expected by central government to be provided by the developer, but on a voluntary basis. English Heritage's efforts are increasingly being directed towards the management needs of archaeological sites and the integration of those needs into strategies to identify, project, manage and record the country's archaeological resource, although its financial resources are dominated by "rescue grants". These grants are designed to secure the recording of the more important archaeological sites which are unavoidably threatened with destruction.

English Heritage acknowledges that developers and local authorities are increasingly recognising their own responsibilities towards archaeological remains affected by development, and knows that their ability to make the right decisions depends critically on the quality and accessibility of information about such remains which survive so that local authorities can improve the quality of their information base and make full use of it as part of the planning process.

In spite of these policies and efforts at providing adequate safeguards, the fact remains that archaeological finds are still being discovered after planning permission has been granted and development works have commenced. Developers are often exposed to public criticism for wishing to proceed with their legitimately obtained permission, whilst archaeologists deplore the imminent destruction of an unexpected find which represents a piece of history.

Several of the *causes célèbre* referred to in paragraph 8.39 above come within this description. PPG 16 deals with this type of experience in a somewhat dismissive way by claiming that its guidance is framed to minimise occasions when totally unexpected problems arise while development is in process. It does however suggest that developers may wish to consider insuring themselves against the risk of a substantial loss whilst safeguarding the interest of historic remains unexpectedly discovered on the site. When sites are found to be of national importance, the Secretary of State for National Heritage has power to schedule remains after consulting with English Heritage. In other cases, it is open to a planning authority or the Secretary of State to revoke a planning permission "if deemed necessary" with the consequential payment of compensation.

[57] *R v. West Oxford DC ex parte Pearce Homes*, [1986] J.P.L., 523.

In the case of the *Rose Theatre*[58] located in Southwark, the Secretary of **8.61** State decided, against public pressure, not to schedule the site (although this was later reversed). Planning permission had already been granted for the development and the owners of the site, Imry Merchant Developers plc, had agreed to fund an archaeological evaluation under the voluntary Code of Practice and to provide time for excavation. Almost at the expiry of the excavation period the remains of the Rose Theatre—one of the four famous Tudor/Jacobean playhouses on London's south bank—which had been destroyed in 1605, were found.[59] The approved scheme would have involved 55 feet piles being driven through the theatre's remains. On the night of the 13/14 May 1989, 500 vigilantes joined hands to keep pile-drivers off the site. The developers agreed to a further postponement of the building work despite financial penalties to which this exposed them, and the Government paid £1 million for the consequences of the delay. The Rose Theatre Trust Co. formed mainly from members of the theatrical profession requested the Secretary of State to schedule the site as an ancient monument. Estimates of the compensation for which the Government would have been liable had that occurred ranged from £5 to £25 million.

After much public and political pressure, the developers redesigned the foundations in a non-damaging fashion, designed a building on stilts in a form which would preserve the theatre site and provided for the remains to be displayed to the public, at an extra cost of £10 million.[60] A combination of these financial and physical factors clearly influenced the Secretary of State's decision at that time not to schedule the site, whereupon the Theatre Trust challenged the decision in the High Court on July 17, 1989. That Court held that the Secretary of State had a broad discretion as to whether he exercised his powers under Schedule 1 of Part I of the Act. The word in the section is "may" schedule. A further point of interest in the *Rose Theatre* High Court case was that the applicants (the Rose Theatre Trust Co) were ruled to have no *locus standi* to apply for judicial review.

Another celebrated archaeological site which revealed unexpected surprises[61] included the remains of a large Roman bath house, built in the first century AD and located underneath a 1960s office block at Huggin Hill—between Little Trinity Lane and Lambeth Hill—where the site was to be redeveloped in 1989. The site had been partly excavated in 1964 and the Museum of London, then being responsible for archaeology, had recorded that the bath house remains were "fragmentary and damaged" and fell into the category of "record, but not worth preserving". The site was scheduled in 1986 and, in 1988, the Hammerson Group sought planning permission to redevelop the 1960s block. An evaluation of the site was undertaken and the developers paid for a full excavation under the terms of the voluntary Code of Practice. This amounted to a five month dig and a £500,000 grant[62] as part of an agreement which included obtaining scheduled monument consent. In the event, the remains were more extensive than had been expected

---

[58] *R v. Secretary of State ex parte Rose Theatre Trust Co* [1990] 1 P.L.R. 39. See also *Archaeology and Development*, Michael Redman; [1990] J.P.L., and *English Heritage Monitor* 1993.

[59] *The Times*, June 2, 1990.

[60] *The Times*, June 23, 1989.

[61] *The Times*, May 12, 1989.

[62] *The Times*, July 31, 1989.

and contained, *inter alia*, an almost complete hypocaust. The prospect of revoking the scheduled monument consent would have involved millions of pounds in compensation. The owners, working with the City planners, agreed to modify their design to protect the surviving remains, at an extra cost of £3 million.

8.62   The sites of new roads can reveal unexpected finds, as was demonstrated in May 1990 when important pre-historic remains including a rare Neolithic henge and Bronze age village were discovered along the route of the Brighton bypass. These extremely rare discoveries were "unknown and unexpected prior to trial trenches being dug at intervals along the road corridor",[63] and after aerial photography and field surveys undertaken by English Heritage, had given no hint of their existence.

The White Paper "Roads for Prosperity—implications for England's archaeological resource"[64] was published in May 1989. This was followed by a report published in February 1990 *Trunk Roads, England: into the 1990s*, which resulted in a claim by English Heritage that the Department of Transport's motorway and trunk road building programme would have a major impact on archaeological remains in England, with over 800 known sites—as well as many others still undiscovered—likely to be destroyed or disturbed. A study undertaken by Environmental Resources Limited on the archaeological implications of this programme estimated that the cost of reducing all the archaeological data from these sites would be in the order of £73 million.[65] These facts were based on the data contained in the Sites and Monuments Records throughout the country, and the Government's road programme was said to have a potentially greater impact on archaeology than any other single development scheme. English Heritage called for a full archaeological assessment of all these sites before the new routes were settled, thus minimising the damage to these remains. In October 1991 the Department of Transport announced that in future it would be directly funding archaeological surveys which are carried out before a trunk road is built or improved. This funding would be given to English Heritage for recording and publication of archaeological sites, and it was hoped that the evaluations might lead to a road being re-aligned to avoid an important site.

The archaeological activities of the late 1980s coincided with the construction boom which occurred in many historic towns and cities throughout the country. In 1986, the Museum of London investigated about a dozen major sites, the figure rose to 33 in 1987 and to 65 in 1988.

The sheer scale of these "threats" and the limited resources available to archaeological units have combined to place the excavation of sites as a "second best" option. The discovery of a major find once planning permission has been given and building operations are in train would incur prohibitive costs in compensation. Calls for automatic scheduling of sites in the event of discoveries of national importance have been met with equally valid claims that stringent laws would lead developers no longer to cooperate with archaeologists and quietly to destroy any discoveries to avoid risk of excavation and the inevitable delays and costs. The dilemma is therefore a difficult one, and to impose statutory controls or to "buy out" the developer once archaeological remains of interest have been found is as

---

[63] *The Times*, May 4, 1990.
[64] *The Planner*, October 1990.
[65] *The Times*, October 16, 1990.

has been seen to be politically unacceptable placing onerous financial burdens on the public purse. PPG 16 therefore adopts the compromise solution of moral persuasion wherever possible. It is inevitable that conflict will sometimes arise when permission is refused because a site is of archaeological interest, or is scheduled as an ancient monument immediately prior to a decision on a planning application. Such a case occurred at Milbourne Port, a village in the South Somerset District,[66] where in 1990 a sheltered housing scheme was proposed, and English Heritage sent its recommendation of refusal just as the Planning Committee meeting was about to start. The site was described as "exceptionally rare and of national importance". The developers were ready to spend £80,000 on an excavation of the site and had paid for the trial tests[67] which subsequently resulted in the Secretary of State deciding to schedule the site. The view was taken by English Heritage that the site should be left untouched until recording methods had improved. In the meantime, the developers lodged an appeal against the planning refusal, which was subsequently withdrawn.

In a report published in 1972 by the Council for British Archaeology for a **8.63** conference entitled "The Erosion of History", it was estimated that there were almost 1000 towns in England, Scotland and Wales which could be considered to be "historic" (which included places which only reached urban status after about 1750). This compares usefully with the more recent estimate[68] of 950 towns existing by the end of the medieval period, which arose out of an assessment by English Heritage in February 1991. At the time of the 1972 publication, nearly 600 of those towns were said to have been faced with development proposals which were likely to harm their archaeology. There is no reason to believe that the picture presented at that time was exaggerated. Indeed, the facts and events of the past two decades suggest that it was probably an under-assessment. The success of "developer funding" was one of the major achievements of the late 1980s, but it has been underwritten by the national and international development companies whose schemes were, during that time, often amongst the most lucrative and in prime locations.

Outside the main commercial centres and in provincial historic towns where sites are less attractive to develop and where financial margins are tighter, it is much more difficult for a local planning authority to persuade a developer to meet the additional costs incurred by archaeological evaluation and restraints, and yet these are the very places where archaeology is largely undisturbed and therefore of special importance. These are the examples where the viability of a scheme could be put into jeopardy, through archaeology, and yet where in other respects the site may be eminently suitable for redevelopment and where the town needs the benefit of the inward investment. A planning refusal in such circumstances might well lead to the developer serving the local authority with a purchase notice[69] on the grounds that the land to which it relates had become "incapable of beneficial use in its existing state".

Just as unexpected archaeological finds can be revealed after building

---

[66] *Building*, June 8, 1990.
[67] *Financial Times*, May 19, 1990.
[68] *Protecting the Archaeology of our Historic Towns, English Heritage Conservation Bulletin*, February 1991.
[69] Town and Country Planning Act 1990, s.137.

work has commenced, there are also cases where developers' contributions to archaeological investigations are out of proportion to be finished results. On a site in Vintner's Place, next to Southwark Bridge, a contribution of £80,000[70] was made to the Museum of London, plus extra costs to support the adjoining ground and the diversion of services amounting to another £200,000. At the end of this exercise "no new discovery was made and nothing will remain visible to the public".

New techniques[71] are emerging which should assist in avoiding these costly and non-productive events; the use of sub-surface radar imaging is currently being developed. Excavators at Sutton Hoo used radar in 1985, but its potential for use in urban situations to assist in locating archaeology is as yet in its infancy. This method has previously been used by construction engineers to locate sub-surface pipes and services. In 1989 it was employed in York to locate features with a precise resolution of tens of centimetres. On a site in Micklegate, the technique was clear enough to pick out the contours of buildings some 10 metres below ground.[72] A profile of the site showed the lower part of a barrel wall, layers of Viking organic debris, a stone Roman wall and various other Roman surfaces. The effect of using this methodology speeded up archaeologists' rescue work and provided information for the developers on the depth and location for the foundations of new buildings. This method has been described as "one more method for gaining extra information which will help to plan excavations much more efficiently".[73] The Ancient Monuments Laboratory of English Heritage exists to help archaeologists obtain the best possible service from modern technology, and this is assisted by research laboratories in several universities.

In spite of the subject of ancient monuments having been the first under the heading of the "built environment" to be protected by legislation, it is still fraught with uncertainties. The voluntary agreements which are supported by the construction industry and endorsed by the Government are, by definition, a means of providing a developer with the option to refuse to co-operate. The art and practice of sound town and country planning in this country depends, even after almost fifty years of legislation, on balancing finely competing demands; never was this more apparent at this time than in the murky waters of archaeology.

13. ARCHAEOLOGICAL AREAS

8.64   Section 33 of the Act contains a provision for the designation and control of operations affecting "areas of archaeological importance". This gives specific powers over areas as opposed to specific monuments. Part II of the Act covers these areas, which are to be designated selectively. This part of the Act was brought into force in April 1982 and provides facilities for rescue archaeology prior to the commencement of development in cases where the archaeological remains of that site may be at risk. So far five areas

---

[70] *Chartered Surveyor*, May 3, 1990 and English Heritage supplement *Science and Technology 1994*.
[71] *Daily Telegraph*, December 11, 1989.
[72] *Annual Report of York Archaeological Trust*, 1989–90.
[73] *Daily Telegraph*, December 11, 1989.

have been designated: in Canterbury, Chester, Exeter, Hereford and York. In a Written Answer to a Parliamentary Question the then Minister for Environment and Countryside said, in July 1990, that English Heritage had advised him that no further areas of archaeological importance should be designated at present until the impact of the Department's planning policy guidance note on *Archaeology and Planning* (PPG 16)had been assessed.[74]

At the time when the Secretary of State designated the five "areas of archaeological importance", rescue archaeology was an accepted preferred option prior to development taking place within these archaeologically sensitive areas. The local archaeologists had no powers of entry to a site other than by a "condition based" approach (see paragraph 8.43) and valuable evidence was lost because developers had no obligation to provide adequate notice of their intended building works or to provide time for evaluation and/or excavation to take place. Rescue archaeology had relied partly upon the powers of the local planning authority to have regard to the desirability of preserving or recording archaeological remains, but mainly on the willingness of developers to permit access to sites for excavation prior to redevelopment. The intention behind areas of archaeological importance was that it required potential developers to give six weeks, notice known as an "Operations Notice"to the local planning authority of any proposal to disturb the ground, tip on it, or flood it. The "investigating authority" (usually the local archaeological unit) then had the power to enter the site and, if necessary, to excavate it for a period of up to four and a half months, before development might proceed. The Act made no financial provision for either the cost of administering the scheme or to the investigating authority for its excavation costs.

A discussion paper issued in 1981 on Part II of the Act, dealing with areas of archaeological importance, envisaged the designated areas as being, in effect, archaeologically expendable, in that the sites would be excavated, the information recorded, and then the archaeological context would be destroyed. The philosophy has now changed, as will be seen from the section on Archaeology in Urban Areas above, and PPG 16 places the emphasis firmly on preservation of the archaeological evidence of a site *in situ*, with excavation being a second best option, and therefore areas of archaeological importance are now of limited value within this revised philosophy.

8.65 The designation of areas of archaeological importance was always intended to be selective and to be reserved in the first instance for areas of great archaeological importance. The five designated areas set out in paragraph 8.64 became effective on September 30, 1984 and these were later said to be "experimental"; PPG 16 reaffirmed the Minister's answer to the House of Commons of July 1990, namely that no more areas would be designated until an assessment of the effects of the PPG had been undertaken, and that assessment was expected to begin in November 1991. The Government suggested, in a consultation paper of April 1994, that this part of the Act would eventually be repealed.

One advantage which the designation of an "area of archaeological importance" had over non-AAI historic towns is that "development" by public services which involved the disturbance of the ground within the designated areas is covered by the "operations notice" procedures. This type of work is "permitted development" under Schedule 2 of the General Per-

---

[74] *Official House of Commons Report*, Issue 1530, column 197, [1990] J.P.L., p. 651.

mitted Development Order 1995 and its predecessor, GDO 1988, and would not normally otherwise be detected. The information gleaned from sewer trenches or other channels can be of value in itself, but can also be a pointer to the existence of archaeological deposits when threats occur to adjoining sites.

Experience in at least one of the five designated areas of archaeological importance has shown that there are important deposits outside these designated areas. This has caused York to adopt a new term ("Area of Archaeological Significance") which includes all of the area of the city outside the area of archaeological importance and associated with it, and requires that development proposals which lie within the AAI or within 100 metres of its boundaries and which are greater than 1 hectare in area are to be subject to an archaeological evaluation. The AAI will principally be used to allow watching briefs and evaluation to be undertaken within a research framework.[75]

(a) Making of Designation Orders

8.66   The basis of this form of control is a designation order made by the Secretary of State, who may from time to time by order designate as an area of archaeological importance any area "which appears to him to merit treatment as such for the purposes of this Act".[76] English Heritage has power to designate such an area within Greater London, and a local authority has a similar power in relation to its own area. The five areas already mentioned have so far been designated; namely the historic centres of Canterbury, Chester, Exeter, Hereford and York. The Secretary of State has power to vary or revoke a designation order, but the power to vary is confined to reducing the area.[77] There is no similar power to make a variation or revocation order by English Heritage or a local authority. There is no appeal against inclusion in a designation order, although, as might be expected, informal discussions with the local authorities were held prior to designation. Schedule 2 of the Act has effect with regard to the making and the variation and revocation of designation orders. There are notification procedures and a requirement of the local authority to submit a designation order to the Secretary of State for confirmation.[78] Finally, a designation order is registrable as a Local Land Charge.[79]

(b) Investigating authorities: Appointments and powers

8.67   The Secretary of State may at any time appoint any person whom he considers to be competent to undertake archaeological investigations and to exercise in relation to any area of archaeological importance, the functions conferred by Part II of the Act.[80] The persons so appointed are known as the

[75] Draft Conservation Policies, *Archaeology*, York City Council, October 1991.
[76] s.33(1) A.M. Archaeological Areas Act 1979.
[77] s.33(4).
[78] Sched. 2, para. 13.
[79] s.33(5).
[80] s.34(1).

"investigating authority", possibly (but not necessarily) an independent archaeological unit or one attached to a university, or perhaps one forming part of the local authority. Appointments of investigating authorities may be cancelled at any time; the Secretary of State must consult with English Heritage and notify each local authority for whose area an investigating authority is appointed, of the appointment and of any cancellation thereof; and an investigating authority may authorise any other person to act on his behalf in exercising the functions conferred by the Act.[81] Investigating authorities have extensive powers of entry to and investigation of sites.[82]

(c) Controls and offences in designated areas

The method by which control is exercised over operations affecting land **8.68** which is included in a designation order is contained in section 35 of the Act which is the kernel of Part II. Section 35 makes it an offence for any person (referred to somewhat tendentiously as "the developer") to carry out or cause or permit to be carried out on designated land, *i.e.* within an area of archaeological importance, any operations involving disturbance of the ground, flooding or tipping without first having served an "operations notice" on the district (or London borough) council in whose area the "site" is situated, and second, having allowed *six weeks* to expire after service of the operations notice. Nowhere in the Regulations is there provision for the amount of information which should be provided with the operations notice. If the "developer" is a local authority, the notice must be served on the Secretary of State. "Site" includes buildings and other structures on the site. The developer must, in the notice, specify the nature of the proposed operations, the estimated date of the commencement of work and a certificate satisfying the provisions of section 36. This in effect is the consent of the person having an interest in the site of the operations or having compulsory purchase rights or it will be issued by a statutory undertaker. An operations notice can be served in respect of operations which have to be carried out after clearance of any site. In these circumstances, the developer must notify the investigating authority immediately on completion of the clearance operations.[83] The investigating authority then has a right to enter and inspect the site, observe any operations, and/or carry out any excavations,[84] but the investigating authority only has a right to excavate the site of the operations if before the end of the period of *four weeks*, beginning with the date of the service of the operations notice, the authority serves notice in the prescribed form of its intention to excavate and serves a copy of that notice on any council served with an operations notice.[85] The period allowed for excavation is a period of four months and two weeks beginning with the date immediately following the end of the *six week* period beginning with the date of the service of the operations notice.

Thus, the developer must serve his notice and must do nothing for *six weeks*. If he does, he commits a criminal offence. If, in the *first four weeks*

[81] s.34(2)(3) and (5).
[82] s.38.
[83] s.35(7).
[84] s.38(1).
[85] s.38(3).

of that six weeks, the investigating authority notify, under section 38, that they intend to inspect or excavate, then the developer is prevented from doing anything until the investigating authority has carried out that work, which cannot be extended beyond the period of four months and two weeks from the end of the six week period. Thus, effectively no development can be delayed by statute beyond six months. Where there is a possibility of a site of archaeological interest being discovered, it is no doubt prudent to write into the standard form of building contract a provision whereby work may be held up for the six months.[86] It will also be noted that there are no emergency powers in the Act equivalent to the building preservation notice procedure which imposes a six months "listed" status on unlisted buildings pending a decision by the Secretary of State. There is no equivalent in ancient monuments legislation to the "stop" notice provisions in general planning law.

The investigating authority may, after six weeks, carry out excavations provided it does not obstruct the execution on the site by the developer of clearance operations.[87] This provision only applies where the period allowed for the excavation begins at a later date than the six weeks beginning with the date of the service of the operations notice. This would only apply where the operations specified in the operations notice are to be carried out after the clearance of the site when, it has been seen, the developer is under an obligation to notify the investigating authority of the completion of the clearance of the site.[88] In practice, there evolves an agreed programme.

(d) Investigation of sites compulsorily acquired

8.69 There is power under section 39 for the investigating authority to investigate in advance of the service of an operations notice on any site which may be acquired compulsorily. There are supplementary powers of entry contained in section 44, and the provision in section 46 in relation to compensation for damage caused by exercise of this power will no doubt be taken into account by the investigating authority before exercising these powers.

(e) Power of entry where Operations Notice served

8.70 Where an Operations Notice is served, section 40 confers powers on a person duly authorised in writing by the Secretary of State to inspect the site and record matters of archaeological or historical interest and a person duly authorised in writing by the Royal Commission on Historical Monuments for similar inspection and recording.

---

[86] But, as to antiquities, fossils and other objects of interest or value, see *e.g.* Clause 34 of the JCT Local Authorities with Quantities 1980, and *Emden on Building Contracts* (December 1986).

[87] s.38(5).

[88] The forms of notice are contained in the *Operations in Areas of Archaeological Importance* (Forms of Notice, etc.) Regulations 1984 (S.I. 1984, No. 1285).

(f) Exemptions from Operations Notice controls

The Secretary of State may by an order[89] direct that section 35 shall not **8.71** apply to the carrying out, or the carrying out by any class or description specified in the order. Thus, operations undertaken in compliance with such an order (an order which is not unlike a permission under the Schedule to the General Permitted Development Order 1995) will not constitute an offence under section 35. The Areas of Archaeological Importance (Notification of Operations) (Exemption) Order 1984 has been made which gives exemption, *inter alia*, to certain operations in connection with agriculture, forestry, landscaping, tunnelling, mining, repair and maintenance of highways, waterways and mains services, and their installation.

(g) Defences to prosecution

In any proceedings for an offence under section 35 for carrying out or **8.72** causing or permitting to be carried out any operations which disturb the ground, it is a defence for the accused to prove that he took all reasonable precautions and exercised all due diligence to avoid or prevent the disturbance of the ground.[90]

In any proceedings under section 35 it is a defence for the accused to prove cither that he did not know and had no reason to believe that the site of the operations was within an area of archaeological importance, or that the operations were urgently necessary in the interests of safety and health and that notice in writing of the need for the operations was given to the Secretary of State as soon as reasonably practicable.[91] It is to be observed that this defence is in contrast to the absolute nature of offences in relation to listed buildings.

(h) Emergency actions prohibiting operations: powers of local authorities

There is a provision contained in section 35(10) whereby a district council **8.73** may institute High Court proceedings for an injunction in relation to an offence under this section in respect of operations on any site wholly or partly within their area if it appears to any such council that any such operations are being, or are about to be, carried out in contravention of section 35, and the site contains or is likely to contain anything of archaeological or historical interest which will be disturbed, damaged, destroyed or removed without proper archaeological investigation.

[89] s.37.
[90] s.37(5).
[91] s.37(6).

(i) Anticipated problems

8.74   A major problem in the present economic climate continues to be the financing of archaeological investigations. There is no mandatory obligation to provide grants, nor can the planning authority impose conditions requiring a financial contribution towards the cost of excavation. The provisions for designating areas of archaeological importance are discretionary unlike, for example the duty on local authorities to keep under review the designation of conservation areas.

14. CROWN LAND[92]

8.75   The constitutional position in this country has afforded the Crown exemption from all statutory provisions, unless they state to the contrary. The Crown is at present largely exempt from planning legislation. Where proposed Crown development affected a scheduled ancient monument or one held in guardianship under the provisions of the 1979 Act, or of any known archaeological remains, the developing department has been required to notify the relevant divisions of the Department of National Heritage or the Welsh Office. In November 1992 the Government issued a consultation paper inviting comments on proposals to remove Crown exemption from the planning system. The principle behind these proposals was that all Crown bodies should be required to apply for planning permission, listed building consent, conservation area consent, and scheduled monument consent, in the normal way. On March 10, 1994 the Planning Minister announced proposals to remove Crown exemption "as soon as a suitable legislative opportunity arises".[93]

15. METAL DETECTORS

8.76   There is a provision in the Act whereby if a person uses a metal detector in a *protected place* without the written consent of English Heritage, he shall be guilty of an offence and liable for a fine not exceeding £200.[94] A *protected place* means any place which is either the site of a scheduled monument or any monument in the ownership or guardianship of the Secretary of State or situated in an area of archaeological importance.[95] It is a defence to the charge to prove that the metal detector was used for a purpose other than detecting or locating objects of archaeological or historical significance. There is a further offence of removing any object of archaeological or historic interest.[96] These provisions form part of the "rights" or the public, and, as such, are considered in detail in Chapter 13.

---

[92] s.50.
[93] *DOE Press Release*, March 10, 1994.
[94] s.42(1).
[95] s.42(2).
[96] s.42(3).

16. TREASURE TROVE

The law of treasure trove which dates back to before 1276[97] was intro- **8.77**
duced by Richard I to fortify his failing revenues. It provides that if articles
of silver or gold in coin, bullion or plate have been concealed in the ground
or other hiding place with a view to later repossession by an owner who can
no longer be traced, such treasure, when subsequently unearthed, belongs to
the Crown. Non-precious metals are not protected in the same way, nor are
items which were not deliberately hidden but merely lost. The narrowness
of the rules has led to the loss to the nation of some important items, such
as the Anglo-Saxon iron and brass helm found in York which was valued at
£500,000 but for which the finder received £50, and the medieval jewel
found near Middleham Castle in North Yorkshire in 1985 which was later
sold for £1.4 million. It is often difficult to establish whether objects were
deliberately hidden or merely lost.[98] Items of gold or silver lost or deposited
without intent to recover are not regarded as treasure trove and are normally returned to the finder. In such cases, the power of the Coroner (to
whom all cases of treasure trove must be referred) is limited, and he cannot
make a statement as to title to the property.

In the case of an ancient solid gold ring dating from the Middle Ages,
uncovered in a field near to the Middleham jewel, a Coroner's jury decided,
in December 1990, that the treasure hunters who unearthed it during a
metal detecting rally could keep it, as it had been lost and was therefore not
treasure trove.[99]

In September 1993[1] the Lowestoft Crown Court decided that "the greatest Roman hoard found in Britain" of 14,780 gold and silver coins, jewellery,
spoons and table decorations, were treasure trove. They were formally
seized by the Crown and were placed on display at the British Museum,
where they had been conserved and catalogued. The value of this treasure
was estimated to be over £1 million and the finder would be entitled to a
reward equal to the market value.

An even larger find of Roman coins and jewellery was dug up in a field in
November 1993[2] at Hoxne, Suffolk, through the use of a metal detector, and
was valued at up to £5 million. This again was declared "treasure trove" and
seized by the Crown. In contrast, another metal detector operating in a public park in Farnham, Surrey[3] unearthed a gold and sapphire Tudor brooch,
and the local council sought to claim the brooch as owners of the land. The
brooch, valued at about £35,000, was declared by the Coroner to have been
lost accidentally rather than buried deliberately, and therefore could not be
claimed by the Crown as treasure trove. The council had tried to pass a by-
law banning the use of metal detectors on its property but was told by the
Home Office that such a restriction was not possible on public land.

---

[97] *Ancient Monuments in the Countryside*, T. Darvill, 1987.
[98] *The Times*, December 13, 1990.
[99] *The Times*, December 13, 1990.
[1] *The Times*, September 4, 1993.
[2] *Daily Mail*, March 2, 1994.
[3] *Sunday Times*, February 20, 1994.

8.78   Under Scottish law all objects of antiquarian value, whatever their material, when found in similar conditions, rank as moveable ancient monuments and are afforded protection, and similar provisions apply in Northern Ireland under the Historic Monuments (Northern Ireland) Act 1971.

A case before the Court of Appeal (*R v. Hancock*, July 1989)[4] involved a collection of coins found at a site in Wanborough, near Guildford, which had been minted between 50 BC and 30 AD and were said to be "unique". The case centred on whether these coins were treasure trove and thus the property of the Crown. Their Lordships were of the view that it was for the jury to determine as part of their findings as to guilt or otherwise of the appellant whether the coins were, in fact, treasure trove and thus the property of the Crown, applying the ordinary burden and standard of proof in a criminal case. Whatever presumptions might be available in civil disputes as to treasure trove, they did not apply to criminal proceedings. The judge had misdirected the jury in advising that all they had to be sure about was that there was a real possibility of the coins being found to be treasure trove, whereas the highest the evidence for the prosecution went on the issue was only that it was possible that coins had been deposited at some time by someone who had intended to retrieve them. The appeal was allowed.[5]

These types of incident have caused concern to many, and especially as it is estimated that metal detecting enthusiasts are responsible for a 70 per cent increase in archaeological finds.

In March 1984[6] the Government accepted the case for reform of the present law relating to treasure trove, and agreed to publish a consultation paper setting out the main options. The paper was intended to look at all types of portable finds and not just those falling within the present definition of treasure trove. This announcement was made to the House of Lords in response to a Private Members Bill, introduced in February 1994 by Lord Perth, which in its present form the Government would not support. The Bill[7] sought to define all objects more than 200 years old as treasure trove whether they were buried with the intention of recovery, buried in a garden, or simply lost. At the time of writing, the debate on an unacceptable means of reforming the law on treasure trove continues.

The responsibility for treasure trove transferred to the Department of National Heritage[8] from H M Treasury from April 1, 1993. The DNH is advised by The Treasure Trove Reviewing Committee, an independent body which was established in 1977, to advise Ministers on the valuation of treasure trove finds. In the financial year ending March 31, 1993, the total value placed on items retained by museums, was £210,457.

The Irish Government has improved the standing of archaeology by introducing in the National Monuments (Amendment) Act 1994, new powers which will enable the State to own all archaeological objects found in the Republic.[9]

---

[4] *The Times*, August 2, 1990.
[5] *Law Report, The Times*, August 3, 1990.
[6] *DNH Press Release*, March 9, 1984.
[7] *The Times*, March 2, 1994.
[8] *DNH Press Release*, October 20, 1993.
[9] *The Times*, January 3, 1995.

17. CRIMINAL OFFENCES

There are a number of criminal offences created in the Act, *e.g.* carrying **8.79**
out works without consent: section 2(10); contravention of public access
regulations: section 19(7); destroying or damaging a protected monument:
section 28(1); carrying out without permission operations in areas of
archaeological importance: section 35(9); issuing a false certificate to
accompany operations notice: section 36(4); using without authority a
metal detector: section 42(5); intentionally obstructing powers of entry:
section 44(8); and failing to give information as to interests in land: section
57(2).

9. Value Added Tax—("VAT")

(a) Introduction

9.01   Until June 1, 1984, work carried out by builders in making alterations (but not repairs) to property was zero rated. The result was that builders could recover the VAT which they suffered on their costs (such as materials purchased), but did not have to add VAT on their charges, so that the work was carried out for the owner of the building entirely free of VAT. This relief from VAT was generally withdrawn from June 1, 1984 but a new relief was introduced for certain work carried out in connection with "protected buildings".

With effect from April 1, 1989 the relief was further restricted with the exclusion of protected commercial and industrial properties from the scope of zero rating. Alterations to such properties are thus liable to VAT at $17\frac{1}{2}$ per cent despite the fact that they are "protected buildings" and the alterations have received listed building consent. This change followed infraction proceedings by the European Commission against the United Kingdom government, which was held to have contravened Community Law.

The relief remains available for listed domestic dwellings and other residential listed buildings as well as some listed properties used for charitable purposes. Such buildings are referred to in this chapter as "qualifying protected buildings".

In outline, zero rating is available for the following supplies:

(i) services of builders in carrying out "approved alterations" to a "qualifying protected building", and goods (such as materials) supplied with those services; and,

(ii) the sale of a "qualifying protected building" (or the grant of a long lease) where this is carried out in the course of a business and the vendor (or grantor of the lease) has substantially reconstructed the building.[1]

[1] V.A.T.A. 1994, Sched. 8, Group 6.

It should be noted that a person carrying out non-approved alterations, or repairs, to a qualifying protected building has to add VAT at 17½ per cent to his charges. The reliefs are hedged with conditions and complications, some of which are covered below. It should particularly be borne in mind that relief is not available for the services of architects, etc., nor for materials supplied by a person not also providing zero rated services, *e.g.* a builders' merchant.

In practical terms, it is often necessary to provide detailed evidence to H. M. Customs and Excise, and obtain appropriate rulings, in order to persuade builders and developers to zero rate their supplies, or to ensure zero rating on a future disposal of a protected building owned by a business. The view of H.M. Customs and Excise in connection with listed buildings are contained in VAT leaflet 708/1/90.

Where a building is open to the public, advice should be taken as to the necessity to register for VAT. If registration is necessary, this will involve not only VAT on the takings, but also a refund of VAT on the expenses of running the house to the extent that they relate to business as opposed to private use. Such apportionment needs to be agreed by H M Customs and Excise. If registration is required, VAT is likely to be due on subsequent sales of many of the items associated with the running of the house (for example, antiques). Removal of items from display can also attract VAT.

(b) Definitions

It will be seen from the above summary that the terms "protected build- **9.02** ing" (or "qualifying protected building" as it is called in this chapter) and "approved alteration" are vital in determining whether relief from VAT is available.

A "qualifying protected building" for the purpose of relief from VAT by way of zero rating is a building which is designed to remain as, or become, a dwelling or number of dwellings or is intended for use solely for a relevant residential or charitable purpose (see below) after reconstruction or alteration, and which in either case is:

    (i) a listed building within the meaning of:

        (a) the Planning (Listed Buildings and Conservation Areas) Act 1990;

        (b) the Town and Country Planning (Scotland) Act 1972; or

        (c) the Planning (Northern Ireland) Order 1991; or is

    (ii) a scheduled monument within the meaning of the Ancient Monuments and Archaeological Areas Act 1979 or the Historic Monuments Act (Northern Ireland) 1971.[2]

A building is designed as a dwelling if it consists of self contained living accommodation, does not have internal access to another dwelling and its separate use to another dwelling and its separate use or disposal is not prohibited by any covenant planning consent, etc.[2a]

---

[2] V.A.T.A. 1994, Sched. 8, Group 6, Note 1.
[2a] V.A.T.A. 1994, Sched. 8, Croup 6, Note (2).

Non-listed buildings in a conservation area or buildings of local interest included in a local authority's non-statutory listing are not "protected buildings" for the purposes of relief from VAT (or for other purposes). They are not listed buildings; they merely have a local significance and may be subject to a degree of protection if they are situate within conservation areas.

Use for a "relevant residential purpose" includes use as:

(1) a residence for the accommodation of children, *e.g.* a home or other institution;

(2) a residence for the accommodation, with personal care, of the elderly, the physically or mentally handicapped, or those dependent on drugs or alcohol;

(3) a hospice;

(4) a building providing residential accommodation for students or school children, *e.g.* halls of residence and dormitories;

(5) a barracks, etc., for members of the armed forces;

(6) a monastery or nunnery; or

(7) an institution which is the sole or main residence of at least 90 per cent of its residents.

Hospitals, prisons, hotels and inns are not eligible for zero rating within this category.[3]

Relevant "charitable use" is defined as use by a charity, being either or both of:

(i) use otherwise than in the course of a business;

(ii) use as a village hall or similar, in providing social or recreational facilities for a local community.[4]

9.03 In general, an "approved alteration" is an alteration for which listed building consent both:

(i) is required, and

(ii) has been obtained.[5]

In the case of buildings on Crown or Duchy land, an approved alteration is one for which listed building consent would have been required had it been situated elsewhere.[6]

If the qualifying protected building is a church and is still used as such, *any* alteration is an approved alteration.[7]

Works of repair or maintenance are never regarded as alterations or as approved alterations.[8] Also incidental alterations to the fabric of the building resulting from repair or maintenance work are excluded from the definition of approved alterations. The distinction between a work of alteration and a work of repair or maintenance has been an area of dispute in the VAT tribunals for many years and has never been fully resolved. In case of doubt, professional advice should be sought.

Where the work consists partly of approved alterations and partly of other

[3] V.A.T.A. 1994, Sched. 8, Group 5, Note 3 and Group 6, Note 3.
[4] V.A.T.A. 1994, Sched. 8, Group 5, Note 4 and Group 6, Note 3.
[5] V.A.T.A. 1994, Sched. 8, Group 6, Note 6.
[6] V.A.T.A. 1994, Sched. 8, Group 6, Note 6(c).
[7] V.A.T.A. 1994, Sched. 8, Group 6, Note 6(a).
[8] V.A.T.A. 1994, Sched. 8, Group 6, Note 6.

works, the charge must be apportioned.[9] Only the part relating to approved alterations may be zero rated. The distinction between approved and non-approved alterations is discussed further at (g) below:

The construction of a separate building within the curtilage of a qualifying protected building is specifically treated as not being an approved alteration.[9a]

EXAMPLE: Builders invoice

To:	Works at XYZ House	£	£ V.A.T.
	Approved alterations	2,000.00	Zero
	Other alterations	1,000.00	175.00
	Repairs	500.00	87.50
		3,500.00	£262.50
	VAT	262.50	
	Total	£3,762.50	

(c) Zero rating for approved alterations

Zero rating is available for:

9.04

(i) services supplied in the course of approved alterations to qualifying protected buildings, other than services of architects, surveyors, and others acting as consultants or in a supervisory capacity[10]; and

(ii) supplies of materials, etc., provided by a person also supplying services which are zero rated as in (i) above, and supplied in connection with those services.[11]

It will be seen from the above that a supply of goods in isolation is incapable of being zero rated, and that there are restrictions on the types of supplies of goods which can be zero rated. Zero rating is generally confined to supplies of materials, and other articles ordinarily installed by builders as fixtures. Specifically excluded from zero rating are supplies of fitted furniture (or materials for the construction thereof) other than kitchen furniture.[12] A VAT liability will therefore arise if, say, fitted wardrobes are provided.

Domestic electrical and gas appliances are also excluded from zero rating, other than space heaters and water heaters and various ventilation and

[9] V.A.T.A. 1994, Sched. 8, Group 6, Note 9.
[9A] V.A.T.A. 1994, Sched. 8, Group 6, Note 10.
[10] V.A.T.A. 1994, Sched. 8, Group 6, Item 2.
[11] V.A.T.A. 1994, Sched. 8, Group 5, Item 3.
[12] V.A.T.A. 1994, Sched. 8, Group 5, Note 22.

safety equipment commonly required under building regulations.[13] Carpets and carpeting material are similarly excluded from zero rating.[14]

The exclusion of zero rating for services of architects, etc., can sometimes be avoided by employing a builder to carry out the overall work on a "design and build" basis, and letting the builder hire the architect.[15] This may be disadvantageous on commercial grounds, as it breaks the contractual link between property owner and professional adviser, and may make it more difficult to obtain recompense if things go wrong.

(d) Residential and charitable buildings

9.05   Special care is needed if the zero rating depends on the use of the listed building for a relevant residential or charitable purpose, *i.e.* if the building is not designed as a dwelling or as a number of dwellings. A builder can only zero rate his supply if he supplies his services to the person or entity who intends to use the building for relevant purposes.[16]

Additionally the user must issue the builder with a certificate in a form specified by H.M. Customs and Excise. The certificate includes a declaration that the building is intended for a relevant use. It must be issued *before* building work starts to ensure zero rating for all approved alterations.[17] If the certificate is issued after a supply has been made zero rating can only be obtained on further supplies after the date of issue (unless concessionary treatment can be negotiated with H.M. Customs and Excise).

The owner of the listed building should take care before issuing a certificate, to ensure that the intended use is, indeed, a qualifying use. If an incorrect certificate is issued, a penalty equal to the amount of tax incorrectly saved can be imposed[18] and the tax will still be due. However, no penalty is due if Customs and Excise, or a VAT Tribunal, can be satisfied that there is a reasonable excuse.[19]

(e) Buildings within grounds

9.06   Special care is needed regarding ancillary buildings. Approved alterations made to the qualifying protected building itself will qualify for zero rating. Zero rating may also be available for approved alterations relating to other buildings within the grounds used in conjunction with a qualifying building.[20] However, zero rating is not available for the construction, from scratch, of such secondary buildings.[21]

If it is desired that the facilities of a qualifying listed building be

---

[13] V.A.T.A. 1994, Sched. 8, Group 5, Note 22.
[14] V.A.T.A. 1994, Sched. 8, Group 5, Note 22.
[15] Leaflet 708/2/90, Para. 11.
[16] V.A.T.A. 1994, Sched. 8, Group 5, Note 12(a).
[17] V.A.T.A. 1994, Sched. 8, Group 5, Note 12(b).
[18] V.A.T.A. 1994, s.62.
[19] V.A.T.A. 1994, s.62(3).
[20] Hardy (MAN/94/591) No. 12, 776.
[21] V.A.T.A. 1994, Sched. 8, Group 6, Note 10.

improved, it will often be preferable (from a VAT point of view) to achieve this by extending the existing building, rather than by erecting new buildings in the grounds.[22]

(f) Sale of a protected building

As indicated above, there is zero rating for the sale of a qualifying pro- **9.07** tected building, or the grant of a long lease over it, by a person who has substantially reconstructed the building.[23]

It should be noted that the sale or lease of a substantially reconstructed commercial or industrial protected building is exempt for VAT purposes. However, under certain circumstances it may be beneficial in terms of VAT recovery to convert the sale into one liable to VAT at $17\frac{1}{2}$ per cent using the option to tax (or election to waive exemption). This is a matter which applies equally to non-listed buildings, and so is not covered in this chapter. It is also an extremely complicated area, and the reader is advised to take professional advice if it may be relevant. The zero rating is only relevant where the supply is made in the course of a business, in which case it will enable the builder or developer to obtain a refund of VAT on expenses incurred in carrying out the works.

No general definition is given as to what is involved in "substantially reconstructing" a building, so this must be interpreted in terms of the general meaning of these words. In the past, H.M. Customs and Excise have been prepared to accept a building as substantially reconstructed if the cost of the works carried out (excluding any repair element) has exceeded half the estimated cost of constructing a similar building from the ground upwards.

The VAT legislation applies two additional, or secondary, tests, one of which must be met before zero rating is available. If at least 60 per cent of the cost of the works involved in carrying out the reconstruction qualifies for zero rating as described above (or would qualify, if the suppliers were VAT registered), then zero rating is available.[24]

Alternatively, zero rating will be granted if all that remains of the original listed building is the external walls and other external features of architectural or historic interest.[25] It should be borne in mind that the general test (of a substantial reconstruction having taken place) must always be met for zero rating to apply. This is scarcely likely to be a problem where the latter of the secondary tests above is relied upon. A further point to remember is that, where the supply for which zero rating is sought consists of the grant of a lease for a period in excess of 21 years, zero rating is only available for the premium or first rental payment.[26] Subsequent rental payments will be

---

[22] See, for instance, *Arbib* (LON/92/1740) No. 11, 486, upheld in the QBD [1995] S.T.C. 490] March 1995.

[23] V.A.T.A. 1994, Sched. 8, Group 6, Item 1.

[24] V.A.T.A. 1994, Sched. 8, Group 6, Note 7(a).

[25] V.A.T.A. 1994, Sched. 8, Group 6, Note 7(b).

[26] V.A.T.A. 1994, Sched. 8, Group 5, Note 14.

consideration for exempt supplies (except in the case of holiday lettings, which are excluded from exemption and so standard rated).[27]

(g) Practical points

9.08 There is often uncertainty whether the conditions of zero rating are met and, more particularly, as to the extent to which work carried out constitutes approved alterations as opposed to other alterations or works of repair or maintenance. The best way of dealing with this uncertainty is by approaching H.M. Customs and Excise for a ruling. Provided that all of the relevant facts are disclosed to H.M. Customs and Excise, a ruling that the work is zero rated will generally be honoured even if it subsequently turns out to have been incorrect.[28] Care should be taken to present the information in writing and to insist on a written ruling, so that there is evidence of the ruling and of the basis on which it was made. The application for a ruling should normally be made to the local VAT office which deals with the building contractor or the developer.

As indicated above an approved alteration means an alteration for which listed building consent was both needed and obtained. In practice, if consent is obtained, H.M. Customs and Excise generally accept that it was needed. When seeking listed building consent, therefore, it is wise to ensure that it embraces as much as possible of the work being undertaken. It is the builder's responsibility to determine the VAT liability of his work and he may well be loath to zero rate approved alterations without evidence to satisfy H.M. Customs and Excise that he was entitled to do so.

9.09 It is therefore advisable to provide the builder with copies of:

(i) either:

  (a) the entry in the relevant statutory list or schedule; or
  (b) the local authority notice issued at the time the building was listed; and

(ii) a copy of the listed building consent or the equivalent scheduled monument consent.

Whilst the proposal must be clearly stated, nevertheless the form of words used in the application for listed building consent, and in the consent itself, can often affect the likelihood of obtaining zero rating. It is often difficult to distinguish between works of alteration and works of repair or maintenance. If the consent uses words like "alteration", "improvement" and "extension", this will generally enhance the chances of obtaining zero rating. The use of words like "repair" and "replacement" tend to colour thinking in the opposite direction, and will almost invariably result in zero rating being denied.

If alterations made to a listed building are incorrectly zero rated without the protection of a ruling from H.M. Customs and Excise, the question arises of who is to bear the unexpected VAT liability which subsequently arises. If the contract for the works was expressed as being for a fixed sum of

---

[27] V.A.T.A. 1994, Sched. 9, Group 1, Note 12.
[28] *Hansard*, July 21, 1978, Col. 426 and 1978 VAT TR 278.

money, with no mention of VAT, the agreed price is taken to include VAT.[29] The legal liability to pay the tax therefore falls on the builder. Where the contract specifies a price "plus VAT if applicable", the builder has the primary liability to pay H.M. Customs and Excise, but can recover the tax from the customer.[30]

10. Churches

1. INTRODUCTION

10.01   The subject of churches within the context of listed buildings raises many interesting and, some would say, anomalous, issues. The first aspect to be addressed is "What is a church?". The answer seems to be a building in regular use for public worship, but this seemingly obvious question and rather simplistic answer becomes more complicated with the passage of time and subsequent legislation.

Churches are included within the lists of buildings of special architectural or historic interest now compiled under section 1 of the Planning (Listed Buildings and Conservation Areas) Act 1990, and contain a high proportion of the most important buildings so listed. The total number of listed building as at December 1994 was 447,043, of which approximately 3 per cent are categorised as "ecclesiastical buildings".[1]

Until 1977 a separate system of listing was used for Anglican churches, when Grade A buildings included churches of "exceptional value" and those retaining their pristine character; Grade B were more modest buildings than Grade A and were often overlaid by subsequent reconstruction, and also included Reformation buildings which were of particular importance but not exceptional; and Grade C buildings were plain buildings which were just of statutory quality. That system has now been superseded, but there are still a few of the older, unrevised, lists in use. Churches are now listed according to merit as Grade I, II*, II using the same criteria as for secular buildings.

---

[1] *English Heritage Monitor 1995.*

2. ECCLESIASTICAL EXEMPTION

The special treatment afforded to churches which are listed buildings **10.02** arises from the events leading up to the Ancient Monuments Consolidation and Amendment Act 1913, when discussions took place as to whether churches and cathedrals should be brought within the scope of that Act. At the time, arguments were advanced and assurances given by the then Archbishop of Canterbury (Archbishop Davidson) on behalf of the Church of England to the effect that the Consistory Courts through the exercise of faculty jurisdiction provided sufficient control. In that debate in 1913, culminating in section 22 of the 1913 Act, it was agreed that all church buildings which were for the time being used for ecclesiastical purposes should not be included in secular control, and this formed the origin of the term "ecclesiastical exemption" which has thereafter been embodied within the Planning Acts.

The Planning (Listed Buildings and Conservation Areas) Act 1990, section 60, continued to uphold the principle of ecclesiastical exemption from listed building control. The phrases used in section 60 of the 1990 Act which relate to proposed works to ecclesiastical buildings, *e.g.* for the demolition, alteration or extension of "any ecclesiastical building which is for the time being used for ecclesiastical purposes", and in section 60(4), for the purposes of section 7–9 of the LBA 1990, "a building shall be taken to be used for the time being for ecclesiastical purposes if it would be so used but for the works in question".

These words were brought into focus through the case of *Attorney* **10.03** *General v. Trustees of the Howard United Reform Church Bedford.*[2] The 18th century non-conformist church in Bedford had ceased to be used for public worship in April 1971, when, in the face of demolition and redevelopment of the site for offices, in May 1971 it was "listed". The church hall and rooms within the curtilage of the church continued to be used for meetings and social gatherings. The question for decision was whether it could lawfully be demolished without listed building consent, and having regard to that, further questions were posed: was it still an ecclesiastical building? and was it "for the time being used for ecclesiastical purposes", or would it have been so used "but for the works"? In March 1973 the Attorney General on the relation of Bedfordshire County Council, as local planning authority, issued a summons for declaring that the church was not within the exemption contained in section 56(1)(a) of the 1971 Act, and also issued an injunction restraining the trustees from demolishing it. Willis J. granted the declaration and held that it was neither an ecclesiastical building nor a building which would have been used for ecclesiastical purposes but for the works. The trustees gave an undertaking that they would not proceed with demolition pending the outcome of the proceedings. The Court of Appeal allowed the appeal by the trustees, and the planning authority appealed to the House of Lords, where they obtained leave to make the submission that "ecclesiastical" in the expression "ecclesiastical building" was equivalent to "Anglican". The basis of that submission was that the reason for the exception had its origins in the 1913 Act at a time when it was thought the faculty jurisdiction system of the Church of England was sufficient to pro-

---

[2] [1975] All E.R. (2) p. 337–346.

tect "ancient monuments". Their Lordships rejected that submission and noted that the 1913 Act also extended to Scotland, and the exception is included in a series of Scottish Town Planning Acts, and they were satisfied that it applied to *all* ecclesiastical buildings. The House of Lords decided that the term "ecclesiastical building" was not confined to a building belonging to the Church of England and the Howard United Reformed Church would remain an ecclesiastical building even if it fell into disuse. The House of Lords also decided that the building was not "being used for ecclesiastical purposes", since it was about to be demolished at the time when the proceedings commenced, and it could not be said that it would have been so used "but for the works" because the trustees intended to demolish the building and redevelop the site for other purposes. The reason for the decision was (according to the speech by Lord Cross) that it could only be said that an ecclesiastical building was used for ecclesiastical purposes "but for the works" if the building was only being partially demolished and that it did not apply to total demolition of a church. That speech by Lord Cross, delivered in May 1975, has exercised the minds and imagination of those seeking ways around the planning laws to avoid having to obtain listed building consent for the partial demolition of a church building. The House of Lords, in the same case, failed to answer the question posed at the outset of this chapter, namely "What is a church?", by stating it was "unnecessary and . . . unwise" to decide whether non-Christian buildings could be regarded as ecclesiastical buildings; whereas in the Court of Appeal, Lawton L.J. had left the question open as to whether synagogues, mosques, and Hindu and Buddhist temples qualified for that description, but Lord Denning M.R. had thought it sufficient that "the building must be owned by the ecclesiastical authorities—and must have some other ecclesiastical attribute marking out as ecclesiastical".[3]

Stephenson L.J., in the Court of Appeal expressed the view that "an ecclesiastical building is a building owned by a Christian church and built or used mainly for religious worship . . . " and he continued by explaining the origin of the word "ecclesia" which has for centuries meant either a Christian congregation or a place where a Christian congregation assembles. He concluded by stating "since the Reformation, it applies to the Church of England and to the different Christian churches which have come into existence in this country."

The *Howard* case established that no listed building consent is required for alteration, extension or partial demolition of a listed ecclesiastical building provided that the ecclesiastical use continued or was suspended only for the duration of the works but that listed building consent is necessary for the total demolition of an ecclesiastical building (except where it is undertaken in pursuance of a pastoral or redundancy scheme (see paragraph 10.21).

10.04   The Church of England itself decided in January 1980, through the General Synod, to appoint a Commission ("the Faculty Jurisdiction Commission") with terms of reference "to review the operation of the Faculty Jurisdiction Measure 1964 and, more generally, to consider how and in what ways the control the Church of England should monitor and, where appropriate, control in the interests both of the Church and of a wider community, the process of maintaining, altering and adapting churches in use

[3] [1974] 3 All E.R. 273 at 276.

for worship, taking account, *inter alia*, of the operation of the Inspection of Churches Measure 1955, the Pastoral Measure 1968 (and the proposed amendment), the ecclesiastical exemption and the making available of State Aid towards the cost of repair and maintenance of churches of historical and architectural interest". That Commission (under the chairmanship of the Bishop of Chichester, and known as the "Chichester Commission") reported to the General Synod of the Church of England in 1984.[4]

On the subject of ecclesiastical exemption from listed building control for churches in use, the Chichester Commission considered the exemption to be sound in principle, and subject to certain reforms in the faculty jurisdiction, beneficial both to the Church and the wider community, and should therefore be retained.

The Government was mindful of the concern of many, especially the conservation bodies, at this special privilege applying to churches, and issued in 1984 a Green Paper for consultation with interested parties entitled "The Ecclesiastical Exemption from Listed Building Control". This eventually led to a statement in the House of Lords in October 1986,[5] during the passage of the Housing and Planning Bill by Lord Skelmersdale, the then Under-Secretary to the Department of the Environment. The noble Lord sought enabling powers to make an order subject to negative resolution to restrict or exclude the operation of exemptions from listed building control as were at that time contained in section 56(1) and section 58(2) of the 1971 Act which became section 60 of the LBA 1990. He reported the acceptance by the Churches Main Committee (an ecumenical body which represents the interests of the principal Christian churches and religious denominations in secular matters of common concern) of normal listed building control over the major partial demolition of a non-Church of England church (such churches already needed consent for their total demolition), if it would materially affect the architectural or historic interest of the building. He quoted such examples as the removal of a spire, tower, or cupola or if the works were otherwise to affect the interest of the building to such an extent that its value as a listed building, or its contribution as an unlisted building in a Conservation Area, would be brought into question; but he confirmed that exemption should continue to apply to proposals which would have a lesser effect.

Lord Skelmersdale also dealt in the same speech with the possibility of **10.05** restricting the exemption to the main church building and not to ancillary buildings forming part of the church complex or within the curtilage, for which he said statutory powers would be needed. He explained the need to define what was a major partial demolition and also the need to consider those cases which arise where services had been transferred to an adjoining building, perhaps a hall or Sunday School, within the curtilage of the main church building, and then the church itself could be demolished, because it would have exemption by reason of being within the curtilage. He left scope for further discussion on this matter but stated that the Government's intention was only to use the statutory powers in respect of curtilage buildings and partial demolition of non-Church of England churches.

[4] *The Continuing Care of Churches and Cathedrals—1984.* A report on the Faculty Jurisdiction Commission.
[5] *Hansard*, October 22, 1986. Also H.L. Deb. Vol. 480; Cols. 608–611; October 13, 1986.

The terms of the agreement announced by Lord Skelmersdale resulted in the insertion of clause 58AA into the Housing and Planning Bill which was enacted in 1986 and is now contained within sub-sections (5) and (6) of section 60 of the LBA 1990, and allows the Secretary of State for National Heritage to restrict the scope of ecclesiastical exemption and to discriminate between different types of building and between different areas and buildings of different denominations.

3. EXCEPTIONS FOR ECCLESIASTICAL BUILDINGS

10.06   A building used or available for use by a minister of religion wholly or mainly as a residence from which to perform the duties of his office is not an ecclesiastical building.[6]

"In relation to the carrying out of works for alterations or extensions to a listed building, the church building shall be taken to be used for the time being for ecclesiastical purposes but for the works in question."[7] The effect of these special powers relating to churches contained in the LBA 1990 is to absolve ecclesiastical buildings from temporary listing by means of a building preservation notice[8]; to remove the control over works for the demolition of a listed building or for its alteration or extension in any manner which would affect its character as a building of special architectural or historic interest[9] of the need to obtain listed building consent[10]; and to the commitment of an offence if such works are executed in relation to a listed building without obtaining such consent.[11] A local planning authority may not by compulsory means acquire a listed ecclesiastical building which is for the time being used for ecclesiastical purposes[12] nor may it execute works which are regarded as urgently necessary for the preservation of a listed ecclesiastical building within its area[13] or take proceedings against any person causing damage to such a building under section 59 of the LBA 1990. Section 60(5) of the 1990 Act gives the Secretary of State for National Heritage powers by order to restrict or exclude some of the above exceptions, and by section 60(6) an order may:

"(a) make provision for buildings generally, for descriptions of buildings or for particular buildings;

  (b) make different provision for buildings in different areas, for buildings of different religious faiths or denominations or according to the use made of the building;

  (c) make such provision in relation to part of a building (including in particular an object or structure falling to be treated as part of the building by virtue of section 1(5)) as may be made in relation to a

---

[6] LBA 1990, s.60(3).
[7] LBA 1990, s.60(1).
[8] LBA 1990, ss.3 and 4.
[9] LBA 1990, s.7.
[10] LBA 1990, s.8.
[11] LBA 1990, s.9.
[12] LBA 1990, ss.47 and 60(1).
[13] LBA 1990, s.54.

building and make different provision for different parts of the same building;

(d) make different provision with respect to works of different descriptions or according to the extent of the works;

(e) make such consequential adaptations or modifications of the operation of any other provision of this Act or the principal Act, or of any instrument made under either of those Acts, as appear to the Secretary of State to be appropriate."

Following public consultation in 1992 the Secretaries of State for National Heritage (and for Wales) announced that an Order would be made to provide that the exemption would apply only to the Church of England and to other denominations and faiths which had set up acceptable internal systems of control embodying the principles set out in the Government's Code of Practice.[14]

The Ecclesiastical Exemption (Listed Buildings and Conservation Areas) **10.07** Order 1994 was duly made under the provisions of sections 60(5) and 75(7) of the LBA 1990 (and came into force on October 1, 1994). The Church of England had already its own procedures which were reformed under the Care of Churches and Ecclesiastical Jurisdiction Measure 1991, sections 14 and 26(1) and (2) and covered works proposed to be carried out in relation to churches other than cathedrals. Faculty Jurisdiction Rules made under this Measure came into force on March 1, 1993 (S.I. 1992 No. 2882) and set out the procedures to be followed where Anglican churches are listed (see paragraph 10.09).

The other denominations which have claimed exemption under the 1994 Order are: the Church in Wales, the Roman Catholic Church, the Methodist Church, the Baptist Church of Great Britain, the Baptist Church of Wales, and the United Reformed Church. Each of these denominations has prepared an acceptable internal system of controls which broadly follows the principles set out in the Government's Code of Practice. The arrangements will be monitored and reviewed after two years.

In a Parliamentary Answer on July 15, 1994,[15] the Secretary of State for National Heritage indicated that he proposed directions "to ensure reasonable parity of treatment between exempted and non-exempted bodies", which would bring within conservation area control tombstones, memorials and monuments not covered by the ecclesiastical exemption but below the current control limit of 113 cubic metres. This extension of control will relate to those tombstones, etc., erected before January 1, 1925. The requirements of sections 7 to 9 of the 1990 Act do not apply to works for the demolition of a redundant building in pursuance of a pastoral or redundancy scheme within the meaning of the Pastoral Measure 1983 when exemption was given by section 2 of the Redundant Churches and other Religious Buildings Act 1969 (see paragraph 10.21).

Under the Ancient Monuments and Archaeological Areas Act 1979 any ecclesiastical building for the time being used for ecclesiastical purposes may not be scheduled as an ancient monument. (See Chapter 8, paragraph 8.03.)

---

[14] PPG 15, para. 8.3.
[15] [1994] J.P.L. 799–800.

4. PLANNING PERMISSION FOR CHURCHES

10.08   In spite of the special privileges relating to listed churches, planning legislation in this country applies in general to ecclesiastical buildings, in the sense that planning permission is required for any development of an ecclesiastical building which amounts to "development" within the requirements of section 55 of the T.C.P.A. 1990. Planning permission is required, for example, for the building of a new church or for an extension, change of use, or other alteration which materially affects the external appearance of the existing church and which is not permitted under the Town and Country Planning (General Permitted Development Order) 1995, or, in the case of a Church of England building, covered by a scheme of redundancy made under the Pastoral Measure 1983 (see paragraph 10.21). Local planning authorities are required by the Planning (Listed Buildings and Conservation Areas) Act 1990 (section 16(2)) to have special regard to the desirability of preserving listed buildings and their setting when considering whether or not to grant planning permission for development. In cases where development affects Grade I or Grade II* listed buildings or their settings, the local planning authority must consult with English Heritage before granting permission.[16] The same consultation procedure applies to churches grade A, B and C in the older lists, and also for any other church (whether Grade II or unlisted) which has received a grant from English Heritage or previously the Department of the Environment, and it is a condition of such a grant that the express approval of English Heritage must be obtained for any subsequent internal or external works which would have a significant effect on the fabric or character of the building. It is worth noting that in assessing planning applications for extensions to existing churches or chapels, the site is often of greater antiquity than the existing building, and may contain remains of an earlier church. Archaeological advice should be obtained at an early stage before a scheme for extension or any building works within the curtilage are planned. The Church of England in each diocese has available the services of a Diocesan archaeological consultant, but other denominations may also be required to provide an archaeological assessment in support of their planning application in accordance with the advice contained in PPG 16.

5. THE FACULTY JURISDICTION OF THE CHURCH OF ENGLAND

10.09   The faculty jurisdiction has its provenance in a distinct system of Church Courts initiated in England by William I in 1072,[17] at which time the major responsibility for property and family law was vested in the Church. In 1857 many of these responsibilities were transferred to secular courts, but the Church Courts retained, *inter alia*, special control over churches within the jurisdiction of the diocesan bishop (or archbishop). Reverting to

---

[16] Direction made by Secretary of State under s.15(5) and para. 82 of Circular 8/87. This remains in force as a "direction" until new directions are issued.
[17] *An Introduction to Legal History*, J.H. Baker, 1979.

the debate in 1913 (see paragraph 10.02); a system was evolved by the Church of England of having diocesan advisory committees for the care of churches, first on a voluntary basis and later, in 1938, in statutory form. Various Measures[18] have been introduced and are now an established and well recognised part of the system whereby the Church of England exercises control over alterations—whether internal or external—and repairs to its buildings. Since 1955 the system has included "quinquennial inspections" of all its churches, and with it has emerged a growing knowledge of its historic churches, their architectural contents and value, and their condition. In the 1970s various inquiries and reviews were undertaken into the subject of repairs and controls over places of worship, and in February 1977 the agreement for State Aid was endorsed by the General Synod of the Church of England, since which time public funded grants have been available, for some listed churches and churches in conservation areas (see paragraph 10.27) [—under the Historic Buildings and Ancient Monuments Act 1953, section 4 (for churches in use) and under the Town and Country Planning (Amendment) Act 1972, section 10—as now contained in section 77 of the LBA 1990—for Churches in Conservation Areas]. These powers relating to churches did not extend to cathedrals, for which separate provision is now made under the Care of Cathedrals Measure 1990 (see paragraph 10.24).

Within the Church of England it is illegal to add to or alter the fabric or contents of churches and churchyards or to change their use without prior diocesan authorisation. The range of matters which require a faculty varies from redecoration or repairs to the sale of moveable objects and the demolition of the fabric.

The concern for listed church buildings in recent years has led many dioceses to exercise their faculty system on similar lines to those applicable to secular listed buildings. This practice was given statutory authority by the Faculty Jurisdiction Rules 1992 (S.I. 1992, no. 2882) which gave a more democratic format to works proposed affecting listed churches. Under Rule 12(3), where it appears to the Chancellor of the Diocese that works for which a faculty is sought: **10.10**

(a) involve alterations to or extension of a church, which is listed under the LBA 1990, to such an extent as is likely to affect its character as a building of special architectural or historic interest, or

(b) affect the archaeological importance of the church or archaeological remains existing within the church or its curtilage; or

(c) involve demolition affecting the exterior of an unlisted church in a conservation area,

The Chancellor shall direct that English Heritage, the local planning authority and any national amenity societies as he deems fit, shall be specially cited.

The general citation of the proposed works shall be displayed in a prominent and visible position outside the church for a period of 28 days, and

[18] A Measure is the name given to ecclesiastical legislation under the Church of England's statutes and has the force of law and the same status as an Act of Parliament. The system is operated by the General Synod, and then proceeds to Parliament under procedures established by the Church of England (Assembly) Powers Act 1919.

shall be published in a newspaper circulating in the locality within 14 days of the Chancellor giving the direction. Provision is made within the Rules for objections to be made, and for these to be heard by the Chancellor.

A further set of Rules (Faculty Jurisdiction (Injunctions and Restoration Orders) Rules 1992)[19] were brought into force on March 1, 1993 and conferred powers upon the Chancellor of any Diocese of the Church of England to grant an injunction to restrain persons from carrying out unauthorised works to a church and to make a restoration order requiring steps to be taken to restore the church, or its churchyard, or some named article belonging to the church.

The Church of England faculty system has been tried, tested, and more recently revised, and although it has not met with universal approval,[20] as an alternative method of dealing with the alteration, extension, or partial demolition of churches within its care, it has been regarded by many as being superior to, and more far reaching than, the secular planning system.

There have been several cases where the ecclesiastical courts have insisted that the power to grant a faculty should be exercised, in relation to listed churches, on similar principles to those applicable in listed building control. Mr Peter Boydell, Q.C. in *Re St Mary's Banbury* (1985) 2 All E.R. 611, as Chancellor, observed that "any proposal to alter the structure of such a building must be approached with the same care and be subject to the same detailed consideration as would be necessary if churches were to lose their ecclesiastical immunity . . . ". In *Re St Stephen's Walbrook* (1987) 2 All E.R. 578, the Court of Ecclesiastical Causes Reserved ruled that "the fact that an ecclesiastical building is listed is a relevant consideration in considering whether to grant a faculty permitting alterations to it . . . " [the Chancellor must have] "full regard to all the circumstances including the interest of the community as a whole in the special architectural or historic attributes of the building and to the desirability of preserving the building and any features of special architectural or historic interest which it possesses."

10.11 The Care of Churches and Ecclesiastical Jurisdiction Measure 1991[21] requires that in every diocese there shall continue to be a Diocesan Advisory Committee to advise on matters affecting places of worship. The DAC must include within its membership persons with knowledge of history, development, and use of church buildings; of Church of England liturgy and worship; architecture, archaeology, art and history, and the care of historic buildings and their contents.

Section 17 of the Measure deals with faculties for demolition of churches, and in sub-section 5 requires that a consistory court shall not grant a faculty in a case where a church is listed or is situated in a conservation area unless the registrar has given notice in writing to:

    (i) the Secretary of State;
    (ii) the local planning authority concerned;
    (iii) English Heritage; and
    (iv) the national amenity societies.

The Diocesan Chancellor, acting as a judge of the consistory court, is

---

[19] S.I. 1992, No. 2884.
[20] *e.g. Minority report in Chichester Commission Report* by Marcus Binney, 1984.
[21] s.2(12) of 1991 Measure.

obliged to consider the advice of these various bodies, and the registrar has to give notice to the Royal Commission on the Historical Monuments of England ("RCHM") providing at least one month before demolition or alteration begins to enable officers of the RCHM to record the church.

The consistory court shall not grant a faculty where demolition is considered necessary, unless it is satisfied, after consultation with the DAC, that when the proposed repair, alteration or reconstruction is completed, the demolition will not materially affect the external or internal appearance of the church or the architectural, archaeological, artistic or historic character of the church.

In the case of emergency partial demolition of churches, the Diocesan Chancellor must be satisfied, in the case of a listed church or one within a conservation area, that it was not practicable to secure safety or health or, as the case may be, the preservation of the building by works of repair or works for affording temporary support or shelter, and that the works to be carried out were limited to the minimum measures immediately necessary. The local planning authority must be given notice in writing describing the urgent works, as soon as is practicable after the works have been carried out, and a copy of the Chancellor's instrument authorising the works shall be sent to the Council for the Care of Churches and to the local planning authority.

In a case[22] brought under section 17 of the Care of Churches and Ecclesiastical Jurisdiction Measure 1991 to demolish a listed building, the Chancellor of the Southwark Consistory Court held that the court needed to know what the pastoral needs of the parish were, what the importance of the listed building was in terms of its architectural or historic interest, what contribution the building made to the area in which it stood, what the cost of the preservation of the building was likely to be, and what possibility, where the church had been almost totally destroyed, there was of rebuilding the church in anything like its original condition. In that case, faculties were granted to demolish the remains of the church tower and north and east walls of St Barnabas' Church, Dulwich, following its serious damage by fire in December 1992. The Chancellor advised the court to begin its consideration of any application by taking into account and giving considerable weight to the role of a church as a local centre of worship and mission and then to go on to approach the proposal with the same care and subject to the same detailed consideration as would be given to an application for listed building consent.

The Church of England has introduced its own Code of Practice 1993 as **10.12** an amplification of the Faculty Jurisdiction Rules 1992 and Faculty Jurisdiction (Injunctions and Restoration Orders) Rules 1993. The Code of Practice recommends parishes to take account of Government advice, as subsequently contained in PPG 15, paragraph 8.4, on repairs and new works, and also of English Heritage's policy statement on "New Work in Historic Churches". Parishes are advised to consult the local planning authority and relevant national amenity societies and English Heritage, if it appears that they will have to be approached later under the terms of the 1992 Rules. All cases will need to go to the Chancellor of the diocese if they involve alterations to, or extension of a listed church to such an extent as is likely to

---

[22] *The Times*, January 20, 1994.

affect its character as a building of special architectural or historic interest; those proposals which affect the archaeological importance of the church or of remains within its curtilage; and those works which involve demolition affecting the exterior of an unlisted church in a conservation area (in this context "demolition" includes "partial demolition"). As we have seen earlier, proposals involving total or partial demolition of a listed church will be discussed with the local planning authority, the national amenity societies and English Heritage.

The Code covers the importance of church archaeology, in relation to the fabric of the church, both above and below ground, together with its historic setting. Having finalised the proposal and passed a resolution to proceed, the parochial church council (PPC) should then seek all consents required under the secular planning option. Certain matters must be referred to the Council for the Care of Churches, which Council may in turn apply to the Chancellor to give evidence in any case it considers appropriate. Objections to a faculty petition may be received from residents of the parish, or from these on the church electoral roll, the Archdeacon, the PCC, the local planning authority, any national amenity society, and any other person or body designated by the Chancellor.

Whilst the "guiding principles" point out that churches exist for the purpose of "the worship of God and the mission of the church", but when considering whether to grant a faculty, the Chancellor will have regard to the desirability of preserving a listed building or its setting, preserving or enhancing the character or appearance of a conservation area, and preserving archaeological remains which are of national importance. Where a church is listed there is a strong presumption against change when it would adversely affect its character as a building of special architecture or historic interest. In a case affecting St Luke's Church, Maidstone, which came before the Court of Arches[23] (see paragraph 10.13) it was stated that in order to rebut that presumption, there had to be evidence of sufficient weight to show a necessity for such a change for some compelling reason, which could include the pastoral well-being of the church. Whether the church was listed or not, a Chancellor should always have in mind not only the religious interests but also the aesthetic, architectural and communal interests relevant to the church in question.

10.13   If demolition is proposed and the church is listed or is situated in a conservation area, the Diocesan Registrar must give notice to the Secretary of State for the Environment,[24] English Heritage, the local planning authority and the relevant national amenity societies. The Chancellor may consider works for partial demolition which are part of a larger programme of repair, alteration or reconstruction but which would not materially affect the church's internal or external appearance or architectural, archaeological, artistic or historic character. There is an appeal procedure which is to the Court of Arches (for the province of Canterbury) and the Chancery Court of York (for the province of York) and a final appeal to the Privy Council.[25]

[23] *The Times*, October 7, 1994. The Court of Arches is an appeal body for the Canterbury province (see para. 10.13).

[24] Circular 20/92, dealing with departmental responsibilities of DNH and DOE.

[25] *The Care of Church and Ecclesiastical Jurisdiction Measure, Code of Practice, article in Law and Practice*, by Dr Richard Morrice. 1993.

6. NON-ANGLICAN CHURCHES

The existence of the system of exemption from listed building control **10.14**
and the way it has evolved has been heavily influenced by the Church of
England on the strength of its own faculty jurisdiction procedures. It has,
however, benefited the non-Anglican churches by conferring on them the
same exemptions but without them having any comparable machinery to
the faculty jurisdiction. To a large extent this has also been influenced by
the fact that until relatively recent times the other denominations (or the
non-Anglican churches) were not expected to possess buildings of listable
quality. Figures available for the end of 1994[26] showed 16,303 listed Anglican churches (of which approximately 3,000 were listed Grade I), but only
about 1,200 listed non-Anglican churches.

Few non-Anglican church authorities until recently had procedures and
safeguards remotely equivalent to the faculty jurisdiction, and there have
been many instances where buildings have been under threat, or even lost,
without consultation in the public arena and without their owners having
had to follow the procedures of listed building control. An example of such a
case was produced by the Roman Catholic church authorities in Liverpool
in 1981, when it was proposed to demolish the Church of St Francis Xavier,
leaving only the tower, the spire and the ornate Sodality Chapel. This 19th-
century church which was listed as a Grade II building, was designed by
Scholes, an important Catholic architect; it was not only a landmark in the
area, but also it contained a fine interior and splendid fittings. The scheme
drawn up by the Roman Catholic diocese would have demolished the body
of the church and redeveloped the site for sheltered housing. The fact that
only part of the building was to be demolished led the church authorities
(with the apparent concurrence of the local authority and the Department of
the Environment) to the view that they benefited from ecclesiastical
exemption and that no listed building consent was required. SAVE Britain's
Heritage took up the case and threatened prosecution if demolition began
before listed building consent had been obtained, arguing that the reasoning
of the House of Lords in the Howard United Reformed Church case (see
paragraph 10.03) extended to cases where demolition, although not total,
was sufficiently substantial to alter or remove the identity of the building.
Circular 23/77 referred to the *Howard* case and stated that "partial demolition" was limited to works which left the identity of the original building
substantially intact. In the event, in the St Francis Xavier case, there was
considerable opposition to the plans for the site, including forceful objection from the Victorian Society, and eventually the Roman Catholic authorities withdrew their proposals and decided that the church would be kept
and essential repairs carried out to allow for it to remain in use.

At or about the same time two other listed church buildings were demo- **10.15**
lished without any application for listed building consent; one was Jesmond
Methodist Church in Newcastle-upon-Tyne (Grade II) and the other was the
auditorium to the Third Church of Christ Scientist in Curzon Street, London, which was demolished, leaving only the facade. There are reports of
interiors of other listed church buildings having been gutted or sold off (or
worse, hacked to bits) for their timber value. In 1986 a former Huguenot

---

[26] *English Heritage Monitor* 1995.

chapel in Fournier Street, Spitalfields[27]—then used as a mosque—had its galleries, panelling, Georgian pews and their fittings, reduced to little pieces by a chain saw, without any record being kept.

Examples such as these had all played a part in the review by the Department of the Environment of "ecclesiastical exemption" in 1984 (see paragraph 10.04) and, amongst other aspects, English Heritage recommended that the buildings of non-Anglican churches should only be treated differently from other secular buildings to the extent that they made suitable new arrangements similar to those of the Anglican church.

Arising from an issue related to a proposal for the partial demolition of a Grade II* Central Chapel in York (which also met with considerable local and national opposition), the governing body of that church sent a "memorial" to the Methodist Conference in 1987[28] "to consider the church's best response to the problems caused by the listing of so many Methodist Church buildings and the destructive way in which such listings can affect the present and future alike of the church, both locally and nationally". As a response, the Property Division of the Methodist Church set up a working party of people experienced in architectural and historic matters, as well as in the life of the church. At the time of the Methodist Church's working party's report there were over 700 listed buildings on their stocks, and a further 847 in conservation areas. The conclusion of the working party was that, for the great majority of their churches, having listed building status presented no obstacles to the work of the church. In the report which arose from that study entitled *A charge to keep?* the effects of ecclesiastical exemption are explained, but it also refers to the agreement of 1986 with the Under-Secretary for the Department of the Environment that partial demolitions which would materially affect the architectural or historic interest of the church should require listed building consent. The Methodist Church, through its Property Division, and indeed all the non-Anglican churches, undertook by this informal agreement to consult their local authorities and, in England, English Heritage, before undertaking any significant external works which remained exempt from listed building control.

Under ecclesiastical exemption all churches were at that time free to alter the inside of a listed building without reference to the local planning authority. In the case of the Methodist Church, such alterations still required the approval of the Property Division and might have been withheld if it was thought that the interior ought to be preserved. Many of the 19th-century chapels owned by the non-conformist churches have especially fine interiors, which are in contrast with their rather plain and austere exteriors. There developed a body of opinion in the 1980s which believed that the freedom of these churches to alter their interiors without formal consent was no longer tenable, and that the liturgical reasons which had been used to justify the exemption from control could no longer be sustained.

Advice on this aspect is contained in paragraph 8.11 of PPG 15, but for churches which qualify for exemption under the Ecclesiastical Exemption (Listed Buildings and Conservation Areas) Order 1994[29], the decision will rest with the particular denomination. In other "non-exempt" church buildings, these internal alterations will be assessed by the local planning auth-

[27] Letter in *The Times*, October 20, 1986, from Chairman of SAVE.
[28] *A Charge to Keep*—A Methodist response to listed buildings and conservation.
[29] S.I. 1994, 1771.

ority on their architectural or historic merits. The PPG gives further advice on the subject of proposals for re-ordering a church interior.[30] The retention of some examples of the replaced furnishings, and other materials such as panelling, should be retained and re-used where possible within the building, but otherwise offered for re-use in a similar context, rather than destroyed.

Paragraph 8.12 of PPG 15 sets out a list of "general considerations" to **10.16** which local planning authorities are advised to give "due weight as material considerations", *i.e.* whether the changes to church interiors are proposed:

(i) are necessitated by a change in the worship needs of the congregation;

(ii) are necessitated by an increase or a reduction in congregation size;

(iii) are directed at accommodating other activities within the building to help ensure its continued viability primarily as a place of worship;

(iv) would involve substantial structural changes, *e.g.* subdivision of important existing spaces;

(v) would involve the removal or destruction of important fixtures and fittings, or are more in the nature of a reversible re-ordering of internal features;

(vi) would involve disturbance of archaeologically important remains below ground.

Modifications were made to the Standing Orders of the Methodist Church at its Conference in 1990 requiring a register to be kept of all chapels, ancillary premises and manses which are officially listed as having architectural or historic interest; instructing the appropriate Methodist district authority when approving any scheme involving a listed building to take into account the significance of its being listed, and before offering a listed building for sale for a secular use to consider the practicality of removing memorials. These were reinforced by further Standing Orders, approved by Conference in June 1994, which, amongst other things, authorised the appointment of a Listed Buildings Advisory Committee in support of the Church's claim to retain ecclesiastical exemption.

In November 1987, the Roman Catholic Bishops' Conference responded to the need to introduce proposals for the care and maintenance of their listed churches (of which there are about 450 in the Roman Catholic Church in the United Kingdom) and churches in conservation areas, by recommending that each diocese should keep an up-to-date register of church buildings that are (a) listed, or (b) in a designated conservation area. Each diocesan finance committee or other body responsible for a listed building was required to have submitted to a specialist diocesan advisory body proposals for maintenance, alterations and decoration of such buildings. All churches or other ecclesiastical buildings in the care of the Roman Catholic Church in England and Wales are now required to be inspected on a minimum five yearly basis.

A central register of listed buildings belonging to the Roman Catholic Church is now kept by the National Catholic Directory, and is compiled by the Committee for Church Art and Architecture. The Bishops' Conference

---

[30] PPG 15, para. 8.11.

decided, in 1989, to create an Art and Architecture Department in each diocese comprising of experts in church building history, architectural practice and pastoral liturgy, and those churches which contain significant works of art should be re-ordered with particular sensitivity, and where appropriate, in consultation with England Heritage. In November 1990 it was agreed by the Bishops' Conference that a sub-committee for Catholic Heritage in Art and History should be formed under the auspices of the Church Art and Architecture Committee, and at the same time a sub-committee was set up to deal with the care of Catholic cathedrals.

The United Synagogue was founded in 1870 and owns the freehold of many fine synagogues in London[31], and due to a combination of declining congregations and the expense of maintaining large buildings, is under pressure to realise its assets and sell off some buildings. In 1987–88 the East London Synagogue in Stepney Green (1877) had been sold to a property developer, and before it could be listed much of the decoration and fittings had been destroyed. Other listed synagogues are under threat and some have been converted into mosques. Such conversions leave the shell intact, but the interior features such as a niche or platform for the ark, the galleries or stained glass, are often stripped. The Jewish community is beginning to be concerned about its heritage in this country as contained in its synagogues and arranged several conferences in 1990–91 to address this problem of building conservation. These are in the order of 30 listed Jewish synagogues.[32]

7. CODE OF PRACTICE

10.17   Under the rules first introduced following public consultation in February 1992, the formal system is now in force[33], whereby for those denominations which possess acceptable internal procedures embodying the principles set out in the Government's Code of Practice, all works for the demolition of a listed ecclesiastical building or for its alteration or extension in any manner which would affect its character as a building of special architectural or historic interest, or works for the demolition of an unlisted ecclesiastical building in a conservation area, may continue to enjoy ecclesiastical exemption and shall be submitted by the local congregation or minister for prior approval of a body which is independent of the local congregation or minister or community proposing the works.

Amongst the factors which this independent "decision-making" body must take into account is the desirability of preserving historic church buildings and the importance of protecting features of architectural merit and historic interest. The "decision-making" body should include or take advice from persons having expert knowledge of historic church buildings.

There should be consultation in the decision-making process with the local planning authority, English Heritage/CADW and the national ame-

---

[31] *Synagogues—Conservation Bulletin, English Heritage*, June 1991.
[32] *English Heritage Monitor 1995.*
[33] Ecclesiastical Exemption (Listed Buildings and Conservation Areas) Order 1994.

nity societies, and normally a period of at least 28 days should be allowed in which these consultees may comment on the proposal. A notice describing the proposed works should be posted on the building in a prominent position outside the building and a similar notice published in a local newspaper inviting comments during the same 28 day period. In the case of demolition, the RCHM should be notified. Any representations received as a result of this publicity should be taken into account before the decision is made, and, along with other factors, are the desirability of preserving historic church buildings and the importance of protecting features of architectural merit and historic interest. Details of the Code of Practice for denominations' internal control system are set out in paragraph 8.4 of PPG 15.

There should be a clear and fair system for settling disputes between the local congregation or community and the decision-making body, and suitable arrangements are expected to be made for dealing with breaches of control, including provision for reinstatement of works which have been carried out without consent. The consultation document expects each church body to ensure that its system is properly enforced and monitored and the Department of National Heritage will wish to discuss these arrangements with them. The Code of Practice will be reviewed two years after making the Order to consider whether it has been successful in securing the proper preservation of historic church buildings. English Heritage wish to be consulted on all works to listed churches in London and all works to Grade I and II* churches elsewhere in the country, and also all works involving demolition of listed churches of any grade in the rest of the country.[34]

10.18 There have always been doubts about the status of buildings within the curtilage of an ecclesiastical building in relation to its exemption from listed building control. PPG 15 (paragraph 8.6) explains the scope of the exemption for those denominations and faiths which have adopted the Code of Practice. The exemption applies to "any church building'" (defined in the PPG as a building whose primary use is as a place of worship); "any object or structure within a church building"; "any object or structure fixed to the exterior of a church building unless the object or structure is itself a listed building", and "any object or structure within the curtilage of a church building which, although not fixed to that building, forms part of the land, unless the object or structure is itself a listed building." "Curtilage buildings" are thus exempt from control if the ecclesiastical building is exempt under the Order.

For those churches or denominations which have not qualified for exemption under the Order, their places of worship will be subject to the normal—secular—listed building and conservation area controls, as from October 1, 1994. Works begun or contracted for before this date will be regarded as exempt. The Secretary of State will continue to have the power to bring within normal listed building or conservation area controls (by a further Order) any individual ecclesiastical building where it seems likely that potentially damaging works will be carried out without the necessary authorisation having been obtained under the "exemption procedures", and without legal sanctions being available internally to the denomination.

---

[34] Circular 8/87, para. 82.

8. CHURCHES IN CONSERVATION AREAS

10.19   The powers to control demolition of buildings within a conservation area are contained within section 74 of the Planning (Listed Buildings and Conservation Areas) Act 1990. Section 74(1) states that "a building in a conservation area shall not be demolished without the consent of the appropriate authority" and under the Act is referred to as "conservation area consent".

There are certain cases to which section 74 does not apply and these are set out in section 75(1) of the LBA 1990, and include:

(a) listed buildings;

(b) ecclesiastical buildings which are for the time being used for ecclesiastical purposes; and

(c) buildings which are scheduled as monuments under section 1 of the Ancient Monuments and Archaeological Areas Act 1979.

This section includes any other buildings which the Secretary of State may direct as may be specified under section 75(2) of the LBA 1990, and according to paragraph 8.10 of PPG 15 it is intended that conservation area control will extend to all memorials, monuments and tombstones erected before 1925, and will be covered by a direction made under this section. This will apply only to those churches and denominations which have not qualified for exemption under the "Code of Practice" (see paragraph 8.4 of PPG 15) and paragraph 10.17 above.

Under section 75(7) of the LBA 1990, the Secretary of State may by order provide for restricting or excluding the operation of subsection (1)(b) in such cases as may be specified in the order. These may:

(a) make provision for buildings generally, for descriptions of building or for particular buildings;

(b) make different provision for buildings in different areas, for buildings of different religious faiths or denominations or according to the use made of the building;

(c) make such provision in relation to a part of a building, including, in particular, an object or structure falling, to be treated as part of the building by virtue of section 1(5) as may be made in relation to a building and make different provision for different parts of the same building;

(d) make different provision with respect to works of different descriptions or according to the extent of the works;

(e) make such consequential adaptations or modifications of the operation of any other provision of this Act or the principal Act, or of any instrument made under either of those Acts, as appear to the Secretary of State to be appropriate.

Section 75(2) of the LBA 1990 gives powers for the Secretary of State to direct that section 74 shall not apply to any description of buildings specified in the direction and those powers of direction may be given either to an individual local planning authority or to local planning authorities generally (section 75(3)) LBA 1990. As in the case of ecclesiastical exemption (see paragraph 10.06), a building used by a minister of religion wholly or mainly as a residence from which to perform his duties of office is not treated as an ecclesiastical building (section 75(5)) LBA 1990.

The various exceptions to the conservation area code are included in the Town and Country Planning (Listed Buildings and Conservation Areas) Regulations 1990 and are set out in full in Chapter 3 and in relation to churches, are contained in the Ecclesiastical Exemption (Listed Buildings and Conservation Areas) Order 1994 (S.I. 1994 No. 1771). So far as they relate to churches, in addition to excluding from conservation area control the two categories referred to above, *i.e.* listed buildings and ecclesiastical buildings which are for the time being used for ecclesiastical purposes, the 1990 Regulations also exclude "a redundant building (within the meaning of the Pastoral Measure 1983) or part of such a building where demolition is in pursuance of a pastoral or redundancy scheme (within the meaning of that Measure)" (see paragraph 10.20).

9. DEMOLITION OF CHURCHES UNDER THE PASTORAL MEASURE

The exemption from secular listed building control under "ecclesiastical **10.20** exemption" is completely separate from the proposals to demolish a redundant church which has been declared redundant under a Pastoral Measure.[35] A redundant church is a consecrated church belonging to the Church of England which has been formally declared redundant because it is no longer needed for worship.

The background to this subject[36] arises from the recommendations from a committee under the chairmanship of Lord Bridges in 1960 with the charge of preserving, in the interest of the nation and the Church of England, those churches of historical and archaeological interest or architectural quality which are no longer required for regular worship. In 1968 a Pastoral Measure established a Fund (known as the Redundant Churches Fund[37]) with the same objectives as were set out in the Bridges Commission and applied to churches for which no suitable alternative use could be found. Consideration of redundancy and alternative use, and vesting of churches in the Fund, is now carried out under procedures laid down under the Pastoral Measure 1983. The Fund is financed jointly by the Department of National Heritage (which contributes 70 per cent of the grant aid) and the Church Commissioners (which contribute 30 per cent of the grant aid) and the system operates on a system of five yearly orders. In the Order made under the Redundant Churches Fund Order 1989, which came into force on April 1, 1989, for the period until March 31, 1994; the aggregate amount of grants that might be paid under the 1989 Order did not exceed £8,700,000. In February 1994 the Secretary of State for National Heritage announced funding of £7.2 million for the Fund over the period 1994–97. Almost 300 churches had been vested in the Fund, and its anticipated annual expenditure was £2.2 million for 1994/95, and £2.5 million for the following two

---

[35] *The Redundant Churches Fund—Facts about the Fund*, 2nd. ed.
[36] *Churches in Retirement*, published by Redundant Churches Fund 1990.
[37] The name of the Fund was changed to the Churches Conservation Trust—April 1994.

years. The Fund's activities are confined to England. The principal aim of the Fund is to conserve and not to restore the buildings in its charge.

10. DECLARATION OF REDUNDANCY— PROCEDURE

10.21   There is a lengthy procedure to be followed before a declaration of redundancy of an Anglican church can be prepared by the Diocesan Pastoral Committee for submission to the Bishop. The committee must first seek the views of the Council for Places of Worship and obtain from them an assessment of the historical and architectural qualities of the building. After consultation with "interested parties" (such as the incumbent, the patron, the parochial church council, the archdeacon, the rural dean and the local planning authority), the Diocesan Pastoral Committee decides whether the proposal should go ahead, and then submits draft proposals to the diocesan bishop, who, if he approves, forwards them to the Church Commissioners for the preparation of a draft Pastoral Scheme to give effect to the proposals. There is still an opportunity for representations to the Church Commissioners to be made about the draft scheme, but if they decide to confirm the scheme it is eventually signed by the Bishop, sealed by the Commissioners and then receives the Royal Assent. After the declaration of redundancy, the church passes into the ownership of the Diocesan Board of Finance and is closed for regular worship. In some cases the Pastoral Scheme will provide for a future use of the church, whereas in other cases the church goes into what is known as a "waiting period" of not less than a year and not more than three years, during which time its care and maintenance is the responsibility of the Diocesan Board of Finance. This gives the Church Commissioners another opportunity to consult about the historic and architectural qualities of the church and it gives the Diocesan Redundant Churches Uses Committee the opportunity of exploring suitable uses for the building. If, after this extensive exercise, the search for a suitable use is unsuccessful, the church can either be vested in the Redundant Churches Fund (the name of which was changed to The Churches Conservation Trust in April 1994), or the Church Commissioners are obliged to issue a scheme for its demolition.

Since the procedures came into operation on the April 1, 1969, 1,468[38] churches have been declared redundant; 787 churches have been found alternative uses, 280 have been taken into the care of the Churches Conservation Trust, and 310 have been demolished. Once a building is vested in the Trust, the Trust becomes the owner and takes over the full responsibility for its care and maintenance. The Trust may authorise occasional uses of a redundant church (which remains consecrated), but its prime objective is to preserve, with public and church money, redundant churches of historic and architectural merit in the interest of the nation and the Church of England. When a church has been declared redundant under the Pastoral Measure, its total or partial demolition is exempt from listed building control by virtue of section 60(7) of the LBA 1990, and from conservation area control by a direction under section 75(2) of that Act.

---

[38] *English Heritage Monitor 1995.*

In a statement to the House of Lords in October 1986 (see paragraph **10.22**
10.04), Lord Skelmersdale also announced that the Church of England had
agreed to greater consultation with the Department of the Environment in
relation to historic churches, and particularly those which it proposed to
demolish under the Pastoral Measure 1983. The Church Commissioners
have agreed always to ask the Secretary of State for the Environment
whether he wished to hold a non-statutory local inquiry if there were
reasoned objections to the proposal by English Heritage, the Advisory Board
for Redundant Churches, the local planning authority, or a national amenity society. The Church Commissioners have undertaken to accept a
recommendation from the Secretary of State following such an inquiry that
the church was of sufficient importance to be vested in the Churches Conservation Trust or to make further efforts to find an alternative use for the
building before using the powers of the Pastoral Measure to demolish. In
considering what recommendation to make, the Secretary of State for the
Environment will take into account the financial implications of retaining
the church building as well as the architectural and historic interest of the
church and other planning and social factors, and will consult with the Secretary of State for National Heritage.[39]

In a review[40] of the Redundant Churches Fund (as it was then known) in
March 1990, Richard Wilding made several recommendations, one of which
included "consideration of an independent charitable trust to look after
redundant churches and chapels not belonging to the Church of England,
financed partly by Government and partly by outside sources". In June
1993, the Secretary of State for National Heritage inaugurated the Historic
Chapels Trust which covers the interests of preserving the best of Roman
Catholic and non-conformist buildings which have no continued ecclesiastical use. This follows from the formation of The Chapel's Society in September 1988.

11. ACQUISITION OF CHURCH LAND

Section 86 of the 1990 Act covers the subject of notices served under the **10.23**
Acquisition of Land Act 1981 in cases where a notice is required to be
served on the owner of land and that land is ecclesiastical property. This
section is limited to ecclesiastical property of the Church of England and all
notices are required to be served on the Church Commissioners. Notices
covered by this section include those required to accompany an application
for listed building consent (section 11), those involving the validity of certain orders, decisions, and directions (sections 62 and 63) and the exercise of
powers relating to Crown land (section 83). The fee simple of any ecclesiastical property shall be treated as being vested in the Church Commissioners, and any compensation is paid to them rather than the local
church authorities, except where the land is diocesan glebe land (section
86(3)), as defined in the Endowments and Glebe Measure 1976.

---

[39] PPG 15 para. 8.15.
[40] *English Heritage Monitor* 1991.

12. CATHEDRALS

10.24   Cathedrals (and also a few churches and chapels which are known as "peculiars")[41] enjoy the benefits of ecclesiastical exemption but are outside the scope of the faculty jurisdiction and are *sui generis*. A Cathedral of the Church of England (of which there are 42) has its own statutes under the provision of the Cathedrals' Measures, and their administration is vested in the Dean (or Provost) and Cathedral Chapter, who are answerable only to the visitation of the Bishop or Archbishop. In 1981 the Cathedrals' Advisory Commission for England was set up by the General Synod in the expectation that all major proposals affecting cathedrals would be referred to it. There was some reluctance by some cathedral chapters to consult the Commission and at the same time there was an increasing concern being voiced by amenity societies and conservationists that this freedom from control created a gap in a system of accountability for works affecting cathedrals and their precincts, and should not be allowed to continue. Several cathedrals demonstrated their independence by setting up Local Advisory Committees (on some of which the Cathedrals Advisory Commission was represented).

The changing role of cathedrals in the wake of the growth of tourism and in their patronage of the arts, coupled with their need to respond to new forms of worship, have brought about changes and alterations on which many felt there was a need for independent, objective and expert advice. These issues were covered in a report of the Faculty Jurisdiction Commission published in 1984 (the Chichester Commission), wherein it was recommended that each cathedral church should be required to appoint a Fabric Advisory Committee to assist the Chapter in the care and maintenance of the fabric of the cathedral and its contents, and to advise on any proposals which are "of significance" and therefore needed to be referred to a higher authority in the form of the Cathedrals' Fabric Commission for England.

The public interest in cathedrals has since been aroused by such incidents as the fire (July 1984) and subsequent restoration of York Minster, the attempt by the Dean and Chapter of Hereford to sell the Mappa Mundi, coupled with many appeals by other cathedrals to undertake much publicised,—and very expensive,—repairs, many of which have been occasioned by the normal deterioration of the passing years, but others by the often destructive work of well-meaning Victorian restorers. The Church of England responded to the conservationists' complaints that alterations to cathedrals

---

[41] The Ecclesiastical Exemption (Listed Buildings and Conservation Areas) Order 1994 provides for continued exemption for ecclesiastical buildings of the various denominations in various categories where insufficient information is currently available *e.g.*, buildings of the Church of England to which the faculty jurisdiction does not extend. These include cathedrals (about which more is said later), but also includes churches known as *peculiars* such as St George's Chapel, Windsor, and the Temple church, both Royal Peculiars: and the colleges of Oxford and Cambridge. The exemption also applies to religious communities of the Church of England and the Roman Catholic Church and school and other institutional chapels. (Source: PPG 15, para. 8.9 and article by Peter Boydell Q.C. *Special Situations— Ecclesiastical Buildings and Ancient Monuments* published as a J.P.L. Occasional Paper in 1977).

were exempt both from the secular controls of the Planning Acts and also to its own faculty jurisdiction governing parish churches, by introducing the Care of Cathedrals Measure 1990. This did not seem initially to be welcomed by some of the Deans and Provosts, but it was later amended and finally procured the approval of the General Synod in November 1989 and received the Royal Assent in July 1990. The Measure came into force on March 1, 1991, and with the Rules which were made under the Measure (The Care of Cathedrals Rules 1990 which set out the form and manner of providing information on proposals affecting cathedrals), is designed to provide safeguards against arbitrary alterations of cathedrals and to provide more public accountability.

The Care of Cathedrals Measure 1990 provides for the administrative **10.25** body of a cathedral (normally the Dean and Chapter) to obtain approval for proposed works on, above, or below, land which is vested in the Chapter of the Cathedral, being works which would materially affect the following aspects:

(i) the architectural, archaeological, artistic or historic character of the cathedral church or any building within the precinct of the cathedral church which is for the time being used for ecclesiastical purposes; or

(ii) the immediate setting of the cathedral church; or

(iii) any archaeological remains within the precinct of the cathedral church.[42]

It also includes proposals governing the sale, loan, or other disposal of any object of the property of the cathedral which is of architectural, archaeological, artistic or historic interest; or any permanent addition to the cathedral which would materially affect the architectural, archaeological, artistic or historic character of the cathedral. These various requirements to obtain approval do not apply to anything done by the administrative body with respect to the ordering of services or the mission of the church, or for works of a temporary nature, or works which do not materially affect the fabric of the cathedral.

The Measure provides for the establishment of the Cathedrals Fabric Commission[43] (consisting of a chairman, vice-chairman and twenty other members) to give advice to the administrative body on all aspects of cathedral churches, ranging from the care, conservation, repair or development of the buildings; the care and study of the architectural, archaeological, artistic or historic interest of the buildings; the educational and research aspects of various cathedrals and their ancillary buildings; and the maintenance of an archive of documents (books, drawings, photographs and other material), relating to the cathedral and the objects in it.

Every cathedral is also required to establish a Fabric Advisory Committee consisting of not less than three nor more than five members appointed by the administrative body of the cathedral, and an equal number of members appointed by the Cathedrals Fabric Commission, being persons with special knowledge of the care and maintenance of historic buildings. This committee is to give advice to the administrative body on the care, conservation, repair or development of the cathedral church, and to consider and

[42] *Care of Cathedrals Measure* 1990, s.2(1)(a)(i)–(iii).
[43] *Care of Cathedrals Measure* 1990, ss.3 and 4.

determine any application made to it by the administrative body of the cathedral church.

The Measure sets out in section 6(1)(a) the nature of the proposals which must be referred to the Cathedrals Fabric Commission and these include[44]:

"(i) the carrying out of works which would permanently alter the fabric of the cathedral church or any building within the precinct of the cathedral church which is for the time being used for ecclesiastical purposes; or

(ii) the demolition of any part of the cathedral church or any such building; or

(iii) the disturbance or destruction of any archaeological remains within the precinct of the cathedral church; or

(iv) the sale, loan or other disposal of any object for the time being designated under section 13(2) of this Measure in relation to the cathedral church or being of outstanding architectural, archaeological, artistic or historic interest . . . ".

Any application for approval of any proposal shall be made, in the form laid down in the Care of Cathedrals Rules 1990, to the Fabric Advisory Committee, although the Cathedral Fabric Commission has power to "call in" (section 6(1)(b)) an application and the Fabric Advisory Committee itself can refer proposals to the Commission, for determination (section 6(2)). The Measure makes provision for publicity to be given to and consultation undertaken on any proposal made by the administrative body so that representations can be made to the Commission.[45] The local planning authority is required (section 7(1)(b)) to be notified of all works or proposals involving planning issues, *i.e.* excluding proposals for the sale, loan or disposal of any designated object. After considering any representations which are received resulting from this publicity, the Fabric Advisory Committee may either approve the proposal, approve it subject to conditions, or refuse to grant approval.

10.26 In a similar way, applications for the approval of the Commission must be publicised and displayed in the prescribed manner, and a notice (under section 8(1)(3)) of them sent to Fabric Advisory Committee and English Heritage, and to national amenity societies[46] (which means the Ancient Monument Society, the Council for British Archaeology, the Georgian Group, the Society for the Protection of Ancient Monuments, the Victorian Society, and such other societies as may from time to time be designated by the Dean of Arches and Auditor, as a national amenity society) in which details shall be provided to these consultees of the proposal and of where it can be inspected and representations made. Again, if the proposal is within the categories contained in section 2(1)(a), a copy of the notice must be sent to the local planning authority. The Commission has similar powers to determine the application as those invested on the Fabric Advisory Committee. A copy of the Commission's decision is required to be sent to the administrative body of the cathedral, the Fabric Advisory Committee, English Heritage, the national amenity societies, the Royal Commission on Historical Monuments for England, and the local planning authority; with

[44] *Care of Cathedrals Measure* 1990, s.6(1)(a)(i)–(iv).
[45] *Care of Cathedrals Measure* 1990, s.7(1)(a).
[46] *Care of Cathedrals Measure* 1990, s.8(3).

a copy of the decision displayed on a notice board in the prescribed manner. Although there are no criteria laid down for determining applications, it is expected that the Commission will adopt similar criteria to those exercised by local planning authorities under listed building control.

There is an appeal procedure[47] for cases where approval to a scheme is refused or granted conditionally by the Fabric Advisory Committee which consists of an appeal to the Commission. There is a further right of appeal to a Commission of Review. The Commission of Review consists of the Dean of Arches and Auditor, a person appointed by the Archbishops of Canterbury and York, being someone who has been a dean, provost or residentiary canon of a cathedral church, and a person appointed by the Secretary of State with special knowledge in church architecture, archaeology, or art (section 10(3)). This review body shall not include anyone who has served on the Cathedrals' Fabric Commission during the preceding five years.

Where an administrative body of a cathedral proposes to make an application for listed building consent in respect of any building, or scheduled monument consent in respect of any building or monument within the precincts of the cathedral church, the chapter clerk of the cathedral is required to notify the Cathedrals' Fabric Commission. Guidance notes on application for approval of proposals made under the Care of Cathedrals Measure have been published by the Cathedrals Advisory Commission for England to assist with the interpretation of the various sections of the Measure.[48]

The Commission may,[49] on a request from the Council for the Care of Churches, give advice to the Council with respect to works which are proposed to be carried out in relation to a church of the Church of England which is not a cathedral church. It may give advice in relation to a cathedral church in Wales, and, in exceptional circumstances, (with special agreements) advice may be given to works proposed to a cathedral of denominations other than one of the Church of England or Church of Wales.

The Care of Cathedrals (Supplementary Provisions) Measure 1994 (No. 2) received Parliamentary approval in July 1994, and provides an enforcement machinery for the Care of Cathedrals Measure 1990. If an act of contravention is committed, or may be proposed to be committed, the bishop can intervene, and, if not satisfied, may authorise proceedings to be instituted in the Vicar-General's Court of the Province in which the cathedral church is situated, for an injunction and/or restoration order against the administrative body.[50]

13. GRANT AID FOR CHURCHES AND CATHEDRALS

In 1971, the General Synod of the Church of England agreed[51] to approach **10.27** the Department of the Environment seeking to obtain financial support from public funds for the repair of churches in use. In 1975 the Government

---

[47] *Care of Cathedrals Measure* 1990, s.9.
[48] *Care of Cathedrals Measure* 1990, s.10.
[49] *Care of Cathedrals Measure* 1990, s.11(1).
[50] *Encyclopedia of Planning Law Bulletin*, September 1994, p. 3.
[51] *Additional Resources for Church Grants—Conservation Bulletin, English Heritage*, October 1988.

announced that it had accepted in principle the case for state aid for places of worship in use. A scheme was announced in 1977 for an initial period of not less than five years. The General Synod agreed to review its faculty jurisdiction system in relation to churches (see paragraph 10.09). Following the 1986 statement in the House of Lords (see paragraph 10.04) which reaffirmed the exemption of ecclesiastical buildings from listed building control, the Church of England responded by agreeing to make improvements to its system of care for both churches and cathedrals in the hope of encouraging English Heritage to continue to make grants available for churches in use.

By 1988 English Heritage was assessing various options on which to spend the increase of £3 million a year from 1990–91 onwards for the existing church grant scheme. It identified four options; to increase expenditure on grants for the conservation of contents of churches (from wall paintings to organ cases); to provide extra resources through what were then known as "section 10" grants from the TICP Amenities Act 1974 (now s. 77 of LBA) for places or worship seriously at risk in conservation areas, and in particular this was designed to benefit non-Anglican churches or chapels which might not have been eligible for grant aid under the normal criteria of being "outstanding"; to use part of the funds to promote a trust which would provide continuing care to look after the best of redundant non-Anglican churches or chapels (on similar lines to the Redundant Churches Fund (see paragraph 10.20), and to fund longer term repair programmes as opposed to urgent and immediate repairs.

In return for the distribution of additional grants, English Heritage would become involved in assessing repairs and alterations to churches, and the Church of England agreed to English Heritage being represented on Diocesan Advisory Committees. The grants to churches in use during 1993–94 amounted to £10.3 million.[52]

In 1988 English Heritage was reported as having considered whether it would be appropriate to extend existing church grants to cathedrals, but at that time concluded that it would not be right to do so. The Church of England agreed, when grants for churches in use were first mooted, that the need of parish churches was much greater then cathedrals. Cathedrals were therefore excluded on the grounds that they had better fund-raising ability. This did not preclude Deans and Chapters from receiving considerable financial help towards the secular buildings in their ownership. This policy has now been changed so that cathedrals may now qualify for receiving grants.

10.28   In its environmental *White Paper* published in September 1990, entitled "This Common Inheritance", the Government accepted the principle of giving state aid for cathedrals. In April 1991[53] details of the new scheme were announced, and under existing legislation the Government agreed to provide English Heritage with an extra £11.5 million over the three years 1991–94 to set up a new grant scheme for cathedrals[54] of all denominations and their ancillary buildings, which included attached cloister walks, attached chapter houses, etc. In March 1993 a further £8 million was pro-

---

[52] *English Heritage Monitor* 1995.
[53] *The Times*, April 4, 1991.
[54] *Cathedrals repair grant scheme, Conservation Bulletin, English Heritage,* June 1991.

mised for 1994–1996.[55] The scheme was to be designed to ensure that urgent repairs were carried out to appropriate standards, and for Anglican cathedrals to run in tandem with the Care of Cathedrals Measure for the care and conservation of cathedral buildings and their contents.

Cathedrals will have to qualify in their own right as buildings of outstanding architectural or historic interest or, by reason of their location in a conservation area. Grants are available[56] only for major structural repairs to historic fabric and associated recording works, and those costing less than £10,000 (exclusive of fees and VAT) will only be accepted in exceptional circumstances. Grant aid will be available[57] towards the conservation of contents of outstanding buildings such as major monuments and works of art historically associated with the building, for example, wall paintings, stained glass and historic fixed fittings such as choir screens and stalls, but organs, bells and clock mechanisms or removable items will not be eligible. Contents costing less than £5,000 (exclusive of fees and VAT) will not normally be eligible for grant aid.

In order to assess the likely cost of the necessary fabric repairs over the decade 1991–2001, English Heritage commissioned[58] a survey of the physical state of English cathedrals so that a priority list of need could be produced. The survey, undertaken by Harry Fairhurst (former chairman of the Cathedral Architects' Association) identified at least £185 million worth of work requiring to be carried out during the ten year period to repair England's 60 cathedrals.

It was announced in November 1994 that English Heritage was offering 30 English cathedrals a total of £4,348,000 for urgent repairs, conservation work and fire prevention in 1995/96. In the first five years of offering grants under the Cathedral Grant Scheme, a total of £23 million had been offered to 53 of England's 61 cathedrals.[59] [60] English Heritage will need to be satisfied that the works for which grant aid has been applied has received consent under the Care of Cathedrals Measure 1990. In the case of Roman Catholic cathedrals (of which there are 18), the prior approval of English Heritage will be required for any future works to cathedrals, except for maintenance and minor repair works and works required for liturgical purposes which are compatible with the historic character and appearance of the building and which are reversible. It will also be a condition of grant aid that these cathedrals obtain a full quinquennial inspection report within two years of a grant offer. Public access to the interior of all cathedrals receiving grant aid, for an average of eight hours a day, will be expected.

14. OTHER CASES

There had been some doubt as to whether ecclesiastical exemption **10.29** extended to consecrated school chapels which are attached to the Church of

---

[55] *Heritage and Renewal*, the Report of the Archbishops' Commission on Cathedrals, November 1994.
[56] Cathedrals Grant Scheme 1991/92—English Heritage Guidance Notes.
[57] Cathedrals repair grant scheme, June 1991.
[58] *Conservation Bulletin, English Heritage*, December 1991.
[59] *English Heritage News Release*, November 9, 1994.
[60] *English Heritage Monitor* 1995.

England. This issue was raised by the Chancellor of the Rochester Consistory Court in Tonbridge School Chapel (No. 1)[61], when he observed that it remained unclear whether the school chapel, which had been badly damaged by fire, was within the Faculty Jurisdiction of the Church of England. The Chancellor proceeded to accept jurisdiction on the basis of the agreement of the parties, who also agreed that although the chapel was a listed building, it fell within ecclesiastical exemption. The Chancellor observed, in this case, that "it does seem to me desirable that an ecclesiastical building should be under one or other form of control, ecclesiastical or secular, rather than both, or possibly, in some cases neither". He expressed the view that the criteria which apply in the case of an application for listed building consent are not precisely the same as those applicable to faculty jurisdiction, pointing out that listed building consent concerns the interior as well as the exterior of the building, and that aesthetics also play a more important part under those controls.[62]

PPG 15, paragraph 8.9 explains that the Ecclesiastical Exemption (Listed Buildings and Conservation Areas) Order 1994 provides for continued exemption for those denominations in various categories where insufficient information is currently available, and gives examples such as those outside the faculty jurisdiction system; Church of England and Roman Catholic religious communities; and schools and other institutional chapels. The intention is that by the end of a limited period all such buildings will either become subject to the normal listed building control or be included within the scope of an exempted denominations internal system of control.

10.30   Consecrated areas of a municipal cemetery were held to be within the scope of section 13 of the Care of Churches and Ecclesiastical Jurisdiction Measure 1991 so as to give the consistory court jurisdiction to order the repair of headstones damaged as part of a local authority clearance programme. The West Norwood Cemetery in London had been laid out in the 19th-century, and in 1965 was acquired by Lambeth Borough Council by means of a compulsory purchase order, as a working cemetery. As part of a landscape improvement scheme in February 1971 the Council proposed a lawn conversion policy, and in 1978 the cemetery was designated as a conservation area. The scheme raised local public controversy and was for a time held in abeyance, until mid–1990, when there was an active resumption of clearance work at the cemetery.

After the 1991 Measure came into force on March 1, 1993, the Archdeacon of Lambeth applied to the consistory court for a restoration order (section 13 of the Measure), after which the Council petitioned for a confirmatory faculty in respect of the works carried out in the consecrated parts of the cemetery and at the same time petitioned for a management scheme under section 10 of the Open Spaces Act 1906. The Archdeacon petitioned for a faculty authorising Lambeth Council to restore the cemetery to its condition prior to the lawn conversion scheme, for which no faculty had been sought or granted. Lambeth Council claimed it had acted under the powers contained in the London County Council (General Powers) Act 1955 for the clearance work of old graves and lawning of Victorian cemeteries.

Sixty seven buildings and monuments within the consecrated area were listed, which meant that the whole of the cemetery was effectively within

---

[61] [1993] 2 All E.R. 350.
[62] [1993] 2 All E.R. 350.

the listing (section 5(1)) of the Planning (Listed Buildings and Conservation Areas) Act 1990, and in this case the curtilage was defined as the cemetery, thus all the memorials which existed before July 1, 1948 (section 5(1)(b) of the 1990 Act) fell within the listing, whether or not they themselves were individually listed. Their removal would have required listed building consent, but such consent had neither been sought nor granted.

A confirmatory faculty was granted by the Chancellor of the Southwark Diocese, because the Open Spaces Act 1906 provided the means for a management scheme to be drawn up and approved by the consistory court, which met the aims of the Lambeth Council, Archdeacon, and the Friends' of West Norwood Cemetery. In granting retrospective permission, the Chancellor required that all future work at the cemetery must be approved by a new consultative committee consisting of representatives from English Heritage, the Victorian Society, and the Friends' of West Norwood Cemetery, who would work closely with the Lambeth Council officers.[63]

[63] *Law report of the Consistory Court, The Times* April 11, 1994, and *South London Press*, March 11, 1994.

11. Rights of Entry

1. IN RELATION TO LISTING AND LISTED BUILDING CONTROLS

11.01 In order to fulfil the various functions authorised by the LBA 1990 and the PCA 1991 in respect of the listing of buildings and the scheduling of monuments, and the exercise of the statutory controls arising from these measures, it is necessary for personnel from Central Government, English Heritage, local authorities, and occasionally others, to have rights of entry to a property.

(a) Entry for compilation of lists of buildings

11.02 Section 88(1) of the LBA 1990 empowers the Secretary of State for National Heritage to permit in writing any duly authorised person at any reasonable time to enter any land for the purpose of surveying any building in connection with a proposal to include the building in a list of buildings of special architectural interest. "Survey" is defined in the *Shorter Oxford Dictionary* as "to examine and ascertain the condition, situation, or value of, formally or officially, *e.g.* the boundaries, tenure, value, etc. of an estate, a building or structure . . . ".

(b) Entry in connection with proposals affecting listed buildings

11.03 Section 88(2) permits any person authorised in writing by the Secretary of State, the local planning authority, or, in the case of a building situated in Greater London, English Heritage, to enter land for the purposes of surveying it in connection with any proposal of the local authority or the Secretary of State in connection with the following various provisions of the LBA 1990.

Section 1–26   —   listing of special buildings
                         —   control of works in respect of listed buildings

	—	applications for listed building consent
	—	the granting of consent subject to conditions
	—	appeals against refusal of listed building consent
	—	revocation and modification of consent
Section 38	—	issuing of listed building enforcement notice
Section 40	—	appeals against listed building enforcement notice
Section 46	—	enforcement by the Secretary of State
Section 48	—	repairs notice
Section 54	—	urgent works to preserve unoccupied listed buildings
Section 55	—	recovery of expenses for above works
Section 60	—	exceptions for ecclesiastical buildings and redundant churches
Section 68	—	reference to English Heritage of planning applications involving listed buildings in Greater London
Section 75	—	control of demolition in conservation areas
Section 76	—	urgent works to preserve unoccupied buildings in conservation areas.

These powers extend to checking if any order or notice has been complied with, and whether an offence has been committed with respect to any building, or whether it is being maintained in a proper state of repair. Comparable powers are granted by section 88(3) in respect of buildings situated in Greater London, where English Heritage is empowered to enter land for various purposes. The definition of the word "land" in the T.C.P.A. 1990 (section 336)[1] includes a building, and therefore the powers contained in section 88 extend the power to enter a building as well as land.

(c) Entry by other persons in connection with valuation

An officer of the Valuation Office may be authorised in writing by a local **11.04** planning authority at any reasonable time to enter the land for the purpose of surveying it, or estimating its value in connection with a claim for compensation payable by the authority under section 27 (for the refusal of consent to alterations, etc., of a listed building); section 28 (where listed

---

[1] s.91 of the LBA 1990 conveys the same meaning of the word "land" as in the principal Act.

building consent is revoked or modified); section 29 (for loss or damage caused by the service of a Building Preservation Notice; or sections 47–52 (acquisition of listed buildings in need of repair, or acquisition by agreement).

In all these functions the following bodies are empowered to exercise the appropriate power of entry; London Borough councils acting as local planning authorities; English Heritage; metropolitan district councils; district planning authorities; National Park authorities; county planning authorities; Norfolk and Suffolk Broads authority; urban development corporations; and housing action trusts.[2]

(d) Penalties for non-co-operation

11.05   Under section 88A[3] of the LBA 1990, if it can be shown to the satisfaction of a Justice of the Peace on sworn information in writing that there are reasonable grounds for entering any land for the purposes of section 88 above, and that admission has been refused or a refusal is reasonably apprehended or the case is a matter or urgency, the Justice may issue a warrant authorising the person to enter the land. A warrant issued under this section authorises entry on one occasion only and that must be within one month from the date of the issue, and at a reasonable hour.[4]

It is an offence under section 325(2) of the principal Act wilfully to obstruct a person exercising powers under this section, but it is not reinforced by any power of arrest. It is however enforceable either by issuing a summons before the Magistrates or by applying for an injunction in the High Court, and a person exercising the right of entry under this section may be entitled to common law remedy of self-help in removing obstructing protesters.[5]

(e) Advance notice of wish to enter property

11.06   Under section 88B of the LBA 1990 an authorised person shall not demand admission as of right unless 24 hours notice has been given to the occupier. The authorised person shall if so required give evidence of his authority and shall state his purpose before entering the property; he may take with him such other persons who may be necessary and he must leave the land as effectively secured against trespass as he found it. Any person who wilfully obstructs an authorised person of a right of entry shall be guilty of an offence and liable on summary conviction to a fine.[6] Any damage to land or chattels caused in exercise of a right of entry is compensa-

---

[2] *Allocation of functions* in commentary on s.88 in *Encyclopedia of Planning Law—Practice.*
[3] s.88A was introduced by Sched. 3, para. 9(2), of the Planning and Compensation Act 1991 and took effect on January 2, 1993.
[4] s.196(B)(3) T.C.P.A. 1990.
[5] *R v. Chief Constable of Devon and Cornwall Constabulary ex p. Central Electricity Generating Board* [1981] 3 All E.R. 826 C.A.
[6] s.88(B)(3).

table by the local planning authority or the Secretary of State who authorised the entry.[7]

(f) Other bodies requiring access to land

The demolition of a listed building is authorised only if, in addition to **11.07** obtaining listed building consent and complying with it, the Royal Commission on the Historical Monuments of England (or, in Wales, the Royal Commission and Ancient and Historical Monuments in Wales) has been notified[8] and provided with the necessary access to enable its officers to record the building. No works of demolition may commence under the consent unless notice has been given of the proposal to execute the works and at least one month's notice reasonable access has been made available to the RCHM for the purposes of recording the building. Section 8(2)(c) requires that "reasonable access to the building has been made available to members or officers of the Royal Commission for the purpose of recording it".

The Secretary of State has also directed, under section 15(5) of the LBA 1990, that other persons as may be specified shall be notified of certain applications made to a local planning authority for listed building consent. The Direction contained in Circular 8/87, paragraph 81, specifies that notice of all applications for consent to demolish a listed building shall be given to the Ancient Monuments Society, the Council for British Archaeology, the Georgian Group, the Society for the Protection of Ancient Buildings, the Victorian Society, and any other society of body nominated by the Secretary of State which can include local amenity societies. These bodies do not appear to have any powers of entry but must rely on the co-operation of the owner and occupier of the property to examine it in relation to the proposal on which their views are sought.

2. IN RELATION TO ANCIENT MONUMENTS AND ARCHAEOLOGICAL AREAS

In order to fulfil the various functions authorised by the LBA 1990 in **11.08** respect of the listing of buildings and the scheduling of monuments, and the exercise of the statutory controls arising from these measures, it is necessary for personnel from Central Government, English Heritage, local authorities, and occasionally others, to have rights of entry to a property.

(a) Entry in process of scheduling a monument

Section 1 of the AMAA 1979 Act places a duty on the Secretary of State **11.09** for National Heritage to compile a schedule of monuments, and section 6(1) of the Act empowers any person authorised in writing by the Secretary of

---

[7] s.196(C)(3) of the T.C.P.A. 1990.
[8] s.8(2)(b) and (c), LBA 1990.

State, at any reasonable time to enter any land for the purpose of inspecting any such scheduled monument to ascertain its condition. There does not appear to be any power conferred on the Secretary of State to enter any land for the purpose of determining whether there is a monument on the land.

(b) Entry in connection with scheduled monument consent

11.10   Section 6(2) of the 1979 Act extends the power of entry to any authorised person who requires to inspect a scheduled monument in connection with an application for scheduled monument consent or for the modification or revocation of a scheduled monument consent and for observing the execution on the land of any works to which such a consent relates.

Any authorised person may enter any land on which scheduled monument consent relates for the purposes of inspecting the land (including any buildings or other structures) with a view to recording any matters of archaeological or historical interest, and observing the execution of those works with a view to examining and recording any objects or other material of archaeological or historical interest discovered during the course of those works.[9]

Similar powers to those conferred by section 6 on the Secretary of State are applicable to persons duly authorised by English Heritage.

(c) Entry by persons in connection with valuation

11.11   Additional powers of entry to a site are granted by section 43 of the 1979 Act for any authorised person for the purpose of surveying it for estimating its value in connection with any proposal to acquire the land or with a claim for compensation. This can include an officer of the Valuation Office who has been duly authorised in writing by the Secretary of State or other authority proposing to make the acquisition.

(d) Entry to an occupied dwellinghouse or other land

11.12   Under section 43 of the 1979 Act a person may not exercise any power of entry to enter a building occupied as a dwellinghouse without the consent of the occupier. Section 44 of the 1979 Act provides that a person may not demand admission as of right to any land which is occupied unless prior notice has been given to the occupier. For the purpose of entry to carry out any works, not less than 14 days notice must be given before the date on which admission is demanded, or in other cases, *e.g.* for the purposes of executing urgent works, not less than 24 hours' notice is required before admission is demanded. In exercising the power of entry the authorised person may take any assistance or equipment reasonably required for his pur-

---

[9] s.6(4)(b), 1979 Act.

pose[10] and he may take away or remove samples of any description as appear to him to be reasonably required for the purposes of archaeological analysis.[11]

(e) Penalties for non-co-operation

Any person who intentionally obstructs a person acting under these powers of entry shall be guilty of an offence and liable to summary conviction. **11.13**

(f) Entry in pursuance of operations notice—Areas of Archaeological Importance

There are a number of powers of entry in connection with activities arising from operations notices under section 35 of the AMAA Act 1979 in respect of Areas of Archaeological Importance, and these are contained in sections 38, 39 and 40 of the 1979 Act. **11.14**

[10] s.44(4) 1979 Act.
[11] s.44(5) 1979 Act.

12. Grant and Loan Facilities

1. INTRODUCTION

12.01   It is perhaps fortunate that the vast majority of listed buildings are gain-
fully and usefully occupied, and that though a large number of ancient
monuments cannot be said to be usefully occupied, some are at least gain-
fully utilised. It is fortunate because in a country which has a wealth of
listed buildings and ancient monuments, there is limited financial assistance available from public sources to help support their maintenance and
repair, although there is no automatic right to a grant. Ever since the early
ancient monuments legislation, successive governments have appeared to
try to avoid shouldering the burden of maintenance and repair, with the
consequence that these burdens have been left to owners of such properties.
Perhaps it is for that reason that some local authorities have not pursued
powers which they have available to them against the owners of listed
buildings quite so vigorously as some would have wished.

Many of those who own or have responsibility for listed buildings wish
that greater funds were available to assist them in the maintenance and
upkeep of their historic buildings. Many contend that there should be, as in
the United States, a greater tax incentive to owners of such buildings.

It should perhaps be noted that in the 17 years from 1976–77 to 1992–93,
English Heritage (and prior to 1984–85, the Historic Buildings Council)
made grants of £309 million.[1]

Successive Parliaments over the last 70 years have recognised that there
must be made available some money in particularly important or deserving
cases. In doing so, however, they have succeeded in creating a web of powers
for the making of grants and loans for historic buildings and areas which are
not readily intelligible.

This chapter seeks to review the current position in respect of grant aid
relating to historic buildings and monuments, conservation areas, buildings
at risk, and churches. We limit our consideration in the main to grant
schemes which are administered either by English Heritage or local authorities. The percentage of grant aid varies according to the type of scheme
and the available funds, and therefore we have not specified this figure. The

---

[1] *English Heritage Monitor 1995.*

scope of each grant or loan is briefly described, together with any specific types of work to which they are applied. Details of the main grants discussed below are available from English Heritage, 23 Savile Row, London W1X 1AB.

The commencement of the National Lottery in 1994 has made available sums undreamed of in the context of mainstream public funding. One of the five areas of spending is on heritage, which could receive up to £320 million a year when the Lottery is fully up and running. The Prime Minister, when he addressed a major conference at English Heritage's 10th anniversary in 1994, was clear that the Government will make no reductions on conventional public spending programmes to take account of awards from the National Lottery.

2. ENGLISH HERITAGE ADMINISTERED GRANT AID

(a) Grants to outstanding buildings

Under section 3A of the Historic Buildings and Ancient Monuments Act **12.02** 1953 (as amended by Schedule 4 of the National Heritage Act 1983), English Heritage is empowered to make grants and loans available for the repair and maintenance of a building, and the upkeep of land, or objects associated with it, individually or as part of a group, which appear to English Heritage to be of *outstanding* historic or architectural interest.

The majority of buildings, grant-aided under this heading, are either scheduled ancient monuments, or buildings listed in the Grade I or II* categories, (or the ecclesiastical equivalent in the older lists), of buildings of special architectural or historic interest. A few Grade II buildings are included where they are considered by English Heritage to be "outstanding" within the meaning of the legislation. Church grants are made only to places of worship in use. Other buildings which are no longer in use for public worship, or are private chapels, are included within the secular grants.

This category of grant aid for the repair of outstanding buildings is judged by national standards and the standard is very high; each case is considered on its merits by English Heritage in the light of the advice from its Historic Buildings Advisory Committee. This type of grant can be extended to associated buildings which are not outstanding in their own right but form part of an outstanding group. Grants are intended for major structural repairs to an agreed and appropriate standard of materials and workmanship. They may occasionally be offered to work on interior features, but the highest priority has been given to structural repairs necessary to save a building. These grants do not cover routine maintenance, or works of alteration, conversion, improvement, or demolition.

A careful financial assessment has to be made by English Heritage to ensure that the building or monument requires the support of a grant, and it will normally be a condition of offering grant aid that an appropriate level of public access will be permitted. The grant may be recoverable if the grantee disposes of his interest in the property by way of sale, exchange or leave, up to ten years.

(b) Grants to buildings in Conservation Areas

12.03   Under sections 77 and 79/80 of the LBA 1990 English Heritage is empowered to make grants or loans for any relevant expenditure which will make a
significant contribution towards the preservation or enhancement of the
character or appearance of any conservation area in England (in Wales,
these grants are dealt with by the Secretary of State after consultation with
the Historic Buildings Council for Wales). These grants are available where
there are agreed schemes or programmes of work, which are often run in
partnership with local authorities. Grants may relate to the costs of repairing historic buildings which contribute to the character of the conservation
area, and for associated environmental improvements. Repair works to
buildings in conservation areas are generally eligible if they relate to the
structure or external appearance. Grants made under this section may be
recovered (section 78 of LBA 1990) in whole or in part, if within ten years of
the grant being made the grantee's interest is disposed of by way of sale,
exchange or lease, for a term of not less than 21 years.

Liability to repay the grant is personal and only enforceable against the
original grantee, except where the grantee's interest has been transferred by
way of *inter vivos* gift, in which case the donee becomes liable for repayment. This type of grant or loan may be made to local authorities, amenity
societies, preservation trusts and individuals.

In April 1994, all local authorities were invited to consider applying to
English Heritage by the end of June for the establishment of new Conservation Area Partnerships, to run from April 1995. These schemes were
introduced to focus joint resources more effectively on areas of greatest
need, and to encourage greater participation by local authorities. By April
1997, Conservation Area Partnership Schemes will be the single formal
means of directing English Heritage funding into conservation areas, apart
from a limited number of specific one-off grants, *e.g.* to outstanding historic
churches, buildings and monuments, or to buildings at risk.

Partnerships will primarily be created between English Heritage and a
local or county authority, although they could be extended to other major
stakeholders providing their aims and interests in the conservation area
coincide with the aims of the scheme. Details of the partnership schemes
are explained in the Conservation Bulletin of English Heritage of November
1994, and in a series of leaflets produced by English Heritage covering
Conservation Area partnership schemes, April 1994.

(c) Town Scheme Grants

12.04   Town schemes are agreements between English Heritage and local authorities, whereby each sets aside funds for grants to historic buildings within
a defined area. Whereas other types of grant schemes concentrate mainly on
historic buildings and conservation areas, Town Schemes have a wider
range of interest and include vernacular buildings which would otherwise
not qualify individually for a grant. They have been successful in bringing
whole historic areas back to life, both in visual terms and economically,.
and whilst initially concentrated on the classic historic cities, are now more
widespread and include smaller towns.

The power to create a Town Scheme is now contained in section 79 of the LBA 1990. Under section 80 of the Act, English Heritage in England (the Secretary of State in Wales) may provide grants to defray all or part of the repair cost for any building within a Town Scheme agreement, if it is situated in a conservation area and appears to be of architectural or historic interest. Grants are recoverable in certain circumstances, under section 78 of the 1990 Act.

Most Town Schemes are set up initially for a period of three years, but their period of operation depends on the needs of the area and the effectiveness of the scheme. Town Scheme grants will eventually be converted into Conservation Area Partnership Schemes by English Heritage—see paragraph (b) above.

(d) Grants towards the cost of local authority acquisition of buildings of special architectural or historic interest

Section 47 of the LBA 1990 enables a local authority, or the Secretary of **12.05** State, to acquire by compulsory means a listed building in need of repair; section 52 of the 1990 Act empowers a local authority to acquire by agreement a building which appears to be of special architectural or historic interest. The building need not be listed, nor need it be in a state of disrepair, nor even in the authority's own area to receive grant aid.

The Historic Buildings and Ancient Monuments Act 1953, sections 5B and 6, confer powers on English Heritage to make grants for the purposes of defraying all or part of a local authority's expenses in acquiring any property under either of these sections.

The following points will be taken into account when considering grant aid under this heading:

(a) whether local acquisition is the only possible way of ensuring that the building is preserved;

(b) whether the building is a viable proposition on the property market; and

(c) whether the intrinsic value of the building justifies the expenditure required to save it.

If the property is subsequently re-sold at a profit, English Heritage may require that a proportion of the grant is repaid.

(e) Grants applicable in London

The Local Government Act 1985 (Schedule 2, paragraph 3(i)) provides **12.06** powers for English Heritage, *inter alia*, "to undertake, or contribute towards, the costs of preserving, maintaining and managing any such building [being a building or place of historic or architectural interest] in Greater London".

The grants available from English Heritage apply to owners of listed buildings within the Greater London area for repair work to enhance and protect the architectural interest of the building and to maintain its historic features. Routine maintenance costs for such works are not eligible.

(f) Grants to scheduled ancient monuments

12.07   English Heritage is empowered under section 24(2) of the Ancient Monuments and Archaeological Areas Act 1979 to provide grant assistance to individual owners of buildings, trusts, companies and local authorities in respect of the preservation, maintenance and management of any ancient monument.

English Heritage may offer management agreements to occupiers of rural monuments and these usually attract small grants based on the acreage covered by the monument and also capital costs.

(g) Grants for "buildings at risk"

12.08   These "buildings at risk" grants are intended to help historic buildings which are in poor condition, particularly those which are not in a proper use and which might otherwise deteriorate before a new use is found. The aim of this type of grant is to provide not only for the necessary repair treatment, but also to ensure that the buildings will be in secure uses which will ensure their survival into the future. A building in this condition is only eligible for grant if it lies in a conservation area, or if it would otherwise be important enough to receive a grant under the Historic Buildings and Ancient Monuments Act 1953, as being of "outstanding" interest. The grants are available to private owners, local authorities, amenity societies, or preservation trusts, and must relate to listed buildings within a conservation area, or if unlisted, the Secretary of State must have authorised the work to be done under the "urgent works" provisions of section 54 of the LBA 1990.

(h) Church and Cathedral Grants

12.09   Government financial aid was first introduced to parish churches in August 1977, and to cathedrals in Autumn 1991.

The special scheme operated by English Heritage to help with repairs to historic religious buildings relates to those in use for public worship of any denomination. The criteria for making this type of grant relies on the historic importance of the building, the urgency of the proposed repairs, and the financial need for support from public funds. Normally only buildings in the Grade I or II* categories are eligible (or categories A and B in the older lists) for grant aid. Exceptionally, buildings outside these gradings may qualify, e.g. 19th-century Church of England churches and non-Anglican churches, if they possess sufficient interest for a special case to be made.

Grants are normally available only for major repairs to the historic fabric of a church and must conform to an appropriate standard of materials and workmanship. There is provision for recovering grants from non-Anglican churches, in the unlikely event that the congregation insisted on carrying out very damaging works against the advice of English Heritage. The Church of England has its own legal system, through the Consistory Courts, to deal with such cases.

Churches may also apply to the Historic Churches Preservation Trust which can make interest-free loans as well as grants. There are also a number of County Trusts whose objectives are to contribute toward church repairs. Whilst most of these bodies are primarily concerned with the structural fabric of the church, the Council for the Care of Churches offers grant aid for church furnishings.

A further source of grant aid was announced in 1994, and is directed at keeping open those churches of architectural and historic merit which must otherwise remain closed for security reasons. This is to be known as the Open Churches Trust.[2] As explained in Chapter 10, redundant historic churches are cared for by the Churches Conservation Trust and its resources are funded on a 70–30 per cent basis by the Government and the Church Commissioners respectively.

(i) Redundant Buildings Grants

This type of grant scheme is operated by The Rural Development Com- **12.10** mission under the Miscellaneous Financial Provisions Act 1983 and relates to conversion schemes of suitable redundant buildings for employment-creating uses. These grants are available to individuals, partnerships, co-operatives or companies and the property must be in a Rural Development Area. The aim is to convert suitable redundant rural buildings (barns, chapels, schools, etc.,) into premises such as workshops, laboratories or factories for light industrial or service occupation by the applicant.

Contact: The Rural Development Commission, 141 Castle Street, Salisbury, SP1 3TP.

(j) Historic Buildings Preservation Trusts

The Architectural Heritage Fund has operated in the United Kingdom **12.11** since 1976 to encourage and finance low-interest loans to enable Building Preservation Trusts to purchase, restore and re-sell historic properties which would otherwise not be of interest on the open market. The principle is for the Fund to provide cheap working capital to charitable bodies to operate a "revolving fund". The loans must be repaid within a specified period.

Contact: The Architectual Heritage Fund, 27 John Adam Street, London WC2N, 6HX.

(k) National Heritage Grants and Loans

The National Heritage Memorial Fund was set up in April 1980 by the **12.12** National Heritage Act 1980 to make grants and loans to eligible recipients for the purpose of assisting them to acquire, maintain or preserve, *inter alia*,

---

[2] *Conservation Bulletin*, November 1994.

any land, building or structure which is in the opinion of the Trustees of outstanding scenic, historic, aesthetic, architectural or scientific interest.

Contact: National Heritage Memorial Fund, 10 St. James' Street, London SW1A 1EF.

3. LOCAL AUTHORITY ADMINISTERED GRANT AID

(a) Grants or loans for repair or maintenance of historic buildings

12.13   Provision was made under section 1 of the Local Authorities (Historic Buildings) Act 1962 and later amended by section 58 of the Town and Country Planning Act 1968 and now contained in section 57 and section 58 of the LPA 1990, for local authorities to make grants for the repair and maintenance of listed buildings, including churches in use, gardens ancillary to those properties, and also unlisted buildings which appear to be of historic or architectural interest. The local authority may offer grant aid to such repair and maintenance work up to 50 per cent. In certain circumstances, the local authority may make an interest free loan rather than a grant, and in that event the authority can at any time indicate that it will not insist on repayment. Applications are made to the relevant local authority.

13. Public Rights— Buildings, Conservation Areas and Ancient Monuments

1. PUBLIC RIGHTS IN RELATION TO THE PROTECTIVE MEASURES

(a) Listing of buildings

Whilst the responsibility for listing buildings rests with the Secretary of **13.01** State for National Heritage, in consultation with English Heritage,[1] it is open to any individual or society at any time to request the Secretary of State to consider the listing of a building. The procedures for listing buildings are set out in Chapter 2. Requests of this nature should be sent to the Listing Branch, Department of National Heritage, 2–4 Cockspur Street, London SW1Y 5DH, and should be accompanied by a justification for adding the building to the list. The supporting information should include a location plan with the position of any nearby listed buildings; recent photographs of the main elevations and any historical data such as its date; function; historical associations; name of architect; contribution to group value of street scene and details of any interior features of interest.

Under section 6 of the LBA 1990 where planning permission is being sought or has been obtained, any person may request the Secretary of State to issue a "certificate of immunity" stating that he does not intend to list the building or buildings involved in the planning application. Once the certificate has been granted the building cannot be listed, nor a building preservation notice issued in respect of it, for at least five years.

---

[1] s. 1(4)(a) of LBA 1990.

A complete set of lists for the whole country is available for public inspection at the National Monuments Record of the Royal Commission on Historical Monuments of England, and each local authority is required to keep a copy of the list relating to its area, available for public inspection (without charge).

(b) Designation of Conservation Areas

The procedures for designating conservation areas is set out in Chapter 3. The general public has no statutory right to be consulted on a proposal to designate a conservation area although, in practice, most local planning authorities now identify their intention of considering such a designation in their Local Plan, which is open to public consultation.

The LBA 1990 (section 71) requires proposals for the preservation and enhancement of a conservation area to be submitted for consideration to a public meeting in the area to which they relate and again, in practice, it is customary for local planning authorities to give wider publicity to their proposals and to consult with local amenity societies, Chambers of Trade, public utilities and the highway authority.

(c) Scheduling of Monuments

The procedures for scheduling of monuments are dealt with in Chapter 8. As with listed buildings, the public has no right to demand the scheduling of a monument, although anyone is free to draw to the attention of the Department of National Heritage a suitable candidate for scheduling.

2. PUBLIC RIGHTS IN RELATION TO THE STATUTORY CONTROLS

(a) Applications for listed buildings consent or conservation area consent

13.02   Where an application is submitted for listed building consent to carry out works (other than works affecting only the interior of a Grade II (unstarred) listed building, or for consent to demolish a non-listed building in a conservation area), the local planning authority is required, under the Planning (Listed Buildings and Conservation Areas) Regulations 1990[2] to publish a notice in a local newspaper and to display a notice—for not less than seven days—on or near the site, and to wait for a period of 21 days to elapse before determining the application. The local planning authority is required to take into account the representations received relating to these forms of publicity. Thus, the public has a right to be notified of the existence of all

---

[2] S.I. 1990, 1519.

listed building applications (except interior works to unstarred Grade II buildings) and certain conservation area applications and to make such comments as are thought fit, and to have them taken into account by the local planning authority before the determination of the application.

Most local planning authorities also publish in the local press a weekly or monthly list of all applications received, and there is therefore ample opportunity for the public to be aware of, and respond to, such applications. Strangely, there is no statutory responsibility for a local planning authority to keep a public register of applications for listed building consent, or conservation area consent as it is obliged to do for applications for planning permission. In practice, however, many authorities do.

(b) Listed building applications "called-in" by the Secretary of State for the Environment

Under sections 12 and 13 of the LBA 1990, if a local planning authority (other than a London borough council, where the application is made by English Heritage) intend to grant listed building consent, they are, subject to certain exceptions, covered by a direction, required first to notify the Secretary of State for the Environment. This requirement also relates to applications subject to building preservation notices, applications for the modification or discharge of conditions, subject to which listed building consent has been granted.[3] This requirement does not apply to applications for conservation area consent.

The notification of the Secretary of State is applicable to all English local planning authorities and presents him with the opportunity to "call-in" the application. He has a period of 28 days beginning with the date of notification to decide whether to direct that the application should be referred to him or to give notice to the local planning authority that he requires further time to consider whether to require such a reference. In the meantime, the local planning authority must not grant listed building consent until the 28 day period has expired and the Secretary of State has stated that he does not intend to "call-in" the application. In arriving at his decision, the Secretary of State will have received copies of all the representations made by the statutory consultees and the general public, to the application. Cases are likely to be called-in where he considers the proposal raises issues of exceptional significance or controversy,[4] and before reaching a decision, the Secretary of State would normally hold a public inquiry.

(c) Planning applications affecting the setting of a listed building

Under section 67(1) of the LPA 1990, where an application for planning permission affects the setting of a listed building, the local planning authority is required to publish details in a local newspaper and provide a period

---

[3] s. 19(3).
[4] PPG 15, para. 3.21.

of 21 days for receiving comments. A site notice on, or near, the land is also required to be displayed for not less than seven days. As in the case of proposals affecting listed buildings, the local planning authority is required, in determining the planning application, to take into account any representations relating to the applications which have been received as a result of the publicity.

In a case of *R. v. South Hereford District Council ex parte* Telton [1989] 3 P.L.R. 81, the High Court quashed a planning permission which had been granted without properly being advertised or notified to English Heritage. The Court decided that the Act did not require that the proposed development would "substantially" affect the setting of a listed building. The decision was upheld in the Court of Appeal ([1990] E.G.C.S. 34).

(d) Appeals concerning applications for listed building consent

13.03   The normal rights of appeal apply where a local planning authority refuses listed building consent or where it grants it subject to conditions. An aggrieved applicant may lodge an appeal with the Secretary of State within six months of the notice of decision, or on the expiration of the prescribed, or agreed, period for reaching a decision (normally eight weeks from the date when the application was lodged with the local planning authority). The same rules relating to appeals apply to applications for conservation area consent. The only person who may appeal is the "aggrieved applicant", although a subsequent owner may continue an appeal lodged by the applicant and may apply to the High Court under section 63 of the LBA 1990 as a "person aggrieved".[5]

Appeals may be dealt with by way of a local public inquiry, a hearing (in effect, an informal inquiry), or by written representations. Under the Town and Country Planning (Inquiry Procedure) Rules 1992[6] and the Town and Country Planning Appeals (Determination by Inspectors) (Inquiry Procedures) Rules 1992[7] the various parties are required to identify the principal issues on which the inquiry should concentrate, thus avoiding needless discussion of matters which are not relevant or can be resolved in advance.

The local planning authority is required to inform, amongst others, any persons who made representations relating to the application. Where the Secretary of State, a local authority or English Heritage have given a direction to the local planning authority which has influenced the decision, the authority is required to inform the sponsor of the inquiry or such other appeal procedure as had been agreed. There is therefore every opportunity for those individuals or bodies who made representations either for or against the application, to repeat or expand on those comments at the time of the appeal.

---

[5] *Times Investments Ltd v. Secretary of State for the Environment, The Times,* June 21, 1990.
[6] S.I. 1992, 2038.
[7] S.I. 1992, 2039.

(e) Applications for scheduled monument consent

Applications for scheduled monument consent (Chapter 8) are made **13.04** direct to the Secretary of State, and his decision is final. However, the 1979 Act[8] requires that before granting scheduled monument consent the Secretary of State shall either:

"(a) cause a public local inquiry to be held; or
(b) afford to the applicant, and to any other person to whom it appears to the Secretary of State expedient to afford it, an opportunity of appearing before and being heard by a person appointed by the Secretary of State for the purpose."[9]

Additionally,

"Before determining whether or not to grant scheduled monument consent on any application therefor the Secretary of State:
(a) shall in every case consider any representations made by any person with respect to that application before the time when he considers his decision thereon (whether in consequence of any notice given to that person in accordance with any requirements of regulations made by virtue of paragraph 2 (of the Schedule) or of any publicity given to the application by the Secretary of State, or otherwise)."[10]

(f) Modification or revocation of scheduled monument consent

There is a similar procedure for an inquiry as in paragraph (e) above.

(g) Operations notices in respect of areas of archaeological importance

These are limited to the five towns which have areas of archaeological importance (Canterbury, Chester, Exeter, Hereford and York) and are dealt with in Chapter 8 and come within section 35 of the Ancient Monuments and Archaeological Areas Act 1979. An "operations notice" required under this section is a notice of intent to undertake works, and not an application for consent to do so. It would appear that the rights associated with this form of notice relate only to the "investigating authority" for the area of archaeological importance, and do not confer any formal rights on the general public to enter a site or make its views known.

---

[8] AMAAA 1979.
[9] AMAAA 1979, Sched. I, para. 3(2) and see para. 8.16 above.
[10] AMAAA 1979, Sched. I, para. 3(3).

3. ACCESS TO BUILDINGS AND SITES

13.05   In the light of the increase in visits made by the general public to historic buildings, churches and sites of historical interest, the legal authority for access to such sites and buildings is of little importance. Visits to historic properties increased by 24 per cent. between 1982 and 1994, and at least 28 historic properties (where a charge was made, and therefore records kept) attracted over 200,000 visitors in 1993. More detailed information about visits to various categories of historic properties are contained in the annually published *English Heritage Monitor*.[11]

(a) Buildings of architectural or historic interest

The inclusion of buildings in lists compiled by the Secretary of State under section 1 of the LBA 1990 confer no public rights of access to either the building or the land on which it stands.

The only circumstances in which public access may be required of an owner of a listed building, or of one which whilst not listed is regarded of local interest, is where a grant (but not a loan) has been made for its repair or maintenance. It can be a condition of the making of a grant that public access should be permitted to the property, or part of it, at such times as the agreement may provide.

Grants made by the Secretary of State under the Historic Buildings and Ancient Monuments Act 1953 (as amended by the National Heritage Act 1983), and by local authorities under section 57 of the LBA 1990, may be subject to public access conditions. English Heritage often give advice on the appropriate form of access conditions when a grant is being considered. There will sometimes be circumstances where the requirement to permit public access would be onerous upon the owner or occupier of the building, to the point where it discourages the acceptance of a grant.

Sometimes the value of the building attracting a grant may lie in its external appearance which can be seen from a street or public place. At other times the building attracting a grant may not be sufficiently large or significant to justify public access. The extent and duration of public access must be clearly decided on the circumstances of each case, and arrangements should be made with the owner to give suitable notice or publicity of the times when public access will be available.

(b) Access to buildings in conservation areas

13.06   Unless a building within a conservation area has received grant aid under section 77 of the LBA 1990, and it was a condition of that grant that public access to the building should be available, there is no right for public access. Even where a grant under this section has been made, the chances are it will have been for external improvement, since this form of grant must relate to

[11] Published by English Tourist Board.

the preservation or enhancement of the character or appearance of the conservation area and would therefore normally be visible to the passing public.

(c) Ancient Monuments and archaeological areas

There is no automatic public right of access to ancient monuments other
than those in the ownership of the Secretary of State, English Heritage or a
local authority. Section 19 of the 1979 Act provides for a general public right
of access under the ownership and guardianship rules. In section 19(4) the
Secretary of State, or the local authority, may prescribe the times when the
public is allowed access to the monument.

The designation of areas of archaeological importance (section 33 of the
1979 Act) does not convey any public rights of access to any such area to
which the public does not normally have access.

(d) Use of metal detectors

The popularity of metal detectors and the growing interest of "treasure
hunting" has given rise to concern to archaeologists, and there is strong evidence of indiscriminate use of metal detectors ruining valuable, unexca-
vated, archaeological sites. This concern caused the introduction of section
42 of the 1979 Act which relates only to areas of archaeological importance
designated under Part II of the Act, and to scheduled monuments and monuments under the ownership or guardianship of the Secretary of State, English Heritage or a local authority. The general offence committed under this
section of the Act is that of using a metal detector in a protected place and is
subject to the defence that the device was being used for a purpose other
than detecting or locating objects of archaeological or historical interest.

Appendix A

DEPARTMENT OF THE ENVIRONMENT   PPG 15

DEPARTMENT OF NATIONAL
HERITAGE   SEPTEMBER 1994

PLANNING POLICY GUIDANCE:

PLANNING AND THE HISTORIC ENVIRONMENT

Planning policy guidance notes set out Government policy on planning issues and provide guidance to local authorities and others on the operation of the planning system. They also explain the relationship between planning policies and other policies which have an important bearing on issues of development and land use. Local planning authorities must take their content into account in preparing their development plans. The guidance may also be material to decisions on individual planning applications and appeals.

This PPG, which is issued jointly by the Secretary of State for the Environment and the Secretary of State for National Heritage, updates the advice in Department of the Environment *Circular 8/87*.

INTRODUCTION

1. This PPG provides a full statement of Government policies for the identification and protection of historic buildings, conservation areas, and other elements of the historic environment. It explains the role played by the planning system in their protection. It complements the guidance on archaeology and planning given in PPG 16.*

2. In addition to normal development controls, the Planning (Listed Buildings and Conservation Areas) Act 1990** provides specific protection for buildings and areas of special architectural or historic interest. In many instances there is a close link between controls over listed buildings and conservation areas and development control decisions. In such cases development and conservation issues will generally need to be considered together.

3. This guidance is not only for local authorities, but also for other public authorities, property owners, developers, amenity bodies and all members of the public with an interest in the conser-

---

* For further details of this and other publications mentioned in the text in italics see the bibliography at Annex D.
** Hereafter referred to as "the Act"; the Town & Country Planning Act 1990 is referred to as "the principal Act".

vation of the historic environment. It updates the advice in Department of the Environment *Circular 8/87*, within the existing legislative framework. The policy content of Circular 8/87 is hereby cancelled, along with all of *Circular 18/88*. The directions in *Circular 8/87* will continue in force until new directions have been made. Such directions will be made at the same time as related changes to the Town and Country Planning General Development Order 1988 (the GDO), and the Planning (Listed Buildings and Conservation Areas) Regulations 1990, and will be the subject of a separate Circular.

4. The guidance given in this PPG should not involve any significant additional expenditure for local planning authorities. New duties placed on authorities by subordinate legislation—eg. directions, the GDO, and the Ecclesiastical Exemption (Listed Buildings and Conservation Areas) Order 1994— are the subject of separate consultation with the local authority associations.

Structure of the PPG

5. Part 1 of the PPG deals with those aspects of conservation policy which interact most directly with the planning system, whose operation is the responsibility of the Secretary of State for the Environment. Decisions on called-in applications for, and appeals against refusals of, listed building or conservation area consent are the responsibility of the Secretary of State for the Environment because of their frequent close links with issues of development control.

6. Part 2 of the PPG deals with aspects of conservation policy which are less directly linked to the planning system, and which are for the most part the responsibility of the Secretary of State for National Heritage.

7. There is however no sharp distinction between the two areas of responsibility. For instance, both Secretaries of State have an interest in policies for the designation and protection of conservation areas; and protection of the wider aspects of the historic environment (eg. historic landscapes) is effected mainly through the operation of the planning system.

8. In Part 1 of the PPG and in Annex B, references to 'the Secretary of State' are, unless otherwise stated, references to the Secretary of State for the Environment; in Part 2 and in Annex A, 'the Secretary of State' refers to the Secretary of State for National Heritage.

PART 1

1. PLANNING AND CONSERVATION

1.1 It is fundamental to the Government's policies for environmental stewardship that there should be effective protection for all aspects of the historic environment. The physical survivals of our past are to be valued and protected for their own sake, as a central part of our cultural heritage and our sense of national identity. They are an irreplaceable record which contributes, through formal education and in many other ways, to our understanding of both the present and the past. Their presence adds to the quality of our lives, by enhancing the familiar and cherished local scene and sustaining the sense of local distinctiveness which is so important an aspect of the character and appearance of our towns, villages and countryside. The historic environment is also of immense importance for leisure and recreation.

The role of the planning system

1.2 The function of the planning system is to regulate the development and use of land in the public interest. It has to take account of the Government's objective of promoting sustainable economic growth, and make provision for development to meet the economic and social needs of the community. As *PPG1* makes clear, planning is also an important instrument for protecting and enhancing the environment in town and country, and preserving the built and natural heritage. The objective of planning processes should be to reconcile the need for economic growth with the need to protect the natural and historic environment.

1.3 The Government has committed itself to the concept of sustainable development—of not sacrificing what future generations will value for the sake of short-term and often illusory gains. This approach is set out in Sustainable Development: The UK Strategy. It is also a key element of the development plan system, as set out in PPG 12. This commitment has particular relevance to the preservation of the historic environment, which by its nature is irreplaceable. Yet the historic environment of England is all-pervasive, and it cannot in practice be preserved unchanged. We must

ensure that the means are available to identify what is special in the historic environment; to define through the development plan system its capacity for change; and, when proposals for new development come forward, to assess their impact on the historic environment and give it full weight, alongside other considerations.

Conservation and economic prosperity

1.4 Though choices sometimes have to be made, conservation and sustainable economic growth are complementary objectives and should not generally be seen as in opposition to one another. Most historic buildings can still be put to good economic use in, for example, commercial or residential occupation. They are a valuable material resource and can contribute to the prosperity of the economy, provided that they are properly maintained: the avoidable loss of fabric through neglect is a waste of economic as well as environmental resources. In return, economic prosperity can secure the continued vitality of conservation areas, and the continued use and maintenance of historic buildings, provided that there is a sufficiently realistic and imaginative approach to their alteration and change of use, to reflect the needs of a rapidly changing world.

1.5 Conservation can itself play a key part in promoting economic prosperity by ensuring that an area offers attractive living and working conditions which will encourage inward investment— environmental quality is increasingly a key factor in many commercial decisions. The historic environment is of particular importance for tourism and leisure, and Government policy encourages the growth and development of tourism in response to the market so long as this is compatible with proper long-term conservation. Further advice on tourist aspects of conservation is given in *PPG 21* and the English Tourist Board's publication *Maintaining the Balance*.

Stewardship: the role of local authorities and others

1.6 The Government urges local authorities to maintain and strengthen their commitment to stewardship of the historic environment, and to reflect it in their policies and their allocation of resources. It is important that, as planning authorities, they adopt suitable policies in their development plans, and give practical effect to them through their development control decisions. As highway authorities too, their policies and activities should reflect the need to protect the historic environment and to promote sustainable economic growth, for roads can have a particular impact at all levels—not only through strategic decisions on the siting of new roads, but also through the more detailed aspects of road building and road maintenance, such as the quality of street furniture and surfaces. Above all, local authorities should ensure that they can call on sufficient specialist conservation advice, whether individually or jointly, to inform their decision-making and to assist owners and other members of the public.

1.7 However, the responsibility of stewardship is shared by everyone—not only by central and local government, but also by business,

voluntary bodies, churches, and by individual citizens as owners, users and visitors of historic buildings. The historic environment cannot be preserved unless there is broad public support and understanding, and it is a key element of Government policy for conservation that there should be adequate processes of consultation and education to facilitate this.

2. DEVELOPMENT PLANS AND DEVELOPMENT CONTROL

2.1 The principal Act (as amended) requires development plans to include policies for 'the conservation of the natural beauty and amenity of the land' and for 'the improvement of the physical environment'. The Town & Country Planning (Development Plan) Regulations 1991 require authorities to have regard to environmental considerations in preparing their plan policies and proposals. The protection of the historic environment, whether individual listed buildings, conservation areas, parks and gardens, battlefields or the wider historic landscape, is a key aspect of these wider environmental responsibilities, and will need to be taken fully into account both in the formulation of authorities' planning policies and in development control.

Development plans

2.2 Structure, local, and unitary development plans are the main vehicle for ensuring that conservation policies are co-ordinated and integrated with other planning policies affecting the historic

407

environment. Imaginative planning policies can not only reduce threats to it, but increase its contribution to local amenity. By including suitable policies in their plans, local authorities can give encouragement to the satisfactory reuse of neglected historic buildings, particularly where major groups of buildings need to be tackled comprehensively, and where other planning factors, such as traffic problems, may be discouraging reuse.

2.3 Section 54A of the principal Act provides that where, in making any determination under the Planning Acts, regard is to be had to the development plan, the determination must be made in accordance with the development plan unless material considerations indicate otherwise. It is therefore important that plans include all the criteria on the basis of which planning decisions will be made. Plans should set out clearly all conservation policies relevant to the exercise of an authority's development control functions, and also policies which are relevant to cases where development and conservation issues are linked and will need to be addressed together.

2.4 The Courts have accepted that section 54A does not apply to decisions on applications for listed building consent or conservation area consent, since in those cases there is no statutory requirement to have regard to the provisions of the development plan. However, authorities should ensure that aspects of conservation policy that are relevant, directly or indirectly, to development control decisions are included—for instance, policies for alterations or extensions to listed buildings that also consti-

tute development (to which section 54A will directly apply). In view of the statutory requirements that authorities should have special regard to the desirability of preserving any listed building or its setting, or any features of special architectural or historic interest which it possesses, and should pay special attention to the desirability of preserving or enhancing the character or appearance of any conservation area in exercising their development control functions, plans should also include policies for works of demolition or alteration which, while not in themselves constituting development, could affect an authority's decision on a related application for planning permission.

2.5 There may be some detailed conservation policies which have no bearing on issues of development control—for instance, policies for the treatment of some internal features of listed buildings where this would not affect consideration of planning applications but might require listed building consent. Other examples may relate to certain types of alteration, repairs, maintenance or decoration. These policies should be presented as supplementary guidance rather than included in the plan itself. Such guidance will carry greater weight to the extent that it has been the subject of public consultation, has been formally adopted by the authority, and is published in a format which gives clear advice and is readily available to the public. Development plans should contain a reference to such policies in the reasoned justification, together with a clear indication of where those policies may be seen in full.

2.6 Full guidance on the preparation of plans is given in *PPG 12*. Structure plans and the first part of unitary development plans provide a statement of the overall strategy for a county, borough or metropolitan district area, and should include conservation of the historic environment as one of their key topics, taking account of any broad strategic objectives or constraints set out in relevant regional planning guidance. The structure plan should provide a broad planning framework, guiding the approach to be adopted in local plans to such issues as the capacity of historic towns to sustain development, the relief of pressure on historic central areas by the identification of opportunities for growth elsewhere, and the provision of transport infrastructure which respects the historic environment.

2.7 Local plans and the second part of unitary development plans should set out more detailed development control policies for an authority's area: they should include both the policies which will apply over the area as a whole, and any policies and proposals which will apply to particular neighbourhoods. Both policies and proposals should be illustrated on the proposals map (see paragraph 7.14 of *PPG 12*).

2.8 Local plans should set out clearly the planning authority's policies for the preservation and enhancement of the historic environment in their area, and the factors which will be taken into account in assessing different types of planning application—for example, proposals for the change of use of particular types of historic building or for new development which would affect their setting. It is important that clear policies are formulated for cases where new development is proposed in order to provide income for the upkeep of historic buildings (see Department of the Environment Circular *16/91*). Plans should also include a strategy for the economic regeneration of rundown areas, and in particular seek to identify the opportunities which the historic fabric of an area can offer as a focus for regeneration. Excessively detailed or inflexible policies concerning individual buildings or groups of buildings should be avoided.

2.9 Plans should set out authorities' broad criteria for the designation of new conservation areas and for the review of existing conservation area boundaries; and, where possible, which particular areas are in mind for both. The process of assessment, detailed definition or revision of boundaries, and formulation of proposals for individual conservation areas (as required by section 71 of the Act) should involve extensive local consultation and should be pursued separately from the local plan process itself. But the plan should provide a policy framework, making clear to the public how detailed assessment documents and statements of proposals for individual conservation areas relate to the plan, and what weight will be given to them in decisions on applications for planning permission and conservation area consent. (See also paragraphs 4.3–4.7, 4.10 and 4.15). Designation strategies should take account of the fact that authorities now have general powers to control the demolition of dwelling houses outside conservation areas (see Department of the Environment *Circular 26/92*).

2.10 English Heritage is a statutory consultee on draft plans, but is also able to offer specialist advice at preparation stage. In conjunction with the Countryside Commission and English Nature, it is also issuing guidance on conservation in strategic and local plans. There will often be advantage in consultation at an early stage in plan preparation with other statutory agencies and with the national amenity societies and local conservation bodies, as well as wider public consultation at the formal deposit stage.

Development control

2.11 The Secretary of State attaches particular importance to early consultation with the local planning authority on development proposals which would affect historic sites and structures, whether listed buildings, conservation areas, parks and gardens, battlefields or the wider historic landscape. There is likely to be much more scope for refinement and revision of proposals if consultation takes place before intentions become firm and timescales inflexible. Local planning authorities should indicate their readiness to discuss proposals with developers before formal planning applications are submitted. They should expect developers to assess the likely impact of their proposals on the special interest of the site or structure in question, and to provide such written information or drawings as may be required to understand the significance of a site or structure before an application is determined. The principle of early consultation should extend to English Heritage and the national amenity societies on cases where a formal planning or listed building consent application

would be notifiable to them by direction or under the GDO.

2.12 It is generally preferable for both the applicant and the planning authority if related applications for planning permission and for listed building or conservation area consent are considered concurrently. Authorities are required by section 66(1) of the Act, in considering whether to grant planning permission for development which affects a listed building or its setting, to have special regard to the desirability of preserving the building or its setting or any features of architectural or historic interest which it possesses. It is unlikely that they will be able to do so effectively unless the planning application is accompanied by a listed building consent application (where the development in question requires one) or at least contains an equivalent amount of information. If an authority is asked to consider a planning application in isolation, a decision on that application cannot be taken as predetermining the outcome of a subsequent application for listed building consent. Authorities are also required by section 72 of the Act, in the exercise in a conservation area of their powers under the Planning Acts (and Part I of the Historic Buildings and Ancient Monuments Act 1953), to pay special attention to the desirability of preserving or enhancing the character or appearance of that area. In the case of unlisted buildings in conservation areas, the Courts have held that consent for the demolition of a building may involve consideration of what is to take its place (see paragraph 4.27)

2.13 Local planning authorities are urged to ensure that they have appropriately qualified specialist advice on any development which, by its character or location, might be held to have an adverse effect on any sites or structures of the historic environment. The need for environmental assessment of major development proposals affecting historic areas should be considered in the light of the advice given in Department of the Environment *Circular 15/88*. Authorities should ensure that the Royal Fine Art Commission is consulted on all planning applications raising conservation issues of more than local importance, and should take the RFAC's views fully into account in reaching their decisions.

2.14 The design of new buildings intended to stand alongside historic buildings needs very careful consideration. In general it is better that old buildings are not set apart, but are woven into the fabric of the living and working community. This can be done, provided that the new buildings are carefully designed to respect their setting, follow fundamental architectural principles of scale, height, massing and alignment, and use appropriate materials. This does not mean that new buildings have to copy their older neighbours in detail: some of the most interesting streets in our towns and villages include a variety of building styles, materials, and forms of construction, of many different periods, but together forming a harmonious group. Further general advice on design considerations which are relevant to the exercise of planning controls is given in Annex A to *PPG 1*.

2.15 Some historic buildings are scheduled ancient monuments, and many which are not scheduled

are either of intrinsic archaeological interest or stand on ground which contains archaeological remains. It is important in such cases that there should be appropriate assessment of the archaeological implications of development proposals before applications are determined; and that, where permission is to be granted, authorities should consider whether adequate arrangements have been made for recording remains that would be lost in the course of works for which permission is being sought. Further advice on archaeology and planning is given in *PPG 16*.

The setting of listed buildings

2.16 Sections 16 and 66 of the Act require authorities considering applications for planning permission or listed building consent for works which affect a listed building to have special regard to certain matters, including the desirability of preserving the setting of the building. The setting is often an essential part of the building's character, especially if a garden or grounds have been laid out to complement its design or function. Also, the economic viability as well as the character of historic buildings may suffer and they can be robbed of much of their interest, and of the contribution they make to townscape or the countryside, if they become isolated from their surroundings, *e.g.* by new traffic routes, car parks, or other development.

2.17 Local planning authorities are required under section 67 of the Act to publish a notice of all applications they receive for planning permission for any development which, in their opinion, affects the setting of a listed build-

411

ing. This provision should not be interpreted too narrowly: the setting of a building may be limited to obviously ancillary land, but may often include land some distance from it. Even where a building has no ancillary land—for example in a crowded urban street—the setting may encompass a number of other properties. The setting of individual listed buildings very often owes its character to the harmony produced by a particular grouping of buildings (not necessarily all of great individual merit) and to the quality of the spaces created between them. Such areas require careful appraisal when proposals for development are under consideration, even if the redevelopment would only replace a building which is neither itself listed nor immediately adjacent to a listed building. Where a listed building forms an important visual element in a street, it would probably be right to regard any development in the street as being within the setting of the building. A proposed high or bulky building might also affect the setting of a listed building some distance away, or alter views of a historic skyline. In some cases, setting can only be defined by a historical assessment of a building's surroundings. If there is doubt about the precise extent of a building's setting, it is better to publish a notice.

Changes of use

2.18 New uses may often be the key to a building's or area's preservation, and controls over land use, density, plot ratio, daylighting and other planning matters should be exercised sympathetically where this would enable a historic building or area to be given a new lease of life. The Secretary of State is not generally in favour of tightening development controls over changes of use as a specific instrument of conservation policy. He considers that, in general, the same provisions on change of use should apply to historic buildings as to all others. Patterns of economic activity inevitably change over time, and it would be unrealistic to seek to prevent such change by the use of planning controls.

2.19 Advice on the planning aspects of re-use and adaption of rural buildings is given in *PPG 7* (paragraph 2.15 and Annex D). English Heritage has also issued guidance entitled *The Conversion of Historic Farm Buildings*. Special considerations apply in *Green Belts* (see *PPG 2*).

Article 4 directions for listed buildings

2.20 Under article 5 of the GDO, directions under article 4 bringing certain categories of permitted development within planning control can be made by local authorities without the need for approval by the Secretary of State if they relate solely to a listed building or to development within the curtilage of a listed building, provided they do not affect the carrying out of development by a statutory undertaker. Authorities are reminded that permitted development rights should not be restricted without good reason; but there will nevertheless be cases where it will be desirable to invoke this power to ensure that the immediate setting of a listed building is protected when minor development is proposed. For example, farm buildings converted to new uses may otherwise generate curtilage developments—such as garages, fuel tanks or fences—

that may not be suitable in an agricultural setting.

Planning controls and other aspects of the historic environment

2.21 Listed buildings and conservation areas are treated in section 3 and 4 below. Other aspects of the historic environment are considered briefly here.

World Heritage Sites

2.22 Details of World Heritage Sites in England are given in paragraph 6.35. No additional statutory controls follow from the inclusion of a site in the World Heritage list. Inclusion does, however, highlight the outstanding international importance of the site as a key material consideration to be taken into account by local planning authorities in determining planning and listed building consent applications, and by the Secretary of State in determining cases on appeal or following call-in.

2.23 Each local authority concerned, taking account of World Heritage Site designation and other relevant statutory designations, should formulate specific planning policies for protecting these sites and include these policies in their development plans. Policies should reflect the fact that all these sites have been designated for their outstanding universal value, and they should place great weight on the need to protect them for the benefit of future generations as well as our own. Development proposals affecting these sites or their setting may be compatible with this objective, but should always be carefully scrutinised for their likely effect on the

site or its setting in the longer term. Significant development proposals affecting World Heritage Sites will generally require formal environmental assessment, to ensure that their immediate impact and their implications for the longer term are fully evaluated (see paragraph 2.13 above).

Historic parks and gardens

2.24 Again no additional statutory controls follow from the inclusion of a site in English Heritiage's Register of Parks and Gardens of Special Historic Interest (see paragraph 6.38), but local planning authorities should protect registered parks and gardens in preparing development plans and in determining planning applications. The effect of proposed development on a registered park or garden or its setting is a material consideration in the determination of a planning application. Planning and highway authorities should also safeguard registered parks or gardens when themselves planning new developments or road schemes.

Historic battlefields

2.25 A similar non-statutory Register of Historic Battlefields is being prepared by English Heritage (see paragraph 6.39). This will not entail additional statutory controls, but, when consultation with landowners and others on the content of the Register is complete, it too will need to be taken into account by local planning authorities. The effects of any development on the limited number of registered sites will form a material consideration to be taken into account in determining planning applications.

413

The wider historic landscape

2.26 Conservation of the wider historic landscape greatly depends on active land management, but there is nevertheless a significant role for local planning authorities. In defining planning policies for the countryside, authorities should take account of the historical dimension of the landscape as a whole rather than concentrate on selected areas. Adequate understanding is an essential preliminary and authorities should assess the wider historic landscape at an early stage in development plan preparation. Plans should protect its most important components and encourage development that is consistent with maintaining its overall historic character. Indeed, policies to strengthen the rural economy through environmentally sensitive diversification may be among the most important for its conservation.

3. LISTED BUILDING CONTROL

3.1 Section 1 of the Act imposes on the Secretary of State for National Heritage a duty to compile or approve lists of buildings of special architectural or historic interest. The Secretary of State's policy for the listing of such buildings is set out in paragraphs 6.10–6.16. Once a building is listed (or is the subject of a building preservation notice), section 7 of the Act provides that consent is normally required for its demolition, in whole or in part, and for any works of alteration or extension which would affect its character as a building of special architectural or historic interest. It is a criminal offence to carry out such works without consent, which should be sought from the local planning authority. This section sets out the main elements of Government policy for listed building controls. Details of the procedures are summarised in Annex B.

3.2 Controls apply to all works, both external and internal, that would affect a building's special interest, whether or not the particular feature concerned is specifically mentioned in the list description. Consent is not normally required for repairs, but, where repairs involve alterations which would affect the character of the listed building, consent is required. Whether repairs actually constitute alterations which require consent is a matter of act and degree which must be determined in each case. Where painting or repainting the exterior or interior of a listed building would affect the building's character, consent is required. Further detailed guidance on alterations to listed buildings, prepared by English Heritage, is given in Annex C. The Secretaries of State commend this guidance and ask all local planning authorities to take it into account in their exercise of listed building and development controls. Whether proposed works constitute alterations or a demolition is again a matter of fact and degree. Fixtures and curtilage buildings—i.e. any object or structure which is fixed to the building, or is within the curtilage and forms part of the land and has done so since before July 1948—are also treated as part of the building for the purposes of listed building control (see paragraphs 3.30–3.36 below).

3.3 The importance which the Government attaches to the protection of the historic environment was explained in paragraphs 1.1–1.7 above. Once lost, listed buildings cannot be replaced; and they can be robbed of their special interest as surely by unsuitable alteration as by outright demolition. They represent a finite resource and an irreplaceable asset. There should be a general presumption in favour of the preservation of listed buildings, except where a convincing case can be made out, against the criteria set out in this section, for alteration or demolition. While the listing of a building should not be seen as a bar to all future change, the starting point for the exercise of listed building control is the statutory requirement on local planning authorities to 'have special regard to the desirability of preserving the building or its setting or any features of special architectural or historic interest which it possesses' (section 16). This reflects the great importance to society of protecting listed buildings from unnecessary demolition and from unsuitable and insensitive alteration and should be the prime consideration for authorities in determining an application for consent.

3.4 Applicants for listed buildings consent must be able to justify their proposals. They will need to show why works which would affect the character of a listed building are desirable or necessary. They should provide the local planning authority with full information, to enable them to assess the likely impact of their proposals on the special architectural or historic interest of the building and on its setting.

General criteria

3.5 The issues that are generally relevant to the consideration of all listed building consent applications are:

i. the importance of the building, its intrinsic architectural and historic interest and rarity, in both national and local terms ('historic interest' is further explained in paragraph 6.11);

ii. the particular physical features of the building (which may include its design, plan, materials or location) which justify its inclusion in the list: list descriptions may draw attention to features of particular interest or value, but they are not exhaustive and other features of importance (eg. interiors) may come to light after the building's inclusion in the list;

iii. the building's setting and its contribution to the local scene, which may be very important, e.g. where it forms an element in a group, park, garden or other townscape or landscape, or where it shares particular architectural forms or details with other buildings nearby;

iv. the extent to which the proposed works would bring substantial benefits for the community, in particular by contributing to the economic regeneration of the area or the enhancement of its environment (including other listed buildings).

3.6 The grading of a building in the statutory lists is clearly a material consideration for the exercise of listed building control. Grades I and II* identify the outstanding architectural or historic interest of a small proportion (about 6%) of all listed buildings. These buildings are of particularly great importance to the nation's built heritage: their significance will generally be beyond dispute. But it should be emphasised that the statutory controls apply equally to all listed buildings, irrespective of grade; and since Grade II includes about 94% of all listed buildings, representing a major element in the historic quality of our towns, villages, and countryside, failure to give careful scrutiny to proposals for their alteration or demolition could lead to widespread damage to the historic environment.

3.7 The following paragraphs deal first with alterations and extensions and then with demolitions, though considerations relevant to the two types of case to some extent overlap. For instance, some of the considerations set out in paragraph 3.19, in relation to demolitions, may also be relevant to substantial works of alteration or extension which would significantly alter the character of a listed building. Since listed building consent applications will often raise the issue of the most appropriate use for a building, the question of use is also discussed here.

Use

3.8 Generally the best way of securing the upkeep of historic buildings and areas is to keep them in active use. For the great majority this must mean economically viable uses if they are to survive, and new, and even continuing, uses will often necessitate some degree of adaptation. The range and acceptability of possible uses must therefore usually be a major consideration when the future of listed buildings or buildings in conservation areas is in question.

3.9 Judging the best use is one of the most important and sensitive assessments that local planning authorities and other bodies involved in conservation have to make. It requires balancing the economic viability of possible uses against the effect of any changes they entail in the special architectural and historic interest of the building or area in question. In principle the aim should be to identify the optimum viable use that is compatible with the fabric, interior, and setting of the historic building. This may not necessarily be the most profitable use if that would entail more destructive alterations than other viable uses. Where a particular compatible use is to be preferred but restoration for that use is unlikely to be economically viable, grant assistance from the authority, English Heritage or other sources may need to be considered.

3.10 The best use will very often be the use for which the building was originally designed, and the continuation or reinstatement of that use should certainly be the first option when the future of a building is considered. But not all original uses will now be viable or even necessarily appropriate: the nature of uses can change over time, so that in some cases the original use may now be less compatible with the building than an alternative. For example, some business or light industrial uses may now require less damaging alterations to historic farm buildings than some types of modern agricultural operation. Policies for development and listed building controls should recognise the need for flexibility where new uses have to be considered to secure a building's survival.

3.11 If a building is so sensitive that it cannot sustain any alterations to keep it in viable economic use, its future may nevertheless be secured by charitable or community ownership, preserved for its own sake for local people and for the visiting public, where possible with non-destructive opportunity uses such as meeting rooms. Many listed buildings subsist successfully in this way—from the great houses of the National Trust to buildings such as guildhalls, churches and windmills cared for by local authorities or trusts—and this possibly may need to be considered. The Secretaries of State attach particular importance to the activities of the voluntary sector in heritage matters: it is well placed to tap local support, resources and loyalty, and buildings preserved in its care can make a contribution to community life, to local education, and to the local economy.

Alterations and extensions

3.12 Many listed buildings are already in well-established uses, and any changes need be considered only in this context. But where new uses are proposed, it is important to balance the effect of any changes on the special interest of the listed building against the viability of any proposed use and of alternative, and possibly less damaging, uses. In judging the effect of any alteration or extension it is essential to have assessed the elements that make up the special interest of the building in question. They may comprise not only obvious visual features such as a decorative facade or, inter-

nally, staircases or decorated plaster ceilings, but the spaces and layout of the building and the archaeological or technological interest of the surviving structure and surfaces. These elements are often just as important in simple vernacular and functional buildings as in grander architecture.

3.13 Many listed buildings can sustain some degree of sensitive alteration or extension to accommodate continuing or new uses. Indeed, cumulative changes reflecting the history of use and ownership are themselves an aspect of the special interest of some buildings, and the merit of some new alterations or additions, especially where they are generated within a secure and committed long-term ownership, should not be discounted. Nevertheless, listed buildings do vary greatly in the extent to which they can accommodate change without loss of special interest. Some may be sensitive even to slight alterations; this is especially true of buildings with important interiors and fittings—not just great houses, but also, for example, chapels with historic fittings or industrial structures with surviving machinery. Some listed buildings are the subject of successive applications for alteration or extension: in such cases it needs to be borne in mind that minor works of indifferent quality, which may seem individually of little importance, can cumulatively be very destructive of a building's special interest.

3.14 As noted above, the listing grade is a material consideration but is not of itself a reliable guide to the sensitivity of a building to alteration or extension. For example, many Grade II buildings are of humble and once common

417

building types and have been listed precisely because they are relatively unaltered examples of a particular building type; so they can as readily have their special interest ruined by unsuitable alteration or extension as can Grade I or II* structures.

3.15 Achieving a proper balance between the special interest of a listed building and proposals for alterations or extensions is demanding and should always be based on specialist expertise; but it is rarely impossible, if reasonable flexibility and imagination are shown by all parties involved. Thus, a better solution may be possible if a local planning authority is prepared to apply normal development control policies flexibly; or if an applicant is willing to exploit unorthodox spaces rather than set a standardized requirement; or if an architect can respect the structural limitations of a building and abandon conventional design solutions in favour of a more imaginative approach. For example, standard commercial office floor-loadings are rarely needed in all parts of a building, and any unusually heavy loads can often be accommodated in stronger areas such as basements. The preservation of facades alone, and the gutting and reconstruction of interiors, is not normally an acceptable approach to the re-use of listed buildings: it can destroy much of a building's special interest and create problems for the long-term stability of the structure.

Demolitions

3.16 While is is an objective of Government policy to secure the preservation of historic buildings, there will very occasionally be cases where demolition is unavoidable. Listed building controls ensure that proposals for demolition are fully scrutinised before any decision is reached. These controls have been successful in recent years in keeping the number of total demolitions very low. The destruction of historic buildings is in fact very seldom necessary for reasons of good planning: more often it is the result of neglect, or of failure to make imaginative efforts to find new uses for them or to incorporate them into new development.

3.17 There are many outstanding buildings for which it is in practice almost inconceivable that consent for demolition would ever be granted. The demolition of any Grade I or Grade II* building should be wholly exceptional and should require the strongest justification. Indeed, the Secretaries of State would not expect consent to be given for the total or substantial demolition of any listed building without clear and convincing evidence that all reasonable efforts have been made to sustain existing uses or find viable new uses, and these efforts have failed; that preservation in some form of charitable or community ownership is not possible or suitable (see paragraph 3.11); or that redevelopment would produce substantial benefits for the community which would decisively outweigh the loss resulting from demolition. The Secretaries of State would not expect consent to demolition to be given simply because redevelopment is economically more attractive to the developer than repair and re-use of a historic building, or because the developer acquired the building at a price that reflected the potential for redevelopment rather than the condition and constraints of the existing historic building.

3.18 Where proposed works would not result in the total or substantial demolition of the listed building or any significant part of it, the Secretaries of State would expect the local planning authority to address the same considerations as it would in relation to an application in respect of alterations or extensions (see paragraphs 3.12 to 3.15 above).

3.19 Where proposed works would result in the total or substantial demolition of the listed building, or any significant part of it, the Secretaries of State would expect the authority, in addition to the general considerations set out in paragraph 3.5 above, to address the following considerations:

i. the condition of the building, the cost of repairing and maintaining it in relation to its importance and to the value derived from its continued use. Any such assessment should be based on consistent and long-term assumptions. Less favourable levels of rents and yields cannot automatically be assumed for historic buildings. Also, they may offer proven technical performance, physical attractiveness and functional spaces that, in an age of rapid change, may outlast the short-lived and inflexible technical specifications that have sometimes shaped new developments. Any assessment should also take account of the possibility of tax allowances and exemptions and of grants from public or charitable sources. In the rare cases where it is clear that a building has been deliberately neglected in the hope of obtaining consent for demolition, less weight should be given to the costs of repair;

ii. the adequacy of efforts made to retain the building in use. The Secretaries of State would not expect listed building consent to be granted for demolition unless the authority (or where appropriate the Secretary of State himself) is satisfied that real efforts have been made without success to continue the present use or to find compatible alternative uses for the building. This should include the offer of the unrestricted freehold of the building on the open market at a realistic price reflecting the building's condition (the offer of a lease only, or the imposition of restrictive covenants, would normally reduce the chances of finding a new use for the building);

iii. the merits of alternative proposals for the site. Whist these are a material consideration, the Secretaries of State take the view that subjective claims for the architectural merits of proposed replacement buildings should not in themselves be held to justify the demolition of any listed building. There may very exceptionally be cases where the proposed works would bring substantial

419

benefits for the community which have to be weighed against the arguments in favour of preservation. Even here, it will often be feasible to incorporate listed buildings within new development, and this option should be carefully considered: the challenge presented by retaining listed buildings can be a stimulus to imaginative new design to accommodate them.

Called-in applications

3.20 The Secretary of State may require applications for listed building consent to be referred to him for decision, but this call-in power has only been exercised in a small number of cases per year in recent years. The policy of the Secretary of State is to be very selective about calling in listed building consent cases.

3.21 Cases are likely to be called in where the Secretary of State considers that the proposals raise issues of exceptional significance or controversy. It may also happen that an application for listed building consent is received by a local planning authority when a related matter (eg. a planning appeal, a called-in planning application or a compulsory purchase order) is being considered by the Secretary of State. Unless it is clear that the listed building consent application can reasonably be dealt with separately, such an application will normally be called in.

Recording buildings

3.22 The Royal Commission on the Historical Monuments of England must be notified of all proposals to demolish listed buildings, and allowed access to buildings which it wishes to record before demolition takes place. There are other circumstances where notification may also be appropriate—for instance, where the exterior of a building is likely to be radically changed as a consequence of major repairs, alteration or extension, or where interior work of significance will be lost, affected by subdivision, or substantially rebuilt.

3.23 Local planning authorities should also consider, in all cases of alteration or demolition, whether it would be appropriate to make it a condition of consent that applicants arrange suitable programmes of recording of features that would be destroyed in the course of the works for which consent is being sought. Authorities should not, however, require applicants to finance such programmes in return for the granting of consent. Nor should applicants expect to be granted consent merely because they have arranged suitable programmes. (For recording of archaeological remains see paragraph 2.15).

3.24 Hidden features of interest are sometimes revealed during works of alteration, especially in older or larger buildings: chimney pieces, fireplaces, early windows and doors, panelling, wattle-and-daub partitions and even wall-paintings may come to light. Applicants for listed building consent should be made aware of this possibility and should seek the advice of the local planning authority when such things are found. If there is any likelihood that hidden features will be revealed, the local planning authority should attach an appropriate condition to the listed building consent to ensure their retention or proper recording, or should require exploratory opening up, with listed building consent as necessary, before considering consent for the main works.

Advice to owners

3.25 Owners of listed buildings should be encouraged to seek expert advice on whether proposed works require listed building consent, and on the best way to carry out any such works to their property. Many will need to obtain professional advice anyway, but the Secretaries of State hope that local planning authorities will give owners informal advice where they can or guide them to other sources where they can get advice for themselves. English Heritage publishes much specialist advice on the care of historic buildings and can sometimes give advice on individual cases, especially where unusual problems are encountered. The national amenity societies are willing to offer advice to individual owners whenever possible. The Royal Commission on the Historical Monuments of England may have a record of a building and its reports and photographs may be available for guidance in understanding the structure and its evolution.

Building and fire legislation; access for disabled people; house renovation grants

3.26 In exercising their responsibilities for the safety of buildings under the building and fire legislation, local planning authorities should deal sympathetically with proposals for the repair or conversion of historic buildings. The Building Regulations should be operated in a way which avoids removal of features which contribute to the character of a listed building and are part of the reason for its being listed. Sufficient flexibility exists within the Building Regulations and Fire Precautions Act systems for authorities to have regard to the possible impact of proposals on the historical or architectural value of a building, and authorities should consult their own conservation officers, or seek expert advice from other sources, when handling difficult situations. It is particularly important that there should be a flexible approach to structural matters, to ensure that any changes are in character with the rest of the building and that there is no unacceptable damage to the fabric. In order to ensure that requirements which are unacceptable in terms of a historic building can be considered as part of a listed building consent application, the precise Building and Fire Regulations requirements should be made explicit *before* an application has been determined. A successful outcome is more likely to be negotiated if the authorities have been consulted from the outset.

3.27 For the longer term, local planning authorities should be aware of the *Report of the Review of the Fire Safety Legislation and Enforcement* which was published on 22 June 1994. The scrutiny was asked to review all legislation for which the Home Office, the Department of the Environment and the Health and Safety Executive have policy responsibility in relation to fire safety; to review the arrangements for enforcing the legislation; and to examine the practicability of bringing policy responsibility for fire safety together in a single department. The Report makes 61 recommendations, but Ministers are committed to full consultation before any proposals for changing the existing arrangements are made.

3.28 It is important in principle that disabled people should have dignified easy access to and within historic buildings. If it is treated as part of an integrated review of access requirements for all visitors or users, and a flexible and pragmatic approach is taken, it should normally be possible to plan suitable access for disabled people without compromising a building's special interest. Alternative routes or re-organizing the use of spaces may achieve the desired result without the need for damaging alterations.

3.29 Where a local planning authority proposes to grant-aid renovation work to a listed house or a house in a conservation area, care should be taken to ensure that standard grant conditions (e.g. for damp proofing or insulation) are not imposed in a way which would be damaging to the historic character of the building. In such cases housing and environmental health departments should consult with the authorities conservation officer or seek expert advice from other sources. Details of grants available are given in the Department of the Environment publication *House Renovation Grants*.

Fixtures and curtilage structures

3.30 It is important to know the extent of a listing, not just to determine whether listed building consent is needed for works, but also to determine the payment of VAT and business rates. List descriptions are for the purposes of identi-

fication and are not a comprehensive or exclusive record of all features—see paragraph 6.19. Section 1(5) of the Act sets out the meaning of a listed building for the purposes of the Act: a listed building is one included in a list compiled or approved by the Secretary of State and includes 'any object or structure fixed to the building' and 'any object or structure within the curtilage of the building which, although not fixed to the building, forms part of the land and has done so since before 1 July 1948'. The Courts have considered in a number of cases in this context the meaning of 'any object or structure fixed to the building' and 'curtilage'.

3.31 The listing of a building confers protection not only on the building, but also on any object or structure fixed to the building which is ancillary to the building. The word 'fixed' has the same connotation as in the law of fixtures. These well-known rules provide that any object or structure fixed to a building should be treated as part of it. It is a test therefore of fact in each case as to whether a structure is free-standing or physically fixed to the building. Generally it would be reasonable to expect some degree of physical annexation, together with indications that the annexation was carried out with the intention of making the object an integral part of the land or building. In the light of this test, items such as chimney-pieces, wall panelling and painted or plastered ceilings will normally be found to be part of the building.

3.32 It may be difficult in some individual cases to decide whether a particular object or structure is a fixture or not. Free-standing

objects, eg. statues, may be fixtures if they were put in place as
part of an overall architectural
design; this could include objects
specially designed or made to fit in
a particular space or room. But
works of art which were placed in
a building primarily to be enjoyed
as objects in their own right, rather
than forming part of the land or the
building, are not likely to be properly considered as fixtures. Each
case must be treated in the light of
its own facts, and owners who are
contemplating works are advised
to contact their local planning
authority first.

3.33 The listing of a building confers protection also on any object
or structure within its curtilage
which forms part of the land and
has done so since before 1 July
1948. Following recent case law,
the Secretary of State for National
Heritage has attempted to consider
individually all the structures and
buildings on a site which can be
construed as separate buildings
and to list those which qualify for
listing. There will still be circumstances, however, where a structure or building forms part of land
which surrounds or is connected to
or serves a listed building, and
landowners and local planning
authorities will need to consider
on the facts of each case whether it
forms part of the land and falls
within the curtilage of the listed
building.

3.34 The principal tests as to
whether an object or structure is
within the curtilage of a listed
building relate to the physical layout of the land surrounding the
listed building at the date of the
statutory listing and the relationship of the structures on the surrounding land to each other.
Changes in ownership, occupation

or use after the listing date will not
bring about the delisting of a building which formed part of the principal building at the date of listing.
The Courts have held that for a
structure or building within the
curtilage of a listed building to be
part of a listed building it must be
ancillary to the principal building,
that is it must have served the purposes of the principal building at
the date of listing, or at a recent
time before the date of listing, in a
necessary or reasonably useful way
and must not be historically an
independent building. Where a
self-contained building was fenced
or walled-of from the remainder of
the site at the date of listing,
regardless of the purpose for which
it was erected and is occupied, it is
likely to be regarded as having a
separate curtilage. The structure or
building must still form part of the
land, and this probably means that
there must be some degree of
physical annexation to the land.

3.35 Considerations which may
assist local planning authorities in
forming their own views, or giving
advice if requested, include:

— the historical indepen-
  dence of the building;
— the physical layout of the
  principal building and
  other buildings;
— the ownership of the buildings now and at the time of
  listing;
— whether the structure
  forms part of the land;
— the use and function of the
  buildings, and whether a
  building is ancillary or subordinate to the principal
  building.

3.36 It is always necessary to recognise, however, that the question
of whether a building, structure or
object is within the curtilage of, or

423

is fixed to, the principal building, unless specifically included in the listing, is in any particular case a matter of fact and ultimately a matter for the Courts. Great caution must, therefore, be exercised in attempting to extrapolate any general principles from recent decisions and this guidance does not purport to be definitive.

Local authority applications

3.37 A county council (where not a local planning authority) is required to make its applications for listed building consent to the relevant district planning authority, which should consider them against the normal criteria. Local planning authorities are normally required to make their own applications to the Secretary of State, whether or not they themselves own the listed building in question. The Secretaries of State ask authorities to deal with their own buildings in ways which will provide examples of good practice to other owners. It is particularly important that every effort should be made to maintain historic buildings in good condition, and to find appropriate new uses for buildings in authority ownership which are no longer in active use. Prompt disposal is important: empty buildings should not be retained on a contingency basis, with all the risk of neglect and disrepair that this can create.

3.38 The Secretary of State will be particularly concerned to ensure that local planning authorities take full account of the policies set out in this PPG, and will not be disposed to grant consent for the demolition of listed buildings in authorities' ownership unless there is clear and convincing evidence that alternative possibilities for new ownership and new uses have been thoroughly explored.

Churches and Crown buildings

3.39 Special provisions apply to ecclesiastical buildings in use for ecclesiastical purposes, which are in some circumstances exempt from listed building and conservation area controls. Details of the arrangements which apply to such buildings are given in section 8.

3.40 The Crown is currently exempt from listed building and conservation area controls; but the Government has undertaken that Crown bodies will normally operate as if these controls did apply (see Department of the Environment *Circular 18/84*). English Heritage should be notified of Crown developments on the same basis as normal applications. Proposals have been published for the removal of Crown exemption in planning and conservation matters; pending the necessary legislation, the arrangements in *Circular 18/84* continue to apply.

3.41 Works by English Heritage on monuments, buildings or land which are owned by or in the care of the Secretary of State for National Heritage and which they are managing on his behalf are treated as Crown development and the procedures in *Circular 18/84* will apply. If English Heritage wishes to carry out works to other listed buildings, or demolish an unlisted building in a conservation area, it must obtain listed building or conservation area consent. The Secretary of State has directed that all such applications should be referred to him. The authority should advertise such applications as they would any other private application and forward any representations received, together with their own comments, to the appropriate regional Government Office.

Listed building consent for works already executed

3.42 Section 8(3) of the Act allows listed building consent to be sought even though the works have already been completed. Applications for consent to retain such works should follow the same procedures as other listed building consent applications and should contain sufficient information (see Annex B paragraph B.3). Local planning authorities should not grant consent merely to recognise a *fait accompli*; they should consider whether they would have granted consent for the works had it been sought before they were carried out, while having regard to any subsequent matters which may be relevant. If the work is not of a suitable type or standard, consent should not normally be given, and the risk of prosecution or enforcement action will remain. If consent is granted, it is not retrospective; the works are authorised only from the date of the consent. A prosecution may still be brought for the initial offence.

Enforcement

3.43 If work is carried out without consent, a local planning authority can issue a listed building enforcement notice (section 38). The notice may (a) require the building to be brought back to its former state; or (b), if that is not reasonably practicable or desirable, require other works specified in the notice to alleviate the effects of the unauthorised works; or (c) require the building to be brought into the state it would have been

in if the terms of any listed building consent had been observed. It was held in the case of *Bath City Council v. Secretary of State for the Environment* ([1983] J.P.L. 737) that this provision could not be used to secure an improvement to a listed building compared to its state before the unauthorised works were carried out. There is a right of appeal to the Secretary of State against a notice; the appeal procedures are generally similar to those for enforcement of development control following the Planning and Compensation Act 1991, although there are no provisions equivalent to a planning contravention notice, nor is there any limitation on the period within which a listed building enforcement notice must be issued. If works subject to a listed building enforcement notice are later authorised under section 8(3), the enforcement notice will cease to have effect in relation to those works, although the liability to prosecution for an offence committed before the date of consent remains. Breach of a listed building enforcement notice is itself an offence, with financial penalties parallel to those for a breach of listed building control.

Prosecutions

3.44 It is a criminal offence to execute, or cause to be executed, without first obtaining listed building consent any works for the demolition, in whole or part, of a listed building or any works of alteration or extension which would affect its special interest, or to fail to comply with the terms of any condition attached to a consent (section 9). This includes the theft of architectural fixtures. The current penalty for conviction in a magistrates' court is a fine of up to

£20,000 or imprisonment for up to six months (or both), whilst on conviction in the Crown Court an unlimited fine or a prison sentence of up to two years (or both) may be imposed. In determining the amount of any fine, a magistrates' court or the Crown Court must have regard to any financial benefit which has accrued or may accrue from the offence.

3.45 In proceedings for an offence under section 9 it is a defence to prove all of the following matters:

    (a) that works to the building were urgently necessary in the interests of safety or health or for the preservation of the building;

    (b) that it was not practicable to secure safety or health or, as the case may be, to preserve the building by works of repair or works for affording temporary support or shelter;

    (c) that the works carried out were limited to the minimum measures immediately necessary; and

    (d) that notice in writing justifying in detail the carrying out of the works was given to the local planning authority as soon as reasonably practicable.

3.46 Anyone—individuals as well as English Heritage and local planning authorities—can start proceedings. English Heritage and planning authorities can also seek injunctions for breaches of listed building control. A prosecution may also be initiated under section 59 where deliberate damage is caused to a listed building by an owner or his agent, for which financial penalties are provided.

3.47 Local planning authorities will obviously need to consider, when faced with a breach of listed building control, whether to take enforcement action or to prosecute or both. Enforcement may be intrinsically desirable for the benefit of the building in question, while the work entailed by enforcement may also represent a sufficient response to the offence. However, unauthorised work may often destroy historic fabric the special interest of which cannot be restored by enforcement. Moreover, well-publicised successful prosecutions can provide a valuable deterrent to wilful damage to, or destruction of, listed buildings, and it is the Secretary of State's policy to encourage proceedings where it is considered that a good case can be sustained.

3.48 Prosecution and enforcement relate to breaches of listed building control that have already occurred. Where such a breach is continuing or there is good reason to suppose it is about to occur, authorities should consider seeking an injunction to stop or prevent it. Since a breach of listed building control (unlike development control) is itself a criminal offence, there is no need or statutory provision for stop notices. Authorities may, of course, find written warnings useful deterrents. Injunctions can be obtained speedily from the Court even where the actual or expected offender is not present before the Court, or indeed where his or her identity is not known; the essential ingredient is to satisfy the Court that the application is soundly based. In the case of an interim injunction the Court would normally ask the applicant to compensate the restrained party for any costs the latter might incur as a result of the interim injunction if the Court refuse to grant a final injunction. Anyone who refuses to comply with an injunction is in contempt of Court and may be fined or imprisoned (or both).

4. CONSERVATION AREAS

4.1 Section 69 of the Act imposes a duty on local planning authorities to designate as conservation areas any 'areas of special architectural or historic interest the character or appearance of which it is desirable to preserve or enhance'. There are now more than 8,000 conservation areas in England. Whilst listing procedures are focused on the protection of individual buildings, conservation area designation is the main instrument available to authorities to give effect to conservation policies for a particular neighbourhood or area. Designation introduces a general control over the demolition of unlisted buildings and provides the basis for policies designed to preserve or enhance all the aspects of character or appearance that define an area's special interest.

Assessment and designation of conservation areas

4.2 It is the quality and interest of areas, rather than that of individual buildings, which should be the prime consideration in identifying conservation areas. There has been increasing recognition in recent years that our experience of a historic area depends on much more than the quality of individual buildings—on the historic layout of property boundaries and thoroughfares; on a particular 'mix' of uses; on characteristic materials;

on appropriate scaling and detailing of contemporary buildings; on the quality of advertisements, shop fronts, street furniture and hard and soft surfaces; on vistas along streets and between buildings; and on the extent to which traffic intrudes and limits pedestrian use of spaces between buildings. Conservation area designation should be seen as the means of recognising the importance of all these factors and of ensuring that conservation policy addresses the quality of townscape in its broadest sense as well as the protection of individual buildings.

4.3 Local planning authorities also have under section 69 a duty to review their areas from time to time to consider whether further designation of conservation areas is called for. In some districts, areas suitable for designation may have been fully identified already; and in considering further designations authorities should bear in mind that it is important that conservation areas are seen to justify their status and that the concept is not devalued by the designation of areas lacking any special interest. Authorities should seek to establish consistent local standards for their designations and should periodically review existing conservation areas and their boundaries against those standards: cancellation of designation should be considered where an area or part of an area is no longer considered to possess the special interest which led to its original designation.

4.4 The more clearly the special architectural or historic interest that justifies designation is defined and recorded, the sounder will be the basis for local plan policies and development control decisions, as well as for the formulation of proposals for the preservation and enhancement of the character or appearance of an area. The definition of an area's special interest should derive from an assessment of the elements that contribute to (and detract from) it. Conservation areas vary greatly, but certain aspects will almost always form the basis for a coherent assessment: the topography—for example, thoroughfares and property boundaries—and its historical development; the archaeological significance and potential; the prevalent building materials; the character and hierarchy of spaces; the quality and relationship of buildings in the area and also of trees and other green features. The assessment should always note those unlisted buildings which make a positive contribution to the special interest of the area. More detailed advice on assessment and on other aspects of the management of conservation areas is set out in English Heritage's guidance note *Conservation Area Practice*.

4.5 The principal concern of a local planning authority in considering the designation of a conservation area should be to form a judgement on whether the area is of special architectural or historic interest the character or appearance of which it is desirable to preserve or enhance. In deciding whether it is desirable to designate, an authority may take into account the resources likely to be required, not only for the administration of conservation area controls, but also for consultation with local residents and formulation of policies for a new area: without follow-up, designation is unlikely to be effective in itself. An authority's justification for designation, as reflected in its assessment of an area's special interest and its character and appearance, is a factor which the Secretary of State will take into account in considering appeals against refusals of conservation area consent for demolition, and appeals against refusals of planning permission (see also paragraph 2.9).

4.6 Given the nature of conservation area controls—essentially controls over demolition; strengthened controls over minor development; and the protection of trees—designation is not likely to be appropriate as a means of protecting landscape features, except where they form an integral part of the historic built environment and that factor needs to be taken into account in considering any planning applications which would affect them. The Courts have held that it is legitimate in appropriate circumstances to include within a conservation area the setting of buildings that form the heart of that area (*R. v. Canterbury City Council ex parte David Halford*, February 1992; CO/2794/1991). Designation is clearly not a proper means of controlling activities (*e.g.* agricultural operations) which do not fall within the definition of development. Designation may well, however, be suitable for historic parks or gardens and other areas of historic landscape containing structures that contribute to their special interest and that fall within the categories subject to conservation area controls. Where there are no other reasons for designating a conservation area, trees may instead be protected by means of a tree preservation order.

4.7 There is no statutory requirement to consult prior to designation or cancellation of designation, but it will be highly desirable that there should be consultation with local residents, businesses and other local interests (eg. amenity bodies) over both the identification of areas and the definition of their boundaries. The greater the public support that can be enlisted for designation before it takes place, the more likely it is that policies for the area will be implemented voluntarily and without the need for additional statutory controls. Local planning authorities should advise English Heritage and the appropriate regional Government Office when conservation areas are designated.

4.8 English Heritage and the Secretary of State for National Heritage also have powers to designate conservation areas, but look to local planning authorities in the first instance to consider the case for designation. English Heritage's powers relate to London only, where they are required to consult the London borough council concerned and to obtain the Secretary of State's consent to designation. The Secretary of State must also consult the authorities concerned before using his powers of designation. His policy is to use his own powers only in exceptional cases, for instance where an area is of more than local interest; or where there is evidence to suggest that an authority's ownership of important buildings may have influenced a decision not to use its own powers, and there is a clear threat to the character or appearance of the area. The Secretary of State may also apply such criteria when requested to approve the use of English Heritage's powers.

Policies for conservation areas

4.9 Section 71 of the Act places a duty on local planning authorities to formulate and publish proposals for the preservation and enhancement of conservation areas. It is important that designation is not seen as an end in itself: policies will almost always need to be developed which clearly identify what it is about the character or appearance of the area which should be preserved or enhanced, and set out the means by which that objective is to be pursued. Clear assessment and definition of an area's special interest and the action needed to protect it will help to generate awareness and encourage local property owners to take the right sort of action for themselves.

4.10 The Act requires proposals for the preservation and enhancement of a conservation area to be submitted for consideration to a 'public meeting' in the area, but wider consultation will almost always be desirable, both on the assessment of special interest and on proposals for the area. Consultation should be undertaken not only with local residents and amenity societies but also with chambers of commerce, public utilities, and the highway authority. The character and appearance of many conservation areas is heavily dependent on the treatment of roads, pavements and other public spaces (see paragraphs 5.13–5.18). It is important that conservation policies are fully integrated with other policies for the area, eg. for shopping and traffic management. Account should also be taken of wider policies (eg. for house renovation grants) which may affect the area's character or appearance. The preparation of local plans provides the best opportunity for integrating conservation policies with wider policies for the area, though a local planning authority's detailed statement of proposals for the conservation area should not itself be part of the development plan (see paragraphs 2.9 above and 4.15 below). Carefully targeted grant schemes using the authority's powers under section 57 of the Act to help with repair and enhancement should also be considered as part of the policy for an area. In certain cases English Heritage Conservation Area Partnership funding may be available.

Vacant premises over shops

4.11 Bringing vacant upper floors back into use, particularly residential use, not only provides additional income and security for the shop owner, but also helps to ensure that what are often important townscape buildings are kept in good repair, it meets a widespread need for small housing units and helps to sustain activity in town centres after working hours. Local planning authorities are urged to develop policies to secure better use of vacant upper premises, eg. by giving careful consideration to planning applications for shop conversions which would eliminate separate accesses to upper floors; by working with housing associations to secure residential conversions; and through the house renovation grant system.

Local information and consultation

4.12 Once policies for a particular area have been formulated, they should be made available to local residents and businesses in leaflet form, setting out clearly why the area has been designated; what its specially valuable features are; how individual householders can help to protect its character and appearance; and what additional controls and opportunities for assistance designation brings with it. Without such information, the support of local residents is not likely to be realised to the full. (English Heritage's guidance note on conservation areas gives advice on such publicity).

4.13 Local planning authorities are asked to consider setting up conservation area advisory committees, both to assist in formulating policies for the conservation area (or for several areas in a particular neighbourhood), and also as a continuing source of advice on planning and other applications which could affect an area. Committees should consist mainly of people who are not members of the authority; local residential and business interests should be fully represented. In addition to local historical, civic and amenity societies, and local chambers of commerce, the authority may wish to seek nominations (depending on the character of the area) from national bodies such as the national amenity societies and the Civic Trust. Authorities should consider whether there is scope for the involvement of local people on a voluntary basis in practical work for the enhancement of an area.

Use of planning powers in conservation areas

4.14 Section 72 of the Act requires that special attention shall be paid in the exercise of planning functions to the desirability of preserving or enhancing the character or appearance of a conservation area. This requirement extends to all powers under the Planning Acts, not only those which relate directly to historic buildings. The desirability of preserving or enhancing the area should also, in the Secretary of State's view, be a material consideration in the planning authority's handling of development proposals which are outside the conservation area but would affect its setting, or views into or out of the area. Local planning authorities are required by section 73 to publish a notice of planning applications for development which would in their opinion affect the character or appearance of a conservation area.

4.15 The status now accorded to the development plan by section 54A of the principal Act makes it particularly important that an authority's policies for its conservation areas, insofar as they bear on the exercise of development controls, should be set out in the local plan. There should also be a clear indication of the relationship between the plan itself and detailed assessment documents or statements of proposals for particular conservation areas, making clear that development proposals will be judged for their effect on the character and appearance of the area as identified in the assessment document.

4.16 Many conservation areas include the commercial centres of the towns and villages of which they form part. While conservation (whether by preservation or enhancement) of their character or appearance must be a major consideration, this cannot realistically take the form of preventing all new development: the emphasis will generally need to be on controlled and positive management of change. Policies will need to be designed to allow the area to remain alive and prosperous, and to avoid unnecessarily detailed controls over businesses and householders, but at the same time to ensure that any new development accords with the area's special architectural and historic interest.

4.17 Many conservation areas include gap sites, or buildings that make no positive contribution to, or indeed detract from, the character or appearance of the area; their replacement should be a stimulus to imaginative, high quality design, and seen as an opportunity to enhance the area. What is important is not that new buildings should directly imitate earlier styles, but that they should be designed with respect for their context, as part of a larger whole which has a well-established character and appearance of its own.

4.18 Local planning authorities will often need to ask for detailed plans and drawings of proposed new development, including elevations which show the new development in its setting, before considering a planning application. In addition to adopted local plan policies, it may be helpful to prepare design briefs for individually important 'opportunity' sites. Special regard should be had for such matters as scale, height, form, massing, respect for the traditional pattern of frontages, vertical or horizontal emphasis, and detailed design (eg. the scale and spacing of window openings, and the nature and quality of materials). General planning standards should be applied sensitively in the interests of harmonising the new development with its neighbours in the conservation area.

4.19 The Courts have recently confirmed that planning decisions in respect of development proposed to be carried out in a conservation area must give a high priority to the objective of preserving or enhancing the character or appearance of the area. If any proposed development would conflict with that objective, there will be a strong presumption against the grant of planning permission, though in exceptional cases the presumption may be overridden in favour of development which is desirable on the ground of some other public interest.

4.20 As to the precise interpretation of 'preserve or enhance', the Courts have held (South Lakeland DC v. Secretary of State for the Environment, [1992] 2 W.L.R. 204) that there is no requirement in the legislation that conservation areas should be protected from all development which does not enhance or positively preserve. Whilst the character and appearance of conservation areas should always be given full weight in planning decisions, the objective of preservation can be achieved either by development which makes a positive contribution to an area's character or appearance, or by development which leaves character and appearance unharmed.

Permitted development in conservation areas

4.21 The GDO requires planning applications for certain types of development in conservation areas which are elsewhere classified as permitted development. These include various types of cladding; the insertion of dormer windows into roof slopes; the erection of satellite dishes on walls, roofs or chimneys fronting a highway; and the installation of radio masts, antennae or radio equipment housing with a volume in excess of two cubic metres (unless the development is carried out in an emergency). The size of house and industrial extensions that may be carried out without specific planning permission is also more restricted.

4.22 On 30 March 1994 the Government announced a new proposal to enable local planning authorities to make directions withdrawing permitted development rights for a prescribed range of development materially affecting some aspects of the external appearance of dwellinghouses, such as doors, windows, roofs and frontages. There would be no requirement to obtain the Secretary of State's approval for such directions, but authorities would have to publicise their proposals in advance and have regard to the views of local people. Further details of these new arrangements will be published by circular shortly.

4.23 The withdrawal of permitted development rights outside these categories will continue to require Article 4 directions for which the Secretary of State's approval is generally needed before they can become effective. The Secretary of State takes the view that permitted development rights should not be withdrawn without clear justification and that, wherever possible, residents in conservation areas should continue to enjoy the same freedom to undertake development as residents elsewhere. He does not consider that the designation of a conservation area in itself automatically justifies making an Article 4 direction. Such directions may, however, have a role to play if they would help to protect features that are key elements of particular conservation areas and do not come within the categories that will be subject to the arrangements set out in paragraph 4.22 above. The Secretary of State will generally be in favour of approving directions in conservation areas where these are backed by a clear assessment of an area's special architectural and historic interest, where the importance to that special interest of the features in question is established, where the local planning authority can demonstrate local support for the direction, and where the direction involves the minimum withdrawal of permitted development rights (in terms of both area and types of development) necessary to achieve its objective.

4.24 Sections 107 and 108 of the principal Act make provision for the payment of compensation in certain circumstances where permitted development rights have been withdrawn by an Article 4 direction or an amendment to the GDO.

Conservation area control over demolition

4.25 Conservation area designation introduces control over the demolition of most buildings within conservation areas (section 74 of the Act); exceptions are specified in section 75 and in the relevant direction. Applications for consent to demolish must be made to the local planning authority or, on appeal or call-in, to the Secretary of State. Procedures are essentially the same as for listed building consent applications. Authorities' own applications must be made to the Secretary of State. Scheduled ancient monuments are exempt from conservation area control: scheduled monument consent for proposed works must be sought from the Secretary of State for National Heritage (see *PPG 16*.)

4.26 In exercising conservation area controls, local planning authorities are required to pay special attention to the desirability of preserving or enhancing the character or appearance of the area in question; and, as with listed building controls, this should be the prime consideration in determining a consent application. In the case of conservation area controls, however, account should clearly be taken of the part played in the architectural or historic interest of the area by the building for which demolition is proposed, and in particular of the wider effects of demolition on the building's surroundings and on the conservation area as a whole.

4.27 The general presumption should be in favour of retaining buildings which make a positive contribution to the character or appearance of a conservation area. The Secretary of State expects that proposals to demolish such buildings should be assessed against the same broad criteria as proposals to demolish listed buildings (paragraphs 3.16–3.19 above). In less clear-cut cases—for instance, where a building makes little or no such contribution—the local planning authority will need to have full information about what is proposed for the site after demolition. Consent for demolition should not be given unless there are acceptable and detailed plans for any redevelopment. It has been held that the decision-maker is entitled to consider the merits of any proposed development in determining whether consent should be given for the demolition of an unlisted building in a conservation area.

4.28 Section 336 of the principal Act states that a building includes 'any part of a building'. The demolition of part of a building should therefore be regarded as falling within the scope of conservation area control. What constitutes a demolition or demolition of part of a building must be a matter of fact and degree, to be decided in the particular case and ultimately by the Courts. Routine works of repair, maintenance or replacement, including work involving such items as doors or windows, would not in the Secretary of State's view normally constitute demolition. Likewise, the removal of internal features, whether replaced or not, would not usually constitute a demolition and for the purposes of conservation area consent would not, in any event, have a material impact on the building's appearance or affect the character or appearance of the area.

4.29 It will often be appropriate to impose on the grant of consent for demolition a condition under section 17(3) of the Act, as applied by section 74(3), to provide that demolition shall not take place until a contract for the carrying out of works of redevelopment has been made and planning permission for those works has been granted. In the past, ugly gaps have sometimes appeared in conservation areas as a result of demolition far in advance of redevelopment.

Leasehold reform

4.30 The extended arrangements for leasehold enfranchisement under the Leasehold Reform, Housing and Urban Development Act 1993 included wider provisions for estate management schemes aimed at maintaining the appearance and amenity of areas currently under a single landlord's control. Schemes can be applied for by landlords or representative bodies such as residents' associations up to 30 October 1995 (in some exceptional cases later with the Secretary of State's agreement) and, when approved, transferred to local planning authorities or specially constituted bodies. Within conservation areas, schemes can by default be promoted by authorities or English Heritage between that deadline and 30 April 1996. The costs of management under such schemes fall to be met by the freeholders. In considering whether to approve a scheme the leasehold valuation tribunal is required to have regard, *inter alia*, to the past development and present character of the area and to architectural or historical considerations. Moreover, in conservation areas, applicants for schemes are required to notify English Heritage and the local planning authority and invite them to make representations to the tribunal. These provisions should enable authorities in appropriate cases to help maintain the appearance of an architecturally unified estate through regulation of the development, use and appearance of property beyond what can be enforced under the planning system (*e.g.* by regulating external decoration and cleaning), and through being able to require proper maintenance and repair of the structure and external elements of the buildings. Further information is available from English Heritage.

Advertisement control

4.31 All outdoor advertisements affect the appearance of the building or the neighbourhood where they are displayed. The main purpose of the advertisement control system is to help everyone involved in the display of outdoor advertising to contribute positively to the appearance of an attractive and cared-for environment. So it is reasonable to expect that the local planning authority's duty to pay special attention to the desirability of preserving or enhancing the character or appearance of a conservation area will result in practice in applying more exacting standards when the authority consider whether to grant consent for a proposed advertisement in such an area.

4.32 In conservation areas it is important for local planning authorities to be sensitive in the use of their powers under the Town & Country Planning (Control of Advertisements) Regulations 1992, because many areas include retail and commercial premises, ranging from small corner-shops to thriving commercial centres. Outdoor advertising is essential to commercial activity in a free and diverse economy, and the success of local businesses will usually help owners and tenants of commercial premises to maintain buildings in good repair and attractive appearance.

4.33 Local planning authorities may wish to adopt advertisement control policies as part of their duty to formulate and publish proposals for the preservation and enhancement of conservation areas. Such policies can inform prospective advertisers about the type of displays likely to prove acceptable in an area; and they should provide a rational and consistent basis for decision-making on all advertisement control

matters, including the serving of discontinuance notices.

4.34 Because of the special interest of most conservation areas, certain categories of 'deemed consent' advertisements which may have a significant visual impact are not permitted for display in a conservation area without the local planning authority's specific consent. But a general prohibition of the display of certain classes of advertisement, or the withdrawal or limitation of those which may be displayed with deemed consent, is not usually justified solely because of designation.

4.35 Attention is drawn to the value of education and co-operation to help prevent unsympathetic advertisements. Local planning authorities may wish to consider mounting programmes, in association with local businesses, to promote advertisement policies by providing advice about the design and siting of suitable displays which respect the character and appearance of an area (either by the publication of design guidelines, the mounting of exhibitions, the setting-up of an advisory service in a Planning Department, or a combination of these approaches).

4.36 Where a local planning authority has pursued this approach, but considers that it has not prevented unsuitable or harmful advertisement displays, the Secretary of State will be prepared to consider making a direction under regulation 7 of the 1992 Regulations referred to above, if the authority can justify it. In seeking such additional control, authorities will be expected to show that they have well-formulated policies for the display of advertisements in the

435

area and that the vigorous use of normal powers of control has proved inadequate. Similarly, when considering whether an advertisement is causing 'substantial injury to amenity', so that its display should be discontinued, the Secretary of State will particularly consider any evidence, on appeal, that the authority have acted in accordance with a well-formulated advertisement control policy.

4.37 Further advice on outdoor advertisement control, including in conservation areas, is given in *PPG 19*.

Trees in conservation areas

4.38 Trees are valued features of our towns and countryside and make an important contribution to the character of the local environment. Under Part VIII of the principal Act, local planning authorities have a power to protect trees and woodlands in the interests of amenity by making tree preservation orders. In addition to this general power, authorities are under a duty to make adequate provision for the preservation and planting of trees when granting planning permission for the development of land. They do this by a combination of planning conditions and tree preservation orders.

4.39 Many trees in conservation areas are the subject of tree preservation orders, which means that the local planning authority's consent must be obtained before they can be cut down, topped or lopped. In addition to these controls, and in view of the contribution that trees can make to the character and appearance of a conservation area, the principal Act makes

special provision for trees in conservation areas which are not the subject of tree preservation orders. Under section 211, subject to a range of exceptions, (including small trees and ones that are dead, dying or dangerous), anyone proposing to cut down, top or lop a tree in a conservation area is required to give six weeks' notice to the local planning authority. The purpose of this requirement is to give the authority an opportunity to consider bringing the tree under their general control by making a tree preservation order in respect of it. Penalties for contravention, which may include a requirement to replant, are similar to those for tree preservation orders. For guidance on these matters see Department of the Environment *Circular 36/78*.

4.40 When considering whether to extend protection to trees in conservation areas, local planning authorities should always take into account the visual, historic and amenity contribution of trees. In some instances new plantings or re-plantings may be desirable where this would be consistent with the character and appearance of the area.

5. TRANSPORT AND TRAFFIC MANAGEMENT

5.1 The Government's commitment to sustainable development entails greater integration of transport with other aspects of land-use planning in order to reduce the need for travel, to moderate future traffic growth, and to minimise the environmental impacts of transport. This may lead to a greater concentration of development on existing centres, including historic towns. In developing policies and projects it is essential, therefore, that local highway and planning authorities take full account of the wider costs of transport choices, including impact on the historic environment.

5.2 Major new transport infrastructure developments can have an especially wide-ranging impact on the historic environment, not just visually and physically, but indirectly, for example, by altering patterns of movement or commerce and generating new development pressures or opportunities in historic areas. Local highway and planning authorities should therefore integrate their activities and should take great care to avoid or minimise impacts on the various elements of the historic environment and their settings.

5.3 The Secretaries of State also attach particular importance to early consultation on traffic management and highway maintenance schemes, and associated development proposals which would affect listed buildings or conservation areas or parks, gardens or battlefields and their settings. Local highway and planning authorities should take great care to assess the impact on existing roads of new projects, eg. for the rerouting of traffic or for pedestrianisation. They are urged to seek the advice of English Heritage, where appropriate, before determining any such proposals.

New traffic routes

5.4 When contemplating a new route, authorities should consider whether the need for it, and any impact on the environment, might be obviated by an alternative package of transport management such as parking and charging policies, park-and-ride schemes, and public transport priority. New roads should not be built just to facilitate more commuting into already congested areas. This is especially true in historic towns where the character and layout cannot easily absorb radical changes such as new roads.

5.5 If a new route is unavoidable, authorities should initially identify any features of the historic environment—including parks, gardens, battlefields and archaeological sites as well as buildings and areas—and evaluate their importance. Wherever possible, new roads (and any other transport infrastructure) should be kept away from listed buildings, conservation areas and other historic sites. However, in each case a suitable balance has to be struck between conservation, other environmental concerns, economics, safety and engineering feasibility. Highway and planning authorities should set common objectives wherever possible and are advised to consult each other about transport proposals affecting historic areas. Such proposals are subject to the same constraints as other major development proposals in areas of protection, and authorities will have to obtain listed building consent or conservation area consent where appropriate. Further advice is given in *PPG 13* on how authorities should seek to manage demand and improve the attractiveness of local centres through their transport and planning policies.

5.6 Where work to listed structures or those in conservation areas, such as historic bridges, is needed to meet new national or European requirements, this

437

should be carried out with great care. Many bridges are of considerable age and represent important features of the cultural heritage. Their survival to this day owes a great deal to the care of past generations, and, where remedial or strengthening works are found to be necessary, proposals should seek to retain the character of these structures for the benefit of future generations. Traditional materials should only be replaced where it can be proved that this is essential in the interests of structural stability. Sympathetic remedial measures, which restore the carrying capacity and extend the life of these structures while retaining their character, are preferable to complete reconstruction, and will normally prove more cost-effective. Authorities are urged to consider sympathetic alterations where necessary to carry heavier traffic, or, where new construction is the only realistic course, to retain and restore the old structure for use by pedestrians and cyclists. Authorities are also urged to exercise flexibility over the design of parapets on historic bridges.

5.7 When the opportunity occurs, the possibility of reusing structures for new transport schemes should always be examined. Disused railway viaducts and bridges provide an environmentally advantageous solution for such schemes, in both rural and urban areas, especially in environmentally sensitive areas. The restoration and conversion of historic structures such as these can be a positive benefit from a transport scheme.

Schemes promoted under the Transport and Works Act 1992

5.8 Since 1 January 1993, when Part I of the Transport and Works Act 1992 came into force, proposals which would have previously been authorised under private Bill procedure have instead had to be authorised by Orders made under that Act. Such proposals include the construction or operation of railways, tramways, trolley vehicle systems, other guided transport systems, inland waterways, and structures interfering with rights of navigation. The Act brings the procedures for authorising such schemes more into line with those which have applied for years to highways projects. If the relevant Secretary of State decides to make an Order under the Act, he may at the same time direct that planning permission be deemed to be granted for the proposal, to the extent to which it involves carrying out any development.

5.9 Where the proposal involves works to a listed building, or demolition of an unlisted building in a conservation area, a separate application must be made to the local planning authority for listed building consent or conservation area consent respectively. The regulations which normally apply to such consent applications are subject to minor modifications so that they may more easily be progressed in parallel with the application for the related order. These changes are set out in the Transport and Works Applications (Listed Buildings, Conservation Areas and Ancient Monuments Procedures) Regulations 1992. An application for listed building or conservation area consent made concurrently with an application for an order under the 1992 Act will automatically be referred by the local planning authority to the Secretary of State for the Environment for his decision, without the need for any specific direction. Where there is need for a public local inquiry, the related applications will be considered at a concurrent inquiry. This means that one Inspector will be able to make mutually compatible recommendations about the different applications.

5.10 A fuller description of these concurrent procedures (together with the procedure for applications under the 1992 Act generally) is set out in the Department of Transport publication *Transport and Works Act 1992: A Guide to Procedures*.

Roads in centres or settlements

5.11 Local highway authorities should take measures to protect the historic environment from the worst effects of traffic. They have powers to create vehicle-restricted areas or pedestrian zones and to introduce traffic-calming measures where appropriate. However, there is increasing recognition that in some historic areas the total exclusion of traffic combined with extensive pedestrianisation can create sterile precincts, particularly at night. In some cases, it may be preferable to consider limited access at selected times for all traffic or particular classes of traffic (eg. buses, trams, service vehicles), or shared streets and other spaces designed to encourage motorists to modify their driving behaviour when mixing with pedestrians. Park and Ride schemes may also have a part to pay in areas where it is desirable to limit car access to historic centres and conservation areas. Advice is available in the English Historic Towns Forum publication *Park and Ride Good Practice Guide*. All these measures, together with

encouraging a variety of uses on the ground floors of developments, can help to increase the attractiveness of town centres, and will also help to meet the policy objectives of *PPG 6* and *PPG 13*, and Department of the Environment *Circular 5/94*.

5.12 Vehicle restrictions and traffic-calming measures can often be effective in reducing the speeds at which people choose to drive. The Department of Transport issues advice on pedestrianisation and a range of traffic-calming features which may be introduced. The Highways (Traffic Calming) Regulations 1993 give authorities the flexibility to use a wide variety of traffic-calming features, in addition to road humps, which can constrain vehicle speeds. These include chicanes, build-outs, pinch points, gateways, rumble devices, islands and overrun areas. However, some designs can be difficult to integrate into an older streetscape and there can be no standard solution. Each feature or device should relate in its design and materials to the overall townscape to ensure that traffic-calming reinforces rather than diminishes local character. Traffic-calming measures using a combination of traditional materials and devices may help to secure the right balance. For instance, the use of traditional cobbles or stone setts may prove effective in keeping down traffic speeds, though they are likely to increase levels of road surface noise; they will also not always find favour with cyclists and disabled people. Authorities should also consult with the emergency services before laying such surfaces to ensure that their response times are not unduly increased. Advice is available to local authorities in the English Historic

Towns Forum publication *Traffic Measures in Historic Towns*. Authorities should consider the extent to which these different kinds of traffic-calming measures need to be signed, and ensure that signing is kept to the minimum necessary to ensure safety and comply with legal requirements.

Floorscape and street furniture

5.13 Floorscape and street furniture often make a vital contribution to the appearance of a conservation area. Traditional stone, or in some cases brick, surfaces and layouts should be retained wherever possible, or reintroduced where there is historical evidence for them. In particular, where there is a tradition of rectangular slab paving, small block paviours and arbitrary new patterns should be avoided. In many small towns and villages, rammed earth, hoggin or aggregate, in modern times finished with tarmac, was always the traditional surface. Tarmac, preferably dressed with a suitable local aggregate, remains an appropriate and inexpensive finish for many conservation areas. Wherever practical, natural earth, hoggin, or aggregate footpaths or drives should be retained and protected for their semi-rural character. If a street is to be pedestrianised, it is important to retain the traditional relationship between footways and carriageway, including kerb lines. Wall-to-wall surfaces are often unsuitable and the scale, texture, colour and laying patterns of any new materials should be sympathetic to the area's appearance.

5.14 In certain circumstances grants may be available from English Heritage towards the cost of street improvement schemes which incorporate the use of traditional paving features. English Heritage's publication *Street Improvements in Historic Areas* offers guidance on the treatment of streets and public open spaces in historic areas, to encourage wider recognition of the important contribution they make to townscape quality. The New Roads and Street Works Act 1991 makes statutory undertakers responsible for carrying out the permanent reinstatement of the highway where they disturb it. They are now required to reinstate the same materials as previously existed, or the closest possible match if the materials cannot be reused. Local authorities play an important role in ensuring that statutory undertakers and their contractors carry out reinstatement to an appropriate specification and timetable.

5.15 Even the smallest towns contain a wealth of street furniture of historic or architectural interest, such as pillar boxes, telephone kiosks, drinking fountains, railings, clocks and many others, often of local distinctiveness. The appearance of historic streets can be improved by preserving or reinstating such items where appropriate (see *Street Improvements in Historic Areas*). Authorities contemplating modern tramway systems should consider the effects that catenary supports and other associated street furniture and electrical equipment may have on historic streetscapes.

5.16 Road signs and markings can also have a significant impact on a street's appearance. These should be of an appropriate character and quality, without unnecessary duplication of signs and posts. Wherever possible signs should be fixed to existing posts or street furniture. Traffic signs are only needed to direct drivers to their desired destinations or to particular facilities, warn them of hazards and indicate mandatory requirements. Signs which do none of these things may not be necessary at all, and much can be done to eliminate sign clutter simply by removing redundant signs, or by combing separate signs onto a single backing board. Regular 'street audits' are valuable and local amenity societies may be able to help with these. Further advice is available in *Traffic Measures in Historic Towns*. Where the Traffic Signs Regulations and the Department of Transport's *Traffic Signs Manual* provide for some degree of flexibility in size, siting and colour, authorities should take advantage of this in historic areas. Parking restriction signs in particular can be sited on buildings where appropriate, thus eliminating the need in many cases for a pole with a single sign. Authorities' attention is drawn to the flexibility permitted in respect of no-waiting lines: a narrower line of a different colour is permitted in environmentally sensitive areas. Consideration should be given to applying waiting restrictions to areas, where appropriate, and removing yellow lines.

5.17 Authorities should seek advice on the selection and positioning of street lighting equipment appropriate to the age and character of the surrounding area. The Department of Transport publication *Road Lighting and the Environment*, for example, provides helpful advice. High pressure sodium lamps (with controlled light spillage) may be preferable in environmentally sensitive areas as they provide a whiter light with a more natural rendition of colour. Off-the-peg 'period' columns and lanterns are not universally appropriate in historic areas. Special designs reflecting established local styles or motifs, or simple modern designs, may be preferable.

5.18 The effects of road works and other transport projects on trees in conservation areas, or trees which form part of the setting of listed buildings, can be particularly damaging. Authorities should stress the need for statutory undertakers and others to take care when excavating, or diverting services, near existing trees in order to avoid damage to roots. Where root damage occurs, this may not show in a tree's health for several years.

PART 2

6. IDENTIFYING AND RECORDING THE HISTORIC ENVIRONMENT

6.1 In its broadest sense, the historic environment embraces all those aspects of the country that reflect the shaping hand of human history. Scarcely any part of England is untouched by the interaction between people and nature which has taken place over thousands of years. Some of the most obvious features of this environment are historic buildings. England is exceptionally rich in these—great churches, houses, and civic buildings—but our understanding of the historic environment now encompasses a much wider range of features, and in particular stresses the relationship between individual buildings, and also the value of historic townscape and landscape as a whole.

6.2 There is growing appreciation not just of architectural set pieces, but of many more structures, especially industrial, agricultural and other vernacular buildings that, although sometimes individually unassuming, collectively reflect some of the most distinctive and creative aspects of English history. More than this, our understanding and appreciation of the historic environment now stretches beyond buildings to the spaces and semi-natural features which people have also moulded, and which are often inseparable from the buildings themselves. For example, the pattern of roads and open spaces and the views they create within historic townscapes may be as valuable as the buildings. In the countryside, the detailed patterns of fields and farms, of hedgerows and walls, and of hamlets and villages, are among the most highly valued aspects of our environment. England is particularly rich in the designed landscapes of parks and gardens, and the built and natural features they contain: the greatest of these are as important to national, and indeed international, culture as are our greatest buildings.

6.3 Processes of classification are necessary for the practical purposes of identifying and protecting individual sites and areas. This is achieved through the statutory systems for scheduling ancient monuments, listing historic buildings and designating conservation areas. Scheduling and listing are undertaken by the Secretary of State; designation of conservation areas is the responsibility of local planning authorities. In addition, English Heritage compiles registers of parks and gardens of special historic interest, and of historic battlefields. Identified in these ways, the historic environment may be protected through the development control system and, in the case of listed buildings and conservation areas, through the complementary systems of listed building and conservation area control.

6.4 The first part of this PPG explained how these control systems work, and how they relate to the broader planning system for development control. This part of the PPG sets out Government policy for the listing of historic buildings, and for the identification of certain other aspects of the historic environment. It also gives guidance on the upkeep of historic buildings, and on the powers available to local authorities and to the Secretary of State to secure repairs to neglected historic buildings.

6.5 Archaeology plays an essential role in informing and widening our understanding of the historic environment. Many important sites and structures of archaeological interest are identified and protected through the statutory schedule of ancient monuments maintained by the Department of National Heritage. The principles of selection are set out in *PPG 16*. Other known sites are included in the National Monuments Record of the Royal Commission on the Historical Monuments of England, and in county sites and monuments records.

Historic buildings

6.6 Historic buildings listed by the Secretary of State under section 1 of the Act are placed in one of three grades to give an indication of their relative importance. The current listing position in England is (to the nearest thousand):—

List Entries (England, 1993)

Grade I	9,000 (2%)
Grade II*	18,000 (4%)
Grade II	416,000 (94%)

443,000

About 500,000 individual buildings are estimated to be protected: some list entries cover several buildings. Some churches in older lists are still Grades A, B and C (which in the context of planning and listed building consent applications should all be treated in the same way as Grade I and II* buildings). Gradings can be changed following revaluation after damage or alteration, or as more evidence of a building's history comes to light.

Identification of buildings for listing

6.7 Buildings are added to the statutory lists in two main ways:

    i. as a result of systematic resurvey or review of particular areas or building types; or

    ii. following proposals from local authorities, amenity societies or other bodies or individuals that particular buildings should be added to the list ('spot listing').

6.8 Before including buildings in the statutory lists the Secretary of State is required to consult English Heritage and such other persons as he may consider appropriate as having special knowledge of, or interest in, buildings of architectural or historic interest. Expert advisers appointed by English Heritage normally visit and report on buildings before they are listed. In the case of systematic resurveys and reviews there will normally be close consultation between English Heritage and the local planning authority before recommendations for listing are submitted to the Secretary of State. Wherever possible the Secretary of State will consider the views of other, but it is not his practice to advertise proposals for new listings.

6.9 The number of listed buildings has increased fourfold since 1970 as a result of 24 years' work to resurvey England's built heritage. Some of the lists deriving from the earlier years of the resurvey are currently being reviewed, but the priority in future will be on more precisely targeted, research-based studies of particular building types which are known to be under-represented in the lists, rather than area surveys.

Principles of selection

6.10 The following are the main criteria which the Secretary of State applies as appropriate in deciding which buildings to include in the statutory lists:

— **architectural interest:** the lists are meant to include all buildings which are of importance to the nation for the interest of their architectural design, decoration and craftsmanship; also important examples of particular building types and techniques (eg. buildings displaying technological innovation or virtuosity) and significant plan forms;

— **historic interest:** this includes buildings which illustrate important aspects of the nation's social, economic, cultural or military history;

— **close historical association:** with nationally important people or events;

— **group value:** especially where buildings comprise an important architectural or historic unity or a fine example of planning (eg. squares, terraces or model villages).

Not all these criteria will be relevant to every case, but a particular building may qualify for listing under more than one of them.

6.11 Age and rarity are relevant considerations, particularly where buildings are proposed for listing on the strength of their historic interest. The older a building is, and the fewer the surviving examples of its kind, the more likely it is to have historic importance. Thus, all buildings built before 1700 which survive in anything like their original condition are listed; and most buildings of about 1700 to 1840 are listed, though some selection is necessary. After about 1840, because of the greatly increased number of buildings erected and the much larger numbers that have survived, greater selection is necessary to identify the best examples of particular building types, and only buildings of definite quality and character are listed. For the same reasons, only selected buildings from the period after 1914 are normally listed. Buildings which are less than 30 years old are normally listed only if they are of outstanding quality and under threat. Buildings which are less than ten years old are not listed.

6.12 The approach adopted for twentieth century listing is to identify key exemplars for each of a range of building types—industrial, educational, residential, etc.—and to treat these exemplars as broadly defining a standard against which to judge proposals for further additions to the list. This approach has already been successfully applied to the interwar period, and English Heritage is now engaged on a three-year research programme to extend it to the post-war period (subject to the '30 year rule' mentioned above). Proposals for listings in each building type will be made as each stage of the research is completed.

Selectivity

6.13 Where a building qualifies for listing primarily on the strength of its intrinsic architectural quality or its group value, the fact that there are other buildings of similar quality elsewhere is not likely to be a major consideration. But, as noted above, the listing of buildings primarily for historical reasons is to a greater extent a comparative exercise, and needs to be selective where a substantial number of buildings of a similar type and quality survive. In such cases the Secretary of State's aim will be to list the best examples of the type which are of special historic interest.

Aesthetic merits

6.14 The external appearance of a building—both its intrinsic architectural merit and any group value—is a key consideration in judging listing proposals, but the special interest of a building will not always be reflected in obvious visual quality. Buildings which are important for reasons of technological innovation, or as illustrating particular aspects of social or economic history, may well have little external visual quality.

Historical associations

6.15 Well-documented historical associations of national importance will increase the case for the inclusion of a building in the statutory list. They may justify a higher grading than would otherwise be appropriate, and may occasionally be the deciding factor. But in the Secretary of State's view there should normally be some quality or interest in the physical fabric of the building itself to justify the statutory protection afforded by listing. Either the building should be of some architectural merit in itself, or it should be well preserved in a form which directly illustrates and confirms its historical associations (eg. because of the survival of internal features). Where otherwise unremarkable buildings have historical associations, the Secretary of State's view is that they are normally best commemorated by other means (eg. by a plaque), and that listing will be appropriate only in exceptional cases.

National and local interest

6.16 The emphasis in these criteria is on national significance, though this cannot be defined precisely. For instance, the best examples of local vernacular building types will normally be listed. But many buildings which are valued for their contribution to the local scene, or for local historical associations, will not merit listing. Such buildings will often be protected by conservation area designation (see paragraphs 4.2 ff). It is also open to planning authorities to draw up lists of locally important buildings, and to formulate local plan policies for their protection, through normal development control procedures. But policies should make clear that such buildings do not enjoy the full protection of statutory listing.

Notifying owners and occupiers

6.17 When a building is included in the statutory list, the Department notifies the appropriate local planning authority. That authority must then notify the owner and occupier of the building. As it is a criminal offence to carry out any works (either to the exterior or interior) which would affect the character of a building once it is listed (unless listed building consent has been obtained), notice of listing must be given to the owner as soon as possible. The statutory notice is prescribed in the Planning (Listed Buildings and Conservation Areas) Regulations 1990. Owners and occupiers are also notified by the Department and sent a copy of the Department's leaflet *What Listing Means*.

Public access to the lists

6.18 A complete set of lists for the whole country is kept available for the public to inspect without charge at the National Monuments Record of the Royal Commission on the Historical Monuments of England. Each local authority also keeps available for inspection (without charge) the lists relating to its own area.

List descriptions

6.19 The lists include a description of each building. This is principally to aid identification. While list descriptions will include mention of those features which led

English Heritage to recommend listing, they are not intended to provide a comprehensive or exclusive record of all the features of importance, and the amount of information given in descriptions varies considerably. Absence from the list description of any reference to a feature (whether external or internal) does not, therefore, indicate that it is not of interest or that it can be removed or altered without consent. Where there is doubt, the advice of the local planning authority should be sought.

Spot listing

6.20 Requests for individual buildings to be spot listed can be made to the Secretary of State at any time. Where the area in question has recently been the subject of resurvey or review, it is important that requests for spot listing draw attention to any new evidence which may not have been available to English Heritage previously, or otherwise explain why the building's special interest may have been overlooked. The Secretary of State recognises that there may be cases where new evidence justifies reconsideration of a previous decision not to list, but he will not generally be disposed to review earlier decisions unless such evidence is provided.

6.21 Difficulties can arise where proposals for spot listing are made at a very late stage of redevelopment proposals, when buildings are under imminent threat of demolition. Spot listing in such cases can often mean delay, sometimes with serious practical and financial consequences for the developer. The Department will consider all requests for spot listing, but it is preferable from all points of view that buildings should be assessed for possible listing before planning permission has been granted for redevelopment. Local planning authorities should draw the Department's attention at the earliest possible stage to any buildings affected by redevelopment proposals (including their own) which appear to them to merit listing. A building preservation notice served by the authority may be a quicker means of protecting a threatened building than a request for spot listing (see paragraph 6.23 below).

6.22 Requests to list buildings should be sent to the Listing Branch, Department of National Heritage, 2–4 Cockspur Street, London SW1Y 5DH. Those sent to English Heritage will be forwarded to the Department. Requests should be accompanied by a justification for adding the building to the list; a location plan (such as an Ordnance Survey map extract) showing, wherever possible, the position of any other listed buildings nearby; clear up-to-date photographic prints of the main elevations of the building; any information about the building (eg. its date); details of specialised function (eg. industrial building); historical associations; the name of the architect (if known); its group value in the street scene; and details of any interior features of interest.

Building preservation notices

6.23 Under Section 3 of the Act district planning authorities and national park authorities have the power to serve building preservation notices in respect of buildings which are not listed, but which they consider are of special architectural or historic interest and are in danger of demolition or alteration in such a way as to affect their character as buildings of such interest. A building preservation notice applies to the building all the provisions of the Act relating to listed buildings (except section 59). It takes effect immediately it is served, and is often a quicker and so more expedient short-term measure than asking the Department to spot list a building.

6.24 A copy of the building preservation notice, a location plan and photographs of the building should be sent to the Department as soon as the notice has been served. The notice remains in force for up to six months, but will lapse if within that period the Department either includes the building in the statutory list or notifies the authority in writing that it does not intend to do so. The authority must notify the owner and occupier if the Department decides not to list the building, and may not serve another building preservation notice in respect of that building within 12 months of the Department's notification.

6.25 In deciding whether to serve a building preservation notice, authorities will realise that they become liable to pay compensation for any loss or damage resulting from the service of a notice which the Secretary of State does not uphold by listing. Neither the Department nor English Heritage can indicate in advance whether the service of a notice in a particular case is likely to result in a listing, though obviously the same general principles of listing, set out above, will apply in these cases as in others. It should not however be assumed that listing will automatically follow the inclusion of a building by English Heritage in a draft list, since that list may be corrected or amended before it is approved.

Requests to de-list buildings

6.26 The Secretary of State is prepared to review listings in the light of new evidence. There is no formal appeal procedure, but owners or others who believe that a listing should be reconsidered should send the evidence to the Department's Listing Branch, together with photographs of the building and a location plan. The evidence must relate to the special architectural or historic interest ascribed to the building: if the objection to listing is (for instance) related to a building's condition and the cost of repairing or maintaining it, or to plans for redevelopment, the appropriate application should be made under the listed building consent procedures described in Annex B. The local authorities concerned and the national amenity societies (listed in Annex A) will be notified by English Heritage of any requests the Department receives to de-list buildings.

6.27 The Secretary of State will not generally entertain an application for de-listing if the building is the subject of an application for listed building consent, or an appeal against refusal of consent, or if action by a local planning authority is in hand because of unauthorised works or neglect. Both listed building consent and enforcement appeal procedures give appellants the right to argue that a building is not of special interest and should be removed from the list. The issue of de-listing should normally be addressed in this way, rather than regarded as a means of avoiding the need for enforcement action.

447

Certificates of immunity from listing

6.28 Provided that planning permission is being sought or has been obtained, any person may ask the Secretary of State to issue a certificate stating that he does not intend to list the building or buildings involved in the planning application. Once a certificate is issued, the building cannot be listed for five years, nor may the local planning authority serve a building preservation notice during that time. However, if he does not grant a certificate, the Secretary of State will normally add the building to the statutory list, and listed building controls will then apply. This procedure gives greater certainty to developers proposing works which will affect buildings which may be eligible for listing: they will know either that they must seek listed building consent in the normal way, or that they have five years to carry out their development without the possibility of disruption by spot listing.

6.29 Because a certificate of immunity is valid for five years, a building is normally completely reassessed when an application for a certificate is made: an earlier assessment might have been based on a restricted inspection, or new information may have come to light since then. It should not be assumed, therefore, that even a recent decision by the Secretary of State not to list a building necessarily means that he will grant a certificate of immunity.

6.30 Even if a certificate of immunity is granted, a building in a conservation area will still normally need consent for demolition. It is not practicable to extend the certificate procedure to provide immunity from the effects of conservation area designation (but conservation area consent is not required where planning permission was granted prior to designation).

6.31 Applications for certificates of immunity should be made to the Department's Listing Branch. There is no application form and no charge. Applicants should supply a copy of the planning application or planning permission, as well as the information requested for spot listing applications (paragraph 6.22).

6.32 Applicants are required to notify the local planning authority in whose area the building is situated of the application at the same time as it is submitted to the Department. In London, applicants must notify English Heritage as well as the London borough council. Applicants should confirm that they have notified these authorities.

6.33 When a certificate is issued, the Department will notify English Heritage and both the district and county council (in London, the London borough council or, if appropriate, the London Docklands Development Corporation). The existence of a certificate and its expiry date should be disclosed in response to enquiries by prospective purchasers of the building or land, together with other information relating to planning matters.

Relationship between listing and scheduling

6.34 Some buildings are scheduled as ancient monuments as well as listed. These are for the most part unoccupied buildings, such as medieval barns or dovecotes, some bridges, and some urban buildings (eg. guildhalls) and industrial monuments. Some areas of overlap reflect the fact that scheduling pre-dated the listing legislation. Where a building is scheduled and listed, scheduling—which introduces closer controls (eg. over repairs) than does listing—takes priority and listed building controls do not apply. For the future, the policy will be to accord buildings and monuments the type of protection which is most appropriate to them, and where possible to avoid over-laps between listing and schedul-ing. The overlap is being addressed in the current national survey of archaeological sites (the Monu-ments Protection Programme) being carried out by English Heri-tage, to evaluate all known archaeological sites in England, review existing schedulings, and identify further sites and monu-ments which may be suitable for scheduling.

World Heritage Sites

6.35 The World Heritage Conven-tion (adopted by UNESCO in 1972) was ratified by the United Kingdom in 1984. The Convention provides for the identification, pro-tection, conservation and presen-tation of cultural and natural sites of outstanding universal value, and requires a World Heritage List to be established under the manage-ment of an inter-governmental World Heritage Committee, which is advised by the International Council on Monuments and Sites (ICOMOS) and the World Conser-vation Union (IUCN). Individual governments are responsible for the nomination of sites, and for ensuring the protection of sites which are inscribed in the List.

There are, at present, ten World Heritage Sites in England:

Durham Cathedral and Castle
Fountains Abbey, St. Mary's Church and Studley Royal Park
Ironbridge Gorge
Stonehenge, Avebury and associated sites
Blenheim Palace and Park
Palace of Westminster and Westminster Abbey
City of Bath
Hadrian's Wall Military Zone
The Tower of London
Canterbury Cathedral (with St. Augustine's Abbey and St. Martin's Church).

6.36 Full details of the operation of the World Heritage Convention, including the selection criteria for cultural and natural sites, are con-tained in the *Operational Guide-lines for the Implementation of the World Heritage Convention*.

6.37 The significance of World Heritage designation for local authorities' exercise of planning controls is set out in section 2 (paragraphs 2.22–2.23). Local plan-ning authorities are also encour-aged to work with owners and managers of World Heritage Sites in their areas, and with other agencies, to ensure that compre-hensive management plans are in place. These plans should:

— appraise the significance and condition of the site;
— ensure the physical conser-vation of the site to the highest standards;
— protect the site and its set-ting from damaging devel-opment;
— provide clear policies for tourism as it may affect the site.

ICOMOS can proved advice and

assistance in carrying forward this work.

Historic parks and gardens

6.38 The Register of Parks and Gardens of Special Historic Interest in England is maintained by English Heritage, to whom all enquiries about its compilation should be made. Sites of exceptional historic interest are assessed as grade I, those of great historic interest as grade II* and those of special historic interest as grade II. The grading of these sites is independent of the grading of any listed building which falls within the area. The Register is under review, with the aim of extending its coverage of parks and gardens deserving protection. (See also paragraph 2.24.)

Historic battlefields

6.39 English Heritage's draft Register of Historic Battlefields, which will be comparable in status with the Parks and Gardens Register, is shortly to be the subject of public consultation. The proposed Register identifies a limited number of areas of historic significance where important battles are sufficiently documented to be located on the ground. They will not be graded. The Register will be periodically reviewed by English Heritage, to whom all enquiries about compilation and content should be addressed. (See also paragraph 2.25.)

The wider historic landscape

6.40 Suitable approaches to the identification of the components and character of the wider historic landscape are being developed by the Countryside Commission (see its *Landscape Assessment Guid-*

ance) and English Heritage (as part of current research on methodology for historic landscape assessment). Appraisals based on assessment of the historic character of the whole countryside will be more flexible, and more likely to be effectively integrated with the aims of the planning process, than an attempt to define selected areas for additional control. It is unlikely therefore to be feasible to prepare a definitive register at a national level of England's wider historic landscape. The whole of the landscape, to varying degrees and in different ways, is an archaeological and historic artefact, the product of complex historic processes and past land-use. It is also a crucial and defining aspect of biodiversity, to the enhancement of which the Government is committed. Much of its value lies in its complexity, regional diversity and local distinctiveness, qualities which a national register cannot adequately reflect.

7. THE UPKEEP AND REPAIR OF HISTORIC BUILDINGS

7.1 Regular maintenance and repair are the key to the preservation of historic buildings. Modest expenditure on repairs keeps a building weathertight, and routine maintenance (especially roof repairs and the regular clearance of gutters and downpipes) can prevent much more expensive work becoming necessary at a later date. It is a common misunderstanding that historic buildings have a fixed lifespan, and that gradual decay of their fabric is inevitable. On the contrary, unless there are intrinsic defects of design or materials, the lifespan of a historic building may be indefinite provided that timely maintenance, and occasional major repairs such as the renewal of roof coverings and other features, are regularly undertaken. Major problems are very often the result of neglect and, if tackled earlier, can be prevented or reduced in scale. Regular inspection is invaluable.

7.2 The effective use of local planning authorities' controls set out in Part 1 is essential, but it will not of itself prevent historic buildings falling into neglect or disuse. The timely use of urgent works and repairs notice powers, described below, should always be considered, but authorities' resources for conservation will be used to best effect if some are devoted to identifying buildings at risk—from neglect or inappropriate changes— as early as possible and providing advice, encouragement and (where appropriate) grants to owners. Monitoring listed buildings, and unlisted buildings which make a positive contribution to conservation areas, by means of simple, regularly updated condition surveys is a valuable element of this approach. Dated photographs will provide a record of changes (and useful evidence in the event of statutory action being needed). Positive involvement of this kind by authorities will help prevent unnecessary loss of historic fabric, not to mention the probable cost and discord of action at a later stage.

7.3 The theft of architectural features, statuary, monuments and specialist materials has increased in recent years, and local authorities and owners are recommended to take precautions to safeguard them, especially when historic buildings are vacant or being refurbished. This may involve careful removal for safe and secure storage on site. Theft is a criminal offence and adequate records and photographs of vulnerable items will help the police recover them if stolen.

Repair

7.4 There is no specific duty on owners to keep their buildings in a good state of repair (though it will normally be in their interests to do so), but local authorities have powers to take action where a historic building has deteriorated to the extent that its preservation may be at risk. These powers take two forms.

Urgent works

7.5 Section 54 of the Act enables a local authority (or English Heritage in London) to carry out urgent works for the preservation of listed buildings in their area after giving notice to the owner. These powers can be used only in respect of an unoccupied building, or the unused part of a partly occupied building. Section 76 of the Act enables the Secretary of State to direct (after consulting English Heritage) that the powers shall apply to an unlisted building in a conservation area if it appears to him that its preservation is important for maintaining the character or appearance of that area. The Secretary of State will consider sympathetically the making of such a direction in respect of an unlisted building which makes a positive contribution to a conservation area. Authorities or members of the public may ask the Secretary of State to make such a direction; such requests should be supported by evidence confirming the importance of the building.

7.6 The Secretary of State can also exercise these powers himself, but under the terms of the legislation he must authorise English Heritage to give notice and carry out the works on his behalf. His policy is to use his powers only in exceptional cases, for instance where a building is of exceptional interest or is in local authority ownership; or where a conservation area is of more than local interest and either the building in question is so important to the area that failure to carry out urgent works to it would seriously damage the character or appearance of the area, or the building, as well as meeting the basic section 76 criterion, in local authority ownership. In all such cases he would normally only consider the use of his powers where the local authority concerned has decided not to take action itself.

7.7 Authorities will note that these powers are confined to *urgent* works: in the Secretary of State's view, their use should be restricted to emergency repairs, for example works to keep a building wind- and weather-proof and safe from collapse, or action to prevent vandalism or theft. The steps taken should be the minimum consistent with achieving this objective, and should not involve an owner in great expense. English Heritage has published *Emergency Repairs—A Handbook* which includes advice on methods of temporary repair.

7.8 Local authorities (or English Heritage in London, or the Secretary of State) may recover from owners the cost of urgent works carried out under these provisions, subject to the owner's right to make representations to the Secretary of State. Representations may be made on the grounds that some or all of the works were unnecessary; that temporary arrangements have continued for an unreasonable length of time; or that amounts are unreasonable or their recovery would cause hardship. The Secretary of State will take all such representations into account before determining the amount to be recovered, and will be particularly concerned to establish whether the works carried out were the minimum required to secure the building's preservation and prevent further deterioration. If an authority intends to attempt to recover the cost of the works, the financial circumstances of the owner should be taken into account at the outset and any sums the authority wishes to recover from an owner should not be unreasonable in relation to his or her means.

Repairs notices

7.9 If a local planning authority (or English Heritage in London) considers that a listed building is not being properly preserved, it may serve a repairs notice on the owner (under section 48 of the Act). This notice must specify the works which the authority considers reasonably necessary for the proper preservation of the building, and must explain the relevant provisions of the legislation, which are described briefly below. These powers are not confined to urgent works or to unoccupied buildings, and authorities should consider their use in cases where protracted failure by an owner to keep a listed building in reasonable repair places the building at risk.

7.10 A House of Lords judgment *Robbins v. Secretary of State for the Environment* ([1989] 1 All E.R. 878) has provided guidance on the nature of the works which may properly be specified in a repairs notice. The judgment held that, while the definition of works reasonably necessary for the proper preservation of the building will always relate to the circumstances of the individual case, and involve judgments about what is reasonable, the word "preservation" has to be given its ordinary meaning in contrast to "restoration", and this imposes an objective limitation which must be applied in considering the scope of works to be specified in a notice. The judgment also made clear that a notice can include works for the preservation of a building having regard to its condition at the date when it was listed: in other words, where a building has suffered damage or disrepair since being listed, the repairs notice procedure can be used to secure the building's preservation as at the date of listing, but should not be used to restore other features. If, however, repairs are necessary to preserve what remains of the rest of the building—for example, to a roof that was defective at the time of listing—it is legitimate, in the Secretary of State's view, to include them in a repairs notice.

7.11 Repairs notice powers may also be exercised by the Secretary of State, but, as with urgent works, his policy is to treat these powers essentially as reserve powers, and to use them only in exceptional circumstances. It is not open to the Secretary of State to authorise the use of repairs notices in respect of unlisted buildings in conservation areas.

Compulsory acquisition of listed buildings in need of repair

7.12 If at least two months have elapsed following the service of a repairs notice, and it appears to the body who served the notice that reasonable steps are not being taken for the proper preservation of the building, they may begin compulsory purchase proceedings. Compulsory purchase orders (CPOs) made by a local planning authority or by English Heritage require the Secretary of State's confirmation, and the Secretary of State must consult English Heritage before making an order himself or confirming an authority's order. In making or confirming an order, the Secretary of State must be satisfied that it is expedient to make provision for the preservation of the building and to authorise its compulsory acquisition for that purpose. The Secretary of State will also need to be satisfied that the means and the resources necessary for securing the building's repair will be available. A listed building CPO may also include land which an authority wishes to acquire for the purposes of access, amenity or management in connection with the building ('relevant land' in the Act).

7.13 The Secretary of State considers that privately owned historic buildings should, wherever possible, remain in the private sector. Local planning authorities are encouraged to identify a private individual or body, such as a building preservation trust, which has access to funds to carry out the necessary repairs and to which the building will be sold on as quickly as possible. Suitable covenants

453

should be negotiated to ensure that repairs will be carried out by a purchaser. Authorities should be aware that where they wish to acquire a listed building and pass it on, 'back to back' deals are possible. These are explained in Department of the Environment *Circular 11/90*, and are set out in regulation 15 of the Local Authorities (Capital Finance) Regulations 1990 as amended. Authorities are reminded that where a historic building is disposed of (either by freehold sale or long lease) within two years of its acquisition (or, where disposal was contracted for, but not implemented, in that period, within three years of acquisition), and the price received on resale is no more than the price paid, use of the capital receipt is unrestricted. Acquisitions under arrangements for immediate onward sale should, therefore, have no adverse financial implications for the authority, though there will clearly be other resource costs involved in securing confirmation of a CPO.

7.14 Any person who has an interest in a listed building which a local planning authority wishes to acquire compulsorily, and who has been served with a notice under the Acquisition of Land Act 1981, may apply to a magistrates' court for an order staying further proceedings on the compulsory purchase order. If an applicant is aggrieved by the decision of the magistrates' court, he or she may appeal to the Crown Court. Authorities should also be aware that where a compulsory purchase order is objected to, and a local public inquiry held (and also where representations against the recovery of expenses for works carried out under section 54 are heard as part of a related planning matter),

the Secretary of State may make an order as to the costs of the parties at the inquiry (see Department of the Environment *Circular 8/93*).

General considerations

7.15 The possible need to follow up with a CPO is clearly something which local planning authorities should take into account when contemplating repairs notice action. But the following are also relevant considerations:

— a recent study (*Listed Building Repairs Notices*) has shown that in over 60% of cases authorisation or formal service of a notice was itself sufficient to prompt owners either to begin repairs or to sell the building in question on to a third party: in only 13% of cases did the matter reach a CPO inquiry;

— the purpose of compulsory purchase is to ensure that reasonable steps are taken for properly preserving a listed building: it is not a requirement that the local authority should itself carry out the repairs or pay for them. Indeed in the Secretary of State's view it is preferable, as stated in paragraph 7.13 above, for the authority to obtain a firm commitment from a private purchaser to repair the building and meet the costs (perhaps with the assistance of any relevant grant-aid available);

— the Act contains provisions for minimum compensation where an owner has deliberately allowed a building to fall into disrepair in order to justify its demolition and secure permission for redevelopment of the site (section 50 of the Act); minimum compensation should however be sought only where there is clear evidence of such an intention;

— where the minimum compensation provisions do not apply, normal market value rules apply (as laid down in the Land Compensation Act 1961); but even here, high costs of repair, combined with limited possibilities for development, may indicate a very low or even nominal value.

Authorities also have powers under section 52 of the Act to acquire land and buildings by agreement.

8. CHURCHES AND THE ECCLESIASTICAL EXEMPTION

8.1 Ecclesiastical buildings are fully subject to planning control, but ecclesiastical buildings which are for the time being used for ecclesiastical purposes are exempt from listed building and conservation area controls, except in so far as the Secretary of State provides otherwise by Order under section 60(5) and 75(7) of the Act. Ecclesiastical exemption does not apply to the residences of ministers of religion (section 60(3)).

8.2 The context of the exemption is provided by an undertaking by the Church of England that its his-

toric buildings would be subject to a separate Church system of control which took account of the historical and architectural importance of churches. This system, known as faculty jurisdiction, has developed over time, in particular in a series of ecclesiastical measures passed by the General Synod and approved by Parliament, and in subordinate arrangements approved by the General Synod; a separate system covers Church of England cathedrals*. The exemption has, however, extended to ecclesiastical buildings of all denominations, not just those of the Church of England.

8.3 Following public consultation in 1992 the Secretary of State, in conjunction with the Secretary of State for Wales, announced that an Order would be made to provide that the exemption would in future apply only to the church of England and to other denominations and faiths which set up acceptable internal systems of control embodying the principles set out in the Government's code of practice. The Ecclesiastical Exemption (Listed Buildings and Conservation Areas) Order 1994 has now been made and is due to come into force on 1 October 1994.

Code of practice for denominations' internal control systems

8.4 The Government's code comprises the following points:

1. proposals for relevant

---

* The Faculty Jurisdiction Measure 1964, the Care of Churches and Ecclesiastical Jurisdiction Measure 1991, the Faculty Jurisdiction Rules 1992, and the Faculty Jurisdiction (Injunctions and Restoration Orders) Rules 1992; and, for cathedrals, the Care of Cathedrals Measure 1990, the Care of Cathedrals (Supplementary Provisions) Measure 1994, and the Care of Cathedrals Rules 1990.

works** should be submitted by the local congregation or minister for the approval of a body independent of them;

2. that body should include, or have arrangements for obtaining advice from, people with expert knowledge of historic church buildings;

3. the decision-making process should provide for:

   (a) consultation with the local planning authority, English Heritage and national amenity societies, allowing them (except in cases of emergency) 28 days to comment;

   (b) the display for the same 28-day period of a notice in a prominent position outside the building describing the proposed works and similarly inviting comments;

   (c) the publication of a similar notice in a local newspaper;

   (d) in cases of demolition, notification of the Royal Commission on the Historical Monuments of England (see also paragraph 3.22).

4. the decision-making body should be required, in considering proposals submitted to it, to take into account any representations made and, along with other factors, the desirability of preserving historic church buildings

and the importance of protecting features of architectural merit and historic interest (including fixtures—see paragraphs 3.13. and 8.11);

5. there should be a clear and fair procedure for settling all disputes between the local congregation or minister and the decision-making body as to whether proposals should proceed;

6. there should be procedures for dealing with any breach of the control system, including provision for reinstatement where works to historic church buildings have been carried out without consent;

7. there should be arrangements for recording how the above procedures were implemented in each case and the nature of the decision taken; for making such records available for public inspection during reasonable hours; and for notifying the decision to the above consultees;

8. there should be arrangements to ensure the proper maintenance of historic church buildings including thorough inspections on a fixed cycle of not more than five years.

So far as a denomination's circumstances permit, these points should be incorporated in legally binding procedures.

8.5 In considering proposals for such works, any effects on the archaeological importance of the

---

** *i.e.* works for the demolition of a listed ecclesiastical building or for its alteration or extension in any manner which would affect its character as a building of special architectural or historic interest; or works for the demolition of an unlisted ecclesiastical building in a conservation area.

church or archaeological remains existing within it or its curtilage should be taken into account along with other relevant factors. Where works of repair or alteration are to be carried out which would affect the fabric of listed churches or churches in conservation areas, denominations should attach any necessary conditions for proper recording in accordance with the principles set out in paragraphs 3.22–3.24 and, in respect of archaeological remains, in paragraph 2.15.

Future scope of the exemption

8.6 For those denominations and faiths which retain the exemption, its scope is reduced by the Order to the following:

— any church building;
— any object or structure within a church building;
— any object or structure fixed to the exterior of a church building, unless the object or structure is itself a listed building;
— any object or structure within the curtilage of a church building which, although not fixed to that building, forms part of the land, unless the object or structure is itself a listed building.

('Church building' is defined as a building whose primary use is as a place of worship.)

8.7 The Order provides continued exemption on this reduced basis (to the extent specified in it) for the Church of England and also for the Church in Wales, the Roman Catholic Church, the Methodist Church, the Baptist Union of Great Britain, the Baptist Union of Wales and the United Reformed Church. Ecclesiastical buildings of these denominations are covered by acceptable internal systems of control broadly conforming to the principles in the Government's code of practice. It is intended to monitor these arrangements and review them after two years. (Further Orders can be made if any other denominations or faiths are subsequently accepted as qualifying.)

8.8 Details of these denominations' arrangements will be published in a separate leaflet circulated to all local authorities. This will include the special arrangements made for Church of England cathedrals where all buildings, objects or structures within an area designated by the Secretary of State for National Heritage, after consulting the Cathedrals Fabric Commission for England, and places of worship and unlisted tombstones and other monuments elsewhere within the cathedral precinct, are exempt. A list of addresses for the denominations concerned, and related bodies, is included in Annex A.

8.9 The Order also provides continued exemption for ecclesiastical buildings of these denominations in various categories where insufficient information is currently available (eg. buildings of Church of England "peculiars", *viz* those outside the faculty jurisdiction system; Church of England and Roman Catholic religious communities; and school and other institutional chapels). The intention is that by the end of a limited period all buildings within these categories will either become subject to the normal local authority controls or be included within the scope of an exempted denomination's internal system of control.

The bodies concerned have been notified of the Order and invited to consider what future arrangements would be appropriate for them.

Exercise of controls over non-exempt church buildings

8.10 For denominations, faiths and independent congregations not listed in the Order, their places of worship will be fully subject to listed building and conservation area control from 1 October 1994. For non-exempt denominations, works begun or contracted for before 1 October 1994 are exempt. Conservation area control will extend to memorials, monuments and tombstones of whatever size erected prior to 1925, in order to bring authorities' controls into alignment with those which will be operated by the denominations listed in the Order; this will be done by a direction made under section 75(2) by the Secretary of State.

8.11 Much of the architectural character and historic interest of places of worship lies in the arrangement and furnishing of their interiors. The great majority of furnishings are likely to be fixed and so form part of the listed building (paragraphs 3.30–3.32), and their architectural coherence and quality will need to be taken into account when considering any proposals for re-ordering. It is probable that some changes have taken place in the past, and before considering further alterations the chronology and completeness of the existing arrangements should be carefully assessed. It is particularly important to identify, and where possible retain, the spatial arrangements and fixtures that belong to the principal period of building. When considering pro-

posals for creating cleared areas for multi-purpose use, the possibility of making fixed seating capable of being dismantled or moved should be investigated. Proper recording in accordance with the principles set out in paragraphs 3.22–3.24 and, in respect of archaeological remains, paragraph 2.15, should always be considered. Where extensive re-ordering takes place, some examples of the replaced furnishings should be retained wherever possible and, where appropriate, materials such as panelling should be re-used within the building or offered for re-use in a similar context, rather than destroyed.

8.12 In considering applications for consent relating to buildings used for worship authorities are advised that, in addition to the general considerations set out in section 3, the following matters (mainly relating to interiors) should be given due weight as material considerations, *viz* whether the changes proposed:

i. are necessitated by a change in the worship needs of the congregation;
ii. are necessitated by an increase or a reduction in congregation size;
iii. are directed at accommodating other activities within the building to help ensure its continued viability primarily as a place of worship;
iv. would involve substantial structural changes, *e.g.* subdivision of important existing spaces;
v. would involve the removal or destruction of important fixtures and fittings, or are more in the nature of a reversible re-

ordering of internal features;

vi. would involve disturbance of archaeologically important remains below ground.

8.13 English Heritage has published guidance entitled *New Works to Historic Churches* which local planning authorities may find useful in respect of buildings of all denominations. The Church of England has published a *Code of Practice on the Care of Churches and Ecclesiastical Jurisdiction Measure* which gives detailed guidance on many of the procedures to be followed and recommended practice under its own system of control (other than for cathedrals).

8.14 The Secretary of State will continue to have the power to bring within normal listed building or conservation area controls by a further Order any individual ecclesiastical building where it seems likely that potentially damaging works will be carried out without the necessary authorisation having been obtained under an exempt denomination's procedures, and without legal sanctions being available to the denomination internally.

Buildings no longer in ecclesiastical use

8.15 In the case of the Church of England total or partial demolitions of a redundant building in pursuance of a pastoral or redundancy scheme under the Pastoral Measure 1983 are exempt from listed building control by virtue of section 60(7) of the Act, and from conservation area control by a direction under section 75(2). The Church Commissioners have, however, agreed to ask the Sec-

retary of State for the Environment whether he wishes to hold a non-statutory public local inquiry into any such proposal for total or partial demolition (which would otherwise fall within the scope of those controls) where English Heritage, the Advisory Board for Redundant Churches, the local planning authority or a national amenity society have lodged reasoned objections. The Church Commissioners have also undertaken to accept a recommendation from the Secretary of State for the Environment following such an inquiry that the church is of sufficient importance to be vested in the Churches Conservation Trust (formerly the Redundant Churches Fund) or, in cases where the recommendation was not that the building should go to the Trust, to make further efforts to find an alternative use and to engage in further consultation with the Secretary of State for the Environment before using the Pastoral Measure powers to demolish. In considering what recommendation he will make, following a non-statutory inquiry, the Secretary of State for the Environment will take into account the financial implications of retaining a church building as well as the architectural and historic interest of the church and other planning and social factors, and will consult the Secretary of State for National Heritage.

8.16 Total demolition by faculty is not exempt but would require listed building and conservation area consent in the normal way, as would total demolition by exempt denominations other than the Church of England. This is because the exemption only applies to a building in ecclesiastical use, and the view of the Courts

459

has been that a building cannot be considered to be in such use if it is being totally demolished. Denominations have been asked to notify the local authority concerned when a church building covered by the exemption ceases to be used primarily for worship. Where total demolition is proposed, denominations may find it useful, before applying to the local planning authority for consent, to see that the proposal has been scrutinised through their normal procedures where these apply.

8.17 Except as mentioned above, Church of England buildings which are no longer in regular ecclesiastical use are fully subject to the normal listed building and conservation area controls once a declaration of redundancy under the Pastoral Measure comes into operation. These controls also cover buildings vested in the Churches Conservation Trust, in most of which church services are still held on an occasional basis. During the waiting period between a declaration of redundancy under the Pastoral Measure and the coming into operation of a redundancy scheme authorities are advised to discuss the application of the controls with the diocesan or parish bodies concerned where the authority is considering taking action under the urgent works provisions of section 54 of the Act or where the diocesan board of finance considers it necessary to remove fixtures for safe keeping under section 49(2) of the Pastoral Measure.

8.18 Many churches, of all denominations, when no longer required for worship may nevertheless have a continuing and valuable contribution to make to the community in terms of architecture, art, social and local or national history. They often occupy central and convenient positions in villages and towns and can, therefore, offer suitable venues for a variety of social and community purposes, such as meetings, concerts, exhibitions, indoor sports and evening classes. Even where the building itself is not worthy of individual listing as of architectural or historic interest, it may nevertheless be a familiar and important feature of an urban or rural landscape—while a surrounding churchyard may possess considerable ecological interest. It is important that once a church becomes redundant no unnecessary delay should occur in finding an alternative use for it. Conversion to another use which preserves the most interesting elements, internal and external, is to be preferred to demolition.

ANNEX A

THE LEGISLATION AND THE MAIN HERITAGE BODIES

A.1 The provisions relating to listed buildings and conservation areas are set out in the Act (as amended) augmented by the Planning (Listed Buildings and Conservation Areas) Regulations 1990* and directions and notifications. Further provisions relating to grants by English Heritage (formally known as the Historic Buildings and Monuments Commission for England) are set out in sections 3A–6 of the Historic Buildings and

* referred to in these Annexes as 'the 1990 Regulations'.

Monuments Act 1953 (as amended) and paragraph 3(1) of Schedule 2 to the Local Government Act 1985.

CENTRAL AND LOCAL GOVERNMENT

A.2 The Secretary of State for National Heritage is responsible for the general legislative and policy framework; for the listing of buildings of special architectural or historic interest; for the exercise of statutory powers to secure repairs to historic buildings and to designate conservation areas; for the scheduling of ancient monuments and for deciding applications for scheduled monument consent; and for the funding of the main heritage agencies.

A.3 Because of their close links with development control, the Secretary of State for the Environment is responsible for deciding called-in applications and appeals against refusals of listed building or conservation area consent, in consultation with the Secretary of State for National Heritage. Further details of the division of responsibility between the two Departments are given in Department of the Environment *Circular 20/92*.

A.4 Local planning authorities (primarily district and borough councils) have the crucial leading role in securing the conservation of the historic environment in their areas. They are responsible for the integration of conservation policy with wider planning policy for their areas, and for the designation of conservation areas. They exercise controls over works to listed buildings and over demolitions in conservation areas. They

have powers to secure the repair of listed buildings which have been allowed to fall into disrepair, and to make grants towards the cost of repairing historic buildings (whether or not listed).

A.5 Authorities should have adequate specialist expertise available to them for the discharge of their responsibilities for listed buildings and conservation policy generally. The availability of advice from English Heritage, and from the national amenity societies on certain categories of listed building consent application, does not relieve authorities of the need to ensure that they have their own expert advice suitably deployed to enable them to deal both with day-to-day casework and with longer-term policy formulation. Whether this expertise should take the form of full-time conservation staff, or the use of consultancy expertise, is a matter for individual authorities to consider. The Secretary of State may direct a district planning authority to submit for approval the arrangements which the authority propose to make to obtain specialist advice in connection with their conservation functions (paragraph 7 of Schedule 4 to the Act).

ENGLISH HERITAGE

A.6 English Heritage was established under section 32 of the National Heritage Act 1983. Its general duties under the Act are:—

(a) to secure the preservation of ancient monuments and historic buildings situated in England;
(b) to promote the preservation and enhancement of the character and appear-

ance of conservation areas situated in England;

(c) to promote the public's enjoyment of, and advance their knowledge of, ancient monuments and historic buildings situated in England and their preservation.

A.7 English Heritage's specific functions involve giving advice in relation to ancient monuments, historic buildings and conservation areas situated in England, including advice to the Secretary of State on the inclusion of buildings in the statutory list of buildings of special architectural or historic interest and the scheduling of ancient monuments; it may make grants and loans in relation to historic buildings, land and gardens, conservation areas, and ancient monuments, and in respect of archaeological investigation. It also compiles registers of parks and gardens of special historic interest, and of historic battlefields, and sponsors surveys of listed buildings at risk.

A.8 With the consent of the Secretary of State, English Heritage may acquire historic buildings, land or gardens, and acquire or become the guardian of ancient monuments. It manages about 400 sites and monuments on behalf of the Secretary of State.

A.9 English Heritage gives advice to local planning authorities on certain categories of listed building consent application which have to be notified to English Heritage, and similarly advises both Secretaries of State on planning and listed building consent applications and appeals and on other matters generally affecting the historic environment.

ROYAL COMMISSION ON THE HISTORICAL MONUMENTS OF ENGLAND (RCHME)

A.10 The RCHME is the national body of survey and record. Its aim is to compile and make available a basic national record of England's historic buildings and ancient monuments for use by individuals and bodies concerned with understanding, conserving and managing the built environment; this information is held in the National Monuments Record.

A.11 The RCHME has a specific responsibility to consider the need for recording and to record listed buildings threatened with total or partial demolition (section 8 of the Act). Works for such demolition are only authorised under the Act if the RCHME has been afforded reasonable access to the building in order to record it.

ROYAL FINE ART COMMISSION (RFAC)

A.12 The RFAC advises Government departments, local planning authorities and other bodies in England and Wales on mainly architectural, town planning and landscape matters. It does so primarily by means of comment on individual major development proposals which are submitted for scrutiny (see paragraph 2.13 above).

NATIONAL HERITAGE MEMORIAL FUND (NHMF)

A.13 The NHMF was established to give financial assistance towards the cost of acquiring, maintaining or preserving land, buildings, works of art and other objects of outstanding interest which are also of importance to the national heritage. The Fund is in the control of independent trustees, and was intended as a memorial to those who have died for the United Kingdom. The Fund operates throughout the United Kingdom and concentrates its activities on securing, through co-operation with other heritage agencies and funding bodies, the retention or preservation of outstanding heritage entities which are perceived to be at risk in some way.

A.14 The NHMF will have responsibility for distributing that part of the proceeds of the National Lottery which will be made available for heritage purposes. It will do so in consultation with other heritage bodies, including English Heritage. Separate guidance on applications etc will be issued in the autumn.

THE NATIONAL AMENITY SOCIETIES

A.15 The six national amenity societies aim to protect different aspects of the built heritage. The societies are:

(a) the Ancient Monuments Society, which is concerned with historic buildings of all ages and types, but with a particular interest in churches;

(b) the Council for British Archaeology, which is concerned with all historic buildings, but with a particular interest in the archaeology of subterranean and standing structures;

(c) the Society for the Protection of Ancient Buildings, which is concerned mainly with structures constructed before 1700, but also with philosophical and technical aspects of conservation;

(d) the Georgian Group, which is concerned with architecture and architecture-related arts between 1700 and 1840;

(e) the Victorian Society, which is concerned with Victorian and Edwardian architecture and architecture-related arts between 1840 and 1914; and

(f) the Twentieth Century Society (formerly the Thirties Society), which is concerned with architecture of the twentieth century in all decades except the first.

The first five of these are required to be notified by local authorities of applications to demolish listed buildings, either in whole or in part; the Twentieth Century Society receives relevant notifications via the Victorian Society.

A.16 The Garden History Society was closely involved in setting up the Register of Historic Parks and Gardens, now maintained by English Heritage. Its work, however, is analogous to that of the national amenity societies mentioned above and it has more experience of dealing with planning applications affecting parks and gardens than any other body.

A.17 Many local amenity societies affiliated to the Civic Trust, and local branches of the national societies, work closely with their local authorities to secure conservation objectives. The Secretaries of State attach particular importance to the activities of the voluntary sector in heritage matters, and hope that local authorities will work in close co-operation with national and local amenity bodies and draw on their expertise to the full.

ARCHITECTURAL HERITAGE FUND (AHF)

A.18 The AHF is a national conservation fund established to give local non-profit-making building preservation trusts access to working capital at favourable rates of interest. Such trusts play a particularly valuable role in renovating and finding new uses for historic buildings at risk from neglect and disrepair. The AHF also gives grants for feasibility studies on potential projects. Its entire capital is at all times available for low-interest loans on a 'revolving fund' basis, since running costs and all non-loan activities to help trusts are paid for out of interest earnings, with some assistance from grants from the Department of National Heritage. The AHF has played a leading part in establishing the United Kingdom Association of Building Preservation Trusts.

CHURCH BODIES

A.19 This annex also contains addresses for the Church of England and the four other denominations for which exemption is to be continued in England (see paragraph 8.7).

A.20 So far as the Church of England is concerned, the Church Commissioners for England have administrative and quasi-judicial duties in connection with pastoral reorganisation and redundant churches (see paragraph 8.15). Where there are plans to demolish a redundant church, the Com-

missioners must consult the Advisory Board for Redundant Churches (which grants the appropriate certificate). Where the Board advises against demolition, a non-statutory public inquiry may be held. The Council for the Care of Churches has certain statutory responsibilities under the Care of Churches and Ecclesiastical Jurisdiction Measure 1991 and the Pastoral Measure 1983 and a significant grant allocating function concerned with the conservation of furnishings and works of art in churches. The Cathedrals Fabric Commission for England gives advice on the care and conservation of cathedrals and determines applications for the approval of proposed works to cathedrals under the Care of Cathedrals Measure 1990 (see paragraph 8.8). The Churches Conservation Trust (formerly the Redundant Churches Fund) is the trustee body for the preservation, in the interests of the nation and of the Church of England, of churches vested in it on account of their historic, archaeological and architectural interest (paragraphs 8.15 and 8.17); it is grant-aided by the Church Commissioners (30 per cent) and the Department of National Heritage (70 per cent).

A.21 The Historic Chapels Trust was set up in 1993 to preserve by acquisition redundant chapels and other places of worship of outstanding architectural or historic interest belonging to Free Church, Roman Catholic, Jewish and other religious bodies. It will normally receive 70 per cent grants from English Heritage for the repair and maintenance of its buildings, raising the remainder privately. The Department of National Heritage also provided support for its setting up.

ADDRESSES OF KEY BODIES
AND ORGANISATIONS

1. **DEPARTMENT OF
   NATIONAL
   HERITAGE**
   2–4 Cockspur Street
   London SW1Y 5DH
   Tel: 0171–211 6000
   Fax: 0171–211 6382

2. **DEPARTMENT OF THE
   ENVIRONMENT**
   2 Marsham Street
   London SW1P 3EB
   Tel: 0171–276 3000
   Fax: 0171–276 3936

3. **ENGLISH HERITAGE**
   23 Savile Row
   London W1X 1AB
   Tel: 0171–973 3000
   Fax: 0171–973 3001

4. **ROYAL COMMISSION
   ON THE
   HISTORICAL
   MONUMENTS OF
   ENGLAND**
   Alexander House
   19 Fleming Way
   Swindon SN1 2NG
   Tel: 01793 414100
   Fortress House
   23 Savile Row
   London W1X 2JQ
   Tel: 0171–973 3500
   Shelley House
   Acomb Road
   York YO2 4HB
   Tel: 01904 784411

5. **ROYAL FINE ART
   COMMISSION**
   7 St James's Square
   London SW1Y 4JU
   Tel: 0171–839 6537

6. **NATIONAL HERITAGE
   MEMORIAL FUND**
   10 St James's Street
   London SW1A 1EF
   Tel: 0171–930 0963

7. **LOCAL AUTHORITY
   ASSOCIATIONS**
   i. **ASSOCIATION OF
      DISTRICT COUNCILS**
      Chapter House
      26 Chapter Street
      London SW1P 4ND
      Tel: 0171–233 6868

   ii. **ASSOCIATION OF
       COUNTY COUNCILS**
       Eaton House
       66a Eaton Square
       London SW1W 9BH
       Tel: 0171–235 1200

   iii. **ASSOCIATION OF
        LONDON AUTHORITIES**
        36 Old Queen Street
        London SW1H 9JF
        Tel: 0171–222 7799

   iv. **ASSOCIATION OF
       METROPOLITAN
       AUTHORITIES**
       35 Great Smith Street
       London SW1P 3BJ
       Tel: 0171–222 8100

   v. **LONDON BOROUGHS
      ASSOCIATION**
      College House
      Great Peter Street
      London SW1P 3LN
      Tel: 0171–799 2477

8. **ASSOCIATION OF
   CONSERVATION
   OFFICERS**
   PO Box 301
   Brighton
   Sussex BN2 1BQ

9. **ASSOCIATION OF
   ARCHAEOLOGICAL
   OFFICERS**
   Planning Department
   Essex County Council
   County Hall
   Chelmsford
   Essex CM1 1LF
   Tel: 01245 492211

10. **ENGLISH HISTORIC TOWNS FORUM**
The Huntingdon Centre
The Vineyards
The Paragon
Bath BA1 5NA
Tel: 01225 469157

11. **JOINT COMMITTEE OF THE NATIONAL AMENITY SOCIETIES**
St. Ann's Vestry Hall
2 Church Entry
London EC4V 5AB
Tel: 0171–236 3934
including:

   i. **ANCIENT MONUMENTS SOCIETY**
St. Ann's Vestry Hall
2 Church Entry
London EC4V 5AB
Tel: 0171–236 3934

   ii. **COUNCIL FOR BRITISH ARCHAEOLOGY**
Bowes Morrell House
111 Walmgate
York YO1 2UA
Tel: 01904 671417

   iii. **SOCIETY FOR THE PROTECTION OF ANCIENT BUILDINGS**
37 Spital Square
London E1 6DY
Tel: 0171–377 1644

   iv. **GEORGIAN GROUP**
37 Spital Square
London E1 6DY
Tel: 0171–377 1722

   v. **VICTORIAN SOCIETY**
1 Priory Gardens
Bedford Park
London W4 1TT
Tel: 0181–994 1019

   vi. **TWENTIETH CENTURY SOCIETY**
58 Crescent Lane
London SW4 9PU
Tel: 0171–793 9898

12. **GARDEN HISTORY SOCIETY**
Station House
Church Lane
Wickwar
Wotton-under-Edge
Gloucestershire GL12 8NB
Tel: 01454 294888

13. **CIVIC TRUST**
17 Carlton House Terrace
London SW1Y 5AW
Tel: 0171–930 0914

14. **ARCHITECTURAL HERITAGE FUND**
27 John Adam Street
London WC2N 6HX
Tel: 0171–925 0199

15. **UNITED KINGDOM ASSOCIATION OF BUILDING PRESERVATION TRUSTS**
c/o The Architectural Heritage Fund
27 John Adam Street
London WC2N 6HX
Tel: 0171–930 1629

16. **THEATRES TRUST**
Doric House
22 Charing Cross Road
London WC2H OHR
Tel: 0171–836 8591

17. **INTERNATIONAL COUNCIL ON MONUMENTS AND SITES**
10 Barley Mow Passage
Chiswick
London W4 4PH
Tel: 0181–994 6477

18. **RELIGIOUS DENOMINATIONS EXEMPTED**
   i. **GENERAL SYNOD OF THE CHURCH OF ENGLAND**
Church House
Great Smith Street
London SW1P 3NZ
Tel: 0171–222 9011

ii. **METHODIST CHURCH**
Property Division
Central Buildings
Oldham Street
Manchester M1 1JQ
Tel: 0161–236 5194

iii. **UNITED REFORMED CHURCH**
c/o Towns, Needham and Co,
Solicitors
6/8 Albert Road
Levenshulme
Manchester M19 3PJ
Tel: 0161–225 0040

iv. **ROMAN CATHOLIC CHURCH**
Catholic Bishops'
Conference of England & Wales
Allington House (1st floor)
136/147 Victoria Street
London SW1E 5LD
Tel: 0171–630 8221

v. **BAPTIST UNION OF GREAT BRITAIN**
c/o Baptist Union
Corporation Ltd
Baptist House
PO Box 44
129 Broadway
Didcot
Oxfordshire
OX11 8RT
Tel: 01235 512077

19. **OTHER RELEVANT CHURCH OF ENGLAND BODIES**
  i. **COUNCIL FOR THE CARE OF CHURCHES**
83 London Wall
London EC2M 5NA
Tel: 0171–638 0971

  ii. **CATHEDRALS FABRIC COMMISSION FOR ENGLAND**
83 London Wall
London EC2M 5NA
Tel: 0171–638 0971

iii. **CHURCH COMMISSIONERS FOR ENGLAND**
1 Millbank
London SW1P 3JZ
Tel: 0171–222 7010

iv. **ADVISORY BOARD FOR REDUNDANT CHURCHES**
Fielden House
Little College Street
London SW1P 3SH
Tel: 0171–222 9603

v. **CHURCHES CONSERVATION TRUST**
89 Fleet Street
London EC4Y 1DH
Tel: 0171–936 2285

20. **HISTORIC CHAPELS TRUST**
29 Thurloe Street
London SW7 2LQ
Tel: 0171–584 6072

ANNEX B

LISTED BUILDING CONTROL PROCEDURES

B.1 The procedures for listed building control are set out in Part I Chapter II of the Act (as amended), the 1990 Regulations, and directions and notifications.

B.2 Guidance on particular points is given below, followed by a summary of the procedures. However, where statutory procedures are involved, the text of the Act and other statutory documents should also be consulted.

1. GUIDANCE ON PARTICULAR POINTS

Applications

B.3 Applications must be made in triplicate on a form issued by the local authority. Section 10(2) of the Act requires that they include sufficient particulars, including a plan, to identify the building in question and such other plans and drawings as are necessary to describe the works for which consent is sought. For all but the simplest work this should normally mean measured drawings of all floor plans and external or internal elevations affected by the work proposed. There should be two sets of such drawings showing the structure before work and the altered structure or new development to replace it after the proposed work. The inclusion of photographs can be particularly helpful—of all elevations in demolition cases, or of the part of the building affected (interior or exterior) in alteration and extension cases. The Act empowers an authority to seek such particulars as it requires and an authority should certainly seek any particulars necessary to ensure that it has a full understanding of the impact of a proposal on the character of the building in question. An authority should not accept an application for consideration until it has sufficient information to provide such understanding.

Granting of consents: demolition

B.4 Section 8(1)–(2) of the Act requires the Royal Commission on the Historical Monuments of England (RCHME) to be allowed at least one month to record a listed building before demolition takes place (unless they indicate that they do not wish to record it). Authorities should make sure that applicants are aware of this requirement. It is helpful if authorities can draw attention to the provisions of the relevant sections in their application forms for listed building consent. All decisions granting consent for demolition should draw attention to the provisions of section 8(1)–(2), and enclose form RCHME (E) for applicants to use to notify RCHME of their proposals (copies are available from RCHME): the decision must also be copied to RCHME themselves.

B.5 Local authorities should avoid authorising demolition to make way for new development unless it is certain that the new development will proceed. This can be done by imposing a condition on the grant of consent providing that demolition shall not take place before a contract for carrying out the works of redevelopment on the site has been made and planning permission has been granted for the redevelopment for which the contract provides.

B.6 Listed buildings acquired for demolition and redevelopment, whether by private owners or local authorities, should be kept in use for as long as possible, or at least kept weather- and vandal-proof until work actually starts. If plans subsequently change, urgent action should be taken to ensure that the building is put into good repair and brought back into suitable use.

B.7 Granting a consent for demolition does not always mean that it will be implemented. But when local authorities know that total demolition has taken place, they should notify the Listing Branch of the Department of National Heritage so that the building can be removed from the list.

Conditions

B.8 The power to impose conditions on a listed building consent

468

is wide, but the Act specifically empowers certain types of condition (section 17). All conditions should of course be necessary, relevant, enforceable, precise and reasonable in all other respects.

B.9 A listed building consent must always be granted subject to a condition that the work to which it relates must be begun not later than five years (or whatever longer or shorter period is considered appropriate in a particular case) from the date on which the consent is granted (section 18). If any consent is granted without a time limit, the five year period will automatically apply. Conditions requiring the preservation of particular features, or the making good of damage caused by works, or the reconstruction of the building (with the use of original materials so far as practicable) may also be imposed. A listed building consent will normally enure for the benefit of the building regardless of ownership, but where appropriate a condition limiting the benefit of the consent to a specified person or persons may be imposed. See also the conditions recommended for restricting premature demolition (paragraph B.5 above) and for recording features or buildings due to be altered or demolished (paragraphs 3.22–3.24).

Later approval of details

B.10 The authority must always be satisfied that it has adequate information to assess the effect of proposed works on the listed building before granting consent: the extent of the work, the method to be used, and the materials involved are all important. However, section 17(2) of the Act permits authorities to impose conditions requiring the sub-

sequent approval of specified details of the works (whether or not these had been set out in the application). This provision is not in any sense an 'outline' listed building consent: it is simply intended to speed up the consideration of applications. It avoids the need for the authority to refuse consent if it is satisfied that the remaining details can safely be left for subsequent approval; but it should never be used unless authorities are satisfied that they have enough details to assess the impact of the proposals on the building as a whole.

Applications for the discharge or variation of a condition

B.11 Conditions should not be varied or discharged lightly. Frequently consent would not be given at all without conditions to safeguard the treatment of the building or to require works to be carried out in a certain way. Nevertheless, occasionally it may become clear that a condition is no longer appropriate (eg. because genuine structural problems arise, or better solutions for the treatment of the building are devised, or other features of interest are revealed once work has started). Section 19 of the Act therefore enables an application to be made by persons with a legal interest in the building which simply seeks a change in the conditions without re-opening the entire question of whether consent should have been granted. In dealing with such an application it is also open to the authority (or the Secretary of State) to add consequential new conditions to the consent.

Appeals

B.12 The procedure for appeals broadly follows that for ordinary

469

planning appeals. There is, however, provision for one additional ground of appeal, namely that the building does not merit its listed status (section 21(4)). Where this argument is advanced the Secretary of State for National Heritage will be consulted.

Purchase Notices

B.13 When listed building consent is refused or granted subject to conditions, any owner of the land may serve a listed building purchase notice on the local authority requiring it to purchase his interest in the land if he can establish that because of the refusal or conditions the land has become 'incapable of reasonably beneficial use' (sections 32–37). The authority must respond within three months; where it proposes not to accept such a notice it must first refer it to the Secretary of State who must give the parties the opportunity of being heard and may then confirm the notice or take other action (see Department of the Environment *Circular 13/83* for more detailed advice.)

Revocation of listed building consent

B.14 An authority may make an order revoking or modifying a listed building consent if it appears expedient to do so, having regard to the development plan and any other material considerations (sections 24–26). Such an order must be advertised; the owner and occupier of the land and all persons who, in the authority's opinion, will be affected by the order must be notified. If all those persons notify the authority in writing that they do not object to the order, it can take effect (unless it relates to a consent granted by the Secretary

of State); but in all other circumstances the order must be sent to the Secretary of State for confirmation. He also has default powers to make such orders. Compensation may be payable for abortive expenditure or other loss or damage caused by the order (section 28).

Compulsory purchase orders which include listed buildings and buildings in conservation areas

B.15 Appendix H to Department of the Environment *Circular 6/85* gives general guidance on the submission of compulsory purchase orders which include listed buildings or buildings in conservation areas. *Circular 5/93* summarises the provisions on compulsory purchase orders made under Housing Act powers.

Dangerous structures

B.16 Local planning authorities may not take any steps with a view to making a dangerous structures order for listed buildings, buildings subject to building preservation notices or buildings in conservation areas without first considering whether they should instead exercise their powers under section 47, 48 or 54 of the Act relating to repairs (section 56). Even when they consider that a dangerous structures order is appropriate, the works specified in such an order relating to such buildings still require listed building consent, except for emergency works authorised under section 78 of the Building Act 1984. Authorities should consider the extent of such an order and in particular whether a building can be made safe with no, or minimal, demolition. Authorities making dangerous structures orders should remind owners of the need to obtain listed building consent—or fulfil the requirements of section 9(3) which provides a defence in the event of prosecution.

II. SUMMARY OF THE PROCEDURES

B.17 The various steps relevant to authorities' handling of listed building consent applications are summarised below. References are to the Act or the 1990 Regulations or to directions made under powers contained in the Act. Authorities should note that some of the steps apply in certain cases only (e.g. in relation to Grade I and Grade II* buildings only).

Procedure	Statutory basis
A. *Initial advertisement and notification of application*	
(1) Advertise in local newspaper	Regulation
(2) Display a notice on or near building concerned	Regulation
(3) Notify English Heritage	Direction
Supporting information (plans, photographs and other relevant documents) should be included and 28 days allowed for comment.	
(4) Notify RCHME and national amenity societies	Direction
The relevant extract from the list description, and appropriate supporting information should be included. Where partial demolition is involved please indicate whether the case will be notified to DOE if the authority propose to grant consent (see step 8 below). 28 days should be allowed for comment.	
B. *Consideration of application*	
(5) Any comments received must be taken into account.	Regulations
(6) Authorities should decide applications as soon as possible after the statutory periods for representations have expired, normally within 8 weeks from receiving a valid application. If they wish to seek the applicant's agreement to an extension of time, they should make clear that he has a right of appeal against failure to take a decision within 8 weeks.	
(7) Authorities are free to *refuse* any application without further reference to any other body.	
C. *Where authority wish to grant consent*	

(8) If outside London, notify DOE Regional Office.

    Authorities are asked to use the attached proforma for this notification. Normally the Secretary of State will aim to decide within 28 days of notification and after consulting English Heritage whether to call in a case but he may extend that time if necessary (under section 13(2)). The authority may wish to ask the applicant whether he is willing to extend the 8 week decision period.

Sections 13(1), 15(1) and (2), Direction

(9) If inside London, notify English Heritage

    English Heritage will notify DOE where it proposes to authorise the granting of consent so that the Secretary of State may consider call-in. Where English Heritage direct the authority to refuse the application, the authority may within 28 days notify DOE to enable the Secretary of State to consider call-in. The Secretary of State will normally aim to reach a decision within 28 days but may extend the time.

Sections 14(1), (2)–(7) Direction

D. *Issue of decision*

(10) The authority has no further jurisdiction if the Secretary of State decides to call in the application

Section 12

(11) Otherwise the authority is free to determine the application (subject in London to any direction given by English Heritage)

(12) Issue reasoned decision in prescribed form.

Regulation

(13) If consent is given for demolition, warn applicant that RCHME must have opportunity to record building.

Section 8(2)(b) and (c)

(14) Copy decision letter to bodies consulted under directions.

Direction

Proforma

PLANNING (LISTED BUILDINGS AND CONSERVATION AREAS) ACT 1990 LISTED BUILDING CONSENT APPLICATIONS: NOTIFICATION TO THE SECRETARY OF STATE FOR THE ENVIRONMENT UNDER SECTION 13(1) OF THE ACT

1. Name of local planning authority:

2. Name and address of listed building:

3. Grade of listed building: I/II*/II

4. This application relates to (please delete whatever does not apply):

Grade I/II*:	alteration/extension/total demolition/partial demolition of principal building only/curtilage building(s) only/both principal and curtilage buildings.
Grade A/B/C Churches:	alteration/extension/total demolition/partial demolition of principal building only/curtilage building(s) only/both principal and curtilage buildings.
Grade II:	total demolition of a principal building/demolition of substantially all of an external elevation of a principal building/ demolition of substantially all of the interior of a principal building

5. The local planning authority resolved to grant consent on

....(date)
subject to the following conditions:

for the following reasons:

6. To assist the Department's consideration of the case the following are attached (please tick boxes as appropriate):

   (a) Copy of the application ☐

   (b) Copy of accompanying plans and drawings ☐

   (c) Copies of representations received ☐

      (i) from the public ☐

      (ii) from national amenity societies, English Heritage or the Royal Commission on the Historical Monuments of England ☐

   (d) Photographs ☐

   (e) Copy of Council's resolution ☐

   (f) Other supporting information (specify) ☐

   ....

7. In case of queries please contact:

   .... (name)

   .... (tel no)

8. Name and position of local planning officer notifying case

   ....

9. Signature: ....

10. Date: ....

ANNEX C
GUIDANCE ON ALTERATIONS TO LISTED BUILDINGS

GENERAL PRINCIPLES

C.1 These guidelines are concerned principally with works that affect the special interest and character of a building and require listed building consent. The range of listed buildings is so great that they cannot be comprehensive, but they do summarise the characteristics and features which make up the special interest of most listed buildings and which should be given full weight in the process of judging listed building consent applications, alongside other considerations—in particular the importance of keeping listed buildings in viable economic use whenever possible (see paragraphs 3.8 ff). Much of what they advise also applies to repairs; they are not however a manual of repair—for which attention is drawn to *The Repair of Historic Buildings: Advice on Principles and Methods* published by English Heritage.

C.2 Each historic building has its own characteristics which are usually related to an original or subsequent function. These should as far as possible be respected when proposals for alterations are put forward. Marks of special interest appropriate to a particular type of building are not restricted to external elements, but may include anything from the orientation, the plan or the arrangement of window openings to small internal fittings. Local planning authorities should attempt to retain the characteristics of distinct types of building, especially those that are particular to their area. The use of appropriate local materials is very desirable. Local planning authorities should encourage their production, and may wish to build up banks of materials to assist appropriate alteration or repair.

C.3 Alterations should be based on a proper understanding of the structure. Some listed buildings may suffer from structural defects arising from their age, methods of construction or past use, but can still give adequate service provided they are not subject to major disturbance. Repairs should usually be low-key, re-instating or strengthening the structure only where appropriate; such repairs may sometimes require listed building consent. New work should be fitted to the old to ensure the survival of as much historic fabric as is practical. Old work should not be sacrificed merely to accommodate the new.

C.4 Information about the history and development of a building will be of value when considering proposed alterations. This may be gained from the physical evidence in the building itself—ghosts of lost features in plaster, rough edges where features have been cut away, empty peg-holes and mortices—which can elucidate the original form or construction. There may also be documentary information, such as early photographs, drawings, written descriptions, or other documents relating to its construction or use.

C.5 Subsequent additions to historic buildings, including minor accretions such as conservatories, porches, balconies, verandas, door dressings, bargeboards or chimneys, do not necessarily detract from the quality of a building.

They are often of interest in their own right as part of the building's organic history. Generally, later features of interest should not be removed merely to restore a building to an earlier form.

C.6 In general the wholesale reinstatement of lost, destroyed or superseded elements of a building or an interior is not appropriate, although, where a building has largely retained the integrity of its design, the reinstatement of lost or destroyed elements of that design could be considered. In such cases there should always be adequate information confirming the detailed historical authenticity of the work proposed. Speculative reconstruction should be avoided, as should the reinstatement of features that were deliberately superseded by later historic additions.

C.7 Modern extensions should not dominate the existing building in either scale, material or situation. There will always be some historic buildings where any extensions would be damaging and should not be permitted. Successful extensions require the application of an intimate knowledge of the building type that is being extended together with a sensitive handling of scale and detail.

EXTERNAL ELEVATIONS

C.8 **Walls** Walls are the main structural fabric of a building. Alterations to wall surfaces are usually the most damaging that can be made to the overall appearance of a historic building. Alterations or repairs to external elevations should respect the existing fabric and match it in materials, texture, quality and colour. Brick or stonework should not normally be rendered unless the surface was rendered originally. It may be necessary to remove more recently applied render if this is damaging the surface beneath. Every effort should be made to retain or re-use facing brickwork, flintwork, stonework, tile or slate hanging, mathematical tiles or weatherboarding. Cob and other earth walling should be carefully maintained and expert advice should be taken if there is a need for repair.

C.9 **Openings** Door and window openings establish the character of an elevation; they should not generally be altered in their proportions or details, especially where they are a conspicuous element of the design. The depth to which window frames are recessed within a wall is a varying historical feature of importance and greatly affects the character of a building: this too should be respected. Rubbed gauged brick or stone voussoir arches should be kept wherever possible or copied and the original design repeated in any new work or repairs. Historic cill and lintel details should be retained.

C.10 **Pointing** The primary feature of a wall is the building material itself and the pointing should normally be visually subservient to it. There are occasions where decorative pointing is used, such as flint galleting, but in general pointing that speaks louder than the walling material is inappropriate. Repointing should usually be no more than a repair—a repeat of the existing mix and appearance— except where the mix is inappropriate or damaging. Any change in the character of the pointing can be visually and physically damaging and requires listed building consent.

C.11 It is important to ensure that repointing does not extend beyond the area where it is necessary. Historic pointing may survive wholly or in part and this should be preserved. New work or repair work should integrate with the existing coursing. Tumbled brick or stonework in gables and patterned and polychrome brickwork are particularly important in this context. Cutting out old mortar with mechanical cutters should not be permitted because it makes the joints unacceptably wide, and may score the masonry above perpend joints.

C.12 **Plaster and render** Existing plaster should not be stripped off merely to expose rubble, brick or timber-framed walls that were never intended to be seen. Refacing of stone, flint, brick or terracotta facades with roughcast, cement render, stick-on stone, Tyrolean render, cement-based paints of other cosmetic treatment that is difficult or impossible to remove should be avoided. This is particularly so where architectural or decorative features would be partially obscured or covered over.

C.13 Traditional lime-based render is generally preferable to cement-rich render. Cement render forms a waterproof barrier that prevents any moisture trapped within the wall from evaporating and tends to drive damp both higher up and further in. This can lead to the breakdown of the wall surface which will, in time, fall away with the render. Cement render also gives distinctive hard sharp edges to quoins and wall on lime has a softer appearance and allows natural evaporation.

C.14 Some historic renders like stucco and Roman cement were intended to have smooth surfaces and sharp edges in imitation of well cut ashlar stonework. These should not be replaced with other types of render. On late 18th and 19th-century stuccoed elevations where there is mock jointing, grooving, rustication or plaster architectural elements like cornices and architraves these should always be retained where possible or carefully copied, never skimmed off. Any new lining out should be matched carefully to the existing.

C.15 Decorative plaster details and plaster features such as pargeting or sgraffito work should not be destroyed. Such features are not always durable and it may be appropriate to reproduce them to complete a decorative scheme. Proper evidence is required for such a scheme of reproduction.

C.16 **Timber frames** With timber-framed buildings, the totality of the structure has to be taken into consideration; *i.e.* walls, roof and internal partitions. Repair to timber frames, including roof structures, should be kept to the essential minimum. Traditional fixing and repair methods should be perpetuated. Proper attention should be given to the in-filling panels which are an integral part of any timber-framed building, and also to the surface of the timbers. The original tool marks are often visible, as well as carpenters' marks, graffiti and smoke-blackening. Such features are always destroyed by sand-blasting and sometimes by painting or other cleaning, which should not normally be permitted.

C.17 **External painting** Painting— or re-painting such as a change of colour—requires listed building consent when it could affect the character of a listed building. Previously unpainted surfaces should not normally be painted over. (An exception to this rule can be made for the sheltercoating of decayed stonework with a lime-based mixture.) In many cases the colour of the paint may be less important than the first application of an unsuitable covering which could be damaging to remove. Cement based or other waterproof and hard gloss paints should not be used on surfaces covered with traditional render. The correct finish for traditional renders and plasters is limewash (although much 19th-century stucco has traditionally been coated in oil paint). When inappropriate paint has been applied, expert advice should be obtained on suitable methods of removal. Repainting with lead-based paints may be historically correct, but is now restricted to Grade I and II* buildings and the intention to use it on any such building must be notified to English Heritage. Downpipes are usually best painted in unobtrusive colours, but lead downpipes should not normally be painted.

C.18 **External cleaning** Cleaning a building usually requires listed building consent. This is not only because cleaning can have a marked effect on the character of buildings, but also because cleaning processes can affect the historic fabric. The cleaning of a building within a homogeneous terrace would obviously affect the appearance of the terrace as a whole. All cleaning methods can cause damage if carelessly handled. Cleaning with water and bristle brushes is the simplest method, although water cleaning can lead to saturation of the walls and out-breaks of rot in timbers. Other methods including abrasive and chemical cleaning can damage wall surfaces and destroy detail. Local planning authorities should satisfy themselves that such cleaning is both necessary and worthwhile to remove corrosive dirt or to bring a major improvement in appearance, and should ensure that cleaning is carried out by specialist firms and under close supervision. Areas not being cleaned should be protected.

C.19 **Wrought and cast iron** The character of wrought iron fittings, railings, lamp-brackets etc is derived from the unique qualities of the material and from traditional smithing techniques. Since wrought iron is now difficult to obtain, old ironwork should be retained wherever possible. It is not possible to copy satisfactorily the character of wrought iron using mild steel. Old cast iron features, including railings, balconies, windows, fire-grates, door furniture and structural beams and columns can be visually and architecturally important. Such features may carry the name of the foundry and the date of casting, thereby adding to the historic interest of the building. Broken cast iron can be repaired and damage should not be regarded as an excuse for removal.

C.20 **Parapets and other features** Parapets (solid or balustraded), pediments, parapeted or coped gables and saddlestones, eaves, cornices and moulded cappings are essential terminal features in the articulation of an elevation. If they have to be replaced, it should be in facsimile and in the same materials.

C.21 **Porches** Porches are sometimes the dominant feature of an

477

elevation; their detailing should always be respected. Open columned porches of the Classical type should not normally be enclosed (eg. with glazed sides and doors to the front), but should be left open. In those instances where new porches are considered acceptable, their design should be undemonstrative and should not challenge the integrity of the facade.

C.22 **Balconies and verandas** Balconies and verandas are very often formal components in the design of an elevation. They should be maintained and repaired; and if they have to be replaced, facsimiles should be erected using matching materials. As with porches they should not normally be enclosed with glazing.

C.23 **Fire escapes** Fire escapes can be very damaging to the external appearance of a building. If an escape is essential it should be inconspicuously located and fixed in such a way as to avoid rust or other staining of the wall surfaces. In many cases there may be alternative ways of ensuring adequate fire protection and means of escape that would require less physical alteration.

C.24 **External plumbing** External plumbing should be kept to a minimum and should not disturb or break through any mouldings or decorative features. A change from cast iron or lead downpipes to materials such as plastic or extruded aluminum sometimes requires listed building consent and should not normally be allowed.

C.25 **Inscriptions and other features** Inscriptions, old lettering, old shop signs, inn sign boards, date plaques and stones, coats of arms, monograms, fire insurance plaques, commemorative or symbolic carvings and statues in niches are part of the history of a building. These features should be retained *in situ* wherever possible. If works require the temporary removal of an interesting feature, it should be put back in its former position. New signs and advertisements will require listed building consent. They should be carefully designed and positioned with appropriate fixings that will not damage the building.

C.26 **Carved details** Carved and other sculptural details such as moulded brickwork and terracotta are an important part of the design and character of buildings that carry them. Where such details are decaying, it is important to record them.

ROOFS

C.27 The roof is nearly always a dominant feature of a building and the retention of its original structure, shape, pitch, cladding and ornament is important.

C.28 Local planning authorities should encourage the retention and development of sources of traditional roofing materials. The cannibalising of other buildings for traditional materials should be discouraged. When a roof is stripped it is important that as much as possible of the original covering is re-used, preferably on the visible slopes, with matching new materials on other slopes.

C.29 **Thatch** Thatched roofs should be preserved, and consent should not be given for their replacement by different roof coverings. Where medieval thatch survives with characteristic smoke blackening on the underside, it should be retained *in situ* and overlaid. When roofs are re-thatched, this should normally be done in a form of thatch traditional to the region, and local ways of detailing eaves, ridges and verges should be followed. Re-thatching roofs that have lost their thatch will require a waiver of building regulations in most cases, since they may not be allowed within 12 metres of a site boundary, but local authorities should be prepared to relax this rule it if does not constitute an unacceptable fire risk to other properties.

C.30 **Slates and tiles** Some slates and all stone slates are laid to diminishing courses. The character of such roof coverings should not be damaged by a radical change in the range of slate sizes. The pattern and coursing of different roofing materials are distinguishing features of different building types and areas of the country. This patterning and coursing should be retained and, where necessary, restored with matching materials.

C.31 **Lead and copper** Both lead and copper are traditional roof coverings and should not normally be replaced by modern substitute materials. Details such as lead rolls, hips and ridges are important visual elements. Any dates or inscriptions in the lead should be preserved.

C.32 **Embellishments to roofs** Towers, turrets, spires, bellcotes and cupolas are not only part of the overall design or indeed sometimes its main feature, but frequently make an important contribution to the townscape or landscape. This is particularly so

with public buildings and churches. Lesser decorative embellishments such as ridge and cresting tiles, iron cresting, finials, gargoyles and spouts, bargeboards, valences, cartouches and statues should also be preserved.

C.33 **Dormers and rooflights** Early dormers, especially of the 17th or 18th-century pedimented type, should be retained and carefully repaired. If beyond repair they should be reconstructed with all details reproduced. Enlargement of existing dormers on principal elevations should normally be avoided.

C.34 Any decision as to whether new dormers or rooflights can be added to a roof must be approached carefully. Historic roof structures must not be damaged by their insertion. New dormers should not upset a symmetrical design of either an individual building or a terrace. Regions have differing traditional types of dormer and these traditions should be respected.

C.35 Where new dormers would be inappropriate to the type of building or proposed position, new rooflights, preferably in flush fittings, may be acceptable, but not on prominent roof slopes.

C.36 **Chimney stacks and pots** Chimney stacks are both formal and functional features of the roofscape and can be important indicators of the date of a building and of the internal planning. In many cases chimneys also perform a vital structural function, and they should normally be retained, even when no longer required. There may, however, be poorly built and positioned later additions that can be removed with advantage. Chimney pots can sometimes be valuable decorative features in their own right, but they are also functional features: plain Georgian and 19th-century pots are often important as part of a traditional roofscape which will be damaged if they are removed.

EXTERNAL DOORS

C.37 **Doors and doorways** Original doorways and any surviving original doors should be retained. Their replacement or defacement is often entirely unnecessary. Domestic and public building door types vary widely and if they have to be replaced their design should be appropriate to the character of the building. Replacement doors should copy the original in the materials, the detail of the design, and the paint finish. Modern off-the-peg doors are not generally acceptable for use in listed buildings, nor are doors with incongruous design features such as integral fanlights. Unpainted hardwood or stained or varnished softwood doors are rarely suitable.

C.38 **Redundant doorways** Doorways that become redundant should in general not be removed. This is particularly the case where a terrace of houses is converted into flats or offices and some of the doors are no longer required: it is most important that they are retained for the sake of the overall design of the terrace.

C.39 **Door detail** Doorcases, door furniture including hinges, knockers and letter-boxes, foot scrapers, fanlights, pediments, columns, pilasters, cornices, consoles and carved or stucco moulded details should not be removed or mutilated but retained even if the doorway is redundant.

WINDOWS

C.40 As a rule, windows in historic buildings should be repaired, or if beyond repair should be replaced "like for like". If listed building consent is given for additional windows it is important that their design, scale and proportion should be sympathetic to the character of the building.

C.41 Within the broad window types such as sash or casement there is a wide variation of detail according to date, function and region. Standardisation to one pattern—such as the many new "Georgian" sashes which adopt early 19th-century details—should be avoided. The thickness and moulding of glazing bars, the size and arrangement of panes and other details should be appropriate to the date of the building or to the date when the window aperture was made.

C.42 If a building has been re-windowed there may be a desire to return to the original glazing pattern. In general the existing windows should be retained, unless they are obviously inappropriate or in very poor condition. There may be some cases, particularly in uniform urban terraces, where a return to earlier glazing patterns following a specific local pattern is appropriate.

C.43 Window types vary according to the region and its building tradition. Mullioned and transomed casement windows continued into the 18th-century in some areas. In the North of England, particularly West Yorkshire and the Pennines, mullioned windows were standard for vernacular buildings until the mid 19th-century: the mullions should therefore not be cut out.

C.44 Leaded and other metal-framed casements in 19th-century and particularly earlier buildings are an increasing rarity and should be repaired or re-leaded rather then replaced.

C.45 Eighteenth and 19th-century fancy glazing bars in geometric Gothic or marginal patterns should be retained wherever possible or copied, whether they are original to the building or later additions.

C.46 Twentieth century mild steel windows were often a design feature of Modern Movement and Art Deco buildings. These should be repaired, or replaced like for like if beyond repair.

C.47 Paint is usually the correct finish for timber windows; staining is not a traditional finish and should not normally be used. However, early windows of oak were commonly limewashed or left unpainted and these should not now be painted but left to weather naturally.

C.48 **Old glass** All old glass is of interest, whether it be stained, painted or etched glass or early plain glass such as crown glass. Great care should be taken to protect old glass during building works. If it is necessary to remove panes to repair the window frames or infrastructure they should be reset. Where external protection for glass is required, it should be reversible and as unobtrusive as possible.

C.49 **Replacement windows** The insertion of factory made standard windows of all kinds, whether in timber, aluminum, galvanised steel or plastic is almost always damaging to the character and appearance of historic buildings. In particular, for reasons of strength the thickness of frame members tends to be greater in plastic or aluminum windows than in traditional timber ones. Modern casements with top-opening or louvred lights or asymmetrically spaced lights are generally unsuitable as replacements for windows in historic buildings. Such alterations should not be allowed. Architects' drawings and specifications should make clear the manner in which new windows are intended to open.

C.50 It is usually impossible to install double-glazed units in existing frames or to replicate existing frames with new sealed units without making noticeable changes to the profiles of glazing bars, styles, and rails. The new glass in such units may also significantly alter the appearance of the window. Such changes are rarely acccptablc in listed buildings. Weather stripping and draught-proofing are visually more innocuous changes as well as thermally efficient and cost-effective. Secondary glazing in a removable inner frame is another acceptable option for some windows.

C.51 Old louvred and panelled external shutters are important features and often contribute to the design of an elevation. Blind-cases and canopies should also be preserved.

SHOP FRONTS

C.52 **Shop fronts and display windows** Wherever shop fronts of merit survive they should be retained. Early 20th-century shop fronts such as those with Art Nouveau or early Art Deco details can be as unusual as 18th or 19th-century examples. Features of value such as blinds in blind boxes, shutters in shutter boxes against an upright and stall-risers are often concealed beneath later facings. Premises where works to shop fronts are proposed should always be inspected and the possible survival of old features checked.

C.53 There are many examples of first floor display windows, and infrequent examples of second floor ones. These date from the late 19th and early 20th-century and give a characteristic appearance which should be preserved. Proposals to remove a modern shopfront to restore an elevation to its previous designed appearance matching the rest of a terrace can usually be encouraged, but should be viewed with caution in cases where the shop front is of interest in itself.

C.54 **Shop blinds and security grilles** Retractable apron blinds covered in canvas are often characteristic features of historic shopfronts and should be retained. Modern plastic canopies are not acceptable.

C.55 External steel roller shutters are not suitable for historic shopfronts. Traditional timber shutters give reasonable protection: laminated glass and internal chain-link screens are modern alternatives. Traditional stall-risers are an effective deterrent to "ram-raiders", as are small shop windows between masonry piers.

C.56 **New shop fronts** New shop fronts should be designed in sympathy with the rest of the elevation and incorporate any ground floor details of interest. Large inserted plate-glass shop fronts without any visual support for the upper part of the premises can have an unfortunate effect, and shop fronts should not extend into the storey above or alter the proportion of first floor windows. Modern materials such as plastics are to be avoided as facings. The fascia board should not be out of scale with the building as a whole and should usually be finished at the top with console brackets and a cornice or other capping. Not only is this the traditional treatment for shop fronts but the cornice provides an architectural division between the modern shop front and the older upper floors.

C.57 Depending on the nature of a proposed commercial or office use, it is very often unnecessary to provide display windows and thus alter an intact ground floor. Existing openings should be retained wherever possible, and if alteration is necessary it should only be to the minimum extent required. Standard corporate shop fronts are seldom appropriate for historic buildings, nor are internally illuminated fascia boxes or signs. The prestige value of listed building premises and their distinctive detailing can be emphasised instead.

INTERIORS

C.58 The plan of a building is one of its most important characteristics. Interior plans and individual features of interest should be respected and left unaltered as far as possible. Internal spaces, staircases, panelling, window shutters, doors and doorcases, mouldings, decorated ceilings, stucco-work, and wall-decorations are part of the special interest of a building and may be its most valuable feature.

C.59 **Walls** Internal walls in old buildings should always be investi-

482

gated with care in advance of alterations in case ancient or interesting features are hidden in the plaster or behind the panelling or other covering. In many cases the partitions themselves are of historic interest. New partitions should be kept to a minimum. They should not cut through mouldings or enriched plaster decoration but be shaped around them to allow for reinstatement at a later date.

C.60 **Plasterwork** All old plain plasterwork should be preserved where possible. Traditional lime and hair plaster has good insulation qualities and is better able to tolerate condensation than modern gypsum plaster. Care should always be taken with works to old plaster, especially when chasing-in electrical wiring, in case there is early decoration. All decorative features from a simple cornice or cove to elaborate wall and ceiling decoration should be preserved.

C.61 **Chimneypieces and chimneybreasts** Good chimneypieces are part of the decorative history of a building and are often central to the design of a room. There is no excuse for their removal if this is simply because a chimney is redundant. In the rare cases where there is no alternative to the removal of a chimneypiece, it should be saved for use in another position and should not be removed from the building. The removal of a later chimneypiece of interest should not normally be allowed even if an earlier open hearth is known to survive behind it. The removal of a chimneybreast is almost never acceptable, not least because it may affect the structural stability of the building.

C.62 **Staircases** The removal or alteration of any historic staircase is not normally acceptable. The stair is often the most considerable piece of design within a building and can be important dating evidence. In retail premises, the removal of the lowest flight of stairs—which will preclude access to and use of upper floors—should not be allowed.

C.63 **Interior paintwork and decoration** A careful choice of both type and colour of paints or wallpapers can make a significant contribution to the appearance and integrity of a historic interior. Inappropriate schemes may, conversely, be visually damaging. In some instances specialist advice should be sought on the original scheme of decoration which may survive beneath later layers. Although strict adherence to historical forms is not normally a requirement in buildings whose interiors are of a "private" rather than a "museum" character, the use of historically appropriate decoration can greatly enhance most listed buildings. Where important early schemes of interior decoration survive, cleaning and conservation rather than renewal may be appropriate. Overpainting, even of deteriorated or discoloured areas of plain colour, may damage or obscure the historical record.

FLOORS

C.64 **Floor surfaces** Floor surfaces are too often disregarded when buildings are refurbished. It is not only marble floors that are important: all types of paving such as stone flags, and pitched cobbles, old brick floors, early concrete, lime ash, and plaster floors, should be respected. This also applies to old boarded floors, especially those with early wide oak or elm boards. All such features should normally be repaired and re-used. When new floorboards are needed, they should be of the same timber, width and thickness as those they are replacing. Great care should be taken when lifting old boards for the installation or repair of services, especially where the boards are tongued or dowelled. The cutting of joists for new services should be kept to a minimum, and any early sound-deadening or fire-proofing between the joists should be preserved.

C.65 **Floor strengthening** Proposals for floor strengthening often form part of refurbishment schemes, and may be dictated by the inflexible requirements of particular clients or funding bodies, demanding the same standards as those applied to new buildings. These are almost always at variance with the architectural and structural integrity of a historic building and should not normally be regarded as a sufficient justification for major alterations. The floors of most historic buildings can be made perfectly adequate for the actual loads they will carry.

C.66 Low-key techniques of stiffening existing floors, or limited strengthening, may often be possible, provided there is minimum disturbance to the overall structural equilibrium, thereby retaining as much existing fabric and structure as possible, as well as, where necessary, improving performance. Repairs should usually be carried out using traditional materials and methods, such as scarfing on new timber. Where more modern techniques are put forward, applicants will need to

show good reason why these are being proposed.

C.67 Often the pressure for floor strengthening and replacement arises from the presence of dry rot within the structural members. Dry rot eradication can rapidly lead to the progressive stripping and dismantling of a building. In every case where remedial works are proposed, the minimum works necessary should be carried out after detailed discussion. The use of new techniques requiring the minimum removal of timber should be encouraged.

MINOR ADDITIONS AND NEW SERVICES

C.68 **Minor additions to listed buildings** There are some standard external fixtures that require listed building consent when they affect the character of a listed building. These include satellite dishes, meter boxes, burglar alarms, security and other floodlighting, video cameras, and central heating and other flues, both standard and balanced. Only undamaging and visually unobtrusive positions for such fixtures should be agreed.

C.69 **Introduction of services to listed buildings** The poorly thought out introduction of services, such as mains electricity, telephone or gas, can be detrimental to the structure, appearance and character of a building. Long runs of surface wiring and any external gas piping should be avoided unless chasing-in would destroy historic fabric. The introduction of new services to historic interiors must also be handled with care, and any false floors or ceilings for concealing services, computer trunking, fibre optics, central heating etc, should be reversible, and not entail alterations to other features such as doors or skirtings.

Appendix B

Circular No. 8/87:
Historic Buildings and
Conservation Areas—
Policy and Procedures

Date of Issue: March 25,
1987

In the Introduction to PPG 15,
paragraph 3 it is explained that the
directions in Circular 8/87 will
continue in force until new *directions* have been made.

We therefore reproduce the
directions from that Circular as
follows:–

29. The Secretary of State for
the Environment, as respects England, under section 28(2B) of the
Town and Country Planning Act
1971 [see now s.67(4) of the Listed
Building Act 1990] and after consultation with the Historic Buildings and Monuments Commission
for England ("the Commission")
hereby notifies local planning
authorities as follows:—

Local planning authorities are
NOT required to send to the Commission any notice relating to an
application for planning permission which—

    (a) affects the setting of a
        Grade II (unstarred) listed
        building situated outside
        Greater London;

    (b) affects the character or
        appearance of a conservation area and which is
        for the development of
        any land by—

        (i) the erection of a new
building or the alteration or extension of
an existing building
where the new building, the part of the
building being
altered, or the extension, is of a cubic
content (ascertained
by external measurement) not exceeding
3,000 cubic metres or
where the area of
ground to be developed does not exceed
1,000 square metres;
or

      (ii) the material change
of use of any building
having a cubic content (ascertained by
external measurement) not exceeding
3,000 cubic metres or
where the area
of ground to be developed does not
exceed 1,000 square
metres; or

    (c) is for the development of
land in Greater London
which in the opinion of
the local planning authority, involves the demolition, in whole or in part,
or the material alteration
of a listed building, which
falls to be notified to the
Commission pursuant to
the provisions of the current General Development Order (at present

article 15(1)(*j*) of the Town and Country Planning General Development Order 1977 (SI 1977, No. 289) (added by SI 1986, No. 435) [see now the 1988 Order, art. 18(1)]).

Notifications

81. The Secretary of State for the Environment as respects England hereby directs that notice of all applications for consent to demolish a listed building and of the decisions taken thereon should be given to the following bodies:— The Ancient Monuments Society, The Council for British Archaeology, The Georgian Group, The Society for the Protection of Ancient Buildings, The Victorian Society, and the Royal Commission on the Historical Monuments of England.

82. The Secretary of State for the Environment as respects England also directs under the powers of paragraphs 7(2) and (3) of Schedule 11 to the 1971 Act [now s.15(5), (6) of the LBA 1990] that local planning authorities shall notify the Historic Buildings and Monuments Commission for England, of all applications for listed building consent in the following categories:

(a) outside Greater London applications to alter, extend or demolish any Grade I or II* building; or

(b) in Greater London (other than the area of the London Docklands Development Corporation), applications to alter, extend or demolish any grade of listed building,

and, in due course, the decisions taken by the authorities thereon.

London Docklands

In the exercise of the powers given by him by section 138 of the Local Government, Planning and Land Act 1980 and of all other powers enabling him in that behalf and after consultation with the London Docklands Development Corporation, the Secretary of State for the Environment hereby directs as follows:—

(1) Where an application for listed building consent or conservation area consent is made to the London Docklands Development Corporation ("the Corporation"), the Corporation shall notify the Historic Buildings and Monuments Commission ("the Commission") of that application and shall not determine such an application until the expiry of a period of 21 days from such notification, shall take into account any representations made by the Commission within such period in respect of that application and shall notify the Commission of their decision on that application.

(2) Where an application for listed building consent is made to the Corporation, paragraph 5 of Schedule 11 to the Town and Country Planning Act 1971 [now s.13(1)–(3) of the LBA 1990] shall apply to that application as if that application was made to a local planning authrity other than a London borough council.

I OUTSIDE GREATER LONDON AND LONDON DOCKLANDS DEVELOPMENT CORPORATION

86. Pursuant to his powers under paragraph 7(1), (1A) and (3) of Schedule 11 to the 1971 Act [now s.15 of the Listed Buildings Act 1990] and to all other powers enabling him in that behalf and after consultation with the Historic Buildings and Monuments Commission for England ("the Commission"), the Secretary of State for the Environment as respects England hereby directs as follows:—

(1) In this direction:—

"principal building" means a building shown in the list compiled under section 54 of the 1971 Act [now s.1 of the Listed Buildings Act 1990] and includes any object of structure fixed to that building but does not include any curtilage building;

"curtilage building" means any object or structure within the curtilage of a principal building which, although not fixed to the principal building, forms part of the land and has done so since before 1 July 1948 and which is treated as part of the principal building by virtue of section 54(9) of the 1971 Act [now s.1(5) of the Listed Buildings Act 1990];

"list description" in relation to a listed building means the detailed description of that building issued by the Department of the Environment in connection with a list compiled by the Secretary of State pursuant to section 54 of the 1971 Act [now ss.1 and 2 of the Listed Buildings Act 1990].

(2) Subject to paragraph (3) below, paragraph 5 of Schedule 11 to the 1971 Act [now s.13 of the Listed Buildings Act 1990] shall not apply to applications for listed building consent for the carrying out of works for the demolition, alteration or extension of a Grade II (unstarred) listed building with the exception of applications of any one of the following descriptions:—

(a) for the total demolition of a principal building;

(b) for the total demolition of a curtilage building where such a building is recorded in the list description, (unless it is expressly stated that it is not of special interes);

(c) (i) Subject to (ii) below, for the demolition of any part of a principal building where the cubic content of that part (as ascertained by external measurement), taken with any other part demolished since the building was listed, exceeds ten per cent. of the cubic content of the building when listed.

(ii) Sub-paragraph (i) above does not apply to applications for the demo-

487

lition of any part of a principal building which;

—was primarily erected before 1 January 1914 provided that the part to be demolished was erected since that date, or

—was primarily erected between 1 January 1914 and 31 December 1939 provided that the part to be demolished was erected after 1 July 1948;

(d) for the total demolition of an elevation of a principal building;

(e) for the demolition of substantially all of the interior of a principal building;

(f) for the demolition (in whole or part) of any object or structure fixed to a prinpal or curtilage building where that object or structure is recorded in the list description (unless it is expressly stated that it is not of special interest);

(g) for the demolition (in whole or in part) of a prinipal or curtilage building where within 5 years of the application a previous application for demolition involving that building was determined by the Secretary of State under paragraph 4 or paragraph 8 of Schedule 11 to the 1971 Act [now ss.12 and 21 of the Listed Buildings Act 1990].

(3) Paragraph (2) above does not apply to applications for consent for the carrying out of works on buildings in respect of which a grant has been made under section 3A or section 4 of the Historic Buildings and Ancient Monuments act 1953, or in respect of which an application for a grant has been made under those provisions but the applicant has not been notified whether it is proposed to make such a grant.

II GREATER LONDON

Pursuant to his powers under paragraph 7(1)), (1A) and (3) of Schedule 11 to the 1971 Act [now s.15 of the Listed Buildingss Act 1990] and to all other powers enabling him in that behalf, and after consultation with the Historic Buildings and Monuments Commission for England ("the Commission") the Secretary of State for the Environment as respects England hereby directs as follows:—

(1) In this direction:—

"principal building" means a building shown in the list compiled under section 54 of the 1971 Act [now s.1 of the Listed Buildings Act 1990] and includes any object or structure fixed to that building but does not include any curtilage building;

"curtilage building" means any object or structure within the curtilage of a principal building which, although not fixed to the principal building. forms part of the land and has done so since before 1 July 1948 and which is treated as part of the principal building by virtue of section 54(9) of the

1971 Act [now s.1(5) of the Listed Buildings Act 1990];

"list description" in relation to a listed building means the detailed description of that building issued by the Department of the Environment in connection with a list compiled by the Secretary of State pursuant to section 54 of the 1971 Act [now ss.1 and 2 of the Listed Buildings Act 1990].

(2) paragraph 6(3) of Schedule 11 to the 1971 Act [now s.14(3) of the Listed Buildings Act 1990] shall not apply to applications for listed building consent for the carrying out of works for:—

(a) the alteration or extension of any listed building;

(b) the demolition of a Grade II (unstarred) listed building with the exception of applications of any one of the following descriptions:—

(i) for the total demolition of a principal building;

(ii) for the total demolition of a curtilage building where such a building is recorded in the list description (unless it is expressly stated that it is not of special interest);

(iii) subject to the exceptions mentioned in this sub-paragraph, for the demolition of any part of a principal building where the cubic content of that part (as ascertained

by external measurement), taken with any other part demolished since the building was listed, exceeds ten per cent. of the cubic content of the building when listed. This sub-paragraph does not apply to applications for the demolition of any part of a principal building which,

—was primarily erected before 1 January 1914 provided that the part to be demolished was erected on or after that date; or

—was primarily erected between 1 January 1914 and 31 December 1939 provided that the part to be demolished was erected after 1 July 1948;

(iv) for the total demolition of an elevation of a principal building;

(v) for the demolition of substantially all of the interior of a principal building;

(vi) for the demolition of any object or structure fixed to a principal or cutilage building where that object or structure is recorded in the list description (unless it is expressly stated that it is not of special interest); or

(vii) for the demolition (in whole or in part) of a principal or curtilage building where within 5 years of the application a previous application involving that demolition was determined by the Secretary of State under paragraph 4 or paragraph 8 of Schedule 11 of the 1971 Act [now ss.12 and 21 of the Listed Buildings Act 1990].

97. In pursuance of his powers under section 277A(4) and (5) of the 1971 Act [now s.75(2), (3) of the Listed Buildings Act 1990] and of all other powers enabling him in that behalf the Secretary of State for the Environment as respects England, hereby directs as follows:—

(1) Section 277A [now s.74 and s.75 of the Listed Buildings Act 1990] shall not apply to the following descriptions of buildings:—

(a) any building with a *total* cubic content not exceeding 115 cubic metres or any part of such building, and in this sub-paragraph "building" does not include part of a building;

(b) any gate, wall, fence or railing which is less than 1 metre high where abutting on a highway (including a public footpath or bridleway) or public open space, or less than 2 metres high in any other case;

(c) any building erected since January 1, 1914 and used, or last used, for the purposes of agriculture or forestry;

(d) any part of a building used, or last used, for an industrial process, provided that such part (taken with any other part which may have been demolished) does not exceed ten per cent. of the cubic content of the original building (as ascertained by external measure-

ment) or 500 square metres of floor space, whichever is the greater;

(e) any building required to be demolished by virtue of an order made under section 51 of the Act [s.102 of the TCPA 1990];

(f) any building required to be demolished by virtue of any provision of an agreement made under section 52 of the Act [see now s.106 of the TCPA 1990];

(g) any building in respect of which the provisions of an enforcement notice served under section 87 [now s.172 of the TCPA 1990], section 96 or section 100 [now s.38 and s.46 of the Listed Buildings Act 1990] of the Act require its demolition, in whole or in part, however expressed;

(h) any building required to be demolished by virtue of a condition of planning permission granted under section 29 of the Act [now s.72 of the TCPA 1990], other than a permission deemed to be granted to a local planning authority by virtue of regulation 4(5) or regulation 5(4) of the Town and Country Planning General Regulations 1976 (S.I. 1976, No. 1419) [since revoked and superseded by S.I. 1992 No. 1489];

(i) any building to which a demolition order made under Part IX of the Housing Act 1985 applies;

(j) any building included in a compulsory purchase order made under the provisions of Part IX of the Housing Act 1985 and confirmed by the Secretary of State;

(k) a redundant building (within the meaning of the Pastoral Measure 1983) or part of such a building where demolition is in pursuance of a pastoral or redundancy scheme (within the meaning of that measure).

(2) In this direction:—

"the Act" means the Town and Country Planning Act 1971;

"forestry" means the growing of a utilisable crop of timber; and

"industrial process" means any process for or incidental to any of the following purposes, namely:—

(a) the making of an article or part of an article, or

(b) the altering, repairing, ornamenting, finishing, cleaning, washing, packing or canning, or adapting for sale, or breaking up, or demolition, of any article, or

(c) without prejudice to the foregoing paragraphs, the getting, dressing or treatment of minerals,

being a process carred out in the course of trade or business, and for the purposes of this definition the expression "article" means an article of any description, including a ship or vessel.

102. The Secretary of State hereby directs, under the powers conferred on him by paragraph 4(1) and (2) of Schedule 11 to the Town and Country Planning Act 1971 [now s.12(1), (2) of the Listed Buildings Act 1990], that all applications for listed building consent made by the Historic Buildings and Monuments Commission for England in respect of the carrying out of works to any building which is in its ownership, guardianship or otherwise under its control or of which it is the prospective pur-

chasers, shall be referred to the Secretary of State instead of being dealt with by the local planning authority. The authority should advertise the application in the usual way and forward any representations received, together with their own comments, to the Department's regional office.

COMMENCEMENT, REVOCATIONS AND CONSEQUENTIALS

154 (1) The Secretary of State for the Environment, as respects England, in exercise of the above mentioned enabling powers relating to the notification and directions set out in this circular, and of all other powers enabling him in that behalf, hereby directs as follows—

(a) the directions contained in this circular shall come into effect on 1 April 1987 ("the commencement date"), but without prejudice to the continued application of the directions referred to in (b) below to listed building consent applications made before that date; and

(b) subject to (a) above, the directions contained in the circulars and letter referred to in paragraph (2) below and paragraph 4 of the direction issued to the London Docklands Development Corporation on 1 July 1986, shall be revoked on the commencement date.

Index

All references are to paragraph numbers

492